Strategies for College Writing

A Rhetorical Reader

ROBERT FUNK
Eastern Illinois University

SUSAN X DAY
Iowa State University

ELIZABETH McMAHAN
Illinois State University

LINDA S. COLEMAN
Eastern Illinois University

PRENTICE HALL, Upper Saddle River, New Jersey 07458

Library of Congress Cataloging-in-Publication Data

Strategies for college writing : a rhetorical reader / Robert Funk . . .
[et al.].
    p.   cm.
  Includes index.
  ISBN 0-13-081224-2
  1. College readers. 2. English language—Rhetoric Problems,
exercises, etc. 3. Report writing Problems, exercises, etc.
I. Funk, Robert.
PE1417.S7654 2000   99–14777
808'.0427—dc21   CIP

Editor-in-Chief: Charlyce Jones Owens
Editorial Director: Leah Jewell
Editorial Assistant: Patricia Castiglione
AVP, Director of Manufacturing
  and Production: Barbara Kittle
Senior Managing Editor: Bonnie Biller
Production Liaison: Fran Russello
Project Manager: Linda B. Pawelchak
Manufacturing Manager: Nick Sklitsis
Prepress and Manufacturing Buyer: Mary Ann Gloriande
Cover Director: Jayne Conte
Cover Design: Kiwi Design
Cover Art: Paul Klee (1879–1940) Swiss. "Color Shapes" 1914.
  Barnes Foundation, Meriod, Pennsylvania/Superstock, Inc.
Marketing Manager: Susan Brekka
Copy Editing: Nancy Menges
Proofreading: Geoffrey Hill

This book was set in 10/12 Times Ten
by The Clarinda Company
and was printed and bound by Courier Companies, Inc.
The cover was printed by Phoenix Color Corp.

Printed in the United States of America
10 9 8 7 6 5 4 3 2 1

ISBN 0-13-081224-2

Prentice-Hall International (UK) Limited, *London*
Prentice-Hall of Australia Pty. Limited, *Sydney*
Prentice-Hall Canada Inc., *Toronto*
Prentice-Hall Hispanoamericana, S.A., *Mexico*
Prentice-Hall of India Private Limited, *New Delhi*
Prentice-Hall of Japan, Inc., *Tokyo*
Pearson Education of Asia Pte. Ltd., *Singapore*
Editora Prentice-Hall do Brasil, Ltda., *Rio de Janeiro*

Contents

◆ ◆ ◆ ◆ ◆

Preface xiii

Thematic Table of Contents xvii

◆ CHAPTER 1
Engaged Reading   1

GETTING STARTED 1
Marking the Text 2
READING WITH A PLAN: WHO? WHAT? WHY?
AND HOW? 2
Deborah Tannen, "Gender Gap in Cyberspace" 4
USING WHO? WHAT? WHY? AND HOW? 9
MAKING THE READING-WRITING CONNECTION 14
Developing the Habit 15

◆ CHAPTER 2
The Reader-Writer Interaction   17

DEVELOPING YOUR WRITING SKILLS 17
CONSTRUCTING AN ESSAY 18
Generating Ideas 18

Making a Plan 20
Organizing Your Ideas 20
Writing a Draft 22
Improving the Draft 24

◆ Checklist for Revising and Editing 25

SAMPLE STUDENT ESSAY WITH AUTHOR'S
   COMMENTS 25

◆ Jennifer Hoff, "Dealing with Death, Coping
   with Life" 25

◆ Using Internet Resources 30

Bruce Maxwell, "Twelve Tips to Search the Internet
   Successfully" 30

INTERNET SOURCES FOR WRITERS 32

◆ CHAPTER 3
Strategies for Discovering and Relating Experiences: Narration   34

INFORMAL DISCOVERY WRITING 35
Anne Frank, "Diary" 35

FOCUSED DISCOVERY WRITING 37
NARRATION: RELATING DISCOVERIES
   TO READERS 38

◆ Student Essay: Tara Coburn, "A Better Place" 38
◆ Writer's Worksop: Responding to a Narrative 40

GETTING STARTED ON A NARRATIVE 40
ORGANIZING A NARRATIVE 41
DEVELOPING A NARRATIVE 41
OPENING AND CLOSING A NARRATIVE 42
USING THE MODEL 43

◆ Checklist for Reading and Writing Narrative Essays 43

Mike Royko, "Jackie's Debut: A Unique Day" 44
   Writing from Reading Assignment 48

Ian Frazier, "Street Scene: Minor Heroism in a Major
   Metropolitan Area" 50

Andre Dubus, "A Quiet Siege: The Death and Life of a Gay Naval Officer" 54

Maxine Hong Kingston, "No Name Woman" 63

George Orwell, "Shooting an Elephant" 76

FURTHER IDEAS FOR USING NARRATION 84

◆ CHAPTER **4**
Strategies for Appealing to the Senses: Description   86

Tracy Kidder, "Mrs. Zajac" 87

◆ Writer's Worksop I: Responding to a Description 89

WRITING FROM READING 90

◆ Student Essay: Ann Moroney, "Lisa" 90

GETTING STARTED ON A DESCRIPTION 92
ORGANIZING A DESCRIPTION 94
DEVELOPING A DESCRIPTION 94
USING THE MODEL 95

◆ Writer's Worksop II: Analyzing a Description 96

◆ Checklist for Reading and Writing Descriptive Essays 96

Mark Twain, "Two Views of the Mississippi" 97
Writing from Reading Assignment 100

Truman Capote, "A Ride Through Spain" 102

Emilie Gallant, "White Breast Flats" 108

Henry Louis Gates, Jr., "In the Kitchen" 116

E. B. White, "Once More to the Lake" 125

FURTHER IDEAS FOR USING DESCRIPTION 133

◆ CHAPTER **5**
Strategies for Making a Point: Exemplification   134

Brent Staples, "Just Walk on By: A Black Man Ponders His Power to Alter Public Space" 135

◆ Writer's Workshop I: Responding to an Exemplification Essay 139

WRITING FROM READING 139

◆ Student Essay: Mark Jones, "Looking Up from the Bottom" 139

GETTING STARTED ON EXEMPLIFICATION 141
ORGANIZING EXEMPLIFICATION 142
DEVELOPING EXEMPLIFICATION 143
OPENING AND CLOSING EXEMPLIFICATION 144
USING THE MODEL 144

◆ Writer's Workshop II: Analyzing an Exemplification Essay 145

◆ Checklist for Reading and Writing Exemplification Essays 145

Sue Hubbell, "On the Interstate: A City of the Mind" 146
    Writing from Reading Assignment 150

Anne Lamott, "Shitty First Drafts" 152

William Greider, "Mock Democracy" 158

Jon D. Hull, "Slow Descent into Hell" 165

Sallie Tisdale, "A Weight That Women Carry" 173

FURTHER IDEAS FOR USING EXEMPLIFICATION 186

◆ CHAPTER **6**
**Strategies for Explaining How Things Work:
Process Analysis   187**

Bud Herron, "Cat Bathing as a Martial Art" 188

◆ Writer's Workshop I: Responding to a Process Analysis 190

WRITING FROM READING 190

◆ Student Essay: James R. Bryans, "Buying Land: Easier Said Than Done" 191

GETTING STARTED ON A PROCESS ANALYSIS 193
ORGANIZING A PROCESS ANALYSIS 193
DEVELOPING A PROCESS ANALYSIS 194
OPENING AND CLOSING A PROCESS ANALYSIS 196
USING THE MODEL 197

◆ Writer's Workshop II: Analyzing Process Writing 197

◆ Checklist for Reading and Writing Process Essays 198

Dereck Williamson, "Wall Covering" 199
    Writing from Reading Assignment 204

Peg Bracken, "Company Menu No. 1" 206

Jessica Mitford, "Embalming Mr. Jones" 211

Garrison Keillor, "How to Write a Personal Letter" 220

Leon Jaroff, "To Hell and Back" 225

Malcolm Gladwell, "The Alzheimer's Strain: How to Accommodate Too Many Patients" 234

FURTHER IDEAS FOR USING PROCESS ANALYSIS 241

◆ CHAPTER **7**
Strategies for Clarifying Meaning: Definition   242

Ellen Goodman, "The Company Man" 243

◆ Writer's Workshop I: Responding to a Definition 245

WRITING FROM READING 245

◆ Student Essay: Megan Quick, "In Tune with His Students" 245

GETTING STARTED ON A DEFINITION 247
ORGANIZING A DEFINITION 249
DEVELOPING A DEFINITION 250
OPENING AND CLOSING A DEFINITION 250
USING THE MODEL 251

◆ Writer's Workshop II: Analyzing a Definition 252

◆ Checklist for Reading and Writing Definition Essays 252

Rebecca Thomas Kirkendall, "Who's a Hillbilly?" 253
   Writing from Reading Assignment 257

Judy Brady, "I Want a Wife" 259

M. F. K. Fisher, " 'Let the Sky Rain Potatoes' " 264

Michel Marriott, "Father Hunger" 269

Andrew Holleran, "The Fear" 277

FURTHER IDEAS FOR USING DEFINITION 286

◆ CHAPTER **8**
Strategies for Organizing Ideas and Experience: Division and Classification   287

Calvin Trillin, "The Extendable Fork" 288

◆ Writers Workshop I: Responding to a Classification 290

WRITING FROM READING 290

◆ Student Essay: Brian Shamhart, "Friend, Foe, or ???" 291

GETTING STARTED ON DIVISION AND
    CLASSIFICATION WRITING 293

ORGANIZING DIVISION AND CLASSIFICATION
    WRITING 294

DEVELOPING DIVISION AND CLASSIFICATION
    WRITING 296

OPENING AND CLOSING DIVISION AND
CLASSIFICATION WRITING 296

USING THE MODEL 297

◆ Writer's Workshop II: Analyzing a Division and Classification
    Essay 298

◆ Checklist for Reading and Writing Division and Classification
    Essays 298

William Lutz, "Doublespeak" 300
    Writing from Reading Assignment 306

Cullen Murphy, "The Power of Two: A New Way of Classifying
    Everyone" 308

Renee Tajima, "Lotus Blossoms Don't Bleed: Images of Asian
    American Women" 314

Phillip Lopate, "What Friends Are For" 323

Lee Smith, "What We Now Know About Memory" 332

FURTHER IDEAS FOR USING DIVISION
    AND CLASSIFICATION 341

◆ CHAPTER 9

Strategies for Examining Connections: Comparison and Contrast   342

Maya Angelou, "Day to Night: Picking Cotton" 343

◆ Writer's Workshop I: Responding to Comparison
    and Contrast 346

WRITING FROM READING 346

◆ Student Essay: Kara Kitner, "Life: It's All About Choices" 346

GETTING STARTED ON COMPARISON
    AND CONTRAST 349
ORGANIZING COMPARISON AND CONTRAST 350
DEVELOPING COMPARISON AND CONTRAST 352
OPENING AND CLOSING COMPARISON
    AND CONTRAST 352
USING THE MODEL 354

◆ Writer's Workshop II: Analyzing Comparison and Contrast 354

◆ Checklist for Reading and Writing Comparison and Contrast
  Essays 354

Denise Noe, "Parallel Worlds: The Surprising Similarities (and
  Differences) of Country-and-Western and Rap" 356
    Writing from Reading Assignment 362

Esmeralda Santiago, "Guavas" 364

Deborah Tannen, "Sex, Lies, and Conversation" 368

Scott Russell Sanders, "Coming from the Country" 376

Andrew Hacker, "Dividing American Society" 388

FURTHER IDEAS FOR USING COMPARISON
    AND CONTRAST 401

◆ CHAPTER **10**
Strategies for Interpreting Meaning:
Cause and Effect   402

E. M. Forster, "My Wood" 403

◆ Writer's Workshop I: Responding to Cause and Effect 405

WRITING FROM READING 406

◆ Student Essay: Ami Krumery, "My Car" 406

GETTING STARTED ON CAUSE AND EFFECT 408
ORGANIZING CAUSE AND EFFECT 409
DEVELOPING CAUSE AND EFFECT 411
OPENING AND CLOSING CAUSE AND EFFECT 412
USING THE MODEL 412

◆ Writer's Workshop II: Analyzing Cause and Effect 413

◆ Checklist for Reading and Writing Cause and Effect Essays 414

Katha Pollitt, "Why Boys Don't Play with Dolls" 415
  Writing from Reading Assignment 419

Kathy A. Svitil, "The Greenland Viking Mystery" 421

Judith Ortiz Cofer, "The Myth of the Latin Woman: I Just Met a Girl Named Maria" 427

Alberto Alvaro Rios, "Becoming and Breaking: Poet and Poem" 435

Scott Russell Sanders, "The Most Human Art: Ten Reasons Why We'll Always Need a Good Story" 443

FURTHER IDEAS FOR USING CAUSE AND EFFECT 450

◆ CHAPTER 11
Strategies for Influencing Opinion: Argument 451

Laurel Robertson, "Bake Your Bread at Home" 452

◆ Writer's Workshop I: Responding to an Argument 455

WRITING FROM READING 455

◆ Student Essay: Sean Stangland, "The Educational Value of Film" 456

GETTING STARTED ON AN ARGUMENT 459
ORGANIZING AN ARGUMENT 460
DEVELOPING AN ARGUMENT 462
OPENING AND CLOSING AN ARGUMENT 462
USING THE MODEL 463

◆ Writer's Workshop II: Analyzing an Argument 463

◆ Checklist for Reading and Writing Argument Essays 464

Lindsy Van Gelder, "Marriage as a Restricted Club" 465
  Writing from Reading Assignment 470

Jeanne A. Heaton, "Tuning in Trouble: Talk TV's Destructive Impact on Mental Health" 472

David Cole, "Five Myths About Immigration" 480

Arlie Russell Hochschild, "Time for Change" 486

Gary Howard, "Whites in Multicultural Education: Rethinking Our Role" 492

FURTHER IDEAS FOR USING ARGUMENT 506

◆ CHAPTER **12**
Combining Strategies: Further Readings   507

"Antonia," "Coming to America, to Clean" (Trans. by Ana Maria Corona) 508

Chang-Rae Lee, "Coming Home Again" 517

Amanda Coyne, "The Long Good-bye: Mother's Day in Federal Prison" 526

Stephanie Coontz, "The Way We Weren't: The Myth and Reality of the 'Traditional' Family" 534

Katha Pollitt, "Let's Get Rid of Sports" 540

Richard Preston, "Back in the Hot Zone" 543

Joy Williams, "The Case Against Babies" 547

IDEAS FOR COMBINING WRITING STRATEGIES 555

Glossary 558

Acknowledgments 571

Index 576

Preface

❖ ❖ ❖ ❖ ❖

Strategies for College Writing emphasizes the interconnectedness of reading and writing by teaching students to read with a writer's eye and to write with a reader's expectations. The book employs a set of innovative and coordinated activities that will enable students to understand their roles as readers and to connect their reading experiences to their own writing. This textbook is a flexible resource. The numerous readings, pedagogical features, and writing topics give instructors the freedom to select from a broad range of assignments and approaches.

A Writer's Approach to Analytical Reading.   The opening chapter, "Engaged Reading," presents an effective and easily practiced procedure for reading nonfiction from a writer's perspective. The chapter applies the familiar journalists' questions—*Who? What? Why? How?*—to the process of reading and analyzing essays. This approach shows students how to evaluate their roles as readers and how to respond, both as readers and writers, to the rhetorical contexts of their reading assignments. To illustrate the procedure, the chapter contains a professional essay, along with the responses of a student using the *Who, What, Why,* and *How* questions to analyze that essay.

A Concise Survey of the Writing Process.   Chapter 2, "The Reader-Writer Interaction," offers practical guidance on the primary tasks of the writing process: discovering, organizing, drafting, revising, and editing. This chapter also demonstrates how students can connect their reading experiences to their roles as writers and how they can appropriate textual strategies from their reading for the essays they write. A sample student essay—based on the *Who, What, Why,* and *How* analysis from Chapter 1— illustrates these connections.

A Contextual Study of Rhetorical Strategies. Chapters 3 through 10 explain and illustrate the strategies that students use to organize and develop their college writing assignments: narration, description, exemplification, process analysis, definition, division and classification, comparison and contrast, cause and effect, and argument. The discussions of the individual strategies include these important pedagogical features:

♦ A **chapter introduction** presents each major rhetorical strategy in the context of a sample professional selection and a student essay written in response to that selection. The accompanying analysis points out how the student's thinking and writing have been shaped and influenced by the reading. These introductions provide advice on how to get started, how to organize material, how to develop content, how to open and close the essay, and how to use the professional model.

♦ Brief **Writer's Workshop** activities, which can be done collaboratively, encourage students to review the key rhetorical points for each strategy by analyzing the two essays in the introduction.

♦ A **Checklist for Reading and Writing** at the end of each introduction sums up the major issues for understanding and applying each strategy.

♦ A detailed **Writing from Reading Assignment** follows the second professional selection in each chapter. Students are given instructions for analyzing the rhetorical strategies of the model essay (using the *Who, What, Why,* and *How* questions) and step-by-step directions for designing an essay written in response to the professional selection.

♦ Four to five additional professional **readings** per chapter provide further examples of each major strategy.

Interactive, Integrated Apparatus. The connection between reading and writing is stressed in the apparatus that accompanies each of the professional selections:

♦ The **pre-reading apparatus** consists of a "preparing to read" question (which can be used as a journal prompt) and an introductory headnote.

◆ The **post-reading apparatus** follows the *Who, What, Why,* and *How* approach established in the opening chapter. It includes "First Responses" (which could also be used for journal writing) and a set of questions that explore ideas and techniques: voice and tone (*Who*), content and meaning (*What*), purpose (*Why*), and style and structure (*How*).

◆ Several **Ideas for Writing** direct students to try their hand at writing a short essay using the ideas and strategies they have examined in the professional selection.

◆ Each chapter ends with **Further Ideas for Using** the strategy. These topics provide ideas for writing longer papers and suggestions for **collaborative writing** and for **combining strategies.**

◆ **Internet Activities.** The post-reading apparatus also includes suggestions for using the resources of the Internet to answer questions about the professional essays and to gather ideas and information for writing essays. A brief, accessible article on Internet use, "Twelve Tips to Search the Internet Successfully," appears at the end of Chapter 2.

This extensive apparatus gives teachers and students a wide variety of choices for exploring the reading-writing connection.

Varied, Thought-Provoking Readings. The sixty-four professional selections have been chosen to illustrate the major rhetorical strategies used in nonfiction writing. They include essays and excerpts of various lengths and cover a wide range of styles and viewpoints. Each chapter begins with two relatively brief readings and then offers longer, more demanding selections for analysis and writing. The topics and issues are intended to engage students and stimulate their thinking. A special effort has been made to appeal to a cross-section of readers by including a number of essays by women and multicultural writers. There is a mix of standard works and new selections.

The ten **student essays** are an important component of the book's pedagogy. They were written by college freshmen and sophomores employing the reading-writing approach that this book teaches. Each student used a professional selection as a model and followed the procedures for engaged reading and process writing that are outlined in the opening chapters. These essays demonstrate how student writers are able to utilize the ideas and strategies they encounter in professional readings by applying and adapting them to their own writing.

Seven **Further Readings** have been gathered in Chapter 12 to illustrate how professional writers combine rhetorical strategies. The first selection in the chapter has been annotated to show how the various methods contribute to the organization and development of the essay.

Other Features. For instructors who want to correlate reading assignments or organize their course around issue-centered units, the **Thematic Table of Contents** groups the readings according to several common themes. The text also contains a **Glossary** of useful rhetorical terms.

◆ ACKNOWLEDGMENTS

We want to extend our thanks to the many people who have helped to develop and produce this book, especially to our editors at Prentice Hall—Leah Jewell and her assistant Vivian Garcia—and the production editor, Linda Pawelchak. We are also grateful for the perceptive criticisms and useful suggestions provided by our reviewers: Judy Burnham, Tulsa Community College; Adelle Mery, University of Texas-Pan American; Elizabeth Metzger, University of South Florida; David Tammer, Eastern Arizona College; Elena Tapia, Eastern Connecticut State University; and Jan Worth, University of Michigan-Flint. Finally, we want to thank the "significant others" in our lives—Bill, Brian, Casey, and Danny—for their patience and support.

Thematic Table of Contents

◆ ◆ ◆ ◆ ◆

◆ SELF AND OTHERS

Identity

Anne Frank, "Diary," p. 35

Andre Dubus, "A Quiet Siege: The Death and Life of a Gay Naval Officer," p. 54

Maxine Hong Kingston, "No Name Woman," p. 63

Ann Moroney, "Lisa" (student essay), p. 90

Mark Jones, "Looking Up from the Bottom" (student essay), p. 139

Sallie Tisdale, "A Weight That Women Carry," p. 173

Brian Shamhart, "Friend, Foe, or ???" (student essay), p. 291

Renee Tajima, "Lotus Blossoms Don't Bleed: Images of Asian American Women," p. 314

Phillip Lopate, "What Friends Are For," p. 323

Kara Kitner, "Life: It's All About Choices" (student essay), p. 346

Ami Krumery, "My Car" (student essay), p. 406

Katha Pollitt, "Why Boys Don't Play with Dolls," p. 415

Judith Ortiz Cofer, "The Myth of the Latin Woman: I Just Met a Girl Named Maria," p. 427

Gary Howard, "Whites in Multicultural Education: Rethinking Our Role," p. 492

Family

Anne Frank, "Diary," p. 35

Tara Coburn, "A Better Place" (student essay), p. 38

Maxine Hong Kingston, "No Name Woman," p. 63

Henry Louis Gates, Jr., "In the Kitchen," p. 116

E. B. White, "Once More to the Lake," p. 125

Ellen Goodman, "The Company Man," p. 243

Michel Marriott, "Father Hunger," p. 269

Laurel Robertson, "Bake Your Bread at Home," p. 452

Chang-Rae Lee, "Coming Home Again," p. 517

Amanda Coyne, "The Long Good-bye: Mother's Day in Federal Prison," p. 526

Stephanie Coontz, "The Way We Weren't: The Myth and Reality of the 'Traditional' Family," p. 534

Community

Mike Royko, "Jackie's Debut: A Unique Day," p. 44

Ian Frazier, "Street Scene: Minor Heroism in a Major Metropolitan Area," p. 50

Andre Dubus, "A Quiet Siege: The Death and Life of a Gay Naval Officer," p. 54

Sue Hubbell, "On the Interstate: A City of the Mind," p. 146

Jon D. Hull, "Slow Descent into Hell," p. 165

Malcolm Gladwell, "The Alzheimer's Strain," p. 234

Rebecca Thomas Kirkendall, "Who's a Hillbilly?" p. 253

Brian Shamhart, "Friend, Foe, or ???" (student essay), p. 291

Phillip Lopate, "What Friends Are For," p. 323

Maya Angelou, "Day to Night: Picking Cotton," p. 343

Scott Russell Sanders, "Coming from the Country," p. 376

Scott Russell Sanders, "The Most Human Art: Ten Reasons Why We'll Always Need a Good Story," p. 443

◆ CULTURAL RELATIONSHIPS

Politics

William Greider, "Mock Democracy," p. 158

Jon D. Hull, "Slow Descent into Hell," p. 165

William Lutz, "Doublespeak," p. 300

Andrew Hacker, "Dividing American Society," p. 388

David Cole, "Five Myths About Immigration," p. 480

Race and Ethnicity

Mike Royko, "Jackie's Debut: A Unique Day," p. 44

Maxine Hong Kingston, "No Name Woman," p. 63

Emilie Gallant, "White Breast Flats," p. 108

Henry Louis Gates, Jr., "In the Kitchen," p. 116

Brent Staples, "Just Walk on By: A Black Man Ponders His Power to Alter Public Space," p. 135

Michel Marriott, "Father Hunger," p. 269

Renee Tajima, "Lotus Blossoms Don't Bleed: Images of Asian American Women," p. 314

Maya Angelou, "Day to Night: Picking Cotton," p. 343

Esmeralda Santiago, "Guavas," p. 364

Andrew Hacker, "Dividing American Society," p. 388

Judith Ortiz Cofer, "The Myth of the Latin Woman: I Just Met a Girl Named Maria," p. 427

Alberto Alvaro Rios, "Becoming and Breaking: Poet and Poem," p. 435

Gary Howard, "Whites in Multicultural Education: Rethinking Our Role," p. 492

Chang-Rae Lee, "Coming Home Again," p. 517

Class and Culture

George Orwell, "Shooting an Elephant," p. 76

Truman Capote, "A Ride Through Spain," p. 102

Sue Hubbell, "On the Interstate: A City of the Mind," p. 146

Jon D. Hull, "Slow Descent into Hell," p. 165

Rebecca Thomas Kirkendall, "Who's a Hillbilly?" p. 253

Denise Noe, "Parallel Worlds: The Surprising Similarities (and Differences) of Country-and-Western and Rap," p. 356

Scott Russell Sanders, "Coming from the Country," p. 376

Kathy A. Svitil, "The Greenland Viking Mystery," p. 421

Lindsy Van Gelder, "Marriage as a Restricted Club," p. 465

David Cole, "Five Myths About Immigration," p. 480

"Antonia," "Coming to America, to Clean" (Trans. by Ana Maria Corona), p. 508

Gender and Sexuality

Deborah Tannen, "Gender Gap in Cyberspace," p. 4

Jennifer Hoff, "Dealing with Death, Coping with Life" (student essay), p. 25

Andre Dubus, "A Quiet Siege: The Death and Life of a Gay Naval Officer," p. 54

Maxine Hong Kingston, "No Name Woman," p. 63

Brent Staples, "Just Walk on By: A Black Man Ponders His Power to Alter Public Space," p. 135

Sallie Tisdale, "A Weight That Women Carry," p. 173

Judy Brady, "I Want a Wife," p. 259

Andrew Holleran, "The Fear," p. 277

Renee Tajima, "Lotus Blossoms Don't Bleed: Images of Asian American Women," p. 314

Deborah Tannen, "Sex, Lies, and Conversation," p. 368

Katha Pollitt, "Why Boys Don't Play with Dolls," p. 415

Judith Ortiz Cofer, "The Myth of the Latin Woman: I Just Met a Girl Named Maria," p. 427

Lindsy Van Gelder, "Marriage as a Restricted Club," p. 465

Arlie Russell Hochschild, "Time for Change," p. 486

Amanda Coyne, "The Long Good-bye: Mother's Day in Federal Prison," p. 526

Science, Health, and Ecology

Bruce Maxwell, "Twelve Tips to Search the Internet Successfully," p. 30

Sallie Tisdale, "A Weight That Women Carry," p. 173

Jessica Mitford, "Embalming Mr. Jones," p. 211

Leon Jaroff, "To Hell and Back," p. 225

Malcolm Gladwell, "The Alzheimer's Strain," p. 234

Andrew Holleran, "The Fear," p. 277

Lee Smith, "What We Now Know About Memory," p. 332

Jeanne A. Heaton, "Tuning in Trouble: Talk TV's Destructive Impact on Mental Health," p. 472

Richard Preston, "Back in the Hot Zone," p. 543

Joy Williams, "The Case Against Babies," p. 547

◆ THE MEANINGFUL LIFE

Education

Tracy Kidder, "Mrs. Zajac," p. 87

James Bryans, "Buying Land: Easier Said Than Done" (student essay), p. 191

Megan Quick, "In Tune with His Students" (student essay), p. 245

Kara Kitner, "Life: It's All About Choices" (student essay), p. 346

Alberto Alvaro Rios, "Becoming and Breaking: Poet and Poem," p. 435

Sean Stangland, "The Educational Value of Film" (student essay), p. 456

Gary Howard, "Whites in Multicultural Education: Rethinking Our Role," p. 492

Work

Tracy Kidder, "Mrs. Zajac," p. 87

Mark Twain, "Two Views of the Mississippi," p. 97

Sue Hubbell, "On the Interstate: A City of the Mind," p. 146

William Greider, "Mock Democracy," p. 158

Dereck Williamson, "Wall Covering," p. 199

Jessica Mitford, "Embalming Mr. Jones," p. 211

Leon Jaroff, "To Hell and Back," p. 225

Ellen Goodman, "The Company Man," p. 243

Megan Quick, "In Tune with His Students" (student essay), p. 245

Maya Angelou, "Day to Night: Picking Cotton," p. 343

Alberto Alvaro Rios, "Becoming and Breaking: Poet and Poem," p. 435

Arlie Russell Hochschild, "Time for Change," p. 486

"Antonia," "Coming to America, to Clean" (Trans. by Ana Maria Corona), p. 508

Places

Tara Coburn, "A Better Place" (student essay), p. 38

Ian Frazier, "Street Scene: Minor Heroism in a Major Metropolitan Area," p. 50

Mark Twain, "Two Views of the Mississippi," p. 97

Truman Capote, "A Ride Through Spain," p. 102

Emilie Gallant, "White Breast Flats," p. 108

E. B. White, "Once More to the Lake," p. 125

Sue Hubbell, "On the Interstate: A City of the Mind," p. 146

Jon D. Hull, "Slow Descent into Hell," p. 165

Malcolm Gladwell, "The Alzheimer's Strain," p. 234

Esmeralda Santiago, "Guavas," p. 364

Scott Russell Sanders, "Coming from the Country," p. 376

E. M. Forster, "My Wood," p. 403

Kathy A. Svitil, "The Greenland Viking Mystery," p. 421

"Antonia," "Coming to America, to Clean" (Trans. by Ana Maria Corona), p. 508

Richard Preston, "Back in the Hot Zone," p. 543

Humor

Anne Lamott, "Shitty First Drafts," p. 152

Bud Herron, "Cat Bathing as a Martial Art," p. 188

Dereck Williamson, "Wall Covering," p. 199

Peg Bracken, "Company Menu No. 1," p. 206

Garrison Keillor, "How to Write a Personal Letter," p. 220

Judy Brady, "I Want a Wife," p. 259

Calvin Trillin, "The Extendable Fork," p. 288

Cullen Murphy, "The Power of Two," p. 308

Katha Pollitt, "Let's Get Rid of Sports," p. 540

Food

Sue Hubbell, "On the Interstate: A City of the Mind," p. 146

Peg Bracken, "Company Menu No. 1," p. 206

M. F. K. Fisher, " 'Let the Sky Rain Potatoes,' " p. 264

Calvin Trillin, "The Extendable Fork," p. 288

Esmeralda Santiago, "Guavas," p. 364

Laurel Robertson, "Bake Your Bread at Home," p. 452

Chang-Rae Lee, "Coming Home Again," p. 517

Writing and Language

Deborah Tannen, "Gender Gap in Cyberspace," p. 4

Anne Lamott, "Shitty First Drafts," p. 152

Garrison Keillor, "How to Write a Personal Letter," p. 220

William Lutz, "Doublespeak," p. 300

Deborah Tannen, "Sex, Lies, and Conversation," p. 368

Scott Russell Sanders, "The Most Human Art: Ten Reasons Why We'll Always Need a Good Story," p. 443

Television, Media, and Entertainment

Renee Tajima, "Lotus Blossoms Don't Bleed: Images of Asian American Women," p. 314

Denise Noe, "Parallel Worlds: The Surprising Similarities (and Differences) of Country-and-Western and Rap," p. 356

Scott Russell Sanders, "The Most Human Art: Ten Reasons Why We'll Always Need a Good Story," p. 443

Sean Stangland, "The Educational Value of Film" (student essay), p. 456

Jeanne A. Heaton, "Tuning in Trouble: Talk TV's Destructive Impact on Mental Health," p. 472

Katha Pollitt, "Let's Get Rid of Sports," p. 540

CHAPTER 1

Engaged Reading

◆ ◆ ◆ ◆ ◆

Like a good conversation, successful reading or writing is a dynamic process, requiring both an articulate speaker and an active listener. The experience of being talked down to or of being listened to without being heard is all too common. These are the conversations people resent or, at best, forget as quickly as possible. By contrast, to enjoy the experience and to learn from it, reader and writer must be aware of each other's needs, abilities, and motives. This chapter will explore the reader-writer relationship from the reader's point of view, outlining the goals of and steps to **engaged reading.** As a more aware reader you will, in turn, improve the style and substance of your own writing.

◆ GETTING STARTED

Being open and focused are essential to a good first reading. Physical surroundings have much to do with these states of mind. Some people demand perfect silence in the early morning hours, a favorite chair, a carton of milk. Others seek out late-night, crowded coffee shops, enjoying the excitement of the busy world around them while being free to shut it out at will. The key is finding a time and place when the reading gets the attention it deserves and needs. Sometimes, of course, favorite settings may not be available, and focus will simply demand greater discipline.

Travelers often feel more comfortable about and well-prepared for trips to unfamiliar places if they study maps and read guide books. Looking ahead at reading selections will provide similar results. An essay's title can sometimes offer immediate access to the writer's subject, goals, and attitudes. Other clues may be gained from notes about the author: what he or she does for a living, other things written by the writer, or comments that he or she might have made about the essay you are about to read. Where the essay was originally published can tell you the kind of reader the author most wanted to reach or help you to judge the reliability of the author's views. Looking out for road signs and roadblocks is a good idea, too. Subheadings, charts, illustrations, footnotes, and definitions of unfamiliar terms may all be included in a reading, and it is useful to know where the help is and when the problems may arise.

Marking the Text

Beginning with pen or pencil in hand is among the best ways to avoid passive reading. Whether you make comments in the margins of a book you plan to keep, stick post-its in texts you plan to sell back, or take notes in a reading journal, you will remember more and understand more fully if you respond as you read. A simple "I disagree!" "Why did she do that?" "thesis?" "This reminds me of that Madonna song" can lead you back to the problem areas and can help you to outline the arguments the author is offering and your responses to them. Quick reminders might include placing question marks next to passages that cause confusion, circling words to look up in the dictionary, or underlining phrases and sentences that identify major ideas or examples. In particularly difficult or complex readings, making brief notes at the end of paragraphs or subsections is a good way to ensure that you understand a main point before moving on to the next.

◆ READING WITH A PLAN: WHO? WHAT? WHY? AND HOW?

Like the journalist always digging to completely understand a story and ever on the lookout for a story to tell, engaged readers ask questions of the things they read, as well as of themselves as they read. The "Who," "What," "Why," and "How" of both the writer and the reader can become a firm foundation for both understanding the reading and using it as a springboard for your own writing. The following questions will enable you to develop the habits of an engaged reader. After studying the questions, you will have the opportunity to practice their effectiveness while reading an essay by Deborah Tannen and then to compare your reactions to a fellow student's in-depth responses to the same essay.

Exploring **Who?**

Writer

Who is the writer or speaker in the reading?

- What personality or voice is he or she projecting and why?
- What is the writer assuming about me by using this voice?

Reader

Who am I as I read this piece?

- How do I respond to this voice? Am I drawn in, turned off, or unaffected?
- Is it a voice I might use effectively in my own writing? How might I do that?

Exploring **What?**

Writer

What primary and secondary ideas does the writer want to convey to me?

Reader

What connection do I have to these ideas?

- How well do I fit as the writer's intended reader? How does this affect my responses?
- Have I had similar ideas, thoughts, feelings, or experiences? How do these help me to understand the primary points?
- Are these ideas I would like to explore in my own writing?

Exploring **Why?**

Writer

Why has the author decided to write on this subject?

- What seem to be the writer's goals or purposes?

Reader

Why do I respond the way I do to this reading? Why might others respond differently?

- ◆ Have the writer's goals been achieved with me as the reader?
- ◆ What is my next step, if any, toward furthering those goals?

Exploring **How?**

Writer

How is the essay organized?

- ◆ What strategies has the writer adopted to best communicate her ideas and achieve her goals?

Reader

How might I adapt these strategies to my own immediate writing goals?

To discover how this approach to reading works, read the following essay and then record your responses to the *Who, What, Why,* and *How* questions. As you read, notice the way an active reader has marked the essay to emphasize major points, remind herself of words to look up, and respond to Tannen's ideas.

Gender Gap in Cyberspace

DEBORAH TANNEN

Deborah Tannen, Professor of Linguistics at Georgetown University, writes academic and popular articles on how men and women communicate with one another. In this essay, which appeared in *Newsweek* in 1994, Tannen focuses attention on the ways in which cyberspace helps to reveal our everyday gender differences to us.

Starts with a mystery   I was a <u>computer pioneer</u>, but I'm still something of a <u>novice</u>. That <u>paradox</u> is telling.

I was the second person on my block to get a computer. The first was my colleague Ralph. It was 1980. Ralph got a Radio Shack TRS-80, I got a used Apple II+. He helped me get started and went on to become (a) (maven,) reading computer magazines, hungering for the new technology he read about, and buying and mastering it as quickly as he could afford. I hung on to old equipment far too long because I dislike giving up what I'm used to, fear making the wrong decision about what to buy, and resent the time it takes to install and learn a new system.

a computerison & contrast?

Me too!

My first Apple came with videogames; I gave them away. Playing games on the computer didn't interest me. If I had free time I'd spend it talking on the telephone to friends.

shows her priorities

Ralph got hooked. His wife was often annoyed by the hours he spent at his computer and the money he spent upgrading it. My marriage had no such strains—until I discovered E-mail. Then I got hooked. E-mail draws me the same way the phone does: it's a souped-up conversation.

Now, a man's point of view?

nice phrase

E-mail deepened my friendship with Ralph. Though his office was next to mine, we rarely had extended conversations because he is shy. Face to face he mumbled so, I could barely tell he was speaking. But when we both got on E-mail, I started receiving long, self-revealing messages; we poured our hearts out to each other. A friend discovered that E-mail opened up that kind of communication with her father. He would never talk much on the phone (as her mother would), but they have become close since they both got on line.

Why, I wondered, would some men find it easier to open up on E-mail? It's a combination of the technology (which they enjoy) and the (obliqueness) of the written word, just as many men will reveal feelings in dribs and drabs while riding in the car or doing something, which they'd never talk about sitting face to face. It's too intense, too bearing-down on them, and once you start you have to keep going. With a computer in between, it's safer.

good question

This sounds familiar!

It was on E-mail, in fact, that I described to Ralph how boys in groups often struggle to get the upper hand whereas girls tend to maintain an appearance of cooperation. And he pointed out that this explained why boys are more likely to be captivated by computers than girls are. Boys are typically motivated by a social structure that says if you don't dominate you will be dominated. Computers, by their nature, balk; you type a perfectly appropriate command and it refuses to do what it should. Many boys and men are incited by this defiance: "I'm going to whip this into line and teach it who's boss! I'll get it to do what I say!" (and if they work hard enough, they always can). Girls and women are more likely to respond, "This thing won't cooperate. Get it away from me!"

All boys & girls?

Uses dialogue for both sides

Yes!

Although no one wants to think of herself as "typical"—how much nicer to be (sui generis) —my relationship to my computer is—gulp—fairly typical for a woman. Most women (with plenty of exceptions) aren't

Main idea?

excited by tinkering with the technology, grappling with the challenge of eliminating bugs or getting the biggest and best computer. These dynamics appeal to many men's interest in making sure they're on the top side of the inevitable who's-up-who's-down struggle that life is for them. E-mail appeals to my view of life as a contest for connections to others. When I see that I have fifteen messages, I feel loved.

"You have mail"

I once posted a technical question on a computer network for linguists and was flooded with long dispositions, some pages long. I was staggered by the generosity and the expertise, but wondered where these guys found the time—and why all the answers I got were from men.

Like coed classrooms and meetings, discussions on E-mail networks tend to be dominated by male voices, unless they're specifically women-only, like single-sex schools. On line, women don't have to worry about getting the floor (you just send a message when you feel like it), but, according to linguists Susan Herring and Laurel Sutton, who have studied this, they have the usual problems of having their messages ignored or attacked. The anonymity of public networks frees a small

Calls on other linguists

number of men to send long, (vituperative,) sarcastic
messages that many other men either can tolerate or actually enjoy, but that turn most women off.   *Why?*

The anonymity of networks leads to another sad
part of the E-mail story: there are men who (deluge)   *Harrass-*
women with questions about their appearance and invi-   *ment?*
tations to sex. On college campuses, as soon as women
students log on, they are bombarded by references to
sex, like going to work and finding pornographic posters
adorning the walls.

Most women want one thing from a computer—to
work. This is significant counterevidence to the claim
that men want to focus on information while women are
interested in rapport. That claim I found was often true
in casual conversation, in which there is no particular information to be conveyed. But with computers, it is
often women who are more focused on information, because they don't respond to the challenge of getting
equipment to submit.

Once I had learned the basics, my interest in
computers waned. I use it to write books (though I   *Use of*
never mastered having it do bibliographies or tables of   *time—*
another
contents) and write checks (but not balance my check-   *main idea*
book). Much as I'd like to use it to do more, I begrudge
the time it would take to learn.

Ralph's computer expertise costs him a lot of time.
Chivalry requires that he rescue (novices) in need, and he
is called upon by damsel novices far more often than

(knaves.) More men would rather study the instruction   *?*

booklet than ask directions, as it were, from another

person. "When I do help men," Ralph wrote (on E-mail,   *Nice use*

of course), "they want to be more involved. I once in-   *of humor*

stalled a hard drive for a guy, and he wanted to be there

with me, wielding the screwdriver and giving his own

advice where he could." Women, he finds, usually are

not interested in what he's doing; they just want him to

get the computer to the point where they can do what   *Is that*

they want.   *true for*
    me?

Which pretty much explains how I managed to be   *Circles*
    back to
a pioneer without becoming an expert.   *intro.*

◆ ◆ ◆

◆ USING WHO? WHAT? WHY? AND HOW?

We asked Jennifer Hoff, a freshman student, to use the *Who, What, Why,* and *How* questions to better understand Tannen as a writer and herself as a reader, digging deeper into her own initial understanding and extending what she learned from her reading into practical lessons for her own writing. Her responses are spontaneous and unedited, meant for her own use rather than to communicate final thoughts to someone else. As you read, compare your responses to Jennifer's.

Exploring Who?

Writer

Who is the writer or speaker in the reading?
The writer or speaker is literally the author of the essay. She is a married woman, writing in first person, and telling of her experiences with computers and men, two elements that communicate and miscommunicate with women in different ways. The speaker is real, not just a made up character. She seems to be sociable, understanding, inquisitive, and capable of a sense of humor.

What personality or voice is he or she projecting and why?

She is projecting a voice of the so-called "typical" woman or what she feels is the personality of a stereotypical woman. She is a mediator in the battle of miscommunication between men and women. She is not trying to say that women are better than men at communicating; they just like to engage in it more. She makes sure to state that not all women follow along the lines of the "typical" woman, but she somewhat stereotypes men innocently only because she is not a man and cannot speak for them. She also has a humorous side to her essay which seems to add comfort to her writing, making it easier to agree with and relate to in some way.

What is the writer assuming about me by using this voice?

The writer is assuming that I am a mature, somewhat educated reader who has experienced miscommunication between genders and can relate to the trouble with engaging in an intimate conversation with the opposite sex. The essay is more for an adult audience. The writer also assumes that I have used a computer and E-mail before.

Reader

Who am I as I read this piece?

I am a female, freshman college student who is eighteen years old. I am a person who can accept or reject her essay, including her views on the differences in communication between men and women and the solutions she sets forth, such as using E-mail.

How do I respond to this voice? Am I drawn in, turned off, or unaffected?

Personally, I am drawn in by this voice. I can relate to her because I like to talk everything out and have that "souped-up conversation." I also like to have that feeling of being loved when I check my E-mail and I see I have new mail. I am that "typical" woman who is happy knowing just enough to get my personal tasks done. I would not find interest in being a computer whiz. I have no problem with asking for help either. Her essay also leaves me with some thoughts to ponder about communication between genders.

Is it a voice I might use effectively in my own writing? How might I do that?

I would like to use her voice and style in my own writing. She tries not to alienate anyone in her writing because she even includes Ralph in her essay as the example for men. She accepts Ralph for who he is. She writes on a personal level but also effectively combines her own opinions on men, women, and their E-mail. I can achieve this voice in my own writing by using language that everyone can relate to and identify with. As I am writing, I could pretend that I am simply talking to someone else, sort of like if someone only heard one side of a conversation. However, just as she used Ralph, I could include other people's opinions so my writing would not come across as offensive or biased.

Exploring **What?**

Writer

What primary and secondary ideas does the writer want to convey to me?

The writer wants me to understand that men and women communicate differently in style, length, and other ways. The writer also presents methods of communication for men and women, such as E-mail. Her secondary ideas revolve around her primary ones; they include many examples of how men and women communicate differently. Most women enjoy long talks, either face to face or on the phone, where they can unleash their feelings, dreams, or maybe just gossip. Women are not interested in being mechanical geniuses and would rather cooperate than compete. Most men fear intimacy or intimate conversations that involve emotions. They like to tackle challenges, such as figuring out a computer, and they hunger for competition. They would rather dominate than feel dominated by asking for directions or for help. However, a secondary idea that the writer also conveys is that not all people fall under the category of these typical men and women, especially women. She also says that E-mail can involve misinterpretation but it can also involve that happy medium of men competing for connection and women just feeling connected to others.

Reader

What connection do I have to these ideas?

I am a woman like the writer and can better understand her viewpoint. I am a very open person and would rather talk everything out and have everything out in the open. Since I started college, I have used E-mail to keep in touch with family and friends who are back home or at different schools. Before college I never really saw a use for E-mail, just as the writer did not see a use for knowing more about computers. I too only use the computer for writing papers and using E-mail. I know how hard it can be to get guys to open up and talk their feelings out. However, I have also known real tough acting guys who open up their feelings over E-mail and never say a sweet word in everyday

*face-to-face communication. I also can relate to the idea of feeling loved with
mail and being let down when I do not see "You have new mail."*

How well do I fit as the writer's intended reader? How does this affect
my responses?

*I think I fit well. She writes for both a male and female audience but
since she is a woman, her essay tends to have a female approach. She is not
male bashing. This aspect leads to different consequences for different readers, depending upon their sex. For me, the consequences are going away entertained and being able to relate to another woman. I also can accept that
men and women communicate differently and you have to roll with it instead
of trying to change who people are. I also have a new interest in an author
that I have just come into contact with and can look to for writing style and
technique.*

Have I had similar ideas, thoughts, feelings, or experiences?

*Yes. I have seen that I have no messages on E-mail and even though I
know that having mail does not determine how many friends I have, I still
may have a feeling of disappointment or loneliness. However, I move on and
minutes later I've forgotten that I did not have mail and I will check my E-
mail later to see if I have to go through the drama of determining how much
I am "loved" by others in this technological world. I am also frequently inde-
cisive like the author stated she was because she fears making a wrong decision. I have also experienced listening to unemotional, insincere male voices
on the phone or in person but then reading E-mail that is full of feeling, excitement, and sincerity from that same person.*

How do these help me to understand the primary points?

*My own experiences and the writer's examples help me to understand
the primary points. I can see that differences in communication not only
occur in my life but in the lives of others as well. I also see that others believe
it is an important enough topic to discuss and elaborate on. I see that in communication, such as between a writer and a reader, connections are made,
whether it be agreeing or disagreeing with someone else's ideas.*

Are these ideas I would like to explore in my own writing?

*Yes, but I think that I would want to at least address the fact that there
were some exceptions to the typical guy the writer portrays. In my writing,
I would like to elaborate on my thoughts and emotions but I also want to
make sure I do not offend anyone. I guess I always want to make everyone
happy or to make sure I have covered everything, sometimes giving too much*

information. I think that if I was writing about the difficulty of communicating between men and women I would want feedback to hear how different people handled different communication problems. My writing, just like the writer of this essay, would be an attempt to find answers or finally be willing to accept the differences between men and women.

Exploring **Why?**

Writer

Why has the author decided to write on this subject?
Her specialty is in sociolinguistics. Therefore, she likes to dwell on the different ways men and women communicate and ways to better those communication lines. Many of her writings focus on communication across genders. Also, communication is an important subject because it connects or disconnects people around the world.

What seem to be the writer's goals or purposes?
The writer's purpose seems to be in combining a simple, entertaining story about a woman's experience with computers with an underlying lesson of how men and women communicate differently and ways they can understand each other better. The writer is not trying to have her essay be a battle between the stereotypical man and woman. She just wants people to relate to her ideas.

Reader

Why do I respond the way I do to this reading? Why might others respond differently?
I think my answer here falls under the same thoughts as given in the Exploring What? reader part.

Have the writer's goals been achieved with me as the reader?
Yes, I was entertained. I definitely could relate to her ideas. I want to be able to understand both men and women better. I also want to be able to express my ideas to other people better.

What is my next step, if any, toward furthering those goals?
My next step would be trying to accept the realization that men and women just are the way they are. I also do not want to follow along that line of having miscommunication make or break my day.

Exploring How?

Writer

How is the essay organized?

The essay is organized as one side of a conversation. She is telling the readers how she sees the communication world. She also brings in expert linguists to back up her ideas. She is descriptive and full of examples to back up her views. She uses parentheses for little additions that tell the reader what she is thinking, to create humor, or to give an extra safety of accepting her essay and opinion by saying that some people or women are exceptions to the so-called typical woman. She tries to not be sexist by bringing in the character of Ralph as the male example. She uses writing techniques such as changing the words "men and women" to "boys and girls," possibly to indicate that communication problems occur throughout life.

What strategies has the writer adopted to best communicate her ideas and achieve her goals?

Many times the writer will start off a section of her essay with a question and then elaborate on an answer through personal examples. Some of her questions remain unanswered as if she is hoping that guys might get back to her with answers to some of her questions, such as why some men find it easier to open up on E-mail, why all the answers she received to her technical questions were from men, and where they found time to answer.

Reader

How might I adapt these strategies to my own immediate writing goals?

I can adapt these strategies by providing a medium for all readers to relate to. I could also pose thought processes for readers to dwell on while elaborating on my own thoughts and opinions. I should try to focus on a specific supporting point but I can also include other ideas around the main idea to make my writing more entertaining and intriguing.

◆ MAKING THE READING-WRITING CONNECTION

How did your reactions to Tannen's essay compare to Jennifer's? As you followed Jennifer's responses, did you notice how she elaborates on her answers, not just stopping with her first thoughts but explaining and looking for concrete examples and additional ideas? You see this when she analyzes

Tannen's assumptions about her reader, for example. Jennifer begins by noting Tannen's assumption of maturity and experience, but then zeros in on specifics, such as computer literacy. Note also that Jennifer's thinking builds on itself as she moves from question to question, with ideas such as the one about the "typical" woman becoming unifying devices or touchstones for her reactions. By the time she asks herself if she can use the kind of voice Tannen has used, Jennifer is really ready to apply what she has learned to how she might achieve her own best writing voice.

Notice, too, that the questions not only require Jennifer to look closely at her own responses, but also prompt her to see how others would respond to Tannen. This exploration leads her to conclude that she might test her thoughts by talking with others, for example, a male friend or fellow student. She might also want to talk with someone not familiar with e-mail. This informal research would expand her understanding of male/female communication and help her to think about her own future writing on the topic and her readers' responses to it. In fact, by the end of the "What?" questions, Jennifer has staked out her own territory on the topic and is ready to look at the "Why?" and "How?" for a more precise sense of purpose and organization.

In the "How" section of her discovery writing, Jennifer very successfully captures Tannen's tone and the overall shape of her essay when she characterizes it as being "one side of a conversation." She also pays close attention to Tannen's use of questions as part of this strategy and to the importance of using personal examples to answer at least some of her questions. By reading Tannen's essay so closely, Jennifer has added to her own bag of writing tricks.

In all but one case, Jennifer attempts to answer questions even when they might at first seem to overlap with other questions or answers already given. Asking questions from several different directions is like looking through a prism—the center is the same, but it becomes slightly different when viewed from each unique angle. By answering these diverse and comprehensive questions, Jennifer has discovered how personal this topic has become and is able to see that the bottom line for her is not wanting "to follow along that line of having miscommunication make or break my day," a clever use of the Clint Eastwood movie line, but also a very specific and important goal.

Developing the Habit

Using the *Who, What, Why,* and *How* questions is one of many ways to better understand what you read and in turn to communicate more effectively with others. It is important at the start to write out your full responses, as Jennifer did, which will make this reading style a habit of mind, so that in future readings you will find yourself asking the questions *as* you read, making the reading process more interesting because you are having active and informed conversation with the author. In future chapters of this book, at the conclusion of each essay, you will find specific *Who, What, Why,* and *How* questions to help you to practice this reading technique and develop in-depth responses. Moreover, engaging in active reading also provides a solid foundation for successful writing, as the next chapter will explain.

■▏ *Internet Activity.* Deborah Tannen has given several interviews that are available online. To learn more about Tannen's research on the relationship between gender and communication, locate some of these interviews and read them. You will find the *Boston Book Review* interview with Tannen at http://www.bookwire.com/bbr/interviews/amy-tannen.html. Your instructor might ask you to report back to the class with information and insights you gathered about Tannen's work.

◆ ◆ ◆ ◆ ◆ ◆ ◆ ◆ C H A P T E R   2 ◆ ◆ ◆ ◆ ◆ ◆ ◆ ◆

The Reader-Writer Interaction

◆ ◆ ◆ ◆ ◆

The connections between reading and writing are strong: in both activities you use language to create meaning. In Chapter 1, you explored the reader-writer relationship from the reader's point of view and saw how writing can help you to understand and remember what you read. In this chapter, you will see how reading can help you to improve your writing.

◆ DEVELOPING YOUR WRITING SKILLS

As you read the essays in this book, you will be shaping and developing your writing skills. Reading can supply you with content for your own writing; you will discover new ideas and new ways of thinking about the world. Even when you already have a topic in mind, reading can help you to come up with the materials to enlarge and support that topic.

As you read, you will also encounter a wide range of writing styles, ways to approach a topic, and methods for organizing and presenting ideas. Most of the time, you don't pay much attention to these features: they just seep into your mind with the rest of the material. But in this textbook, you will examine the reading-writing connection more consciously than you have probably done before. By asking questions about the texts you read (Why did the author begin this way? What is the point of this comparison? How does this example work?), you will see how a writer puts an essay together; and that knowledge will help you to plan and develop your own essays.

◆ CONSTRUCTING AN ESSAY

Writing an essay is a lot like building a house. A writer fits separate pieces of meaning together to make an understandable statement. If you want to write well, you need to learn the basic skills of constructing an essay.

Despite differences in education and personality, most writers follow a remarkably similar process of *discovering, organizing, drafting, revising,* and *editing.* Whether building a single paragraph or a ten-page article, successful writers usually follow a series of steps that go roughly like this:

1. Find a topic, generate ideas, and collect information. (Discovering)
2. Focus on a central idea and map out an approach. (Organizing)
3. Write a first draft. (Drafting)
4. Rework and improve the draft. (Revising)
5. Proofread and correct mechanical errors. (Editing)

If you follow these steps, you will be able to write more productively and more easily. The process will give you a sense of direction for producing a well-written essay. But keep in mind that this sequence is only a general guide. The steps often overlap and loop around. The important point to remember is that writing is done in stages; successful writers take the time to construct their essays step by step and to polish and finish their work.

Generating Ideas

One of the most difficult challenges of writing is coming up with a topic. Even when you are responding to a reading, you still have to decide what to say about it. As you saw in Chapter 1, the *Who, What, Why,* and *How* questions not only help you to gain a better understanding of what you read, but they also unlock your own thinking about a topic and lead you to discover ideas and viewpoints to write about. Writing out your responses to the *Who, What, Why,* and *How* questions will produce a wide range of thoughts and impressions that you can draw on for your own essays. These questions will also lead you to examine and perhaps adopt a writer's strategies and techniques. Thinking about **audience, purpose, tone,** organization, and use of language will help you to make important decisions about the style and approach you want to use in your writing.

As you review your responses to the *Who, What, Why,* and *How* questions, try to identify a subject area that appeals to you. Many writers begin with a general topic, which they narrow and refine as they work. One good way to sift through a broad topic is to do some brainstorming about it.

Brainstorming involves making a list of everything you can think of about a topic. You might list feelings, ideas, facts, examples, personal experiences, problems—anything that comes to mind. There is no need to write in sentences; just jot down words and phrases. Don't try to organize your thoughts; just list them as they occur to you. If you give yourself a time limit, you'll find that ideas come faster that way. You can also brainstorm with classmates or friends. You'll discover that their ideas help to trigger more of yours. When you've finished brainstorming, reread your list and mark promising ideas.

Having read "Gender Gap in Cyberspace" in Chapter 1, Jennifer Hoff wanted to write about the differences in the way males and females go about performing some activity, so she used brainstorming to look for a specific area to focus on.

```
what do men and women talk about?
how do they behave differently in some situations?
at parties
on dates
at concerts
at sports events
when talking to members of the opposite sex
when talking to members of the same sex
one-on-one vs. in groups
with their parents and families
on the telephone
in classes or in the dorm
at church or at weddings or funerals
do men have heart-to-heart talks?
gossip, small talk
jokes and pranks—any differences?
```

Making this list helped Jennifer to identify several specific situations she could use. The brainstorming also stirred up memories of some observations she had made at the time of her grandmother's death. She now had an idea she could focus on for her essay: the different ways that men and women behave at funerals.

If brainstorming doesn't help you to settle on a topic, you can try other strategies: talking into a tape recorder, discussing ideas with your instructor or classmates, interviewing someone with expertise in the subject, or rereading your answers to the *Who, What, Why,* and *How* questions. You can also try shifting the focus of your topic or coming up with a different one. The point is to keep working until you can find something you'd like to write about.

Making a Plan

Once you have reviewed your responses to the *Who, What, Why,* and *How* questions and done some brainstorming to find a topic, you need to decide on a specific focus for your paper. One way to find direction for your writing is to ask yourself, "What point do I want to make?" The answer to this question will lead you to your main idea, or **thesis.** After you decide what point you want to make, then you can sort through your notes and decide which details to use and which ones to toss.

A thesis says something *about* the subject of an essay. As a reader, your job is to discover the writer's thesis. The answers to the *What* and *Why* questions will direct you to a writer's main ideas. As a writer, your job is to provide a clear thesis for your readers. Look at the difference between a subject and a thesis in these examples:

Subject: Differences in the ways men and women use computers
Thesis: Men want to master a computer's technology; women just want the thing to work.

Subject: Communication styles of males and females
Thesis: Males often struggle to get the upper hand in a conversation, while women tend to maintain an appearance of cooperation.

You can, of course, change or refine your thesis as the paper develops, but having an idea of what you want to say makes the actual writing considerably easier.

Organizing Your Ideas

Having a plan or scratch outline to follow makes you less likely to wander from your main idea and allows you to concentrate on one idea at a time as you write. You can begin by making a list of all the points you want to cover in your essay. Review the list and cross off any ideas that don't fit or points that are too similar to other points. Then revise your list, putting the ideas in the order that you plan to cover them. Specific organizational strategies will be discussed in later chapters; but, in general, if there is no chronology (time order) involved or there are no steps that belong in a certain order, begin with a fairly important and interesting point to get your readers' attention, and end with your strongest point to leave your audience feeling that you have said something worthwhile. The following brief outline is based on the thesis that Jennifer Hoff devised after arranging her brainstorming ideas:

> *Thesis:* Since people respond to death in the same way they cope with life, men and women handle it differently.

1. Opening—grandma's death
   Phone calls from friends:
   Jim's was short and disappointing to me
   Jane was more interested and supporting (over the phone)

2. My friends at the wake
   Jim showed up but didn't say much, but joked with my dad
   Jane didn't show—said she couldn't handle "that sort of thing"

3. My realization: men and women react to death in different ways
   Differing reactions depend on how they deal with life

4. Men and women at the wake
   Actions: women hugged and kissed; men shook hands, nodded
   Conversation: men talked about sports, jobs; women talked about other people

5. At the funeral
   People continued their roles
   Men were strong and silent
   Women held on to others, cried openly

6. Each gender has specific traits: my friends as examples
   Jim—supportive but not willing to be intimate
   Jane—supportive but too emotional to show up

7. Women: treat life like a soap opera
   Interested in other people's business (gossip)
   Ruled by emotions but provide comfort
8. Men: less social and outgoing
   Put others at ease—helps put themselves at ease
   Want to keep emotions in check but helps them to do
      what needs to be done
9. Conclusion—both ways of dealing with life and death
   are effective

Writing a Draft

If you have an outline or plan to work from, you shouldn't have any trouble producing the first draft of your paper. Getting started is probably the hardest part. Don't worry about writing a perfect introduction at this point. Remember that you are writing a *draft:* you can revise it later when you have a clearer, stronger sense of where the paper is headed. The main goal is to get your ideas down on paper in a reasonably complete form.

One good reason for giving yourself plenty of time to write an essay is that you may get stuck or feel you are running out of ideas. When that happens, try rereading what you have already written. Writing is a back-and-forth process; writers frequently read through what they've already written to find clues about what to write next. You can also return to the discovery step in the process to explore the topic further and gather more ideas. Start by reviewing your responses to the *Who, What, Why,* and *How* questions; this material may provide the inspiration that you are looking for. If you still need help, consider using one or more of these methods for generating additional material for your draft:

1. *Freewriting.* Start with the idea or point you are stuck on. Put it at the top of the page or computer screen. Then, write nonstop for a limited period of time, usually five to ten minutes. Don't worry about grammar, punctuation, or spelling; focus on recording your thoughts as they come to you. The most important thing is to keep writing as fast as you can without stopping. After you finish, reread what you have written, and underline anything you might be able to use. If you want to pursue an idea that surfaces in the freewriting, copy the key sentence on another sheet of paper or computer screen, and take off from it for another five or ten minutes. You can repeat this step as many times as you need to—as long as you think it's productive and helps you to advance the topic you're writing about.

2. *Clustering.* This is a visual way of generating ideas. Because it's nonlinear, you may find that it frees you from conventional patterns of thinking and enables you to probe ideas more deeply and creatively. Choose a single word or phrase that seems to be the focus of what you want to explore, write it in the center of a full sheet of paper, and draw a circle around it. Surround that focus idea with related words and phrases that you connect to it with lines (like spokes in a wheel). If some of the satellite ideas lead to more specific clusters, write them down as well. The following example (Figure 2–1) shows how Jennifer Hoff used clustering to develop the last section of her essay, "Dealing with Death, Coping with Life."

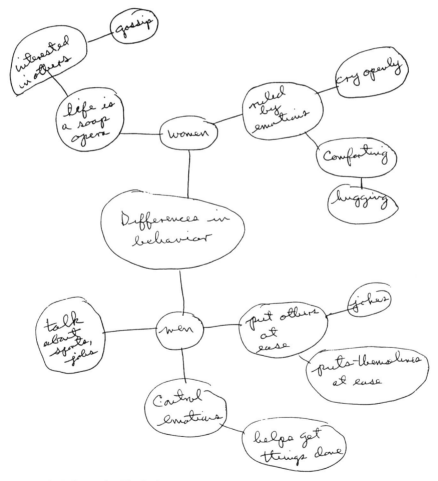

Figure 2–1 Sample Clustering

3. *Questioning.* Try to look at your essay from the readers' point of view by using some of the *Who, What, Why,* and *How* questions. Ask yourself questions like these: "Who is my main audience? What readers do I want to reach? What specific purpose do I have in regard to those readers? What primary and secondary points do I want to make? What explanations and information do my readers need to understand my points? How do I want my readers to perceive me?" Returning to these basic issues should stimulate your thinking and put you back on track with your draft.

As you work on your draft, keep a spare piece of paper alongside you. Writers often think of just-right words or details they want to use somewhere else in an essay, and you can jot these down on the spare page as they occur to you. Don't trust your busy memory to retrieve such inspirations later. Even when you compose on the computer, you need a pen and pad at your side to record useful thoughts and fleeting ideas.

Improving the Draft

When you have finished the first draft, set it aside, at least overnight, so you can look at it in a new light. This process of looking at your draft again is called **revising,** and the term literally means "re-seeing." In fact, you want to try to see your work now with different eyes—the eyes of a reader.

When revising your draft, concentrate on making major improvements in content and organization. Save the smaller changes for the editing stage. Ask yourself these questions:

◆ Have I made my thesis clear to the readers?
◆ Does the introduction get the readers' attention?
◆ Are there any points that the readers might not understand?
◆ Do I need to give the readers more reasons and examples?
◆ Have I shown the readers how every point relates to the thesis?
◆ Does the conclusion tie everything together for the readers?

When you are satisfied with the changes you've made to improve content and organization, you can move on to matters of sentence structure, spelling, word choice, punctuation, capitalization, and mechanics. This is the **editing** stage, and you cannot skip it. Readers quickly become annoyed by writing that is full of errors.

The following checklist gives additional suggestions that will help you revise and edit your first draft.

◆ ◆ ◆ *Checklist for Revising and Editing* ◆ ◆ ◆

1. Let your work sit for a day to clear your head and increase your chances of spotting problems.
2. Read your draft out loud, or ask someone to read it to you. Listen for anything that sounds unclear or incomplete or awkward.
3. Ask some reliable readers to look over your draft and suggest improvements.
4. Don't try to do everything at once: deal with big problems first, and save time to take a break when you need one.
5. Slow down when you edit: look at each word and punctuation mark individually, and watch for mistakes that you know you usually make.

◆ SAMPLE STUDENT ESSAY WITH AUTHOR'S COMMENTS

Here is the final draft of the essay that Jennifer Hoff wrote about the differences in male and female behavior at her grandmother's funeral. Jennifer's comments in the margin call attention to some of the strategies she used in presenting her ideas.

```
Jennifer Hoff
English 1092, Section 2
20 April 1998


          Dealing with Death, Coping with Life

    My grandma's death came as something
of a shock to my family. I was pretty
shaken up by this unfortunate event. Two
of my friends happened to call me even
before they knew of my family's loss. My
friend Jim called right after I found
out that my grandma had passed away. He
talked to me slowly, sensing something
```

I start with the examples of my two friends.

was wrong, but he seemed hesitant to come right out and ask what the problem was. I told him about my grandma, expecting some kind of comforting response. But he simply said, "I'm sorry. I'll let you go. If there is anything I can do just let me know, okay? 'Bye." I did not understand why he was in such a rush to get off the phone with me.

Shortly afterwards my friend Jane called. She also sensed that something was wrong, but she was quick to ask what the matter was. After I told her my grandma had passed away, her immediate response was, "Are you okay? I'll be right over." She wanted to know everything that happened and how all my family members were coping. I told her that I would talk to her later because I had to be with my family at the moment. However, I was glad to know that my friend was truly interested in our loss.

A few days later, sitting at the funeral home greeting people I knew and people I never saw before, I was longing to see the face of a friend. I didn't really expect my friends to attend the wake, but I was hoping someone might come to raise my spirits. Finally, a friend did show up. It was Jim, who came with his mom. At first he didn't say much, talking only when his mom or I said something first. But when my dad joined in our conversation, he and Jim took turns telling jokes. Like most of the guys at the wake, my dad and Jim acted as sources of comic relief, trying to create an atmosphere of humor and lightheartedness. Their behavior told people, "Hey, no matter what has happened, everything is fine."

In this ¶, I wanted to show the differences in Jane's reactions.

This ¶ shifts to the funeral home and how my friends behaved.

I start to focus on gender differences here.

As for my female friends, I'm sure they would have given me endless empathy, if any of them had shown up! I wondered how Jane could seem so concerned about my family but then never bother to attend the wake and give her support. She later explained to me that she wanted to come and was all ready to walk out the door, but she just could not handle "that sort of thing." I thought it curious that Jane said she could not handle a part of life that every person is inevitably bound to experience.

In this ¶ I continue to develop the differences.

My reaction to Jane leads to my main idea.

As I continued to observe those people behind the signatures on the guest list, I noted their behavior as they engaged in conversation. I also thought about my friends' reactions, and it began to dawn on me that the way people react to death seems to mirror the way they cope with life. And men and women respond quite differently.

In this ¶ I was ready to state my thesis.

All the guests approached my grieving family with the usual "sorry about so and so" speech. Most of the women offered a hug and sometimes even a kiss on the cheek. Most of the men seemed to feel that a handshake or a simple nod of the head would suffice. After these initial greetings, the conversations continued to differ just as the approaches did. The men sneaked away to corners of the room and poured their hearts out talking about sports or their jobs. My dad and his co-workers talked about which football teams would win this year. I also heard my older brother and his friend challenge each other to some sort of athletic contest. By contrast, the women stayed together in the middle of the room and discussed

In this ¶ I provide support by directly comparing the two styles of conversation.

which family members turned out to be losers and which ones had not bothered to show up. I heard my aunt say, "Did you see how all of Uncle Ed's kids showed up in jeans?" My mom commented on my grandma's appearance: "Doesn't her make-up look nice? The undertaker did a wonderful job on her." Other women agreed and also discussed her clothes and the floral arrangements in the funeral home.

At the funeral the next day, everyone fulfilled their expected duties. A few selected men, looking strong and steady, were pallbearers, wearing white gloves as they carried the heavy casket. I thought the white gloves seemed to portray them as knights or heroes completing their acts of chivalry and civic duty. The rest of the congregation followed behind, some--mostly women-- clutching the arms of another person for comfort. Most of these women were crying openly. However, I did not see any men shed tears (although some man must have cried secretly because I heard someone in the distance say, "I never saw him cry before").

I guess each gender has its own specific characteristics or tendencies. Both sexes put restrictions on what they can or want to do emotionally in life. Jim and Jane would be supportive as long as it didn't exceed their personal limits. Jim would be there for me only if we did not have a serious, intimate conversation. Jane would be there for me as long as she could keep her composure and not have an emotional breakdown. I could see in my friends the same personality differences I saw in the men and women at the funeral home.

This ¶ offers more support by comparing behavior at the funeral.

In this ¶ I make generalizations about the differences I observed.

Most women treat life as a soap opera. Every aspect of life is a big deal and something to talk about. I realized this when the women at the wake seemed to be concerned with everyone else but themselves. Basically, they were all gossiping. They were also dominated by their emotions. For many women, tears are a natural reaction to both good and bad circumstances. Even my friend Jane let her emotions control her: she could not handle the emotions that she felt at wakes and funerals, so she stayed at home. Being ruled by emotions, however, is not always a bad thing. Women's open expressions of feeling can be a major source of comfort. Most women at the wake did not think twice about giving a hug to anyone, man or woman. These women may have gossiped about those same people afterwards, but only because their personalities are prone to dwell on every aspect of life, especially the social parts. They simply get caught up in everyone's business while trying to deal with their own personal concerns.

In the next two ¶s I discuss the pros and cons of the differences.

Men tend to approach life a little differently. They take a back seat during the social transactions that women feed on. They would rather be the heroes who rescue the women from their emotions by making them laugh, as my dad and Jim did, or by carrying the heavy casket and taking the burden off others. By supplying comic relief, men also help put themselves at ease, suppressing the emotions on the verge of being unleashed. Most men are not being insincere when they don't ask what is wrong or when they give a handshake instead of a hug. They just seem to have

a hands-off approach to the emotions
mixed in with life. But a man's choice
not to let his emotions rule him is not
altogether unfortunate. For instance, my
friend Jane might have shown up at the
wake if she were a male. By containing
their emotions, men gain the control
they need to carry out the difficult jobs
that need to be done in difficult
situations.

My observations are far from
conclusive. People are more complicated
than they appear to be. But I saw human
beings facing the death of a loved one
in the same way they handle life. Women
follow their emotions; men rein them in.
Both reactions seem to work.

In my conclusion
I acknowledge
the limits of my
ideas and sum up
my main point.

◆ ◆ ◆ ▇ **Using Internet Resources** ◆ ◆ ◆

Throughout this book, you will find suggestions for using sources from the Internet to help you with your reading and your writing. The following article gives you some practical advice on how to make your Internet searches more efficient and more productive.

Twelve Tips to Search the Internet Successfully

BRUCE MAXWELL

Bruce Maxwell is the author of *How to Find Health Information on the Internet* and *How to Access the Federal Government on the Internet*. This article appeared in the November 6–8, 1998, edition of *USA Weekend*.

Trying to navigate the World Wide Web without help is like trying to   1
do research in a library that has no librarians, a jumble of card catalogs list-
ing just a fraction of the collection, and 320 million books.

To flounder less and learn more in your maiden voyages on the Web,   2
follow these tips.

ONE: If your subject is broad (cancer, archaeology, politics), start with a directory—such as Yahoo! (http://www.yahoo.com)—that categorizes Web sites by subject. Just pick the most likely subject, then drill down through layers of subcategories until you find what you want.

TWO: If your subject is narrow (such as a particular bed-and-breakfast you want to try), choose a search engine: AltaVista (http://altavista.digital.com), HotBot (http://www.hotbot.com), Excite (http://www.excite.com), Infoseek (http://www.infoseek.com) or Northern Light (http://www.nlsearch.com).

THREE: For comprehensive research, use several search engines or try a meta-search engine such as MetaCrawler (http://www. metacrawler.com) that simultaneously queries numerous engines.

FOUR: Before using a search engine, read any instructions it offers. Yes, these documents can be snoozers. But each engine has its quirks, and knowing them will help you craft a more accurate search.

FIVE: When choosing keywords for a search engine, select six to eight words to help narrow your search. If you type just one or two words, you'll likely get thousands or even millions of documents. Use nouns whenever possible, and put the most important words first. Put a "+" before any word you want to include, and a "−" before any word you want to exclude (this works with most engines).

SIX: To increase your search's accuracy, use phrases instead of single words. Put quotation marks around the phrase.

SEVEN: Many search engines will let you refine the results of your initial query. Do it.

EIGHT: When you find a good Web site about your topic, check whether it provides links to similar sites.

NINE: You may be able to guess the address of specific sites. Many are "www," a period, the name or acronym of the site's operator, a period and three letters denoting the site's type. Thus: www.microsoft.com (commercial), www.fbi.gov (federal government) and www.harvard. edu (education).

TEN: Double-check your spelling. You'd be amazed at how many people misspell words in their queries.

ELEVEN: Keep in mind that even if you type a precise query, many of the documents returned won't be applicable. Computers (and search engines) aren't perfect.

TWELVE: Remember: The Internet does not contain the sum of all knowledge. You may still need to hit the library.

Where to Get Searching Help

Many excellent searching guides and sites are available on the Internet. Among the best: 3

> Tutorial: Guide to Effective Searching of the Internet. <http://thewebtools.com/searchgoodies/tutorial.htm>
>
> Yahoo! How to Search the Web. <http://www.yahoo.com/Computers_and_Internet/Internet/World_Wide_Web/Searching the_Web/How_to_Search_the_Web/>
>
> Search Engine Watch. <http://searchenginewatch.com>
>
> How to Search the World Wide Web: A Tutorial for Beginners and Non-Experts. <http://www.ultranet.com/~egrlib/tutor.htm>
>
> The Spider's Apprentice: How to Use Web Search Engines. <http://www.monash.com/spidap.html>
>
> Searching the Internet. <http://wwwscout.cs.wisc.edu/scout/toolkit/searching/>

◆ ◆ ◆

◆ ◆ ◆ Internet Sources for Writers ◆ ◆ ◆

The following Web sites and online services provide help for writers at all stages of the writing process:

- ◆ *The University of Victoria's Hypertext Writer's Guide* will help you through the basics of the writing process and answer questions about essays, paragraphs, sentences, words, and documentation. <http://webserver.maclab.comp.uvic.ca/writersguide/Pages/StartHere.html>
- ◆ *Paradigm Online Writing Assistant,* by Chuck Gilford, offers helpful advice on writing various types of papers. It contains sections on discovering, organization, and editing. <http://www.idbsu.edu/english/cguilfor/paradigm/>
- ◆ *Writer's Web* contains sections for generating ideas, drafting and organizing, focusing and connecting ideas, creating and supporting an argument, editing a draft, punctuation, sentence structure and mechanics,

editing for clarity and style, documentation, and using sources effectively. <http://www.urich.edu/~writing/wweb.html>

♦ *The Able Writer: A Rhetoric and Handbook,* by Dr. John P. Broderick of Old Dominion University, is filled with advice and exercises to help you learn the basics of writing papers. <http://www.odu.edu/~jpb/ablewriter.html>

♦ *Guide to Grammar and Writing,* from Capital Community-Technical College, gives advice on writing at the sentence, paragraph, and essay level. <http://webster.comment.edu/HP/pages/darling/original.thm>

♦ *Composition Site on the World Wide Web* lists links to a wide variety of topics about writing and composition. If the other sites don't have the answers you're looking for, then try this one. <http://www.geocities.com/Athens/Oracle/4184/>

CHAPTER 3

Strategies for Discovering and Relating Experiences

Narration

◆ ◆ ◆ ◆ ◆

Narrative writing tells what happens over time.

◆ Writers use narrative to bring ideas and experiences to life.

◆ Effective narrations are organized according to time or logic.

◆ Writers must decide when to summarize events and when to narrate them in detail.

Among the oldest and most powerful ways people come to understand their own lives and to communicate with one another is through the sharing of their stories. This chapter introduces you first to **discovery writing,** a method of recording thoughts and experiences for one's own enjoyment or future use. Although such writing might lead a writer to any number of the formal strategies explor0ed in this book, **narration** is a logical starting point because it depends so extensively on the memories and details that are uncovered in the pages of a diary or class journal.

◆ INFORMAL DISCOVERY WRITING

Novelist Virginia Woolf called the ideas generated in her writer's diary "the diamonds of the dustheap." Like most good writers, she recognized the importance of having a place to think regularly about her life and the world around her. In the diary, she was free to let her mind wander in its own way and time. In addition to the everyday pleasure of writing without worrying about a reader's feelings or judgments, it was in this diary that many of her stories were born and took shape.

A diary is one of the many forms of discovery writing. Like freewriting and brainstorming, keeping a diary is an unstructured process in which writers are able to explore past or present experience for its value to them—and possibly, later, to others. Among the most famous of diaries is holocaust victim Anne Frank's, which she began before she went, at age thirteen, into hiding with her family to escape Nazi persecution. Here is her first entry, written on June 14, 1942:

> I'll begin from the moment I got you [her diary], the moment I saw you lying on the table among my other birthday presents. (I went along when you were bought, but that didn't count.)
>
> On Friday, June 12, I was awake at six o'clock, which isn't surprising, since it was my birthday. But I'm not allowed to get up at that hour, so I had to control my curiosity until quarter to seven. When I couldn't wait any longer, I went to the dining room, where Moortje (the cat) welcomed me by rubbing against my legs.
>
> A little after seven I went to Daddy and Mama and then to the living room to open my presents, and *you* were the first thing I saw, maybe one of my nicest presents. . . .

Throughout the three years before her death in the Nazi concentration camps, Anne turned to her diary, and through it to an imagined friend, Kitty, to reflect on and shape her adolescent self-image:

> I hope I will be able to confide everything to you, as I have never been able to confide to anyone, and I hope you will be a great source of comfort and support.

And later she added:

> So far you truly have been a great source of comfort to me, and so has Kitty, whom I now write to regularly. This way of keeping a diary

is much nicer, and now I can hardly wait for those moments when I'm able to write in you.

Oh, I'm so glad I brought you along!

Anne's diary was often the place where she tried to work out her relationship with her mother. Here is a longer entry, from January 2, 1944, a year and a half after she went into hiding:

> This morning, when I had nothing to do, I leafed through the pages of my diary and came across so many letters dealing with the subject of "Mother" in such strong terms that I was shocked. I said to myself, "Anne, is that really you talking about hate? Oh, Anne, how could you?"
>
> I continued to sit with the open book in my hand and wonder why I was filled with so much anger and hate that I had to confide it all to you. I tried to understand the Anne of last year and make apologies for her, because as long as I leave you with these accusations and don't attempt to explain what prompted them, my conscience won't be clear. I was suffering then (and still do) from moods that kept my head under water (figuratively speaking) and allowed me to see things only from my own perspective, without calmly considering what the others—those whom I, with my mercurial temperament, had hurt or offended—had said, and then acting as they would have done.
>
> I hid inside myself, thought of no one but myself and calmly wrote down all my joy, sarcasm and sorrow in my diary. Because this diary has become a kind of memory book, it means a great deal to me, but I could easily write "over and done with" on many of its pages.
>
> I was furious at Mother (and still am a lot of the time). It's true, she didn't understand me, but I didn't understand her either. Because she loved me, she was tender and affectionate, but because of the difficult situations I put her in, and the sad circumstances in which she found herself, she was nervous and irritable, so I can understand why she was often short with me.
>
> I was offended, took it far too much to heart and was insolent and beastly to her, which, in turn, made her unhappy. We were caught in a vicious circle of unpleasantness and sorrow. Not a very happy period for either of us, but at least it's coming to an end. I didn't want to see what was going on, and I felt very sorry for myself, but that's understandable too.
>
> Those violent outbursts on paper are simply expressions of anger that, in normal life, I could have worked off by locking myself in my room and stamping my foot a few times or calling Mother names behind her back.

The period of tearfully passing judgment on Mother is over. I've grown wiser and Mother's nerves are a bit steadier. Most of the time I manage to hold my tongue when I'm annoyed, and she does too; so on the surface, we seem to be getting along better. But there's one thing I can't do, and that's to love Mother with the devotion of a child.

I soothe my conscience with the thought that it's better for unkind words to be down on paper than for Mother to have to carry them around in her heart.

Although Anne Frank was never able to grow into adulthood and complete her goal of becoming a writer, she kept her diary with that future in mind. Clearly there were many diamonds she might have polished later.

◆ FOCUSED DISCOVERY WRITING

In preparation for exploring and later narrating a relationship of her own, Tara Coburn, a freshman student, was asked to read these selections from Anne's diary. While she might simply have used the ideas in the diary to do some brainstorming or freewriting of her own, Tara instead used a few simple *Who, What,* and *Why* questions to take a closer look at Anne's diary and to better understand her own responses to Anne's ideas. This approach to discovery writing remains informal, meant primarily for the writer's own use, but because it is more directed, it helps a writer to progress toward fuller understanding of the topic, as well as to more focused attention on how and why that topic might be of interest to others.

Starting with *Who,* Tara found Anne to be "caring, sincere, and natural," someone that she "would like to be friends with." Of Anne's tone, she concluded that it "reminds me of the tone I have used when I write letters or e-mail to friends, especially if I have exciting news." Based on this comfort and familiarity, Tara also found herself drawn to the use of a diary for working out personal problems, especially the challenge of a daughter sorting out her feelings about her mother. More specifically, in Anne's movement back and forth between self-criticism and feeling "wiser and more mature," Tara found a comforting model for handling her own relationship with her mother:

> Even though most teenagers are not as isolated
> as Anne was, some still do not have supportive
> friends to whom they can tell their problems. A
> majority of teens would identify with Anne's
> feelings about her mother. I feel the same way,

```
sometimes. I regret some things that I said and
did now that I am older, in the same way Anne
looked upon her past.
```

She also identified in the diary an important purpose for doing discovery writing:

```
    Anne is challenging herself to become a better
person. She is disturbed by the ways she has acted
in the past, and she wants to behave differently.
Anne realized that she has been unfair, vicious,
and unloving at times. At the time that she is
writing the third passage, Anne is a very
different person from the person she was before.
She wants to continue to change for the better.
```

◆ NARRATION: RELATING DISCOVERIES TO READERS

Narration is the challenge of plucking an uncut or rough diamond out of the dustheap of our personal experiences and turning it into an essay that others will find entertaining and meaningful. After reading Anne Frank's diary for the *Who, What,* and *Why,* Tara took a close look at the *How* and then, using Anne as a model, she did her own discovery writing. Finally, she decided to write the following essay about her own mother. As you read her essay, be sure to underline major ideas and note your responses or observations about her writing style in the margins.

```
                    A Better Place

    The phrase "be careful what you wish for" really    1
started to make sense to me when I was sixteen. I had
always wished that my parents would stop fighting. When
they announced that they were getting a divorce,
though, I regretted ever hoping for it. Later that
year, when my mother moved into an apartment, the
relationship between us began to change drastically.
During the first few weeks that she was gone, I handled
these changes very badly. I thought that my
relationship with my mother was doomed. Gradually,
however, my expectations became more realistic and my
```

perspective broadened. I now realize that the divorce
has actually brought my mother and me to a better
place.

Before my parents even began considering divorce, 2
my ties with my mother were not as strong as I wanted
them to be. We tried to become close, but our
relationship always took a backseat to the
relationship between my parents. Near the end of their
marriage, not a day went by that they did not have a
major fight. The constant turmoil and distractions in
the house kept both of us from becoming close with
each other. Because of the stress and unhappiness in
our lives, our relationship was never more than a
shallow bond.

Even though the situation between us was not what 3
I wanted, the changes after the divorce hit me very
hard. For a while, I thought that I was dealing with
them well. It was not until the night that my mother
moved out that I panicked. I remember standing outside
where she had dropped me off when I suddenly realized
that I was going into a house where my mother did not
live. Feelings of betrayal and abandonment that I had
kept hidden began to overwhelm me. As I began to cry,
I turned to her and started screaming. I told her that
she did not love me and she was going to forget about
me. I knew that I did not mean what I said, but I
could not help myself. The pain of that loss really
deafened me from hearing how awful I sounded, and I
said a lot that I wish I had not.

Because I have had time to reflect on that night, I 4
have come to realize that I reacted very irrationally.
It was my own stubborn selfishness that prevented me
from realizing that our new situation was a chance to
become closer. This opportunity became clear to me one
day when I was visiting my mother's apartment. My
father called to talk to her, and soon after, the
distantly familiar sounds of shouting started coming
from the other room. I was shocked. It had been a
pleasantly long time since I had heard them fight. That
was a major turning point in my view of my mother
because I could see how calmer, friendlier
environments made both of our lives better. I see now

that my mother was trying to help both of us while I
was busy feeling sorry for myself. In the end, a lot
of the hurt subsided from both of us, and I was able
to see that she really made a wise choice.

Seeing my relationship with my mother from both of   5
our perspectives not only made me feel better, but it
also changed how I treat my mother. Before I judge her
actions, I try to remind myself that she has gone
through a lot. She and I are very different people,
and I have accepted that I will not always agree with
her. This was probably one of the most valuable things
that I have discovered. I never really knew her before
the divorce because our lives were so hectic.
Communicating with her is much easier now, so I have
gotten to know her better. We are different people,
but I really like the person that she is. We have fun
together. Our relationship is how I had always wanted
it to be; it just needed space.

◆ ◆ ◆ Writer's Workshop ◆ ◆ ◆
Responding to a Narrative

Before looking more closely at Tara's essay as an example of narration, analyze your responses to her story using the *Who, What, Why,* and
How questions in Chapter 1 (pp. 3–4). You might want to compare your answers to those of your classmates by discussing them in small groups or by
passing your answers around to two or three other students.

◆ GETTING STARTED ON A NARRATIVE

Most narratives are lively stories that bring the writer's experience to
life through vivid language and concrete detail. After doing either informal
or structured discovery writing, a writer seeks a more specific **purpose** for
turning a memory into a narrative essay, or, in reverse, he or she may begin
with an idea to be explained and the narration becomes a method for illustrating or convincing the reader. In both cases, narratives offer readers insights that have been gained from experience and that in turn might be of
value to others. For Tara, the memory of her evolving relationship with her
mother made her realize how much closer they have become, an insight
which gives her a valuable thesis to share with others her age. For columnist

Mike Royko, a childhood memory of the day Jackie Robinson integrated major league baseball in Chicago becomes an opportunity to make the abstract idea of prejudice very human and real.

◆ ORGANIZING A NARRATIVE

Who are the best storytellers you know? Which ones put you to sleep? Narratives are often thought to be especially easy because events can be simply retold as they happened, in **chronological order.** From experience, though, we know that a good narrative writer often improves on real life by adding to, deleting from, or reordering events. Such changes make the stories clearer in our minds and give them greater drama and energy.

Having a definite purpose helps a writer to organize a narrative according to time (for example, from morning to night) or in a logical sequence of events. Choosing the right framework for the story and the right events is key to success. Tara decided to describe her evolving relationship with her mother by stages: before, during, and after the divorce. This approach organizes her changing feelings toward her mother and thus unifies the story and her purpose for recounting it. Writer George Orwell uses the events surrounding his shooting of an elephant—and within the events the distinctly different responses of various people to these scenes—to underscore his complex thesis: "it gave me a better glimpse than I had had before of the real nature of imperialism—the real motives for which despotic governments act."

Writers also have the option to rearrange events and time, using **flashbacks** or digressions, for example, to provide contrast between then and now or to fill in information a reader needs to understand an event. Tara's memory of the shouting matches between her parents provides a vivid contrast to the "calmer, friendlier" post-divorce reality.

◆ DEVELOPING A NARRATIVE

Developing a narrative involves careful decision making. Some parts of the story must be summarized to capture only the important elements, while others must be drawn in very specific detail for emphasis. In each section of her essay, Tara provides an overview of her feelings during that time and concretely explains the experiences that led to these feelings. Yet in some cases, she recalls a very specific interaction with her mother to really drive her point home. It is in these scenes—for example, walking alone into the house for the first time—that Tara rises to the challenge of bringing ideas to life through careful phrasing and precise detail. She wasn't simply afraid; she "panicked." Showing us her tears and her screams helps us to sympathize with her conclusion that "I said a lot that I wish I had not."

Another very effective way to develop a narrative is to use carefully selected dialogue that captures the tone of a conversation or perhaps the personality of a person in the story. In telling the story of "The Death and Life of a Gay Naval Officer," Andre Dubus writes the following two lines from a conversation he had with a crew member:

> "Did y'all know about him?"
> "We all knew. We didn't care. We would have followed him into hell."

These short, emotional sentences capture both the personality of the crew and an essential component of Dubus's purpose for writing.

◆ OPENING AND CLOSING A NARRATIVE

Before writing, narrative writers must determine whether to state their thesis directly or let their story speak for itself. Some writers, such as Maxine Hong Kingston, prefer to begin and end their essays with the start and close of the events, implying their purpose in the way they select scenes and phrase their descriptions:

> "You must not tell anyone," my mother said, "what I am about to tell you. In China your father had a sister who killed herself. She jumped into the family well. We say that your father has all brothers because it is as if she had never been born."

This dramatic opening brings the reader immediately into the story, leaving the specific purpose for telling this story open-ended. Others, such as Tara, use the introduction to establish their thesis and provide the reader with a reason for being interested in their personal story. Conclusions in these essays can pose a challenge. In her original draft, for example, Tara included this paragraph as a conclusion:

> Unfortunately, for my mother and I to find
> balance in our relationship, we first had to
> separate. More families like mine are splitting
> up, and I am sure that I am not the only teenager
> to react badly, at first. Divorce is always

```
unfortunate, but does not have to be an ending,
like I first thought. It can be an opportunity for
members of a family to build on their
relationships and improve themselves, like my
mother and I have. Though I said and did some
things that I regret, we have come closer.
Although making mistakes is not pleasant, I am
glad that I have learned from the ones I have
made.
```

When she reread the draft, though, Tara realized that these ideas had already been conveyed in the story and in her paragraph-by-paragraph analysis of her feelings, so she cut what had become a second conclusion.

◆ USING THE MODEL

As a result of reading Anne Frank's diary and then answering several questions about it, Tara ended up writing an essay with a topic and purpose very similar to Anne's. Both young women write about their pasts from the perspective of their presents. Their greater maturity allows both to see events from their own as well as their mothers' points of view. Having read both Anne's and Tara's stories, you might want to use this same multiple perspective to examine other topics or other relationships—for example, the development of a sympathetic relationship with a friend or coach or teacher you used to find difficult to like or understand.

◆ ◆ ◆ Checklist for Reading and Writing ◆ ◆ ◆ Narrative Essays

1. Is the purpose for telling this story made clear? Has it been achieved?
2. Has a conscious decision been made about which events to include or exclude and how best to organize them? Are connections between scenes or paragraphs made clear?
3. Do readers have enough information about people, places, and times to understand the scenes included and the ideas communicated?
4. Are the scenes made lively through language appealing to the reader's senses of smell, touch, sight, and sound?
5. Would any additional concrete details add clarity to a scene or support to an idea within the essay?

◆ ◆ ◆ PREPARING TO READ

Have you ever experienced a single event that significantly changed an opinion you had about a person or a group of people? Did you realize the importance of the event at the time?

◆ ◆ ◆

Jackie's Debut: A Unique Day

MIKE ROYKO

When Chicago native Mike Royko, a life-long newspaper journalist, died in 1997, he was a columnist for the *Chicago Tribune*. Throughout his career, his sharp-tongued observations about everyday urban life brought him national recognition, including a Pulitzer Prize. On October 15, 1972, writing for the *Chicago Daily News* on the death of major league baseball great Jackie Robinson, Royko dug into his childhood memories and record-ed a snapshot view of the complex reality of American race relations.

1   All that Saturday, the wise men of the neighborhood, who sat in chairs on the sidewalk outside the tavern, had talked about what it would do to baseball.

2   I hung around and listened because baseball was about the most im-portant thing in the world, and if anything was going to ruin it, I was wor-ried.

3   Most of the things they said, I didn't understand, although it sounded terrible. But could one man bring such ruin?

4   They said he could and would. And the next day he was going to be in Wrigley Field for the first time, on the same diamond as Hack, Nicholson, Cavarretta, Schmidt, Pafko, and all my other idols.

5   I had to see Jackie Robinson, the man who was going to somehow wreck everything. So the next day, another kid and I started walking to the ball park early.

6   We always walked to save the streetcar fare. It was five or six miles, but I felt about baseball the way Abe Lincoln felt about education.

7   Usually, we could get there just at noon, find a seat in the grandstands and watch some batting practice. But not that Sunday, May 18, 1947.

By noon, Wrigley Field was almost filled. The crowd outside spilled off 8 the sidewalk and into the streets. Scalpers were asking top dollar for box seats and getting it.

I had never seen anything like it. Not just the size, although it was a 9 new record, more than 47,000. But this was 25 years ago, and in 1947 few blacks were seen in the Loop, much less up on the white North Side at a Cub game.

That day, they came by the thousands, pouring off the northbound Ls 10 and out of their cars.

They didn't wear baseball-game clothes. They had on church clothes 11 and funeral clothes—suits, white shirts, ties, gleaming shoes, and straw hats. I've never seen so many straw hats.

Big as it was, the crowd was orderly. Almost unnaturally so. People 12 didn't jostle each other.

The whites tried to look as if nothing unusual was happening, while 13 the blacks tried to look casual and dignified. So everybody looked slightly ill at ease.

For most, it was probably the first time they had been that close to 14 each other in such great numbers.

We managed to get in, scramble up a ramp and find a place to stand 15 behind the last row of grandstand seats. Then they shut the gates. No place remained to stand.

Robinson came up in the first inning. I remember the sound. It wasn't 16 the shrill, teen-age cry you now hear, or an excited gut roar. They applauded, long, rolling applause. A tall middle-aged black man stood next to me, a smile of almost painful joy on his face, beating his palms together so hard they must have hurt.

When Robinson stepped into the batter's box, it was as if someone 17 had flicked a switch. The place went silent.

He swung at the first pitch and they erupted as if he had knocked it 18 over the wall. But it was only a high foul that dropped into the box seats. I remember thinking it was strange that a foul could make that many people happy. When he struck out, the low moan was genuine.

I've forgotten most of the details of the game, other than that the 19 Dodgers won and Robinson didn't get a hit or do anything special, although he was cheered on every swing and every routine play.

But two things happened I'll never forget. Robinson played first, and 20 early in the game a Cub star hit a grounder and it was a close play.

Just before the Cub reached first, he swerved to his left. And as he got 21 to the bag, he seemed to slam his foot down hard at Robinson's foot.

It was obvious to everyone that he was trying to run into him or spike 22 him. Robinson took the throw and got clear at the last instant.

I was shocked. That Cub, a home-town boy, was my biggest hero. It   23
was not only an unheroic stunt, but it seemed a rude thing to do in front of
people who would cheer for a foul ball. I didn't understand why he had
done it. It wasn't at all big league.

I didn't know that while the white fans were relatively polite, the Cubs   24
and most other teams kept up a steady stream of racial abuse from the
dugout. I thought all they did down there was talk about how good
Wheaties are.

Later in the game, Robinson was up again and he hit another foul ball.   25
This time it came into the stands low and fast, in our direction. Somebody in
the seats grabbed for it, but it caromed off his hand and kept coming. There
was a flurry of arms as the ball kept bouncing, and suddenly it was between
me and my pal. We both grabbed. I had a baseball.

The two of us stood there examining it and chortling. A genuine,   26
major-league baseball that had actually been gripped and thrown by a Cub
pitcher, hit by a Dodger batter. What a possession.

Then I heard a voice say: "Would you consider selling that?"   27

It was the black man who had applauded so fiercely.   28

I mumbled something. I didn't want to sell it.   29

"I'll give you $10 for it," he said.   30

Ten dollars. I couldn't believe it. I didn't know what $10 could buy be-   31
cause I'd never had that much money. But I knew that a lot of men in the
neighborhood considered $60 a week to be good pay.

I handed it to him, and he paid me with ten $1 bills.   32

When I left the ball park, with that much money in my pocket, I was   33
sure that Jackie Robinson wasn't bad for the game.

Since then, I've regretted a few times that I didn't keep the ball. Or   34
that I hadn't given it to him free. I didn't know, then, how hard he probably
had to work for that $10.

But Tuesday I was glad I had sold it to him. And if that man is still   35
around, and has that baseball, I'm sure he thinks it was worth every cent.

FIRST RESPONSES

How might you have responded to being in the stands at this game?
What would you have done with the caught baseball? Have you been called
on to make any similar decisions in your life?

TAKING A CLOSER LOOK

Exploring *Who:* Voice and Tone

1. How did the young boy's feelings about his baseball heroes change in the course of this baseball game? How does the adult Royko view his boyhood attitudes? Identify two or three places where he makes these two different points of view most clear.
2. What tone of voice does Royko use when he opens with the warnings of "the wise men of the neighborhood"? When do you realize his current feelings about these elders? Are there other attitudes expressed in the early paragraphs that can be read differently after you have finished the essay?
3. What reactions does Royko hope you will have toward his boyhood ideas and actions? What does he expect of you as you read? How did you respond, for example, when the boy thinks, "I had to see Jackie Robinson, the man who was going to somehow wreck everything"?

Exploring *What:* Content and Meaning

1. What did you learn about the game of baseball in 1947 from reading this essay? About Chicago? Was this new information for you? Why or why not?
2. What did you learn about black and white interaction at that time? Did any of the behaviors of the white or black players or spectators surprise you? Is race still an issue in sports? For the players? For the crowds?
3. How well did the essay prepare you for understanding the two major events during the game—the close play and the foul ball? How did you feel when the Cub player swerved into Robinson? Did you understand why the boy sold the ball to the black man?

Exploring *Why:* Purpose

1. Royko is generally known for his critical attitude toward human frailties. Remembering that the essay was written the day Robinson died, how do you think Royko hoped readers would respond to his experience? Has remembering the event been valuable for Royko himself? How does paragraph 34 help to answer that question?
2. If the black man to whom he sold the ball read Royko's essay, would he agree with Royko's conclusion? Can you name a few ways in

which this black fan would remember things differently about this day?

3. ▣ *Using the Internet.* Visit the Negro League Baseball Online Archives (http://www.nc5.infi.net/moxie/nlb/nlb.html) or the Negro League's Web site (http://www.blackbaseball.com/). What did you know about this league before visiting the Web site? How does this additional information add to your reading of Royko's essay?

Exploring *How:* Style and Strategy

1. You have looked closely at many of the details Royko includes in his essay. What did he exclude? Why? Why does the essay begin and end where it does? For example, how would the essay be different if it began with the Cub player's running into Robinson?

2. Why did Royko give so many details about how the black spectators were dressed? Which of your senses does Royko appeal to in paragraphs 16 to 18? What is the effect on your feelings about the game that day?

3. Why does Royko tell us that he "felt about baseball the way Abe Lincoln felt about education"?

WRITING FROM READING ASSIGNMENT

Mike Royko's narrative captures a pivotal moment in his own and the nation's growth toward maturity. Lack of experience with people who are different from us is one of our many youthful limitations. Its consequence is often prejudice, which affects how we think and act. The following assignment uses Royko's essay as a model and assists you in writing a narrative about a specific and direct experience you had with someone or something you were unfamiliar with, perhaps even prejudiced against. You might, for example, consider a time you had to play on the same basketball team with a student from a different school, went on a field trip with a person from another country, or worked with a critically ill or elderly person while volunteering at a hospital.

A. Begin by doing some freewriting or brainstorming to discover a topic. Explore what you felt at the time of the experience, as well as what you are feeling as you remember the scenes. Did you realize at the time that your attitudes were changing? What do you think you learned from the experience?

B. After you have identified the story you wish to recount and one or two specific insights you gained from the interaction, reread the Royko essay to look carefully at how he narrates his story and when and where he makes clear his reasons for writing about this experience. Go back to your topic and make a list of all the events or scenes in your story, and then do some additional brainstorming to recall all the details you can associate with each scene. Jot them down. Now write a working thesis for your essay.

C. Royko sets a context for the story he is about to tell by revealing his naive understanding of the racist attitudes of the day. He also invites the readers to come along with him as he finds out "what it would do to baseball." Do you need to provide a similar introduction for your readers? How else might you arouse readers' interest in your story and help them to focus on what you believe is important about the change you are about to narrate? Write a draft introduction.

D. Royko has organized his essay in chronological order, from the day before the game until he leaves the park. Like Tara Coburn's essay, Royko's reveals a progression in his attitudes—before, during, and after the game. Find a logical pattern for the sequence of events in your narrative. Decide if you want to present all the events in order or if you need flashbacks or digressions to help clarify an idea or provide essential information. Write an outline or list of scenes for your essay. Think carefully about what you are including as well as what you are leaving out.

E. Royko's point of view is largely that of a fifteen-year-old boy, but his adult voice sometimes intervenes. In paragraph 24, for example, he shares with us what he now knows was going on in the dugout that he couldn't have known as a boy. Decide what point of view you will use and when and if you will vary that point of view. Now write a draft of your essay.

F. As you discovered in question 2 under "Exploring *How*," Royko uses sounds to draw his readers into the scene. Use specific detail and description to bring your scenes to life. You might use analogy, such as Royko's to Abe Lincoln, to help your readers understand more fully the ideas behind your story.

G. Take a close look at your conclusion before writing your final draft. Have you avoided the pitfall Tara fell into when she wrote her double conclusion? Be sure insights you gained from your experience are clear to your readers.

◆ ◆ ◆ PREPARING TO READ

Have you ever witnessed a dramatic or startling public event, such as an accident or a fire? How did the people around you react? How did you react?

◆ ◆ ◆

Street Scene: Minor Heroism in a Major Metropolitan Area

IAN FRAZIER

Journalist Ian Frazier (b. 1951, Cleveland, Ohio) writes frequently for both *The Atlantic Monthly* and *The New Yorker.* He is perhaps best known for his biting humor in books such as *Coyote v. Acme* (1996), for which he received the first Thurber House Award for American Humor in 1997. At the core of all his writing, however, is a connection of particular people to particular places, from an assembled cast of varied characters who evoke the complex spirit of the *Great Plains* (1989) to his own *Family* (1994), pieced together in a memory book to create "a meaning that would defeat death." The following essay first appeared in *The Atlantic Monthly* in February 1995.

On a Saturday morning I left my Brooklyn apartment to shop for a   1
dinner party and saw a crowd—baseball caps, legs straddling bicycles, an arm holding a lamp stand with a dangling price tag—around a person on the sidewalk. I was almost at my doorstep; I went closer, and saw a woman lying on her back with her lips turned into her mouth and her eyes neither open nor closed. Her hair was gray, her face the same color as the pavement. A slight, brown-haired woman was giving her mouth-to-mouth resuscitation, while a well-built brown-skinned man with hair close-cropped like a skullcap was performing chest massage. He and the woman giving mouth-to-mouth were counting, "One, two, three, four, *five.*" Then he would pause and she would breathe into the woman's mouth.

A police car drove up and a young Hispanic cop got out. He went over   2
to the woman and talked to the pair trying to revive her. Someone pointed out to him the woman's son, a tall, gangly man who stood nearby, kind of bobbing up and down and nodding to himself. The cop patted the son on the

arm and spoke to him. A large, lumpy-faced man with his pants high on his waist said to me, "The ambulance will never come. They never come when you call anymore. They don't care. In New York nobody cares. People are so arrogant on the street in Manhattan. I call New York a lost city. Used to be a great city, now it's a lost city. People are nicer out west or upstate. I went to Methodist Hospital and the nurse wouldn't talk to me. I told her right to her face . . ." After a minute I realized it made no difference if I listened to him or not. The pair at work on the woman paused for a moment while the man asked if anyone had a razor so he could cut the woman's shirt. Someone found a pocket knife. He bent over his work again. Minutes passed. The cop asked if he was getting tired and he said he wasn't. Sirens rose in the distance, faded. Then one rose and didn't fade, and in the next second an Emergency Medical Service truck from Long Island College Hospital pulled up. The chest-massage guy didn't quit until the EMS paramedic took over; then he straightened up, looked at the truck, and said, "Long *Island?* Fuckin' Methodist is only three blocks away."

The EMS guys put the woman on a stretcher and lifted her into the   3 back of the truck. Hands gathered up a few items the woman had dropped on the sidewalk; someone pointed out her false teeth. The woman who had been giving mouth-to-mouth bent over and picked up the teeth. She paused just a second before touching them. I thought this was from squeamishness; then I saw it was from care. Gently she handed the teeth to one of the paramedics. Then she and the chest-massage guy parted without a word, or none that I saw. The guy walked toward his car, a two-tone Pontiac. Apparently he had just been driving by; its door was still open. I went up to him and thanked him for what he had done. I shook his hand. His strength went right up my arm like a warm current. I ran after the woman, who was now well down the block. I tapped her shoulder and she turned around and I said thank you. Her eyes were full of what had just happened. There were tears on her upper cheeks. She said something like, "Oh, of course, don't mention it." She was a thin-faced white woman with Prince Valiant hair and a green windbreaker—an ordinary-looking person, but glowingly beautiful.

The EMS guys and the cop worked on the woman in the back of the   4 truck with the doors open. The crowd dispersed. The son crouched inside the truck holding the IV bottle for a while; then he stood outside again. Eventually the cop got out of the back of the truck. The son climbed in, the EMS guys closed the doors, and the truck drove off with sirens going. The cop sat in his car. The window was down. I walked over and asked, "Excuse me—did they ever get a pulse?" He winced slightly at the nakedness of my question. A pause. Then he shook his head. "Nahhh. Not really."

I went to the park across the street. A bunch of kids were hang-   5 ing around the entrance jawing back and forth at each other. In my neighborhood there is a gang called NAB, or Ninth Avenue Boys. Newspaper stories say they've done a lot of beatings and robberies nearby. From a few feet away I heard one kid say to another, "You shut your stupid fuckin' chicken-breath mouth." I felt as strong as the strangers I had just talked to. I walked through the kids without fear.

◆ ◆ ◆

FIRST RESPONSES

Would you have stopped to help this woman? What motivates good Samaritans? What causes others not to act?

TAKING A CLOSER LOOK

Exploring *Who:* Voice and Tone

1. What were Frazier's feelings about the people and events he witnessed? At what point in the essay did you discover his attitudes? Why does he wait so long to reveal them? Did they change as a result of his experience?

2. In paragraph 3, when the woman who has been helping grasps the victim's false teeth, Frazier remarks, "She paused just a second before touching them. I thought this was from squeamishness; then I saw it was from care." What effect does this observation have on your understanding of Frazier's thinking about this woman?

3. How does Frazier expect you to respond when he concludes, "I walked through the kids without fear"? What in your experience or in the essay led to your feelings about his own minor act of heroism?

Exploring *What:* Content and Meaning

1. What is Frazier's definition of heroism? How many other responses to the victim does Frazier describe? What human strengths and weaknesses are suggested by these responses?

2. What impressions of the police, the paramedics, and the city does the essay create?

3. Were you surprised when Frazier went up and thanked the man and woman who had tried to save the victim? What was his motive and what did he gain from his spontaneous act?

Exploring *Why:* Purpose

1. Why would Frazier believe that this personal experience and insight would be valuable to his readers?
2. ■▯ *Using the Internet.* With one of the Internet search engines, use the keyword "heroism" to find other articles on acts of heroism, and compare the definitions. Based on these examples, how would you define the term? Has this reading changed how you might react in a crisis?

Exploring *How:* Style and Strategy

1. How directly does Frazier define heroism? How would the essay have changed if he had decided instead to include a direct thesis in his introduction and an analytical conclusion?
2. Look closely at paragraph 1 for the ways that people and actions are described. How well can you picture the crowd around the woman receiving CPR? Which of your senses does Frazier appeal to, and why?
3. Did you notice Frazier's occasional use of very brief sentences? Look, for example, at the line "Minutes passed" toward the end of paragraph 2. What are the effects of this sentence at this point in the action? Can you find other such sentences in paragraph 4?
4. Frazier intentionally included only a few bits and pieces of dialogue. Why, and with what effect?

IDEAS FOR WRITING A NARRATIVE

1. Narrate a crisis that you experienced, either as a direct participant or as an observer. Use concrete detail and dialogue to support the actions you recount.
2. Recall a time when you had to overcome a fear in order to accomplish a goal—for example, conquering a fear of heights to go on a hiking trip with friends. As you tell this story, concentrate on your changing feelings through the course of the experience.
3. Tell the story of a time when you witnessed (or displayed) courage.

◆ ◆ ◆ **PREPARING TO READ**

Who do you see when you think of a veteran Navy pilot? Where do these images come from?

◆ ◆ ◆

A Quiet Siege: The Death and Life of a Gay Naval Officer

ANDRE DUBUS

Louisiana native Andre Dubus (1936–1999) spent his teaching and writing careers in Massachusetts, the setting of most of his books. Primarily a short story writer and essayist, Dubus, like Flannery O'Connor, wrote to achieve a fuller understanding of the relationship between violence and morality. He received numerous prestigious awards and fellowships, including the PEN/Malamud Award, the Guggenheim, and the MacArthur. His more recent works include the story collection *Dancing After Hours* (1996) and the personal essays gathered in *Broken Vessels* (1991). "A Quiet Siege" appeared in *Harper's* magazine in June 1993.

He was a Navy pilot in World War II and in Korea, and when I knew   1
him in 1961 for a few months before he killed himself he was the Commander of the Air Group aboard the USS *Ranger,* an aircraft carrier, and we called him by the acronym CAG. He shot himself with his .38 revolver because two investigators from the Office of Naval Intelligence came aboard ship while we were anchored off Iwakuni in Japan and gave the ship's captain a written report of their investigation of CAG's erotic life. CAG was a much-decorated combat pilot, and his duty as a commander was one of great responsibility. The ship's executive officer, also a commander, summoned CAG to his office, where the two investigators were, and told him that his choices were to face a general court-martial or to resign from the Navy. Less than half an hour later CAG was dead in his stateroom. His body was flown to the United States; we were told that he did not have a family, and I do not know where he was buried. There was a memorial service

aboard ship, but I do not remember it; I only remember a general sadness like mist in the passageways.

I did not really know him. I was a first lieutenant then, a career Marine; two years later I would resign and become a teacher. On the *Ranger* I was with the Marine detachment; we guarded the planes' nuclear weapons stored belowdecks, ran the brig, and manned one of the antiaircraft gun mounts. We were fifty or so enlisted men and two officers among a ship's crew of about 3,000 officers and men. The Air Group was not included in the ship's company. They came aboard with their planes for our seven-month deployment in the western Pacific. I do not remember the number of pilots and bombardier-navigators, mechanics and flight controllers, and men who worked on the flight deck, but there were plenty of all, and day and night you could hear planes catapulting off the front of the deck and landing on its rear. 2

The flight deck was 1,052 feet long, the ship weighed 81,000 tons fully loaded, and I rarely felt its motion. I came aboard in May for a year of duty, and in August we left our port in San Francisco Bay and headed for Japan. I had driven my wife and three young children home to Louisiana, where they would stay during the seven months I was at sea, and every day I longed for them. One night on the voyage across the Pacific I sat in the wardroom drinking coffee with a lieutenant commander at one of the long tables covered with white linen. The wardroom was open all night because men were always working. The lieutenant commander told me that Soviet submarines tracked us, they recorded the sound of our propellers and could not be fooled by the sound of a decoy ship's propellers, and that they even came into San Francisco Bay to do this; our submarines did the same with Soviet carriers. He said that every time we tried in training exercises to evade even our own submarines we could not do it, and our destroyers could not track and stop them. He said, "So if the whistle blows we'll get a nuclear fish up our ass in the first thirty minutes. Our job is to get the birds in the air before that. They're going to Moscow." 3

"Where will they land afterward?" 4

"They won't. They know that." 5

The voyage to Japan was five or six weeks long because we did not go directly to Japan; the pilots flew air operations. Combat units are always training for war, but these men who flew planes, and the men in orange suits and ear protectors who worked on the flight decks during landings and takeoffs, were engaging in something not at all as playful as Marine field exercises generally were. They were imperiled. One pilot told me that from his fighter-bomber in the sky the flight deck looked like an aspirin tablet. On the passage to Japan I became friendly with some pilots, drinking coffee in 6 the wardroom, and I knew what CAG looked like because he was CAG. He had dark skin and alert eyes, and he walked proudly. Then in Japan I sometimes drank with young pilots. I was a robust twenty-five-year-old, one of two Marine officers aboard ship, and I did not want to be outdone at anything by anyone. But I could not stay with the pilots; I had to leave them in the bar, drinking and talking and laughing, and make my way back to the ship to sleep and wake with a hangover. Next day the pilots flew; if we did not go to sea, they flew from a base on land. Once I asked one of them how he did it.

"The pure oxygen. Soon as you put on the mask, your head clears."   7

It was not simply the oxygen, and I did not understand any of these   8 wild, brave, and very efficient men until years later when I read Tom Wolfe's *The Right Stuff.*

It was on that same tour that I saw another pilot die. I worked below-   9 decks with the Marine detachment, but that warm gray afternoon the entire ship was in a simulated condition of war, and my part was to stand four hours of watch in a small turret high above the ship. I could move the turret in a circular way by pressing a button, and I looked through binoculars for planes or ships in the 180-degree arc of our port side. On the flight deck planes were taking off; four could do this in quick sequence. Two catapults launched planes straight off the front of the ship, and quickly they rose and climbed. The third and fourth catapults were on the port side where the flight deck angled sharply out to the left, short of the bow. From my turret I looked down at the ship's bridge and the flight deck. A helicopter flew low near the ship, and planes were taking off. On the deck were men in orange suits and ear protectors; on both sides of the ship, just beneath the flight deck, were nets for these men to jump into, to save themselves from being killed by a landing plane that veered or skidded or crashed. One night I'd inspected a Marine guarding a plane on the flight deck; we had a sentry there because the plane carried a nuclear bomb. I stepped from a hatch into the absolute darkness of a night at sea and into a strong wind that lifted my body with each step. I was afraid it would lift me off the deck and hurl me into the sea, where I would tread water in that great expanse and depth while the ship went on its way; tomorrow they would learn that I was missing. I found the plane and the Marine; he stood with one arm around the cable that held the wing to the deck.

In the turret I was facing aft when it happened: men in orange were at   10 the rear of the flight deck, then they sprinted forward, and I rotated my turret toward the bow and saw a plane in the gray sea and an orange-suited pilot lying facedown in the water, his parachute floating beyond his head, moving toward the rear of the ship. The plane had dropped off the port deck and now water covered its wing, then its cockpit, and it sank. The pilot was behind the ship; his limbs did not move, his face was in the sea, and his parachute was filling with water and starting to sink. The helicopter hovered low and a sailor on a rope descended from it; he wore orange, and I watched him coming down and the pilot floating and the parachute sinking beneath the waves. There was still some length of parachute line remaining when the sailor reached the pilot; he grabbed him; then the parachute lines tightened their pull and drew the pilot down. There was only the sea now beneath the sailor on the rope. Then he ascended.

I shared a stateroom with a Navy lieutenant, an officer of medical ad- 11 ministration, a very tall and strong man from Oklahoma. He had been an enlisted man, had once been a corpsman aboard a submarine operating off the coast of the Soviet Union, and one night their periscope was spotted, destroyers came after them, and they dived and sat at the bottom and listened by sonar to the destroyers' sonar trying to find them. He told me about the sailor who had tried to save the pilot. In the dispensary they gave him brandy, and the sailor wept and said he was trained to do that job, and this was his first time, and he had failed. Of course he had not failed. No man could lift another man attached to a parachute filled with water. Some people said the helicopter had not stayed close enough to the ship while the planes were taking off. Some said the pilot was probably already dead; his plane dropped from the ship, and he ejected himself high into the air, but not high enough for his parachute to ease his fall. This was all talk about the mathematics of violent death; the pilot was killed because he flew airplanes from a ship at sea.

He was a lieutenant commander, and I knew his face and name. As he 12 was being catapulted, his landing gear on the left side broke off and his plane skidded into the sea. He was married; his widow had been married before, also to a pilot who was killed in a crash. I wondered if it were her bad luck to meet only men who flew; years later I believed that whatever in their spirits made these men fly also drew her to them.

I first spoke to CAG at the officers' club at the Navy base in Yoko- 13 suka. The officers of the Air Group hosted a party for the officers of the ship's company. We wore civilian suits and ties, and gathered at the club to drink. There were no women. The party was a matter of protocol, probably a tradition among pilots and the officers of carriers; for us young officers it meant getting happily drunk. I was doing this with pilots at the bar when one of them said, "Let's throw CAG into the pond."

He grinned at me, as I looked to my left at the small shallow pond with 14 pretty fish in it; then I looked past the pond at CAG, sitting on a soft leather chair, a drink in his hand, talking quietly with two or three other commanders sitting in soft leather chairs. All the pilots with me were grinning and saying yes, and the image of us lifting CAG from his chair and dropping him into the water gave me joy, and I put my drink on the bar and said, "Let's go."

I ran across the room to CAG, grabbed the lapels of his coat, jerked him up from his chair, and saw his drink spill onto his suit; then I fell backward to the floor, still holding his lapels, and pulled him down on top of me. There was no one else with me. He was not angry yet, but I was a frightened fool. I released his lapels and turned my head and looked back at the laughing pilots. Out of my vision the party was loud, hundreds of drinking officers who had not seen this, and CAG sounded only puzzled when he said, "What's going on?"

He stood and brushed at the drink on his suit, watching me get up from the floor. I stood not quite at attention but not at ease either. I said, "Sir, I'm Marine Lieutenant Dubus. Your pilots fooled me." I nodded toward them at the bar, and CAG smiled. "They said, 'Let's throw CAG into the pond.' But, sir, the joke was on me."

He was still smiling.

"I'm very sorry, sir."

"That's all right, Lieutenant."

"Can I get the Commander another drink, sir?"

"Sure," he said, and told me what he was drinking, and I got it from the bar, where the pilots were red-faced and happy, and brought it to CAG, who was sitting in his chair again with the other commanders. He smiled and thanked me, and the commanders smiled; then I returned to the young pilots and we all laughed.

Until a few months later, on the day he killed himself, the only words I spoke to CAG after the party were greetings. One night I saw him sitting with a woman in the officers' club, and I wished him good evening. A few times I saw him in the ship's passageways; I recognized him seconds before the features of his face were clear: he had a graceful, athletic stride that dipped his shoulders. I saluted and said, "Good morning, sir" or "Good afternoon, sir." He smiled as he returned my salute and greeting, his eyes and voice mirthful, and I knew that he was seeing me again pulling him out of his chair and down to the floor, then standing to explain myself and apologize. I liked being a memory that gave him sudden and passing amusement.

On a warm sunlit day we were anchored off Iwakuni, and I planned to go with other crew members on a bus to Hiroshima. I put on civilian clothes and went down the ladder to the boat that would take us ashore. I was not happily going to Hiroshima; I was going because I was an American, and I felt that I should look at it and be in it. I found a seat on the rocking boat, then saw CAG in civilian clothes coming down the ladder. There were a few seats remaining, and he chose the one next to me. He asked me where I was going, then said he was going to Hiroshima, too. I was relieved and grateful;

while CAG was flying planes in World War II, I was a boy buying savings stamps and bringing scrap metal to school. On the bus he would talk to me about war, and in Hiroshima I would walk with him and look with him, and his seasoned steps and eyes would steady mine. Then from the ship above us the officer of the deck called down, "CAG?"

CAG turned and looked up at him, a lieutenant junior grade in white 24 cap and short-sleeved shirt and trousers.

"Sir, the executive officer would like to see you." 25

I do not remember what CAG said to me. I only remember my disap- 26 pointment when he told the boat's officer to go ashore without him. All I saw in CAG's face was the look of a man called from rest back to his job. He climbed the ladder, and soon the boat pulled away.

Perhaps when I reached Hiroshima CAG was already dead; I do not re- 27 member the ruins at ground zero or what I saw in the museum. I walked and looked, and stood for a long time at a low arch with an open space at the ground, and in that space was a stone box that held the names of all who died on the day of the bombing and all who had died since because of the bomb. That night I ate dinner ashore, then rode the boat to the ship, went to my empty room, climbed to my upper bunk, and slept for only a while, till the quiet voice of my roommate woke me: "The body will be flown to Okinawa."

I looked at him standing at his desk and speaking into the telephone. 28

"Yes. A .38 in the temple. Yes." 29

I turned on my reading lamp and watched him put the phone down. 30 He was sad, and he looked at me. I said, "Did someone commit suicide?"

"CAG." 31

"CAG?" 32

I sat up. 33

"The ONI investigated him." 34

Then I knew what I had not known I knew, and I said, "Was he a ho- 35 mosexual?"

"Yes." 36

My roommate told me the executive officer had summoned CAG to 37 his office, shown him the report, and told him that he could either resign or face a general court-martial. Then CAG went to his room. Fifteen minutes later the executive officer phoned him; when he did not answer, the executive officer and the investigators ran to his room. He was on his bunk, shot in the right temple, his pilot's .38 revolver in his hand. His eyelids fluttered; he was unconscious but still alive, and he died from bleeding.

"They *ran*?" I said. "They *ran* to his room?" 38

Ten years later one of my shipmates came to visit me in Massachu- 39 setts; we had been civilians for a long time. In my kitchen we were drinking beer, and he said, "I couldn't tell you this aboard ship, because I worked in the legal office. They called CAG back from that boat you were on because he knew the ONI was aboard. His plane was on the ground at the base in Iwakuni. They were afraid he was going to fly it and crash into the sea and they'd lose the plane."

All 3,000 of the ship's crew did not mourn. Not every one of the hundreds of men in the Air Group mourned. But the shock was general and hundreds of men did mourn, and each morning we woke to it, and it was in our talk in the wardroom and in the passageways. In the closed air of the ship it touched us, and it lived above us on the flight deck and in the sky. One night at sea a young pilot came to my room; his face was sunburned and sad. We sat in desk chairs, and he said, "The morale is very bad now. The whole Group. It's just shot."

"Did y'all know about him?"

"We all knew. We didn't care. We would have followed him into hell."

Yes, they would have followed him; they were ready every day and every night to fly with him from a doomed ship and follow him to Moscow, to perish in their brilliant passion.

◆ ◆ ◆

FIRST RESPONSES

Do you understand CAG's shipmates' sadness? Can you connect their feelings to a loss you have experienced in your life?

TAKING A CLOSER LOOK

Exploring *Who:* Voice and Tone

1. What were Dubus's feelings about CAG before the suicide? What does Dubus mean when he says, "Then I knew what I had not known I knew"? Did Dubus's feelings change as a result of CAG's death, or of his being forced to acknowledge that CAG was gay?

2. How does the fact that Dubus was not himself a pilot affect his relationship to the people and events in this story?

3. How much does Dubus expect you to know about life on-board a ship and about the experience of being gay in the military?

4. What emotions did you experience as you read this narrative?

Exploring *What:* Content and Meaning

1. Describe the relationship among the Navy pilots. How does Dubus's description of the pilot he saw die contribute to your understanding of their bond?

2. What kind of a person was CAG? How did his men feel about him as a commander? How does CAG's response to the practical joke that Dubus played on him contribute to your feelings about CAG? Why does the author call him CAG, and not use his name?

3. Why did CAG commit suicide? Does this action fit with the kind of man you saw emerge during the essay? How did you feel about his decision? Have you had any personal experiences that helped you to understand it?

Exploring *Why:* Purpose

1. What clues does the title "A Quiet Siege" offer to Dubus's motives for writing this essay and his attitude toward its topic?

2. *Using the Internet.* The military's "Don't Ask, Don't Tell" policy regarding gays in the military was very much in the news in early 1993. How might that have influenced Dubus to write this essay? Did it influence your reading of the essay? Using the National Gay and Lesbian Task Force Web site (http://www.ngltf.org/), clarify the current status of the legal challenges to that policy.

3. Dubus associates his trip to Hiroshima with CAG's death. Did linking these two events affect your response to the issues Dubus wants you to consider?

Exploring *How:* Style and Strategy

1. Paragraph 1 is a brief overview of the story Dubus is about to narrate. Reread the paragraph. How does the tone of the paragraph prepare you for the essay as a whole? How would the essay be different if it had begun with paragraph two, saving the essential events and information until later in the story?

2. In many ways you learn more about Dubus than about CAG in this essay. In paragraph 3, for example, we learn that during the long months at sea, Dubus "longed" for his wife and three young children. Why does he choose to include this? Does it in any way help you to understand CAG, too?

3. At the end of paragraph 1, Dubus writes, "I only remember a general sadness like mist in the passageways." What **figure of speech** is he using here, and why?

4. How many different strategies does Dubus use in paragraph 22 to describe CAG's appearance and personality?

IDEAS FOR WRITING A NARRATIVE

1. Write an essay narrating a personal experience that taught you something about a social problem that had not previously touched your life in a direct way (gay bashing, sexism, racial discrimination, domestic violence, drunk driving, homelessness, child abuse, or unemployment, for example).

2. Have you ever done something you regret out of fear or because of social pressures? Narrate that story so that readers understand your original motives, the result of the experience, and what you feel about the action now.

3. Tell the story of a time when you or someone else was treated unjustly.

◆ ◆ ◆ **PREPARING TO READ**

Did one of your parents or grandparents ever tell you a story about his or her own life in order to teach you a lesson or to help you to make a decision in your own life? Did the story have the desired effect on you?

◆ ◆ ◆

No Name Woman

MAXINE HONG KINGSTON

Maxine Hong Kingston's fiction and essays have brought the unique experiences of west-coast Chinese-American subculture into national view. Born in 1940 in Stockton, California, to first generation Chinese immigrant parents, Kingston earned a degree in English literature from the University of California, Berkeley. Her autobiographical novel *The Woman Warrior,* from which "No Name Woman" is drawn, won a National Book Critics Circle Award in 1976. *China Men* (1980), a work of historical fiction, won the American Book Award, and her contemporary novel *Tripmaster Monkey* (1990) won the PEN West Award.

"You must not tell anyone," my mother said, "what I am about to tell   1
you. In China your father had a sister who killed herself. She jumped into the family well. We say that your father has all brothers because it is as if she had never been born.

"In 1924 just a few days after our village celebrated seventeen hurry-   2
up weddings—to make sure that every young man who went 'out on the road' would responsibly come home—your father and his brothers and your grandfather and his brothers and your aunt's new husband sailed for America, the Gold Mountain. It was your grandfather's last trip. Those lucky enough to get contracts waved goodbye from the decks. They fed and guarded the stowaways and helped them off in Cuba, New York, Bali, Hawaii. 'We'll meet in California next year,' they said. All of them sent money home.

"I remember looking at your aunt one day when she and I were dress-   3
ing; I had not noticed before that she had such a protruding melon of a stomach. But I did not think, 'She's pregnant,' until she began to look like other pregnant women, her shirt pulling and the white tops of her black

pants showing. She could not have been pregnant, you see, because her husband had been gone for years. No one said anything. We did not discuss it. In early summer she was ready to have the child, long after the time when it could have been possible.

"The village had also been counting. On the night the baby was to be   4
born the villagers raided our house. Some were crying. Like a great saw, teeth strung with lights, files of people walked zigzag across our land, tearing the rice. Their lanterns doubled in the disturbed black water, which drained away through the broken bunds. As the villagers closed in, we could see that some of them, probably men and women we knew well, wore white masks. The people with long hair hung it over their faces. Women with short hair made it stand up on end. Some had tied white bands around their foreheads, arms, and legs.

"At first they threw mud and rocks at the house. Then they threw eggs   5
and began slaughtering our stock. We could hear the animals scream their deaths—the roosters, the pigs, a last great roar from the ox. Familiar wild heads flared in our night windows; the villagers encircled us. Some of the faces stopped to peer at us, their eyes rushing like searchlights. The hands flattened against the panes, framed heads, and left red prints.

"The villagers broke in the front and the back doors at the same time,   6
even though we had not locked the doors against them. Their knives dripped with the blood of our animals. They smeared blood on the doors and walls. One woman swung a chicken, whose throat she had slit, splattering blood in red arcs about her. We stood together in the middle of our house, in the family hall with the pictures and tables of the ancestors around us, and looked straight ahead.

"At that time the house had only two wings. When the men came back   7
we would build two more to enclose our courtyard and a third one to begin a second courtyard. The villagers pushed through both wings, even your grandparents' rooms, to find your aunt's, which was also mine until the men returned. From this room a new wing for one of the younger families would grow. They ripped up her clothes and shoes and broke her combs, grinding them underfoot. They tore her work from the loom. They scattered the cooking fire and rolled the new weaving in it. We could hear them in the kitchen breaking our bowls and banging the pots. They overturned the great waist-high earthenware jugs; duck eggs, pickled fruits, vegetables burst out and mixed in acrid torrents. The old woman from the next field swept a broom through the air and loosed the spirits-of-the-broom over our heads. 'Pig.' 'Ghost.' 'Pig,' they sobbed and scolded while they ruined our house.

"When they left, they took sugar and oranges to bless themselves.   8
They cut pieces from the dead animals. Some of them took bowls that were not broken and clothes that were not torn. Afterward we swept up the rice

and sewed it back up into sacks. But the smells from the spilled preserves lasted. Your aunt gave birth in the pigsty that night. The next morning when I went up for the water, I found her and the baby plugging up the family well.

"Don't let your father know that I told you. He denies her. Now that you have started to menstruate, what happened to her could happen to you. Don't humiliate us. You wouldn't like to be forgotten as if you had never been born. The villagers are watchful."   9

Whenever she had to warn us about life, my mother told stories that ran like this one, a story to grow up on. She tested our strength to establish realities. Those in the emigrant generations who could not reassert brute survival died young and far from home. Those of us in the first American generations have had to figure out how the invisible world the emigrants built around our childhoods fit in solid America.   10

The emigrants confused the gods by diverting their curses, misleading them with crooked streets and false names. They must try to confuse their offspring as well, who, I suppose, threaten them in similar ways—always trying to get things straight, always trying to name the unspeakable. The Chinese I know hide their names; sojourners take new names when their lives change and guard their real names with silence.   11

Chinese-Americans, when you try to understand what things in you are Chinese, how do you separate what is peculiar to childhood, to poverty, insanities, one family, your mother who marked your growing with stories, from what is Chinese? What is Chinese tradition and what is the movies?   12

If I want to learn what clothes my aunt wore, whether flashy or ordinary, I would have to begin, "Remember Father's drowned-in-the-well sister?" I cannot ask that. My mother has told me once and for all the useful parts. She will add nothing unless powered by Necessity, a riverbank that guides her life. She plants vegetable gardens rather than lawns; she carries the odd-shaped tomatoes home from the fields and eats food left for the gods.   13

Whenever we did frivolous things, we used up energy; we flew high kites. We children came up off the ground over the melting cones our parents brought home from work and the American movie on New Years' Day—*Oh, You Beautiful Doll* with Betty Grable one year, and *She Wore a Yellow Ribbon* with John Wayne another year. After the one carnival ride each, we paid in guilt; our tired father counted his change on the dark walk home.   14

Adultery is extravagance. Could people who hatch their own chicks and eat the embryos and the heads for delicacies and boil the feet in vinegar for party food, leaving only the gravel, eating even the gizzard lining—could such people engender a prodigal aunt? To be a woman, to have a daughter   15 in starvation time was a waste enough. My aunt could not have been the lone romantic who gave up everything for sex. Women in the old China did not choose. Some man had commanded her to lie with him and be his secret evil. I wonder whether he masked himself when he joined the raid on her family.

Perhaps she encountered him in the fields or on the mountain where the daughters-in-law collected fuel. Or perhaps he first noticed her in the marketplace. He was not a stranger because the village housed no strangers. She had to have dealings with him other than sex. Perhaps he worked an adjoining field, or he sold her the cloth for the dress she sewed and wore. His demand must have surprised, then terrified her. She obeyed him; she always did as she was told.   16

When the family found a young man in the next village to be her husband, she stood tractably beside the best rooster, his proxy, and promised before they met that she would be his forever. She was lucky that he was her age and she would be the first wife, an advantage secure now. The night she first saw him, he had sex with her. Then he left for America. She had almost forgotten what he looked like. When she tried to envision him, she only saw the black and white face in the group photograph the men had had taken before leaving.   17

The other man was not, after all, much different from her husband. They both gave orders: she followed. "If you tell your family, I'll beat you. I'll kill you. Be here again next week." No one talked sex, ever. And she might have separated the rapes from the rest of living if only she did not have to buy her oil from him or gather wood in the same forest. I want her fear to have lasted just as long as rape lasted so that the fear could have been contained. No drawn-out fear. But women at sex hazarded birth and hence lifetimes. The fear did not stop but permeated everywhere. She told the man, "I think I'm pregnant." He organized the raid against her.   18

On nights when my mother and father talked about their life back home, sometimes they mentioned an "outcast table" whose business they still seemed to be settling, their voices tight. In a commensal tradition, where food is precious, the powerful older people made wrongdoers eat alone. Instead of letting them start separate new lives like the Japanese, who could become samurais and geishas, the Chinese family, faces averted but eyes glowering sideways, hung on to the offenders and fed them leftovers. My aunt must have lived in the same house as my parents and eaten at an outcast table. My mother spoke about the raid as if she had seen it, when she and my aunt, a daughter-in-law to a different household, should not have been living together at all. Daughters-in-law lived with their husbands' parents, not their own; a synonym for marriage in Chinese is "taking a daughter-in-law." Her husband's parents could have sold her, mortgaged   19 her, stoned her. But they had sent her back to her own mother and father, a mysterious act hinting at disgraces not told me. Perhaps they had thrown her out to deflect the avengers.

She was the only daughter; her four brothers went with her father, husband, and uncles "out on the road" and for some years became western men. When the goods were divided among the family, three of the brothers took land, and the youngest, my father, chose an education. After my grandparents gave their daughter away to her husband's family, they had dispensed all the adventure and all the property. They expected her alone to keep the traditional ways, which her brothers, now among the barbarians, could fumble without detection. The heavy, deep-rooted women were to maintain the past against the flood, safe for returning. But the rare urge west had fixed upon our family, and so my aunt crossed boundaries not delineated in space.   20

The work of preservation demands that the feelings playing about in one's guts not be turned into action. Just watch their passing like cherry blossoms. But perhaps my aunt, my forerunner, caught in a slow life, let dreams grow and fade and after some months or years went toward what persisted. Fear at the enormities of the forbidden kept her desires delicate, wire and bone. She looked at a man because she liked the way the hair was tucked behind his ears, or she liked the question-mark line of a long torso curving at the shoulder and straight at the hip. For warm eyes or a soft voice or a slow walk—that's all—a few hairs, a line, a brightness, a sound, a pace, she gave up family. She offered us up for a charm that vanished with tiredness, a pigtail that didn't toss when the wind died. Why, the wrong lighting could erase the dearest thing about him.   21

It could very well have been, however, that my aunt did not take subtle enjoyment of her friend, but, a wild woman, kept rollicking company. Imagining her free with sex doesn't fit, though. I don't know any women like that, or men either. Unless I see her life branching into mine, she gives me no ancestral help.   22

To sustain her being in love, she often worked at herself in the mirror, guessing at the colors and shapes that would interest him, changing them frequently in order to hit on the right combination. She wanted him to look back.   23

On a farm near the sea, a woman who tended her appearance reaped a reputation for eccentricity. All the married women blunt-cut their hair in flaps about their ears or pulled it back in tight buns. No nonsense. Neither style blew easily into heart-catching tangles. And at their weddings they displayed themselves in their long hair for the last time. "It brushed the backs of my knees," my mother tells me. "It was braided, and even so, it brushed the backs of my knees."   24

At the mirror my aunt combed individuality into her bob. A bun could   2⁵
have been contrived to escape into black streamers blowing in the wind or
in quiet wisps about her face, but only the older women in our picture
album wear buns. She brushed her hair back from her forehead, tucking the
flaps behind her ears. She looped a piece of thread, knotted into a circle between her index fingers and thumbs, and ran the double strand across her
forehead. When she closed her fingers as if she were making a pair of shadow geese bite, the string twisted together catching the little hairs. Then she
pulled the thread away from her skin, ripping the hairs out neatly, her eyes
watering from the needles of pain. Opening her fingers, she cleaned the
thread, then rolled it along her hairline and the tops of the eyebrows. My
mother did the same to me and my sisters and herself. I used to believe that
the expression "caught by the short hairs" meant a captive held with a de-
pilatory string. It especially hurt at the temples, but my mother said we were
lucky we didn't have to have our feet bound when we were seven. Sisters
used to sit on their beds and cry together, she said, as their mothers or their
slave removed the bandages for a few minutes each night and let the blood
gush back into their veins. I hope that the man my aunt loved appreciated a
smooth brow, that he wasn't just a tits-and-ass man.

Once my aunt found a freckle on her chin, at a spot that the almanac   26
said predestined her for unhappiness. She dug it out with a hot needle and
washed the wound with peroxide.

More attention to her looks than these pullings of hairs and pickings   27
at spots would have caused gossip among the villagers. They owned work
clothes and good clothes, and they wore good clothes for feasting the new
seasons. But since a woman combing her hair hexes beginnings, my aunt
rarely found an occasion to look her best. Women looked like great sea
snails—the corded wood, babies, and laundry they carried were the whorls
on their backs. The Chinese did not admire a bent back; goddesses and war-
riors stood straight. Still there must have been a marvelous freeing of beauty when a worker laid down her burden and stretched and arched.

Such commonplace loveliness, however, was not enough for my aunt.   28
She dreamed of a lover for the fifteen days of New Year's, the time for families to exchange visits, money, and food. She plied her secret comb. And
sure enough she cursed the year, the family, the village, and herself.

Even as her hair lured her imminent lover, many other men looked at   29
her. Uncles, cousins, nephews, brothers would have looked, too, had they
been home between journeys. Perhaps they had already been restraining
their curiosity, and they left, fearful that their glances, like a field of nesting
birds, might be startled and caught. Poverty hurt, and that was their first reason for leaving. But another, final reason for leaving the crowded house was
the never-said.

She may have been unusually beloved, the precious only daughter, spoiled and mirror-gazing because of the affection the family lavished on her. When her husband left, they welcomed the chance to take her back from the in-laws; she could live like the little daughter for just a while longer. There are stories that my grandfather was different from other people, "crazy ever since the little Jap bayoneted him in the head." He used to put his naked penis on the dinner table, laughing. And one day he brought home a baby girl, wrapped up inside his brown western-style greatcoat. He had traded one of his sons, probably my father, the youngest, for her. My grandmother made him trade back. When he finally got a daughter of his own, he doted on her. They must have all loved her, except perhaps my father, the only brother who never went back to China, having once been traded for a girl.   30

Brothers and sisters, newly men and women, had to efface their sexual color and present plain miens. Disturbing hair and eyes, a smile like no other, threatened the ideal of five generations living under one roof. To focus blurs, people shouted face to face and yelled from room to room. The immigrants I know have loud voices, unmodulated to American tones even after years away from the village where they called their friendships out across the fields. I have not been able to stop my mother's screams in public libraries or over telephones. Walking erect (knees straight, toes pointed forward, not pigeon-toed, which is Chinese-feminine) and speaking in an inaudible voice, I have tried to turn myself American-feminine. Chinese communication was loud, public. Only sick people had to whisper. But at the dinner table, where the family members came nearest one another, no one could talk, not the outcasts nor any eaters. Every word that falls from the mouth is a coin lost. Silently they gave and accepted food with both hands. A preoccupied child who took his bowl with one hand got a sideways glare. A complete moment of total attention is due everyone alike. Children and lovers have no singularity here, but my aunt used a secret voice, a separate attentiveness.   31

She kept the man's name to herself throughout her labor and dying; she did not accuse him that he be punished with her. To save her inseminator's name she gave silent birth.   32

He may have been somebody in her own household, but intercourse with a man outside the family would have been no less abhorrent. All the village were kinsmen, and the titles shouted in loud country voices never let kinship be forgotten. Any man within visiting distance would have been neutralized as a lover—"brother," "younger brother," "older brother"—one hundred and fifteen relationship titles. Parents researched birth charts probably not so much to assure good fortune as to circumvent incest in a population that has but one hundred surnames. Everybody has eight million relatives. How useless then sexual mannerisms, how dangerous.   33

As if it came from an atavism deeper than fear, I used to add   3.
"brother" silently to boys' names. It hexed the boys, who would or would
not ask me to dance, and made them less scary and as familiar and deserv-
ing of benevolence as girls.

But, of course, I hexed myself also—no dates. I should have stood up,   3.
both arms waving, and shouted out across libraries, "Hey, you! Love me
back." I had no idea, though, how to make attraction selective, how to control its direction and magnitude. If I made myself American-pretty so that
the five or six Chinese boys in the class fell in love with me, everyone else—
the Caucasian, Negro, and Japanese boys—would too. Sisterliness, dignified
and honorable, made much more sense.

Attraction eludes control so stubbornly that whole societies designed   3€
to organize relationships among people cannot keep order, not even when
they bind people to one another from childhood and raise them together.
Among the very poor and the wealthy, brothers married their adopted sisters, like doves. Our family allowed some romance, paying adult brides
prices and providing dowries so that their sons and daughters could marry
strangers. Marriage promises to turn strangers into friendly relatives—a
nation of siblings.

In the village structure, spirits shimmered among the live creatures,   37
balanced and held in equilibrium by time and land. But one human being
flaring up into violence could open up a black hole, a maelstrom that pulled
in the sky. The frightened villagers, who depended on one another to maintain the real, went to my aunt to show her a personal, physical representation of the break she made in the "roundness." Misallying couples snapped
off the future, which was to be embodied in true offspring. The villagers
punished her for acting as if she could have a private life, secret and apart
from them.

If my aunt had betrayed the family at a time of large grain yields and   38
peace, when many boys were born, and wings were being built on many
houses, perhaps she might have escaped such severe punishment. But the
men—hungry, greedy, tired of planting in dry soil, cuckolded—had been
forced to leave the village in order to send food-money home. There were
ghost plagues, bandit plagues, wars with the Japanese, floods. My Chinese
brother and sister had died of an unknown sickness. Adultery, perhaps only
a mistake during good times, became a crime when the village needed food.

The round moon cakes and round doorways, the round tables of grad-   39
uated size that fit one roundness inside another, round windows and rice
bowls—these talismans had lost their power to warn this family of the law:
A family must be whole, faithfully keeping the descent line by having sons
to feed the old and the dead who in turn look after the family. The villagers
came to show my aunt and lover-in-hiding a broken house. The villagers

were speeding up the circling of events because she was too shortsighted to see that her infidelity had already harmed the village, that waves of consequences would return unpredictably, sometimes in disguise, as now, to hurt her. This roundness had to be made coin-sized so that she would see its circumference: Punish her at the birth of her baby. Awaken her to the inexorable. People who refused fatalism because they could invent small resources insisted on culpability. Deny accidents and wrest fault from the stars.

After the villagers left, their lanterns now scattering in various directions toward home, the family broke their silence and cursed her. "Aiaa, we're going to die. Death is coming. Death is coming. Look what you've done. You've killed us. Ghost! Dead Ghost! Ghost! You've never been born." She ran out into the fields, far enough from the house so that she could no longer hear their voices, and pressed herself against the earth, her own land no more. When she felt the birth coming, she thought that she had been hurt. Her body seized together. "They've hurt me too much," she thought. "This is gall, and it will kill me." With forehead and knees against the earth, her body convulsed and then relaxed. She turned on her back, lay on the ground. The black well of sky and stars went out and out forever; her body and her complexity seemed to disappear. She was one of the stars, a bright dot in blackness, without home, without a companion, in eternal cold and silence. An agoraphobia rose in her, speeding higher and higher, bigger and bigger; she would not be able to contain it; there would be no end to fear. 40

Flayed, unprotected against space, she felt pain return, focusing her body. This pain chilled her—a cold, steady kind of surface pain. Inside, spasmodically, the other pain, the pain of the child, heated her. For hours she lay on the ground, alternately body and space. Sometimes a vision of normal comfort obliterated reality: She saw the family in the evening gambling at the dinner table, the young people massaging their elders' backs. She saw them congratulating one another, high joy on the mornings the rice shoots came up. When these pictures burst, the stars drew yet further apart. Black space opened. 41

She got to her feet to fight better and remembered that old-fashioned women gave birth in their pigsties to fool the jealous, pain-dealing gods, who do not snatch piglets. Before the next spasms could stop her, she ran to the pigsty, each step a rushing out into emptiness. She climbed over the fence and knelt in the dirt. It was good to have a fence enclosing her, a tribal person alone. 42

Laboring, this woman who had carried her child as a foreign growth that sickened her every day, expelled it at last. She reached down to touch the hot, wet, moving mass, surely smaller than anything human, and could 43 feel that it was human after all—fingers, toes, nails, nose. She pulled it up on to her belly, and it lay curled there, butt in the air, feet precisely tucked one under the other. She opened her loose shirt and buttoned the child inside. After resting, it squirmed and thrashed and she pushed it up to her breast. It turned its head this way and that until it found her nipple. There, it made little snuffling noises. She clenched her teeth at its preciousness, lovely as a young calf, a piglet, a little dog.

She may have gone to the pigsty as a last act of responsibility: She would protect this child as she had protected its father. It would look after her soul, leaving supplies on her grave. But how would this tiny child without family find her grave when there would be no marker for her anywhere, neither in the earth nor the family hall? No one would give her a family hall name. She had taken the child with her into the wastes. At its birth the two of them had felt the same raw pain of separation, a wound that only the family pressing tight could close. A child with no descent line would not soften her life but only trail after her, ghostlike, begging her to give it purpose. At dawn the villagers on their way to the fields would stand around the fence and look.   44

Full of milk, the little ghost slept. When it awoke, she hardened her breasts against the milk that crying loosens. Toward morning she picked up the baby and walked to the well.   45

Carrying the baby to the well shows loving. Otherwise abandon it. Turn its face into the mud. Mothers who love their children take them along. It was probably a girl; there is some hope of forgiveness for boys.   46

"Don't tell anyone you had an aunt. Your father does not want to hear her name. She has never been born." I have believed that sex was unspeakable and words so strong and fathers so frail that "aunt" would do my father mysterious harm. I have thought that my family, having settled among immigrants who had also been their neighbors in the ancestral land, needed to clean their name, and a wrong word would incite the kinspeople even here. But there is more to this silence: They want me to participate in her punishment. And I have.   47

In the twenty years since I heard this story I have not asked for details nor said my aunt's name; I do not know it. People who comfort the dead can also chase after them to hurt them further—a reverse ancestor worship. The real punishment was not the raid swiftly inflicted by the villagers, but the family's deliberately forgetting her. Her betrayal so maddened them, they saw to it that she would suffer forever, even after death. Always hungry, always needing, she would have to beg food from other ghosts, snatch and steal it from those whose living descendants give them gifts. She would have to fight the ghosts massed at crossroads for the buns a few thoughtful citizens leave to decoy her away from village and home so that the ancestral spirits   48 could feast unharassed. At peace, they could act like gods, not ghosts, their descent lines providing them with paper suits and dresses, spirit money, paper houses, paper automobiles, chicken, meat, and rice into eternity—essences delivered up in smoke and flames, steam and incense rising from each rice bowl. In an attempt to make the Chinese care for people outside the family, Chairman Mao encourages us now to give our paper replicas to the spirits of outstanding soldiers and workers, no matter whose ancestors they may be. My aunt remains forever hungry. Goods are not distributed evenly among the dead.

My aunt haunts me—her ghost drawn to me because now, after fifty 49 years of neglect, I alone devote pages of paper to her, though not origamied into houses and clothes. I do not think she always means me well. I am telling on her, and she was a spite suicide, drowning herself in the drinking water. The Chinese are always very frightened of the drowned one, whose weeping ghost, wet hair hanging and skin bloated, waits silently by the water to pull down a substitute.

◆ ◆ ◆

FIRST RESPONSES

Which story about the aunt's relationship with her baby's father do you most want to believe? Why? Does that choice affect your response to the aunt's death?

TAKING A CLOSER LOOK

Exploring Who: Voice and Tone

1. How does Kingston feel about her aunt? About her mother? About being both Chinese and American? Why does she believe that narrating the events which led to her attitudes and feelings will be valuable to her readers, too?
2. What tone of voice does Kingston use when she writes in paragraph 25, "I hope that the man my aunt loved appreciated a smooth brow, that he wasn't just a tits-and ass man"? What does the sentence tell you about Kingston?
3. How much does Kingston expect readers to know about the Chinese culture? Does she include experiences or feelings that anyone, regardless of nationality, can relate to?

4. ▟▌ *Using the Internet.* The University of Minnesota has established a Maxine Hong Kingston Web site at htttp://english.cla.umn.edu/lkd/vgf/authors/maxinehongkingston. Does the information provided there add to your understanding of Kingston's perspective in "No Name Woman"? How?

Exploring *What:* Content and Meaning

1. Why did the villagers attack Kingston's family's home? Reread paragraph 39 to see if it gives you additional insight into their reasons. Find evidence that Kingston has some sympathy for their motives.
2. Could this essay have been written by a man? Why or why not? How would it be diffcrent if one of Kingston's brothers tried to retell the mother's story about the aunt?
3. What does Kingston mean when she says, "Carrying the baby to the well shows loving"? How has Kingston prepared you to understand her point?

Exploring *Why:* Purpose

1. Kingston directly reveals her mother's reason for narrating her aunt's story: "Now that you have started to menstruate, what happened to her could happen to you." How did you respond to this warning? What are Kingston's reasons for telling us this same story?
2. What does Kingston mean when she says in the conclusion, "I do not think she [her aunt] always means me well"? What risks does she face in telling us this story? Have you ever repeated a story that you were asked not to share with anyone?

Exploring *How:* Style and Strategy

1. Kingston writes, "Unless I see her life [her aunt's] branching into mine, she gives me no ancestral help." Does this explain why she writes multiple versions of her aunt's story? What sources does Kingston use to piece together the interpretations she creates? Paragraph 19 might offer you some answers to this question.
2. Read paragraphs 4 and 5 and identify the **similes** (comparisons using *like* or *as*). How do these comparisons add to your understanding of the scene Kingston is describing?
3. Kingston uses vivid, descriptive language to bring her scenes to life. Look at one of the major scenes, either the villagers' attack or the

childbirth, and identify Kingston's use of concrete detail and appeal to the senses to achieve her desired affect on the reader.

IDEAS FOR WRITING A NARRATIVE

1. Write a narrative in which you tell the story of an important moment in your life from your own point of view. Then rewrite the story from the point of view of someone else involved in the story.
2. Narrate a story that reveals a time you felt torn between two roles that you hold—for example, daughter versus sister, employee versus friend, or student versus friend.
3. Tell the story of a time when you were happy or unhappy with your family life.

◆ ◆ ◆ PREPARING TO READ

Did you ever have to perform an extremely difficult or distasteful task? Why did you feel you had to do it? How did you feel afterward?

◆ ◆ ◆

Shooting an Elephant

GEORGE ORWELL

Novelist, essayist, and critic, George Orwell (pen name of Eric Blair, 1903–1950) was born in India, where his father was in the civil service. He was educated at Eton but was financially unable to go on to Oxford or Cambridge. Instead he spent five years with the Imperial Police in Burma. Orwell is widely regarded as one of the finest satirists of the twentieth century. His most famous novels are *Animal Farm,* a scathing attack on communism, and *1984,* a chilling depiction of a totalitarian society. Several of his best essays, including the one you're about to read, draw upon his experiences in Burma.

In Moulmein, in Lower Burma, I was hated by large numbers of 1 people—the only time in my life that I have been important enough for this to happen to me. I was subdivisional police officer of the town, and in an aimless, petty kind of way anti-European feeling was very bitter. No one had the guts to raise a riot, but if a European woman went through the bazaars alone somebody would probably spit betel juice over her dress. As a police officer I was an obvious target and was baited whenever it seemed safe to do so. When a nimble Burman tripped me up on the football field and the referee (another Burman) looked the other way, the crowd yelled with hideous laughter. This happened more than once. In the end the sneering yellow faces of young men that met me everywhere, the insults hooted after me when I was at a safe distance, got badly on my nerves. The young Buddhist priests were the worst of all. There were several thousands of them in the town and none of them seemed to have anything to do except stand on street corners and jeer at Europeans.

All this was perplexing and upsetting. For at that time I had already 2 made up my mind that imperialism was an evil thing and the sooner I chucked up my job and got out of it the better. Theoretically—and secretly, of course—I was all for the Burmese and all against the oppressors, the

British. As for the job I was doing, I hated it more bitterly than I can perhaps make clear. In a job like that you see the dirty work of Empire at close
quarters. The wretched prisoners huddling in the stinking cages of the lock-
ups, the grey, cowed faces of the longterm convicts, the scarred buttocks of
the men who had been flogged with bamboos—all these oppressed me with
an intolerable sense of guilt. But I could get nothing into perspective. I was
young and ill-educated and I had had to think out my problems in the utter
silence that imposed on every Englishman in the East. I did not even know
that the British Empire is dying, still less did I know that it is a great deal
better than the younger empires that are going to supplant it. All I knew
was that I was stuck between my hatred of the empire I served and my rage
against the evil-spirited little beasts who tried to make my job impossible.
With one part of my mind I thought of the British Rajas as an unbreakable
tyranny, as something clamped down, in *saecula saeculorum,* upon the will
of prostrate peoples; with another part I thought that the greatest joy in the
world would be to drive a bayonet into a Buddhist priest's guts. Feelings
like these are the normal by-products of imperialism; ask any Anglo-Indian
official, if you can catch him off duty.

    One day something happened which in a roundabout way was en-   3
lightening. It was a tiny incident in itself, but it gave me a better glimpse
than I had had before of the real nature of imperialism—the real motives
for which despotic governments act. Early one morning the subinspector at
a police station at the other end of town rang me up on the phone and said
that an elephant was ravaging the bazaar. Would I please come and do
something about it? I did not know what I could do, but I wanted to see
what was happening and I got on to a pony and started out. I took my rifle,
an old .44 Winchester and much too small to kill an elephant, but I thought
the noise might be useful *in terrorem.* Various Burmans stopped me on the
way and told me about the elephant's doings. It was not, of course, a wild
elephant, but a tame one which had gone "must." It had been chained up, as
tame elephants always are when their attack of "must" is due, but on the
previous night it had broken its chain and escaped. Its mahout, the only person who could manage it when it was in that state, had set out in pursuit, but
had taken the wrong direction and was now twelve hours' journey away,
and in the morning the elephant had suddenly reappeared in the town. The
Burmese population had no weapons and were quite helpless against it. It
had already destroyed somebody's bamboo hut, killed a cow, and raided
some fruit stalls and devoured the stock; also it had met the municipal rub-
bish van and, when the driver jumped out and took to his heels, had turned
the van over and inflicted violences upon it.

    The Burmese subinspector and some Indian constables were waiting   4
for me in the quarter where the elephant had been seen. It was a very poor

quarter, a labyrinth of squalid bamboo huts, thatched with palmleaf, winding all over a steep hillside. I remember that it was a cloudy, stuffy morning at the beginning of the rains. We began questioning the people as to where the elephant had gone and, as usual, failed to get any definite information. That is invariably the case in the East; a story always sounds clear enough at a distance, but the nearer you get to the scene of events the vaguer it becomes. Some of the people said that the elephant had gone in one direction, some said that he had gone in another, some professed not even to have heard of any elephant. I had almost made up my mind that the whole story was a pack of lies, when we heard yells a little distance away. There was a loud, scandalized cry of "Go away, child! Go away this instant!" and an old woman with a switch in her hand came round the corner of a hut, violently shooing away a crowd of naked children. Some more women followed, clicking their tongues and exclaiming; evidently there was something that the children ought not to have seen. I rounded the hut and saw a man's dead body sprawling in the mud. He was an Indian, a black Dravidian coolie, almost naked, and he could not have been dead many minutes. The people said that the elephant had come suddenly upon him round the corner of the hut, caught him with its trunk, put its foot on his back, and ground him into the earth. This was the rainy season and the ground was soft, and his face had scored a trench a foot deep and a couple of yards long. He was lying on his belly with arms crucified and head sharply twisted to one side. His face was coated with mud, the eyes wide open, the teeth bared and grinning with an expression of unendurable agony. (Never tell me, by the way, that the dead look peaceful. Most of the corpses I have seen looked devilish.) The friction of the great beast's foot had stripped the skin from his back as neatly as one skins a rabbit. As soon as I saw the dead man I sent an orderly to a friend's house nearby to borrow an elephant rifle. I had already sent back the pony, not wanting it to go mad with fright and throw me if it smelled the elephant.

The orderly came back in a few minutes with a rifle and five cartridges,   5
and meanwhile some Burmans had arrived and told us that the elephant was in the paddy fields below, only a few hundred yards away. As I started forward practically the whole population of the quarter flocked out of the houses and followed me. They had seen the rifle and were all shouting excitedly that I was going to shoot the elephant. They had not shown much interest in the elephant when he was merely ravaging their homes, but it was different now that he was going to be shot. It was a bit of fun to them, as it would be to an English crowd; besides they wanted the meat. It made me vaguely uneasy. I had no intention of shooting the elephant—I had merely sent for the rifle to defend myself if necessary—and it is always unnerving to have a crowd following you. I marched down the hill, looking and feeling

a fool, with the rifle over my shoulder and an ever-growing army of people jostling at my heels. At the bottom, when you got away from the huts, there was a metalled road and beyond that a miry waste of paddy fields a thousand yards across, not yet ploughed but soggy from the first rains and dotted with coarse grass. The elephant was standing eight yards from the road, his left side towards us. He took not the slightest notice of the crowd's approach. He was tearing up bunches of grass, beating them against his knees to clean them and stuffing them into his mouth.

I had halted on the road. As soon as I saw the elephant I knew with   6
perfect certainty that I ought not to shoot him. It is a serious matter to shoot a working elephant—it is comparable to destroying a huge and costly piece of machinery—and obviously one ought not to do it if it can possibly be avoided. And at that distance, peacefully eating, the elephant looked no more dangerous than a cow. I thought then and I think now that his attack of "must" was already passing off; in which case he would merely wander harmlessly about until the mahout came back and caught him. Moreover, I did not in the least want to shoot him. I decided that I would watch him for a little while to make sure that he did not turn savage again, and then go home.

But at that moment, I glanced round at the crowd that had followed   7
me. It was an immense crowd, two thousand at the least and growing every minute. It blocked the road for a long distance on either side. I looked at the sea of yellow faces above the garish clothes—faces all happy and excited over this bit of fun, all certain that the elephant was going to be shot. They were watching me as they would watch a conjuror about to perform a trick. They did not like me, but with the magical rifle in my hands I was momentarily worth watching. And suddenly I realized that I should have to shoot the elephant after all. The people expected it of me and I had got to do it. I could feel their two thousand wills pressing me forward, irresistibly. And it was at this moment, as I stood there with the rifle in my hands, that I first grasped the hollowness, the futility of the white man's dominion in the East. Here was I, the white man with his gun, standing in front of the unarmed native crowd—seemingly the leading actor of the piece; but in reality I was only an absurd puppet pushed to and fro by the will of those yellow faces behind. I perceived in this moment that when the white man turns tyrant it is his own freedom that he destroys. He becomes a sort of hollow, posing dummy, the conventionalized figure of a sahib. For it is the condition of his rule that he shall spend his life in trying to impress the "natives," and so in every crisis he has got to do what the "natives" expect of him. He wears a mask, and his face grows to fit it. I had got to shoot the elephant. I had committed myself to doing it when I sent for the rifle. A sahib has got to act like a sahib; he has got to appear resolute, to know his own mind and do definite

things. To come all that way, rifle in hand, with two thousand people marching at my heels, and then to trail feebly away, having done nothing—no, that was impossible. The crowd would laugh at me. And my whole life, every white man's life in the East, was one long struggle not to be laughed at.

But I did not want to shoot the elephant. I watched him beating his bunch of grass against his knees, with that preoccupied grandmotherly air that elephants have. It seemed to me that it would be murder to shoot him. At that age I was not squeamish about killing animals, but I had never shot an elephant and never wanted to. (Somehow it always seems worse to kill a large animal.) Besides, there was the beast's owner to be considered. Alive, the elephant was worth at least a hundred pounds; dead, he would only be worth the value of his tusks, five pounds, possibly. But I had got to act quickly. I turned to some experienced-looking Burmans who had been there when we arrived, and asked them how the elephant had been behaving. They all said the same thing: He took no notice of you if you left him alone, but he might charge if you went too close to him.   8

It was perfectly clear to me what I ought to do. I ought to walk up to within, say, twenty-five yards of the elephant and test his behavior. If he charged, I could shoot; if he took no notice of me, it would be safe to leave him until the mahout came back. But also I knew that I was going to do no such thing. I was a poor shot with a rifle and the ground was soft mud into which one would sink at every step. If the elephant charged and I missed him, I should have about as much chance as a toad under a steamroller. But even then I was not thinking particularly of my own skin, only of the watchful yellow faces behind. For at that moment, with the crowd watching me, I was not afraid in the ordinary sense, as I would have been if I had been alone. A white man mustn't be frightened in front of "natives"; and so, in general, he isn't frightened. The sole thought in my mind was that if anything went wrong those two thousand Burmans would see me pursued, caught, trampled on, and reduced to a grinning corpse like that Indian up the hill. And if that happened it was quite probable that some of them would laugh. That would never do. There was only one alternative. I shoved the cartridges into the magazine and lay down on the road to get a better aim.   9

The crowd grew very still, and a deep, low, happy sigh, as of people who see the theatre curtain go up at last, breathed from innumerable throats. They were going to have their bit of fun after all. The rifle was a beautiful German thing with cross-hair sights. I did not then know that in shooting an elephant one would shoot to cut an imaginary bar running from ear-hole to ear-hole. I ought, therefore, as the elephant was sideways on, to have aimed straight at his ear-hole; actually I aimed several inches in front of this, thinking the brain would be further forward.   10

When I pulled the trigger I did not hear the bang or feel the kick—one   11
never does when a shot goes home—but I heard the devilish roar of glee
that went up from the crowd. In that instant, in too short a time, one would
have thought, even for the bullet to get there, a mysterious, terrible change
had come over the elephant. He neither stirred nor fell, but every line of his
body had altered. He looked suddenly stricken, shrunken, immensely old, as
though the frightful impact of the bullet had paralyzed him without knocking him down. At last, after what seemed a long time—it might have been
five seconds, I dare say—he sagged flabbily to his knees. His mouth slob-
bered. An enormous senility seemed to have settled upon him. One could
have imagined him thousands of years old. I fired again into the same spot.
At the second shot he did not collapse but climbed with desperate slowness
to his feet and stood weakly upright, with legs sagging and head drooping. I
fired a third time. That was the shot that did for him. You could see the
agony of it jolt his whole body and knock the last remnant of strength from
his legs. But in falling he seemed for a moment to rise, for as his hind legs
collapsed beneath him he seemed to tower upward like a huge rock top-
pling, his trunk reaching skywards like a tree. He trumpeted, for the first
and only time. And then down he came, his belly towards me, with a crash
that seemed to shake the ground even where I lay.

I got up. The Burmans were already racing past me across the mud. It   12
was obvious that the elephant would never rise again, but he was not dead.
He was breathing very rhythmically with long rattling gasps, his great
mound of a side painfully rising and falling. His mouth was wide open. I
could see far down into caverns of pale pink throat. I waited a long time for
him to die, but his breathing did not weaken. Finally, I fired my two remaining shots into the spot where I thought his heart must be. The thick blood
welled out of him like red velvet, but still he did not die. His body did not
even jerk when the shots hit him, the tortured breathing continued without
a pause. He was dying, very slowly and in great agony, but in some world remote from me where not even a bullet could damage him further. I felt I
had got to put an end to that dreadful noise. It seemed dreadful to see the
great beast lying there, powerless to move and yet powerless to die, and not
even to be able to finish him I sent back for my small rifle and poured shot
after shot into his heart, and down his throat. They seemed to make no impression. The tortured gasps continued as steadily as the ticking of a clock.

In the end I could not stand it any longer and went away. I heard later   13
that it took him half an hour to die. Burmans were bringing dahs and baskets even before I left, and I was told they had stripped his body almost to
the bones by the afternoon.

Afterwards, of course, there were endless discussions about the shoot-   14
ing of the elephant. The owner was furious, but he was only an Indian and

could do nothing. Besides, legally I had done the right thing, for a mad elephant has to be killed, like a mad dog, if its owner fails to control it. Among the Europeans opinion was divided. The older men said I was right, the younger men said it was a damn shame to shoot an elephant for killing a coolie, because the elephant was worth more than any damn Coringhee coolie. And afterwards I was very glad that the coolie had been killed; it put me legally in the right and it gave me sufficient pretext for shooting the elephant. I often wondered whether any of the others grasped that I had done it solely to avoid looking a fool.

◆ ◆ ◆

FIRST RESPONSES

Do you think Orwell should have killed the elephant? What other choices did he have? Do you sympathize with him? Do you sympathize with the elephant?

TAKING A CLOSER LOOK

Exploring *Who:* Voice and Tone

1. What attitude does Orwell have toward the Burmese people? How do they feel about him? How might the incident have ended if he had had other Europeans with him when he encountered the elephant?
2. How does Orwell want to present himself in paragraphs 6 through 9? How did you respond to this section of the essay?
3. Orwell says he shot the elephant "solely to avoid looking a fool." What do you think of this admission? Have you ever felt you had to go against your instincts to avoid looking foolish?

Exploring *What:* Content and Meaning

1. Where is Burma, and what was Orwell doing there?
2. What is Orwell's thesis? Where does he state it?
3. ■ *Using the Internet.* Orwell uses the word *imperialism* several times. What does it mean? Using an Internet search engine, do a keyword search for *imperialism,* and see if you can find any current or recent events where the term is applicable.

4. List the reasons Orwell considers when he tries to decide what to do. Do any of these reasons seem suspect?

5. Why does Orwell say, "I was very glad that the coolie had been killed" (paragraph 14)?

Exploring *Why:* Purpose

1. Is Orwell trying to justify his actions? Or does he have a different purpose? To what extent is this essay an exploration of the author's beliefs?

2. A **parable** is defined as "an illustrative story that teaches a lesson." In what ways is this essay a parable?

Exploring *How:* Style and Strategy

1. Where does the narrative begin? Why does Orwell take so long to get to the central incident? How did you react to this long introduction?

2. Why does the author use Latin phrases? What effect did these have on you?

3. Why does he enclose some remarks in parentheses (paragraphs 4 and 8)?

4. Why didn't Orwell use any dialogue in this essay? What does he lose by omitting dialogue? What does he gain?

5. What effect do the graphic details of the dead man and the dying elephant have on your reactions to the essay? Could Orwell have accomplished his purpose without including these details?

6. How does Orwell build tension after he shoots the elephant?

IDEAS FOR WRITING A NARRATIVE

1. Narrate an experience that led you to a realization about your place in the world around you (for example, as a white person, as a woman, as a midwesterner, as a youth, or as a college student). Explain what you learned and how it changed your social or political outlook.

2. Write a narrative about a time when you felt isolated or outnumbered. Describe the situation and also your feelings.

3. Write an essay about a time when you resisted group pressure to do something that went against your values.

◆ FURTHER IDEAS FOR USING NARRATION

1. Write a narrative about a time when you surprised yourself—for example, by being more courageous, more fearful, smarter or dumber, more conservative or liberal, or more outgoing or introverted than you usually are. Be sure to establish why you were surprised. Imply rather than state why you behaved (or thought or felt) differently from your ordinary expectations.

2. Situations at school and work, as well as relationships with family and friends, can force us into making difficult ethical choices—for example, telling a truth that will help one person but hurt another or feeling forced to share information that was told you in confidence. Once made, however, these decisions offer us a foundation for positive future action. Narrate an experience in which, for better or worse, you learned a valuable ethical lesson.

3. Watch a movie with a child of eight or under. A few hours later, or the next day, ask the child to tell you the story of the movie you saw together, and audiotape the narrative. Write an essay considering the differences between the child's narrative and one you might give (for example, if you were writing a film review). Discuss what you learned about narrating experience from this exercise. (As an alternative, you could do this exercise with someone older than you are or someone from a clearly different cultural background from yours.)

4. Read "Coming to America, to Clean," a narrative reprinted in Chapter 12. Interview someone about his or her immigrant experience, and edit the interview into a narrative essay.

5. COLLABORATIVE WRITING. In a small group, brainstorm and create a set of interview questions that will help you elicit material for writing a vivid narrative based on another person's experience. You might decide to focus on interviewing someone who has gone through a certain era or type of experience—for example, a person in a rock and roll band, someone who was a footsoldier in a war, a person who has written a book, someone who witnessed an historic event, or even someone who has gone through a more ordinary life event such as giving birth, getting fired, winning or losing an important contest. Then, each group member can use the questions, perform the interview, and write a narrative based on it.

6. ▪️ *Using the Internet.* There are numerous sites and resources for writers on the Internet. To get some ideas for writing a narrative, visit

a Web site like the StoryTellers Challenge (http://storyteller. simplenet.com/), which gives topics in the form of "challenges." On the "Truer Than Fiction" page you will find suggestions for writing nonfiction, as well as sample essays from other writers. Another useful site to look at for narrative writing is Storyteller.net at http://www. storyteller.net. The "Story of the Week" page might spark some ideas.

CHAPTER 4

Strategies for Appealing to the Senses

Description

◆ ◆ ◆ ◆ ◆

Descriptive writing tells how something looks, acts, sounds, feels, smells, or tastes.

◆ Writers use description to present information and express feelings.

◆ Extended descriptions convey a dominant impression of the subject.

◆ Effective descriptions employ specific details, images, and comparisons.

You use **descriptions** all the time. In talking with your friends or writing to your family, you describe where you've been, what you saw, who you went out with. Good descriptions add life and interest to any conversation or piece of writing.

Although you seldom need to make description the basis for an entire essay, virtually everything you write includes descriptive details. They enliven narratives, clarify explanations, perk up examples, sharpen comparisons, and add vigor to arguments. No matter what you have to say, accurate and effective descriptions will help you say it better.

In the following selection, Tracy Kidder describes in detail a dedicated fifth-grade teacher. The student essay that follows takes a similar look at an oddly appealing childhood chum. Both pieces are filled with first-rate examples of descriptive writing.

Mrs. Zajac

TRACY KIDDER

Tracy Kidder is an award-winning author of nonfiction books about houses, computers, and nursing homes. In 1988, he spent nine months in the fifth-grade class of Mrs. Zajac and her twenty students. What follows is the opening section of the book he wrote about this experience, entitled *Among School Children*.

Mrs. Zajac wasn't born yesterday. She knows you didn't do your best 1
work on this paper, Clarence. Don't you remember Mrs. Zajac saying that if you didn't do your best, she'd make you do it over? As for you, Claude, God forbid that you should ever need brain surgery. But Mrs. Zajac hopes that if you do, the doctor won't open up your head and walk off saying he's almost done, as you just said when Mrs. Zajac asked you for your penmanship, which, by the way, looks like who did it and ran. Felipe, the reason you have hiccups is, your mouth is always open and the wind rushes in. You're in fifth grade now. So, Felipe, put a lock on it. Zip it up. Then go get a drink of water. Mrs. Zajac means business, Robert. The sooner you realize she never said everybody in the room has to do the work except for Robert, the sooner you'll get along with her. And . . . Clarence, Mrs. Zajac knows you didn't try. You don't just hand in junk to Mrs. Zajac. She's been teaching an awful lot of years. She didn't fall off the turnip cart yesterday. She told you she was an old-lady teacher.

She was thirty-four. She wore a white skirt and yellow sweater and 2
a thin gold necklace, which she held in her fingers, as if holding her own reins, while waiting for children to answer. Her hair was black with a hint of Irish red. It was cut short to the tops of her ears, and swept back like a pair of folded wings. She had a delicately cleft chin, and she was short—the children's chairs would have fit her. Although her voice sounded

conversational, it had projection. She had never acted. She had found this voice in classrooms.

Mrs. Zajac seemed to have a frightening amount of energy. She strode   3
across the room, her arms swinging high and her hands in small fists. Taking her stand in front of the green chalkboard, discussing the rules with her new class, she repeated sentences, and her lips held the shapes of certain words, such as "homework," after she had said them. Her hands kept very busy. They sliced the air and made karate chops to mark off boundaries. They extended straight out like a traffic cop's, halting illegal maneuvers yet to be perpetrated. When they rested momentarily on her hips, her hands looked as if they were in holsters. She told the children, "One thing Mrs. Zajac expects from each of you is that you do your best." She said, "Mrs. Zajac gives homework. I'm sure you've all heard. The old meanie gives homework." *Mrs. Zajac.* It was in part a role. She worked her way into it every September.

At home on late summer days like these, Chris Zajac wore shorts or   4
blue jeans. Although there was no dress code for teachers here at Kelly School, she always went to work in skirts or dresses. She dressed as if she were applying for a job, and hoped in the back of her mind that someday, heading for job interviews, her students would remember her example. Outside school, she wept easily over small and large catastrophes and at sentimental movies, but she never cried in front of students, except once a few years ago when the news came over the intercom that the Space Shuttle had exploded and Christa McAuliffe had died—and then she saw in her students' faces that the sight of Mrs. Zajac crying had frightened them, and she made herself stop and then explained.

At home, Chris laughed at the antics of her infant daughter and egged   5
the child on. She and her first-grade son would sneak up to the radio when her husband wasn't looking and change the station from classical to rock-and-roll music. "You're regressing, Chris," her husband would say. But especially on the first few days of school, she didn't let her students get away with much. She was not amused when, for instance, on the first day, two of the boys started dueling with their rulers. On nights before the school year started, Chris used to have bad dreams: her principal would come to observe her, and her students would choose that moment to climb up on their desks and give her the finger, or they would simply wander out the door. But a child in her classroom would never know that Mrs. Zajac had the slightest doubt that students would obey her.

The first day, after going over all the school rules, Chris spoke to them   6
about effort. "If you put your name on a paper, you should be proud of it," she said. "You should think, This is the best I can do and I'm proud of it and

I want to hand this in." Then she asked, "If it isn't your best, what's Mrs. Zajac going to do?"

Many voices, most of them female, answered softly in unison, "Make   7
us do it over."

"*Make you do it over,*" Chris repeated. It sounded like a chant.   8

"Does anyone know anything about Lisette?" she asked when no one   9
answered to that name.

Felipe—small, with glossy black hair—threw up his hand.   10

"Felipe?"   11

"She isn't here!" said Felipe. He wasn't being fresh. On those first few   12
days of school, whenever Mrs. Zajac put the sound of a question in her
voice, and sometimes before she got the question out, Felipe's hand shot up.

In contrast, there was the very chubby girl who sat nearly motionless   13
at her desk, covering the lower half of her face with her hands. As usual,
most of their voices sounded timid the first day, and came out of hiding
gradually. There were twenty children. About half were Puerto Rican. Almost two-thirds of the twenty needed the forms to obtain free lunches.
There was a lot of long and curly hair. Some boys wore little rattails. The
eyes the children lifted up to her as she went over the rules—a few eyes
were blue and many more were brown—looked so solemn and so wide that
Chris felt like dropping all pretense and laughing. Their faces ranged from
dark brown to gold, to pink, to pasty white, the color that Chris associated
with sunless tenements and too much TV. The boys wore polo shirts and T-
shirts and new white sneakers with the ends of the laces untied and tucked
behind the tongues. Some girls wore lacy ribbons in their hair, and some
wore pants and others skirts, a rough but not infallible indication of religion—the daughters of Jehovah's Witnesses and Pentecostals do not wear
pants. There was a lot of prettiness in the room, and all of the children
looked cute to Chris.

◆ ◆ ◆

◆ ◆ ◆ Writer's Workshop I ◆ ◆ ◆
Responding to a Description

Use the *Who, What, Why,* and *How* questions (see pp. 3–4) to explore
your own understanding of the ideas and writing strategies employed by
Tracy Kidder in "Mrs. Zajac." Your instructor may ask you to record these
responses in a journal or bring them to class to use in small group discussions.

◆ WRITING FROM READING

After reading this excerpt from Tracy Kidder's book, freshman Ann Moroney explored her reactions to the description of Mrs. Zajac, using the *Who, What, Why,* and *How* questions. She was impressed with the way Kidder brought his subject to life and wondered if she could do the same with someone she knew. She decided to write about a childhood friend and began to brainstorm for ideas. This is the essay she eventually produced.

Ann Moroney
English 1092
February 14, 1998

Lisa

She was a mousy little thing. Barely taller than a   1
yardstick, she didn't appear to be capable of hurting
a fly. Instead of looking directly at you when she was
talking, she stared slightly to the left with big,
distant blue eyes through spiky brown bangs that never
seemed to get washed properly. Her left eye twitched a
little; it seemed to bother her because she was
constantly wiping at it with a grimy finger. Every once
in a while she tugged at long brown wisps of unkempt
hair that floated across her face. Sometimes it was
almost as if she was mesmerized by the hair and not
really paying attention to what she was saying; her
eyes actually lit up and she looked like her thoughts
were going a mile a minute, each one there and gone
before she knew it. Then she came back to Earth and
realized she was still speaking, and her eyes returned
to their usual shade of lifeless blue. This cycle
would repeat itself until you were so frustrated with
her fidgeting and distractions that you had to leave;
yet, the next day you went to play with her because
she was your next door neighbor, your built-in pal.
She was fun to play with as long as she didn't talk to
you too much.

When you were over at Lisa's house, you always had 2
something to do. That's why the neighborhood kids
liked to play with her. She had the sandbox, the pool,
the biggest trees, the swing set and slide. She had a
big house and everywhere you looked was something just
waiting for kids to get into. The paint was always
peeling and the stone patio blocks were broken and
shifted; you had to be careful so you didn't stub your
toe on them. Inside, there were piles of clothes and
boxes strewn about, but somehow that didn't bother the
kids; they played hide-and-seek in the filth. The
furniture tended to moan and groan under new weight
when you sat down, as if it would fall apart if it had
to support one more person. The carpet was scratchy
and dusty, and when you moved the beds, there was a
rectangle of perfectly new carpet underneath. Despite
the poor conditions, you always left her house happy,
even though the dust and dirt started to get to you
and after a while you couldn't breathe anymore.

The most interesting parts of Lisa's house were 3
the floors; you could always find sharp as well as
colorful objects all over. With things like metal
paper clips to little broken plastic pieces,
ammunition for an unexpected war was never out of
reach. You sometimes left her house with holes in your
socks and maybe even in your feet.

Lisa wore skirts in the wintertime and pants in 4
the summertime: "So I don't ruin my skirts," she said.
Her shirt usually had stains around the edges of her
sleeves as if she had rammed her hands into mounds of
mud and didn't bother to pull them back. Her pants
were worn in the knees and the hems were torn; they
were the most likely victims of a hard day's work in
the sandbox. But somehow, they looked a little
shabbier than the pants the other kids in the
neighborhood wore, like they had been recycled from an
older brother or sister. Every once in a while, you
would see her in newer-looking pants, but that was
short lived because the next day they looked just as
worn-out as the rest of her wardrobe. She wore
splotchy white boy-socks that looked as if they'd been

accidentally washed with the black ones. She seldom wore shoes, and when she did they were standard, run-of-the-mill K-mart shoes. But they were the best looking articles of clothing on her.

"Hey Lisa, I know something you don't know!" one   5
of the neighborhood kids said to Lisa in a sing-song voice. "Look at your slide." There was a great big crack that ran from the ladder to the ground. The slide was unusable. "Tommy did it. He tried to slide on his feet, and he fell on his butt. He told us not to tell. And he already went home."

A screen door slammed. "Lisa Marie, who broke the   6
slide?"

"Tommy did."   7

"Don't lie to me, young lady. Tommy isn't even   8
here. Now, who broke the slide?"

"Tommy did!"   9

"Did you see him do it?"   10

"No. But—"   11

"No *buts,* and quit lying to me. How could you   12
accuse one of your friends of such a thing? You probably did it yourself!"

"But Mom—"   13

"I said no *buts!* Get in your room this instant.   14
You're grounded. And your friends all have to go home now."

With a pathetic look on her face, Lisa turned to   15
her friends and sighed. She forced a smile and began saying that she would come over as soon as she could, but the kids were already walking out the gate, chattering to themselves about what they were going to do now. Lisa stopped and just watched them go. Then she turned and went in the house.

"Hey, Mom? When will I be off grounding? 'Cause my   16
friends are really going to miss me."

◆ GETTING STARTED ON A DESCRIPTION

People write descriptions for two reasons: (1) to present information accurately and clearly, and (2) to convey their feelings about the subject. The first kind of description is an *objective* one; the second is *expressive.*

Ann Moroney decided she wanted to follow Tracy Kidder's lead and express her feelings about the person she would be describing. She began by reviewing her responses to the *Who, What, Why,* and *How* of Kidder's description. Then she put her recollections down on paper, sorting out the confused emotions she had about her childhood friend Lisa. Here are some excerpts from the freewriting Ann did about her subject:

> I always felt sorry for Lisa, I was one of the many neighborhood kids that would be at her house, not for her but for her toys, but for some reason I still felt bad about how the rest of the kids treated her. I still treated her like a person. I was nice to her because I wanted to be that way, no matter how annoying she was. I still played with her. She was more my friend than anyone else's just because she lived right next door.
>
> Looking back on her I think Lisa was a bit mentally slow. No doubt it had something to do with her upbringing, but in my opinion she needed special care. She was a year younger than me but her habits and mannerisms were more the toddler-type speed. She had speech problems, a lisp and stuttering slightly. When you're a kid you don't see these things as serious or treatable. You see them as things that set her apart from the rest and you label her "weird," "strange," and "outcast." She's not really a friend, but a person that needs help. And treat her like that. Sometimes in a negative, bad, degrading way.

After writing down her feelings about Lisa and thinking about the impressions she wanted to convey, Ann then made a list of details and examples she might use in writing her description:

tiny, rather dirty
neighborhood kids basically used her
had good toys but not good important things—house, clothes, hygiene
sort of "out of it" a lot
let herself be led around
kids broke her toys & she took the blame

sandbox—sand always out of the box
broken slide—Tommy
Andrea & Amy decapitating Barbie dolls

◆ ORGANIZING A DESCRIPTION

Some descriptions can be arranged spatially—top to bottom, left to right, near to far, back to front, and so on, like the movement of a camera filming a room or scene. But there's no built-in approach (like presenting a narrative in chronological order) that will work for many descriptions. A writer has to tailor the arrangement of details to suit the subject. To get some ideas for organizing her descriptive essay, Ann looked at how Tracy Kidder arranged his material. She made this rough outline of his description:

¶1: Quotes Mrs. Zajac talking to her class
¶2: Describes her clothes and physical appearance
¶3: Describes her movements and gestures in the classroom
¶4: Describes how she dresses, behaves at home vs. dress and behavior at school
¶5: Shows her at home with her family
¶s 6-12: Shows her interacting with her students (dialogue)
¶13:Gives information about some of her students and how she feels about them

Looking over this list, Ann saw how Kidder broke his description down into subtopics, or chunks of related information. She decided to take a similar approach by focusing on four areas: Lisa's appearance and mannerisms, her dress and hygiene, her environment, and the way the kids took advantage of her. With this rough plan in mind, Ann was ready to write her first draft.

◆ DEVELOPING A DESCRIPTION

Effective descriptions depend on language that appeals to the readers' senses. As Ann was working on her draft, she looked back at Tracy Kidder's description and noted that he relies heavily on **images**—words and phrases that prompt the reader to see, hear, smell, taste, and feel what the author is describing. For example, he mentions colors to help his readers visualize what Mrs. Zajac looks like: "She wore a white skirt and yellow sweater and a thin gold necklace, which she held in her fingers, as if holding her own reins. . . . Her hair was black with a hint of Irish red." He also describes the details of her movements in visual terms: "She strode across the room, her arms swinging high and her hands in small fists." Ann noticed, too, that Kidder uses a lot of comparisons, describing one thing in terms of another. Most of them are **similes,** which use *like* or *as*: Mrs. Zajac's hair "swept back like a pair of folded wings"; "her hands looked as if they were in holsters." But some of them are **metaphors,** which don't use *like* or *as* but imply a comparison by talking about one item as if it were another. For instance, instead of writing that Mrs. Zajac used her hands *like* a knife or *as* a karate master would, Kidder simply says they "sliced the air and made karate chops to mark off boundaries." He also suggests that Mrs. Zajac is like an actress in a play: "It was in part a role. She worked her way into it every September."

Ann also liked the use of conversation and dialogue to create scenes that let the reader hear Mrs. Zajac and see how she interacts with her family and her students. Ann was especially impressed with the way Kidder combines physical details with comments about Mrs. Zajac's beliefs and philosophy of teaching: "She dressed as if she were applying for a job, and hoped in the back of her mind that someday, heading for job interviews, her students would remember her example." Ann decided she would try to use both of these strategies in developing her description.

◆ USING THE MODEL

As you have seen, Tracy Kidder's essay helped Ann in several ways: it encouraged her to try writing a description of a person she felt strongly about; it suggested how she might organize her material; and it showed her how to use descriptive language effectively. But Ann didn't just copy Kidder's approach. For one thing, she didn't write about someone she admired; she chose, instead, to describe someone for whom she had mixed feelings. She also decided not to begin with a long monologue, the way Kidder does, and she ended her essay with dialogue, a technique that Kidder uses—but in a different way. In other words, Ann used Kidder as a model, but she also retained her independence as a writer.

The selections in the rest of this chapter illustrate how description can be used to shape and develop an essay. If you work with them the way that Ann worked with Kidder's example, you will discover many first-rate ideas and strategies for writing your own descriptions.

◆ ◆ ◆ *Writer's Workshop II* ◆ ◆ ◆
Analyzing a Description

Working individually or with a small group of classmates, read through Ann Moroney's essay "Lisa," and respond to the following questions:

1. Identify as many images, similes, and metaphors as you can. Which ones are most effective? Are there any that don't work for you?
2. What feelings do the descriptions convey? What is the author's attitude toward her subject? Is that attitude clear and consistent? What could she do to improve her depiction of Lisa?
3. Why does Ann use "you" in her essay? Why doesn't she use "I"?
4. Why does Ann end with a dialogue? Do you think this is an effective way to conclude? What other kind of ending could she have written?

◆ ◆ ◆ *Checklist for Reading and Writing* ◆ ◆ ◆
Descriptive Essays

1. What is the purpose of the description? Is it clear?
2. Is the description objective or expressive? If objective, are the details accurate and complete? If expressive, what feelings does it convey?
3. Is the material arranged appropriately? Do the parts of the description work together?
4. Is the language concrete and vivid? Does the description contain images that appeal to the senses? Are the comparisons fresh and effective?

◆ ◆ ◆ PREPARING TO READ

Have you ever visited a place (like a school, a neighborhood, a vacation spot) that you hadn't seen for a while and noticed that it looked very different from the way you remembered it? Had the place changed or had you?

◆ ◆ ◆

Two Views of the Mississippi

MARK TWAIN

Before becoming Mark Twain, America's most beloved humorist, Samuel Clemens (1830–1910) was a riverboat pilot, a journalist, and an unsuccessful gold miner. He said late in his life that those days on the river were the happiest he ever spent. In *Life on the Mississippi* he explains how he became a pilot and learned to "read" the river. In the following passage, Twain tells of one drawback to that otherwise rewarding experience.

The face of the water, in time, became a wonderful book—a book that   1
was a dead language to the uneducated passenger but which told its mind to me without reserve, delivering its most cherished secrets as clearly as if it uttered them with a voice. And it was not a book to be read once and thrown aside, for it had a new story to tell every day. Throughout the long twelve hundred miles there was never a page that was void of interest, never one that you could leave unread without loss, never one that you would want to skip, thinking you could find higher enjoyment in some other thing. There never was so wonderful a book written by man, never one whose interest was so absorbing, so unflagging, so sparklingly renewed with every reperusal. The passenger who could not read it was charmed with a peculiar sort of faint dimple on its surface (on the rare occasions when he did not overlook it altogether) but to the pilot that was an *italicized* passage; indeed it was more than that, it was a legend of the largest capitals with a string of shouting exclamation-points at the end of it, for it meant that a wreck or a rock was buried there that could tear the life out of the strongest vessel that ever floated. It is the faintest and simplest expression the water ever makes, and the most hideous to a pilot's eye. In truth, the passenger who could not read this book saw nothing but all manner of pretty pictures in it, painted by

the sun and shaded by the clouds, whereas to the trained eye these were not pictures at all, but the grimmest and most dead-earnest of reading matter.

Now when I had mastered the language of this water, and had come to know every trifling feature that bordered the great river as familiarly as I knew the letters of the alphabet, I had made a valuable acquisition. But I had lost something, too. I had lost something which could never be restored to me while I lived. All the grace, the beauty, the poetry, had gone out of the majestic river! I still keep in mind a certain wonderful sunset which I witnessed when steamboating was new to me. A broad expanse of the river was turned to blood; in the middle distance the red hue brightened into gold, through which a solitary log came floating black and conspicuous; in one place a long, slanting mark lay sparkling upon the water; in another the surface was broken by boiling, tumbling rings, that were as many-tinted as an opal; where the ruddy flush was faintest was a smooth spot that was covered with graceful circles and radiating lines, ever so delicately traced; the shore on our left was densely wooded, and the somber shadow that fell from this forest was broken in one place by a long, ruffled trail that shone like silver; and high above the forest wall a clean-stemmed dead tree waved a single leafy bough that glowed like a flame in the unobstructed splendor that was flowing in the sun. There were graceful curves, reflected images, woody heights, soft distances; and over the whole scene, far and near, the dissolving lights drifted steadily, enriching it every passing moment with new marvels of coloring.

I stood like one bewitched. I drank it in, in a speechless rapture. The world was new to me, and I had never seen anything like this at home. But as I have said, a day came when I began to cease from noting the glories and charms which the moon and sun and the twilight wrought upon the river's face; another day came when I ceased altogether to note them. Then, if that sunset scene had been repeated, I should have looked upon it without rapture, and should have commented upon it, inwardly, after this fashion: "This sun means that we are going to have wind to-morrow; that floating log means that the river is rising, small thanks to it; that slanting mark on the water refers to a bluff reef which is going to kill somebody's steamboat one of these nights, if it keeps on stretching out like that; those tumbling 'boils' show a dissolving bar and a changing channel there; the lines and circles in the slick water over yonder are a warning that that troublesome place is shoaling up dangerously; that silver streak in the shadow of the forest is the 'break' from a new snag, and he has located himself in the very best place he could have found to fish for steamboats; that tall dead tree, with a single living branch, is not going to last long, and then how is a body ever going to get through this blind place at night without the friendly old landmark?"

No, the romance and beauty were all gone from the river. All the value any feature of it had for me now was the amount of usefulness it could furnish toward compassing the safe piloting of a steamboat. Since those days, I have pitied doctors from my heart. What does the lovely flush in a beauty's cheek mean to a doctor but a "break" that ripples above some deadly disease? Are not all her visible charms sown thick with what are to him the signs and symbols of hidden decay? Does he ever see her beauty at all, or doesn't he simply view her professionally and comment upon her unwholesome condition all to himself? And doesn't he sometimes wonder whether he has gained most or lost most by learning his trade? 4

◆ ◆ ◆

FIRST RESPONSES

Do you agree that gaining knowledge takes away the appreciation of beauty? Have you ever had a learning experience that robbed you of a childhood illusion? Have you had the opposite experience—when learning increased your appreciation for something?

TAKING A CLOSER LOOK

Exploring *Who:* Voice and Tone

1. Have you read any books and stories by Mark Twain? How does this selection compare with his other works?
2. What does Twain think about passengers? How do you respond to the way he talks about passengers?
3. What attitude toward the river does Twain have? What attitude does he expect his readers to have?

Exploring *What:* Content and Meaning

1. How is the Mississippi River like a book? What is the "language" of the river?
2. What did Twain lose by learning to be a riverboat pilot? What did he gain?
3. Why does Twain feel sorry for doctors? Can you think of other professionals who might lose as much as they gain by learning their trades?

4. ◼️ *Using the Internet.* Have you ever been on a riverboat? Do you understand all the terms and details about the river that Twain uses? For information about this subject, search the Internet using "riverboat pilots" as the keywords, or visit the Mississippi River Home Page (http://www.greatriver.com) for an interview with a modern riverboat pilot.

Exploring *Why:* Purpose

1. Is Twain writing primarily for passengers, or is he writing for other pilots?
2. What is the main point of this selection? Is Twain providing you with information, or is he trying to persuade you of something?
3. Why does Twain include the detailed description of the sunset in paragraph 2? What feelings does the description evoke in you? Do you think your feelings are the same as Twain's?

Exploring *How:* Style and Strategy

1. Why does Twain compare the river to a book? How does he extend that description throughout the selection? Find words and phrases that continue the book metaphor.
2. Point out other comparisons that Twain uses to develop his description. Are these **similes** (comparisons that use *like* or *as*), or are they **metaphors** (implied comparisons that declare one thing to be another)?
3. Twain also personifies the river—that is, he gives it human characteristics. Find phrases and sentences that involve **personification.** Why does the author use this figure of speech?
4. What transitional phrases and sentences match up the parts of the description?
5. Why does Twain conclude with comments about doctors? Why do you think he decided to end this way? Would you have written a different conclusion?

WRITING FROM READING ASSIGNMENT

People often feel warm and sentimental about the past. Do you have any fond memories of the "good old days"? The main point of this writing assignment is to develop an expressive description of something or someone from your past that has been replaced—but not necessarily by something better.

A. First, reread "Two Views of the Mississippi," paying special attention to the feelings that the descriptions convey. Also, review your responses to the previous *Who, What, Why,* and *How* questions.

B. Then think of a person, place, or thing that you miss. Brainstorm a list of details and examples that you might use to describe your subject; freewrite about your feelings for the subject and the impression you want to present to your audience.

C. Begin your draft by letting your readers know that you have a fine, new whatever—best friend, favorite restaurant, music teacher, TV series, racing bike, sports car, designer jeans, neighborhood bakery—but that the new model doesn't measure up to what you had before.

D. Then, describe your former favorite. Use plenty of precise details, vivid images, and figurative comparisons, as Mark Twain does in his second paragraph, to appeal to your readers' senses. Show your readers what makes you feel the way you do about this past treasure.

E. Next, make a transition similar to Twain's—"But as I have said . . ." Or write your own: "After Lauren moved to California, I began to hang out with Megan; and although we've become really close, I still miss my former best buddy."

F. Now describe your replacement, focusing on its shortcomings—the ways in which it doesn't live up to the item you miss. Follow the same order in presenting the failings as you did in describing the virtues. (Look at how Twain uses exactly the same order in telling the two ways he saw the river. In his third paragraph, he begins with the sunset, then mentions the log, then the slanting mark on the water, then the "tumbling boils," then the lines and circles, then the streak in the shadow, and finally the dead tree—just as he did in his second paragraph.)

G. In your conclusion, express again the way you feel about having to make do with the unsatisfactory replacement and your longing to have the old one back.

You could write this same essay about a person or thing that has been replaced by someone or something a whole lot better.

◆ ◆ ◆ PREPARING TO READ

Have you seen any travelogues or travel programs on the Discovery Channel, or read any travel magazines or brochures? What kinds of descriptions and information do you expect to find in such materials?

◆ ◆ ◆

A Ride Through Spain

TRUMAN CAPOTE

Born Truman Steckfus Persons on September 30, 1924, in New Orleans, Capote then began his childhood in Monroeville, Alabama, with a batch of eccentric relatives he would later immortalize in his writing. Although he gained success with his lyrical novels and polished short stories, such as *Other Voices, Other Rooms* (1948) and *Breakfast at Tiffany's* (1958), Capote is best known for his "nonfiction novel" *In Cold Blood* (1966). This breathtaking account of two psychopaths who murdered a family in Kansas was made into a Hollywood film in 1968 and a television movie in 1996. Capote also wrote brilliant biographical profiles and travel sketches for magazines like *Cosmopolitan* and *The Saturday Evening Post*. The following essay first appeared in *The New Yorker* in 1946.

Certainly the train was old. The seats sagged like the jowls of a bull- 1
dog, windows were out and strips of adhesive held together those that were left; in the corridor a prowling cat appeared to be hunting mice, and it was not unreasonable to assume his search would be rewarded.

Slowly, as though the engine were harnessed to elderly coolies, we 2
crept out of Granada. The southern sky was as white and burning as a desert; there was one cloud, and it drifted like a traveling oasis.

We were going to Algeciras, a Spanish seaport facing the coast of 3
Africa. In our compartment there was a middle-aged Australian wearing a soiled linen suit; he had tobacco-colored teeth and his fingernails were unsanitary. Presently he informed us that he was a ship's doctor. It seemed curious, there on the dry, dour plains of Spain, to meet someone connected with the sea. Seated next to him there were two women, a mother and daughter. The mother was an overstuffed, dusty woman with sluggish, disapproving eyes and a faint mustache. The focus for her disapproval fluctuated; first, she

eyed me rather strongly because as the sunlight fanned brighter, waves of heat blew through the broken windows and I had removed my jacket—which she considered, perhaps rightly, discourteous. Later on, she took a dislike to the young soldier who also occupied our compartment. The soldier, and the woman's not very discreet daughter, a buxom girl with the scrappy features of a prizefighter, seemed to have agreed to flirt. Whenever the wandering cat appeared at our door, the daughter pretended to be frightened, and the soldier would gallantly shoo the cat into the corridor: this by-play gave them frequent opportunity to touch each other.

4   The young soldier was one of many on the train. With their tasseled caps set at snappy angles, they hung about in the corridors smoking sweet black cigarettes and laughing confidentially. They seemed to be enjoying themselves, which apparently was wrong of them, for whenever an officer appeared the soldiers would stare fixedly out the windows, as though enraptured by the landslides of red rock, the olive fields and stern stone mountains. Their officers were dressed for a parade, many ribbons, much brass; and some wore gleaming, improbable swords strapped to their sides. They did not mix with the soldiers, but sat together in a first-class compartment, looking bored and rather like unemployed actors. It was a blessing, I suppose, that something finally happened to give them a chance at rattling their swords.

5   The compartment directly ahead was taken over by one family: a delicate, attenuated, exceptionally elegant man with a mourning ribbon sewn around his sleeve, and traveling with him, six thin, summery girls, presumably his daughters. They were beautiful, the father and his children, all of them, and in the same way: hair that had a dark shine, lips the color of pimientos, eyes like sherry. The soldiers would glance into their compartment, then look away. It was as if they had seen straight into the sun.

6   Whenever the train stopped, the man's two youngest daughters would descend from the carriage and stroll under the shade of parasols. They enjoyed many lengthy promenades, for the train spent the greatest part of our journey standing still. No one appeared to be exasperated by this except myself. Several passengers seemed to have friends at every station with whom they could sit around a fountain and gossip long and lazily. One old woman was met by different little groups in a dozen-odd towns—between these encounters she wept with such abandon that the Australian doctor became alarmed: why no, she said, there was nothing he could do, it was just that seeing all her relatives made her so happy.

7   At each stop cyclones of barefooted women and somewhat naked children ran beside the train sloshing earthen jars of water and furrily squalling *Agua! Agua!* For two pesetas you could buy a whole basket of dark runny figs, and there were trays of curious white-coated candy doughnuts that

looked as though they should be eaten by young girls wearing Communion dresses. Toward noon, having collected a bottle of wine, a loaf of bread, a sausage and a cheese, we were prepared for lunch. Our companions in the compartment were hungry, too. Packages were produced, wine uncorked, and for a while there was a pleasant, almost graceful festiveness. The soldier shared a pomegranate with the girl, the Australian told an amusing story, the witch-eyed mother pulled a paper-wrapped fish from between her bosoms and ate it with a glum relish.

Afterward everyone was sleepy; the doctor went so solidly to sleep   8 that a fly meandered undisturbed over his open-mouthed face. Stillness etherized the whole train; in the next compartment the lovely girls leaned loosely, like six exhausted geraniums; even the cat had ceased to prowl, and lay dreaming in the corridor. We had climbed higher, the train moseyed across a plateau of rough yellow wheat, then between the granite walls of deep ravines where wind, moving down from the mountains, quivered in strange, thorny trees. Once, at a parting in the trees, there was something I'd wanted to see, a castle on a hill, and it sat there like a crown.

It was a landscape for bandits. Earlier in the summer, a young Eng-   9 lishman I know (rather, know of) had been motoring through this part of Spain when, on the lonely side of a mountain, his car was surrounded by swarthy scoundrels. They robbed him, then tied him to a tree and tickled his throat with the blade of a knife. I was thinking of this when without preface a spatter of bullet fire strafed the dozy silence.

It was a machine gun. Bullets rained in the trees like the rattle of cas-   10 tanets, and the train, with a wounded creak, slowed to a halt. For a moment there was no sound except the machine gun's cough. Then, "Bandits!" I said in a loud, dreadful voice.

"Bandidos!" screamed the daughter.   11

"Bandidos!" echoed her mother, and the terrible word swept through   12 the train like something drummed on a tom-tom. The result was slapstick in a grim key. We collapsed on the floor, one cringing heap of arms and legs. Only the mother seemed to keep her head; standing up, she began systematically to stash away her treasures. She stuck a ring into the buns of her hair and without shame hiked up her skirts and dropped a pearl-studded comb into her bloomers. Like the cryings of birds at twilight, airy twitterings of distress came from the charming girls in the next compartment. In the corridor the officers bumped about yapping orders and knocking into each other.

Suddenly, silence. Outside, there was the murmur of wind in leaves, of   13 voices. Just as the weight of the doctor's body was becoming too much for me, the outer door of our compartment swung open, and a young man stood there. He did not look clever enough to be a bandit.

"Hay un médico en el tren?" he said, smiling.   14

The Australian, removing the pressure of his elbow from my stomach,   15
climbed to his feet. "I'm a doctor," he admitted, dusting himself. "Has someone been wounded?"

"Si, Señor. An old man. He is hurt in the head," said the Spaniard, who   16
was not a bandit: alas, merely another passenger. Settling back in our seats,
we listened, expressionless with embarrassment, to what had happened. It
seemed that for the last several hours an old man had been stealing a ride
by clinging to the rear of the train. Just now he'd lost his hold, and a soldier,
seeing him fall, had started firing a machine gun as a signal for the engineer
to stop the train.

My only hope was that no one remembered who had first mentioned   17
bandits. They did not seem to. After acquiring a clean shirt of mine which he
intended to use as a bandage, the doctor went off to his patient, and the mother, turning her back with sour prudery, reclaimed her pearl comb. Her daughter and the soldier followed after us as we got out of the carriage and strolled
under the trees, where many passengers had gathered to discuss the incident.

Two soldiers appeared carrying the old man. My shirt was wrapped   18
around his head. They propped him under a tree and all the women clustered about vying with each other to lend him their rosary; someone
brought a bottle of wine, which pleased him more. He seemed quite happy,
and moaned a great deal. The children who had been on the train circled
around him, giggling.

We were in a small wood that smelled of oranges. There was a path,   19
and it led to a shaded promontory; from here, one looked across a valley
where sweeping stretches of scorched golden grass shivered as though the
earth were trembling. Admiring the valley, and the shadowy changes of light
on the hills beyond, the six sisters, escorted by their elegant father, sat with
their parasols raised above them like guests at a *fête champêtre.* The soldiers
moved around them in a vague, ambitious manner; they did not quite dare
to approach, though one brash, sassy fellow went to the edge of the
promontory and called, *"Yo te quiero mucho."* The words returned with the
hollow sub-music of a perfect echo, and the sisters, blushing, looked more
deeply into the valley.

A cloud, somber as the rocky hills, had massed in the sky, and the grass   20
below stirred like the sea before a storm. Someone said he thought it would
rain. But no one wanted to go: not the injured man, who was well on his way
through a second bottle of wine, nor the children who, having discovered
the echo, stood happily caroling into the valley. It was like a party, and we all
drifted back to the train as though each of us wished to be the last to leave.
The old man, with my shirt like a grand turban on his head, was put into a
first-class carriage and several eager ladies were left to attend him.

In our compartment, the dark, dusty mother sat just as we had left her.   21
She had not seen fit to join the party. She gave me a long, glittering look.
"Bandidos," she said with a surly, unnecessary vigor.

The train moved away so slowly butterflies blew in and out the windows.   22

◆ ◆ ◆

FIRST RESPONSES

Do you think you would have enjoyed taking this train ride through
Spain? Why or why not? Have you had any travel experiences that are similar in any way to the one described in this essay?

TAKING A CLOSER LOOK

Exploring *Who*: Voice and Tone

1. What does Capote think of the train he's riding in? What does he
   think of the people who are traveling with him? How do you know
   what he's thinking about them?
2. Why doesn't the author ever identify himself or explain the purpose
   of his trip? What information does he give about himself? What role
   does he play in the events that he describes?
3. How do you react to the author's voice in this essay? Do you find any
   of his descriptions humorous? Do any of them capture your interest?
   Would you like to visit any of the places described in the essay?

Exploring *What*: Content and Meaning

1. When Capote collected some of his nonfiction writings, he included
   this essay under the heading of "local color." What details of local
   Spanish color do you see?
2. What impressions of the people on the train do you get from this
   essay? What's their attitude toward train travel and toward one another? Is it the same as the author's? as yours?
3. How much knowledge of Spanish geography do you need to understand this essay? What do you learn about Spain from reading it?
4. What do the phrases *fête champêtre, Yo te quiero mucho,* and *Hay un
   médico en el tren* mean? Why doesn't Capote translate them for his
   readers?

Exploring *Why:* Purpose

1. Is the author more interested in describing the people or telling a story? Why does he include the incident with the bandits?
2. How does Capote feel when it turns out that there aren't any bandits? How did you feel? Were you surprised or disappointed?
3. ▆▊ *Using the Internet.* How do Capote's descriptions differ from the ones you would find in popular travel magazines? Do you suppose the Spanish tourist bureau approved of this essay? Do you think Capote cared? To help answer these questions, visit a Web site like the one for the Tourist Office of Spain (http://okspain.org/), and browse through their promotional materials.

Exploring *How:* Style and Strategy

1. Find descriptive details that appeal to each of the five senses: smell, taste, sound, sight, and touch. Which ones make the description particularly lively? How many visual images involve colors?
2. Capote wrote that "A Ride Through Spain" was "a lark; buoyed along by its anecdotal nature, it skimmed off the end of a Black Wing pencil in a matter of hours." Did you feel this sense of ease and playfulness when you were reading it? What words, phrases, and details contribute to the light, breezy style?
3. Locate five comparisons that Capote uses to describe humans and five more that describe the physical surroundings. Which ones put a picture in your mind? Which ones are playful and fanciful?
4. Which is the most memorable description in the essay? Explain why it appeals to you.

IDEAS FOR WRITING A DESCRIPTION

1. Describe a trip that you took. Use sensory details that reveal the feelings you have about that trip, but do not name the emotions themselves.
2. Go to some place (a restaurant, library, mall, park, or laundromat, for example) where you can observe people without being noticed. Make a list of details about several of the people you see there; choose details that appeal to the senses. Then develop those details into a series of descriptive profiles. Use figurative images to create a **dominant impression** of each person you describe.
3. Describe a bus, air, or train terminal.

◆ ◆ ◆ PREPARING TO READ

Do you believe that spirits can inhabit a place? Do you know a place that is haunted or has some mystery surrounding it? How do you explain such places and beliefs?

◆ ◆ ◆

White Breast Flats

EMILIE GALLANT

Emilie Gallant is a member of the Piegan tribe of Canada. She was born in Alberta and received a degree from the University of Calgary. This essay first appeared in *A Gathering of Spirits* (1984), an anthology of drawings, poems, stories, and other writings by Native American women. In this selection, Gallant describes a place filled with childhood memories about a way of life that no longer exists.

As one grows older, and the past recedes swiftly as a bird, wings extended in the wind, there are people and places whose contours, caught through the clouds of memory, take on the dimensions of myth. For me, one such place is White Breast Flats on the Piegan Reserve in southwest Alberta where the plains give way to the foothills, the Rockies loom near, and the great obelisk Chief Mountain stands powerfully at the entrance to northern Montana. White Breast Flats is a name known only to a few. My grandfather, Otohkostskaksin (Yellow Dust), was the one who told me that name, and recently, when I read the name in a book, I felt a special joy. Seeing it in print, so many years and miles later, seemed to establish the place as fact, and it opened again the pages of that precious time in my past.

White Breast Flats was occupied solely by my grandparents, and on occasion by my mother. It was located on the first bottomland north of the Old Man River on the west end of the reserve, and the land that rose behind it—the valley wall I suppose you could call it—reached its highest point there, a half-mile from bottom to top, two miles in span. That valley wall was laced with a maze of foot-trails, and there were bushes aplenty of saskatoon, whiteberries, gooseberries, chokecherries, and bullberries. There were also wild turnips and cactusberries there. All of these berries gave nourishment to my sisters, to my brother, and to me as we played or just wandered through.

The bottomland stretched from the base of the hill towards the river 3
for a mile and a half at its farthest point and a quarter of a mile at its closest.
The one-roomed log house my grandparents lived in was situated about a
half a mile from the hill and about two hundred feet from the river. The Old
Man has probably eaten away the spot where the house stood, for the bank
crept a little closer each year. The trees there were of several varieties, but
other than the willows, cottonwoods, chokecherry, saskatoon, and pussy willows, I am still unable to name the trees that made up the forest. Where
there were no trees, the grasses grew wild and rampant, and I can still see
fields of yellow and white sweet clover and the ever-present and venomous
purple thistles which stabbed at us with their thorns every chance they got.

We were brought up to fear bears; and although I never saw a bear 4
while I was growing up, I was always on the lookout for the one which I was
sure was waiting for me to relax my guard. The most fearsome thing I ever
saw was a snake. I was afraid of water, and the river bank we clambered down
to reach the green, swirling currents was dotted with holes which I thought
were the homes of deadly and poisonous snakes. My sisters were both strong
swimmers and enjoyed swimming across the river, but I would churn inwardly with fear as I watched them splash and drift away, bantering and yelling
with abandon. And there I would be, standing first on one dirt-caked rock
with a dried-up water spider stuck to it, and moving to another, sometimes
walking in the water up to my knees very cautiously and carefully, for the
rocks were slippery. Sometimes a fish would awake and swim off suddenly,
making my heart jump and my throat constrict with a scream I held in. The
river was a malevolent thing to me, never friendly. I watched warily for the
mythical water-being which I was convinced lived somewhere in the green-
est, deepest part. It had to. Otherwise, where did all the foam come from
which flecked the river's surface; it had to be the water-being's spittle.

One particular day, I was standing on the river's edge again, watching 5
my two sisters, whom I resented and admired for their fearlessness, when I
slipped and fell into the water. It was in the evening and the sun's last rays
had turned the river into a golden, glinting, and somehow not so perilous
place. I imagined that the water below the surface where the water-being
lived was illuminated. In a matter of minutes the warmth of the day was exchanged for the coolness of the evening. My skin prickled with goosebumps
from the chill, and I decided to put on my cotton dress until the two mer-
maids left the water. I picked up my dress and almost died with fright! A big
snake slithered out of my dress. I screamed, and my mother, who had been
washing and rinsing clothes some distance away, came running, and I got to
ride her piggyback all the way home. I even had her throw my dress in the
river, something I always remember, for we were very poor and could ill
afford to throw clothing away.

There were plants that my grandmother would collect for her medici- 6
nal and everyday purposes. She would hang mint to dry in bunches from a
line tied across the length of the room, close to the ceiling. I loved the smell
of it, and although I didn't care for mint tea then, I do now. It's not only the
taste that I enjoy; it's the remembering of moments of my childhood. Every
so often I happen upon a cup of wild mint tea, and the bitterness of it, if the
tea is made too strong, brings me back to my mother's house when I was
probably five or six years old and deathly ill—or so I remember, because my
grandmother was summoned. She was a medicine woman and had in her
possession all kinds of herbs and roots with which she brought back to
health anyone who was ailing. She came into the house on a cold, winter
day, bundled up with shawls and blankets. The snowy wind whipped the log
house until chinks of the limestone plaster were peeled off and swept away
in the storm. My mother kept plugging up the cracks with rags to keep the
snow from being blasted inside. The wet snow that stuck to my grandmother's wraps hissed as it hit the stove. She carried a flour sack, and from this
she took out a bag made from fawn hide, spotted and with the little hooves
on it. Inside the bag she had wrapped still other small bundles, and she took
out something greasy and rubbed my chest. On top of that she placed a
layer of dried leaves. Ritually she spat on these, and covered the leaves with
a hot cloth. She gave me a drink of an awful-tasting brew, and I wouldn't
have drunk it if she hadn't been the one to give it to me. She then chanted
holy songs, her voice a little frail and weak at first but gaining strength and
fullness until the sound was a soothing prayer. She had a sacred rattle made
from rawhide and painted with red ochre; this she shook in time with the ca-
dence of her voice. She closed her eyes as she sang, and as I watched her I
saw that she had painted her face with the red ochre, and the hair that
framed her face was tinted with it. After her song, she prayed that my health
be restored and I be blessed with a long and happy life. From a little buck-
skin bag rubbed with the sacred red ochre, she took some paint that had the
consistency of uncooked pastry but which became oily when she rubbed it
in her hand. This she rubbed on my face and then she left, leaving some
brew and plants for my mother to administer to me. She also left an orange
in plain sight that I could have when I was well enough. Oranges during the
Second World War were rare, and not seen unless at a feast.

Sometimes I can detect the smell of sweetgrass when there is none 7
around. I've grown to know that is only my grandparents coming to visit me.
Sweetgrass—an appropriate name for a special plant. Sweetgrass is the incense the old Indians used to honor the Creator, and the burning of it was a
daily occurrence in my grandparents' home. Each morning my grandfather
would get up and make the fire in the stove and as soon as the warmth made
getting up comfortable, my grandmother would rise and they would pray

together. He would burn incense to greet the Creator, and to give thanks for life and health of family and friends, and to ask for guidance in living the day, as well as for help in some special need. Then they shared a song between them and a smoke on their pipe from chunk tobacco.

A quarter of a mile east of the house and just where the woods began 8 was a spring. This was where my grandfather got our drinking water. He used a wooden stoneboat to haul it. The stoneboat was constructed of two logs at the bottom; they were the runners, smooth and heavy. On top of them were wide planks of board, bolted onto the logs. The planks were so old I used to sit and scratch them with my fingernails and a papery, powdery substance would come off the wood. Grandfather would hitch up the team, and we children tagged along, jumping on and off the stoneboat with our dogs barking happily behind us until we reached the spring. He tied the team to a tree above the spring and carried two pails to bring the water back to the old metal-girded wooden barrel. He would make twenty or thirty trips until the barrel was full, and then he would put a canvas cover over it and tie the cover on with a rope. Once the water was brought home, my grandmother would have a drink of it first, then set about to making a pot of tea.

A slow-moving stream which leaked off the river and eased by the 9 spring was a refrigerator for butter, meat, and the seasonal garden vegetables. The vegetables came from my grandfather's garden at the base of the hill. Everything grew in abundance there: carrots, rhubarb, turnips, onion, radishes, lettuce, potatoes, and sugar beets. It was neat and ordered, with its straight rows and well-tended mounds of earth. It was fascinating to watch the steam rising from the garden after my grandfather watered it or after a rainfall or shower. I thought a mysterious creature, perhaps a cousin of the water-being, inhabited the earth, and the steam was its breath just as the flecks of foam in the river were the water-being's spittle. I never hung around the garden alone.

The stream that adjoined the spring was the home of a thousand min- 10 nows. We would catch some in a jar and take them home, and although we fed them flies and bread, they always died. Long-legged water spiders glided silently around the stream and the little frogs of grey, green, or brown jumped noiselessly, even when they landed in the water. Only our big, clumsy dogs would ruin the silent stream with their panting, lolling tongues as they splashed in, sitting right in the water to have a drink. Then they would shake their wet bodies mightily until it seemed as though it was raining. Our shouts of anger and surprise would usually result in their jumping on us with friendly licks and muddy paws. Surprisingly, of all the dogs we had (it seems they were all shaggy) the only one I remember is Pete. Pete, the short-haired hound with long legs, a tail like a whip, and shiny ears, one of which would sometimes get stuck inside out or underside up, was blacker than the deepest badger hole we dared to peep into, and he had white, laughing teeth and a rosy, wet tongue.

There was a faded, creaking ghost house on top of the hill. It had two stories and no windows or doors, just openings from which whitemen ghosts watched passersby. It used to belong to a white man I knew only as Inopikini, which means Long Nose. We would go to the ghost house in broad daylight, always in the protective company of my mother and grandmother. The wind was always blowing through the house, flapping wallpaper, rattling floorboards, shingles, and window casings. It was a wonderful, mysterious, scary place to go poking around in. It had lots of rooms, small ones and big ones. There were old curly shoes, clothing of all kinds, pieces of furniture, bits of toys, stray dishes, cracked cups without handles, and faded pictures still in their frames. We never took anything, because then Inopikini would haunt us until we returned what we had taken, or else, if he was a real mean ghost, he would twist our faces. 11

There was a trapdoor in one room which we never dared to open because we were sure something stayed down there, but we would stomp across it, each one stomping harder than the last but always with mother or grandmother in the room. After we verbally challenged the ghosts who had the guts to come out and meet us face to face, we would climax our visit by scaring only ourselves and stampede off in hysterical screams, our bodies prickling and our eyes wild with fear, not daring to look back lest we see Inopikini hot on our trail. 12

I always expected to see a tall, emaciated man with hair all over his skin and blood around his nostrils and perhaps little horns growing out of his head. He was always garbed, in my imagination, in the cracked, curly boots he left in his house and his body covered with the rags scattered about through the rooms. 13

Summer reminds me of my grandmother mashing cherries in her tipi, which was erected as soon as it was warm enough to sleep outside. My old grandmother used to herd us up the hill to dig for turnips and pick berries for some upcoming feast, but those were the times we wished berries didn't grow. It was always a hot day when we yearned to be down by the spring and we quarreled amongst ourselves and sneaked away. 14

On hot summer days when I wearied of playing or had nothing to do, I would go and ask my grandmother to check my head because it was itchy. She would put aside whatever she was doing and check my head, all the while telling me stories until I fell asleep. Sometimes when I didn't fall asleep soon enough for her, she would tell me to erase a cloud by rubbing my hands together and concentrating on that cloud. I demolished many a 15 cloud. My grandmother was a tireless old woman who never rested. She was always busy beading, fixing deerskins, fixing berries (drying, mashing, sorting), repairing clothing, cooking, sweeping, washing clothes and minding us kids. She would gather wood on a big piece of canvas and carry it home on her back or drag it behind her. Then she would sit at the woodpile and chop wood with her hatchet, which she also used for butchering the deer my grandfather killed.

I haven't been to White Breast Flats for a long time now, too long. The log house and outer buildings have long been dismantled and carried away for firewood, and the paths and roads are overcome by weeds. Only the descendants of the magpies, gophers, rabbits, and frogs have reclaimed their ancestral grounds. Perhaps a rusted wagon wheel or a skeletal haymower tells a hanging eagle that people once lived here. White Breast Flats will not happen again; it only lives in the longings and hearts of Ippisuwahs, Piiksi Kiipipi Pahtskikaikana, and Itsinakaki, the grandchildren whose voices once rang clear and echoed through its secret places.

16

◆ ◆ ◆

FIRST RESPONSES

Did reading this essay cause you to recall any childhood memories of your own? If so, what are they, and how do they seem to relate to this essay? If not, can you explain why the essay didn't trigger any memories?

TAKING A CLOSER LOOK

Exploring *Who:* Voice and Tone

1. What is Gallant's attitude toward White Breast Flats and the memories she has of that place? Is her tone what you would expect of someone recalling her childhood? She says she hasn't been back to White Breast Flats for a long time. Why do you suppose that is?
2. Does Gallant change her voice in this essay? Does she maintain the voice of an adult looking back, or does she shift her tone as she moves back into her memories?
3. Is this essay written primarily for Native Americans? Can other readers identify with Gallant's memories? Do you?

Exploring *What:* Content and Meaning

1. The author says that people and places from the past "take on the dimensions of myth." What does she mean? Do you feel that your past has taken on mythic dimensions?
2. What rituals of her tribe does Gallant describe? Are there similar rituals in your family or community? Why or why not?
3. What connections between nature and human beings does the author establish?
4. What point does the last paragraph make about White Breast Flats?
5. ▇▐ *Using the Internet.* Find a Web site that shows this landscape; look for the Chief Mountain or the Piegan Reserve in southwest Alberta, Canada. Did you visualize this place in the same way when you were reading Gallant's essay?

Exploring *Why:* Purpose

1. What is Gallant's reason for writing about the people and places of her past?
2. Is this an informative essay? Does the author want to do more than share information? Why does she make so many references to spirits, ghosts, and supernatural forces?
3. How do you think Gallant wants you to respond to her recollections? Did she succeed?

Exploring *How:* Style and Strategy

1. Gallant opens her essay with two images: the past receding "swiftly as a bird, wings extended in the wind," and the "contours" of people and places "caught through the clouds of memory." Why does she begin with these metaphors? What tone do they set for her essay?
2. Find other examples of similes, metaphors, and images. Are they effective? What feelings do they evoke?
3. At several points, the author lists the names of plants, bushes, trees, and vegetables. Why does she enumerate the specific names of these items? What effect is she trying to create?
4. In paragraph 5, Gallant briefly recounts the incident with the snake and her dress. How many other incidents does she narrate in this essay? Do these brief narratives blend in well with the descriptions?

IDEAS FOR WRITING A DESCRIPTION

1. Write a three- or four-paragraph description of a solitary experience you once had—for example, being alone with nature, going to the movies by yourself, taking a long trip by yourself, being alone in a crowd, staying home alone for the first time, or taking a long relaxing bath. Try to convey the dominant feelings of the experience, whether it was positive or negative, tedious or exhilarating, scary or refreshing.

2. Smells and tastes can trigger strong memories. Write an essay that describes some of the distinctive smells and tastes from your past; describe the memories they evoke.

3. Write an essay describing a place or situation in which you feel physically quite uncomfortable or unusually comfortable. Consider, for instance, waiting to see the dentist, or relaxing in your room—but you can think of more interesting situations than those. Try to include details that will enable your readers to feel the experience.

◆ ◆ ◆ PREPARING TO READ

Is there any part of your physical appearance that you'd like to change? How far would you go to improve your looks?

◆ ◆ ◆

In the Kitchen

HENRY LOUIS GATES, JR.

Henry Louis Gates, Jr., was born in 1950 in Keyser, West Virginia. He was educated at Yale University and earned his doctorate from Cambridge University in 1979. Gates is one of the nation's leading scholars in African American studies. He has taught at Yale, Cornell, and Duke universities; since 1991, he has been the chair of the Afro-American Studies program at Harvard. The editor and author of numerous works of literary criticism and cultural theory, Gates has also written a memoir of his youth in West Virginia—*Colored People* (1994). The following selection is the fourth chapter in that book.

We always had a gas stove in the kitchen, though electric cooking be- 1
came fashionable in Piedmont, like using Crest toothpaste rather than Colgate, or watching Huntley and Brinkley rather than Walter Cronkite. But
for us it was gas, Colgate, and good ole Walter Cronkite, come what may. We
used gas partly out of loyalty to Big Mom, Mama's mama, because she was
mostly blind and still loved to cook, and she could feel her way better with
gas than with electric.

But the most important thing about our gas-equipped kitchen was 2
that Mama used to do hair there. She had a "hot comb"—a fine-toothed
iron instrument with a long wooden handle—and a pair of iron curlers that
opened and closed like scissors: Mama would put them into the gas fire until
they glowed. You could smell those prongs heating up.

I liked what that smell meant for the shape of my day. There was an in- 3
timate warmth in the women's tones as they talked with my mama while she
did their hair. I knew what the women had been through to get their hair
ready to be "done," because I would watch Mama do it to herself. How that
scorched kink could be transformed through grease and fire into a magnificent head of wavy hair was a miracle to me. Still is.

Mama would wash her hair over the sink, a towel wrapped round her   4
shoulders, wearing just her half-slip and her white bra. (We had no shower
until we moved down Rat Tail Road into Doc Wolverton's house, in 1954.)
After she had dried it, she would grease her scalp thoroughly with blue
Bergamot hair grease, which came in a short, fat jar with a picture of a beautiful colored lady on it. It's important to grease your scalp real good, my
mama would explain, to keep from burning yourself.

Of course, her hair would return to its natural kink almost as soon as   5
the hot water and shampoo hit it. To me, it was another miracle how hair so
"straight" would so quickly become kinky again once it even approached
some water.

My mama had only a few "clients" whose heads she "did"—and did, I   6
think, because she enjoyed it, rather than for the few dollars it brought in.
They would sit on one of our red plastic kitchen chairs, the kind with the
shiny metal legs, and brace themselves for the process. Mama would stroke
that red-hot iron, which by this time had been in the gas fire for half an hour
or more, slowly but firmly through their hair, from scalp to strand's end. It
made a scorching, crinkly sound, the hot iron did, as it burned its way
through damp kink, leaving in its wake the straightest of hair strands, each
of them standing up long and tall but drooping at the end, like the top of a
heavy willow tree. Slowly, steadily, with deftness and grace, Mama's hands
would transform a round mound of Odetta kink into a darkened swamp of
everglades. The Bergamot made the hair shiny; the heat of the hot iron gave
it a brownish-red cast. Once all the hair was as straight as God allows kink
to get, Mama would take the well-heated curling iron and twirl the straightened strands into more or less loosely wrapped curls. She claimed that she
owed her strength and skill as a hairdresser to her wrists, and her little finger would poke out the way it did when she sipped tea. Mama was a southpaw, who wrote upside down and backwards to produce the cleanest,
roundest letters you've ever seen.

The "kitchen" she would all but remove from sight with a pair of   7
shears bought for this purpose. Now, the *kitchen* was the room in which we
were sitting, the room where Mama did hair and washed clothes, and where
each of us bathed in a galvanized tub. But the word has another meaning,
and the "kitchen" I'm speaking of now is the very kinky bit of hair at the
back of the head, where the neck meets the shirt collar. If there ever was
one part of our African past that resisted assimilation, it was the kitchen.
No matter how hot the iron, no matter how powerful the chemical, no matter how stringent the mashed-potatoes-and-lye formula of a man's
"process," neither God nor woman nor Sammy Davis, Jr., could straighten
the kitchen. The kitchen was permanent, irredeemable, invincible kink.
Unassimilably African. No matter what you did, no matter how hard you

tried, nothing could dekink a person's kitchen. So you trimmed it off as best you could.

When hair had begun to "turn," as they'd say, or return to its natural   8
kinky glory, it was the kitchen that turned first. When the kitchen started creeping up the back of the neck, it was time to get your hair done again. The kitchen around the back, and nappy edges at the temples.

Sometimes, after dark, Mr. Charlie Carroll would come to have his   9
hair done. Mr. Charlie Carroll was very light-complected and had a ruddy nose, the kind of nose that made me think of Edmund Gwenn playing Kris Kringle in *Miracle on 34th Street*. At the beginning, they did it after Rocky and I had gone to sleep. It was only later that we found out he had come to our house so Mama could iron his hair—not with a hot comb and curling iron but with our very own Proctor-Silex steam iron. For some reason, Mr. Charlie would conceal his Frederick Douglass mane under a big white Stetson hat, which I never saw him take off. Except when he came to our house, late at night, to have his hair pressed.

(Later, Daddy would tell us about Mr. Charlie's most prized piece of   10
knowledge, which the man would confide only after his hair had been pressed, as a token of intimacy. "Not many people know this," he'd say in a tone of circumspection, "but George Washington was Abraham Lincoln's daddy." Nodding solemnly, he'd add the clincher: "A white man told me." Though he was in dead earnest, this became a humorous refrain around the house—a "white man told me"—used to punctuate especially preposterous assertions.)

My mother furtively examined my daughters' kitchens whenever we   11
went home for a visit in the early eighties. It became a game between us. I had told her not to do it, because I didn't like the politics it suggested of "good" and "bad" hair. "Good" hair was straight. "Bad" hair was kinky. Even in the late sixties, at the height of Black Power, most people could not bring themselves to say "bad" for "good" and "good" for "bad." They still said that hair like white hair was "good," even if they encapsulated it in a disclaimer like "what we used to call 'good.' "

Maggie would be seated in her high chair, throwing food this way and   12
that, and Mama would be cooing about how cute it all was, remembering how I used to do the same thing, and wondering whether Maggie's flinging her food with her left hand meant that she was going to be a southpaw too. When my daughter was just about covered with Franco-American Spaghet-tiOs, Mama would seize the opportunity and wipe her clean, dipping her head, tilted to one side, down under the back of Maggie's neck. Sometimes, if she could get away with it, she'd even rub a curl between her fingers, just to make sure that her bifocals had not deceived her. Then she'd sigh with satisfaction and relief, thankful that her prayers had been answered. No

kink . . . yet. "Mama!" I'd shout, pretending to be angry. (Every once in a while, if no one was looking, I'd peek too.)

I say "yet" because most black babies are born with soft, silken hair. 13 Then, sooner or later, it begins to "turn," as inevitably as do the seasons or the leaves on a tree. And if it's meant to turn, it *turns,* no matter how hard you try to stop it. People once thought baby oil would stop it. They were wrong.

Everybody I knew as a child wanted to have good hair. You could be 14 as ugly as homemade sin dipped in misery and still be thought attractive if you had good hair. Jesus Moss was what the girls at Camp Lee, Virginia, had called Daddy's hair during World War II. I know he played that thick head of hair for all it was worth, too. Still would, if he could.

My own hair was "not a bad grade," as barbers would tell me when 15 they cut my head for the first time. It's like a doctor reporting the overall results of the first full physical that he has given you. "You're in good shape" or "Blood pressure's kind of high; better cut down on salt."

I spent much of my childhood and adolescence messing with my hair. 16 I definitely wanted straight hair. Like Pop's.

When I was about three, I tried to stick a wad of Bazooka bubble gum 17 to that straight hair of his. I suppose what fixed that memory for me is the spanking I got for doing so: he turned me upside down, holding me by my feet, the better to paddle my behind. Little *nigger,* he shouted, walloping away. I started to laugh about it two days later, when my behind stopped hurting.

When black people say "straight," of course, they don't usually mean 18 "straight" literally, like, say, the hair of Peggy Lipton (the white girl on *The Mod Squad*) or Mary of Peter, Paul and Mary fame; black people call that "stringy" hair. No, "straight" just means not kinky, no matter what contours the curl might take. Because Daddy had straight hair, I would have done *anything* to have straight hair—and I used to try everything to make it straight, short of getting a process, which only riffraff were dumb enough to do.

Of the wide variety of techniques and methods I came to master in the 19 great and challenging follicle prestidigitation, almost all had two things in common: a heavy, oil-based grease and evenly applied pressure. It's no accident that many of the biggest black companies in the fifties and sixties made hair products. Indeed, we do have a vast array of hair grease. And I have tried it all, in search of that certain silky touch, one that leaves neither the hand nor the pillow sullied by grease.

I always wondered what Frederick Douglass put on *his* hair, or Phillis 20 Wheatley. Or why Wheatley has that rag on her head in the little engraving in the frontispiece of her book. One thing is for sure: you can bet that when

Wheatley went to England to see the Countess of Huntingdon, she did not stop by the Queen's Coiffeur on the way. So many black people still get their hair straightened that it's a wonder we don't have a national holiday for Madame C. J. Walker, who invented the process for straightening kinky hair, rather than for Dr. King. Jheri-curled or "relaxed"—it's still fried hair.

I used all the greases, from sea-blue Bergamot, to creamy vanilla   21
Duke (in its orange-and-white jar), to the godfather of grease, the formidable Murray's. Now, Murray's was some *serious* grease. Whereas Bergamot was like oily Jell-O and Duke was viscous and sickly sweet, Murray's was light brown and *hard*. Hard as lard and twice as greasy, Daddy used to say whenever the subject of Murray's came up. Murray's came in an orange can with a screw-on top. It was so hard that some people would put a match to the can, just to soften it and make it more manageable. In the late sixties, when Afros came into style, I'd use Afro-Sheen. From Murray's to Duke to Afro-Sheen: that was my progression in black consciousness.

We started putting hot towels or washrags over our greased-down   22
Murray's-coated heads, in order to melt the wax into the scalp and follicles. Unfortunately, the wax had a curious habit of running down your neck, ears, and forehead. Not to mention your pillowcase.

Another problem was that if you put two palmfuls of Murray's on   23
your head, your hair turned white. Duke did the same thing. It was a challenge: if you got rid of the white stuff, you had a magnificent head of wavy hair. Murray's turned kink into waves. Lots of waves. Frozen waves. A hurricane couldn't have blown those waves around.

That was the beauty of it. Murray's was so hard that it froze your hair   24
into the wavy style you brushed it into. It looked really good if you wore a part. A lot of guys had parts *cut* into their hair by a barber, with clippers or a straight-edge razor. Especially if you had kinky hair—in which case you'd generally wear a short razor cut, or what we called a Quo Vadis.

Being obsessed with our hair, we tried to be as innovative as possible.   25
Everyone knew about using a stocking cap, because your father or your uncle or the older guys wore them whenever something really big was about to happen, secular or sacred, a funeral or a dance, a wedding or a trip in which you confronted official white people, or when you were trying to look really sharp. When it was time to be clean, you wore a stocking cap. If the event was really a big one, you made a new cap for the occasion.

A stocking cap was made by asking your mother for one of her hose,   26
and cutting it with a pair of scissors about six inches or so from the open end, where the elastic goes up to the top of the thigh. Then you'd knot the cut end, and behold—a conical-shaped hat or cap, with an elastic band that you pulled down low on your forehead and down around your neck in the back. A good stocking cap, to work well, had to fit tight and snug, like a

press. And it had to fit that tightly because it *was* a press: it pressed your hair with the force of the hose's elastic. If you greased your hair down real good and left the stocking cap on long enough—*voilà:* you got a head of pressed-against-the-scalp waves. If you used Murray's, and if you wore a stocking cap to sleep, you got a *whole lot* of waves. (You also got a ring around your forehead when you woke up, but eventually that disappeared.)

And then you could enjoy your concrete 'do. Swore we were bad, too, with all that grease and those flat heads. My brother and I would brush it out a bit in the morning, so it would look—ahem—"natural." 27

Grown men still wear stocking caps, especially older men, who generally keep their caps in their top drawer, along with their cuff links and their see-through silk socks, their Maverick tie, their silk handkerchief, and whatever else they prize most. 28

A Murrayed-down stocking cap was the respectable version of the process, which, by contrast, was most definitely not a cool thing to have, at least if you weren't an entertainer by trade. 29

Zeke and Keith and Poochie and a few other stars of the basketball team all used to get a process once or twice a year. It was expensive, and to get one you had to go to Pittsburgh or D.C. or Uniontown, someplace where there were enough colored people to support a business. They'd disappear, then reappear a day or two later, strutting like peacocks, their hair burned slightly red from the chemical lye base. They'd also wear "rags" or cloths or handkerchiefs around it when they slept or played basketball. Do-rags, they were called. But the result was *straight* hair, with a hint of wave. No curl. Do-it-yourselfers took their chances at home with a concoction of mashed potatoes and lye. 30

The most famous process, outside of what Malcolm X describes in his *Autobiography* and maybe that of Sammy Davis, Jr., was Nat King Cole's. Nat King Cole had patent-leather hair. 31

"That man's got the finest process money can buy." That's what Daddy said the night Cole's TV show aired on NBC, November 5, 1956. I remember the date because everyone came to our house to watch it and to celebrate one of Daddy's buddies' birthdays. Yeah, Uncle Joe chimed in, they can do shit to his hair that the average Negro can't even *think* about—secret shit. 32

Nat King Cole was *clean*. I've had an ongoing argument with a Nigerian friend about Nat King Cole for twenty years now. Not whether or not he could sing; any fool knows that he could sing. But whether or not he was a handkerchief-head for wearing that patent-leather process. 33

Sammy Davis's process I detested. It didn't look good on him. Worse still, he liked to have a fried strand dangling down the middle of his forehead, shaking it out from the crown when he sang. But Nat King Cole's hair 34 was a thing unto itself, a beautifully sculpted work of art that he and he alone should have had the right to wear.

The only difference between a process and a stocking cap, really, was   35
taste; yet Nat King Cole—unlike, say, Michael Jackson—looked *good* in his process. His head looked like Rudolph Valentino's in the twenties, and some say it was Valentino that the process imitated. But Nat King Cole wore a process because it suited his face, his demeanor, his name, his style. He was as clean as he wanted to be.

I had forgotten all about Nat King Cole and that patent-leather look   36
until the day in 1971 when I was sitting in an Arab restaurant on the island of Zanzibar, surrounded by men in fezzes and white caftans, trying to learn how to eat curried goat and rice with the fingers of my right hand, feeling two million miles from home, when all of a sudden the old transistor radio sitting on top of a china cupboard stopped blaring out its Swahili music to play "Fly Me to the Moon" by Nat King Cole. The restaurant's din was not affected at all, not even by half a decibel. But in my mind's eye, I saw it: the King's sleek black magnificent tiara. I managed, barely, to blink back the tears.

◆ ◆ ◆

FIRST RESPONSES

Do you and your friends want to have good hair? Do you agree with Gates that people can be ugly and still be thought attractive if they have good hair? Is hair really that important?

TAKING A CLOSER LOOK

Exploring *Who:* Voice and Tone

1. How does Gates feel about black people getting their hair straightened? He says that in his childhood and adolescence he "definitely wanted straight hair." Do you think he still does?
2. Is Gates writing primarily for African American readers? In what ways is this topic of interest to all audiences?
3. What do you think about people who wear wigs or hair pieces? Do you have the same opinion of the people Gates writes about in this essay?

Exploring *What:* Content and Meaning

1. What is the "kitchen"? What does Gates mean when he says, "If there ever was one part of our African past that resisted assimilation, it was the kitchen"?
2. In paragraph 11, Gates says that in the early 1980s "good" hair was straight and "bad" hair was kinky. Is that distinction still true today?
3. Who are Frederick Douglass and Phillis Wheatley? Why does Gates wonder what they put on their heads (paragraph 20)?
4. What is "a process"? Why was it not considered "cool" to have one? Why was it all right for entertainers to have one?
5. What does Nat King Cole represent to Gates? Why does he use him as a reference point?

Exploring *Why:* Purpose

1. Why did Gates choose to write about this topic? Is he making some comment about himself? about the African-American community? Is it the kind of topic you'd ever write about?
2. Does Gates have a political agenda in writing about this topic? Do you think he wants you to take sides on the straight vs. kinky question? What *do* you think about this issue?
3. ▪️ *Using the Internet.* Visit the African American Web Connection (http:// www.aawc.com/aawc.html) or a similar Web site to see if you can find out the latest opinions on the topic of kinky hair.

Exploring *How:* Style and Strategy

1. Why does Gates begin by describing the kitchen in his boyhood home? How does he use this setting to move into the main topic of this essay? Is this transition effective?
2. Gates describes several different methods for straightening kinky hair. What details and images does he use to help you visualize these procedures and their effects? Which ones did you find most effective?
3. Where is there humor in this essay? How do you respond to these humorous touches? Do you think they're appropriate?
4. Why does Gates conclude with an anecdote about Nat King Cole? Do you like this ending?

IDEAS FOR WRITING A DESCRIPTION

1. Write a detailed description of someone you know (a friend, class-mate, or relative), but don't reveal the person's name or identity. Then show your description to others who also know the person to see if they recognize your subject.

2. Describe some ritual or routine (exercise, diet, grooming methods, beauty practices) that you follow to improve your health or appear-ance. Use descriptive words and phrases to convey how you feel about this activity.

3. ■ *Using the Internet.* People send messages about themselves by the way they wear their hair. Describe several distinctive hairstyles (crewcut, colorful dyes, buns, ponytails, mohawks, lacquered spikes, etc.), and explain why you think people adopt them. Or describe the current favorite in hairdos, and explain why it's popular. Do a search on the Internet (keywords: "hair styles") to see what you can find out about the latest hair fashions.

◆ ◆ ◆ PREPARING TO READ

Did you have a favorite getaway place as a child? Why was this place special? How did it make you feel?

◆ ◆ ◆

Once More to the Lake

E. B. WHITE

For more than fifty years, Elwyn Brooks White (1899–1985) was a regular contributor to *The New Yorker* and *Harper's* magazines. His feature articles, editorials, and commentaries earned him recognition as one of America's most incisive and witty essayists. He also wrote two highly acclaimed children's books, *Stuart Little* (1945) and *Charlotte's Web* (1952). The following personal essay first appeared in *Harper's* in 1941.

One summer, along about 1904, my father rented a camp on a lake in 1
Maine and took us all there for the month of August. We all got ringworm from some kittens and had to rub Pond's Extract on our arms and legs night and morning, and my father rolled over in a canoe with all his clothes on; but outside of that the vacation was a success and from then on none of us ever thought there was any place in the world like that lake in Maine. We returned summer after summer—always on August 1st for one month. I have since become a salt-water man, but sometimes in summer there are days when the restlessness of the tides and the fearful cold of the sea water and the incessant wind that blows across the afternoon and into the evening make me wish for the placidity of a lake in the woods. A few weeks ago this feeling got so strong I bought myself a couple of bass hooks and a spinner and returned to the lake where we used to go, for a week's fishing and to revisit old haunts.

I took along my son, who had never had any fresh water up his nose 2
and who had seen lily pads only from train windows. On the journey over to the lake I began to wonder what it would be like. I wondered how time would have marred this unique, this holy spot—the coves and streams, the hills that the sun set behind, the camps and the paths behind the camps. I was sure that the tarred road would have found it out and I wondered in what other ways it would be desolated. It is strange how much you can

remember about places like that once you allow your mind to return into the grooves that lead back. You remember one thing, and that suddenly reminds you of another thing. I guess I remembered clearest of all the early mornings, when the lake was cool and motionless, remembered how the bedroom smelled of the lumber it was made of and the wet woods whose scent entered through the screen. The partitions in the camp were thin and did not extend clear to the top of the rooms, and as I was always the first up I would dress softly so as not to wake the others, and sneak out into the sweet outdoors and start out in the canoe, keeping close along the shore in the long shadows of the pines. I remembered being very careful never to rub my paddle against the gunwale for fear of disturbing the stillness of the cathedral.

The lake had never been what you would call a wild lake. There were   3 cottages sprinkled about the shores, and it was in farming country although the shores of the lake were quite heavily wooded. Some of the cottages were owned by nearby farmers, and you would live at the shore and eat your meals at the farmhouse. That's what our family did. But although it wasn't wild, it was a fairly large and undisturbed lake and there were places in it which, to a child at least, seemed infinitely remote and primeval.

I was right about the tar: It led to within half a mile of the shore. But   4 when I got back there, with my boy, and we settled into a camp near a farmhouse and into the kind of summertime I had known, I could tell that it was going to be pretty much the same as it had been before—I knew it, lying in bed the first morning, smelling the bedroom, and hearing the boy sneak quietly out and go off along the shore in a boat. I began to sustain the illusion that he was I, and therefore, by simple transposition, that I was my father. This sensation persisted, kept cropping up all the time we were there. It was not an entirely new feeling, but in this setting it grew much stronger. I seemed to be living a dual existence. I would be in the middle of some simple act, I would be picking up a bait box or laying down a table fork, or I would be saying something, and suddenly it would be not I but my father who was saying the words or making the gesture. It gave me a creepy sensation.

We went fishing the first morning. I felt the same damp moss covering   5 the worms in the bait can, and saw the dragonfly alight on the tip of my rod as it hovered a few inches from the surface of the water. It was the arrival of this fly that convinced me beyond any doubt that everything was as it always had been, that the years were a mirage and there had been no years. The small waves were the same, chucking the rowboat under the chin as we fished at anchor, and the boat was the same boat, the same color green and the ribs broken in the same places, and under the floorboards the same fresh-water leavings and debris—the dead hellgrammite, the wisps of moss, the rusty discarded fishhook, the dried blood from yesterday's catch. We stared silently at the tips of our rods, at the dragonflies that came and went. I lowered the tip of mine into the water, tentatively, pensively dislodging the fly, which darted two feet away, poised, darted two feet back, and came to rest again a little farther up the rod. There had been no years between the ducking of this dragon-fly and the other one—the one that was part of memory. I looked at the boy, who was silently watching his fly, and it was my hands that held his rod, my eyes watching. I felt dizzy and didn't know which rod I was at the end of.

We caught two bass, hauling them in briskly as though they were   6 mackerel, pulling them over the side of the boat in a businesslike manner without any landing net, and stunning them with a blow on the back of the head. When we got back for a swim before lunch, the lake was exactly where we had left it, the same number of inches from the dock, and there was only the merest suggestion of a breeze. This seemed an utterly en-chanted sea, this lake you could leave to its own devices for a few hours and come back to, and find that it had not stirred, this constant and trustworthy body of water. In the shallows, the dark, watersoaked sticks and twigs, smooth and old, were undulating in clusters on the bottom against the clean ribbed sand, and the track of the mussel was plain. A school of minnows swam by, each minnow with its small individual shadow, doubling the at-tendance, so clear and sharp in the sunlight. Some of the other campers were in swimming, along the shore, one of them with a cake of soap, and the water felt thin and clear and unsubstantial. Over the years there had been this person with the cake of soap, this cultist, and here he was. There had been no years.

Up to the farmhouse to dinner through the teeming, dusty field, the   7 road under our sneakers was only a two-track road. The middle track was missing, the one with the marks of the hooves and splotches of dried, flaky manure. There had always been three tracks to choose from in choosing which track to walk in; now the choice was narrowed down to two. For a moment I missed terribly the middle alternative. But the way led past the tennis court, and something about the way it lay there in the sun reassured me; the tape had loosened along the backline, the alleys were green with plantains and other weeds, and the net (installed in June and removed in September) sagged in the dry noon, and the whole place steamed with mid-day heat and hunger and emptiness. There was a choice of pie for dessert, and one was blueberry and one was apple, and the waitresses were the same country girls, there having been no passage of time, only the illusion of it as in a dropped curtain—the waitresses were still fifteen; their hair had been washed, that was the only difference—they had been to the movies and seen the pretty girls with the clean hair.

Summertime, oh summertime, pattern of life indelible, the fade-proof   8
lake, the woods unshatterable, the pasture with the sweetfern and the ju-
niper forever and ever, summer without end; this was the background, and
the life along the shore was the design, the cottages with their innocent and
tranquil design, their tiny docks with the flagpole and the American flag
floating against the white clouds in the blue sky, the little paths over the
roots of the trees leading from camp to camp and the paths leading back to
the outhouses and the can of lime for sprinkling, and at the souvenir counters at the store the miniature birch-bark canoes and the post cards that
showed things looking a little better than they looked. This was the American family at play, escaping the city heat, wondering whether the newcomers in the camp at the head of the cove were "common" or "nice,"
wondering whether it was true that the people who drove up for Sunday
dinner at the farmhouse were turned away because there wasn't enough
chicken.

It seemed to me, as I kept remembering all this, that those times and   9
those summers had been infinitely precious and worth saving. There had
been jollity and peace and goodness. The arriving (at the beginning of August) had been so big a business in itself, at the railway station the farm
wagon drawn up, the first smell of the pine-laden air, the first glimpse of the
smiling farmer, and the great importance of the trunks and your father's
enormous authority in such matters, and the feel of the wagon under you
for the long ten-mile haul, and at the top of the last long hill catching the
first view of the lake after eleven months of not seeing this cherished body
of water. The shouts and cries of the other campers when they saw you, and
the trunks to be unpacked, to give up their rich burden. (Arriving was less
exciting nowadays, when you sneaked up in your car and parked it under a
tree near the camp and took out the bags and in five minutes it was all over,
no fuss, no loud wonderful fuss about trunks.)

Peace and goodness and jollity. The only thing that was wrong now, re-   10
ally, was the sound of the place, an unfamiliar nervous sound of the outboard motors. This was the note that jarred, the one thing that would
sometimes break the illusion and set the years moving. In those other sum-
mertimes all motors were inboard; and when they were at a little distance,
the noise they made was a sedative, an ingredient of summer sleep. They
were one-cylinder and two-cylinder engines, and some were make-and-
break and some were jump-spark, but they all made a sleepy sound across
the lake. The one-lungers throbbed and fluttered, and the twin-cylinder
ones purred and purred, and that was a quiet sound too. But now the
campers all had outboards. In the daytime, in the hot mornings, these motors made a petulant, irritable sound; at night, in the still evening when the
afterglow lit the water, they whined about one's ears like mosquitoes. My

boy loved our rented outboard, and his great desire was to achieve single-handed mastery over it, and authority, and he soon learned the trick of choking it a little (but not too much), and the adjustment of the needle valve. Watching him I would remember the things you could do with the old one-cylinder engines with the heavy flywheel, how you could have it eating out of your hand if you got really close to it spiritually. Motor boats in those days didn't have clutches, and you would make a landing by shutting off the motor at the proper time and coasting in with a dead rudder. But there was a way of reversing them, if you learned the trick, by cutting the switch and putting it on again exactly on the final dying revolution of the flywheel, so that it would kick back against compression and begin reversing. Approaching a dock in a strong following breeze, it was difficult to slow up sufficiently by the ordinary coasting method, and if a boy felt he had complete mastery over his motor, he was tempted to keep it running beyond its time and then reverse it a few feet from the dock. It took a cool nerve, because if you threw the switch a twentieth of a second too soon you could catch the flywheel when it still had speed enough to go up past center, and the boat would leap ahead, charging bull-fashion at the dock.

We had a good week at the camp. The bass were biting well and the 11
sun shone endlessly, day after day. We would be tired at night and lie down in the accumulated heat of the little bedrooms after the long hot day and the breeze would stir almost imperceptibly outside and the smell of the swamp drift in through the rusty screens. Sleep would come easily and in the morning the red squirrel would be on the roof, tapping out his gay routine. I kept remembering everything, lying in bed in the mornings—the small steamboat that had a long rounded stern like the lip of a Ubangi, and how quietly she ran on the moonlight sails, when the older boys played their mandolins and the girls sang and we ate doughnuts dipped in sugar, and how sweet the music was on the water in the shining night, and what it had felt like to think about girls then. After breakfast we would go up to the store and the things were in the same place—the minnows in a bottle, the plugs and spinners disarranged and pawed over by the youngsters from the boys' camp, the Fig Newtons and the Beeman's gum. Outside, the road was tarred and cars stood in front of the store. Inside, all was just as it had always been, except there was more Coca-Cola and not so much Moxie and root beer and birch beer and sarsaparilla. We would walk out with a bottle of pop apiece and sometimes the pop would backfire up our noses and hurt. We explored the streams, quietly, where the turtles slid off the sunny logs and dug their way into the soft bottom; and we lay on the town wharf and fed worms to the tame bass. Everywhere we went I had trouble making out which was I, the one walking at my side, the one walking in my pants.

One afternoon while we were there at that lake a thunderstorm came   12
up. It was like the revival of an old melodrama that I had seen long ago with
childish awe. The second-act climax of the drama of the electrical distur-
bance over a lake in America had not changed in any important respect.
This was the big scene, still the big scene. The whole thing was so familiar,
the first feeling of oppression and heat and a general air around camp of not
wanting to go very far away. In midafternoon (it was all the same) a curious
darkening of the sky, and a lull in everything that had made life tick; and
then the way the boats suddenly swung the other way at their moorings with
the coming of a breeze out of the new quarter, and the premonitory rumble.
Then the kettle drum, then the snare, then the bass drum and cymbals, then
crackling light against the dark, and the gods grinning and licking their
chops in the hills. Afterward the calm, the rain steadily rustling in the calm
lake, the return of light and hope and spirits, and the campers running out in
joy and relief to go swimming in the rain, their bright cries perpetuating the
deathless joke about how they were getting simply drenched, and the children screaming with delight at the new sensation of bathing in the rain, and
the joke about getting drenched linking the generations in a strong inde-
structible chain. And the comedian who waded in carrying an umbrella.

When the others went swimming my son said he was going in too. He   13
pulled his dripping trunks from the line where they had hung all through
the shower, and wrung them out. Languidly, and with no thought of going
in, I watched him, his hard little body, skinny and bare, saw him wince slightly as he pulled up around his vitals the small, soggy, icy garment. As he
buckled the swollen belt suddenly my groin felt the chill of death.

◆ ◆ ◆

FIRST RESPONSES

How do you feel about the author and the revelation he makes in the
final paragraph? Can you identify with his situation? Explain why you feel
the way you do.

TAKING A CLOSER LOOK

Exploring *Who:* Voice and Tone

1. How old was the author when he wrote this essay? How much does
   his age matter to his attitude and state of mind?

2. How would you describe the author's mood at the beginning of the essay? How has his mood changed in the end? What were you feeling as you read this essay? Did your feelings change?
3. What age group is White addressing in this essay? Are you part of the audience that White is writing to? Can people who have never been to the Maine woods relate to this essay?
4. How did White's son feel about the trip to the lake? Can you be sure that White is conveying his son's impressions, or is the author projecting his own memories?

Exploring *What:* Content and Meaning

1. Explain the illusion that White describes in paragraph 4. How does he explain this sensation to himself? Have you ever had a similar sensation?
2. What role does time play in this essay? Find images and references that bring out the theme of time's passing.
3. What is the point of the discussion of inboard and outboard motors (paragraph 10)?
4. Explain the last sentence. Does it raise an issue that concerns you?

Exploring *Why:* Purpose

1. In what sense is the author writing this essay for himself? What feelings is he trying to come to terms with?
2. ▆▆ *Using the Internet.* How would a travel agent's description of the lake be different from White's? Find a travel agency's Web site on the Internet to see what kinds of information they give. What details and impressions does White include that a travel brochure would not? Why does he include this kind of material?
3. Do you think this essay contains a message or a lesson? What is it? Have you had any experiences that might communicate the same point?

Exploring *How:* Style and Strategy

1. Point out images that re-create the sights, sounds, smells, and tastes of White's childhood visit. How effectively do these images communicate the quality of memory?

2. What do you think of White's reference to the lake as "this holy spot" and a "cathedral" (paragraph 2)?

3. This essay is both a description and a comparison. How closely related are the two strategies? In what ways does the description contribute to the comparison?

4. Describe the impact of the final paragraph. Is this the way you expected the essay to end? How would you have concluded an essay like this?

IDEAS FOR WRITING A DESCRIPTION

1. Describe the perfect place to escape to, real or imagined.

2. Describe yourself as you think your parents see you. What qualities do they like? Which ones would they like you to change?

3. Describe a place that has a strong appeal (either positive or negative) to you. Include sensory details that will help reveal your feelings, but do not name the emotions themselves.

◆ FURTHER IDEAS FOR USING DESCRIPTION

1. Write a two-part description of the same person, place, or object. In the first part, give an objective description; in the second part, present an expressive (subjective) description by using details and sensory images to convey your feelings about the subject. Choose something or someone you can describe in detail.

2. Think of a setting that is quite familiar to you but probably unknown to your classmates. Write an essay in which you try to convey the experience of being in that setting, as several writers in this chapter do. You might want to consider nature, family, school, and solitary settings in choosing your topic.

3. Attempt to describe, in concrete, sensory terms, a certain feeling—such as grief, happiness, hope, boredom, or mistrust. Try to evoke the feeling without labeling it.

4. COLLABORATIVE WRITING. Go to an art exhibit with a small group of classmates. Choose which works each of you will describe for an exhibit catalog. Together, organize your descriptions and revise them for a consistent style and tone. Then collaboratively write a paragraph or two of introduction for the catalog.

5. COMBINING STRATEGIES. Combine narrative and description to write an account of an experience that changed you in some important way. Do not *tell* your readers explicitly what the change was, but let the description-narration clearly *show* how you were changed.

6. ■▯ *Using the Internet.* Describe a memorable vacation you had. Assume that your readers have not visited this place. Use the Internet to refresh your memory and gather more details for your description. If you went to the Black Hills, for instance, you could browse the Black Hills Information Web at http://www.blackhills-info.com/.

Strategies for Making a Point

Exemplification

◆ ◆ ◆ ◆ ◆

> **Exemplification writing explains and clarifies a generalization through illustration.**
>
> ◆ Writers use examples that are appropriate, relevant, and sufficiently detailed.
> ◆ Effective exemplification connects examples logically and clearly to the thesis and to one another.

You began using exemplification at a very early age. When your mother or father wouldn't let you ride your bike more than a block from the house, you probably informed them that your best friend had been going two whole blocks safely for at least the last month. Successful writers, too, make their points, or at least make them clearer and more interesting, by providing **examples.**

Exemplification, like narration and description, may be the focus of an entire essay, or it may be employed to bring other writing strategies to life. A *Sports Illustrated* story on the various community service activities of Michael Jordon or Rebecca Lobo reminds us that many athletes can and do provide positive role models for young people. And an in-depth example of a successful project at your current job may very well convince a prospective employer that you are the best candidate. Examples are, in a way, the "show" part of "show and tell." When writers simply tell readers their point, the result can be the kind of dense, dry, confusing essay that needs to be read and reread. Lively, clear, appropriate illustrations, however, ensure that readers will understand a step in a process, remember an essential trait in a definition, distinguish clearly one category from another, or visualize the consequence of an action.

Journalist Brent Staples turned to his own experience as a black man to create the following essay, which exemplifies the look, the feel, and the consequences of racism. After reading about Staples's experience, student writer Mark Jones looked at his own life to understand the nature of stereotypes. His essay follows Mr. Staples's.

Just Walk on By: A Black Man Ponders His Power to Alter Public Space

BRENT STAPLES

Born in 1951 to a poor and troubled family, Brent Staples earned a Ph.D. in psychology from the University of Chicago and has since established himself as a respected reporter and editorial writer with the *New York Times*. The following selection was originally published in *Ms.* magazine in 1986 and appeared as part of Staples's coming-of-age memoir, *Parallel Time: Growing Up in Black and White* (1994).

My first victim was a woman—white, well dressed, probably in her early twenties. I came upon her late one evening on a deserted street in Hyde Park, a relatively affluent neighborhood in an otherwise mean, impoverished section of Chicago. As I swung onto the avenue behind her, there seemed to be a discreet, uninflammatory distance between us. Not so. She cast back a worried glance. To her, the youngish black man—a broad six feet two inches with a beard and billowing hair, both hands shoved into the pockets of a bulky military jacket—seemed menacingly close. After a few more quick glimpses, she picked up her pace and was soon running in earnest. Within seconds she disappeared into a cross street.

That was more than a decade ago. I was 22 years old, a graduate stu- 2
dent newly arrived at the University of Chicago. It was in the echo of that
terrified woman's footfalls that I first began to know the unwieldy inheritance I'd come into—the ability to alter public space in ugly ways. It was
clear that she thought herself the quarry of a mugger, rapist, or worse. Suffering a bout of insomnia, however, I was stalking sleep, not defenseless
wayfarers. As a softy who is scarcely able to take a knife to a raw chicken—
let alone hold it to a person's throat—I was surprised, embarrassed, and dismayed all at once. Her flight made me feel like an accomplice in tyranny. It
also made it clear that I was indistinguishable from the muggers who occasionally seeped into the area from the surrounding ghetto. That first encounter, and those that followed, signified that a vast, unnerving gulf lay
between nighttime pedestrians—particularly women—and me. And I soon
gathered that being perceived as dangerous is a hazard in itself. I only needed to turn a corner into a dicey situation or crowd some frightened, armed
person in a foyer somewhere, or make an errant move after being pulled
over by a policeman. Where fear and weapons meet—and they often do in
urban America—there is always the possibility of death.

In that first year, my first away from my hometown, I was to become 3
thoroughly familiar with the language of fear. At dark, shadowy intersec-
tions in Chicago, I could cross in front of a car stopped at a traffic light and
elicit the *thunk, thunk, thunk, thunk* of the driver—black, white, male or
female—hammering down the door locks. On less traveled streets after
dark, I grew accustomed to but never comfortable with people who crossed
to the other side of the street rather than pass me. Then there were the standard unpleasantries with police, doormen, bouncers, cab drivers, and others
whose business it is to screen out troublesome individuals *before* there is
any nastiness.

I moved to New York nearly two years ago and I have remained an 4
avid night walker. In central Manhattan, the near-constant crowd cover
minimizes tense one-on-one street encounters. Elsewhere—visiting friends
in SoHo, where sidewalks are narrow and tightly spaced buildings shut out
the sky—things can get very taut indeed.

Black men have a firm place in New York mugging literature. Norman 5
Podhoretz in his famed (or infamous) 1963 essay, "My Negro Problem—and
Ours," recalls growing up in terror of black males; they "were tougher than
we were, more ruthless," he writes—and as an adult on the Upper West Side
of Manhattan, he continues, he cannot constrain his nervousness when he
meets black men on certain streets. Similarly, a decade later, the essayist and
novelist Edward Hoagland extols a New York where once "Negro bitterness
bore down mainly on other Negroes." Where some see mere panhandlers,
Hoagland sees "a mugger who is clearly screwing up his nerve to do more

than just *ask* for money." But Hoagland has "the New Yorker's quick-hunch posture for broken-field maneuvering," and the bad guy swerves away.

I often witness that "hunch posture," from women after dark on the   6
warrenlike streets of Brooklyn where I live. They seem to set their faces on neutral and, with their purse straps strung across their chests bandolier style, they forge ahead as though bracing themselves against being tackled. I understand, of course, that the danger they perceive is not a hallucination. Women are particularly vulnerable to street violence, and young black males are drastically overrepresented among the perpetrators of that violence. Yet these truths are no solace against the kind of alienation that comes of being ever the suspect, against being set apart, a fearsome entity with whom pedestrians avoid making eye contact.

It is not altogether clear to me how I reached the ripe old age of 22   7
without being conscious of the lethality nighttime pedestrians attributed to me. Perhaps it was because in Chester, Pennsylvania, the small, angry industrial town where I came of age in the 1960s, I was scarcely noticeable against a backdrop of gang warfare, street knifings, and murders. I grew up one of the good boys, had perhaps a half-dozen fist fights. In retrospect, my shyness of combat has clear sources.

Many things go into the making of a young thug. One of those things   8
is the consummation of the male romance with the power to intimidate. An infant discovers that random flailings send the baby bottle flying out of the crib and crashing to the floor. Delighted, the joyful babe repeats those motions again and again, seeking to duplicate the feat. Just so, I recall the points at which some of my boyhood friends were finally seduced by the perception of themselves as tough guys. When a mark cowered and surrendered his money without resistance, myth and reality merged—and paid off. It is, after all, only manly to embrace the power to frighten and intimidate. We, as men, are not supposed to give an inch of our lane on the highway; we are to seize the fighter's edge in work and in play and even in love; we are to be valiant in the face of hostile forces.

Unfortunately, poor and powerless young men seem to take all this   9
nonsense literally. As a boy, I saw countless tough guys locked away; I have since buried several, too. They were babies, really—a teenage cousin, a brother of 22, a childhood friend in his mid-twenties—all gone down in episodes of bravado played out in the streets. I came to doubt the virtues of intimidation early on. I chose, perhaps even unconsciously, to remain a shadow—timid, but a survivor.

The fearsomeness mistakenly attributed to me in public places often   10
has a perilous flavor. The most frightening of these confusions occurred in the late 1970s and early 1980s when I worked as a journalist in Chicago. One day, rushing into the office of a magazine I was writing for with a deadline

story in hand, I was mistaken for a burglar. The office manager called security and, with an ad hoc posse, pursued me through the labyrinthine halls, nearly to my editor's door. I had no way of proving who I was. I could only move briskly toward the company of someone who knew me.

Another time I was on assignment for a local paper and killing time 11 before an interview. I entered a jewelry store on the city's affluent Near North Side. The proprietor excused herself and returned with an enormous red Doberman pinscher straining at the end of a leash. She stood, the dog extended toward me, silent to my questions, her eyes bulging nearly out of her head. I took a cursory look around, nodded, and bade her good night. Relatively speaking, however, I never fared as badly as another black male journalist. He went to nearby Waukegan, Illinois, a couple of summers ago to work on a story about a murderer who was born there. Mistaking the reporter for the killer, police hauled him from his car at gunpoint and but for his press credentials would probably have tried to book him. Such episodes are not uncommon. Black men trade tales like this all the time.

In "My Negro Problem—and Ours," Podhoretz writes that the ha- 12 tred he feels for blacks makes itself known to him through a variety of avenues—one being his discomfort with that "special brand of paranoid touchiness" to which he says blacks are prone. No doubt he is speaking here of black men. In time, I learned to smother the rage I felt at so often being taken for a criminal. Not to do so would surely have led to madness—via that special "paranoid touchiness" that so annoyed Podhoretz at the time he wrote the essay.

I began to take precautions to make myself less threatening. I move 13 about with care, particularly late in the evening. I give a wide berth to nervous people on subway platforms during the wee hours, particularly when I have exchanged business clothes for jeans. If I happen to be entering a building behind some people who appear skittish, I may walk by, letting them clear the lobby before I return, so as not to seem to be following them. I have been calm and extremely congenial on those rare occasions when I've been pulled over by the police.

And on late-evening constitutionals along streets less traveled by, I 14 employ what has proved to be an excellent tension-reducing measure: I whistle melodies from Beethoven and Vivaldi and the more popular classical composers. Even steely New Yorkers hunching toward nighttime destinations seem to relax, and occasionally they even join in the tune. Virtually everybody seems to sense that a mugger wouldn't be warbling bright, sunny selections from Vivaldi's *Four Seasons*. It is my equivalent of the cowbell that hikers wear when they know they are in bear country.

◆ ◆ ◆

◆ ◆ ◆ *Writer's Workshop I* ◆ ◆ ◆
Responding to an Exemplification Essay

Use the *Who, What, Why,* and *How* questions (see pp. 3–4) to explore your own understanding of the ideas and the writing strategies employed by Brent Staples in "Just Walk on By." Your instructor may ask you to record these responses in a journal or bring them to class to use in small group discussions.

◆ WRITING FROM READING

The *Who, What, Why,* and *How* questions helped freshman Mark Jones understand Brent Staples's successful strategies for exemplifying what all Americans lose when they act on stereotypes or are victimized by them. Mark soon recognized that this very difficult and abstract problem, one many people distance themselves from, had been made clear and immediate through Staples's honest and detailed revelation of his specific feelings and concrete actions. After freewriting to identify a stereotype that affects how other people might see him, Mark wrote the following essay.

```
Mark Jones
English 1090
May 2, 1998
```

Looking Up from the Bottom

You see me walking down the street, and this is   1
your visual description: tall (6' 4 1/2"); thin, but
not skinny; blonde hair; clean, somewhat dressy
clothes; casual air, grinning. Who is this kid, you
ask? A snotty, arrogant, rich white boy? A hard
working, upwardly mobile citizen? And what made him
who he is? Might he be a last-born child? Bingo. By
putting me into a birth-order stereotype, you have hit
the nail on the head.

Being the "baby of the family" can't describe   2
everything about me--no stereotype in the world could
do that. But one's position within the family does

predict possible personality traits. Oldest child, only child, middle child, and youngest child are four spots on the birth order spectrum and each has its own tendencies. Since I fit the youngest category, I will explore that one. As with each of the family roles, there are two sides to the attributes a youngest sibling may have. The good attributes and the bad attributes are both form fitting to me, and I wear them like a true youngest child.

A youngest born is said to be outgoing and eager   3 to help. Volunteering at the local hospital and coaching a younger age soccer team are examples of ways that I fit this stereotype. Youngest children are also supposed to be charming, engaging, fun loving, affectionate, and able to get along easily with others. I exemplify many of these traits as well. Most of my jobs have allowed me to interact with people. As an assistant carpenter, I ran into college kids and homeowners who were often angry at what had happened to their houses or apartments, and I needed to use my charm to calm them down. I have also been a lifeguard, a job that required me to confront people who didn't obey the rules and to set them straight (which was harder when they were a lot bigger than I was). In these job-related scenarios my people skills came in handy. Of course, I would much rather be out with my friends playing pool or engaged in a sport than doing work or writing a paper. Being an open and carefree youngest child affects both my work and play.

Now for the bad part. The youngest born child can 4 be manipulative, blame others, and show off. These negative attributes may result from our having been spoiled, and, as a result, we may not be taken seriously. I have many of these problems. I hate to take the blame for anything, so I will shift it wherever I can: to the next person on the project, the computer, the traffic, fate, whatever. But, if the thing done deserves praise, hey, I'm right there basking in it. I'm not spoiled to the extreme, but of course it is better to have something done for you than to do it yourself, isn't it? Mom enjoys doing my laundry, right? My most obvious trait is being a class

clown type personality. There are a few lengths I
won't go to to get a laugh, but those are way out
there. If you were to ask any teacher I have had or
any one of my friends, he or she will say I have a
sense of humor unparalleled by others. If a neighbor's
tree turned up decorated in toilet paper, or, after
gym class, if one of the guys found a new set of
bright pink laces in the shoes in his locker,
everybody knew who was probably to blame! See, right
there I'm showing off, so the traits run deep.

In this world we have numerous stereotypes which   5
range from the dangerous to the merely annoying, based
on a person's race or the amount of hair a person has,
for example. Luckily, the birth order stereotype
doesn't apply a solely negative label to a person such
as more troubling stereotypes do--hick, snob, ghetto-
boy, schmoozer, for example. And, since the birth
order stereotype is an average accumulation of traits,
each individual has a unique combination. Oh, if you
like this paper, you are probably the youngest in your
family.

◆ GETTING STARTED ON EXEMPLIFICATION

When you have an idea to *explain,* a point to *clarify,* or an opinion to
convince someone of, you need to begin a search for the best examples to
support your **generalization.** This central idea, or **thesis,** will probably be a
work-in-progress at this point, too. Although you should have a **purpose** for
writing in mind, its exact scope and phrasing will be made clearer when the
illustrations you decide on have been gathered.

At this stage, you must decide how to best "show" the generalization
you wish to "tell." The source of your examples will depend on the assignment and your thesis. If your writing will focus on personal experience, then
brainstorming, freewriting, or one of the more structured discovery systems
discussed in Chapter 2 is the best starting point. After he had decided to write
about being a youngest child, Mark made a simple list of exemplary traits:
outgoing, eager, open, carefree, a bit spoiled, a show-off. He then did some
brainstorming to come up with illustrations of these parts of his personality,
which led him to the jobs he'd held as well as the practical jokes he'd played.

For both Mark and Brent Staples, all the necessary examples were right
at their fingertips, so the challenge was to take the time to find an *appropriate*

number, to ensure that each was *relevant* to the point he wanted to make, and to remember or describe the example in *sufficient detail* to make it clear and convincing for the reader. There are times when one extended, in-depth example will be all that is needed to support the thesis. Staples, however, knew that some readers might be skeptical about his claims, so that the single opening incident had to be followed up with similar experiences in different times and places. His instincts also led him to go beyond his own experience and to recall other black men who had been victimized by race stereotyping. Readers might dismiss his experiences as unique, but together with those of other professional black men, they form a persuasive body of evidence.

If the assignment or your thesis requires examples that don't arise from your own experience, getting started may involve doing research at the library or interviewing people with direct experience with or expertise on your topic. Mark, for example, might have interviewed others who were the youngest in their families, or looked for case studies on the subject gathered by psychologists or pediatricians. Staples's experiences could have been presented in a slightly different context had he identified writings by white women who describe their reactions to stranger contact with members of a different race. Had he expanded his purpose in this way, his thesis—"It was in the echo of that terrified woman's footfalls that I first began to know the unwieldy inheritance I'd come into—the ability to alter public space in ugly ways"—would need to be expanded to include the two points of view.

◆ ORGANIZING EXEMPLIFICATION

Time and space provide the basic starting points for organizing narrative and descriptive essays. The thesis and purpose direct the plan for an essay developed through examples. Whether you use one extended example or a series of examples to make your point, some intentional and thoughtful sequence, which is revealed through **transitional words and phrases,** is needed to avoid turning your essay into a loosely strung together list.

Staples's thesis implies a persuasive purpose: to illustrate a problem, to give examples of the consequences, and to provide evidence of the precautions he takes to avoid both the problem and the consequences. His essay, therefore, divides into three parts, with appropriate examples given in each section. Mark, on the other hand, wishes to explain both the good and the bad sides to being a youngest child, so he clusters his examples into pro and con paragraphs and provides appropriate transitional sentences. Paragraph 4, for example, begins with "Now for the bad part," signaling his change in direction and the topic which unifies the examples that follow.

In the essays that follow, you will see writers employ a number of additional organizing methods. Sue Hubbell, for example, uses geography to organize "On the Interstate: A City of the Mind." Her thesis—"In the early morning there is a city of the mind that stretches from coast to coast, from border to border"—offers a built-in plan for the essay, with each scene of truck stop life coming from a different part of the country. You'll notice when you read her essay that she went a step further in her organization and provided descriptions of similar items and kinds of people at each location.

Extended examples require equally careful planning. If the example is a story, narrative strategies might be used. Or if the example is a place, descriptive methods are helpful. In the case of William Greider's "Mock Democracy," the essay is organized so that each paragraph introduces a different aspect of the professional life of a typical public relations man who illustrates specifically and quite concretely the difficult and abstract qualities of the term (mock democracy) that Greider is defining.

◆ DEVELOPING EXEMPLIFICATION

Once the organization is decided upon, and you have selected the likely examples to be used and determined where each might best be placed, you must think about the level of specificity and amount of detail to be provided in each section of the paper. There is no magic formula for deciding how fully to develop examples, but giving full consideration to your readers' needs and attitudes can be a big help. Readers familiar with your example may need to be reminded of only a name, a time, or a place to bring the entire experience back to them. Someone with little information on your topic or who is skeptical about your generalization requires more extended information. Staples uses a mixture of approaches to development along a spectrum from the general to the very specific. The introduction is at the most concrete end of the range. We see one particular woman, his "first victim," and the setting; and we feel her unique fear as she "cast back a worried glance." Paragraph 5, by contrast, generalizes about the typical reactions Staples encounters in an attempt to convince us that such fears are broadly exhibited.

Each of Mark's body paragraphs moves from a generalized example of his personality, for example his people skills, to a concrete illustration, such as his diplomatic role in calming hostile tenants. Professional writers such as Sallie Tisdale know that readers can relate more fully to her personal struggle with weight if she uses recognizable popular examples such as Michelle Pfeiffer and if she draws on popular magazines to make her point that our modern age considers the "well-fed" female body to be a size 8.

◆ OPENING AND CLOSING EXEMPLIFICATION

Because exemplification essays are developed around a central generalization, their introductions are usually organized to introduce this thesis and provide readers with an immediate sense of this topic's interest or usefulness to them. Another common strategy is to begin with a provocative example, as Staples does. Notice, however, that very early in the second paragraph, Staples provides a thesis to connect this example to a broader purpose. By contrast, knowing that an essay about him might not be of obvious interest to a reader, Mark draws his **audience** in by using a series of questions a typical person might pose.

The conclusion to an essay developed through examples generally returns the reader to the generalization in order to ensure the success and clarity of the writer's purpose. Mark's generally positive exploration of the usefulness of stereotypes requires him to refine his initial thesis in his conclusion, pointing out that stereotypes remain a complicated and sometimes troubling topic. Staples uses a different approach. His closing completes his three-part purpose, leaving readers with the sounds of whistled Mozart to challenge racist assumptions about individual personalities and accomplishments.

Writer Jon Hull's conclusion to "Slow Descent into Hell" illustrates another more subtle and indirect approach. The reader's exposure to the real people who live and die homeless in America is framed by an introduction and conclusion that focuses on the same man, George. While the essay begins with some hope for this human being who insists on staying clean and who evades the chronic alcoholism of his peers, in the end, when George returns to McDonald's washroom, the reader has seen far too many examples of failure to remain so optimistic.

◆ USING THE MODEL

Both Brent Staples and Mark Jones chose to explore the nature of stereotypes. Staples realized that before he could challenge the dangerous effects of racist assumptions, he would first have to convince readers of its continued existence. Examples fulfilled that goal and, in turn, provided evidence of racism's consequences. Mark decided on a less serious approach to the same topic, but he turned to Staples's essay for its method of carefully examining a personal experience in relation to popularly held views. Is there something about your life that either reinforces or challenges a common notion or assumption? Would it make an interesting essay?

◆ ◆ ◆ *Writer's Workshop II* ◆ ◆ ◆
Analyzing an Exemplification Essay

Working individually or with a small group of classmates, read through Mark Jones's essay "Looking Up from the Bottom," and respond to the following questions.

1. Why did Mark put his positive examples before the negative ones? How else might Mark have organized his essay?
2. Do you agree that some stereotypes can be useful? Did Mark convince you that he's a typical youngest child? If not, would more examples have helped?
3. Did you see enough of Mark's "people skills" to understand what he meant by that term?
4. Is the topic sentence in paragraph 4 appropriate? For example, did he really see being a class clown as a negative trait? Try rewriting the topic sentence.
5. Was Mark's use of questions an effective way to introduce his essay? Did he create an interest in sibling stereotypes?

◆ ◆ ◆ *Checklist for Reading and Writing* ◆ ◆ ◆
Exemplification Essays

1. Is there a clear, unifying thesis? Do all examples explain or clarify that generalization?
2. Does each paragraph have a topic sentence or a clear central focus?
3. Is there a logical order for the body paragraphs? Are the examples within each paragraph arranged coherently? Are there transitions to help direct readers from one example to the next?
4. Are there a sufficient number of examples, and are they appropriate for the paper?
5. Are examples developed in enough detail to be interesting and useful?

◆ ◆ ◆ **PREPARING TO READ**

Sometimes while traveling, we get brief and fascinating glimpses into other people's lives. Is there a particularly interesting stranger or bit of overheard conversation that has stayed with you long after the trip was over? What makes this memory so vivid?

◆ ◆ ◆

On the Interstate: A City of the Mind

SUE HUBBELL

Whether writing about toothpicks or life on an Ozark farm, journalist and essayist Sue Hubbell finds natural history in everyday life. Formerly a regular contributor to *The New Yorker,* she now writes for *Natural History, Vogue,* and *Smithsonian.* Hubbell has also written two books on insects: *Broadside from the Other Order: A Book of Bugs* (1993) and *A Book of Bees . . . And How to Keep Them* (1988). At one time a trucker herself, Hubbell recorded part of her life on the road in "On the Interstate," which appeared in *Time* in 1985. An expanded essay on trucker life appears in her collection *Far Flung Hubbell* (1995), which has been described as "wigged out journeys" written in a "calm, tongue-firmly-in-cheek prose."

In the early morning there is a city of the mind that stretches from 1
coast to coast, from border to border. Its cross streets are the interstate highways, and food, comfort, companionship are served up in its buildings, the truck stops near the exits. Its citizens are all-night drivers, the truckers, and the waitresses at the stops.

In the daylight the city fades and blurs when the transients appear, 2
tourists who merely want a meal and a tank of gas. They file into the carpeted dining rooms away from the professional drivers' side, sit at the Formica tables set off by imitation cloth flowers in bud vases. They eat and are gone, do not return. They are not a part of the city and obscure it.

It is 5 A.M. in a truck stop in West Virginia. Drivers in twos, threes and 3
fours are eating breakfast and talking routes and schedules.

"Truckers!" growls a manager. "They say they are in a hurry. They 4
complain if the service isn't fast. We fix it so they can have their fuel

pumped while they are eating and put in telephones on every table so they can check with their dispatchers at the same time. They could be out of here in half an hour. But what do they do? They sit and talk for two hours."

The truckers are lining up for seconds at the breakfast buffet (all you 5 can eat for $3.99—biscuits with chipped-beef gravy, fruit cup, French toast with syrup, bacon, pancakes, sausage, scrambled eggs, doughnuts, Danish, cereal in little boxes).

The travel store at the truck stop has a machine to measure heartbeat 6 in exchange for a quarter. There are racks of jackets, belts, truck supplies, tape cassettes. On the wall are paintings for sale, simulated wood with likenesses of John Wayne or a stag. The rack by the cash register is stuffed with Twinkies and chocolate Suzy Qs.

It is 5 A.M. in New Mexico. Above the horseshoe-shaped counter on 7 panels where a menu is usually displayed, an overhead slide show is in progress. The pictures change slowly, allowing the viewer to take in all the details. A low shot of a Peterbilt, its chrome fittings sparkling in the sunshine, is followed by one of a bosomy young woman, the same who must pose for those calendars found in autoparts stores. She almost has on clothes, and she is offering to check a trucker's oil. The next slide is a side view of a whole tractor-trailer rig, its 18 wheels gleaming and spoked. It is followed by one of a blond bulging out of a hint of cop clothes writing a naughty trucker a ticket.

The waitress looks too tired and too jaded to be offended. The jaws of 8 the truckers move mechanically as they fork up their eggs-over-easy. They stare at the slides, glassy eyed, as intent on chrome as on flesh.

It is 4 A.M. in Oklahoma. A recycled Stuckey's with blue tile roof calls 9 itself simply Truck Stop. The sign also boasts showers, scales, truck wash and a special on service for $88.50. At a table inside, four truckers have ordered a short stack and three eggs a piece, along with bacon, sausage and coffee (Trucker's Superbreakfast—$3.79).

They have just started drinking their coffee, and the driver with the 10 Roadway cap calls over the waitress, telling her there is salt in the sugar he put in his coffee. She is pale, thin, young, has dark circles under her eyes. The truckers have been teasing her, and she doesn't trust them. She dabs a bit of sugar from the canister on a finger and tastes it. Salt. She samples sugar from the other canisters. They have salt too, and she gathers them up to replace them. Someone is hazing her, breaking her into her new job. Her eyes shine with tears.

She brings the food and comes back when the truckers are nearly 11 done. She carries a water jug and coffeepot on her tray. The men are ragging her again, and her hands tremble. The tray falls with a crash. The jug breaks. Glass, water and coffee spread across the floor. She sits down in the booth, tears rolling down her cheeks.

"I'm so tired. My old man . . . he left me," she says, the tears coming 12
faster now. "The judge says he's going to take my kid away if I can't take
care of him, so I stay up all day and just sleep when he takes a nap and the
boss yells at me and . . . and . . . the truckers all talk dirty . . . I'm so
tired."

She puts her head down on her arms and sobs luxuriantly. The truck- 13
ers are gone, and I touch her arm and tell her to look at what they have left.
There is a $20 bill beside each plate. She looks up, nods, wipes her eyes on
her apron, pockets the tips and goes to get a broom and a mop.

It is 3:30 A.M. in Illinois at a glossy truck stop that offers all mechani- 14
cal services, motel rooms, showers, Laundromat, game room, TV lounge,
truckers' bulletin board and a stack of newspapers published by the Association of Christian Truckers. Piped-in music fills the air.

The waitress in the professional drivers' section is a big motherly- 15
looking woman with red hair piled in careful curls on top of her head. She
correctly sizes up the proper meal for the new customer at the counter.
"Don't know what you want, honey? Try the chicken-noodle soup with a
hot roll. It will stick to you like you've got something, and you don't have to
worry about grease."

She has been waitressing 40 years, 20 of them in this truck stop. As she 16
talks she polishes the stainless steel, fills mustard jars, adds the menu inserts
for today's special (hot turkey sandwich, mashed potatoes and gravy, pot of
coffee— $2.50).

"The big boss, well, he's a love, but some of the others aren't so hot. 17
But it's a job. Gotta work somewhere. I need a day off though. Been working six, seven days straight lately. Got shopping to do. My lawn needs
mowing."

Two truckers are sitting at a booth. Their faces are lined and leathery. 18
One cap says HARLEY-DAVIDSON, the other COORS.

Harley-Davidson calls out, "If you wasn't so mean, Flossie, you'd have 19
a good man to take care of you and you wouldn't have to mow the damn
lawn."

She puts down the mustard jar, walks over to Harley-Davidson and 20
Coors, stands in front of them, hands on wide hips. "Now you listen here,
Charlie, I'm a good enough woman for any man, but all you guys want are
chippies."

Coors turns bright red. She glares at him. "You saw my ex in here last 21
Saturday night with a chippie on his arm. He comes in here all the time with
two, three chippies just to prove to me what a high old time he's having. If
that's a good time, I'd rather baby-sit my grandkids."

Chippies are not a topic of conversation that Charlie and Coors wish 22
to pursue. Coors breaks a doughnut in two, and Charlie uses his fork to

make a spillway for the gravy on the double order of mashed potatoes that accompanies his scrambled eggs.

Flossie comes back to the counter and turns to the new customer in   23 mirror shades at this dark hour, a young trucker with cowboy boots and hat. "John boy. Where you been? Haven't seen you in weeks. Looks like you need a nice omelet. Cook just made some of those biscuits you like too."

I leave a tip for Flossie and pay my bill. In the men's room, where I am   24 shunted because the ladies' is closed for cleaning, someone has scrawled poignant words: NO TIME TO EAT NOW.

◆ ◆ ◆

FIRST RESPONSES

Have you ever worked a job that brought you into regular contact with people like these waitresses or truckers? How would you handle those truckers' demands, practical jokes, and one-liners if you were a waitress or manager?

TAKING A CLOSER LOOK

Exploring *Who:* Voice and Tone

1. How directly is Sue Hubbell involved in the events in this essay? How might the essay have changed if she had not been a trucker herself?
2. In paragraph 12, why does the waitress choose to turn to Hubbell to share her complaints?
3. How would you describe Hubbell's responses to the truckers? the waitresses? Can you find any humor in this essay?
4. Reread paragraph 2. What does the writer mean when she describes the tourists as "transients"? What is she implying about most of her readers here? Have you ever been a truck stop transient?

Exploring *What:* Content and Meaning

1. What do these truck stop scenes tell you about daily life as a trucker? as a waitress? How has it reinforced or changed your attitudes toward these jobs and the people who hold them? You might want to start by looking at the food they eat.

2. What are the differences between the young waitress in Oklahoma and the "motherly-looking" waitress in Illinois? If you look closely, can you also find similarities?

3. Why is the waitress described as sobbing "luxuriantly" in paragraph 13? Do you understand why she feels as she does at such a moment?

4. In paragraphs 18 to 22, what is the effect of referring to the two truckers as Harley-Davidson and Coors? What is a "chippie"? What does the word tell us about Flossie?

Exploring *Why:* Purpose

1. Do Hubbell's examples convince you that there is a "city of the mind" at these truck stops? Do they make you want to spend some time at truck stops? Is that Hubbell's purpose?

2. What does the word "poignant" mean in the concluding paragraph? Why has Hubbell used it to describe the men's room graffiti? Why is this the final impression Hubbell wishes to leave us with?

3. ▇▐ *Using the Internet.* How would the truckers and waitresses described here respond to Hubbell's view of them? Using one of the Internet search engines, locate a trucker's site to analyze the ways in which other writers discuss the issues of interest to truckers.

Exploring *How:* Style and Strategy

1. Why does Hubbell describe four different truck stops? What subpoints do the examples have in common?

2. What view of the truckers is suggested by paragraphs 7 and 8? Why is this New Mexico truck stop included as the second example rather than as the third or fourth one?

3. Why is the cowboy trucker in paragraph 23 included in the essay? Don't we already have a pretty clear image of Flossie and this truck stop?

4. Hubbell uses quite a bit of dialogue. Why? Select any example, and describe how your feelings about the scene would change without the dialogue.

WRITING FROM READING ASSIGNMENT

"On the Interstate" offers a behind-the-scenes look at a place and a life that many Americans pass by every day. In this writing assignment, gather examples from your experience to reveal a place, job, or person that you know well but that others may know only on the surface or, perhaps, that others misunderstand because of their lack of experience.

A. Begin by brainstorming about places, jobs, and people that you know especially well and would like others to know or understand better— for example, camp counselors' bunk houses, the duties of a golf caddie, grunge music fans.

B. Select a topic, and write a tentative generalization that you would like to offer your readers about this topic. What do you want them to know, and why might they be interested in knowing it?

C. Having settled on a topic, do some additional brainstorming, freewriting, or clustering to come up with as many examples as you can to support your purpose for writing. At this point, you might review the kinds of major examples that make up "On the Interstate." Hubbell uses different examples of the same kind of place in different locations. She might have shown us the same truck stop on different days—or even at different times. Consider all your choices. Do you have enough examples to prove your point?

D. After you have a sufficient number of suitable examples, do some freewriting on *each* example to recall as many details as possible. Look at the concrete examples in paragraphs 5 and 6 of "On the Interstate," and also think about your reactions to the dialogue in that essay. How much will your readers already know and how much information will they need to see the people or places you are exemplifying?

E. Now that you have your examples, turn your working generalization into a thesis and write a draft of an introduction. Reread the first paragraph of "On the Interstate." Do you, too, want to preview the subtopics you will develop? What other approach might grab the readers' interest in your topic and keep them reading?

F. In the previous *How* questions, you considered the order of Hubbell's examples. What sequence will best serve your purpose and your readers' needs?

G. In each of her examples, Hubbell includes the same types of people and descriptions of the settings. What will your examples have in common? How do these points support your thesis?

H. After you complete a draft of your essay, return to the "Checklist for Reading and Writing Exemplification Essays" (p. 145), and evaluate how fully your examples complete the purpose with which you began your project.

◆ ◆ ◆ **PREPARING TO READ**

When you imagine your favorite writer sitting down to begin writing, what do you see him or her doing, feeling, thinking? How does this compare with your experience as a writer?

◆ ◆ ◆

Shitty First Drafts

ANNE LAMOTT

Anne Lamott is equally at home as a writer of fiction and nonfiction. Her most recent novel, *Crooked Little Heart* (1997), returns to the young heroine of an earlier novel, *Rosie* (1983), who is a talented young tennis pro. Rosie's athletic ability and privilege add to instead of protecting her from life's challenges. Lamott's alcoholism and struggles as a single mom and professional writer have been the focus of her nonfiction, including her autobiographical book *Operating Instructions: A Journal of My Son's First Year* (1993) and *Bird by Bird: Some Instructions on Writing and Life* (1995), from which "Shitty First Drafts" is taken.

Shitty first drafts. All good writers write them. This is how they end up   1
with good second drafts and terrific third drafts. People tend to look at successful writers, writers who are getting their books published and maybe even doing well financially, and think that they sit down at their desks every morning feeling like a million dollars, feeling great about who they are and how much talent they have and what a great story they have to tell; that they take in a few deep breaths, push back their sleeves, roll their necks a few times to get all the cricks out, and dive in, typing fully formed passages as fast as a court reporter. But this is just the fantasy of the uninitiated. I know some very great writers, writers you love who write beautifully and have made a great deal of money, and not *one* of them sits down routinely feeling wildly enthusiastic and confident. Not one of them writes elegant first drafts. All right, one of them does, but we do not like her very much. We do not think that she has a rich inner life or that God likes her or can even stand her. (Although when I mentioned this to my priest friend Tom, he said you can safely assume you've created God in your own image when it turns out that God hates all the same people you do.)

Very few writers really know what they are doing until they've done it. 2
Nor do they go about their business feeling dewy and thrilled. They do not
type a few stiff warm-up sentences and then find themselves bounding
along like huskies across the snow. One writer I know tells me that he sits
down every morning and says to himself nicely, "It's not like you don't have
a choice, because you do—you can either type or kill yourself." We all often
feel like we are pulling teeth, even those writers whose prose ends up being
the most natural and fluid. The right words and sentences just do not come
pouring out like ticker tape most of the time. Now, Muriel Spark is said to
have felt that she was taking dictation from God every morning—sitting
there, one supposes, plugged into a Dictaphone, typing away, humming. But
this is a very hostile and aggressive position. One might hope for bad things
to rain down on a person like this.

For me and most of the other writers I know, writing is not rapturous. 3
In fact, the only way I can get anything written at all is to write really, really
shitty first drafts.

The first draft is the child's draft, where you let it all pour out and then 4
let it romp all over the place, knowing that no one is going to see it and that
you can shape it later. You just let this childlike part of you channel whatever voices and visions come through and onto the page. If one of the characters wants to say, "Well, so what, Mr. Poopy Pants?" you let her. No one is
going to see it. If the kid wants to get into really sentimental, weepy, emotional territory, you let him. Just get it all down on paper, because there may
be something great in those six crazy pages that you would never have gotten to by more rational, grown-up means. There may be something in the
very last line of the very last paragraph on page six that you just love, that is
so beautiful or wild that you now know what you're supposed to be writing
about, more or less, or in what direction you might go—but there was no
way to get to this without first getting through the first five and a half pages.

I used to write food reviews for *California* magazine before it folded. 5
(My writing food reviews had nothing to do with the magazine folding, although every single review did cause a couple of canceled subscriptions.
Some readers took umbrage at my comparing mounds of vegetable puree
with various ex-presidents' brains.) These reviews always took two days to
write. First I'd go to a restaurant several times with a few opinionated, articulate friends in tow. I'd sit there writing down everything anyone said that
was at all interesting or funny. Then on the following Monday I'd sit down at
my desk with my notes, and try to write the review. Even after I'd been
doing this for years, panic would set in. I'd try to write a lead, but instead I'd
write a couple of dreadful sentences, xx them out, try again, xx everything
out, and then feel despair and worry settle on my chest like an x-ray apron.

It's over, I'd think, calmly; I'm not going to be able to get the magic to work this time. I'm ruined. I'm through. I'm toast. Maybe, I'd think, I can get my old job back as a clerk-typist. But probably not. I'd get up and study my teeth in the mirror for a while. Then I'd stop, remember to breathe, make a few phone calls, hit the kitchen and chow down. Eventually I'd go back and sit down at my desk, and sigh for the next ten minutes. Finally I would pick up my one-inch picture frame, stare into it as if for the answer, and every time the answer would come: all I had to do was to write a really shitty first draft of, say, the opening paragraph. And no one was going to see it.

So I'd start writing without reining myself in. It was almost just typing, just making my fingers move. And the writing would be *terrible*. I'd write a lead paragraph that was a whole page, even though the entire review could only be three pages long, and then I'd start writing up descriptions of the food, one dish at a time, bird by bird, and the critics would be sitting on my shoulders, commenting like cartoon characters. They'd be pretending to snore, or rolling their eyes at my overwrought descriptions, no matter how hard I tried to tone those descriptions down, no matter how conscious I was of what a friend said to me gently in my early days of restaurant reviewing. "Annie," she said, "it is just a piece of *chicken*. It is just a bit of *cake*."

But because by then I had been writing for so long, I would eventually let myself trust the process—sort of, more or less. I'd write a first draft that was maybe twice as long as it should be, with a self-indulgent and boring beginning, stupefying descriptions of the meal, lots of quotes from my black-humored friends that made them sound more like the Manson girls than food lovers, and no ending to speak of. The whole thing would be so long and incoherent and hideous that for the rest of the day I'd obsess about getting creamed by a car before I could write a decent second draft. I'd worry that people would read what I'd written and believe that the accident had really been a suicide, that I had panicked because my talent was waning and my mind was shot.

The next day, though, I'd sit down, go through it all with a colored pen, take out everything I possibly could, find a new lead somewhere on the second page, figure out a kicky place to end it, and then write a second draft. It always turned out fine, sometimes even funny and weird and helpful. I'd go over it one more time and mail it in.

Then, a month later, when it was time for another review, the whole process would start again, complete with the fears that people would find my first draft before I could rewrite it.

Almost all good writing begins with terrible first efforts. You need to start somewhere. Start by getting something—anything—down on paper. A friend of mine says that the first draft is the down draft—you just get it down. The second draft is the up draft—you fix it up. You try to say what you have to say more accurately. And the third draft is the dental draft, where you check every tooth, to see if it's loose or cramped or decayed, or even, God help us, healthy.

What I've learned to do when I sit down to work on a shitty first draft 11 is to quiet the voices in my head. First there's the vinegar-lipped Reader Lady, who says primly, "Well, *that's* not very interesting, is it?" And there's the emaciated German male who writes these Orwellian memos detailing your thought crimes. And there are your parents, agonizing over your lack of loyalty and discretion; and there's William Burroughs, dozing off or shooting up because he finds you as bold and articulate as a houseplant; and so on. And there are also the dogs: let's not forget the dogs, the dogs in their pen who will surely hurtle and snarl their way out if you ever *stop* writing, because writing is, for some of us, the latch that keeps the door of the pen closed, keeps those crazy ravenous dogs contained.

Quieting these voices is at least half the battle I fight daily. But this is 12 better than it used to be. It used to be 87 percent. Left to its own devices, my mind spends much of its time having conversations with people who aren't there. I walk along defending myself to people, or exchanging repartee with them, or rationalizing my behavior, or seducing them with gossip, or pretending I'm on their TV talk show or whatever. I speed or run an aging yellow light or don't come to a full stop, and one nanosecond later am explaining to imaginary cops exactly why I had to do what I did, or insisting that I did not in fact do it.

I happened to mention this to a hypnotist I saw many years ago, and 13 he looked at me very nicely. At first I thought he was feeling around on the floor for the silent alarm button, but then he gave me the following exercise, which I still use to this day.

Close your eyes and get quiet for a minute, until the chatter starts up. 14 Then isolate one of the voices and imagine the person speaking as a mouse. Pick it up by the tail and drop it into a mason jar. Then isolate another voice, pick it up by the tail, drop it in the jar. And so on. Drop in any high-maintenance parental units, drop in any contractors, lawyers, colleagues, children, anyone who is whining in your head. Then put the lid on, and watch all these mouse people clawing at the glass, jabbering away, trying to make you feel like shit because you won't do what they want—won't give them more money, won't be more successful, won't see them more often. Then imagine that there is a volume-control button on the bottle. Turn it all the way up for a minute, and listen to the stream of angry, neglected, guilt-mongering voices. Then turn it all the way down and watch the frantic mice lunge at the glass, trying to get to you. Leave it down, and get back to your shitty first draft.

A writer friend of mine suggests opening the jar and shooting them all   15
in the head. But I think he's a little angry, and I'm sure nothing like this
would ever occur to you.

◆ ◆ ◆

FIRST RESPONSES

When you write your first drafts, do you hear voices similar to the ones
Lamott describes in paragraph 11? What names might you give your voices?

TAKING A CLOSER LOOK

Exploring *Who:* Voice and Tone

1. Were you surprised by the title of this essay? How did it affect your interest in reading the rest of the essay? Did Lamott turn out to be the
   kind of person the title led you to expect?
2. Why does Lamott include the parenthetical comments in paragraphs
   1 and 5? What impression of her do they create?
3. Lamott draws examples from her friends and from other professional
   writers. Why not rely on her own opinions and experiences?

Exploring *What:* Content and Meaning

1. What does Lamott mean when she says "writing is not rapturous"? Why
   would anyone think it was? Does the essay convince you that it is not?
2. What is involved in writing a "child's draft"? Have you been encouraged to write such drafts before? If not, is it something you feel you
   might enjoy and benefit from?
3. Why did Lamott "hit the kitchen" and have to "remember to breathe"
   while she was writing the drafts of her food reviews? Have you ever
   had this experience? How does it make you feel to know that Lamott
   acts in these ways?
4. ◼️ *Using the Internet.* The Inkspots Internet site has a "quotes for
   writers" link at http://192.41.39.106/bt/craft/quotes.html, where you
   will find advice from writers such as C. J. Cherryh, who offers her version of "shitty first drafts": "It is perfectly okay to write garbage—as
   long as you edit brilliantly." Visit the site. Do all the writers agree with
   Lamott and Cherryh?

Exploring *Why:* Purpose

1. The subtitle of the book this essay appears in is "Some Instructions on Writing and Life." What relationship does Lamott see between "shitty first drafts" and life in general?

2. Are you the "uninitiated" reader Lamott describes in paragraph 1 of the essay? What does this tell you about whom Lamott expects to read her book?

3. What is a Dictaphone? Why does Lamott imagine Muriel Spark using one? And why does she "hope for bad things to rain down on" Spark?

4. What does Lamott mean in paragraph 7 when she says she has learned to "trust the process"? What in your writing process do you count on each time you sit down to write?

Exploring *How:* Style and Strategy

1. Why does Lamott offer readers the extended example of writing her food reviews? What does it add to your understanding of draft writing that had not been learned by that point in her essay? How would the essay change if she had begun with this extended example?

2. How many **similes** (comparisons using *like* or *as*) can you find in paragraph 2? What is Lamott's purpose for using so many in the same paragraph?

3. What feeling is Lamott trying to capture when she uses this series of short sentences in the middle of paragraph 5: "I'm ruined. I'm through. I'm toast"?

IDEAS FOR WRITING AN EXEMPLIFICATION ESSAY

1. Write an essay using examples to show the behind-the-scenes realities of a task that you know especially well—preparing for a recital or athletic event, being a volunteer nurse's aid, making Big Macs.

2. Is there a person you know who is exceptional in some way? Write an essay demonstrating how and why this person is an exceptional example. If you know more than one person who is exceptional, you might use multiple examples instead.

3. Write an essay in which you warn speakers, conversationalists, teachers, or writers about a certain practice or usage that bothers you. Give examples to support your point.

◆ ◆ ◆ PREPARING TO READ

Have you ever written to an elected official to express an opinion on a piece of legislation? What were your expectations? If you have not written such a letter yet, would you consider doing so? Why or why not?

◆ ◆ ◆

Mock Democracy

WILLIAM GREIDER

Political analyst William Greider hopes to convince average Americans that national and global events really do affect each and every one of them. He is a regular contributor to *Rolling Stone Magazine* and has produced a number of books, which include *Secrets of the Temple: How the Federal Reserve Runs the Country* (1987) and *One World, Ready or Not: The Manic Logic of Global Capitalism* (1997). In *Who Will Tell the People: The Betrayal of American Democracy* (1992), from which the following essay is taken, Greider calls attention to what he believes is a crisis in America but offers suggestions for how to return democracy to the people.

In a democracy, everyone is free to join the argument, or so it is said in   1
civic mythology. In the modern democracy that has evolved, that claim is nearly meaningless. During the last generation, a "new politics" has enveloped government that guarantees the exclusion of most Americans from the debate—the expensive politics of facts and information.

A major industry has grown up in Washington around what might be   2
called "democracy for hire"—business firms and outposts of sponsored scholars devoted to concocting facts and opinions and expert analysis, then aiming them at the government. That is the principal function of all those enterprises along Washington's main boulevards like K Street—the public-relations agencies, the direct-mail companies and opinion-polling firms. All these work in concert with the infrastructure of think tanks, tax-exempt foundations and other centers that churn out reams of policy ideas for the political debate. Most are financed by corporate interests and wealthy benefactors. The work of lobbyists and lawyers involves delivering the material to the appropriate legislators and administrators.

Only those who have accumulated lots of money are free to play in   3
this version of democracy. Only those with a strong, immediate financial

stake in the political outcomes can afford to invest this kind of money in manipulating the governing decisions. Most Americans have neither the personal ability nor the wherewithal to compete on this field.

The contours of this barrier are embedded in the very texture of   4
everyday political debate itself. Citizens have been incapacitated, quite literally, because they do not speak the language. Modern methodologies of persuasion have created a new hierarchy of influence over government decision—a new way in which organized money dominates the action while the unorganized voices of citizens are inhibited from speaking. A lonely congressman, trying to represent the larger public interest, finds himself arrayed against an army of authorities—working for the other side.

Beyond the fact of unequal resources, however, lies a more troubling   5
proposition: that democracy is now held captive by the mystique of "rational" policymaking, narrow assumptions about what constitutes legitimate political evidence. It is a barrier of privilege because it effectively discounts authentic political expressions from citizens and elevates the biases and opinions of the elites.

This mystique, not surprisingly, is embraced and exalted by well-   6
educated citizens of most every persuasion, the people who are equipped with professional skills and expertise, including the dedicated reformers who attempt to speak for the larger public. After all, it is the basis for their own primacy in political action. Yet the premise of rationality, as the evidence demonstrates, is deeply flawed and routinely biased in its applications.

For those who are active every day in the conventional politics of gov-   7
erning, this proposition may not be so easy to grasp. Indeed, it will seem quite threatening to some of them, for it challenges their own deeply held beliefs about how politics is supposed to work and puts in question the meaning of their own political labors. Ordinary citizens, those who are distant from power, will have much less difficulty seeing the truth of the argument—that information-driven politics has become a convenient reason to ignore them.

Jack Bonner, an intense young denizen of K Street, has the squirrelly   8
enthusiasm of a salesman who can't stop talking about his product because he truly believes in it. What Bonner's firm sells is democracy, not the abstract version found in textbooks, but the living, breathing kind that occurs when people call up a senator and tell him how to vote. Bonner & Associates packages democratic expression and sells it to corporate clients—drug manufacturers and the cosmetic industry, insurance companies and cigarette makers and the major banks.

Jack Bonner's firm is an exotic but relatively small example of the   9
vast information industry that now surrounds the legislative debate and

government in general. You want facts to support the industry's lobbying claims? It pumps out facts. You want expert opinions from scholars? It has those in abundance from the think tanks corporate contributors underwrite. You want opinion polls? It hires polling firms to produce them. You want people—live voters who support the industry position? Jack Bonner delivers them.

When the Senate was debating the new clean-air legislation in 1990,   10
certain wavering senators received pleas from the grassroots on the question of controlling automobile pollution. The Big Brothers and Big Sisters of the Mahoning Valley wrote to Senator John Glenn of Ohio. Sam Nunn of Georgia heard from the Georgia Baptist Convention and its 1.2 million members. The Easter Seal Society of South Dakota lobbied Senator Thomas A. Daschle. The Delaware Paralyzed Veterans Association contacted Senator William V. Roth, Jr.

These groups and some others declared their opposition to the pend-   11
ing clean-air amendment that would compel the auto industry to improve the average fuel efficiency of its cars substantially. The measure would both conserve energy and reduce the carbon-dioxide pollution that is the main source of global warming. These citizen organizations were persuaded to take a stand by Bonner & Associates, which informed them, consistent with the auto industry's political propaganda, that tougher fuel standards would make it impossible to manufacture any vehicles larger than a Ford Escort or a Honda Civic.

Vans and station wagons, small trucks and high-speed police cruisers,   12
they were told, would cease to exist. The National Sheriffs Association was aroused by the thought of chasing criminals in a Honda Civic. The Nebraska Farm Bureau said rural America would be "devastated" if farmers tried to pull a trailer loaded with livestock or hay with a Ford Escort.

For twenty years, whenever the government has attempted to improve   13
auto safety or environmental protection through new regulation, the auto industry has always made similar groans—satisfying tougher standards would be impossible without dire social and economic consequences. The industry warnings have always proved to be false, but the innocent citizens recruited to speak for Detroit probably didn't know this history.

Jack Bonner was thrilled by their expressions of alarm and so was the   14
auto industry that paid him for them. Bonner's fee, which he coyly described as somewhere between $500,000 and $1 million, was for scouring six states for potential grassroots voices, coaching them on the "facts" of the issue, paying for the phone calls and plane fares to Washington and hiring the hall for a joint press conference.

"On the clean-air bill, we bring to the table a third party—'white hat'   15
groups who have no financial interest," Bonner explained. "It's not the auto

industry trying to protect its financial stake. Now it's senior citizens worried about getting out of small cars with walkers. Easter Seal, Multiple Sclerosis—a lot of these people have braces, wheelchairs, walkers. It's farm groups worrying about small trucks. It's people who need station wagons to drive kids to Little League games. These are groups with political juice and they're white hot."

In the textbook version of democracy, this activity is indistinguishable from any other form of democratic expression. In actuality, earnest citizens are being skillfully manipulated by powerful interests—using "facts" that are debatable at best—in a context designed to serve narrow corporate lobbying strategies, not free debate. Bonner & Associates does not start by looking for citizens whose self-interest might put them on the auto industry's side. It starts with a list of the senators whose votes the auto industry needs. Then the firm forages among those senators' constituents for willing bodies.   16

"We sit down with the lobbyists and ask: How much heat do you want on these guys?" Bonner explained. "Do you want ten local groups or two hundred groups? Do you want one hundred phone calls from constituents or a thousand phone calls?"   17

Bonner's K Street office has a "boiler room" with three hundred phone lines and a sophisticated computer system, resembling the phone banks employed in election campaigns. Articulate young people sit in little booths every day, dialing around America on a variety of public issues, searching for "white hat" citizens who can be persuaded to endorse the political objectives of Mobil Oil, Dow Chemical, Citicorp, Ohio Bell, Miller Brewing, U.S. Tobacco, the Chemical Manufacturers Association, the Pharmaceutical Manufacturers Association and dozens of other clients.   18

This kind of political recruiting is expensive but not difficult. Many of the citizens are no doubt flattered to be asked, since ordinary Americans are seldom invited to participate in a personal way in the larger debates, even by the national civic organizations that presumably represent them. In a twisted sense, Jack Bonner does what political parties used to do for citizens—he educates and agitates and mobilizes.   19

Since members of Congress are not naive, they understand the artificiality well enough. They know that many of the 400 million pieces of mail they receive each year are contrived by interested parties of one kind or another. Hearing authentic voices from the grassroots, however, provides them with a valuable defense on controversial votes, especially when a senator intends to vote with the auto-industry lobbyists and against cleaner air. Public opinion, as every senator knows, is with the air.   20

"Obviously," Bonner said, "you target senators inclined to go your way but who need some additional cover. They need to be able to say they've heard from people back home on this issue. Or we target people   21

who are genuinely undecided. It's not a good use of money to target senators who are flat opposed or who are already for you."

Corporate grassroots politics, as Bonner likes to emphasize, is really   22
borrowed from the opposition—the citizen "public interest" organizations,
especially in the environmental movement, who first perfected the technique of generating emotional public responses with factual accusations.
"Politics turns on emotion," Bonner said. "That's why industry has lost in
the past and that's why we win. We bring emotion to the table."

The democratic discourse is now dominated by such transactions—   23
information and opinion and scholarly expertise produced by and for the
self-interested sponsors. Imagine Bonner's technique multiplied and elabo-
rated in different ways across hundreds of public issues and you may begin
to envision the girth of this industry. Some firms produce artfully designed
opinion polls, more or less guaranteed to yield results that suggest public
support for the industry's position. Some firms specialize in coalition building—assembling dozens or hundreds of civic organizations and interest
groups in behalf of lobbying goals.

This is democracy and it costs a fortune. Democracy-for-hire smothers   24
the contemporary political debates and, while it does not always prevail,
relatively few Americans have the resources to hire a voice for themselves.
David Cohen of the Advocacy Institute, which trains citizens in how to
lobby for their causes, recognizes a kind of class system emerging in the political process itself. "We are moving to a system," he said, "where there are
two different realms of citizens—a society in which those with the resources
are going to have the ability to dominate the debate and outcomes while
others are not going to be able to draw on the tools of persuasion." If democratic expression is reduced to a question of money, then those with
money will always have more.

In previous times, reformers wrote devastating critiques about the   25
"capture" of government regulatory agencies by the industries they were
supposed to regulate. The Civil Aeronautics Board became the puppet of the
airlines. The Bureau of Mines was owned by the coal industry. The Federal
Communications Commission belonged to the broadcasters. The occasional
exposés sometimes produced reforms though the basic problem endured.

Now, however, it is not an exaggeration to say that democracy itself   26
has been "captured." The forms of expression, the premises and very language of debate, not to mention the rotating cadres of experts and managers, are now owned in large measure by relatively few interests, much the
way that powerful industries came to own regulatory agencies. Democracy
is held captive, not just by money, but by ideas—the ideas that money buys.

◆ ◆ ◆

FIRST RESPONSES

What are your impressions of Jack Bonner? How do you feel about his job and about the people who hire him? Is it a job you might take?

TAKING A CLOSER LOOK

Exploring *Who:* Voice and Tone

1. What is the effect of Greider's use of the term "democracy for hire" in the second paragraph? What does it tell you about Greider's attitude toward his topic?
2. Can you tell from reading this essay what Greider's personal political affiliation is? Does it matter?
3. Would you have preferred a more objective tone of voice in "Mock Democracy"? What would be lost and what would be gained?

Exploring *What:* Content and Meaning

1. Why does Greider call our popular belief about democracy a "civic mythology"? What comes to mind when you hear the term "mythology"? How does this view compare to the way democracy was discussed in your high school classes or even in your home?
2. How responsible are elected officials for the current situation? Are you surprised to learn of their cooperation with public relations agencies and opinion-polling firms? Why or why not?
3. How is what Jack Bonner and his colleagues do different from what the average citizen might do to persuade an elected official? Do you think his tactics are legal? Do you think they're ethical?
4. ▮▯ *Using the Internet.* Using one of the Internet search engines, such as Alta Vista or Yahoo, enter the keywords "government public relations" and visit the sites of several of the public relations firms. How do the firms' presentations of their goals and tactics compare to Greider's?

Exploring *Why:* Purpose

1. Greider describes current political debate as reflecting a "class system." Why does he believe this concept should disturb his readers? What does this assumption tell us about the people Greider hopes to reach with his ideas?

2. Reread paragraph 22. Who first used these techniques of political influence? Does that change your opinion of groups such as Bonner's? How would you judge these techniques if they were used to support a bill you agreed with?

3. In "Preparing to Read," you were asked about your own participation in the democratic process. Has this essay changed your feelings about when and how you might become involved?

Exploring *How:* Style and Strategy

1. If "Jack Bonner's firm is an exotic but relatively small example," why did Greider use it as an extended example of the problem he hopes to define? What other types of examples does Greider provide throughout the essay to support his argument?

2. The major example of the type of activity Jack Bonner is involved in is his lobbying against a clean-air bill. Why did Greider select this topic? How might you have responded to a call from Bonner's firm about this bill?

3. What purpose does paragraph 16 serve? Why is it located at this point in the essay?

4. What is a "denizen"? What effect does this term and the others used to describe Jack Bonner in paragraph 8 have on your initial reaction to him? Does the essay convince you that these are fair descriptions?

IDEAS FOR WRITING AN EXEMPLIFICATION ESSAY

1. Write an essay in which you use examples to illustrate the essential characteristics of a job you have held. You might use yourself as a single extended example or use several different people who hold the job to draw attention to the variety of ways to approach the job.

2. Is there a person or a group of people who exhibit a character trait (such as generosity, loyalty, honesty, or positive work habits) that you admire? Write an essay using examples to show your reader the behaviors that have led to your admiration.

3. Many areas of our lives are guided by rules or principles. Your household probably has ground rules; scientific experimentation follows principles; your school has course requirements; your job has certain guidelines and expectations; your business transactions involve regulations. Use examples to explain and describe the rules or principles guiding one area of your life.

◆ ◆ ◆ **PREPARING TO READ**

Have you ever spent time with a person who you were previously distant from or perhaps afraid of because of a significant difference between your life and the other person's? What similarities did you find as you got to know the person? How did the experience change you?

◆ ◆ ◆

Slow Descent into Hell

JON D. HULL

Like most journalists working for popular magazines, *Time* correspondent Jon Hull has written about many of today's most pressing issues—the Middle East, gun control, Baby Jessica, and inner city gang rituals. To prepare to write the following essay, Hull lived briefly on the streets of Philadelphia, where he met George, Red, and Gary, people he hoped his readers would also come to know as dramatic examples of the frightening cycle of homelessness.

A smooth bar of soap, wrapped neatly in a white handkerchief and tucked safely in the breast pocket of a faded leather jacket, is all that keeps George from losing himself to the streets. When he wakes each morning from his makeshift bed of newspapers in the subway tunnels of Philadelphia, he heads for the rest room of a nearby bus station or McDonald's and begins an elaborate ritual of washing off the dirt and smells of homelessness: first the hands and forearms, then the face and neck and finally the fingernails and teeth. Twice a week he takes off his worn Converse high tops and socks and washes his feet in the sink, ignoring the cold stares of well-dressed commuters. 1

George, 28, is a stocky, round-faced former high school basketball star who once made a living as a construction worker. But after he lost his job just over a year ago, his wife kicked him out of the house. For a few weeks he lived on the couches of friends, but the friendships soon wore thin. Since then he has been on the street, starting from scratch and looking for a job. "I got to get my life back," George says after rinsing his face for the fourth time. He begins brushing his teeth with his forefinger. "If I don't stay clean," he mutters, "the world ain't even going to look me in the face. I just couldn't take that." 2

George lives in a world where time is meaningless and it's possible to   3
go months without being touched by anyone but a thug. Lack of sleep, food
or conversation breeds confusion and depression. He feels himself slipping
but struggles to remember what he once had and to figure out how to get it
back. He rarely drinks alcohol and keeps his light brown corduroy pants
and red-checked shirt meticulously clean. Underneath, he wears two other
shirts to fight off the cold, and he sleeps with his large hands buried deep
within his coat pockets amid old sandwiches and doughnuts from the soup
kitchens and garbage cans.

Last fall he held a job for six weeks at a pizza joint, making $3.65 an   4
hour kneading dough and clearing tables. Before work, he would take off
two of his three shirts and hide them in an alley. It pleases him that no one
knew he was homeless. Says George: "Sure I could have spent that money
on some good drink or food, but you gotta suffer to save. You gotta have
money to get out of here and I gotta get out of here." Some days he was
scolded for eating too much of the food. He often worked without sleep,
and with no alarm clock to wake him from the subways or abandoned tenements, he missed several days and was finally fired. He observes, "Can't get
no job without a home, and you can't get a home without a job. They take
one and you lose both."

George had $64 tucked in his pocket on the evening he was beaten   5
senseless in an alley near the Continental Trailways station. "Those damn
chumps," he says, gritting his teeth, "took every goddam penny. I'm gonna
kill 'em." Violence is a constant threat to the homeless. It's only a matter of
time before newcomers are beaten, robbed, or raped. The young prey on
the old, the big on the small, and groups attack lonely individuals in the
back alleys and subway tunnels. After it's over, there is no one to tell about
the pain, nothing to do but walk away.

Behind a dumpster sits a man who calls himself Red enjoying the last   6
drops of a bottle of wine called Wild Irish Rose. It's 1 A.M., and the ther-
mometer hovers around 20 degrees, with a biting wind. His nickname comes
from a golden retriever his family once had back in Memphis, and a sparkle
comes to his eyes as he recalls examples of the dog's loyalty. One day he
plans to get another dog, and says, "I'm getting to the point where I can't
talk to people. They're always telling me to do something or get out of their
way. But a dog is different."

At 35, he looks 50, and his gaunt face carries discolored scars from the   7
falls and fights of three years on the streets. An upper incisor is missing, and
his lower teeth jut outward against his lower lip, giving the impression that
he can't close his mouth. His baggy pants are about five inches too long and
when he walks, their frayed ends drag on the ground. "You know something?" he asks, holding up the bottle. "I wasn't stuck to this stuff until the

cold got to me. Now I'll freeze without it. I could go to Florida or some-place, but I know this town and I know who the creeps are. Besides, it's not too bad in the summer."

Finishing the bottle, and not yet drunk enough to sleep out in the cold,   8
he gathers his blanket around his neck and heads for the subways beneath city hall, where hundreds of the homeless seek warmth. Once inside, the game of cat-and-mouse begins with the police, who patrol the maze of tun-nels and stairways and insist that everybody remain off the floor and keep moving. Sitting can be an invitation to trouble, and the choice between sleep and warmth becomes agonizing as the night wears on.

For the first hour, Red shuffles through the tunnels, stopping occasion-   9
ally to urinate against the graffiti-covered walls. Then he picks a spot and stands for half an hour, peering out from the large hood of his coat. In the distance, the barking of German shepherds echoes through the tunnels as a canine unit patrols the darker recesses of the underground. Nearby, a young man in a ragged trench coat stands against the wall, slapping his palms against his sides and muttering, "I've got to get some paperwork done. I've just got to get some paperwork done!" Red shakes his head. "Home sweet home," he says. Finally exhausted, he curls up on the littered floor, lying on his side with his hands in his pockets and his hood pulled all the way over his face to keep the rats away. He is asleep instantly.

Whack! A police baton slaps his legs and a voice booms, "Get the hell   10
up, you're outta here. Right now!" Another police officer whacks his night-stick against a metal grating as the twelve men sprawled along the tunnel crawl to their feet. Red pulls himself up and walks slowly up the stairs to the street, never looking back.

Pausing at every pay phone to check the coin-return slots, he makes   11
his way to a long steam grate whose warm hiss bears the acrid smell of a dry cleaner's shop. He searches for newspaper and cardboard to block the mois-ture but retain the heat. With his makeshift bed made, he curls up again, but the rest is short-lived. "This s.o.b. use to give off more heat," he says, staring with disgust at the grate. He gathers the newspapers and moves down the block, all the while muttering about the differences among grates. "Some are good, some are bad. I remember I was getting a beautiful sleep on this one baby and then all this honking starts. I was laying right in a damn drive-way and nearly got run over by a garbage truck."

Stopping at a small circular vent shooting jets of steam, Red shakes his   12
head and curses: "This one is too wet, and it'll go off sometimes, leaving you to freeze." Shaking now with the cold, he walks four more blocks and finds another grate, where he curls up and fishes a half-spent cigarette from his pocket. The grate is warm, but soon the moisture from the steam has soaked his newspapers and begins to gather on his clothes. Too tired to find another

grate, he sets down more newspapers, throws his blanket over his head and
sprawls across the grate. By morning he is soaked.

At the St. John's Hospice for Men, close to the red neon marquees of   13
the porno shops near city hall, a crowd begins to gather at 4 P.M. Men and
women dressed in ill-fitting clothes stamp their feet to ward off the cold and
keep their arms pressed against their sides. Some are drunk; others simply
talk aloud to nobody in words that none can understand. Most are loners
who stand in silence with the sullen expression of the tired and hungry.

A hospice worker lets in a stream of women and old men. The young   14
men must wait until 5 P.M., and the crowd of more than 200 are asked to
form four rows behind a yellow line and watch their language. It seems an
impossible task. A trembling man who goes by the name Carper cries,
"What goddam row am I in!" as he pulls his red wool hat down until it covers his eyebrows. Carper has spent five to six years on the streets, and thinks
he may be 33. The smell of putrid wine and decaying teeth poisons his
breath; the fluid running from his swollen eyes streaks his dirty cheeks before disappearing into his beard. "Am I in a goddam row? Who the hell's
running the rows?" he swears. An older man with a thick gray beard informs
Carper he is in Row 3 and assures him it is the best of them all. Carper's
face softens into a smile; he stuffs his hands under his armpits and begins
rocking his shoulders with delight.

Beds at the shelters are scarce, and fill up first with the old, the very   15
young, and women. Young men have little hope of getting a bed, and some
have even come to scorn the shelters. Says Michael Brown, 24: "It stinks to
high heaven in those places. They're just packed with people and when the
lights go out, it's everybody for themselves." Michael, a short, self-described
con man, has been living on the streets three years, ever since holding up a
convenience store in Little Rock. He fled, fearing capture, but now misses
the two young children he left behind. He says he is tired of the streets and
plans to turn himself in to serve his time.

Michael refuses to eat at the soup kitchens, preferring to panhandle   16
for a meal: "I don't like to be around those people. It makes you feel like
some sort of crazy. Before you know it, you're one of them." He keeps a tear
in the left seam of his pants, just below the pocket; when he panhandles
among commuters, he tells them that his subway fare fell out of his pants.
When that fails, he wanders past fast-food outlets, waiting for a large group
eating near the door to get up and leave. Then he snatches the remaining
food off the table and heads down the street, smiling all the more if the food
is still warm. At night he sleeps in the subway stations, catnapping between
police rounds amid the thunder of the trains. "Some of these guys sleep
right on the damn floor," he says. "Not me. I always use two newspapers and
lay them out neatly. Then I pray the rats don't get me."

It was the last swig of the bottle, and the cheap red wine contained 17
flotsam from the mouths of three men gathered in a vacant lot in northeast
Philadelphia. Moments before, a homeless and dying man named Gary had
vomited. The stench and nausea were dulled only by exhaustion and the
cold. Gary, wheezing noisily, his lips dripping with puke, was the last to
drink from the half-gallon jug of Thunderbird before passing it on, but no
one seemed to care. There was no way to avoid the honor of downing the
last few drops. It was an offer to share extended by those with nothing, and
there was no time to think about the sores on the lips of the previous
drinkers or the strange things floating in the bottle or the fact that it was
daybreak and time for breakfast. It was better to drink and stay warm and
forget about everything.

Though he is now dying on the streets, Gary used to be a respectable 18
citizen. His full name is Gary Shaw, 48, and he is a lifelong resident of
Philadelphia and a father of three. He once worked as a precision machin-
ist, making metal dies for casting tools. "I could work with my eyes closed,"
he says. "I was the best there was." But he lost his job and wife to alcohol.
Now his home is an old red couch with the springs exposed in a garbage-
strewn clearing amid abandoned tenements. Nearby, wood pulled from
buildings burns in a 55-gallon metal drum while the Thunderbird is passed
around. When evening falls, Gary has trouble standing, and he believes his
liver and kidneys are on the verge of failing. His thighs carry deep burn
marks from sleeping on grates, and a severe beating the previous night has
left bruises on his lower back and a long scab across his nose. The pain is apparent in his eyes, still brilliant blue, and the handsome features of his face
are hidden beneath a layer of grime.

By 3 A.M., Gary's back pains are unbearable, and he begins rocking 19
back and forth while the others try to keep him warm. "Ah, please God help
me. I'm f---ing dying, man. I'm dying." Two friends try to wave down a patrol
car. After 45 minutes, a suspicious cop rolls up to the curb and listens impa-
tiently to their plea: "It's not drugs, man, I promise. The guy was beat up bad
and he's dying. Come on, man, you've got to take us to the hospital." The
cop nods and points his thumb toward the car. As Gary screams, his two
friends carefully lift him into the back seat for the ride to St. Mary Hospital.

In the emergency room, half an hour passes before a nurse appears 20
with a clipboard. Address: unknown. No insurance. After an X-ray, Gary is
told that a bone in his back may be chipped. He is advised to go home, put
some ice on it and get some rest. "I don't have a goddam home!" he cries,
his face twisted in pain. "Don't you know what I am? I'm a goddam bum,
that's what, and I'm dying!" After an awkward moment, he is told to come
back tomorrow and see the radiologist. The hospital pays his cab fare back
to the couch.

Gary returns in time to share another bottle of Thunderbird, and the   21
warm rush brings his spirits up. "What the hell are we doing in the city?"
asks Ray Kelly, 37, who was once a merchant seaman. "I know a place in
Vermont where the fishing's great and you can build a whole damn house in
the woods. There's nobody to bother you and plenty of food." Gary inter-
rupts to recall fishing as a boy, and the memories prior to his six years on the
street come back with crystal clarity. "You got it, man, we're all getting out
of here tomorrow," he says with a grin. In the spirit of celebration, King, a
34-year-old from Puerto Rico, removes a tube of glue from his pocket with
the care of a sommelier, sniffs it and passes it around.

When the sun rises, Ray and King are fast asleep under a blanket on   22
the couch. Gary is sitting at the other end, staring straight ahead and breathing heavily in the cold air. Curling his numb and swollen fingers around the
arm of the couch, he tries to pull himself up but fails. When another try fails,
he sits motionless and closes his eyes. Then the pain hits his back again and
he starts to cry. He won't be getting out of here today, and probably not tomorrow either.

Meanwhile, somewhere across town in the washroom of a McDonald's,   23
George braces for another day of job hunting, washing the streets from his
face so that nobody knows where he lives.

◆ ◆ ◆

FIRST RESPONSES

What choices has George made about how to live his life on the
streets? Did he have other options? What choices might you make in his
situation?

TAKING A CLOSER LOOK

Exploring *Who:* Voice and Tone

1. Although Hull spent time with these men, he does not include himself
   as part of this story. Why? Do you still feel that you know something
   about Hull's attitudes?
2. In paragraph 1, Hull describes George as "ignoring the cold stares of
   well-dressed commuters." Would you have stared as well? Why has
   Hull included this detail so early in the essay?
3. In paragraph 16, when Michael says, "I don't like to be around those
   people," who is he talking about? Hull seems to be providing his

readers with a strong sense of the **irony** to be found in street life. Are there other examples of such ironies in the essay?

Exploring *What:* Content and Meaning

1. In paragraph 3, Hull tells his readers that "it's possible to go months without being touched by anyone but a thug." Can you imagine this kind of separation from friends and family? How does it make you feel about these men?
2. George and Red, like many of the men on the streets, "are loners who stand in silence." Find examples of how George and Red and the others attempt to maintain their individuality. What other survival tactics have these men developed?
3. Would you call Gary and his friends a community? What do these men share? What are the pros and cons of this advanced stage of homelessness?

Exploring *Why:* Purpose

1. What surprised you about these men and what reinforced the views you already held? How does what you learned make you feel about your own life and future?
2. "Descent into Hell" begins and ends with George. By the time you return to George in the last paragraph, what have you learned to change your expectations for or attitudes toward him?
3. Who is responsible for Gary's health problems? Where else could Red sleep than on the grate? Do you understand why the police and the medical staff responded as they did?
4. *Using the Internet.* A Ph.D. student in philosophy has created a Web site for homeless people that he calls Vagrant Gaze. He provides single shot disposable cameras to individuals who live on the streets, and places their photographs on the Web site. Visit Vagrant Gaze (http://perfekt/~vagrant/homeless.htm) and look at these self-created images. How do they correspond to the images created by Hull, and to those in your own mind?

Exploring *How:* Style and Strategy

1. Hull begins with George as his first example rather than with Red or Gary. Why? What differences and similarities do you see between George, Red, and Gary? Is there a clear reason for the order of the three major examples?

2. Why did Hull choose to give three extended examples of homelessness rather than several more short examples?

3. What specific sights, sounds, smells, and feelings do you most remember from the essay? Why does Hull go into such specific sensory detail?

4. Why does Hull include only men as examples in this essay?

5. Gary tells the emergency room nurse, "I don't have a goddam home . . . Don't you know what I am? I'm a goddam bum, that's what, and I'm dying!" Why does Hull take the chance of including dialogue such as this that may be objectionable to some people?

IDEAS FOR WRITING AN EXEMPLIFICATION ESSAY

1. Think of a time when you found yourself in a situation you never expected to be in. Write an essay showing how you behaved in this situation. If appropriate, include how others reacted to you in this situation, as well.

2. Write an essay using examples to explain an incident in which you or someone you know was treated unfairly. Describe both the unfair treatment and the reactions to it. You might choose to analyze the causes or let the situation speak for itself.

3. Think of a situation or circumstance that makes you feel insecure or frightened or tense. Write an essay using examples to describe this situation and explain its effect on you.

◆ ◆ ◆ PREPARING TO READ

How often do you weigh yourself? What emotions do you feel when you do? Do you freely share your weight with others?

◆ ◆ ◆

A Weight That Women Carry

SALLIE TISDALE

Journalist and creative writing teacher Sallie Tisdale writes on nature, travel, and public institutions for a wide range of popular magazines, including *Audubon, Antioch Review, Harper's,* and the *New York Times Magazine.* Calling on her early training as a nurse, Tisdale investigated public health problems in two early books, *The Sorcerer's Apprentice: Tales of a Modern Hospital* (1986) and *Harvest Moon: Portrait of a Nursing Home* (1987). In her most recent books, *Stepping Westward: The Long Search for Home in the Pacific Northwest* (1991) and *Talk Dirty to Me: An Intimate Philosophy of Sex* (1994), Tisdale focuses on her personal understanding of two other significant ethical concerns—ecology and sexuality. "A Weight That Women Carry" appeared in 1993 in *Harper's.*

I don't know how much I weigh these days, though I can make a good   1
guess. For years I'd known that number, sometimes within a quarter pound, known how it changed from day to day and hour to hour. I want to weigh myself now; I lean toward the scale in the next room, imagine standing there, lining up the balance. But I don't do it. Going this long, starting to break the scale's spell—it's like waking up suddenly sober.

By the time I was sixteen years old I had reached my adult height of   2
five feet six inches and weighed 164 pounds. I weighed 164 pounds before and after a healthy pregnancy. I assume I weigh about the same now; nothing significant seems to have happened to my body, this same old body I've had all these years. I usually wear a size 14, a common clothing size for American women. On bad days I think my body looks lumpy and misshapen. On my good days, which are more frequent lately, I think I look plush and strong; I think I look like a lot of women whose bodies and lives I admire.

I'm not sure when the word "fat" first sounded pejorative to me, or   3
when I first applied it to myself. My grandmother was a petite woman, the

only one in my family. She stole food from other people's plates, and hid the debris of her own meals so that no one would know how much she ate. My mother was a size 14, like me, all her adult life; we shared clothes. She fretted endlessly over food scales, calorie counters, and diet books. She didn't want to quit smoking because she was afraid she would gain weight, and she worried about her weight until she died of cancer five years ago. Dieting was always in my mother's way, always there in the conversations above my head, the dialogue of stocky women. But I was strong and healthy and didn't pay too much attention to my weight until I was grown.

It probably wouldn't have been possible for me to escape forever. It doesn't matter that whole human epochs have celebrated big men and women, because the brief period in which I live does not; since I was born, even the voluptuous calendar girl has gone. Today's models, the women whose pictures I see constantly, unavoidably, grow more minimal by the day. When I berate myself for not looking like—whomever I think I should look like that day, I don't really care that no one looks like that. I don't care that Michelle Pfeiffer doesn't look like the photographs I see of Michelle Pfeiffer. I want to look—think I should look—like the photographs. I want her little miracles: the makeup artists, photographers, and computer imagers who can add a mole, remove a scar, lift the breasts, widen the eyes, narrow the hips, flatten the curves. The final product is what I see, have seen my whole adult life. And I've seen this: even when big people become celebrities, their weight is constantly remarked upon and scrutinized; their successes seem always to be *in spite of* their weight. I thought my successes must be, too.

I feel myself expand and diminish from day to day, sometimes from hour to hour. If I tell someone my weight, I change in their eyes: I become bigger or smaller, better or worse, depending on what that number, my weight, means to them. I know many men and women, young and old, gay and straight, who look fine, whom I love to see and whose faces and forms I cherish, who despise themselves for their weight. For their ordinary, human bodies. They and I are simply bigger than we think we should be. We always talk about weight in terms of gains and losses, and don't wonder at the strangeness of the words. In trying always to lose weight, we've lost hope of simply being seen for ourselves.

My weight has never actually affected anything—it's never seemed to mean anything one way or the other to how I lived. Yet for the last ten years I've felt quite bad about it. After a time, the number on the scale became my totem, more important than my experience—it was layered, metaphorical, *metaphysical,* and it had bewitching power. I thought if I could change that number I could change my life.

In my mid-twenties I started secretly taking diet pills. They made me feel strange, half-crazed, vaguely nauseated. I lost about twenty-five pounds, dropped two sizes, and bought new clothes. I developed rituals and taboos around food, ate very little, and continued to lose weight. For a long time afterward I thought it only coincidental that with every passing week I also grew more depressed and irritable.

I could recite the details, but they're remarkable only for being so common. I lost more weight until I was rather thin, and then I gained it all back. It came back slowly, pound by pound, in spite of erratic and melancholy and sometimes frantic dieting, dieting I clung to even though being thin had changed nothing, had meant nothing to my life except that I was thin. Looking back, I remember blinding moments of shame and lightning-bright moments of clearheadedness, which inevitably gave way to rage at the time I'd wasted—rage that eventually would become, once again, self-disgust and the urge to lose weight. So it went, until I weighed exactly what I'd weighed when I began.   8

I used to be attracted to the sharp angles of the chronic dieter—the caffeine-wild, chain-smoking, skinny women I see sometimes. I considered them a pinnacle not of beauty but of will. Even after I gained back my weight, I wanted to be like that, controlled and persevering, live that under-fed life so unlike my own rather sensual and disorderly existence. I felt I should always be dieting, for the dieting of it; dieting had become a rule, a given, a constant. Every ordinary value is distorted in this lens. I felt guilty for not being completely absorbed in my diet, for getting distracted, for not caring enough all the time. The fat person's character flaw is a lack of narcissism. She's let herself go.   9

So I would begin again—and at first it would all seem so . . . easy. Simple arithmetic. After all, 3,500 calories equal one pound of fat—so the books and articles by the thousands say. I would calculate how long it would take to achieve the magic number on the scale, to succeed, to win. All past failures were suppressed. If 3,500 calories equal one pound, all I needed to do was cut 3,500 calories out of my intake every week. The first few days of a new diet would be colored with a sense of control—organization and planning, power over the self. Then the basic futile misery took over.   10

I would weigh myself with foreboding, and my weight would determine how went the rest of my day, my week, my life. When 3,500 calories didn't equal one pound lost after all, I figured it was my body that was flawed, not the theory. One friend, who had tried for years to lose weight following prescribed diets, made what she called "an amazing discovery." The real secret to a diet, she said, was that you had to be willing to be hungry *all the time*. You had to eat even less than the diet allowed.   11

I believed that being thin would make me happy. Such a pernicious, enduring belief. I lost weight and wasn't happy and saw that elusive happiness   12 disappear in a vanishing point, requiring more—more self-disgust, more of the misery of dieting. Knowing all that I know now about the biology and anthropology of weight, knowing that people naturally come in many shapes and sizes, knowing that diets are bad for me and won't make me thin— sometimes none of this matters. I look in the mirror and think: Who am I kidding? *I've got to do something about myself.* Only then will this vague discontent disappear. Then I'll be loved.

For ages humans believed that the body helped create the personality, from the humors of Galen to W. H. Sheldon's somatotypes. Sheldon distinguished between three templates—endomorph, mesomorph, and ectomorph—and combined them into hundreds of variations with physical, emotional, and psychological characteristics. When I read about weight now, I see the potent shift in the last few decades: the modern culture of dieting is based on the idea that the personality creates the body. Our size must be in some way voluntary, or else it wouldn't be subject to change. A lot of my misery over my weight wasn't about how I looked at all. I was miserable because I believed I was bad, not my body. I felt truly reduced then, reduced to being just a body and nothing more.   13

Fat is perceived as an *act* rather than a thing. It is antisocial, and curable through the application of social controls. Even the feminist revisions of dieting, so powerful in themselves, pick up the theme: the hungry, empty heart; the woman seeking release from sexual assault, or the man from the loss of the mother, through food and fat. Fat is now a symbol not of the personality but of the soul—the cluttered, neurotic, immature soul.   14

Fat people eat for "mere gratification," I read, as though no one else does. Their weight is *intentioned,* they simply eat "too much," their flesh is lazy flesh. Whenever I went on a diet, eating became cheating. One pretzel was cheating. Two apples instead of one was cheating—a large potato instead of a small, carrots instead of broccoli. It didn't matter which diet I was on; diets have failure built in, failure is in the definition. Every substitution— even carrots for broccoli—was a triumph of desire over will. When I dieted, I didn't feel pious just for sticking to the rules. I felt condemned for the act of eating itself, as though my hunger were never normal. My penance was to not eat at all.   15

My attitude toward food became quite corrupt. I came, in fact, to subconsciously believe food itself was corrupt. Diet books often distinguish between "real" and "unreal" hunger, so that *correct* eating is hollowed out, unemotional. A friend of mine who thinks of herself as a compulsive eater says she feels bad only when she eats for pleasure. "Why?" I ask, and she says, "Because I'm eating food I don't need." A few years ago I might have admired that. Now I try to imagine a world where we eat only food we need,   16 and it seems inhuman. I imagine a world devoid of holidays and wedding feasts, wakes and reunions, a unique shared joy. "What's wrong with eating a cookie because you like cookies?" I ask her, and she hasn't got an answer. These aren't rational beliefs, any more than the unnecessary pleasure of ice cream is rational. Dieting presumes pleasure to be an insignificant, or at least malleable, human motive.

I felt no joy in being thin—it was just work, something I had to do. But   17 when I began to gain back the weight, I felt despair. I started reading about the "recidivism" of dieting. I wondered if I had myself to blame not only for needing to diet in the first place but for dieting itself, the weight inevitably regained. I joined organized weight-loss programs, spent a lot of money, listened to lectures I didn't believe on quack nutrition, ate awful, processed diet foods. I sat in groups and applauded people who'd lost a half pound, feeling smug because I'd lost a pound and a half. I felt ill much of the time, found exercise increasingly difficult, cried often. And I thought that if I could only lose a little weight, everything would be all right.

When I say to someone, "I'm fat," I hear, "Oh, no! You're not *fat!*   18 You're just—" What? Plump? Big-boned? Rubenesque? I'm just *not thin.* That's crime enough. I began this story by stating my weight. I said it all at once, trying to forget it and take away its power; I said it to be done being scared. Doing so, saying it out loud like that, felt like confessing a mortal sin. I have to bite my tongue not to seek reassurance, not to defend myself, not to plead. I see an old friend for the first time in years, and she comments on how much my fourteen-year-old son looks like me—"except, of course, he's not chubby." "Look who's talking," I reply, through clenched teeth. This pettiness is never far away; concern with my weight evokes the smallest, meanest parts of me. I look at another woman passing on the street and think, "At least I'm not *that* fat."

Recently I was talking with a friend who is naturally slender about a   19 mutual acquaintance who is quite large. To my surprise my friend reproached this woman because she had seen her eating a cookie at lunchtime. "How is she going to lose weight that way?" my friend wondered. When you are as fat as our acquaintance is, you are primarily, fundamentally, seen as fat. It is your essential characteristic. There are so many presumptions in my friend's casual, cruel remark. She assumes that this woman should diet all the time—and that she *can.* She pronounces whole categories of food to be denied her. She sees her unwillingness to behave in this externally prescribed way, even for a moment, as an act of rebellion. In his story "A Hunger Artist," Kafka writes that the guards of the fasting man were "usually butchers, strangely enough." Not so strange, I think.

I know that the world, even if it views me as overweight (and I'm not   20 sure it really does), clearly makes a distinction between me and this very big woman. I would rather stand with her and not against her, see her for all she is besides fat. But I know our experiences aren't the same. My thin friend assumes my fat friend is unhappy because she is fat: therefore, if she loses weight she will be happy. My fat friend has a happy marriage and family and a good career, but insofar as her weight is a source of misery, I think she would be much happier if she could eat her cookie in peace, if people would shut up and leave her weight alone. But the world never lets up when you are her size; she cannot walk to the bank without risking insult. Her fat is seen as perverse bad manners. I have no doubt she would be rid of the fat if she could be. If my left-handedness invited the criticism her weight does, I would want to cut that hand off.

In these last several years I seem to have had an infinite number of   21 conversations about dieting. They are really all the same conversation—weight is lost, then weight is gained back. This repetition finally began to sink in. Why did everyone sooner or later have the same experience? (My friend who had learned to be hungry all the time gained back all the weight she had lost and more, just like the rest of us.) Was it really our bodies that were flawed? I began reading the biology of weight more carefully, reading the fine print in the endless studies. There is, in fact, a preponderance of evidence disputing our commonly held assumptions about weight.

The predominant biological myth of weight is that thin people live   22 longer than fat people. The truth is far more complicated. (Some deaths of fat people attributed to heart disease seem actually to have been the result of radical dieting.) If health were our real concern, it would be dieting we questioned, not weight. The current ideal of thinness has never been held before, except as a religious ideal; the underfed body is the martyr's body. Even if people can lose weight, maintaining an artificially low weight for any period of time requires a kind of starvation. Lots of people are naturally thin, but for those who are not, dieting is an unnatural act; biology rebels. The metabolism of the hungry body can change inalterably, making it ever harder and harder to stay thin. I think chronic dieting made me gain weight—not only pounds, but fat. This equation seemed so strange at first that I couldn't believe it. But the weight I put back on after losing was much more stubborn than the original weight. I had lost it by taking diet pills and not eating much of anything at all for quite a long time. I haven't touched the pills again, but not eating much of anything no longer works.

When Oprah Winfrey first revealed her lost weight, I didn't envy her.   23 I thought, She's in trouble now. I knew, I was certain, she would gain it back; I believed she was biologically destined to do so. The tabloid headlines blamed it on a cheeseburger or mashed potatoes; they screamed OPRAH PASSES 200 POUNDS, and I cringed at her misery and how the world wouldn't let up, wouldn't leave her alone, wouldn't let her be anything else. How dare the world do this to anyone? I thought, and then realized I did it to myself.

The "Ideal Weight" charts my mother used were at their lowest   24 acceptable-weight ranges in the 1950s, when I was a child. They were based on sketchy and often inaccurate actuarial evidence, using, for the most part, data on northern Europeans and allowing for the most minimal differences in size for a population of less than half a billion people. I never fit those weight charts, I was always just outside the pale. As an adult, when I would join an organized diet program, I accepted their version of my Weight Goal as gospel, knowing it would be virtually impossible to reach. But reach I tried; that's what one does with gospel. Only in the last few years have the weight tables begun to climb back into the world of the average human. The newest ones distinguish by gender, frame, and age. And suddenly I'm not off the charts anymore. I have a place.

A man who is attracted to fat women says, "I actually have less specif-   25 ic physical criteria than most men. I'm attracted to women who weigh 170 or 270 or 370. Most men are only attracted to women who weigh between 100 and 135. So who's got more of a fetish?" We look at fat as a problem of the fat person. Rarely do the tables get turned, rarely do we imagine that it might be the viewer, not the viewed, who is limited. What the hell is wrong with *them,* anyway? Do they believe everything they see on television?

My friend Phil, who is chronically and almost painfully thin, admitted   26 that in his search for a partner he finds himself prejudiced against fat women. He seemed genuinely bewildered by this. I didn't jump to reassure him that such prejudice is hard to resist. What I did was bite my tongue at my urge to be reassured by him, to be told that I, at least, wasn't fat. That over the centuries humans have been inclined to prefer extra flesh rather than the other way around seems unimportant. All we see now tells us otherwise. Why does my kindhearted friend criticize another woman for eating a cookie when she would never dream of commenting in such a way on another person's race or sexual orientation or disability? Deprivation is the dystopian ideal.

My mother called her endless diets "reducing plans." Reduction, the   27 diminution of women, is the opposite of feminism, as Kim Chernin points out in *The Obsession.* Smallness is what feminism strives against, the smallness that women confront everywhere. All of women's spaces are smaller than those of men, often inadequate, without privacy. Furniture designers distinguish between a man's and a woman's chair, because women don't spread out like men. (A sprawling woman means only one thing.) Even our voices are kept down. By embracing dieting I was rejecting a lot I held dear, and the emotional dissonance that created just seemed like one more necessary evil.

A fashion magazine recently celebrated the return of the "well-fed"   28
body; a particular model was said to be "the archetype of the new womanly
woman . . . stately, powerful." She is a size 8. The images of women presented to us, images claiming so maliciously to be the images of women's
whole lives, are not merely social fictions. They are *absolute* fictions; they
can't exist. How would it feel, I began to wonder, to cultivate my own real
womanliness rather than despise it? Because it was my fleshy curves I wanted to be rid of after all. I dreamed of having a boy's body, smooth, hipless,
lean. A body rapt with possibility, a receptive body suspended before the
storms of maturity. A dear friend of mine, nursing her second child, weeps at
her newly voluptuous body. She loves her children and hates her own moth-
erliness, wanting to be unripened again, to be a bud and not a flower.

Recently I've started shopping occasionally at stores for "large   29
women," where the smallest size is a 14. In department stores the size 12 and
14 and 16 clothes are kept in a ghetto called the Women's Department. (And
who would want that, to be the size of a woman? We all dream of being "ju-
niors" instead.) In the specialty stores the clerks are usually big women and
the customers are big, too, big like a lot of women in my life—friends, my sister, my mother and aunts. Not long ago I bought a pair of jeans at Lane
Bryant and then walked through the mall to the Gap, with its shelves of
generic clothing. I flicked through the clearance rack and suddenly remembered the Lane Bryant shopping bag in my hand and its enormous weight,
the sheer heaviness of that brand name shouting to the world. The shout is
that I've let myself go. I still feel like crying out sometimes: Can't I feel *satisfied?* But I am not supposed to be satisfied, not allowed to be satisfied. My
discontent fuels the market; I need to be afraid in order to fully participate.

American culture, which has produced our dieting mania, does more   30
than reward privation and acquisition at the same time: it actually associates them with each other. Read the ads: the virtuous runner's reward is a
new pair of $180 running shoes. The fat person is thought to be impulsive,
indulgent, but insufficiently or incorrectly greedy, greedy for the wrong
thing. The fat person lacks ambition. The young executive is complimented
for being "hungry"; he is "starved for success." We are teased with what we
will have if we are willing to *have not* for a time. A dieting friend, avoiding
the food on my table, says, "I'm just dying for a bite of that."

Dieters are the perfect consumers: they never get enough. The dieter   31
wistfully imagines food without substance, food that is not food, that begs
the definition of food, because food is the problem. Even the ways we *don't
eat* are based in class. The middle class don't eat in support groups. The poor
can't afford not to eat at all. The rich hire someone to not eat with them in
private. Dieting is an emblem of capitalism. It has a venal heart.

The possibility of living another way, living without dieting, began to   32
take root in my mind a few years ago, and finally my second trip through
Weight Watchers ended dieting for me. This last time I just couldn't stand
the details, the same kind of details I'd seen and despised in other programs, on other diets: the scent of resignation, the weighing-in by the quarter pound, the before and after photographs of group leaders prominently
displayed. Jean Nidetch, the founder of Weight Watchers, says, "Most fat
people need to be hurt badly before they do something about themselves."
She mocks every aspect of our need for food, of a person's sense of enti-
tlement to food, of daring to *eat what we want*. Weight Watchers refuses to
release its own weight charts except to say they make no distinction for
frame size; neither has the organization ever released statistics on how
many people who lose weight on the program eventually gain it back. I
hated the endlessness of it, the turning of food into portions and exchanges,
everything measured out, permitted, denied. I hated the very idea of "maintenance." Finally I realized I didn't just hate the diet. I was sick of the way
I acted on a diet, the way I whined, my niggardly, penny-pinching behavior.
What I liked in myself seemed to shrivel and disappear when I dieted.
Slowly, slowly I saw these things. I saw that my pain was cut from whole
cloth, imaginary, my own invention. I saw how much time I'd spent on
something ephemeral, something that simply wasn't important, didn't
matter. I saw that the real point of dieting is dieting—to not be done with
it, ever.

I looked in the mirror and saw a woman, with flesh, curves, muscles, a   33
few stretch marks, the beginnings of wrinkles, with strength and softness in
equal measure. My body is the one part of me that is always, undeniably,
here. To like myself means to be, literally, shameless, to be wanton in the
pleasures of being inside a body. I feel *loose* this way, a little abandoned, a
little dangerous. That first feeling of liking my body—not being resigned to
it or despairing of change, but actually *liking* it—was tentative and guilty
and frightening. It was alarming, because it was the way I'd felt as a child,
before the world had interfered. Because surely I was wrong; I knew, I'd
known for so long, that my body wasn't all right this way. I was afraid even
to act as though I were all right: I was afraid that by doing so I'd be acting
a fool.

For a time I was thin. I remember—and what I remember is nothing   34
special—strain, a kind of hollowness, the same troubles and fears, and no
magic. So I imagine losing weight again. If the world applauded, would this
comfort me? Or would it only compromise whatever approval the world
gives me now? What else will be required of me besides thinness? What
will happen to me if I get sick, or lose the use of a limb, or, God forbid,
grow old?

By fussing endlessly over my body, I've ceased to inhabit it. I'm trying   35
to reverse this equation now, to trust my body and enter it again with a
whole heart. I know more now than I used to about what constitutes
"happy" and "unhappy," what the depths and textures of contentment are
like. By letting go of dieting, I free up mental and emotional room. I have
more space, I can move. The pursuit of another, elusive body, the body
someone else says I should have, is a terrible distraction, a sidetracking that
might have lasted my whole life long. By letting myself go, I go places.

Each of us in this culture, this twisted, inchoate culture, has to choose   36
between battles: one battle is against the cultural ideal, and the other is
against ourselves. I've chosen to stop fighting myself. Maybe I'm tilting at
windmills; the cultural ideal is ever-changing, out of my control. It's not a
cerebral journey, except insofar as I have to remind myself to stop counting,
to stop thinking in terms of numbers. I know, even now that I've quit dieting
and eat what I want, how many calories I take in every day. If I eat as I
please, I eat a lot one day and very little the next; I skip meals and snack at
odd times. My nourishment is good—as far as nutrition is concerned, I'm in
much better shape than when I was dieting. I know that the small losses and
gains in my weight over a period of time aren't simply related to the number of calories I eat. Someone asked me not long ago how I could possibly
know my calorie intake if I'm not dieting (the implication being, perhaps,
that I'm dieting secretly). I know because calorie counts and grams of fat
and fiber are embedded in me. I have to work to not think of them, and I
have to learn to not think of them in order to really live without fear.

When I look, *really* look, at the people I see every day on the street,   37
I see a jungle of bodies, a community of women and men growing every
which way like lush plants, growing tall and short and slender and round,
hairy and hairless, dark and pale and soft and hard and glorious. Do I look
around at the multitudes and think all these people—all these people who
are like me and not like me, who are various and different—are not loved
or lovable? Lately, everyone's body interests me, every body is desirable in
some way. I see how muscles and skin shift with movement; I sense a cornucopia of flesh in the world. In the midst of it I am a little capacious and
unruly.

I repeat with Walt Whitman, "I dote on myself . . . there is that lot of   38
me, and all so luscious." I'm eating better, exercising more, feeling fine—and
then I catch myself thinking, *Maybe I'll lose some weight.* But my mood
changes or my attention is caught by something else, something deeper,
more lingering. Then I can catch a glimpse of myself by accident and think
only: That's me. My face, my hips, my hands. Myself.

◆ ◆ ◆

FIRST RESPONSES

Do you agree with Tisdale that weight is one of the first things we notice about other people? Does it affect how you judge a stranger? Is it a significant part of your feelings about your friends and family members?

TAKING A CLOSER LOOK

Exploring *Who:* Voice and Tone

1. What addiction is Tisdale comparing her weight obsession to in paragraph 1? What first impression does this comparison give you of Tisdale?
2. Because Tisdale's attitudes have changed over the years, she speaks in a number of different voices in this essay. How many can you identify? What emotions characterize each of these periods of her life, and how do you respond to each of them? For example, what is Tisdale feeling when she says, "Rarely do the tables get turned, rarely do we imagine that it might be the viewer, not the viewed, who is limited. What the hell is wrong with *them?*" How does her tone affect your response to the idea she is presenting?
3. In paragraph 9, when Tisdale says, "The fat person's character flaw is a lack of narcissism. She's let herself go," whose point of view is she expressing?
4. Tisdale ends her essay by claiming Walt Whitman as a role model for her current self-image. Is he a good choice? Why does she quote from him instead of simply mentioning him?

Exploring *What:* Content and Meaning

1. What celebrities besides Oprah have been popular *"in spite of"* their weight? Are they primarily male or female? What limits has weight placed on their career choices?
2. If Tisdale knows that Michelle Pfeiffer's image is created by make-up and photographers, why does she still feel she should be able to look like Pfeiffer? How does she know many of her readers share this desire?
3. Do you agree with Tisdale's claim that "My weight has never actually affected anything—it never seemed to mean anything one way or the other to how I lived"? How do food and your weight affect your everyday life?

4. Tisdale now sees a "jungle of bodies" when she walks down the street. How does this contrast with the desire for control and order she had as a dieter? Which Tisdale would you rather have as a friend?

5. ▣ *Using the Internet.* In June of 1998, the federal government changed the ideal weight charts. Using the Internet, find the National Heart, Lung and Blood Institute site (www.nhlbi.nih.gov/nhlb:/nhlb:.htm) where this chart can be found. Next locate at least one popular magazine article (in *Time* or *Newsweek,* for example) on the release of this chart and how it compares to earlier charts. What would Tisdale say about the changes?

Exploring *Why:* Purpose

1. Why does Tisdale describe her process of coming to terms with her weight as a battle? How have the combatants and the sites of the battles changed over the years?

2. Paragraphs 8 and 10 capture Tisdale's dieting cycles. What does she feel are the social and biological causes for these cycles? Had you already heard about the effect of dieting on metabolism? Does this medical fact affect your attitudes toward your own or other people's weight?

3. Why does Tisdale see a friend feeling "bad only when she eats for pleasure" as "inhuman"? Do you agree with her?

4. How has weight affected Tisdale's friendships? How optimistic is she about changing such behaviors?

Exploring *How:* Style and Strategy

1. How does Tisdale justify using primarily only her own experience to prove what she believes is a widespread American problem? How else might she have developed her thesis?

2. Tisdale uses a number of **euphemisms** for the word fat—for example, "stocky" and "plump." Why? Can you think of other examples of common words for people we consider overweight?

3. What does "recidivism" mean in paragraph 17? Why does she use such a technical word here?

4. Why does Tisdale hate Weight Watchers' use of the term "maintenance"? In what other contexts do you use that word? How might that use affect your feelings about yourself if you were on a diet?

IDEAS FOR WRITING AN EXEMPLIFICATION ESSAY

1. Write an essay using examples to trace a change in your attitude toward something about yourself or your family. Show each stage of your feelings as clearly and objectively as possible, and provide a clear explanation for the changes that have taken place.

2. Do people make assumptions about you when they first see you because of some aspect of your physical appearance? Write an essay in which you use examples of such responses to analyze the effects of first impressions.

3. Write an essay illustrating the fact that appearances can be deceiving.

◆ FURTHER IDEAS FOR USING EXEMPLIFICATION

1. As a child, your parents probably started their sentences with the comment, "When you grow up you'll understand that. . . ." Were they right? Write an essay using examples from your experience to explain how you learned the truth or error of one or more of their warnings.

2. ■ *Using the Internet.* Write an essay using your own experiences, as well as those of people you know, to exemplify the pros and cons of family vacations. Use an Internet search engine to visit the sites of typical vacation destinations, such as the Grand Canyon and Disneyland, to gather additional ideas. In your essay, consider both the parents' and the children's points of view.

3. COLLABORATIVE WRITING. Meet with a small group of other students to compare notes on your past experiences with writing. Discuss the attitudes and feelings about writing that have resulted from these experiences. Include personal writing, school assignments, and work-related tasks. After the discussion session, write an essay using past experience to explain your current thoughts and feelings about writing, including any changes you have experienced in these attitudes.

4. COMBINING STRATEGIES. After spending a few hours watching any of the many video TV channels, such as MTV, VH1, BET, or CMT, write an essay explaining what you believe are the most common attitudes toward women in the music videos shown on that channel—pop, rock, rap, or country. As you present your examples, remember that your readers may or may not have seen these videos, so you will need to narrate events and describe lyrics as appropriate.

5. COMBINING STRATEGIES. Narrate one particular interaction you had with someone you know well who is in a position of authority—a teacher, a pastor, or a judge, for example. Concentrate on how this particular interaction exemplifies the nature of your relationship with that person.

Strategies for Explaining How Things Work

Process Analysis

◆ ◆ ◆ ◆ ◆

Process writing tells how to do something or how something functions.

◆ Process writing is used to give directions and explain behaviors.

◆ Effective process writing is organized according to time or logic.

◆ Writers must decide what background information is needed, what steps to include, and what pitfalls to mention.

Communicating directions so that almost anyone can understand them is a difficult task, as you know if you've ever tried to do it. Explaining a process is quite similar; after you've performed a certain job over and over, it's hard to explain to someone else exactly how it's done. And when a child asks, "Where does the rain come from?" most people would rather come up with a cute story than grapple with the workings of nature.

But knowing how to provide an orderly, step-by-step explanation of how something is done or how it works is a valuable skill. For instance, if you're a political science major, you might be asked to explain how a bill gets passed in Congress or how the Electoral College works. If you're taking a science class, you might have to explain how photosynthesis works or recount the steps followed in an experiment. If you're taking physical education, you might be asked to write out the process for treating a sports injury or for improving a tennis serve. Sometimes the explanation may be just part of a larger essay or on-the-job report. For example, proposing a solution to your company's mail problems should include an account of how the current mail system works before addressing the changes to be made.

Often, **process writing** proceeds step by step: how to wash a dog, how to make English muffins, or how to change a light switch. But another version of process writing describes a process that is not necessarily **chronological:** designing a home for Alzheimer's patients or explaining how to keep your brain in top shape to avoid Alzheimer's. The second variety doesn't lend itself to easy step-by-step organization, so you have to sort out your points and arrange them in a **logical** way. Both kinds of process writing also involve analysis, since you must analyze your material thoroughly before you begin writing about it.

In the following essay, humorist Bud Herron calls upon his own harrowing experience to advise cat owners how to bathe a cat and come out alive. Student writer James R. Bryans read the cat bathing piece and arranged his own more serious essay following Herron's model.

Cat Bathing as a Martial Art

BUD HERRON

We have been unable to locate any information about Bud Herron—and we've looked everywhere. We found this piece posted on the Internet during the summer of 1997 and decided then to include it in this text. Perhaps Mr. Herron has since expired from cat-inflicted wounds.

Some people say cats never have to be bathed. They say cats lick   1
themselves clean. They say cats have a special enzyme of some sort in their saliva that works like new, improved Wisk—dislodging the dirt where it hides and whisking it away.

I've spent most of my life believing this folklore. Like most blind be-   2
lievers, I've been able to discount all the facts to the contrary: the kitty

odors that lurk in the corners of the garage and dirt smudges that cling to the throw rug by the fireplace. The time comes, however, when a man must face reality, when he must look squarely in the face of massive public sentiment to the contrary and announce: "This cat smells like a port-a-potty on a hot day in Juarez." When that day arrives at your house, as it has at mine, I have some advice you might consider as you place your feline friend under your arm and head for the bathtub:

◆ Know that although the cat has the advantage of quickness and lack   3
of concern for human life, you have the advantage of strength. Capitalize on that advantage by selecting the battlefield. Don't try to bathe him in an open area where he can force you to chase him. Pick a very small bathroom. If your bathroom is more than four feet square, I recommend that you get in the tub with the cat and close the sliding-glass doors as if you were about to take a shower. (A simple shower curtain will not do. A berserk cat can shred a three-ply rubber curtain quicker than a politician can shift positions.)

◆ Know that a cat has claws and will not hesitate to remove all the   4
skin from your body. Your advantage here is that you are smart and know how to dress to protect yourself. I recommend canvas overalls tucked into high-top construction boots, a pair of steel-mesh gloves, an army helmet, a hockey face mask, and a long-sleeved flak jacket.

◆ Prepare everything in advance. There is no time to go out for a   5
towel when you have a cat digging a hole in your flak jacket. Draw the water. Make sure the bottle of kitty shampoo is inside the glass enclosure. Make sure the towel can be reached, even if you are lying on your back in the water.

◆ Use the element of surprise. Pick up your cat nonchalantly, as if to   6
simply carry him to his supper dish. (Cats will not usually notice your strange attire. They have little or no interest in fashion as a rule. If he does notice your garb, calmly explain that you are taking part in a product testing experiment for J. C. Penney.)

◆ Once you are inside the bathroom, speed is essential to survival. In   7
a single liquid motion, shut the bathroom door, step into the tub enclosure, slide the glass door shut, dip the cat in the water, and squirt him with shampoo. You have begun one of the wildest 45 seconds of your life.

◆ Cats have no handles. Add the fact that he now has soapy fur, and the   8
problem is radically compounded. Do not expect to hold on to him for more

than two or three seconds at a time. When you have him, however, you must remember to give him another squirt of shampoo and rub like crazy. He'll then spring free and fall back into the water, thereby rinsing himself off. (The national record for cats is three latherings, so don't expect too much.)

◆ Next, the cat must be dried. Novice cat bathers always assume this   9
part will be the most difficult, for humans generally are worn out at this point and the cat is just getting really determined. In fact, the drying is simple compared to what you have just been through. That's because by now the cat is semi-permanently affixed to your right leg. You simply pop the drain plug with your foot, reach for your towel and wait. (Occasionally, however, the cat will end up clinging to the top of your army helmet. If this happens, the best thing you can do is to shake him loose and to encourage him toward your leg.) After all the water is drained from the tub, it is a simple matter to just reach down and dry the cat.

In a few days the cat will relax enough to be removed from your leg.   10
He will usually have nothing to say for about three weeks and will spend a lot of time sitting with his back to you. He might even become psycho-ceramic and develop the fixed stare of a plaster figurine. You will be tempted to assume he is angry. This isn't usually the case. As a rule he is simply plotting ways to get through your defenses and injure you for life the next time you decide to give him a bath. But at least now he is clean.

◆ ◆ ◆

◆ ◆ ◆ Writer's Workshop I ◆ ◆ ◆
Responding to a Process Analysis

Use the *Who, What, Why,* and *How* questions (see pp. 3–4) to explore your own understanding of the ideas and writing strategies employed by Bud Herron in "Cat Bathing as a Martial Art." Your instructor may ask you to record these responses in a journal or bring them to class to use in small group discussions.

◆ WRITING FROM READING

After applying the *Who, What, Why,* and *How* questions to Herron's essay, freshman James R. Bryans chose to explain a process less dangerous than cat bathing—buying land. While he adopts a tone more serious than

Herron's, he does include some humor in his essay, and he follows essentially the same structure—a two-paragraph introduction giving background material; a step-by-step chronological account of the process; and a one-paragraph conclusion. Here is Jim's essay.

James R. Bryans
Eng. 101
April 17, 1998

Buying Land: Easier Said Than Done

There are times in a man's life when he wants   1
something so badly he can taste it. This obsession may
lead a normally sane man to undertake a course of
action he would not normally take. For me, this
obsession was the desire to own my own piece of
property.

Little did I know, as an 18-year-old, prospective   2
land baron, that I would have to go through a tedious,
complicated process to achieve my goal. All I wanted
was 13 acres of woods that my grandfather and his
three siblings owned. I believed that all I would have
to do was say, "Hey, I'd like to buy your land." Then
I'd sign a deed and that would be that.

First of all, I wasn't sure that my Aunt Pauline   3
and my Uncle Virgil would want to sell this land that
had belonged to their grandparents. My grandfather,
and my Uncle Lloyd, I thought, would just give me
their stake in the land for nothing. As it turned out,
the four of them had discussed the matter and decided
to sell the land. I offered to buy it, and they
agreed. This part was what I thought was to be the
hardest, but I was so wrong.

I had to get the papers from Aunt Pauline. These   4
papers included the old "abstract of title," often
referred to as simply an abstract, which is a history
of ownership of a piece of real estate. Also, I was
given an old deed--a document that certifies a person's
legal ownership to a plot of land and includes

information regarding township, section, range, lot numbers, and so forth--and some other pieces of paper. Well, this was simple enough so far.

The next order of business was to go to see the lawyer. Unfortunately, a person cannot buy property without going to a lawyer, and this, of course, is a considerable expense. He took my papers and told me that new ones would have to be drawn up. I did not see anything wrong with the old ones, myself, but I still had to wait for a new abstract and a new deed to be prepared.

Once the deed was prepared, I had to get the signatures of all the sellers on it. Each of these signatures had to be witnessed by a notary public, a person who can legally certify a document's authenticity, but does not have to be an attorney. So, my father, who has a notary public's license, went to my grandfather and to Aunt Pauline, who lived in our area. But the other two owners, Uncle Virgil and Uncle Lloyd, lived out of state--one in Florida and the other in Missouri. Fortunately, my father decided he wanted to see his kinfolk anyway, so he just went for a visit and took the deed with him. He returned with all of the necessary signatures and notarization.

When all of this signing and notarizing was done, there was still a recording fee to pay. Now, what this is, is a similar thing to the Stamp Act that made the American Colonists mad enough to revolt. I had to pay to have my deed stamped, showing that the state would recognize me as the legal owner, and the fee for this stamp made me eligible to pay property taxes. In other words, I had to pay a tax to be able to pay taxes. But if I had neglected to pay the recording fee, I would not officially be the owner of my land, which would have defeated the purpose of owning land, I do believe.

In conclusion, my journey to the status of land owner was a long, complex, and expensive one. It took time, patience, and of course, money. Buying land requires a knowledge of the system that one may truly obtain only by going through the system. A lawyer is usually more than happy to help with the process--for a price. In fact, the only way to buy land legally

without a lawyer is to be one. In the end, though, I
am very glad that I bought that land. Maybe someday I
will be able to buy some more. And, next time, I'll
know what to expect.

◆ GETTING STARTED ON A PROCESS ANALYSIS

Before beginning to explain a process in writing, you'll want to consider your prospective readers. Sizing up your **audience** is crucial if you are
explaining a technical process, like how to replace a hard drive. You need to
judge how much—or how little—your readers already know about the complex insides of a personal computer. If you don't give enough background
information, you'll lose the beginners at the outset, and they may remain
permanently lost. But if you give too much background, the more experienced users may become impatient, skip along, and maybe miss some vital
step. Probably it's better to err on the side of providing more background
information than some readers need rather than to risk confusing the
novices.

If your process is not complex, figuring out your audience is easier.
Bud Herron, for instance, has an easily identifiable audience—cat owners.
He may even engage a few readers who don't care for cats but can appreciate the humor anyway. But he's basically writing for people who know
how cats behave, and therein lies much of his humor. Similarly, Jim Bryans
doesn't have to worry about whether his readers have ever bought land before because, as he complains, you can't do it without a lawyer anyway. So,
Jim addresses his advice to anyone who might be interested in buying a
piece of land.

◆ ORGANIZING A PROCESS ANALYSIS

The basic organizing principle behind process writing involves time.
You are usually involved with relating a series of events, and these events
may not float through your mind in the same order they should appear in
your written work. Your readers will be frustrated and confused by **flashbacks** or detours to supply information you should have covered earlier.
Therefore, the scratch outline takes on great importance in this type of writing. A blank piece of unlined paper will help you get started. On this page,
list the steps or stages of the process as you think of them—only be sure to
space the items widely apart. In the spaces, you can add points you forgot
the first time through. When you get to the end of your process, read

through the steps while visualizing the process to pinpoint anything you may have forgotten.

If you'll glance back at Herron's essay, you'll notice that following his two introductory paragraphs establishing the need for cat bathing, his main points (using his own phrasing) go like this:

- ◆ selecting the battlefield
- ◆ dress to protect yourself
- ◆ prepare everything in advance
- ◆ use the element of surprise
- ◆ speed is essential
- ◆ cats have no handles (hard to hold onto)
- ◆ the cat must be dried

As you can see, the essay follows essentially the order in which the contest between cat and cat-bather will take place, in case anyone wants to risk life and limb by following this advice.

If you'll look again at James Bryans's essay, you'll see that he organizes his material in the same way Herron does. After a two-paragraph introduction stating his desire to "become a prospective land baron," Jim presents his main points this way:

- ◆ arranges to buy the land
- ◆ gets deed and abstract
- ◆ hires a lawyer
- ◆ obtains signatures of sellers
- ◆ pays recording fee

There are, of course, those other sorts of process papers that do not lend themselves to this easy chronological organization—topics like "How to choose a personal computer" or "How to live within your means." For such subjects, you must figure out a clear, **logical arrangement** that suits your material.

◆ DEVELOPING A PROCESS ANALYSIS

Developing a process essay simply involves explaining each step fully and clearly while keeping your audience in mind. But here are some guidelines that are especially important if you are giving instructions about a mechanical or technical process.

◆ *Define terms.* In parentheses or in a concise sentence, define any word that would be unfamiliar to most of your readers, like "motherboard" or "gigabyte," in explaining how to upgrade your computer—or any common word that you're using in an unfamiliar way, like "rubber" or "vulnerable," in explaining how to keep score in bridge. Just after using the legal term *abstract,* Jim Bryans briefly defines it: "an abstract, which is a history of ownership of a piece of real estate." He later defines *notary public* as "a person who can legally certify a document's authenticity, but does not have to be an attorney."

◆ *Be specific.* Remember that in writing, you must make yourself clear without those gestures you use to make yourself understood when speaking. Instead of saying, "Strip the insulation back *a little bit* on a piece of wire"—and then showing your listener a short space between your thumb and forefinger—you need to write, "Strip the insulation back *1-inch* on a piece of wire." Notice that Bud Herron is not content with just telling a prospective cat-bather to wear heavy clothes. He specifically recommends "canvas overalls tucked into high-top construction boots, a pair of steel-mesh gloves, an army helmet, a hockey face mask, and a long-sleeved flak jacket."

◆ *Include reasons.* You can often help your readers better understand the process by explaining the reasons for taking certain steps. Bud Herron, after advising his readers "to prepare everything in advance," explains why: because, "There is no time to go out for a towel when you have a cat digging a hole in your flak jacket."

◆ *Include* **don'ts.** If there happens to be a common—or uncommon but disastrous—mistake that people can make in following the process, you had better warn your readers. For instance, "Do not stick your fingers in the fusebox unless you have pulled out the main fuse" is handy advice. Bud Herron cautions, "Don't try to bathe [your cat] in an open area where he can force you to chase him." He later warns, "Do not expect to hold on to him for more than two or three seconds at a time," so that we understand the need to wash rapidly.

◆ *Mention possible pitfalls.* Whenever things are likely to go wrong despite your careful directions, let your readers know about it. When describing the process of making bread, for instance, you should note that if the water is too hot, it will kill the yeast and the dough won't rise. Jim Bryans advises us that although paying the double tax seems unfair, it is absolutely necessary: "If I had neglected to pay the recording fee,

I would not officially be the owner of my land." Bud Herron's process is full of pitfalls—some quite dire: "A berserk cat can shred a three-ply rubber curtain quicker than a politician can shift positions"; "Know that a cat has claws and will not hesitate to remove all the skin from your body"; "Make sure the towel can be reached, even if you are lying on your back in the water."

◆ OPENING AND CLOSING A PROCESS ANALYSIS

By the time your readers finish your first paragraph, they should know what process you are going to describe. To open a "how-to" process paper, you may reassure your readers by giving your credentials—telling them why they should listen to *you* on this subject. Jim Bryans begins by telling of his desire to own a piece of land and cites as credentials his experience in land buying.

You might begin by mentioning the advantages of knowing how to perform this process. Bud Herron opens by refuting the accepted wisdom that cats do not need bathing by telling us about his cat who is desperately dirty. Thus, he convinces us of the value of reading his instructions. We know from the humorous tone that he grossly exaggerates on all counts, but still his advice could be followed by anyone cocky enough to try washing a full-grown cat with claws intact.

Another common element of process introductions is a list of materials involved. In a how-to paper, it is convenient for the readers to have all the necessary items named in one place. If they are going to follow directions for washing the cat, they should be told (as Herron tells his readers) to collect the soap and towels before they collect the cat; otherwise, the beast will bolt while they are gone. If you decide to include such a list, double-check to make sure you do not leave anything out.

A truly impressive closing is hard to come by in process writing, but here are a few ideas that may help. You can enumerate the advantages of knowing the process, as Jim Bryans does in his final paragraph. Be sure, of course, that you are not just repeating the introduction. In his conclusion, Jim takes a parting shot at lawyers, declares that he's glad he bought the land, and says that he hopes to repeat the process again someday. You can speculate on the results of completing the process, as Bud Herron does. He concludes that the cat may be angry about his mistreatment, but usually isn't. "As a rule he is simply plotting ways to get through your defenses and injure you for life the next time you decide to give him a bath." And his final short, emphatic sentence provides a word of comfort: "But at least now he is clean."

With some topics, you can mention related or complementary processes that your reader might be interested in. If you have just explained how to design a raised-bed vegetable garden, you could close with the suggestion that your readers might like to try the same technique with a butterfly garden. Or if all else fails, you can give your readers a few cheery words of encouragement. Just one warning: do not mindlessly insist that a process is "fun and easy" when you know it is not. You might lose your credibility. Try "difficult but rewarding" instead.

◆ USING THE MODEL

Although both Bud Herron and Jim Bryans explain processes, their essays are quite different. Herron writes in a humorous tone giving step-by-step instructions. Bryans, after reading that model, chose a serious approach to a slightly different kind of process. His advice about buying land involves not so much steps as stages that occur over a long period of time, but he follows the same chronological organization that Herron does. Because his topic involves legal jargon, Jim also includes several definitions that were not necessary in the model explaining how to bathe a cat. Have you ever done something unusual for a person your age, like buying land? Or do you know how to perform well some difficult task, like cat bathing? Or do you know how to do something that others might like to learn how to do, like constructing a picnic table or designing a butterfly garden? Would it make an interesting essay?

◆ ◆ ◆ *Writer's Workshop II* ◆ ◆ ◆
Analyzing Process Writing

Working individually or with a group of classmates, read through James Bryans's essay "Buying Land: Easier Said Than Done" and respond to the following questions.

1. What do you find out about the topic of the essay in the first two paragraphs? Is the thesis stated or implied?
2. Do you think you would be able to follow this process if you decided to buy a piece of land? Are the steps clear? Are there questions you might like to ask the author?
3. How are transitions made between paragraphs? Are there transitional words or phrases within paragraphs?
4. What strategy does Bryans use in his conclusion? Can you think of a more effective one?

◆ ◆ ◆ *Checklist for Reading and Writing* ◆ ◆ ◆
Process Essays

1. Can you identify the process or the purpose of the essay in the introduction?
2. Is there enough background information so that readers will be able to understand the process? Or is there perhaps too much?
3. If the process requires equipment or materials, are these listed at the beginning? Is everything necessary included?
4. Are the steps given in chronological order? Are any steps missing? Are reasons given when understanding the reasons for doing a step would be helpful?
5. Is the process easy to follow or would more transitional devices help? Or, if there are too many transitions, which ones could be omitted?
6. Are all unfamiliar terms defined? Are all instructions specific enough?
7. If there are any *don't*s or pitfalls involved in this process, are these mentioned?
8. Does the ending give readers a sense of closure?

◆ ◆ ◆ **PREPARING TO READ**

Have you ever watched a Laurel and Hardy slapstick comedy in which these two try to perform manual labor—like building a house or hanging wallpaper? Have you ever tried to hang wallpaper yourself? Was your work satisfactory, or could you imagine yourself signing on as one of the Three Stooges?

◆ ◆ ◆

Wall Covering

DERECK WILLIAMSON

A freelance journalist who writes with humor about life and its ironies, Dereck Williamson lives in New Jersey and publishes articles in many popular magazines. He also writes amusing do-it-yourself books full of useful, tongue-in-cheek advice. The following selection, which first appeared in *The Saturday Review,* is taken from *The Complete Book of Pitfalls: A Victim's Guide to Repairs, Maintenance, and Repairing the Maintenance* (1971).

1   Over the years, starting even before Adolf Hitler, paperhanging has gotten a million laughs. In the movies, great rolls of paper curl up over people who fall off ladders covered with paste as dogs chase cats around the room. It's what advertising copy writers call "a laff riot."

2   People who have done their own wallpapering rarely even chuckle at the antics on the silver screen. They remember great rolls of curling paper causing them to fall off ladders on dogs and cats covered with paste. (Never mind what modifies what, you picky grammarians; *everything* was covered with paste.)

3   In recent years the job of wall decorating has become a little easier, but paperhanging is still nothing to be sneezed at. Especially when you're trying to line up the edges.

4   The most difficult job is preparing the surface. The very thought makes the brain cringe. So many more jobs would get done around the home if you didn't have to "prepare the surface" first. By the time you get a surface prepared, all enthusiasm for the project at hand has disappeared. Remember Uncle Percy who invited you and all the other kids for a Sunday drive? As you gathered around he said, "First we must wash the car. . . ."

Many people have such severe hang-ups about preliminary work that 5
they flee from place to place all their lives, leaving a trail of unprepared surfaces behind them. Or else they tackle the job without preparing the surface. That's possible in a paperhanging project, but it's not a good idea.
Chances are you'll run into trouble. Putting new paper on old paper is risky
unless the old paper is still adhering firmly. And you know it isn't. Deep in
your heart you know the old paper is loose and cracked and awful.

Too many layers of wallpaper can give a closed-in feeling. Many city 6
apartments have been papered over so many times that there's no room in
the rooms. A good rule of thumb is that if both elbows touch walls—and
you're standing in the room the long way—you should remove all the old
wallpaper and start all over again. However, if you have unusually long elbows, you might possibly get away with one more layer of paper.

To remove old layers of wallpaper you need old clothes, a wide putty 7
knife, and a compulsive urge to destroy. You loosen up the paper either by
soaking it with hot water or using a wallpaper steamer. You rent the latter at
a paint store, not a shipping office.

Do-it-yourself books say the job is messy, but that it goes fast once you 8
start. Only the first part is true. Have you ever heard of a messy job going
fast? You'll be steaming and soaking and scraping and slopping and slush-
ing and slogging around that room for days. Only two things will relieve the
boredom. The first is the layer by layer discovery of what hideous taste the
previous tenants had. The other is the prospect of finding a million dollar
bill or an original Van Gogh between the wall and first layer of paper, a logical hiding place for money and paintings.

As you wield the scraper, be careful not to gouge the walls. Not only 9
will the Van Gogh be ruined, but you'll have to fill up the holes before you
put on the new paper.

Cracks and holes should be filled with spackling compound and sand- 10
ed smooth after dry. The next step is to apply a coat of wall size, a gluelike
substance which seals the surface and also fills in small depressions. Like
your ears and eyes.

Materials you'll need for papering are a paste brush and bucket, a 11
sponge, a plumb line, chalk, a stepladder, a yardstick, scissors, razor blades, a
smoothing brush, a seam roller, and the same putty knife you used for wall-
gouging.

Instructions that come with the wallpaper tell you that a long, clean, 12
flat work surface is essential for preparing the paper. The illustration shows
a smiling man standing at a banquet table, brushing paste on an endless
strip of paper. He is wearing a necktie. Do you know anybody who wears a
necktie when he applies wallpaper paste?

Face the fact that paperhanging is a grubby job, and that you won't　13
have enough space to work in. If you're lucky, you'll find room someplace to
set up a lone card table, and you'll make do with that. Afterward, the table
won't be any good for card-playing. Each time you shuffle, the bottom card
will stick to the table. You'll have to play with an incomplete deck, stopping
every few hands to steam and scrape cards.

There are formulas for estimating the amount of paper you'll need,　14
but they don't take into account dog and cat damage. Your best bet is to
supply the dealer with your room dimensions, plus window and door mea-
surements, and a list of household pets. The dealer will give you enough
rolls of paper to do the room. Make sure he has more of the same pattern
on hand.

Start papering next to a door. (Don't paper over the door.) From the　15
door frame, measure out a distance of one inch less than the width of the
paper, and make a mark. Then, using the chalked plumb line, snap a perfectly
vertical line against the wall. Then go to bed. That's quite enough for one day.

When you return to the room several months later, maybe someone　16
will have already papered it. Or taken away the rolls of paper and applied a
decent coat of whitewash. If not, you've got to start hanging the wallpaper.

Cut off a piece from the roll the distance from floor to ceiling plus　17
about eight inches to allow trimming on the top and bottom. Then lay the
paper face down on the work table and start brushing paste on the back, as
the remainder of the roll falls off the table into the fresh bucket of paste.

After plucking out the roll and flinging it against the wall in a blind　18
rage, finish applying paste to the first strip and then start on exposed parts
of your body. Remove your clothes and cover yourself completely with
paste. Now you are ready to (1) go out in the street and dance, or (2) apply
the first strip of paper to the wall. If you choose to be dull and hang paper,
here's the technique:

Carefully line up the first strip so the edge touches the chalk line, and　19
smooth it out against the wall. It helps if you apply the paste on one half of
the paper's length first, fold it over loosely paste side to paste side, and then
do the same thing with the other half. It also helps if you don't lose your
head as you're trying to hold the paper up against the wall and unfold it at
the same time.

Once the paper is lined up, use a smoothing brush or damp sponge to　20
flatten out the strip and remove bubbles and wrinkles. Then carefully trim
off the top and bottom with a razor blade, and wipe off the excess paste.

Some paper comes with untrimmed edges, and you use a long straight-　21
edge to trim off the selvage. That's done while the paper is on the table.
Next time, get smart and buy paper already trimmed.

Each succeeding layer of paper is applied to the wall just a tiny bit away 22
from the preceding one, and then sort of nudged over in place so it matches
up. Press the edges down with the seam roller. Before you put paste on the
next strip, the books say to hold it up against the wall to make sure it will
match up with the other piece. To do this, just pull the roll apart until one
hand is up against the ceiling molding and the other hand is against the base-
board. Then go out in the kitchen and eat a bunch of bananas.

Save leftover strips and use them around windows and doors. Remove 23
wall fixtures and switch plates, paper over them, and then cut out the openings later if you can find them. Some people carefully paper each individual
switch plate, making sure it exactly fits in with the wall pattern. This type of
person Simonizes the inside of his glove compartment, and fills unused peg-
board holes with Plastic Wood.

One kind of paper comes with the paste already applied. You put a 24
water trough on the floor, soak each precut strip in the water for a minute,
then slowly pull one end out of the trough, unrolling the paper and climbing
the ladder and scratching your nose and lighting a cigarette. The trough gets
moved along the floor as you apply successive strips. Try to keep your feet
out of it.

When you come to the corner, take the paper around to the next wall 25
about an inch. Before starting on the new wall, make another chalk mark if
you can find the plumb bob under all that rubble.

In order to paper ceilings it takes two people, both insane. If you're 26
thinking of papering your ceiling you don't need instructions, you need a
doctor.

◆ ◆ ◆

FIRST RESPONSES

Do you think Williamson has ever hung wallpaper? Do you think you
could put up wallpaper following his directions? Would you want to?

TAKING A CLOSER LOOK

Exploring *Who:* Voice and Tone

1. Point out some examples of exaggeration that contribute to the
   essay's humorous tone. What other sources of humor do you find in
   the essay?
2. Who is the intended audience for this piece?

3. How much knowledge does Williamson presume his readers will have of tools and techniques?
4. Are there any words you think he should have defined, even for this audience?

Exploring *What:* Content and Meaning

1. What is the hardest thing about wallpapering? What happens if you skip that difficult step?
2. In several places Williamson offers good advice for making the job go more smoothly. What are a couple of these tips?
3. What is the problem with the standard formulas for estimating how much paper is needed for a wallpapering job?
4. What are a couple of *don't*s that Williamson mentions? What are a couple of pitfalls? Where does he include a definition?

Exploring *Why:* Purpose

1. Can you tell from the first three introductory paragraphs what Williamson's purpose is? Does he state his thesis or imply it?
2. Locate a couple of places where the author provides reasons for doing or not doing something. Find one example that is seriously intended to help readers understand the process and one that is included just to add to the humor.
3. Paragraph 21 about trimming off selvages is out of place chronologically. Where does it belong in the step-by-step account? Why did Williamson not put it there? Were you bothered by the lapse in chronology? If not, why not?
4. Could you really put up wallpaper following these directions? What elements resemble the format of serious instructions? What elements do not?

Exploring *How:* Style and Strategy

1. How does Williamson attempt to get you interested in reading about wallpapering in his first three paragraphs?
2. In two different places (paragraphs 7 and 11), Williamson gives us lists of needed equipment. Why doesn't he follow the standard advice for process writing and provide a single list at the beginning?
3. Find two examples of the kind of precise language customarily used in explaining a process.

4. In paragraph 8, he includes a list of six items in a series separated not by commas, in the usual way, but by *and*s. Try inserting *and*s in place of the commas in the long series in paragraph 11. Does the strategy work there? Why or why not? Now try inserting *and*s to replace the commas in the short series in the opening sentence of paragraph 12.

5. How do you think the technique works there? Can you generalize about what a writer achieves with this strategy? How often do you think it can be used and still be effective?

WRITING FROM READING ASSIGNMENT

In a decidedly humorous tone, "Wall Covering" provides directions and advice for hanging wallpaper. For this writing assignment, think of some process or procedure that you know well enough to explain to others—either seriously or with tongue in cheek. Perhaps you know how to do something that most people don't, like glass blowing or wind surfing. Or maybe you're especially skillful at doing some familiar task, like simonizing a car or making an omelet. Or maybe you're knowledgeable about a process that will help people save money, like negotiating a good price on a new car.

A. Begin by thinking through the process chronologically, from start to finish, jotting down on a piece of paper the steps you go through. Be sure to leave plenty of space between the steps.

B. Then, go over the process again in your mind, focusing this time on any pitfalls or *don't*s or any bits of advice or reasons that might prove useful. Add these in the open spaces where they belong in the time frame. If your explanation would benefit from examples, like those Williamson uses, brainstorm for ideas and write them in where they belong.

C. Now, check over your list of steps or stages one more time to be sure you haven't left anything out.

D. Begin your essay, as Williamson does, by discussing how people normally respond to your process—finding it too difficult, too boring, too time-consuming, too comical, or too puzzling. Then let them know that the task is not impossible if they follow your instructions.

E. Now present your process, step by step, following your plan. Be sure to include sufficient reasons, examples, and advice. And don't forget the *don't*s and pitfalls.

F. Close by offering encouragement or by mentioning the advantages of learning this skill.

G. Read over what you've written to see whether you've used any words your readers might not be familiar with. If so, define them briefly. Then consult the "Checklist for Reading and Writing Process Essays" (p. 198) to see how well you have fulfilled the criteria for good process writing.

♦ ♦ ♦ **PREPARING TO READ**

Have you ever found yourself in the middle of a set of instructions that were missing a step? What did you do? Or perhaps you've had the misfortune to be served a dish prepared by a cook who has suffered this regrettable experience. How did the food taste?

♦ ♦ ♦

Company Menu No. 1

PEG BRACKEN

Peg Bracken (b. 1918) writes witty light verse and humorous articles about domestic life in the suburbs. Her pieces have appeared in popular magazines—*Good Housekeeping, Woman's Day,* and *The Ladies Home Journal.* About her bestseller, *The I Hate to Cook Book* (1960), she writes, "Some women, it is said, like to cook. This book is not for them. This book is for those of us who want to fold our dishwater hands around a dry martini instead of a wet flounder, come the end of a long hard day." The following excerpt is from chapter 6, entitled "Company's Coming—or Your Back's to the Wall." As you read through the following recipes, decide whether you think you could whip up a meal for company using these directions.

COMPANY MENU NO. 1

Chicken-Artichoke Casserole
Plain Baked Potatoes
Sliced Fresh Tomatoes
Irish Coffee

Chicken-Artichoke Casserole

3-pound cut-up fryer (or equal weight of chicken pieces)
1½ teaspoons salt
1½ teaspoons paprika
¼ teaspoon pepper
6 tablespoons butter

¼ pound mushrooms, cut in large pieces
12- to 15-ounce can artichoke hearts
2 tablespoons flour
⅔ cup chicken consommé or bouillon
3 tablespoons sherry

Salt, pepper, and paprika the chicken pieces. Then brown them pretti- 1
ly in four tablespoons of the butter and put them in a big casserole. Now put
the other two tablespoons of butter into the frying pan and sauté the mushrooms in it five minutes. Then sprinkle the flour over them and stir in the
chicken consommé and the sherry. While this cooks five minutes, you may
open the can of artichokes and arrange them between the chicken pieces.
Then pour the mushroom-sherry sauce over them, cover, and bake at 375
degrees for forty minutes.

You can fix this in the morning, or the day before.   2

Put your middle-sized baking potatoes in the oven twenty minutes be- 3
fore you put the casserole in, and things will come out even.

That chicken-artichoke arrangement is not only quite good, it's very 4
pretty. But I'd like to mention here that it is unwise to expect your company meals to look *precisely* like the company meals you see in the full-
color spreads everywhere. In this connection, I have news for you: food
photographers do not play fair and square. It was once my privilege to
watch a beef stew being photographed in the studio of a major food pho-
tographer. It was a superb stew—the gravy glistening richly, the beef
chunks brown and succulent and in beautiful juxtaposition to the bright
carrots and the pearly onions. I can make a respectable beef stew myself,
but my gravy is never that gorgeous, and my onions invariably sink as
though torpedoed. I inquired about this and discovered that the gravy had
been dyed, and the onions had been propped up on toothpicks! Moreover,
that very same morning, they told me they'd had to lacquer a lobster. There
you have it.

Irish Coffee

This is a real triple threat: coffee, dessert, and liqueur all in one, and 5
what else can make that statement? To make Irish Coffee, you needn't fuss
with dessert, dessert plates, dessert forks, coffeepot, sugar bowl, creamer,
demitasse cups, wee spoons, liqueur bottles, and liqueur glasses. You
merely need Irish whiskey, instant coffee, hot water, sugar, and whipping
cream (which you can whip before dinner, if you like), and to contain it,
Irish whiskey glasses. These are stemmed goblets holding seven to eight
fluid ounces. (The stems are important, because they'd otherwise be too hot
to hold.)

Put one and a half ounces of Irish whiskey into each glass. Add one 6
and a half teaspoons of granulated sugar. Add one and a half teaspoons of
instant coffee. Fill to within half an inch of the brim with hot water and stir.
Now, on top float the whipped cream, which should be thick but not stiff.

(One half of a cup of cream, before whipping, is about right for four Irish Coffees.) And serve.

Obviously, the saving here in money, time, dishwashing, and wear and tear on the leg muscles is phenomenal. And last but not least, people don't sit around drinking Irish Coffee until the cock crows. Because it is rich, one is enough. It serves as a pleasant punctuation mark to the evening, and, because it also has a slight somniferous effect on many people, your guests may eventually go home.   7

Salude! Not to mention *bon soir.*   8

FIRST RESPONSES

Did Peg Bracken's account of the deception involved in food photography remind you of some mildly deceptive practice you discovered by accident—like catching the tooth fairy in the act or finding out that an attractive person is wearing implants and a hairpiece? Explain how this revelation made you feel.

TAKING A CLOSER LOOK

Exploring *Who:* Voice and Tone

1. Describe the tone of Bracken's writing. What specific words and phrases convey her tone?
2. How do you think Bracken envisioned the readers of her cookbook? In other words, what kind of cooks was she writing it for?
3. Did you feel included in her audience? If so, why? If not, why not?
4. What is the level of her language—formal, informal, or colloquial? Point out words, phrases, or perhaps whole sentences to support your answer.

Exploring *What:* Content and Meaning

1. What, according to Bracken, are the main advantages of serving Irish Coffee instead of dessert?
2. Look up the following terms in a college dictionary and explain what they mean in the context of Bracken's remarks: somniferous, Salude, *bon soir.*
3. Have you read other cookbooks? How are Bracken's instructions different?

Exploring *Why:* Purpose

1. Peg Bracken explains her purpose in her introduction. She writes,

   > Now about this book: its genesis was a luncheon with several good friends, all of whom hate to cook but have to. At that time, we were all unusually bored with what we had been cooking and, therefore, eating. For variety's sake, we decided to pool our ignorance, tell each other our shabby little secrets, and toss into the pot the recipes we swear by instead of at.

   Without adopting her humorous tone, summarize her purpose in a single sentence.

2. What warning does Bracken include after explaining how to make and serve Irish Coffee (paragraph 5)?

3. Do you think perhaps she might have included a few more warnings— or at least more explicit instructions—in these two recipes? What details would you add if you were asked to revise these recipes for an audience of novice cooks?

4. ■ *Using the Internet.* Look at several of the recipes on the Cooking.Com Web site on the Internet (http://www.cooking.com/ recipes/rehome.asp). How does the attitude toward cooking expressed there differ from Peg Bracken's? How are the instructions different? Or, if you prefer, select one of Julia Child's cookbooks from your library, and compare the tone and the instructions you find there to Bracken's.

Exploring *How:* Style and Strategy

1. Point out specific words, phrases, or details that contribute to the warm, chatty tone of this selection. What unusual word choices do you find interesting?

2. Why do you think Bracken includes the little digression letting us know that "food photographers do not play fair and square" (paragraph 4)?

3. Bracken includes a simile (paragraph 4) and a metaphor (paragraph 7) in these cooking instructions. Find these figures of speech and analyze their effectiveness.

4. Paragraph 4 departs from the process organization of the rest of the selection. What strategy is used in developing this paragraph?

IDEAS FOR WRITING A PROCESS ANALYSIS

1. Write a recipe for success—in studying for an exam, in playing a sport, in applying make-up, in washing a dog. Choose an activity that requires the use of some equipment, as cooking does. Arrange your points chronologically, beginning with a list of items you need to assemble before you begin.

2. Explain how to perform some fairly simple but tricky task—a task requiring some expertise, like building a campfire, starting a fire in a fireplace, kicking a football through goal posts, ironing a man's dress shirt, or making a flaky pie crust from scratch.

3. Think of something you can make, and explain the process so that someone else can make it.

◆ ◆ ◆ PREPARING TO READ

Have you ever attended a funeral at which the body was displayed? What was your reaction? Did you think the deceased looked "life-like"? Did you notice what the casket looked like? Did you pay any attention to the clothing of the deceased?

◆ ◆ ◆

Embalming Mr. Jones

JESSICA MITFORD

Born in England to a prominent family, Jessica Mitford (1917–1996) spoke of herself as uneducated because, having always been privately tutored by governesses, she had no diplomas. She became an American citizen in 1944 and began an illustrious career as an investigative journalist—a muckraker, as she described her vocation. In her influential exposé of the funeral industry, *The American Way of Death* (1963), from which the following excerpt is taken, she ridicules the irrational and expensive process of preparing corpses for viewing.

1 The drama begins to unfold with the arrival of the corpse at the mortuary.

2 Alas, poor Yorick! How surprised he would be to see how his counterpart of today is whisked off to a funeral parlor and is in short order, sprayed, sliced, pierced, pickled, trussed, trimmed, creamed, waxed, painted, rouged, and neatly dressed—transformed from a common corpse into a Beautiful Memory Picture. This process is known in the trade as embalming and restorative art, and is so universally employed in the United States and Canada that the funeral director does it routinely, without consulting corpse or kin. He regards as eccentric those few who are hardy enough to suggest that it might be dispensed with. Yet no law requires embalming, no religious doctrine commends it, nor is it dictated by considerations of health, sanitation, or even of personal daintiness. In no part of the world but in Northern America is it widely used. The purpose of embalming is to make the corpse presentable for viewing in a suitably costly container; and here too the funeral director routinely, without first consulting the family, prepares the body for public display.

Is all this legal? The processes to which a dead body may be subjected are after all to some extent circumscribed by law. In most states, for instance, the signature of next of kin must be obtained before an autopsy may be performed, before the deceased may be cremated, before the body may be turned over to a medical school for research purposes; or such provision must be made in the decedent's will. In the case of embalming, no such permission is required nor is it ever sought. A textbook, *The Principles and Practices of Embalming,* comments on this: "There is some question regarding the legality of much that is done within the preparation room." The author points out that it would be most unusual for a responsible member of a bereaved family to instruct the mortician, in so many words, to *"embalm"* the body of a deceased relative. The very term *embalming* is so seldom used that the mortician must rely upon custom in the matter. The author concludes that unless the family specifies otherwise, the act of entrusting the body to the care of a funeral establishment carries with it an implied permission to go ahead and embalm.   3

Embalming is indeed a most extraordinary procedure, and one must wonder at the docility of Americans who each year pay hundreds of millions of dollars for its perpetuation, blissfully ignorant of what it is all about, what is done, how it is done. Not one in ten thousand has any idea of what actually takes place. Books on the subject are extremely hard to come by. They are not to be found in most libraries or bookshops.   4

In an era when huge television audiences watch surgical operations in the comfort of their living rooms, when, thanks to the animated cartoon, the geography of the digestive system has become familiar territory even to the nursery school set, in a land where the satisfaction of curiosity about all matters is a national pastime, the secrecy surrounding embalming can, surely, hardly be attributed to the inherent gruesomeness of the subject. Custom in this regard has within this century suffered a complete reversal. In the early days of American embalming, when it was performed in the home of the deceased, it was almost mandatory for some relative to stay by the embalmer's side and witness the procedure. Today, family members who might wish to be in attendance would certainly be dissuaded by the funeral director. All others, except apprentices, are excluded by law from the preparation room.   5

A close look at what does actually take place may explain in large measure the undertaker's intractable reticence concerning a procedure that has become his major *raison d'être.* Is it possible he fears that public information about embalming might lead patrons to wonder if they really want this service? If the funeral men are loath to discuss the subject outside the trade, the reader may, understandably, be equally loath to go on reading at this point. For those who have the stomach for it, let us part the formaldehyde curtain. . . .   6

The body is first laid out in the undertaker's morgue—or rather, Mr. 7
Jones is reposing in the preparation room—to be readied to bid the world
farewell.

The preparation room in any of the better funeral establishments has 8
the tiled and sterile look of a surgery, and indeed the embalmer-restorative
artist who does his chores there is beginning to adopt the term "dermasur-
geon" (appropriately corrupted by some mortician-writers as "demisur-
geon") to describe his calling. His equipment, consisting of scalpels, scissors,
augers, forceps, clamps, needles, pumps, tubes, bowls and basins, is crudely
imitative of the surgeon's, as is his technique, acquired in a nine- or twelve-
month post-high-school course in an embalming school. He is supplied by
an advanced chemical industry with a bewildering array of fluids, sprays,
pastes, oils, powders, creams, to fix or soften tissue, shrink or distend it as
needed, dry it here, restore the moisture there. There are cosmetics, waxes,
and paints to fill and cover features, even plaster of Paris to replace entire
limbs. There are ingenious aids to prop and stabilize the cadaver: a Van-Pose
Head Rest, the Edwards Arm and Hand Positioner, the Repose Block (to
support the shoulders during the embalming), and the Throop Foot Positioner, which resembles an old-fashioned stocks.

Mr. John H. Eckels, president of the Eckels College of Mortuary Sci- 9
ence, thus describes the first part of the embalming procedure: "In the
hands of a skilled practitioner, this work may be done in a comparatively
short time and without mutilating the body other than by slight incision—so
slight that it scarcely would cause serious inconvenience if made upon a living person. It is necessary to remove the blood, and doing this not only
helps in the disinfecting, but removes the principal cause of disfigurements
due to discoloration."

Another textbook discusses the all-important time element: "The ear- 10
lier this is done, the better, for every hour that elapses between death and
embalming will add to the problems and complications encountered. . . ."
Just how soon should one get going on the embalming? The author tells us,
"On the basis of such scanty information made available to this profession
through its rudimentary and haphazard system of technical research, we
must conclude that the best results are to be obtained if the subject is embalmed before life is completely extinct—that is, before cellular death has
occurred. In the average case, this would mean within an hour after somatic
death." For those who feel that there is something a little rudimentary, not
to say haphazard, about this advice, a comforting thought is offered by another writer. Speaking of fears entertained in early days of premature
burial, he points out, "One of the effects of embalming by chemical injection, however, has been to dispel fears of live burial." How true; once the
blood is removed, chances of live burial are indeed remote.

To return to Mr. Jones, the blood is drained out through the veins and   11
replaced by embalming fluid pumped in through the arteries. As noted in
The Principles and Practices of Embalming, "every operator has a favorite
injection and drainage point—a fact which becomes a handicap only if he
fails or refuses to forsake his favorites when conditions demand it." Typical
favorites are the carotid artery, femoral artery, jugular vein, subclavian vein.
There are various choices of embalming fluid. If Flextone is used, it will produce a "mild, flexible rigidity. The skin retains a velvety softness, the tissues
are rubbery and pliable. Ideal for women and children." It may be blended
with B. and G. Products Company's Lyf-Lyk tint, which is guaranteed to reproduce "nature's own skin texture . . . . the velvety appearance of living
tissue." Suntone comes in three separate tints: Suntan; Special Cosmetic
Tint, a pink shade "especially indicated for young female subjects"; and
Regular Cosmetic Tint, moderately pink.

About three to six gallons of a dyed and perfumed solution of   12
formaldehyde, glycerin, borax, phenol, alcohol, and water is soon circulating
through Mr. Jones, whose mouth has been sewn together with a "needle directed upward between the upper lip and gum and brought out through the
left nostril," with the corners raised slightly "for a more pleasant expression." If he should be bucktoothed, his teeth are cleaned with Bon Ami and
coated with colorless nail polish. His eyes, meanwhile, are closed with flesh-
tinted eye caps and eye cement.

The next step is to have at Mr. Jones with a thing called a trocar. This   13
is a long, hollow needle attached to a tube. It is jabbed into the abdomen,
poked around the entrails and chest cavity, the contents of which are
pumped out and replaced with "cavity fluid." This done, and the hole in the
abdomen sewn up, Mr. Jones's face is heavily creamed (to protect the skin
from burns which may be caused by leakage of the chemicals), and he is
covered with a sheet and left unmolested for a while. But not for long—
there is more, much more, in store for him. He has been embalmed, but not
yet restored, and the best time to start the restorative work is eight to ten
hours after embalming, when the tissues have become firm and dry.

The object of all this attention to the corpse, it must be remembered,   14
is to make it presentable for viewing in an attitude of healthy repose. "Our
customs require the presentation of our dead in the semblance of normal-
ity . . . unmarred by the ravages of illness, disease or mutilation," says Mr.
J. Sheridan Mayer in his *Restorative Art.* This is a rather large order since
few people die in the full bloom of health, unravaged by illness and un-
marked by some disfigurement. The funeral industry is equal to the challenge: "In some cases the gruesome appearance of a mutilated or
disease-ridden subject may be quite discouraging. The task of restoration
may seem impossible and shake the confidence of the embalmer. This is the

time for intestinal fortitude and determination. Once the formative work is begun and affected tissues are cleaned or removed, all doubts of success vanish. It is surprising and gratifying to discover the results which may be obtained."

The embalmer, having allowed an appropriate interval to elapse,   15 returns to the attack, but now he brings into play the skill and equipment of sculptor and cosmetician. Is a hand missing? Casting one in plaster of Paris is a simple matter. "For replacement purposes, only a cast of the back of the hand is necessary; this is within the ability of the average operator and is quite adequate." If a lip or two, a nose or an ear should be missing, the embalmer has at hand a variety of restorative waxes with which to model replacements. Pores and skin texture are simulated by stippling with a little brush, and over this cosmetics are laid on. Head off? Decapitation cases are rather routinely handled. Ragged edges are trimmed, and head joined to torso with a series of splints, wires and sutures. It is a good idea to have a little something at the neck—a scarf or high collar—when time for viewing comes. Swollen mouth? Cut out tissue as needed from inside the lips. If too much is removed, the surface contour can easily be restored by padding with cotton. Swollen necks and cheeks are reduced by removing tissue through vertical incisions made down each side of the neck. "When the deceased is casketed, the pillow will hide the suture incisions . . . as an extra precaution against leakage, the suture may be painted with liquid sealer."

The opposite condition is more likely to present itself—that of emaci-   16 ation. His hypodermic syringe now loaded with massage cream, the embalmer seeks out and fills the hollowed and sunken areas by injection. In this procedure the backs of the hands and fingers and the under-chin area should not be neglected.

Positioning the lips is a problem that recurrently challenges the inge-   17 nuity of the embalmer. Closed too tightly they tend to give a stern, even disapproving expression. Ideally, embalmers feel, the lips should give the impression of being every so slightly parted, the upper lip protruding slightly for a more youthful appearance. This takes some engineering, however, as the lips tend to drift apart. Lip drift can sometimes be remedied by pushing one or two straight pins through the inner margin of the lower lip and then inserting them between the two upper front teeth. If Mr. Jones happens to have no teeth, the pins can just as easily be anchored in his Armstrong Face Former and Denture Replacer. Another method to maintain lip closure is to dislocate the lower jaw, which is then held in its new position by a wire run through holes which have been drilled through the upper and lower jaws at the midline. As the French are fond of saying, *il faut soffrir pour être belle.*

If Mr. Jones has died of jaundice, the embalming fluid will very likely   18
turn him green. Does this deter the embalmer? Not if he has intestinal
fortitude. Masking pastes and cosmetics are heavily laid on, burial gar-
ments and casket interiors are color-correlated with particular care, and
Jones is displayed beneath rose-colored lights. Friends will say, "How *well*
he looks." Death by carbon monoxide, on the other hand, can be rather a
good thing from the embalmer's viewpoint: "One advantage is the fact that
this type of discoloration is an exaggerated form of a natural pink coloration." This is nice because the healthy glow is already present and needs
but little attention.

The patching and filling completed, Mr. Jones is now shaved, washed,   19
and dressed. Cream-based cosmetic, available in pink, flesh, suntan, bru-
nette, and blond, is applied to his hands and face, his hair is shampooed and
combed (and, in the case of Mrs. Jones, set), his hands manicured. For the
horny-handed son of toil special care must be taken; cream should be applied to remove ingrained grime, and the nails cleaned. "If he were not in
the habit of having them manicured in life, trimming and shaping is advised
for better appearance—never questioned by kin."

Jones is now ready for casketing (this is the present participle of the   20
verb "to casket"). In this operation his right shoulder should be depressed
slightly "to turn the body a bit to the right and soften the appearance of
lying flat on the back." Positioning the hands is a matter of importance, and
special rubber positioning blocks may be used. The hands should be cupped
slightly for a more lifelike, relaxed appearance. Proper placement of the
body requires a delicate sense of balance. It should lie as high as possible in
the casket, yet not so high that the lid, when lowered, will hit the nose. On
the other hand, we are cautioned, placing the body too low "creates the impression that the body is in a box."

Jones is next wheeled into the appointed slumber room where a few   21
last touches may be added—his favorite pipe placed in his hand or, if he was
a great reader, a book propped into position. (In the case of little Master
Jones a Teddy bear may be clutched.) Here he will hold open house for a
few days, visiting hours 10 A.M. to 9 P.M.

◆ ◆ ◆

FIRST RESPONSES

Have you ever been involved in planning a funeral? How rational was
your thinking at the time? Did you or anyone else question the suggestions
of the person "selling" the services? What was the family's reaction when
the bill came? How would you feel about pre-planning a funeral?

TAKING A CLOSER LOOK

Exploring *Who:* Voice and Tone

1. Clearly, Mitford is serious in her criticism of the practice of making a corpse "presentable for viewing in an attitude of healthy repose" (paragraph 14), but most people would not describe her tone as serious. Why not? What adjectives would you choose to describe Mitford's tone—that is, her attitude toward her topic?

2. Most readers find this piece quite funny, despite its grim subject matter. Point out several examples of humor and explain what makes it funny. For instance, in paragraph 18, Mitford observes that "Death by carbon monoxide, on the other hand, can be rather a good thing from the embalmer's viewpoint." That statement is humorous because of the abrupt contrast between what the reader expects and what the embalmer expects. Death by carbon monoxide is definitely not "rather a good thing" for most of us average readers.

Exploring *What:* Content and Meaning

1. Who was the "poor Yorick" alluded to at the begining of the second paragraph?

2. What does Mitford say is the purpose of embalming?

3. In paragraph 5, we are told that "All others, except apprentices, are excluded by law from the preparation room." Why do you think a law was passed preventing family members from being present while embalming takes place?

4. Did you learn more about embalming than you really wanted to know? Why do you think Mitford included so many gruesome details?

5. Explain this metaphor at the end of paragraph 6: "Let us part the formaldehyde curtain. . . ." What does it mean, and how does it function as a transition?

6. Mitford makes it clear that embalming is not required either by law or by religious doctrine. Why, then, do you think people continue to pay exorbitant prices for extravagant funerals that sometimes the family cannot even easily afford?

Exploring *Why:* Purpose

1. Why do you think Mitford wrote this piece? What was she hoping to accomplish?

2. What is her purpose in mentioning and quoting from textbooks like *The Principles and Practices of Embalming?*
3. Do you agree with Mitford when she says that "the secrecy surrounding embalming can, surely, hardly be attributed to the inherent gruesomeness of the subject" (paragraph 5)? What does Mitford think is the reason for the secrecy? Can you think of anything else that might account for this lack of knowledge by the public?
4. Did you find Mitford's satirical approach effective?

Exploring *How:* Style and Strategy

1. After a fairly long introduction, in which Mitford questions the whole practice of embalming, she begins an explanation of the process involved in preparing a body for public viewing. But several times she departs from her step-by-step account to provide relevant information. Explain why she includes the digression in paragraph 8, for instance.
2. Successful **satire** hinges largely on appropriate word choice. Comment on the effect Mitford achieves with these words and phrases: "whisked off" (paragraph 2); "sprayed, sliced, pierced, pickled, trussed, trimmed, creamed, waxed, painted, rouged, and neatly dressed" (paragraph 2); "a suitably costly container" (paragraph 2); "blissfully ignorant" (paragraph 4); "to have at Mr. Jones" (paragraph 13); "returns to the attack" (paragraph 15); "head off?" (paragraph 15); "the patching and filling completed" (paragraph 19).
3. Besides the usual transitional words used in process writing *(first, to return to, the next step is, is now, next),* Mitford uses several rhetorical questions. Find three of these questions and explain how they function.
4. In paragraph 14, Mitford quotes textbook author J. Sheridan Mayer as saying, "This is the time for intestinal fortitude and determination." In paragraph 18, she repeats his "intestinal fortitude" phrase. What does she achieve with this echo?
5. How does Mitford subtly echo her introduction in her conclusion? Comment on her verbal strategies in the final paragraph. In other words, how does her word choice make the ending effective?

IDEAS FOR WRITING A PROCESS ANALYSIS

1. With a group of classmates, discuss some social ritual that can make people uncomfortable—like family reunions, holiday dinners, or class reunions. Jot down details as they come to you during this brain-

storming session. Then organize your ideas chronologically, and write a satire similar to Jessica Mitford's, in which you criticize or make fun of the process people typically are expected to go through on these occasions.

2. ■▯ *Using the Internet.* Mitford's essay was influential in modifying the business practices of the funeral industry and in prompting alternative funeral plans. Locate the Web site of the Funeral and Memorial Societies of America (http://www.funerals.org/ famsa/) for information about burial societies. Then write an account of the process you might go through today if you were using the help of a burial society to plan the funeral of Mr. Jones.

3. Think of a modern custom or practice that you approve of. Write an essay in which you analyze the way the custom or practice proceeds. Following Mitford's model, explain the process clearly while conveying your attitude toward it at the same time.

◆ ◆ ◆ PREPARING TO READ

How do you feel when you receive a letter? Does anyone regularly write to you? To whom do you write, and why? Do you send your letters through cyberspace, or do you use "snail mail"?

◆ ◆ ◆

How to Write a Personal Letter

GARRISON KEILLOR

Garrison Keillor, host of *A Prairie Home Companion* on National Public Radio, is famous for his spoken essays reporting on the "News from Lake Wobegon," a make-believe Minnesota town where "all the men are strong, all the women are good-looking, and all the children are above average." Listeners are delighted by the charming quirkiness of the everyday lives of Lake Wobegon's citizens. In the following essay, reprinted from his book, *We Are Still Married* (1989), Keillor gives advice and encouragement to letter writers in the same warm, neighborly voice that characterizes his popular radio show.

We shy persons need to write a letter now and then, or else we'll dry   1
up and blow away. It's true. And I speak as one who loves to reach for the phone, dial the number, and talk. The telephone is to shyness what Hawaii is to February; it's a way out of the woods. *And yet:* a letter is better.

Such a sweet gift—a piece of handmade writing, in an envelope that is   2
not a bill, sitting in our friend's path when she trudges home from a long day spent among wahoos and savages, a day our words will help repair. They don't need to be immortal, just sincere. She can read them twice and again tomorrow: *You're someone I care about, Corinne, and think of often, and every time I do, you make me smile.*

We need to write; otherwise nobody will know who we are. They will   3
have only a vague impression of us as A Nice Person, because, frankly, we don't shine at conversation, we lack the confidence to thrust our faces forward and say, "Hi, I'm Heather Hooten; let me tell you about my week." Mostly we say "Uh-huh" and "Oh really." People smile and look over our shoulder, looking for someone else to meet.

So a shy person sits down and writes a letter. To be known by another   4
person—to meet and talk freely on the page—to be close despite distance.

To escape from anonymity and be our own sweet selves and express the music of our souls.

Same thing that moves a giant rock star to sing his heart out in front of 123,000 people moves us to take ballpoint in hand and write a few lines to our dear Aunt Eleanor. *We want to be known.* We want her to know that we have fallen in love, that we quit our job, that we're moving to New York, and we want to say a few things that might not get said in casual conversation: *Thank you for what you've meant to me. I am very happy right now.* 5

The first step in writing letters is to get over the guilt of *not* writing. You don't "owe" anybody a letter. Letters are a gift. The burning shame you feel when you see unanswered mail makes it harder to pick up a pen and makes for a cheerless letter when you finally do. *I feel bad about not writing, but I've been so busy,* etc. Skip this. Few letters are obligatory, and they are *Thanks for the wonderful gift* and *I am terribly sorry to hear about George's death* and *Yes, you're welcome to stay with us next month.* Write these promptly if you want to keep your friends. Don't worry about the others, except love letters, of course. When your true love writes *Dear Light of My Life, Joy of My Heart, O Lovely Pulsating Core of My Sensate Life,* some response is called for. 6

Some of the best letters are tossed off in a burst of inspiration, so keep your writing stuff in one place where you can sit down for a few minutes and—*Dear Roy, I am in the middle of an essay but thought I'd drop you a line. Hi to your sweetie too*—dash off a note to a pal. Envelopes, stamps, address book, everything in a drawer so you can write fast when the pen is hot. 7

A blank white 8″ × 11″ sheet can look as big as Montana if the pen's not so hot—try a smaller page and write boldly. Get a pen that makes a sensuous line, get a comfortable typewriter, a friendly word processor—whichever feels easy to the hand. 8

Sit for a few minutes with the blank sheet of paper in front of you, and meditate on the person you will write to, let your friend come to mind until you can almost see her or him in the room with you. Remember the last time you saw each other and how your friend looked and what you said and what perhaps was unsaid between you, and when your friend becomes real to you, start to write. 9

Write the salutation—*Dear You*—and take a deep breath and plunge in. A simple declarative sentence will do, followed by another and another. Tell us what you're doing and tell it like you were talking to us. Don't think about grammar, don't think about style, don't try to write dramatically, just give us your news. Where did you go, who did you see, what did they say, what do you think? 10

If you don't know where to begin, start with the present: *I'm sitting at*   11
the kitchen table on a rainy Saturday morning. Everyone is gone and the
house is quiet. Let your simple description of the present moment lead to
something else; let the letter drift gently along.

The toughest letter to crank out is one that is meant to impress, as we   12
all know from writing job applications; if it's hard work to slip off a letter to
a friend, maybe you're trying too hard to be terrific. A letter is only a report
to someone who already likes you for reasons other than your brilliance.
Take it easy.

Don't worry about form. It's not a term paper. When you come to the   13
end of one episode, just start a new paragraph. You can go from a few lines
about the sad state of pro football to the fight with your mother to your
fond memories of Mexico to your cat's urinary-tract infection to a few
thoughts on personal indebtedness and on to the kitchen sink and what's in
it. The more you write, the easier it gets, and when you have a True True
Friend to write to, a *compadre,* a soul sibling, then it's like driving a car; you
just press on the gas.

Don't tear up the page and start over when you write a bad line—try   14
to write your way out of it. Make mistakes and plunge on. Let the letter
cook along and let yourself be bold. Outrage, confusion, love—whatever is
in your mind, let it find a way to the page. Writing is a means of discovery, always, and when you come to the end and write *Yours ever* or *Hugs and
Kisses,* you'll know something you didn't when you wrote *Dear Pal.*

Probably your friend will put your letter away, and it'll be read again a   15
few years from now—and it will improve with age. And forty years from
now, your friend's grandkids will dig it out of the attic and read it, a sweet
and precious relic of the ancient Eighties that gives them a sudden clear
glimpse of you and her and the world we old-timers knew. You will have
then created an object of art. Your simple lines about where you went, who
you saw, what they said, will speak to those children, and they will feel in
their hearts the humanity of our times.

You can't pick up a phone and call the future and tell them about our   16
times. You have to pick up a piece of paper.

FIRST RESPONSES

After reading Keillor's essay, are you encouraged to write a letter
to a friend or loved one instead of making a phone call? Explain why or
why not.

TAKING A CLOSER LOOK

Exploring *Who:* Voice and Tone

1. In his opening sentence, Keillor adopts the persona (the voice and characteristics) of a shy person. What does he achieve by assuming that role?
2. What three adjectives would you choose to best describe his tone?
3. Did you feel included in Keillor's audience? Explain why or why not.
4. Does this writing style strike you as formal or informal? Point out words and phrases that influenced your decision. Why do you think Keillor made this choice about level of formality?

Exploring *What:* Content and Meaning

1. *Using the Internet.* Why does Keillor think we should write letters instead of just make phone calls? Do you think he would consider an e-mail message as valuable as a letter written on paper? Take a look at the Web site called A Beginner's Guide to Effective E-mail (http://enterprise.powerup.com.au/htmlxp/pu/emailhow.htm), and compare the suggestions there with Keillor's. Do you find any common ground?
2. What does Keillor suggest are the main problems people have in getting around to writing letters? Do you think that perhaps e-mail would help avoid some of these problems?
3. After telling his readers in paragraph 6 that "Few letters are obligatory," Keillor names three kinds that are. What are they? Have you ever written any of these kinds of letters? If so, which kind was the hardest to write?
4. In general, his advice in paragraphs 8 through 14 applies to the kind of writing you are doing in this class. But, if you were going to revise that section as instruction to help a classmate, what would you change or leave out—besides the *Dear Pal* and the *Hugs and Kisses* parts? What two important steps would you need to add at the end to keep your classmate from flunking the course?

Exploring *Why:* Purpose

1. What would you say is Keillor's main point in this essay?
2. Why do you think Keillor cares whether people write letters or not?

3. Do you think his strategy of addressing himself primarily to shy people was a wise choice, given his purpose?

4. If you are not a shy person, did you find the essay convincing?

Exploring *How:* Style and Strategy

1. Keillor mentions several fictitious persons in this essay *(Corinne, Heather Hooten, our dear Aunt Eleanor).* What does he achieve with this strategy?

2. Make a brief list of Keillor's pieces of advice. What is the reasoning behind the order he uses? Explain how this organization suits his purpose.

3. What is the purpose of the lines and phrases printed in italics? Were you confused by them or do you think this was a clever strategy?

4. Locate five sentences of six words or fewer, and explain what Keillor achieves with each one.

IDEAS FOR WRITING A PROCESS ANALYSIS

1. In the reading, Keillor advocates writing a letter, even when a phone call is possible. Write an essay in which you promote doing something in the old-fashioned way even though new ways are available. Think about writing by hand rather than on a word processor, baking bread, sewing clothes, building furniture, doing math without a calculator, walking to work, mowing the lawn, raking the leaves, or rowing your boat using only person-power.

2. Try writing a letter to a friend, using Keillor's advice if you want. At the same time, take notes on how you go about performing the task. Record the thoughts and feelings that you experience along the way as well as the techniques you use. Then write an essay recounting the process of writing the letter. Put direct quotations from the letter in italics to illustrate your points.

3. Keillor asserts that "writing is a means of discovery" (paragraph 14). Write an essay about a piece of writing you once did (or tried to do) that led you to an unexpected discovery. The discovery could be about yourself, about the writing process, about the subject matter, about the intended audience, about the assignment, or about a combination of things.

◆ ◆ ◆ PREPARING TO READ

Did you ever suffer a small, deep burn or a serious sunburn? Can you still remember how it felt? Can you, then, imagine the pain involved in an extensive third-degree burn in which the flesh is cooked?

◆ ◆ ◆

To Hell and Back

LEON JAROFF

Prominent science writer Leon Jaroff (b. 1927) founded *Discover* magazine in 1980. He is presently science editor of *Time* magazine and has received a number of awards for his scientific reporting. The following article explains the process that teams of specialists follow in treating burn patients; it first appeared in a special supplement to *Time* magazine (Fall, 1997).

It happens in an instant, but the scars and psychological damage can last a lifetime. An inquisitive child pulls at the handle of a pot on the stove and is scalded by a cascade of boiling water. A smoker falls asleep with a lighted cigarette and is badly burned when the bedding catches fire. An eruption of caustic chemicals engulfs a worker, eating away skin and flesh. A blast of superheated air burns a fire fighter's face and damages his lungs. 1

Some 1.25 million Americans suffer burns every year. Most of them quickly recover, both physically and mentally, with permanent damage limited to a small scar or two. But more than 50,000 burn victims require hospitalization annually, and 5,000 die of their injuries. 2

For the more severely burned, life hangs in the balance as they fight to survive the loss of large portions of the skin's protective covering, which keeps body temperature normal and internal organs properly hydrated. Many of the survivors continue to suffer psychologically, not only from varying degrees of disfigurement but also from frightening and debilitating flashbacks of their ordeal. 3

To deal with the many consequences of severe burns, a growing number of major hospitals have established burn centers, staffed by the medical equivalent of police SWAT teams, that accommodate every need of critically injured burn victims. America's busiest burn unit is at Manhattan's New York Hospital-Cornell Medical Center and consists of some 100 doctors, nurses, therapists, social workers and dieticians who treat 1,300 patients a 4 year in the unit's 46-bed facility. "The name of the game in burns is team-work," says Dr. Roger Yurt, the unit's director since 1995.

Yurt, 52, began specializing in burn treatment while he was a doctor in 5
the U.S. Army. Since he took over the burn unit, he has expanded the team
to include highly specialized nurses and even a chaplain, who ministers not
only to patients and their families but also to staff members, who are exposed daily to unnerving sights and suffering.

A few team members are particularly motivated by the fact that they 6
too were once burn victims. Others, like Dr. Harvey Himel, a plastic surgeon
on the team, are attracted by a long-term association with the patients. "It's
the real partnership with the patients that I treasure," Himel says. "I always
feel that I'm connecting with them." That connection can last for years.
Himel follows his patients from their most desperate moments immediately after a burn, through skin grafts, follow-up visits and sometimes through
reconstructive and cosmetic surgery.

The New York burn specialists and their patients are benefiting from 7
some remarkable recent advances in operating-room techniques and a
more sophisticated understanding of how the body reacts to severe burns.
"Patients who 20 or 30 years ago would have died now survive the injury,"
says Lisa Staiano-Coico, dean of research at Cornell University Medical
College and the team's wound-healing specialist. "Now the issue becomes
one of how do we ameliorate the burn wound, how do we improve the rate
of healing with less scarring. Now it's gone beyond survival."

As recently as the 1970s, a middle-aged patient with 40% of his body 8
burned had a 1-in-2 chance of survival if his respiratory system had escaped
damage. Today someone who has as much as 70% of his body burned can
expect the same odds. And the average hospital stay for a severely burned
patient is considerably less than the old rule of thumb, which was one day
for every 1% of the body burned.

First-degree burns, which are the least dangerous because they in- 9
volve only the outer, epidermal, layer of the skin, usually do not require
hospitalization. Thin as a sheet of paper, the epidermis consists of about five
layers of cells. The cells in the deepest layers constantly reproduce, pushing
older layers to the surface, where they slough off after two weeks or so. Thus
while first-degree burns appear red and swollen and are painful to the
touch, they usually heal on their own.

Second- and third-degree burns, the kind treated by the New York 10
team, call for much more care and, often, extended hospital stays. Penetrating
below the epidermis, second-degree burns reach into the upper layer of the
dermis, a thin layer of cells 1 to 3 mm thick that contains blood vessels, nerves,
hair follicles and sweat glands. This upper portion can slowly regenerate and

heal if damaged. But if the burn is third degree and destroys the dermis down to fat and muscle, skin grafts are needed for effective healing.

When the skin suffers a deep third-degree burn, two major regulatory 11 systems go awry. The body loses its ability to control its temperature, causing burn patients to shiver even in temperatures as high as 75° F. Consequently, burn-unit rooms are often kept around 90° F, and a burn team's first priority is to warm the patients with heated fluids or heat shields suspended above the patient's bed.

Another major concern is the loss of fluid. When deep burns cover a 12 large area of the body and the skin no longer provides an effective barrier against infection, the immune system goes into overdrive to ward off invading germs. It floods the injured areas with blood and plasma carrying immune cells, which cause extensive inflammation and swelling. In some cases the swelling is severe enough to interfere with breathing, and the patient must be put on a ventilator.

The massive immune response can also cause fluid to leak from blood 13 vessels throughout the body. This leads not only to dehydration and deterioration of vital organs but also to a dangerous drop in blood pressure, which can result in shock. Indeed, many patients admitted to burn units are already in shock and unable to feel the pain that would be overwhelming if they were conscious.

Even when a patient is conscious, though, the burn team must focus 14 first not on painkillers but on stabilizing the blood pressure. The New York team accomplishes this by pumping as much as 8 gal. of a salt fluid into his veins in the first 24 hours of treatment, a process that can cause the patient temporarily to gain as much as 60 lbs.

"There is clearly a period at least early on where patients are not 15 getting any type of pain relief," explains director Yurt. "It's too risky. You don't want to give them too much morphine. Otherwise they'll drop their blood pressure." Once the blood pressure stabilizes, however, doctors can begin dripping morphine directly into the veins, gradually increasing the dosage if the pain persists. Still, Yurt admits, "we can never relieve the pain completely."

The need to balance these concerns when both time and care are crit- 16 ical was evident to *Time* reporter Alice Park, who observed members of the New York Hospital-Cornell burn team as they attended a 26-year-old woman who had been terribly burned on her face and upper torso by acid thrown on her by her male companion's former girlfriend:

7:47 A.M. After the nurses gently unwind the temporary loose gauze 17 twined around her head, neck and chest, the woman is anesthetized, a breathing tube is placed in her mouth, and her temperature and blood pressure are monitored. While surgeon Alain Polynice finds her blood pressure to be within normal bounds, he notes that her temperature is slightly lower than desired, calls engineering to ask that the room temperature be raised. Then he places a bubbled heat blanket between her legs.

8:10 A.M. The surgical assistant begins washing the woman's left leg   18
with a soapy solution, sterilizing it so that swatches of it can later be peeled away to graft onto her chest and neck.

8:14 A.M. Himel snaps some pictures of the patient's chest and the   19
right side of her face. He is especially concerned about the patient's nose and right ear. "It's likely that she will lose that ear and have to have another one constructed for her next spring," he says.

8:25 A.M. Using an instrument resembling a vegetable peeler, Himel   20
begins peeling back the hardened, white, dead skin on the woman's burned chest. "I know I've reached healthy skin if there's bleeding," he says. After a few thin layers have been removed, blood begins to ooze. While Polynice mops it up, Himel continues to peel away at dead skin until he reaches the fat and muscle layer underneath.

8:43 A.M. "The skin has been so damaged by the acid that it's lique-   21
fied," says Himel. It begins to stick to the razor-sharp peeler, which he wipes repeatedly to keep it clean.

8:50 A.M. Himel has moved his attention from the woman's chest to   22
her neck and discovers that the acid has burned all the way through the dermis on the right side. He carefully slices away the damaged tissue.

9:40 A.M. Having removed all the dead skin from the chest and neck,   23
Himel holds the patient's left thigh taut while the surgical assistant uses an electric-powered device to peel away two foot-long strips of the epidermis and the upper part of the dermis from the woman's left leg.

9:50 A.M. As the surgical assistant uses a razor to make tiny pinpricks   24
along the entire length of each skin strip, Himel explains, "Pinpricks will allow the fluids and blood to seep out and any bacterial growth to leave the wound bed."

9:53 A.M. Displaying jigsaw-puzzle finesse, Himel and Polynice   25
arrange and rearrange the strips over the patient's neck and chest, trying for a placement that will leave as few visible seams as possible. Finally they decide on two strips laid lengthwise, beginning under her chin and ending at the base of her neck.

9:57 A.M. Polynice begins stapling the grafts to the adjoining healthy   26
skin. In tricky areas, he resorts to tiny steel clips that he squeezes closed with surgical forceps.

10:10 A.M. Himel decides he wants to graft two separate pieces of skin   27
onto the woman's chest so that they meet in a seam between the breasts. He is concerned that a single band of skin might contract when it heals.

Needing more skin, he measures for it by placing a piece of gauze over the remaining uncovered area.

10:30 A.M. Using skin sections taken from the patient's inner thigh, 28 Himel deftly sutures the pieces together on her chest.

10:35 A.M. The surgical assistant places wound dressings over the 29 donor sites on the thigh, which should heal enough in two weeks to provide additional donor skin if needed.

10:50 A.M. Winding down the procedure, Himel injects a saline solu- 30 tion under the skin grafts to irrigate the wounds before nurses cover them with an antibiotic and a gauze dressing. He takes his final photos of the grafted areas, which are now neatly covered with skin lined by shiny staples.

10:52 A.M. Himel wants no head movement that could retard healing, 31 so two physical therapists arrive, dip a large, heat-sensitive plastic sheet into a warm fluid to make it flexible, place it on the woman's chest and begin to cut and mold it to her chin.

11:07 A.M. The therapists wrap the woman's chest, first in gauze, then 32 in an Ace bandage.

11:20 A.M. Removing the breathing tube, the anesthesiologist awakens 33 the woman, who clenches her fists, moans and begins to shiver. The nurses cover her with a prewarmed blanket while Himel makes a note to the intensive-care staff, stressing that he does not want her blood pressure to exceed 130 systolic. If it did, she might bleed through her sutures.

11:27 A.M. More than 3½ hours after entering the operating room, the 34 woman is wheeled out to the intensive-care unit to begin what will likely be more than a year of recovery and additional surgery.

Because the patient's acid burns, while severe, were confined to her 35 face, neck and chest, skin taken from elsewhere on her body could be used for grafts. "Most people still get their own skin grafts because it's what your body accepts most readily," says Himel. But for many patients with more widespread damage, the healthy skin that remains is insufficient to cover their wounds. For those patients, New York Hospital maintains a skin bank, which provides its burn team with a large store of frozen cadaver skin. Unlike the patient's own skin, cadaver skin is soon rejected by the immune system, which recognizes it as foreign. But it survives long enough to protect the wound from bacteria and viruses while stimulating the patient's own skin to grow.

The skin bank owes its success to hospitals throughout New York 36 State that call the New York Hospital-Cornell burn team whenever they receive consent to release a newly deceased cadaver. Nancy Gallo, director of the bank, immediately dispatches a pair of assistants to the calling hospital and books an operating room, where the assistants take blood from the body for later tests for infectious diseases, then peel away skin from the back, chest and legs of the cadaver. Keeping the skin iced and in a sterile jar, they race it back to New York Hospital where, frozen in liquid nitrogen, it can keep for as long as five years. But before it can be judged suitable and released for grafting, two months of testing are required.

Still, skin banks are sometimes depleted, and the New York burn   37 team, like other burn units, is turning more and more to substitutes for cadaver skin. Cornell's Staiano-Coico was part of the first research team to report success with grafts grown in culture from bits of cadaver skin, and describes them as "biological Band-Aids to provide growth factors to the wound to help increase the healing process." Other groups have used skin taken from raised blisters on unrelated, live donors and cultured into sheets in the laboratory. In both procedures, only the patient's cells remain in the healed wound after about two weeks.

Commercial skin substitutes for both the epidermis and dermis are   38 also becoming widely available. One epidermal substitute is made of silicone, whereas the dermal varieties can consist of nylon or of collagen taken from cows, pigs or cadavers. Explains Staiano-Coico: "A lot of the dermal substitutes are like scaffolds, so the body can come in and use that matrix to rebuild its own dermis." Eventually, as healing takes place, the artificial structures are absorbed or surgically removed.

The New York burn team abounds with other specialists. Within a day   39 after surgery, a physical therapist visits a burn patient to see whether the injury has affected the fingers, knees, ankles or other joints. If it has, the therapist begins guiding the patient through some simple daily exercises that involve working the joints to prevent natural shrinkage and the resulting loss of flexibility that can occur as the body heals.

Another team member, Joyce Scheimberg, is one of the few social   40 workers to be found in any hospital trauma unit. Yet her presence makes good sense. Since house fires are the most common cause of burns in the U.S., many victims have lost their homes and most of their belongings. Other family members may also have been injured in the blaze. "Everyone who comes in here is an emergency situation," says Scheimberg, who acts as the liaison between the patient and his family, the hospital staff, insurance companies, lawyers, emergency community services and other pertinent agencies. In her role, Scheimberg is all too aware that the burn victim may not recover—or at least may not recover enough to return to the job. "You don't know what the future will bring," she says, "but we at the burn unit are all eternal optimists."

That optimism pervades the New York Hospital-Cornell Medical   41 Center burn unit, and more often than not, it is justified by the sight of recovered burn patients ready once more to lead normal lives.

◆ ◆ ◆

FIRST RESPONSES

Were you put off by the grisly and graphic descriptions in this article? If not, why do you think you weren't shocked?

TAKING A CLOSER LOOK

Exploring *Who:* Voice and Tone

1. Does the writer seem emotionally involved in the material being presented?
2. Can you come up with a word to describe Jaroff's tone—his attitude toward his subject matter?
3. Why are the surgeons allowed to speak in their own words—in direct quotations?
4. Does the writer try to involve you emotionally in the material? What about the opening paragraph? Is its tone different from the rest of the essay?

Exploring *What:* Content and Meaning

1. Jaroff defines three different degrees of burns. Name these and explain what happens to the body in each one.
2. Why is it necessary to withhold morphine, even from seriously burned patients?
3. Why do surgeons prick the harvested skin before grafting it over the burn?
4. What is a skin bank? Describe what happens to the cadaver skin and other "dermal substitutes" after grafting.
5. Why are members of the burn unit "eternal optimists"? Do you think this attitude helps them in their work?

Exploring *Why:* Purpose

1. What is the purpose of introducing the readers to Dr. Yurt and other team members in the second, third, and fourth paragraphs?
2. Why does Jaroff include definitions of the three types of burns and their effects on the body?

3. What does he achieve by providing a step-by-step account of the process of treating a specific patient in the operating room? Why is the exact time of day included for each step of the procedure?

4. Jaroff carefully provides enough transitions so that we can easily follow his often technical explanations. At the very end of the article, look at the transition between paragraphs 39 and 40, and explain how it functions.

Exploring *How:* Style and Strategy

1. In writings of this length, the thesis won't necessarily be stated in the first paragraph. Reread the opening paragraphs until you come to a statement of the main idea of the article. What is the paragraph number? Where within that paragraph is the thesis placed?

2. What is Jaroff's strategy in the opening paragraph? How does he go about catching your interest?

3. If you were reading an account of these same medical advances in the *Journal of the American Medical Association,* you would probably have great difficulty understanding it. How does Jaroff make sure his material won't go over your head?

4. Even though he's dealing with technical material, Jaroff employs several imaginative figures of speech: *burn centers, staffed by the medical equivalent of police* SWAT *teams* (paragraph 4); *razor-sharp peeler* (paragraph 21); *jigsaw-puzzle finesse* (paragraph 25); *biological Band-Aids* (paragraph 37). Explain how these phrases, in context, help clarify what is being described.

IDEAS FOR WRITING A PROCESS ANALYSIS

1. Think of some familiar process that involves a schedule for which you can assign a time to move from one step to the next. These times don't need to be as exact as those Jaroff supplies for the operating room procedure, but they can be if you follow a precise schedule. Consider explaining your exercise routine, for instance, or your daily study schedule; or you could describe how you shower and shave in the morning, or how you give yourself a manicure. Model your account on paragraphs 17 through 34 of Jaroff's article.

2. ■ *Using the Internet.* Locate information about first aid for burn victims. You might consult Active First Aid Online (http://www. parasolemt.com.au/afa/) or the Mayo Clinic Health Oasis (http://www. mayohealth.org/mayo/library/htm/firstaid.htm). Using the information

that you find, write a three-part essay explaining how to give first aid to a victim of first-degree burns, of second-degree burns, and of third-degree burns.

3. Think about and record the feelings you experienced after a particularly striking event or discovery—a death, news of a pregnancy, an unexpectedly failed exam, a revealed secret. Then write an essay explaining the sequence of those emotions and how you felt afterward.

◆ ◆ ◆ PREPARING TO READ

Have you ever visited a nursing home—what used to be called an "old folks home"? What kind of place was it? How did you feel about being there?

◆ ◆ ◆

The Alzheimer's Strain: How to Accommodate Too Many Patients

MALCOLM GLADWELL

Malcolm Gladwell, who has a talent for making difficult concepts both interesting and understandable in crisp, graceful prose, publishes articles in numerous national magazines. The essay reprinted here first appeared in *The New Yorker* in October 1997.

Alzheimer's patients cannot sit still. This is one of the facts that make   1
caring for them so difficult. A normal, healthy adult can be fully entertained watching television, reading a book, or holding a conversation, but for someone who no longer has the ability to absorb the meaning of words and images stillness represents a kind of prison. So people with Alzheimer's tend to wander. They walk along the walls of houses and nursing homes, in an abstracted, ceaseless, and sometimes obsessive attempt to escape from their deprivation. They wander up stairs and through doors and down hallways and into the rooms of others, rummaging through drawers and closets, randomly opening and closing cabinets, looking for things they cannot articulate and may never find. When some dementia specialists at Presbyterian SeniorCare, a nonprofit long-term-care group in Western Pennsylvania, set out several years ago to design the ideal Alzheimer's facility, then, their first goal was to create a safe, familiar environment in which residents could move around.

The wandering problem, prosaic though it sounds, is one of the hard-   2
est new questions facing the American health-care system. About half of the million six hundred thousand Americans in nursing homes today suffer from Alzheimer's or other forms of dementia. Most of those homes, however, are designed for people who are physically impaired and mentally

healthy, not physically healthy and mentally impaired. For years, nursing homes coped with this mismatch by simply tying down their Alzheimer's patients, strapping them to their beds or wheelchairs to keep them from roaming. Or they employed what are euphemistically referred to as "chemical restraints," because following the wanderers around to make sure they didn't head out into the street or trip and fall or walk into someone else's room was too much trouble. These methods were not particularly humane. Nor did they make much financial sense, since the patients who do not get exercise end up sicker, and cost more in the long run, than those who are allowed to walk around. Since nursing-home care now costs about sixty billion dollars a year—and within twenty years will cost more than double that—these considerations are far from trivial. Barring a medical miracle, in fact, by the middle of the next century there will be as many Americans with Alzheimer's as currently reside in the state of Pennsylvania.

Solving the wandering problem is surprisingly difficult, however. The SeniorCare group, for example, didn't want to build what their architect, David Hoglund, refers to as a "psychiatric racetrack"—a building that would channel all wandering into a purposeless monitored loop. They wanted to create a space that allowed for movement with meaning, that allowed patients to explore and then—just as important—allowed them to find their way home again. At the same time, the SeniorCare group couldn't just create a meandering walkway lined with gadgets and pictures and bright colors to grab and hold the wanderers' attention, because the paradox of Alzheimer's is that the very stimulation its victims seek is the one thing they cannot handle.

Alzheimer's represents human development in reverse. It is what happens when a disease implacably unravels a lifetime of neurological connections, beginning with those which govern higher cognitive functions and then steadily moving backward along the developmental path, until all that are left are the most basic and primal of emotions and instincts. Memory goes first, then comprehension and language. Those are the obvious signs of dementia. What goes at the same time, though, is the ability to sort and arrange and choose from all the information that the human environment presents. Most people can stand in the middle of a crowded cocktail party, focus intently on the conversation in front of them, and screen out all the other words in the room. A person with Alzheimer's cannot do that. No information is privileged. Everything counts. New faces startle. Large crowds become intimidating. Paranoia and hostility are commonplace. An Alzheimer's ward in a traditional nursing home is full of shouts and cries and screams, the sounds of fright and breakdown. People with Alzheimer's often say that what they are looking for in their relentless searches is "home," by which they mean a place of familiarity and certainty. They are driven to explore, but what they find often terrifies them. The ideal environment for an Alzheimer's patient, the Pittsburgh team realized, must engage but not overwhelm.

There were other requirements as well. In fact, the list was so long, and   5
so many of its requirements were contradictory, that the task seemed almost impossible. The home had to be flexible, because the second of the many paradoxes of Alzheimer's is that as the disease strips people of their identity it makes them more individualistic. "We've got people who get up every morning at two," Beth L. Deely, the director of Alzheimer's programs for Presbyterian SeniorCare, told me. "We have people who sleep for twenty-four hours, then are awake for forty-eight. We've got one gentleman who consumes most of his food after nine at night." One of the reasons for heavily medicating people with Alzheimer's is to impose a regimen on them, but if the Pittsburgh team wasn't going to use any restraints then it had to fashion a facility that could respond to all the patients' idiosyncrasies at once. And it couldn't look like a traditional nursing home or hospital, because there are few things that frighten and agitate someone in full cognitive retreat as much as hospitals do. To someone with Alzheimer's, a nurse's voice on an intercom is a terrifying disembodied presence; a long, straight hallway is a navigational impossibility; a white coat might be a subconscious trigger of a lifetime of medical crises. The perfect home had to be flexible, and it couldn't look like an institution. In short, it had to be better than a traditional nursing home. Yet—and this went without saying—if it wasn't also cheaper than a traditional nursing home it would be forgotten the minute it was built.

Several years ago, after exhaustive planning, Presbyterian SeniorCare   6
opened Woodside Place, in the Pittsburgh suburb of Oakmont. Within a year, it won five architectural awards. It has been studied by architects and long-term-care experts from around the world, and it is credited with sparking an entirely new movement in nursing-home design. Recently, a group of researchers from the University of Pittsburgh and Carnegie Mellon University completed a three-year study of Woodside and concluded that the residents there have a slower rate of deterioration than residents at traditional nursing homes, that they stay physically active longer, that they spend three times as much time socializing with other residents, that their families visit more often, and, to top it off, that the costs of caring for them run somewhere around twenty per cent *less* than normal. "It is clear," the researchers' report noted, "that Woodside Place serves a population that was not well served before."

The complex sits on a small wooded lot, behind a larger nursing home,   7
on Presbyterian SeniorCare's Oakmont campus. It is patterned after a traditional Pennsylvanian Shaker village. There are three high-roofed, gray-shingled houses, all linked to a large main building and surrounded by a

white picket fence. Each house has ten bedrooms, with private bathrooms, off a central hallway; a kitchen; and a courtyard. The main building has a series of public rooms—a music room, a television room, a meeting hall—surrounded by a corridor lined with big picture windows. The buildings are mostly carpeted, and are painted in soothing greens, blues, and pinks. There are quilts on the walls and the furniture is solid and old-fashioned. On the day that I visited, some of the residents were bowling in the hallways, a man was taking an art class in one of the kitchens, and other residents were sitting in deck chairs along the main corridor, looking out the windows.

Woodside Place has only thirty-six beds. "We didn't want a Texas-size   8
facility," Beth Deely said. After all, if Woodside was going to be comforting and nonthreatening, it couldn't be large, and this was the smallest number of residential units that could be maintained economically. Separating the residents into three houses of twelve each was an attempt to make Woodside seem smaller still. Among the last faculties to desert a person with Alzheimer's are the sense of smell and the ability to recognize and draw comfort from familiar faces, and both those facts drove the design of the individual houses. They aren't served by a central nurse's station, for example, as they would be in a typical nursing home. Each house always has a staff member on duty, who provides a soothing anchor. And the staff members don't work in an office—which would, of course, seem out of place in an institution striving to feel like a home—but in the kitchens, which are wide open on the sides, so cooking smells can circulate through the house. "We tried to integrate the staff into the house," David Hoglund said. "The kitchen is hearth and home." Moreover, separate kitchens enable the staff to be far more flexible. Originally, the idea had been to bring food to Woodside Place from the large central kitchens in the neighboring nursing home. That would have been cheaper, but it would have meant that all meals had to be provided on a schedule, which is fine for normal adults but not for Alzheimer's patients. The individual kitchens allow the staff to serve meals around the clock. "We have some people who have five or six breakfasts before lunch," Deely said. "We're not going to say 'Don't you remember you just had breakfast?' That's when people with Alzheimer's get frustrated. We don't have that regimental mind-set."

For the wanderers, the corridor around the main building leads past the   9
front entrance (which is locked to residents) and toward two large glass doors opening onto the fenced-in garden. There are a number of walkways in the garden, and all of them are circular, so the wanderer never has to face the anxiety of coming to a dead end. The idea of lining the interior corridor with floor-to-ceiling windows was controversial, because some felt that opening the building up to the outside would provide too much stimulus. But Hoglund thought it worth the risk. Plus, he took steps to control what the

residents would see. "You've got to watch what you plant," he says. "If a tree or a shrub gets too big, or its cone gets shaped like an evergreen's, it sways in the wind and looks like a person." The windows also create shadows in the evening, which is a problem. "The residents misperceive them," Deely told me. "They think people are out to get them." There is a recessed light along the inside edge of the corridor ceiling which eliminates most of the shadows, but not all of them. Deely says it's a trade-off, because the windows allow for precisely the kind of stimulation that the residents crave. "In the spring, we have an Easter-egg hunt in the garden, and kids come in and run all over," she said. "The residents love it. They gather at the windows to watch."

That kind of balance between familiarity and stimulation is in evidence all over the building. The hallways leading from the houses to the main building, for example, have floors of blue ceramic tiles decorated with a muted-red geometric pattern. Why tiles? Because the other hallways are carpeted, so the sudden change from carpet to tile provides a welcome moment of novelty, and also a subtle auditory cue telling the wanderers that they have arrived in a public area. Why the pattern? Because a plain tile would look institutional. But why muted red? "We didn't want a profound color change, because people might think that the pattern was an object, and try to pick it up. Or they might think it's a hole in the floor," Deely said as she mimed an elderly patient stepping gingerly to avoid each pattern. "That might make it very difficult to walk there." 10

Woodside is by no means perfect. Hoglund concedes that he made plenty of mistakes—mostly because the facility was the first of its kind—and he has tried to correct them in subsequent designs. He regrets, for example, having put the main doorway in full sight of the bank of corridor windows. The residents are drawn to it when they see visitors coming into the building, and they approach the door and try to get out, only to find that they can't. It's an unfortunate source of frustration. He also thinks that he should have differentiated the three houses more clearly. Alzheimer's patients need a lot of help finding their way back to their own rooms, and the color differences between the houses are too subtle to serve as a guide. What tends to happen is that a resident knows where his room is, relative to the other rooms off his hallway, but he goes to the wrong house. "At this point, there are probably two or three people in the wrong room," Deely told me when I visited. (In a similar facility in Maryland that Hoglund designed recently, he made the houses as distinct as possible. One, the Baltimore House, is decorated in Federal style, with a brick courtyard and a sundial. A second, the Eastern Shore House, is decorated with contemporary furniture. The third, the Carroll County House, has a strong rural theme and an herb garden in the back.) 11

Hoglund adds that he'd change the position of the bathroom in each bedroom, to help resolve Woodside's chronic problem with incontinence. 12

Right now the toilets aren't visible from the hallways, which is good, because it affords privacy for those who forget to close the door. But neither are the toilets visible from the beds, which is bad, since it would help if the residents had a reminder in the middle of the night of what a bathroom is for. Of course, there may be a limit to how many of the problems posed by Alzheimer's can be solved through intelligent design. "Our men pee a lot in the corners," Deely said ruefully. "What we really need to do is figure out how to design a building without corners."

◆ ◆ ◆

FIRST RESPONSES

Have you ever known anyone with Alzheimer's disease? Who took care of this person? Was the care a burden to the family, either physically or financially?

TAKING A CLOSER LOOK

Exploring *Who:* Voice and Tone

1. Do you think the writer of this piece is involved in caring for Alzheimer's patients? How does he convince us that he knows what he's talking about?
2. Most of us would not expect to be engaged by an article about designing facilities for Alzheimer's patients. How does Gladwell make the topic interesting?
3. Identifying the tone of an article like this one is more difficult than recognizing a humorous, satirical, or nostalgic essay, but can you come up with a word to describe Gladwell's tone?

Exploring *What:* Content and Meaning

1. In the past, how were Alzheimer's patients kept from wandering?
2. What three functions of the brain do Alzheimer's patients lose first?
3. Describe several features of the new design employed in building Woodside Place, and explain their benefits to the patients.
4. Because the designer of Woodside Place was implementing a totally new concept in patient care, he discovered he had made "plenty of mistakes." What features would he change in planning his next Alzheimer's facility?

Exploring *Why:* Purpose

1. The process involved in this selection is a social one—a "how to" sort of process. State what process is being explained here.
2. What do you think Gladwell was trying to accomplish in this essay?
3. Why does he include so many direct quotations?

Exploring How: Style and Strategy

1. Discuss Gladwell's strategy in crafting his opening sentence: is it an effective opening? Why or why not?
2. How about the three sentences that conclude the essay: do they make a good conclusion? Explain why or why not.
3. Gladwell uses several imaginative phrases that add interest to his crisp, clean style. Discuss what the following phrases mean in context: "a psychiatric racetrack" (paragraph 3); "in full cognitive retreat" (paragraph 5); "a Texas-size facility" (paragraph 8); "a soothing anchor" (paragraph 8).
4. Reread paragraph 10 and comment on the way the following strategies function in achieving coherence: a transition that works by echoing an idea; a pure transitional phrase; a series of rhetorical questions.

IDEAS FOR WRITING A PROCESS ANALYSIS

1. Write an essay about the process of getting used to some new condition of life: a move, an illness, an office reorganization, marriage, prison, career change, or additions to the family, for example.
2. Write about a time when you had an opportunity to do something you might want to do but that might also conflict with your principles—like cheating on your partner, helping a friend get an abortion, deciding to sue for divorce, or shoplifting an inexpensive trinket. Trace your thought process as you made your decision.
3. *Using the Internet.* Find a health Web site (http://www.mayohealth.org/mayo/library/htm) and call up information on Alzheimer's, diabetes, breast cancer, arthritis, or any other chronic ailment. After studying this information, write an essay explaining what symptoms people with this disease suffer, what their present options are for treatment, and what new drugs and/or treatments are in the pipeline.

◆ ◆ ◆

◆ FURTHER IDEAS FOR USING PROCESS ANALYSIS

1. Using Dereck Williamson's essay as a model, provide the *real* instructions for some task you have found to be more difficult than the directions or instructions admitted.

2. Using Malcolm Gladwell's "The Alzheimer's Strain" as a model, write about a process that needs logical (instead of chronological) organization. Consider some self-improvement advice, like how to quit smoking or how to stop procrastinating or how to become a better listener. Or provide advice for improving relationships, like how to win the approval of your spouse's (or lover's) parents or how to get your mate to help with the housework.

3. ▣ *Using the Internet.* Find out about funeral customs in another country by searching the Internet. (Your library's online catalog can also direct you to appropriate articles or books.) Write an essay in which you analyze the process described in your source, and use it as the basis for agreeing or disagreeing with Jessica Mitford's opinion of American funeral practices.

4. COLLABORATIVE WRITING. With a small group of fellow students, think of some established process that could use improvement—like grading, registration, income tax, courtship, or weddings. Take notes while the group brainstorms to figure out how a preferable arrangement would function. Then, after the discussion, write an essay proposing the new process and explaining how it would work.

5. COMBINING STRATEGIES. Think of some process that can be done several different ways, like preparing food, for instance. Which is better? Fried, baked, or broiled? Decide which way you think is best. Then write an essay arguing that although there are several ways to fix this food (or perform this process), the way you are about to explain is the best way. Then explain the process and present your reasons for considering it the best choice.

6. Find a complicated set of instructions, like those for programming a VCR. Study them until you figure them out. Then write a new set of instructions that a novice user would find easy to follow.

◆ ◆ ◆ ◆ ◆ ◆ ◆ ◆ CHAPTER 7 ◆ ◆ ◆ ◆ ◆ ◆ ◆ ◆

Strategies for Clarifying Meaning

Definition

◆ ◆ ◆ ◆ ◆

Definitions explain the meanings of words, concepts, objects, or phenomena.

◆ Writers use definitions to clarify, evaluate, and increase awareness.

◆ Extended definitions explore the nature of complex subjects and controversial terms.

◆ Effective definitions include specific characteristics, examples, analogies, and contrasts.

If Harvey tells you he's going to leave work at 5:30 P.M., mail a package at the post office, stop by the ATM for some cash, go to the liquor store for some wine, pick up a pizza at the Italian Village, and get home in time for dinner at 6:00, you may conclude that he's not very bright. On the other hand, this same person may be the author of three books on molecular biology, a well-known scientist you admire for his mental ability. Do you think Harvey is intelligent or not? The answer to this question is a matter of **definition;** it all depends on what you mean by "intelligent."

Defining exactly what we mean is essential to clear and productive communication. After all, one person's "protest march" might be another person's "street riot." Indeed, many of our national debates about such issues as "affirmative action," "sexual harassment," "political correctness," "free speech," "multiculturalism," and "the right to die" turn on what people mean by these terms.

Writers also use definition to explore ideas and evaluate principles. In the essay that follows, Ellen Goodman explains what it means to be a "workaholic" by focusing on a single individual whose life and behavior define the condition. The detailed description of Phil not only *shows* what a workaholic is, but it also conveys Goodman's reservations about such people.

The Company Man

ELLEN GOODMAN

A syndicated columnist whose writing appears in over four hundred newspapers, Ellen Goodman began her career in journalism in 1963, the year after she graduated from Radcliffe College. She started as a reporter and feature writer for the *Detroit Free Press* and then moved to the *Boston Globe,* where she has been publishing her weekly syndicated column, "At Large," since 1971. Goodman's strong interest in social changes continues to play the central role in her work. She writes about family, politics, ethics, generation gaps, abortion, and the ever-changing status of women. Her columns have been praised for their keen observations and incisive wit, and she has won a number of writing awards, including the 1980 Pulitzer Prize for Distinguished Commentary.

He worked himself to death, finally and precisely, at 3:00 A.M. Sunday morning. 1

The obituary didn't say that, of course. It said that he died of a coronary thrombosis—I think that was it—but everyone among his friends and acquaintances knew it instantly. He was a perfect Type A, a workaholic, a classic, they said to each other and shook their heads—and thought for five or ten minutes about the way they lived. 2

This man who worked himself to death finally and precisely at 3:00 A.M. Sunday morning—on his day off—was fifty-one years old and a vice-president. He was, however, one of six vice-presidents, and one of three who might conceivably—if the president died or retired soon enough—have moved to the top spot. Phil knew that. 3

He worked six days a week, five of them until eight or nine at night,   4
during a time when his own company had begun the four-day week for
everyone but the executives. He worked like the Important People. He had
no outside "extracurricular interests," unless, of course, you think about a
monthly golf game that way. To Phil, it was work. He always ate egg salad
sandwiches at his desk. He was, of course, overweight, by 20 or 25 pounds.
He thought it was okay, though, because he didn't smoke.

On Saturdays, Phil wore a sports jacket to the office instead of a suit,   5
because it was the weekend.

He had a lot of people working for him, maybe sixty, and most of them   6
liked him most of the time. Three of them will be seriously considered for
his job. The obituary didn't mention that.

But it did list his "survivors" quite accurately. He is survived by his   7
wife, Helen, forty-eight years old, a good woman of no particular marketable skills, who worked in an office before marrying and mothering. She
had, according to her daughter, given up trying to compete with his work
years ago, when the children were small. A company friend said, "I know
how much you will miss him." And she answered, "I already have."

"Missing him all these years," she must have given up part of herself   8
which had cared too much for the man. She would be "well taken care of."

His "dearly beloved" eldest of the "dearly beloved" children is a hard-   9
working executive in a manufacturing firm down South. In the day and a
half before the funeral, he went around the neighborhood researching his
father, asking the neighbors what he was like. They were embarrassed.

His second child is a girl, who is twenty-four and newly married. She   10
lives near her mother and they are close, but whenever she was alone with
her father, in a car driving somewhere, they had nothing to say to each other.

The youngest is twenty, a boy, a high-school graduate who has spent the   11
last couple of years, like a lot of his friends, doing enough odd jobs to stay in
grass and food. He was the one who tried to grab at his father, and tried to
mean enough to him to keep the man at home. He was his father's favorite.
Over the last two years, Phil stayed up nights worrying about the boy.

The boy once said, "My father and I only board here."   12

At the funeral, the sixty-year-old company president told the forty-   13
eight-year-old widow that the fifty-one-year-old deceased had meant much
to the company and would be missed and would be hard to replace. The
widow didn't look him in the eye. She was afraid he would read her bitterness and, after all, she would need him to straighten out the finances—the
stock options and all that.

Phil was overweight and nervous and worked too hard. If he wasn't at   14
the office, he was worried about it. Phil was a Type A, a heart-attack natural. You could have picked him out in a minute from a lineup.

So when he finally worked himself to death, at precisely 3:00 A.M. Sunday morning, no one was really surprised.   15

By 5:00 P.M. the afternoon of the funeral, the company president had   16
begun, discreetly of course, with care and taste, to make inquiries about his replacement. One of three men. He asked around: "Who's been working the hardest?"

◆ ◆ ◆

◆ ◆ ◆ Writer's Workshop I ◆ ◆ ◆
Responding to a Definition

Use the *Who, What, Why,* and *How* questions (pp. 3–4) to explore your own understanding of the ideas and writing strategies used by Ellen Goodman in "The Company Man." Your instructor may ask you to record these responses in a journal or bring them to class to use in small group discussions.

◆ WRITING FROM READING

After reading "The Company Man," freshman Megan Quick used the *Who, What, Why,* and *How* questions to explore her understanding of Goodman's ideas and to develop material for writing a similar essay. Megan asked herself several questions about a possible topic: "Do I know someone who stands for a certain quality? Is this someone I dislike or admire? Is it someone I know well enough to write about?" These questions led her to focus on her high school music teacher, Mr. Woods. The definition essay she wrote about him follows.

```
Megan Quick
English 1091
November 8, 1997


                In Tune with His Students

     He walked into his students' lives in the fall of    1
1994. Though the students could not have known it
then, their new band director would have a profound
effect on their lives in just a few short years. He
would share in their thoughts and feelings, in their
```

successes and disappointments. He would be the perfect example of dedication and inspiration.

    Derek Woods is an educator and a friend to his students. He is involved in their lives both personally and professionally. Students look to Mr. Woods for advice about friendships, dating, family conflicts, career decisions, college choices, and music. To some, he is a counselor, to others he is a mentor, but mostly he is just a great teacher and friend. When he's feeling sentimental, he calls his students his "kids"--all fifty of them. When he's invited to a student party, he usually comes. Other times Mr. Woods helps to arrange the get-togethers himself. At the end of the marching band season, he takes the section leaders out for lunch as a reward for all their hard work. When students have performed well or achieved a personal success, he will congratulate them publicly. He will also let them know if they are not performing up to their potential. After the senior band members graduate, he tells them he does not want to see them back in their hometown working at dead-end jobs--because they have more potential than that. Mr. Woods believes in his students and knows they can be successful if they try. 2

    Accomplishing goals is important to Mr. Woods. His practices are intense, yet fun. On a regular basis, Mr. Woods puts the band through such unusual activities as group hugs, four-count jumping jacks, and massage lines (where the band stands in single file lines and the members massage the person standing in front of them). Other favorite activities include march-offs (a drill where Mr. Woods gives marching commands until only the person who has made no mistakes is left) and leprechaun kicks (executed by clicking the ankles together in midair). Leprechaun kicks are performed only on joyous or special occasions. Yet somehow Mr. Woods manages to keep the students focused. Before every competition and after every practice, Mr. Woods gives the entire band a pep talk. He must be doing something right because he has led the marching band to two consecutive state titles. 3

One of Mr. Woods's goals is to make his students the   4
best they can be. He cares about their well-being, their
success in life. Mr. Woods applies several philosophies
in his quest for student excellence. He insists that
"The band is only as good as its worst player." He also
says, "If you are going to play a wrong note, play it
with confidence"--but never make the same mistake twice.
On the marching field, he is constantly reminding the
students to "Give 110% at all times!" He shows them how
music unifies people of all races, colors, genders, and
ages. Music is a powerful tool, and Mr. Woods instills
the desire in his students to use their musical
abilities to create positive benefits.

His obvious enthusiasm for his subject and his   5
interest in his students have caused many of them to
develop a lifelong interest in music. He has inspired
some students, like me, to major in music education;
others he has encouraged to become professional
musicians. Those students did not know what they were
getting into the day they met Derek Woods; but ask any
of them, and they will tell you that they are glad he
stepped into their lives.

◆ GETTING STARTED ON A DEFINITION

A good definition can be reassuring or troubling: it can focus your readers' thinking and ease their minds, or it can shake up their long-held views and little-considered opinions. Either way, definition concerns meaning and therefore has a place in almost every mode of writing.

The first decision you have to make is what kind of definition you're going to use. Your choice, of course, depends on your **purpose** and how much you think your readers need to know.

Sometimes a short definition is enough to introduce a key term or clarify some technical language that your readers may not know. Short definitions can sometimes be handled by adding a word or two in parentheses after the term, like this:

> If you want your yogurt to yog (thicken), start with a fresh culture.

Miscommunication occurs when reader and writer do not share the same idea about a word's denotation (direct meaning) or connotation (emotional associations).

If there is no apt synonym, you can add a sentence, using the traditional three-part definition, which goes like this: (1) the *term* to be defined, (2) the *class* to which it belongs, and (3) *specific differences* to distinguish it from other members of its class. This formula may sound dry and academic, but it produces efficient one-sentence definitions:

TERM	CLASS	SPECIFIC DIFFERENCES
A friend	is a person	you know, like, and trust.
Intelligence	is the capacity	to acquire and apply knowledge.

You can leave these single-sentence definitions as they are, or you can expand the third part if you think your readers need more information.

When it comes to controversial, abstract, or complex words, you may decide to write an **extended definition.** Extended definition is a kind of explanatory writing that investigates the nature and significance of a term. Writers use extended definitions for one or more of the following reasons:

1. *To explain an abstraction or concept.* An abstraction—like intelligence or compassion or prejudice—is an idea that cannot be directly observed. Its meaning has to be understood indirectly from observable evidence. Ellen Goodman makes the concept of a "workaholic" understandable by describing the actions and behavior of a specific person.

2. *To provide an interpretation of a controversial term.* Any discussion of "family values" or "reverse discrimination" or "the right to life" must include an extended definition of how you are using and applying the phrase.

3. *To increase awareness of a new concept or a poorly understood term.* You might explain the meaning and nature of a term your readers probably don't understand at all, like "hypertext" or "feudalism." Or you might give your readers a new outlook on a familiar word—like "fear" or "wife"—by redefining it for them in a new way, as Andrew Holleran and Judy Brady do in essays in this chapter.

Following Ellen Goodman's lead, Megan Quick decided she would describe someone who exemplifies the abstract qualities of "dedication" and "inspiration." She brainstormed a list of points to use in her essay and began to write her first draft.

◆ ORGANIZING A DEFINITION

As you have seen, definitions come in all sizes and serve many different purposes. We cannot give you a set formula for writing an extended definition. Since you can use a number of strategies—description, narration, exemplification, comparison/contrast, classification—to develop a definition, you will be able to follow the organizational patterns that govern these techniques. Megan Quick began with the idea of writing an expressive description of Mr. Woods. Her first brainstorming list included a collection of descriptive details and narrative examples. As she worked on her first draft, she discovered that she could limit her discussion to those points that defined Mr. Woods's dedication and showed how he inspired his students. In other words, the definition provided a focus for her thinking and helped her to manage her presentation.

It's always a good idea to center your thoughts and supporting materials on a single controlling idea—a **thesis.** You don't have to state this idea in a thesis sentence, although doing so can be helpful to your readers. What is important is that you let this idea direct your writing. Here are several thesis sentences from the essays in this chapter. Notice how each one makes a definite assertion about the general subject and, at the same time, conveys the writer's point of view.

> [I]n our increasingly urban society, rural Americans have been unable to escape from hillbilly stigma, which is frequently accompanied by labels like "white trash," "redneck," and "hayseed." These negative stereotypes are as unmerciful as they are unfounded. (Rebecca Kirkendall, "Who's a Hillbilly?")

> But this general panic [about AIDS], this unease, this sense that the world is out of control and too intimately connected, is not *all* the Fear among homosexuals. The Fear among homosexuals is personal, physical, and real. (Andrew Holleran, "The Fear")

> What is so devastating for so many of us in search of our Black fathers is the realization that many of them are utter failures at nurturing us. And now, as many of us are fathers ourselves, we also find ourselves struggling with the identical phenomenon in relation to our own sons. . . . (Michel Marriott, "Father Hunger")

◆ DEVELOPING A DEFINITION

You can develop an extended definition by using any of the strategies discussed in this book. For example, if you wanted to define "sportsmanship," you could *narrate* an incident that illustrates the quality; *describe* how sportsmanship makes people feel and behave; *contrast* a good sport with a sore loser; give *examples* that reveal the nature of good sportsmanship; *classify* competitors into cheaters, arrogant winners, and good sports; or explain the *effects* of good sportsmanship on a team. You could also combine several of these strategies.

The most common methods of defining are these:

1. *Attributing characteristics.* A true friend is loyal, sensitive, and has a sense of humor.
2. *Providing examples.* A true friend will stay with your children while you go to a party.
3. *Using analogies.* A true friend is a safe port in a storm or a cross between a therapist and a pet who can cook.
4. *Explaining through contrasts.* A true friend is not just an old acquaintance or a jogging partner or a buddy at work.

As she worked on her definition essay, Megan Quick consulted Ellen Goodman's description of a workaholic. She observed that Goodman includes details about Phil's job, his physical appearance, and his habits. She also noticed that Goodman shows how Phil's behavior affected others and how other people reacted and related to Phil. Megan used these same strategies in developing her enlightening description of Mr. Woods.

◆ OPENING AND CLOSING A DEFINITION

A good way to begin an extended definition of something is to define its key terms. For example, "Before we can identify the best living jazz musicians, we must agree on a definition of *jazz.*" Or you can open with a three-part, one-sentence definition—"a true friend is someone you can trust and depend on"—and then expand on the specific characteristics mentioned in the last part.

You'll notice that a number of essays in this chapter open with narrative examples. Ellen Goodman and Megan Quick both begin with a specific event: Phil's death, Mr. Woods's arrival. Michel Marriott ("Father Hunger") uses a story about a trip to Cuba to introduce his subject; Rebecca

Kirkendall ("Who's a Hillbilly?") narrates an incident from her past; and Judy Brady ("I Want a Wife") combines a classification statement with a brief anecdote about a recently divorced friend. By contrast, M. F. K. Fisher ("Let the Sky Rain Potatoes") uses provocative questions to set up her definition: "There are two questions which can easily be asked about a potato: What is it, and Why is it?" And Andrew Holleran ("The Fear") plunges right into his topic: "The Fear is of course unseemly—as most fear is."

The conclusion of an extended definition often sums up the main characteristics of the term and emphasizes the significance of the definition. That's how many of the essays in this chapter end. Megan Quick, for example, cites Mr. Woods's enthusiasm for music, his interest in his students, and his inspiration—and then closes with an echo of her opening sentence. Andrew Holleran sums up the essence of his definition of the Fear with this powerful ending:

> The Fear . . . feeds on the Imagination. And the moment you know someone who faces this disease daily with composure, calm, humor, and his or her own personality intact, you realize how deforming, how demeaning, how subject to the worst instincts Fear is.

◆ USING THE MODEL

As you have seen, reading and analyzing Ellen Goodman's essay helped Megan Quick in a number of ways. First of all, she got her topic and her basic approach from Goodman: to describe a person she knows who exemplifies certain abstract qualities. Megan also picked up pointers from Goodman's essay on where to look for relevant examples and how to use them to develop her ideas. But she did not follow Goodman in every way. For one thing, Megan's purpose was to hold up Mr. Woods as an admirable example, not to criticize him, as Goodman does with her subject. Megan also decided to conclude with a more conventional summary of her main points, a strategy that Goodman does not employ.

We all know people who seem to represent a certain quality or value. Think of someone whose life defines for you some abstraction like ambition, determination, loyalty, enthusiasm, or procrastination. Or perhaps you know somebody who is the perfect example of a perfectionist, a bore, a fanatic, a disciplinarian, a hopeless romantic, a con artist, a deadbeat, or something similar. Talk to other people who know this same person and get their views. Then write a definition essay in which you use this individual as your primary example to illustrate that quality.

◆ ◆ ◆ *Writer's Workshop II* ◆ ◆ ◆
Analyzing a Definition

Working individually or with a small group of classmates, read through Megan Quick's essay "In Tune with His Students," and respond to the following questions.

1. What is Megan's purpose for writing this essay? Does she make her purpose clear in the beginning?
2. Do the examples support Megan's thesis? Which examples are the most effective? Are there any that are incomplete or ineffective? How would you improve them?
3. How does Megan organize her description? Did you find it easy to follow?
4. Do you like the opening and the closing? Would you change them? If so, how?
5. What attitude about Mr. Woods does Megan convey? Does she convince you of her evaluation? Why or why not?

◆ ◆ ◆ *Checklist for Reading and Writing* ◆ ◆ ◆
Definition Essays

1. What term or concept is being defined? Does the essay focus clearly on this term or concept?
2. What is the purpose of the definition—to clarify, evaluate, or increase awareness?
3. How is the definition developed? Are there enough details, specific characteristics, examples, analogies, and contrasts?
4. Who is the intended audience? How would the essay be different if written for a different audience? What details and explanations would be added or deleted?
5. Is the organization clear?
6. Does the essay begin and end appropriately and effectively?

◆ ◆ ◆ **PREPARING TO READ**

Where do you live now—in the city, the suburbs, or the country? What do you like and dislike about where you live? Would you prefer to live somewhere else? Why or why not?

◆ ◆ ◆

Who's a Hillbilly?

REBECCA THOMAS KIRKENDALL

Rebecca Thomas Kirkendall was a doctoral student at the University of Missouri when this essay was first published in *Newsweek* magazine in November 1995. In some ways, her essay is a counterdefinition because it takes issue with the term *hillbilly*. But in attacking the assumptions behind the use of the term, Kirkendall also proposes a more accurate description of what it really means to be part of the rural culture of the Ozarks.

I once dated a boy who called me a hillbilly because my family has 1 lived in the Ozarks in southern Missouri for several generations. I took offense, not realizing that as a foreigner to the United States he was unaware of the insult. He had meant it as a term of endearment. Nonetheless, it rankled. I started thinking about the implications of the term to me, my family and my community.

While growing up I was often surprised at the way television belittled 2 "country" people. We weren't offended by the self-effacing humor of *The Andy Griffith Show* and *The Beverly Hillbillies* because, after all, Andy and Jed were the heroes of these shows, and through them we could comfortably laugh at ourselves. But as I learned about tolerance and discrimination in school, I wondered why stereotypes of our lifestyle went unexamined. Actors playing "country" people on TV were usually comic foils or objects of ridicule. Every sitcom seemed to have an episode where country cousins, wearing high-water britches and carrying patched suitcases, visited their city friends. And movies like *Deliverance* portrayed country people as backward and violent.

As a child I laughed at the exaggerated accents and dress, never imag- 3 ining that viewers believed such nonsense. Li'l Abner and the folks on *Hee Haw* were amusing, but we on the farm knew that our work did not lend itself to bare feet, gingham bras and revealing cutoff jeans.

Although our nation professes a growing commitment to cultural   4
egalitarianism, we consistently oversimplify and misunderstand our rural
culture. Since the 1960s, minority groups in America have fought for ac-
knowledgment, appreciation and, above all, respect. But in our increasingly
urban society, rural Americans have been unable to escape from the hillbilly stigma, which is frequently accompanied by labels like "white trash,"
"redneck" and "hayseed." These negative stereotypes are as unmerciful as
they are unfounded.

When I graduated from college, I traveled to a nearby city to find   5
work. There I heard wisecracks about the uneducated rural folk who lived a
few hours away. I also took some ribbing about the way I pronounced certain words, such as "tin" instead of "ten" and "agin" for "again." And my expressed desire to return to the country someday was usually met with scorn,
bewilderment or genuine concern. Co-workers often asked, "But what is
there to *do?*" Thoreau may have gone to Walden Pond, they argued, but he
had no intention of staying there.

With the revival of country music in the early 1980s, hillbillyness was   6
again marketable. Country is now big business. Traditional country
symbols—Minnie Pearl's hat tag and Daisy Mae—have been eclipsed by the
commercially successful Nashville Network, Country Music Television, and
music theaters in Branson, Mo. Many "country" Americans turned the negative stereotype to their advantage and packaged the hillbilly legacy.

Yet with successful commercialization, the authentic elements of   7
America's rural culture have been juxtaposed with the stylized. Country
and Western bars are now chic. While I worked in the city, I watched with
amazement as my Yuppie friends hurried from their corporate desks to
catch the 6:30 line-dancing class at the edge of town. Donning Ralph Lauren jeans and ankle boots, they drove to the trendiest country bars, sat and
danced together and poked fun at the local "hicks," who arrived in pickup
trucks wearing Wrangler jeans and roper boots.

Every summer weekend in Missouri the freeways leading out of our   8
cities are clogged with vacationers. Minivans and RVs edge toward a clear
river with a campground and canoe rental, a quiet lake resort or craft show
in a remote Ozark town. Along these popular vacation routes, the rural
hosts of convenience stores, gift shops and corner cafes accept condescension along with personal checks and credit cards. On a canoeing trip not
long ago, I recall sitting on the transport bus and listening, heartbroken, as
a group of tourists ridiculed our bus driver. They yelled, "Hey, plowboy,
ain't ya got no terbacker fer us?" They pointed at the young man's
sweat-stained overalls as he, seemingly unaffected by their insults, single-
handedly carried their heavy aluminum canoes to the water's edge. That
"plowboy" was one of my high-school classmates. He greeted the tourists

with a smile and tolerated their derision because he knew tourism brings dollars and jobs.

America is ambivalent when it comes to claiming its rural heritage. 9 We may fantasize about Thomas Jefferson's agrarian vision, but there is no mistaking that ours is an increasingly urban culture. Despite their disdain for farm life—with its manure-caked boots, long hours, and inherent financial difficulties—urbanites rush to imitate a sanitized version of this lifestyle. And the individuals who sell this rendition understand that the customer wants to experience hillbillyness without the embarrassment of being mistaken for one.

Through it all, we Ozarkians remind ourselves how fortunate we are 10 to live in a region admired for its blue springs, rolling hills and geological wonders. In spite of the stereotypes, most of us are not uneducated. Nor are we stupid. We are not white supremacists, and we rarely marry our cousins. Our reasons for living in the hills are as complex and diverse as our population. We have a unique sense of community, strong family ties, a beautiful environment, and a quiet place for retirement.

We have criminals and radicals, but they are the exception. Our 11 public-education system produces successful farmers, doctors, business professionals, and educators. Country music is our favorite, but we also like rock and roll, jazz, blues, and classical. We read Louis L'Amour, Maya Angelou, and *The Wall Street Journal.* And in exchange for living here, many of us put up with a lower standard of living and the occasional gibe from those who persist in calling us "hillbillies."

FIRST RESPONSES

Why do people use terms like "hillbilly" or "hick"? Can you think of two or three well-known labels for urban residents? Are they as unfair and unfounded as *hillbilly?* Why or why not?

TAKING A CLOSER LOOK

Exploring *Who:* Voice and Tone

1. What is Kirkendall's personal agenda in writing about this topic? How does she make it clear that she has a personal stake in this discussion?
2. Is the author writing for herself or on behalf of a larger community? How would you describe the community she's writing about?

3. Is Kirkendall angry? Is she being defensive? Describe the tone you detect in her writing.

4. How do you respond to the author's survey of attitudes toward rural people? Do you think she is criticizing or challenging you in any way?

Exploring *What:* Content and Meaning

1. What evidence does Kirkendall present to support her claim that rural people are negatively stereotyped? Do you agree with her claim?

2. How have some rural people turned the negative stereotype to their advantage? Does the author approve of this commercialization of the country image?

3. What does Kirkendall mean when she says, "America is ambivalent when it comes to claiming its rural heritage" (paragraph 9)?

4. ◼▯ *Using the Internet.* What do you know about the Ozarks? Visit a Web site on the Internet that gives information about this part of the country. What does the Web site tell you about the culture and people of this region? Does the presentation of the information confirm or refute what Kirkendall says in her essay?

Exploring *Why:* Purpose

1. Why does the author refer to television shows and movies in the first three paragraphs of her essay? Do you know the references she makes?

2. Kirkendall refers to "a growing commitment to cultural egalitarianism" in American society. What is "cultural egalitarianism"? Why does the author introduce this idea?

3. What does Kirkendall hope to accomplish with this essay? Does she expect you to alter your attitudes and opinions? Has she succeeded?

Exploring *How:* Style and Strategy

1. Locate the author's use of personal examples to illustrate her points. What is the effect of including these incidents? What other kinds of examples does she use?

2. Kirkendall uses sophisticated words like *stigma, egalitarianism, eclipsed, legacy, ambivalent, juxtaposed, condescension, derision, inherent,*

urbanites, geological, and *supremacists.* How does this vocabulary—along with the references to Thoreau, Louis L'Amour, Maya Angelou, and *The Wall Street Journal*— advance the point of her essay?

3. Reread the last two paragraphs. What is the point of this last section of the essay? Why does Kirkendall include them?

WRITING FROM READING ASSIGNMENT

Sometimes writers, like Rebecca Kirkendall, feel that the accepted definitions do not define a word or term accurately or fairly, so they offer a redefinition that fits their purposes better. In this writing assignment, your goal is to offer a counterdefinition of some word or phrase that you think needs to be clarified or redefined.

A. Begin by identifying a term that you want to write about. You might, like Kirkendall, use a word that carries negative connotations you want to challenge and correct. Think of some term like *jock, Yuppie, activist, liberal, conservative, feminist, politician, capitalist, socialist,* or *atheist.* Or you could define what people in your community or area are really like (as opposed to what others may think).

B. Consult other people who might have varying points of view about their understanding of the word or phrase. Be sure to ask them if the term carries any negative connotations for them. Then do some brainstorming or freewriting to get your points and ideas down on paper.

C. Try to think of a relevant anecdote; then use it to set up your counterdefinition, as Kirkendall does in the opening paragraph of her essay. You could also use a dictionary definition to begin your discussion, pointing out that it gives the basic meaning but doesn't deal with the connotations you propose to focus on. If appropriate, you might consult The Online Slang Dictionary (http://www.umr.edu/~wrader/slang.html) or the WWWebster Dictionary (http://www.m-w.com/dictionary) to help you get started.

D. Provide examples of people who use the term in a negative or inaccurate way. You might draw on television programs and films, as Kirkendall does, to illustrate why the word needs to be redefined.

E. After establishing the current use of the term, state the main point and purpose of your essay. Look at paragraph 4 in "Who's a Hillbilly?" to see how Kirkendall presents her thesis.

F. Discuss the problems or consequences of continuing to use the word or phrase inaccurately. Include any evidence you have that some change in usage has already taken place, as Kirkendall does in paragraphs 6 through 8 of her essay.

G. Once you have demonstrated that the word or phrase is being misused and that its misuse is unfair or misleading, then present your counterdefinition. Give details, examples, and explanations to make your point. Reread paragraphs 10 and 11 of "Who's a Hillbilly?" for an example.

◆ ◆ ◆ PREPARING TO READ

What tasks does a wife typically perform around the house? What are the typical tasks that a husband does? If both of them are working outside the home, who has the harder job at home?

◆ ◆ ◆

I Want a Wife

JUDY BRADY

Born in 1937, Judy Brady received a B.F.A. in painting from the University of Iowa in 1962. She married in 1960 and is the mother of two daughters. As a freelance writer, Brady has written essays on union organizing, abortion, and the role of women in American society. Motivated by her own struggle with cancer, she edited a collection of articles entitled *1 in 3: Women with Cancer Confront an Epidemic* (1991). The following essay, written after eleven years of marriage and before Brady separated from her husband, first appeared in 1971 in *Ms.* magazine. It has been widely reprinted ever since.

1   I belong to that classification of people known as wives. I am A Wife. And, not altogether incidentally, I am a mother.

2   Not too long ago a male friend of mine appeared on the scene from the Midwest fresh from a recent divorce. He had one child, who is, of course, with his ex-wife. He is obviously looking for another wife. As I thought about him while I was ironing one evening, it suddenly occurred to me that I, too, would like to have a wife. Why do I want a wife?

3   I would like to go back to school so that I can become economically independent, support myself, and, if need be, support those dependent upon me. I want a wife who will work and send me to school. And while I am going to school I want a wife to take care of my children. I want a wife to keep track of the children's doctor and dentist appointments. And to keep track of mine, too. I want a wife to make sure my children eat properly and are kept clean. I want a wife who will wash the children's clothes and keep them mended. I want a wife who is a good nurturant attendant to my children, arranges for their schooling, makes sure that they have an adequate social life with their peers, takes them to the park, the zoo, etc. I want a wife who takes care of the children when they are sick, a wife who arranges to be

around when the children need special care, because, of course, I cannot miss classes at school. My wife must arrange to lose time at work and not lose the job. It may mean a small cut in my wife's income from time to time, but I guess I can tolerate that. Needless to say, my wife will arrange and pay for the care of the children while my wife is working.

I want a wife who will take care of *my* physical needs. I want a wife who will keep my house clean. A wife who will pick up after my children, a wife who will pick up after me. I want a wife who will keep my clothes clean, ironed, mended, replaced when need be, and who will see to it that my personal things are kept in their proper place so that I can find what I need the minute I need it. I want a wife who cooks the meals, a wife who is a *good* cook. I want a wife who will plan the menus, do the necessary grocery shopping, prepare the meals, serve them pleasantly, and then do the cleaning up while I do my studying. I want a wife who will care for me when I am sick and sympathize with my pain and loss of time from school. I want a wife to go along when our family takes a vacation so that someone can continue to care for me and my children when I need a rest and a change of scene. 4

I want a wife who will not bother me with rambling complaints about a wife's duties. But I want a wife who will listen to me when I feel the need to explain a rather difficult point I have come across in my course of studies. And I want a wife who will type my papers for me when I have written them. 5

I want a wife who will take care of the details of my social life. When my wife and I are invited out by my friends, I want a wife who will take care of the babysitting arrangements. When I meet people at school that I like and want to entertain, I want a wife who will have the house clean, will prepare a special meal, serve it to me and my friends, and not interrupt when I talk about the things that interest me and my friends. I want a wife who will have arranged that the children are fed and ready for bed before my guests arrive so that the children do not bother us. I want a wife who takes care of the needs of my guests so that they feel comfortable, who makes sure that they have an ashtray, that they are passed the hors d'oeuvres, that they are offered a second helping of the food, that their wine glasses are replenished when necessary, that their coffee is served to them as they like it. And I want a wife who knows that sometimes I need a night out by myself. 6

I want a wife who is sensitive to my sexual needs, a wife who makes love passionately and eagerly when I feel like it, a wife who makes sure that I am satisfied. And, of course, I want a wife who will not demand sexual attention when I am not in the mood for it. I want a wife who assumes the complete responsibility for birth control, because I do not want more children. I want a wife who will remain sexually faithful to me so that I do not have to clutter up my intellectual life with jealousies. And I want a wife 7 who understands that my sexual needs may entail more than strict adherence to monogamy. I must, after all, be able to relate to people as fully as possible.

If, by chance, I find another person more suitable as a wife than the wife I already have, I want the liberty to replace my present wife with another one. Naturally, I will expect a fresh, new life; my wife will take the children and be solely responsible for them so that I am left free.   8

When I am through with school and have acquired a job, I want my wife to quit working and remain at home so that my wife can more fully and completely take care of a wife's duties.   9

My God, who *wouldn't* want a wife?   10

FIRST RESPONSES

Brady wrote this essay almost thirty years ago. Is it still relevant today? Have changes in gender roles made Brady's views outdated? Or are her points still valid?

TAKING A CLOSER LOOK

Exploring *Who:* Voice and Tone

1. Why does Brady identify herself as a wife and a mother at the beginning of the essay? Is this information important?
2. What assumptions did Brady probably make about her audience (readers of *Ms.* magazine in 1971)? Do you think she can make the same assumptions about you?
3. What evidence is there that the author is being ironic or sarcastic? Look at her use of italics, and think about the way she uses these words: *proper* and *pleasantly* (paragraph 4), *bother* and *necessary* (paragraph 6), *demand* and *clutter up* (paragraph 7), *suitable* and *free* (paragraph 8).
4. Do you think Brady intends to provoke a reaction from her readers? What is your reaction? How do your own experiences (as a husband, wife, child, boyfriend, girlfriend, etc.) affect your responses?

Exploring *What:* Content and Meaning

1. Sum up in one sentence what Brady means by the term *wife.* Does this kind of wife actually exist?

2. Make a list of the specific duties of the wife described in this essay. How many general categories are covered?
3. What does Brady say about the sexual expectations and behavior of husbands? Do you agree with her?
4. Would you want a spouse or partner like the one described in this essay? Do you think Brady really does?

Exploring *Why:* Purpose

1. Is Brady's purpose to explain a wife's duties, to complain about her own situation, to attack or poke fun at men, to call attention to society's treatment of women, or what?
2. Is the author trying to present a realistic and fair definition of a *wife?* Explain.
3. What part does exaggeration play in this essay? Why would a writer use exaggeration?
4. Brady never uses any pronouns to refer to the wife. Why not?

Exploring *How:* Strategy and Style

1. Why are the words *A Wife* capitalized in the first paragraph?
2. Why does Brady include the story about a male friend who visits her? Is it significant that he is looking for another wife?
3. Give at least two reasons for the frequent repetition of the words "I want a wife."
4. According to what principles does Brady organize the details of her definitions into paragraphs? Why does she end with the point about the wife quitting work and remaining at home (paragraph 9)?
5. What is the effect of the rhetorical question at the very end? How does this conclusion sum up her main point?

IDEAS FOR WRITING A DEFINITION

1. Write an essay similar to Brady's, defining a word that denotes a social relationship: *husband, friend, lover, mother, father, brother, grandparent, son, daughter, roommate, neighbor, mentor, partner, confidant.* Define the term indirectly by showing what such a person does or should do. You can adopt a serious tone or an ironic one, as Brady does.
2. Go to your local bookstore, and review the text of greeting cards designed for wives, husbands, or mothers. Using ideas and examples you

find, write an essay that defines a wife, a husband, or a mother as viewed by the greeting card industry.

3. *Using the Internet.* Visit the Web site for the National Partnership for Women and Families (http://www.nationalpartnership.org/), and examine some of their articles about work and family. Then write an essay in which you expand on your answers to the questions in the First Responses section: Are Brady's views still relevant today? Have changes in gender roles made Brady's views outdated? Are her points still valid?

◆ ◆ ◆ **PREPARING TO READ**

Do you have a favorite food? How would you describe this food to someone who hasn't eaten it? Can you explain why it's your favorite?

◆ ◆ ◆

"Let the Sky Rain Potatoes"
—The Merry Wives of Windsor

M. F. K. FISHER

Mary Frances Kennedy Fisher, born in 1909 in California, was a renowned memoirist and essayist. She had written six books and translated a seventh before she became known to a wide reading public. Five of these early books, written between 1937 and 1949, were collected as *The Art of Eating* (1954); in them, she combined personal observations with literate writing about food, expanding her subject to encompass needs and pleasures of all sorts. Fisher alternated between living in France and in the wine regions of California. She produced more than sixteen books of essays, poetry, and memoirs before her death in 1992. The following selection from *The Art of Eating* demonstrates her keen wit and her unusual approach to writing about food.

There are two questions which can easily be asked about a potato: 1
What is it, and Why is it?

Both these questions are irritating to a true amateur. The answers to 2
the first are self-evident: a potato is a food, delicious, nourishing, and so on.
The second question is perhaps too impertinent even to be answered, although many a weary housewife has felt like shouting it to the high heavens if her family has chanced to be the kind that takes for granted the daily appearance of this ubiquitous vegetable.

A dictionary will say that a potato is a farinaceous tuber used for food. 3
An encyclopedia will cover eight or nine large pages with a sad analysis of its origins, modes of cultivation, and diseases, some of which are enough in themselves to discourage any potato enthusiast who might read them carefully.

Between these two extremes of definition is a story interesting even to   4
one who is not overly fond of potatoes as a food. There are romance and
color, and the fine sound of brave names in its telling.

In Peru, the Spanish found *papas* growing in the early 1500s, and the   5
monk Hieronymus Cardán took them back with him to his own people. The
Italians liked them, and then the Belgians.

About that time, Sir Walter Raleigh found a potato in the American   6
South, and carried it back to his estate near Cork. Some say it was a yam
he had, thought strongly aphrodisiac by the Elizabethans. Some say it
was a white potato. A German statue thanks Raleigh for bringing it to
Europe. On the other hand, the Spanish claim recognition for its European
introduction.

No matter what its origin, eat it, eat it, urged the British Royal Society.   7
But for many decades its cultivation made but little progress.

By the time it had become important as a food, especially for poor   8
people, its diseases also had matured, and in 1846 potato blight sent thousands of hungry Irishmen to their graves, or to America.

Warts and scabs and rusts and rots did their work, too, and men   9
worked hard to breed new varieties of potatoes before newer plagues
seized them. Great Scott, the Boston Comrade, Magnum Bonum, Rhoder-
ick Dhu, and Up-to-Date, Ninetyfold: these and many hundreds more filled
pots around the world, and still do.

But no matter the name; a spud's a spud, and by any other name it   10
would still be starchy, and covered with dusty cork for skin, and, what's
worse, taken for granted on every blond-head's table.

If the men are darker, it is pastas in slender strings they'll eat, or tubes,   11
always farinaceous, as the dictionary says; but more often on Anglo-Saxon
fare the potato takes place before any foreign macaroni or spaghetti.

It is hard sometimes to say why. A potato is good when it is cooked   12
correctly. Baked slowly, with its skin rubbed first in a buttery hand, or boiled
in its jacket and then "shook," it is delicious. Salt and pepper are almost always necessary to its hot moist-dusty flavor. Alone, or with a fat jug of rich
cool milk or a chunk of fresh Gruyère, it fills the stomach and the soul with
a satisfaction not too easy to attain.

In general, however, a potato is a poor thing, poorly treated. More   13
often than not it is cooked in so unthinking and ignorant a manner as to
make one feel that it has never before been encountered in the kitchen, as
when avocados were sent to the Cornish Mousehole by a lady who heard
months later that their suave thick meat had been thrown away and the
stones boiled and boiled to no avail.

"Never have I tasted such a poor, flaccid, gray sad mixture of a mess,"   14
says my mother when she tells of the potatoes served in Ireland. And who

would contradict her who has ever seen the baked-or-boiled in a London Lyons or an A.B.C.?

The Irish prefer them, evidently, to starvation, and the English, too. 15 And in mid-western Europe, in a part where dumplings grow on every kitchen-range, there are great cannon balls of them, pernicious as any shrapnel to a foreign palate, but swallowed like feathery egg-whites by the natives.

They are served with goose at Christmas, and all around the year. 16 They are the size of a toddling child's round head. They are gray, and exceedingly heavy. They are made painstakingly of grated raw potato, molded, then boiled, then added to by molding, then boiled again. Layer after layer is pressed on, cooked, and cooled, and finally the whole sodden pockmarked mass is bounced in bubbling goose broth until time to heave it to the platter.

Forks may bend against its iron-like curves, stomachs may curdle in a 17 hundred gastric revolutions; a potato dumpling is more adamantine. It survives, and is served to ever-renewing decades of hungry yodelling mouths.

In itself, this always fresh desire for starch, for the potato, is important. 18 No matter what its form, nor its national disguise, the appetite for it is there, impervious to the mandates of dictators or any other blight.

Perhaps its most insidious manifestation is that Anglo-Saxons take it 19 for granted. A meal for them includes potatoes in some form; it always has, therefore it always will. And no revolt, no smoldering rebellion of the meal-planner, can change this smug acceptance.

Most important, however, is the potato's function as a gastro- 20 nomic complement. It is this that should be considered, to rob it of its dangerous monotony, and clothe it with the changing mysterious garment of adaptability.

Although few realize it, to be complementary is in itself a compliment. 21 It is a subtle pleasure, like the small exaltation of a beautiful dark woman who finds herself unexpectedly in the company of an equally beautiful blonde. It is what a great chef meant once when he repulsed a consolation.

He was a Frenchman, summoned to London when King Edward VII 22 found that his subjects resented his dining more in Paris than at home.

This great cook one day prepared a dish of soles in such a manner that 23 the guests at Edward's table waited assuredly for a kingly compliment. He was summoned. Their mouths hung open in sated expectation.

"The Château Yquem," said Edward VII, "was excellent." 24

Later the master chef shrugged, a nonchalance denied by every mus- 25 cle in his pleased face.

"How could my dish have had a greater compliment?" he demanded, 26 calmly. "His Majesty knows, as I do, that when a dish is perfect, as was my sole tonight, the wine is good. If the dish is lower than perfection, the wine, lacking its complement, tastes weak and poor. So—you see?"

Although there are few ways of preparing potatoes to make them approach the perfection of a royal plate of fish, and none I know of to make them worth the compliment of a bottle of Château Yquem, they in their own way are superlative complements. And it is thus, as I have said, that they should be treated.   27

If, French fried, they make a grilled sirloin of beef taste richer; if, mashed and whipped with fresh cream and salty butter, they bridge the deadly gap between a ragout and a salad; if, baked and pinched open and bulging with mealy snowiness, they offset the fat spiced flavor of a pile of sausages—then and then alone should they be served.   28

Then they are dignified. Then they are worthy of a high place, not debased to the deadly rank of daily acceptance. Then they are a gastronomic pleasure, not merely "tubers used for food."   29

◆ ◆ ◆

FIRST RESPONSES

Do you think potatoes are dignified? Has Fisher's essay made you think differently about French fries and baked potatoes?

TAKING A CLOSER LOOK

Exploring *Who:* Voice and Tone

1. How would you describe the author of this selection? What sense of her intellect and personality do you get from the language she uses?
2. How does Fisher convince you that she knows a lot about potatoes? List some of the details and facts that establish her expertise on the subject.
3. What is Fisher's attitude toward potatoes? Is her tone always serious?
4. Could you write an essay about a vegetable? What would you write about?

Exploring *What:* Meaning and Content

1. Fisher begins by asking two questions about a potato: what is it? and why is it? What answers does she give to each question?

2. Fisher says the potato is a "ubiquitous vegetable." What does she mean? Do you agree?
3. According to Fisher, what is a potato's most important function? When, and only when, should potatoes be served?
4. What does the word *gastronomic* mean?

Exploring *Why*: Purpose

1. Fisher mentions three times that the potato is "taken for granted." Why does she repeat this point? What does it have to do with her purpose?
2. Has Fisher convinced you that potatoes are "a gastronomic pleasure" and "worthy of a high place" on the menu?

Exploring *How*: Style and Structure

1. Why does Fisher include the dictionary definition of a potato? Why does she summarize its history?
2. Find examples of the figurative language Fisher uses to describe potatoes. Why does she use this kind of language?
3. Reread paragraphs 13 through 16. Why does the author include these details?
4. What's the point of the anecdote about the French chef and the excellent wine, Château Yquem (paragraphs 21 through 26)?

IDEAS FOR WRITING A DEFINITION

1. Describe and define a food that you love, one that you think other people should try. If you want a challenge, write about a vegetable that many people don't like—such as cauliflower, broccoli, squash, or spinach.
2. Write a humorous essay about your favorite snack food. Adopt a formal or academic tone, and use irony and exaggeration to explain its nutritional, social, and economic benefits.
3. ◼ *Using the Internet.* Locate a Web site that gives information about ethnic foods and international cuisine. A site like The Global Gastronomer: Cuisines of the World (http://www.cs.yale.edu/homes/hupfer/global) will give you links to recipes, food history, and food lore of all regions on the globe. Choose a food or a style of cooking, and gather facts and details about it. Then write an essay that introduces an audience of your peers to some new gastronomic pleasure.

◆ ◆ ◆ **PREPARING TO READ**

What kind of relationship do you have with your father or mother? Is he or she warm, loving, and easy to talk to, or do you have a hard time expressing your feelings for each other? Do you get along well, or do you seem to fight all the time? How do you think you might get to know your father or mother better? Do you care to?

◆ ◆ ◆

Father Hunger

MICHEL MARRIOTT

Michel Marriott is a reporter for the *New York Times;* he has also written for *Newsweek* magazine. His areas of interest have included political corruption, street hustles, youth violence, gang activity, exercise machines, and rap music stars. Most recently, he has written a series of articles about the effects of the Internet on business and the arts. In the following essay, which first appeared in *Essence* magazine in 1990, Marriott explores the meaning of the phrase "father hunger."

Once, not too many years ago, I looked up from the scribble on my reporter's pad and stared into the hyperanimated face of Fidel Castro—and I saw my father. As part of a delegation of African-American journalists invited to Cuba in 1986, I counted myself lucky to be among the teeming Caribbeans crammed onto a dusty soccer field just outside a knot of empty shops, crowded flats and stands of sugarcane. Moreover, I felt a stab of surprise that I had somehow stepped, flesh and blood, into my father's dream. 1

Long disenchanted with what he called the "trick bag" of the United States, my father reveled in the sheer bravado of the Cuban revolution, its elevation of the Brown and Black to real power. He often talked, half jokingly, of course, of retiring someday to that island republic and having Uncle Sam send his Social Security checks to Havana. 2

In recognition of the special significance my journey might hold for him, I presented Dad with a gift on my return. To my disappointment, however, he barely accepted the carefully framed photograph I had taken of Castro and inscribed with words of tribute to my father's courage as a free-thinker. 3

Why is it so difficult for us? I asked myself some weeks later when I   4
discovered the picture pitched against a mound of disarray on my father's
desk. After so many years of being buffeted by swirling currents of father-
son tensions, intermittent hostilities and redeeming love, *why*, I mused, *does
it remain so hard for us—two Black men—to, well, just get along?* There had
been times when we had hurled hurtful words at each other like poison-
tipped spears. We had even, in dizzying and terrifying fits of machismo, both
reached for guns, prepared to shoot each other if need be.

Why wasn't it like television, where dads wore suits and ties to the   5
dinner table and were ever ready to lend an ear or dispense fatherly advice
with a knowing grin? Where was Fred MacMurray in blackface?

The truth is that for millions of Black men, our relationships with our   6
fathers represent lifetimes of unfinished business. Much too often our most
obvious models—from whom we begin to fashion our distinctive sense of a
masculine identity—are marginal to our lives because of our fathers' physical or emotional absence from home. The issue is not new or exclusive to
African-American men. James Herzog, a Harvard University Medical
School assistant professor of psychiatry, coined the phrase "father hunger"
to describe the psychological condition young children endure when long
separated from their fathers. English professor Andrew Merton of the University of New Hampshire wrote in a 1986 article in *New Age* magazine of
many men whose lives have been profoundly shaped and troubled by failures of intimacy with their fathers. Quoting author Samuel Osherson, Merton wrote: "The psychological or physical absence of fathers from their
families is one of the great underestimated tragedies of our times."

What is so devastating for so many of us in search of our Black fathers   7
is the realization that many of them were utter failures at nurturing us. And
now, as many of us are fathers ourselves, we also find ourselves struggling
with the identical phenomenon in relation to our own sons—as if this difficulty were inherent in our Black condition, as if it somehow passes from
generation to generation in a recessive gene that we peculiarly carry. But, of
course, it's sociological, not biological.

"The masculine role has clearly restricted our ability to relate to chil-   8
dren," write Joseph H. Pleck and Jack Sawyer of American men in general,
in their 1974 collection *Men and Masculinity*. "Our drive toward getting
ahead means we often find little time or energy for being with children;
moreover, we may project our own strivings for success upon them."

In the case of too many Black men, however, it is more likely that we   9
project upon our sons our fear and profound sense of powerlessness and
vulnerability in a society that daily crushes many of us. Countless Black
boys, as a consequence, grow up in a tangle of fatherly love and loathing for
what lies ahead for little Michael, little Jamil.

For example, my father would bristle with indignation whenever he   10
discovered my brother and me, as young boys, watching Saturday-morning
cartoons. "You don't have time for that bullshit," he'd say in a tone so sharp
our child-joy would expire on the spot. "The white man wants you to look at
Bugs Bunny while he's figuring out better ways to beat you. You better
learn some math, read a book."

There'd be no hugs given or "good mornings" spoken. There was al-   11
ways so much harshness, a sternness very much like that I saw years later
captured in Troy Maxson's rage and reason in August Wilson's play *Fences*.
When Troy's teenage son, Cory, asks him why he doesn't like him, Troy re-
sponds with fury: "I done give you everything I had to give you. I gave you
your life! Me and your mama worked that out between us. And liking your
black ass wasn't part of the bargain. Don't you try and go through life worrying about if somebody like you or not. You best be making sure they
doing right by you." Similarly, growing up with my father, at the time a factory worker at a synthetic-rubber manufacturing plant in Louisville, Kentucky, was like growing up in boot camp, training for the inevitable clashes
with white racism and domination that waited just outside the nest of our
segregated neighborhood.

Yet I identified with my father. I marveled at his strength—not mere-   12
ly muscular, since he was never a particularly large man. I was in awe of his
accordionlike ability to expand on demand, to pump up his nerve and face
down anyone who threatened him or his wife or three boys, whether a landlord, a police officer, or a teacher who shirked responsibility. In that way,
among many, I wanted to be like him: smart, tough, the relentless warrior.

James P. Comer, M.D., an African-American professor of child psychi-   13
atry at the Yale University Child Study Center, says that while the concept
of role modeling may sound like a cliché, it is nevertheless "very real" and
necessary. "Kids are here without a road map, and you are like that map to
them," he points out. According to Samuel Osherson in his popular 1986
book *Finding Our Fathers,* the need to "identify with father creates the crucial dilemma for boys. [Father is] often a shadowy figure at best, difficult to
understand." The result can often be a troubling psychological limbo, explains Osherson, in which boys as young as three years old begin pulling
away from their mothers but have no clear male model to identify with.

I've never forgotten the unshed tear in the voice of my best friend   14
when I first asked him about his father, a man I'd never heard him talk
about. Until that afternoon some years ago, my buddy had seemed to be a
product of his mother's labors alone, a bloom from a self-pollinating black
orchid.

But there was a man, from whom my friend's features had borrowed   15
heavily. He had never married his mother. My buddy's only contact with

the man was when, as a boy, he occasionally sat in the cluttered back room of the man's television-repair shop, a place cooled during the Philadelphia summers by an open door and the warm, breathy air of buzzing electric fans. After being told by his mother that the man in the shop was his father, one day my friend stoked up his nerve and asked the man if this was true.

"You're not any boy of mine," he replied, my friend told me. Wounded   16 deeply, he never returned to the shop. Some years later his father died, a bridge between knowing and not knowing a part of himself forever swept away.

After having dozens of recent conversations with Black men about   17 their relationships with their fathers, a common element emerges, regardless of age: Like a primal impulse, the men who have had injured relations with their fathers are busy trying to heal them. Those who enjoy mutually satisfying, rich and rewarding relationships—if not the exaggerated bliss of *The Cosby Show*—find them invaluable. In an interview with astronaut Colonel Frederick Drew Gregory shortly before he became the first African-American to command a spacecraft in the late 1980s, he spoke with me at length about his father as mentor and role model. It was his father, he said, who inspired him to reach for heights that many, Black and white, would consider unattainable. James Comer writes lovingly of his late father in his 1988 book *Maggie's American Dream: The Life and Times of a Black Family.*

Comer, the father of a grown son and daughter, says it is not surprising   18 that many Black men are trying to better understand and appreciate their fathers. "They realize what they have missed," he says. "In some cases there is a struggle for independence that can lead to a difficult relationship," though, he adds, "even bad times can be important once you have reestablished a good relationship." But at any time, Comer emphasizes, "it is important to reestablish the relationship."

Unfortunately that may be more problematic for boys born in the   19 closing years of the twentieth century, since the numbers of African-American families headed by women continue to be substantial. And with alarming regularity, Black fathers are relegating themselves to being ghost dads of sorts: Many are lost to the streets, prisons, to successful careers or to legacies of poor relationships with their own fathers, who had troubles with *their* fathers.

"Imagine what it must be like to have a part of you not there," says   20 Terry M. Williams, author and sociologist at Yale, of boys who don't know or know well their fathers. "You think, *So where can I find it?*" Having the father present in the son's life is key, stresses Williams, even "if his role is not that strong."

Williams, author of the 1989 book *The Cocaine Kids: The Inside Story* 21
of a Teenage Drug Ring, in which he chronicles some four years of observing a young crew of cocaine dealers in New York City, says many young men of color perceive themselves as being in a state of war. "They are acting out and trying to find a way to be men, through tough crews and homeboy networks. You can't deny that these are some of the negative sides of not having fathers around."

Williams, who has two sons, suggests that more Black men be more at- 22
tentive to their roles as fathers and also reach out to be mentors and role models for other boys. Without positive role models, it is obvious that boys may turn to crime or antisocial behavior, says Williams.

As my own son nears his teenage years, I worry if our relationship will 23
hold. His mother and I divorced when he was hardly a year old. But I have worked hard through the years to keep our father-son links strong and supportive, despite the hundreds of miles that separate us for most of the year. At the close of every telephone conversation, I tell him I love him. And he is careful to tell me he loves me, something my father has never been able to bring himself to say.

I love my father. Some of that love stems from my culture's obligation 24
to honor him because he is my father. Yet another, much larger, part of that love flows from my understanding of him, my empathy with his life and wounds as a proud Black man dangling from a leafless tree of opportunities denied. At 63, my father is a man of enormous talents and, in his own estimation, of humble accomplishments. Many demons still stir in his soul.

For the past ten years we have moved, gently, to resolve our conflicts, 25
to settle into roles reassigned to us by time and growth. In the last few years he has let me hug him when I see him now, which is all too infrequently. I, on the other hand, have reined in my juvenile urges to compete with him, to prove in battles of wit and wile that I am as much a man as he is.

For the last three years I've pulled out the same card of bright colors 26
and upbeat prose I bought for Father's Day. But each year something prevents me from sending it. Procrastination abounds, moving me to return the card to my top drawer, more determined to actually send it to him the next year. Yet, as I wrote this article in the late summer, a process that forced me to refocus my feelings about Pop, I got out the card, signed it "I love you" and sent it homeward. I hope its arrival, though odd, will signal to him anew my homage to our connections, both involuntary and voluntary, both of the blood and of the heart.

I want my father to know that with each morning look into the bath- 27
room mirror, I see a little more of his face peering through mine. Life's journey is circular, it appears. The years don't carry us away from our fathers—they return us to them.

If we are lucky, we will have our memories of them. If we are luckier   28
still and work hard for it, we can enjoy with them laughter and tears of
recognition, enjoy loving embraces of mutual appreciation and respect.

With each day, I feel luckier.   29

◆ ◆ ◆

FIRST RESPONSES

Do you think the "psychological or physical absence of fathers from
their families is one of the great underestimated tragedies of our times"?
Why is it difficult for fathers to express their love for their sons?

TAKING A CLOSER LOOK

Exploring *Who:* Voice and Tone

1. In the opening sentence, Marriott reveals that he's a reporter. What
   other information about himself does he divulge in the essay?
2. Marriott doesn't mention his mother—and mentions his wife only
   once. Why doesn't he say more about them? Is this an oversight or an
   intentional omission?
3. Is Marriott writing only for African-American males? Why should
   other people read this essay and care about the issues it raises?
4. How did your background (race, age, gender) affect the way you responded to the author's ideas and feelings about fatherhood?

Exploring *What:* Content and Meaning

1. What is "father hunger"? Try defining it in several sentences.
2. Where does the author state his thesis? Where does he reinforce and
   restate his main point?
3. According to Marriott, why do African-American fathers frequently
   abandon their sons?
4. In paragraph 25, the author talks about his "juvenile urges to compete
   with" his father. What does he mean? Do you have any experiences or
   observations that help you to understand this idea?
5. *Using the Internet.* Find a review of one of the books that Marriott
   cites in his essay—*Men and Masculinity; Finding Our Fathers; Maggie's
   American Dream;* or *The Cocaine Kids.* Do any of the reviews touch on

the issue of father-son relationships? If so, do they support Marriott's ideas? If not, why do you think they don't mention this topic? You can find links to book reviews at several online bookstores; the BookWire site (http://www.bookwire.com/) includes a list. Or look at the Web version of *The Quarterly Black Review of Books* (http://www.bookwire.com/qbr/qbr.html).

Exploring *Why:* Purpose

1. Why is Marriott "in search of" his father? Was writing this essay a part of that search? See paragraph 26.
2. What does the author say about his own fathering skills? What does his relationship with his own son have to do with his reasons for writing this essay?
3. Reread the last six paragraphs. Notice that in this section, Marriott calls his father "Pop" for the first and only time in the essay. Why does he use the term at this point? Why does he say he feels "luckier" with each day?

Exploring *How:* Strategy and Style

1. Why does Marriott begin with an anecdote about Fidel Castro? How does this narrative provide a lead-in to his central idea?
2. Why are the sentences in paragraph 4 in italics?
3. Look at the kinds of evidence Marriott uses to support his thesis; notice how he combines personal experience with expert opinion. Which do you find more persuasive—the quotations from writers and the mention of celebrities or the author's own experiences?
4. Why does the author include the extended example about his best friend (paragraphs 14 through 17)? How did you respond to the father's statement, "You're not any boy of mine"? Do you understand why the father said this?

IDEAS FOR WRITING A DEFINITION

1. Think about all the benefits of a mother's love. Then, imagine how your life would have been different if deprived of that love. Write an essay defining "mother hunger."
2. Write an essay defining the distinctive qualities of your family as you were growing up. What were the recurrent themes or persistent issues

within your family during this time in your life? Have they changed now that you are older? Why or why not?

3. A number of situation comedies on television depict fathers who are raising children without a mother in the family. Analyze two or three of these sitcoms, and write an essay evaluating how realistically these family situations are being presented. Or explain the appeal of such programs.

◆ ◆ ◆ PREPARING TO READ

What is your biggest fear? How do you deal with it? Does it ever make you behave in irrational and unpleasant ways?

◆ ◆ ◆

The Fear

ANDREW HOLLERAN

Andrew Holleran (b. 1934) is the author of three novels about gay life: *Dancer from the Dance* (1978), *Nights in Aruba* (1983), and *The Beauty of Men* (1996). His collection of essays, *Ground Zero* (1988), deals with the public and personal issues surrounding AIDS. A former resident of New York City, he now lives in Florida. In the following essay, which appeared in a 1989 collection of writers' responses to the AIDS crisis, Holleran examines the anxiety and distrust that grip people who are at risk from infection by the AIDS virus.

The Fear is of course unseemly—as most fear is. People behave at   1
worst with demonic cruelty—at best oddly. Even among those who are good-hearted, the madness breaks out in small ways that bring friendships of long standing to an abrupt end. When the plague began and the television crews of certain TV stations refused to work on interviews with people with AIDS, I wanted to get their names, write them down, publish them on a list of cowards. When the parents in Queens picketed and refused to send their kids to school; when they kicked Ryan White out of class in Indiana; when people called in to ask if it was safe to ride the subway; when Pat Buchanan called for a quarantine of homosexuals; when they burned down the house in Arcadia, Florida, I felt a thrilling disgust, a contempt, an anger at the shrill, stupid, mean panic, the alacrity with which people are converted to lepers and the lepers cast out of the tribe, the fact that if Fear is contemptible, it is most contemptible in people who have no reason to fear.

Even within the homosexual community, however, there was despica-   2
ble behavior: men who would not go to restaurants, hospital rooms, wakes, for fear that any contact with other homosexuals might be lethal. At dinner one night in San Francisco in 1982, a friend said, "There's a crack in the glass," after I'd taken a sip of his lover's wine, and took the glass back to the kitchen to replace it—a reaction so swift it took me a moment to realize

there was no crack in the glass; the problem was my lips' touching it—homosexual lips, from New York: the kiss of death. I was furious then, but the behavior no longer surprises me. AIDS, after all, belongs to the Age of Anxiety. My friend was a germophobe to begin with, who, though homosexual himself, after five years in San Francisco, had come to loathe homosexuals. The idea that they could now kill him, or his lover, fit in. AIDS fed on his free-floating anxiety about the rest of modern life: the fertilizers, pesticides, toxic wastes, additives in food, processing of food, steroids given cattle, salmonella in chickens, killer bees moving up from Brazil, Mediterranean fruit fly, poisoned water, lead in our pipes, radon in our homes, asbestos in our high schools, danger of cigarette smoke, mercury in tuna, auto emissions in the air, Filipinos on the bus, Mexicans sneaking across the border. The society that could make sugar sinister was ready, it would seem, to panic over AIDS, so that when Russia put out the disinformation in its official press that AIDS was the work of a germ-warfare laboratory run by the Pentagon, it was only repeating a charge made by homosexuals convinced that AIDS is a right-wing program to eradicate queers.

God only knows what AIDS will turn out to be, years and years from 3 now—perhaps, in 2005, "Sixty Minutes" will reveal it *was* a CIA foul-up. But this general panic, this unease, this sense that the world is out of control and too intimately connected, is not *all* the Fear is among homosexuals. The Fear among homosexuals is personal, physical, and real. It is easy enough to dismiss the idea that the CIA set out to exterminate homosexuals; it is not easy to dismiss the fact that—having lived in New York during the seventies as a gay man—one can reasonably expect to have been infected. "We've all been exposed," a friend said to me in 1981 on the sidewalk one evening before going off to Switzerland to have his blood recycled—when "exposed" was still the word to spare the feelings of those who were, someone finally pointed out, "infected." The idea—that everyone had been swimming in the same sea—made little impression on us at the time; nor did I grasp the implications—because then the plague was still so new, and its victims so (relatively) few, that most homosexuals could still come up with a list of forty to fifty things to distinguish their past, their habits, from those of the men they knew who had it. Now, five years later, that list is in shreds; one by one those distinguishing features or habits have been taken away, and the plague reveals itself as something infinitely larger, more various, more random, than was suspected at the start—as common as the flu—indeed, the thing the doctors are predicting a repeat of: the Spanish influenza following World War I.

Predictions like these, above all, intensify the Fear, to the point that 4 one tenses when a news story comes on the evening news about AIDS—and wonders: What new sadistic detail? What new insoluble problem? One looks away when the word is in the newspaper headline and turns to the comics instead. One hopes the phone will not ring with news of yet another friend diagnosed, because one can always trace a flare-up of the Fear—an AIDS anxiety attack: that period when you are certain you have *It,* and begin making plans for your demise—to some piece of news, or several, that came through the television or the telephone. Sometimes they are so numerous, and all at once, that you are undone—like the man walking down the boardwalk on Fire Island with a friend one evening on their way to dance, who, after a quiet conversation at dinner, suddenly threw himself down on the ground and began screaming: "We're all going to die, we're all going to die!" He did. Sometimes it hits like that. It appears in the midst of the most ordinary circumstances—like the man on that same beach, who in the middle of a cloudless summer afternoon turned to my friend and said: "What is the point of going on?" ("To bear witness," my friend responded.) The Fear is there all the time, but it comes in surges, like electricity— activated, triggered, almost always by specific bad news.

　　The media are full of bad news, of course—the stories of break- 5 throughs, of discoveries, of new drugs seem to have subsided now into a sea of disappointment. They do not sound the note of relief and hope and exultation they once did—that dream that one evening you would be brushing your teeth, and your roommate, watching the news in the living room, would shout: "It's over!" and you would run down the hall and hear the Armistice declared. Instead, the media carry the *pronunciamientos* of the Harvard School of Public Health, the World Health Organization, dire beyond our wildest nightmares: What began as a strange disease ten or twelve homosexuals in New York had contracted becomes the Black Death. Of course, journalists, as Schopenhauer said, are professional alarmists, and have only fulfilled their usual role: scaring their readers. They are scaring them so that the readers will protect themselves, of course; they are at the same time inducing despair in those already infected. There's the dilemma: They're all watching the same TV, reading the same newspapers.

　　After a while, the Fear is so ugly you feel like someone at a dinner 6 party whose fellow guests are being taken outside and shot as you concentrate politely on your salad. There is the school of thought that says the Fear is a form of stress, and stress enhances the virus. Like the man so afraid of muggers he somehow draws them to him, the Fear is said to make itself come true, by those who believe in mind control. As a friend of mine (so fearful of the disease he refused to have sex for four years) said, "I got everything I resisted." So one becomes fearful even of the Fear. The Fear can be so wearing, so depressing, so constant that a friend who learned he had AIDS said, on hearing the diagnosis, "Well, it's a lot better than worrying about it."

He also said, "I wasn't doing anything anyone else wasn't." Which ex-   7
plains the Fear more succinctly than anything else: Tens of thousands were
doing the same thing in the seventies. Why, then, should some get sick and
not others? Isn't it logical to expect everyone will, eventually? The Fear is
so strong it causes people to change cities, to rewrite their pasts in order to
imagine they were doing less than everyone else; because the most unnerving thing about the plague is its location in the Past, the Time allotted to it.

Were AIDS a disease which, once contracted, brought death within   8
forty-eight hours of exposure, it would be a far more easily avoided
illness—but because it is not—because it is invisible, unknown, for such a
long period of time, because it is something people got before they even
knew it existed (with each passing year, the Time Lag gets longer), the Fear
of AIDS is limitless. Who has not had sex within the last seven years—once?
(The nun in San Francisco who got AIDS from a blood transfusion given
her during an operation to set her broken leg, and died, her superiors said,
without anger or bitterness.) (The babies who get it in the womb.) There's a
memory—of an evening, an incident—to justify every Fear. And nothing
exists that will guarantee the fearful that even if they are functioning now,
they will not get caught in the future. The phrase that keeps running
through the fearful mind is: Everyone was healthy before he got sick. One
has to have two programs, two sets of responses, ready at all times: (a) Life,
(b) Death. The switch from one category to the other can come at any moment, in the most casual way. At the dentist's, or putting on your sock. Did
that shin bruise a little too easily? Is that a new mole? Is the sinus condition
that won't go away just a sinus condition? Do you feel a bit woozy standing
at the kitchen sink? Do you want to lie down? Is the Fear making you
woozy, or the virus? Have you had too many colds this past spring to be just
colds? Thus the hyperconsciousness of the body begins. Your body—which
you have tended, been proud of—is something you begin to view with suspicion, mistrust. Your body is someone you came to a party with and you'd
like to ditch, only you promised to drive him home. Your body is a house—
there's a thief inside it who wants to rob you of everything. Your body could
be harboring It, even as you go about your business. This keeps you on edge.
You stop, for instance, looking in mirrors. Or at your body in the shower—
because the skin, all of a sudden, seems as vast as Russia: a huge terrain, a
monumental wall, on which tiny handwriting may suddenly appear. The
gums, the tongue, the face, the foot, the forearm, the leg: *billions* of cells
waiting to go wrong. Because you read that sunburn depresses the immune
system, you no longer go out in the sun. You stay in the house—as if already
an invalid—you cancel all thoughts of traveling in airplanes because you
heard flights can trigger the pneumonia and because you want to be home
when it happens, not in some hotel room in Japan or San Diego.

And so the Fear constricts Life. It suffocates, till one evening its prey   9
snaps—gets in the car and drives to the rest stop, or bar, or baths to meet another human being; and has sex. Sometimes has sex; sometimes just talks
about the Fear, because a conversation about the danger of sex sometimes
replaces sex itself. The Fear is a god to which offerings must be made before
sex can commence. Sometimes it refuses the offering. If it does not, it takes its
share of the harvest afterward. Sex serves the Fear more slavishly than anything. Even safe sex leads to the question: Why was I even doing something
that *required* condoms? The aftermath of sex is fear *and* loathing. AIDS is a
national program of aversion therapy. Sex and terror are twins. Death is a
hunk, a gorgeous penis. And fear is self-centered, is above all personal, and
you vent your terror before you realize how insensitive this is. One day you
spill out your fears about the sex you had to a friend who—you realize too
late—has had AIDS for a couple of years now. He has lived with his own fear
for two years. Your friend merely listens calmly, says what you did does not
seem unsafe, and then remarks: "What I'm getting from what you've been
saying is that you're still afraid." Of course, you want to reply, *of course* I'm
still afraid! "But you have no reason to be," he says, from the height, the emi-
nence of his own fear, digested, lived with, incorporated into his own life by
now. "If you don't have it now, you won't." (Your other friend has told you,
"The doctors think we're about to see a second wave of cases, the ones who
contracted it in 1981.") Going home on the subway, your fear takes the form
of superstition: He should never have said that! He himself had said (a remark you've never forgotten) that he was diagnosed just at the point when—
after three years of abstinence—he thought he had escaped. It's the Time
Lag, of course, the petri dish in which the Fear thrives. Of course, you are
afraid; every male homosexual who lived in New York during the seventies is
scared shitless. And a bit unstable, withdrawn, and crazy. The tactlessness of
venting your fear to a friend who already has been diagnosed is symptomatic
of this behavior. People who are afraid are seldom as considerate as those
who are unafraid. The ironic thing about my last visit to New York was that
the two men I knew who have AIDS were cheerful, calm, gracious, well behaved. Those who did not were nervous wrecks: depressed, irritable, isolated,
withdrawn, unwilling to go out at night, in bed by ten under a blanket, with
terror and a VCR. The Fear is not fun to live with, though when shared, it can
produce occasional, hysterical laughter. The laughter vanishes, however, the
moment you leave the apartment building and find yourself alone on the
street. Falls right off your face as you slip instantly back into the mood you
were in before you went to visit your friend. The Fear breeds depression. The
depression breeds anger. (Not to mention the anger of people who have it
toward those who don't. Why me? Why should *he* escape?) Friendships
come to an end over incidents which would have been jokes before. People

withdraw from each other so they don't have to go through the suffering of each other's illness. People behave illogically: One night a friend refuses to eat from a buffet commemorating a dead dancer because so many of the other guests have AIDS ("They shouldn't have served finger food"), but he leaves the wake with a young handsome Brazilian who presumably doesn't, goes home, and has sex. We all have an explanation for our private decisions, our choices of what we will do and what we won't; we all have a rationale for our superstitions. Most of it is superstition, because that is what the Fear produces and always has. Some of it is just muddled thinking, like the nightclub patrons in Miami who said they did not worry about AIDS there because it cost ten dollars to get in. And some of it is perfectly rational, like that which convinces people they should not take the Test because they would rather not live with the knowledge they have antibodies to the virus. (Today, the news announces a home test that will tell you in three minutes if you do, or don't; not much time for counseling!)

The Test is the most concentrated form of the Fear that there is— 10 which is why people are advised not to take it if they think they will have trouble handling the results. Why should we know? The fact is things are happening in our bodies, our blood, all the time we know nothing of, the hole in the dike of our immune systems may appear at any moment, and is always invisible, silent, unadvertised.

When does a person begin to develop cancer? When does a tumor 11 start to grow? When does the wall of the heart begin to weaken? Do you want to know? With AIDS, there is presumably something in hiding, in the brain, the tissues, waiting for some moment to begin its incredibly fast and protean reproduction. It may be waiting—or reproducing—as I type this. This is the Fear that is finally selfish. That is perhaps worse in the imagining than in the reality. This is what makes you think: I must know, I can't bear this, I'll take the Test. So you drive over one hot afternoon to do it, thinking of the letter from a woman whose nephew just died at home of AIDS: "Tony even tested Negative two months before he died." What fun. You feel as if you are driving not toward the county health department but the Day of Judgment. In my right hand, I give you Life, in my left, Death. What will you do, the voice asks, when you find out? How will you live? How do people with AIDS drive the car, fall asleep at night, face the neighbors, deal with solitude? The stupendous cruelty of this disease crashes in upon you. And so you bargain with God. You apologize, and make vows. Ask, How could this have happened? How could I have reached this point? Where did I make the turn that got me on *this* road? Every test you have ever taken, written or oral—the book reports; the thesis examinations; the spelling bees; those afternoons walking home from school as far as you could before turning the page of your test to see the grade, on a corner where no one could see your reaction; the day you got drafted; the day you found out whether you were going to Vietnam—all pale, or come back, in one single concentrated tsunami of terror at this moment.

In eighteenth-century Connecticut, Jonathan Edwards preached a   12 sermon called "Sinners in the Hands of an Angry God," which was so terrifying that women in the congregation fainted. Some things never change. The Fear, like the sermon, feeds on the Imagination. And the moment you know someone who faces this disease daily with composure, calm, humor, and his or her own personality intact, you realize how deforming, how demeaning, how subject to the worst instincts Fear is.

◆ ◆ ◆

FIRST RESPONSES

If you thought you were at risk for getting AIDS, would you get tested? Do you think it's better to know you have an incurable disease, or would you prefer not to know? Explain your thinking.

TAKING A CLOSER LOOK

Exploring *Who:* Voice and Tone

1. Does Andrew Holleran ever say he has AIDS? Why doesn't he reveal this fact?
2. Do you know anyone with AIDS? How might the answer to this question affect your response to the essay?
3. Does the author himself give in to the madness that he equates with the Fear? Where do you see evidence of that? How does that perception color your response to the author and his essay?
4. Do you have to be at risk of getting AIDS to understand and appreciate this essay? Point out several passages that illustrate the way fear, of any sort, affects people in general.

Exploring *What:* Content and Meaning

1. Identify and describe several of Holleran's attitudes toward the behavior of various fearful people.
2. Holleran says that "the most unnerving thing" about AIDS is "its location in the Past." What does he mean?

3. How does the Fear constrict life? Have you had any experiences with fear that shed light on this phenomenon? (See the fears that Holleran lists in paragraph 2.)

4. How does fear produce superstitions? Can you cite additional examples that confirm this point?

Exploring *Why:* Purpose

1. Why does the essay focus on the experience of fear rather than on AIDS?

2. What is Holleran's purpose? Do you think he wants to elicit sympathy and understanding for people with AIDS? Does he have a more general purpose?

3. Reread the last sentence. What is the point of this ending? How does it sum up Holleran's main message?

4. What have you learned from reading this essay?

Exploring *How:* Style and Structure

1. Why is the word *fear* sometimes capitalized? What is the difference between "fear" and "the Fear"? Why are other words—like Life, Time Lag, the Past, and the Test—capitalized?

2. At first, Holleran writes in the third person (talking *about* people and their behavior). In paragraph 4, he begins with the indefinite third-person pronoun *one* ("One looks away . . . . One hopes the phone will not ring . . . .") but then brings in the pronoun *you* ("that period when you are certain you have It"), which he uses more frequently as the essay progresses. Why does he use *you?* Does he mean *you* the reader? Could he be referring to himself?

3. Look at Holleran's examples. Which ones are taken from his own experience, and which ones has he gotten from other people? Can you always tell? Is there any reason why Holleran would mix the two kinds of examples (personal and hearsay)?

4. Find several examples of metaphors and analogies in the essay. Which ones catch your attention and make you think?

5. Look at the way Holleran uses parentheses. Does he follow the standard practice of putting parentheses around supplemental material, minor digressions, and afterthoughts? Or does he use parentheses to achieve emphasis?

IDEAS FOR WRITING A DEFINITION

1. Write an essay in which you explore the effects of a powerful emotion, like love, hate, anger, joy, guilt, or jealousy. Use the techniques that Holleran uses—examples, descriptions, quotations, explanations, and analogies—to show how much an emotion can affect people.

2. Write an essay in which you use examples to define an abstract term like *racism, sexism, discrimination, homophobia, prejudice, intolerance, bigotry,* or *injustice.*

3. ■ *Using the Internet.* Since Andrew Holleran wrote "The Fear" in 1989, many things about the AIDS epidemic have changed: new therapies, better testing, more education, greater support for people with AIDS, changes in insurance coverage, more pubic awareness. Write an essay entitled "The Hope," in which you define and discuss some of the positive aspects of recent developments in the AIDS crisis. You will find lots of information about AIDS on the Internet to use in your essay. These five Web sites are especially useful: (1) The HIV/AIDS Index Page, prepared by the U.S. Food and Drug Administration (http://www.fda.gov/oashi/aids/hiv.html); (2) The HIV InfoWeb (http:// www.infoweb.org/); (3) HIV InSite, a project of the University of California San Francisco (http://hivinsite.ucsf.edu/); (4) The Gay Men's Health Crisis (GMHC) Website (http://www.gmhc.org/); and (5) HIV/AIDS Education and Prevention, a Web site prepared by Vanderbilt University Medical Center (http://www.mc.vanderbilt.edu/resources/interests/aids.edu.html/).

◆ ◆ ◆

◆ FURTHER IDEAS FOR USING DEFINITION

1. Recent research has shown that the birth of a baby causes serious tensions and strains on the new parents' relationship because of the enormous amount of extra work and stress involved in caring for a newborn. Why, then, do you think that most people—including the prospective parents—continue to think of a new baby as a total bundle of joy and often suffer a rude awakening when the baby comes home? Write an essay defining several of the powerful *pronatal influences* in our society, especially influences from the advertising and entertainment industries.

2. For an audience of people from another culture, define *situation comedy, fast food, soap opera, aroma therapy, homecoming weekend,* or another term that labels a cultural phenomenon.

3. COMBINING STRATEGIES. Write an essay that gives your classmates a vivid sense of a place from your past—your high school, neighborhood, home town, favorite hangout. What was valued most there? What activities were most important? Define the flavor and character of this place by citing examples, describing characteristics, narrating brief stories, explaining qualities, making analogies, and drawing contrasts about particular features and key individuals.

4. COLLABORATIVE WRITING. The purpose of this assignment is to write an article that defines and makes recommendations about a common problem such as procrastination, poor study skills, an eating disorder, self-centeredness, shopping addiction, or the doormat syndrome. Get together with a group of fellow students, and identify a problem that you think is worth writing about. It may help to focus the group's thinking if you assume that you are going to submit this article to your school newspaper or some other student publication. Brainstorm a list of characteristics, examples, and details that define the problem; make another list of recommendations that you can offer to solve the problem. Then write the article, individually or as a group.

5. ■▯ *Using the Internet.* Choose someone you find especially interesting—an athlete, businessperson, entertainer, or public figure. Through a computer search, locate several online articles or Web pages about that person. (Find substantial articles, not just gossip items.) Using facts and details from these sources, write an essay in which you define the unique traits that have made this person successful. Assume your audience will be readers of a popular publication like *Parade* or *USA Today.* Be sure to give appropriate credit to your sources.

Strategies for Organizing Ideas and Experience

Division and Classification

◆ ◆ ◆ ◆ ◆

Division and classification writing imposes or reveals order and makes ideas more understandable.

◆ Writers use division and classification to present information in a systematic way.

◆ Meaningful division and classification includes a reason or makes a point.

◆ Writers should establish a clear basis for their divisions and make sure their classification system is consistent, complete, significant, and accurate.

The next time you get ready to do your laundry, look on the back of the detergent box. There you will see directions for sorting your clothes according to the temperature of the water that you should use. The directions may read something like this:

FOR BEST CLEANING RESULTS

Sort and select temperature and begin filling washer with water.

Hot	Warm	Cold
White cottons	Bright colors	Dark colors
Colorfast pastels	Permanent press	Colors that could bleed
Diapers	Knits	Delicates
Heavily soiled items		Stains like blood and chocolate

Do you follow a procedure like this when you do your laundry? Why do you suppose the detergent makers put directions like this on the back of the box?

As our example shows, separating and arranging things helps us to accomplish tasks more efficiently and more effectively. This process of "sorting things out" also helps us to clarify our thinking and understand our feelings.

Many writing tasks lend themselves to grouping information into categories. For example, you might write a paper for psychology class on the various ways people cope with the death of a loved one. For a course in economics you might write about the three basic types of unemployment *(frictional, structural,* and *cyclical)*. This approach—called **division** and **classification**—enables you to present a body of information in an orderly way. In the following essay, columnist Calvin Trillin comments humorously on human nature by classifying eaters according to how they eat off of other people's plates.

The Extendable Fork

CALVIN TRILLIN

Born in Kansas City, Missouri, in 1935, Calvin Trillin was educated at Yale University. He began his career in journalism as a reporter for *Time* magazine and then became a columnist for *The New Yorker.* More recently, he has written a nationally syndicated newspaper column and staged a one-man show off-Broadway. He has also published two novels, four collections of his reporting, several books of humorous essays, and a best-selling memoir, *Remembering Denny* (1993).

In our house, news that the extendable fork had been invented was   1
greeted with varying degrees of enthusiasm. I think it's fair to say that I
was the most enthusiastic of all. I eat off of other people's plates. My wife
was mildly enthusiastic. She figures that if I use an extendable fork I'm less
likely to come away from the table with gravy on my cuff.

People who eat off of other people's plates can be categorized in four   2
types—The Finisher, The Waif, The Researcher and The Simple Thief. I
might as well admit right here at the beginning that I am all four.

The Finisher demonstrates concern that food may be left uneaten   3
even though the starving children your mother told you about are still hungry. Once the pace of eating begins to slacken off a bit, he reaches across to
spear a roast potato off of someone's plate a nanosecond after saying, "If
you're not planning to finish these . . ."

The long reach eater I think of as The Waif often doesn't order much   4
himself at a restaurant, claiming that he's not terribly hungry or that he's
trying to lose weight. Then, he gazes at his dinner companions' plates, like a
hungry urchin who has his nose pressed up against the window of a restaurant where enormously fat rich people are slurping oysters and shoveling
down mounds of *boeuf bourguignon*. Occasionally, he murmurs something
like, "That looks delicious." Answering "Actually, it's not all that good" does
not affect him—although it may slow down the Researcher, who, as he extends his fork usually says something like, "I'm curious how they do these
fried onions."

The Simple Thief simply waits for his dining companions to glance   5
away, then confidently grabs what he wants. If he's desperate, he may actually take measures to distract them, saying something like, "Is it my imagination, or could that be Michael Jackson and Lisa Marie Presley at the table
over by the door?"

That sort of subterfuge is not necessary, by the way, if the plate I have   6
singled out as a target is my wife's. She does not object to my sampling—a
reflection, I've always thought, of her generous heart. In fact, I have said in
the past that if a young groom on his honeymoon reaches over for the first
time to sample his bride's fettuccine only to be told "Don't you like what
you're having?" or "There really isn't that much of this," he knows he's in
for a long haul.

Actually, my wife might be called a Finisher herself. If we're having   7
fried chicken, she will stare at what's on my plate after I have indeed finished. "Look at all the chicken you left," she'll say. Or "There's a ton of meat
still on that chicken."

Oddly enough, this is precisely the sort of thing that I heard from my   8
mother, who was also fond of saying that I didn't "do a good job" on the
chicken. The way my wife eats chicken is to eat every speck of meat off the

bones, so that the chicken looks as if it had been staked out on an anthill by a tribe of crazed chicken torturers. She treats a lobster the same way.

I eat more the way a shark eats—tearing off whatever seems exposed   9 and easy to get at. I have suggested, in fact, that in fried-chicken or lobster restaurants we could economize by getting only one order, which I could start and my wife could finish.

My wife's approach to finishing does not, of course, require an extend-   10 able fork, but I intend to be an early customer myself. According to an item in the *New York Times,* the fork is nearly two feet long when fully opened. It's being marketed under the name of Alan's X-Tenda Fork.

I might have chosen another name, but this one is, I'll admit, evoca-   11 tive. For me, it conjures up visions of a Limbaugh-sized man named Alan sitting in a restaurant with friends and family. He seems to be engaging in normal conversation, but his tiny eyes dart from plate to plate; occasionally, with a fork as quick as the strike of an adder, he helps with the finishing.

In fact, I can imagine Alan inventing other needed implements—a   12 sort of vacuum tube, for instance, that can suck up french fries from three feet away. I can see him improving on Alan's X-Tenda Fork. He might in-stall a tiny tape recorder in it, so when you pulled it out to its full length and moved it quickly across the table a voice said, "If you're not planning to fin-ish these . . ."

◆ ◆ ◆

◆ ◆ ◆ *Writer's Workshop I* ◆ ◆ ◆
Responding to a Classification

Use the *Who, What, Why,* and *How* questions (pp. 3–4) to explore your own understanding of the ideas and writing strategies used by Calvin Trillin in "The Extendable Fork." Your instructor may ask you to record these respon-ses in a journal or bring them to class to use in small group discussions.

◆ WRITING FROM READING

Freshman Brian Shamhart enjoyed reading "The Extendable Fork" and thought he would like to write a similar essay. He explored Trillin's ideas and strategies by writing out responses to the *Who, What, Why,* and *How* questions, and then wrote the following essay that classifies friends, enemies, and the people in between.

Brian Shamhart
Eng. 1091
November 10, 1997

Friend, Foe, or ???

Many people divide their acquaintances into two   1
groups: friends and enemies. In actuality, a couple
of groups get left out of this two-part division.
I'm referring to the *Wanna-bes* and the *Hafta-bes.*
These two categories cover more people than any
person's friends and enemies categories combined. As
we explore various groups, I encourage you to think
about the people you know; re-examine your friends
and enemies, and if need be, move them to a different
classification. Then see how many are left in the
original categories when you are done. Who knows?
You might never look at certain people the same way
again.

Enemies are not hard to identify. They do   2
everything in their power to get you in trouble. If
the opportunity arises, they put you down, talk behind
your back, and try to make you look bad. No matter how
likable you are, you cannot avoid having enemies.
Somewhere, sometime, somebody is going to resent you
or be jealous of you or feel threatened by you; and
you will have an enemy. My advice for dealing with
enemies is to learn to live with them.

As with enemies, identifying friends should not   3
cause many problems. But you must realize that
qualifying as a true friend requires a lot of
dedication and loyalty. True friends include only
those who will always be there for you, standing by
your side through any situation. When you're in
trouble, true friends will help you out as much as
possible. Most important, true friends want to see you
succeed, no matter what the cost is to them. No amount
of money or type of bribe will keep them from standing
by your side. True friends are the people you love and
admire more than anyone else.

It might be hard to see how a person can be   4
considered something else, but the *Wanna-bes* and the
Hafta-bes do exist. Pay close attention because I am
about to describe what types of people belong in these
odd categories. Once you have an understanding of who
might fit into these other groups, your individual list
of friends and enemies should be shortened
dramatically.

The *Wanna-bes* are people who try to be friends   5
with everyone. Inevitably, this approach to friendship
leads to conflicts and suspicion. Imagine trying to be
friends with your best friend and your best friend's
enemy at the same time. To complicate things further,
imagine that you show no preference--as if they were
both your best friends. Every time you were with one
of them, the other one would get jealous. This
jealousy could easily lead to ugly thoughts, mean
words, and eventually, the loss of everyone's trust.
You simply cannot depend on a *Wanna-be* as a friend.
You never know whose side they would take between you
and your enemies if push came to shove, and you would
always wonder what they're telling your enemies.
These are the problems you face when dealing with a
Wanna-be.

The *Hafta-bes* are the people you have to be   6
friends with. First and foremost, this group includes
relatives. Some might seem like friends, some might
seem like enemies, but all of them are *Hafta-bes*
because you have to at least try to be friends with
them. Throughout history, in-laws have been considered
one of the hardest groups of people to get along with.
But they are relatives, and must be considered members
of the *Hafta-bes*. Bosses make up another subgroup of
Hafta-bes. No matter how much you hate your boss, you
have to remain on friendly terms because your job
depends on it. Of course, if you were to get fired,
that boss could change from a *Hafta-be* to an enemy
very easily and quickly.

Well, has thinking about these two new categories   7
shortened your original list very much? Are you
thinking about some people in a new light? I guarantee

that I am. By enlarging my perspective, I can more
accurately gauge just where the people I know fit in.
I hope that this discussion has also helped you to
value your friends more fully. Maybe now you can
look at them, and see just how much they really mean
to you.

◆ GETTING STARTED ON DIVISION AND CLASSIFICATION WRITING

Dividing and classifying forces you to think clearly about a topic. By breaking a subject down into its distinct parts, or categories, you can look at it more closely and decide what to say about each part. For example, if you are writing an essay about effective teaching styles, you might begin by dividing the teachers you have had into the "good" ones and the "bad" ones. You could then break those broad categories down further into more precise ones: teachers who held your interest, teachers who knew their subject, teachers who made you do busy work, and so forth. As you develop each category, you have to think about the qualities that impressed you, and this thought process leads you to a better understanding of the topic you are writing about. You may end up writing only about the good teachers, but dividing and classifying the examples will help you to organize your thinking.

Most things can be classified or divided in more than one way, depending on the reason for making up the groups. In the laundry example, for instance, you are told to sort the clothes according to the temperature of the water. Putting bright colors with knits doesn't make any sense if you don't know the reason—or basis—for the category: *items to be washed in cold water.*

As you begin to divide and classify a topic, try to come up with a sound basis for formulating your categories. For example, if you are writing about friends, you could group them according to how close you are to them, as Phillip Lopate does in "What Friends Are For." But you could also group them according to other principles: how long you have known them, what you have in common with them, or how much time you spend with the people in each group. Calvin Trillin's four types of eaters are based, humorously, on their motives for taking food from other people's plates. The important thing is to choose a workable principle and stick with it.

Merely putting facts or ideas into different groups isn't necessarily meaningful. You must consider your purpose for using division and classification. Look at these sentences that classify for no apparent reason:

1. There are five kinds of friends in most of our lives.
2. People deal with their spare money in four basic ways.

How could you give a purpose to these ideas? You would have to add a *reason* or declare a *point* for the categories. Here are some revisions that give purpose to these two classifications:

1.   a. There are five kinds of friends in most of our lives, and each kind is important in its own way.
     b. Most of us have five kinds of friends, and each one drives us crazy in a special way.
2.   a. People deal with their spare money in four ways that reflect their overall attitudes toward life.
     b. People deal with their spare money in four ways, only one of which is truly constructive.

You should also recognize the difference between useful and useless ways of classifying. Sorting your clothes by brand name probably won't help you get the best cleaning results when doing the laundry. And dividing teachers into those who wear glasses and those who don't is not a very useful way to approach an essay on effective teaching styles. However, classifying teachers into those who lecture, those who use a question-discussion format, and those who run small-group workshops might be productive, mainly because such groupings would allow you to discuss the teachers' philosophies, their attitudes toward students, and their effectiveness in the classroom.

◆ ORGANIZING DIVISION AND CLASSIFICATION WRITING

Ideally, your subject will divide naturally into parallel, meaningful categories, and these categories will slip conveniently into well-developed paragraphs of roughly equal length. Ideally. In reality, that seldom happens. You will probably have to rethink and reorganize the groups or types you first come up with. Here are a couple of important questions to ask about your categories:

1. *Does the basis of the division shift?* If you can see a problem with the following classification system, you already understand this point.

Types of Teachers

a. Teachers who lecture
b. Teachers who lead discussion
c. Teachers who have a sense of humor
d. Teachers who run workshops
e. Teachers who never hold office hours

Notice that three types of teachers (a, b, and d) are grouped according to the way they run their classes, but two types (c and e) are defined by some other standard. You can see the confusion these shifting groups cause: Can teachers who lecture have a sense of humor? Don't those who use workshops hold office hours?

2. *Are the groups parallel or equal in rank?* The following classification illustrates a problem of rank:

Kinds of Popular Music

a. Easy listening
b. Country and western
c. Rock and roll
d. Ice-T

Although Ice-T does represent a type of popular music distinct from easy listening, country, and rock, the category is not parallel with the others: it is far too small. It should be "rap," with Ice-T used as an example.

After making sure that your categories are logical and consistent, you need to consider how to arrange them. The order in which you first thought of them may not be necessarily the best. Your groups might lend themselves to chronological order (according to time). In an essay about horror films, for example, you might begin with classic mass destruction movies (like *The Blob* and *War of the Worlds*), then move to the supernatural thrillers that came next *(The Exorcist* and *Rosemary's Baby),* and end with the slasher style of more recent movies (*The Texas Chainsaw Massacre* and the *Friday the Thirteenth* series).

A classification of the parts of a machine or process may be arranged spatially—top to bottom, left to right, inside to outside. An essay on types of people, like gamblers, might be organized by size—from the group with the fewest members to the group with the most. Consider arranging by degree, too: least important to most important, simple to complex, or mildly irritating to totally repulsive. When you organize by degree, you might want to put your strongest category last for emphasis.

◆ DEVELOPING DIVISION AND CLASSIFICATION WRITING

Once you have established and organized the categories for your discussion, you need to think about the details that will define and describe the groups, the examples that will support your claims about the groups, and the explanations that will make your purpose clear to your readers. As usual, you can use your favorite invention techniques—brainstorming, freewriting, clustering, questioning—to generate the material you will need to develop and explain your classification system. As you are planning and drafting the content for your essay, you should also address these questions:

1. *Can I handle the subject and its divisions in the number of words that I want?* Entire books have been written on heroes and their qualities and the types that exist. If you want only a 750-word paper, you should probably narrow your categories to "Types of Heroes on Popular TV Shows" or "Barney Fife's Heroic Qualities." On the other hand, if you find that you'll be able to devote fewer than fifty words to each group you've chosen, that is nature's way of telling you to consolidate categories or change topics.

2. *Does my classification cover everything I claim it covers?* If, for instance, you know some teachers who sometimes lecture and sometimes use small groups, you can't pretend these people don't exist just to make your categories tidy. At least mention exceptions, even if you don't give them as much space as the major categories.

3. *Am I presenting stereotypes?* When you write about types of behavior or put people into groups, you run the risk of oversimplifying the material. The best way to avoid this problem is to use plenty of specific examples. You can also point out exceptions and describe variations; such honesty shows that you have been thinking carefully about the topic.

◆ OPENING AND CLOSING DIVISION AND CLASSIFICATION WRITING

Somewhere in the opening you need to let your readers know just what you are dividing and classifying and why: several ways to handle criticism, four kinds of friends, three types of stress, or three levels of intelligence, for example. Here are some strategies for introducing your categories:

1. *Pose a problem.* Simply presenting the problem to be discussed may set an appropriate context for some topics: "Affluent city dwellers are faced with the dilemma of choosing what kind of housing to live in—a rented apartment, a mortgaged condominium, or a single-family house." Then you present the information on these options in the body of your paper.
2. *State your purpose.* Indicate the point or value of your classification system: "As a child, I was the victim of baby-sitting blues until I learned to classify the behavior of my sitters and cope with each type differently."
3. *Set a historical context.* Renee Tajima takes this approach in the first few paragraphs of her essay "Lotus Blossoms Don't Bleed" (page 314), pointing out that "Images of Asian women [in the movies] have remained consistently simplistic and inaccurate during the sixty years of largely forgettable screen appearances."
4. *Begin with a pertinent anecdote.* Lee Smith uses this strategy to draw readers into his essay about types of memory (page 332): "The alarm finally goes off in your head around 3 P.M. Your face flushes and your hands plow through the papers on your desk. You have accidentally stood someone up for lunch. It gets worse. You can't remember who. And still worse: You can't recall where you left your glasses, so you can't look up the name in your appointment book."

The closing of a division and classification essay is a good place to review your categories and draw some final conclusions about the ideas or behaviors you have been describing. That's how Brian Shamhart closes his essay about friends and enemies: "I hope that this discussion has also helped you to value your friends more fully. Maybe now you can look at them, and see just how much they really mean to you." You can also look into the future to suggest the longer-term implications of your topic, as Lee Smith does in the last two paragraphs of "What We Now Know About Memory," where he writes about the new class of drugs that may prove to be "the easy, safe, and effective way to freshen old memories."

◆ USING THE MODEL

After reading Calvin Trillin's essay, Brian Shamhart decided that he would also write about some form of human behavior. Classification is primarily an organizational strategy, so it was natural that Brian based his discussion on the structure that he found in "The Extendable Fork." Noting that Trillin divides eaters into four categories, Brian divided his subjects into two primary groups and two groups that fall in between. Although Brian's essay is not as lighthearted as "The Extendable Fork," some of the humor of Trillin's essay found its way into Brian's writing, especially in his names and descriptions of the in-between groups—the *Wanna-bes* and the *Hafta-bes.*

You can probably think of some form of human behavior that can be divided into informative and revealing types—for instance, the way different people walk to class or eat pizza or study for a test or move on the dance floor. You could consider the ways people approach their work, style their hair, arrange their closets, discipline their children, or shop for groceries. Figure out three or four valid categories into which you can group the people who engage in the behavior; establish a clear basis for grouping them; decide what your purpose is; and write an essay that comments on the foibles and distinctions of human nature.

◆ ◆ ◆ Writer's Workshop II ◆ ◆ ◆
Analyzing a Division and Classification Essay

Working individually or with a small group of classmates, read through Brian Shamhart's essay "Friend, Foe, or ???" and respond to the following questions:

1. What is Brian's purpose for writing this essay? Does he make his purpose clear in the beginning?
2. What do you think of Brian's division of people into four groups? Is his classification reasonable and useful? Is it complete, or do you think there are other in-between groups that he could have discussed?
3. Does Brian define and explain his groups sufficiently? Does he provide enough details and examples to support his judgments about each category?
4. Is the conclusion of Brian's essay satisfactory? Why or why not?

◆ ◆ ◆ Checklist for Reading and Writing ◆ ◆ ◆
Division and Classification Essays

1. What is being divided and classified? What is the basis for the groupings?
2. Who are the intended readers? What purpose does the division and classification serve for these readers?

3. Are the categories clearly defined? Do they shift? Do they cover what they claim to cover? Are they parallel?

4. Are the categories clearly arranged? Are any subgroups clearly distinguished from the main groups?

5. Does the division into groups lead to stereotyping? Are exceptions and variations noted and explained?

◆ ◆ ◆ **PREPARING TO READ**

Have you ever tried to read a lease agreement, a credit card contract, or an insurance policy? How would you describe the language in these documents? Did you get the feeling that you were not supposed to understand what you were reading?

◆ ◆ ◆

Doublespeak

WILLIAM LUTZ

A professor of English at Rutgers University, William Lutz has long spoken out against the "conscious use of language as a weapon or tool by those in power." Lutz is the editor of *The Doublespeak Review* and has written extensively on the topic of deceptive and evasive language. His most recent book is *The New Doublespeak: Why No One Knows What Anyone's Saying Anymore* (1996). The following selection is taken from an earlier book, *Doublespeak: How Government, Business, Advertisers, and Others Use Language to Deceive You* (1989).

There are no potholes in the streets of Tucson, Arizona, just "pavement deficiencies." The Reagan Administration didn't propose any new taxes, just "revenue enhancement" through new "user's fees." Those aren't bums on the street, just "nongoal oriented members of society." There are no more poor people, just "fiscal underachievers." There was no robbery of an automatic teller machine, just an "unauthorized withdrawal." The patient didn't die because of medical malpractice, it was just a "diagnostic misadventure of a high magnitude." The U.S. Army doesn't kill the enemy anymore, it just "services the target." And the doublespeak goes on. 1

Doublespeak is language that pretends to communicate but really doesn't. It is language that makes the bad seem good, the negative appear positive, the unpleasant appear attractive or at least tolerable. Doublespeak is language that avoids or shifts responsibility, language that is at variance with its real or purported meaning. It is language that conceals or prevents thought; rather than extending thought, doublespeak limits it. 2

Doublespeak is not a matter of subjects and verbs agreeing; it is a matter of words and facts agreeing. Basic to doublespeak is incongruity, the incongruity between what is said or left unsaid, and what really is. It is the 3 incongruity between the word and the referent, between seem and be, between the essential function of language—communication—and what doublespeak does—mislead, distort, deceive, inflate, circumvent, obfuscate.

How to Spot Doublespeak

How can you spot doublespeak? Most of the time you will recognize   4
doublespeak when you see or hear it. But, if you have any doubts, you can identify doublespeak just by answering these questions: Who is saying what to whom, under what conditions and circumstances, with what intent, and with what results? Answering these questions will usually help you identify as doublespeak language that appears to be legitimate or that at first glance doesn't even appear to be doublespeak.

First Kind of Doublespeak

There are at least four kinds of doublespeak. The first is the eu-   5
phemism, an inoffensive or positive word or phrase used to avoid a harsh, unpleasant, or distasteful reality. But a euphemism can also be a tactful word or phrase which avoids directly mentioning a painful reality, or it can be an expression used out of concern for the feelings of someone else, or to avoid directly discussing a topic subject to a social or cultural taboo.

When you use a euphemism because of your sensitivity for someone's   6
feelings or out of concern for a recognized social or cultural taboo, it is not doublespeak. For example, you express your condolences that someone has "passed away" because you do not want to say to a grieving person, "I'm sorry your father is dead." When you use the euphemism "passed away," no one is misled. Moreover, the euphemism functions here not just to protect the feelings of another person, but to communicate also your concern for that person's feelings during a period of mourning. When you excuse yourself to go to the "rest room," or you mention that someone is "sleeping with" or "involved with" someone else, you do not mislead anyone about your meaning, but you do respect the social taboos about discussing bodily functions and sex in direct terms. You also indicate your sensitivity to the feelings of your audience, which is usually considered a mark of courtesy and good manners.

However, when a euphemism is used to mislead or deceive, it becomes   7
doublespeak. For example, in 1984 the U.S. State Department announced that it would no longer use the word "killing" in its annual report on the status of human rights in countries around the world. Instead, it would use the phrase "unlawful or arbitrary deprivation of life," which the department claimed was more accurate. Its real purpose for using this phrase was simply to avoid discussing the embarrassing situation of government-sanctioned

killings in countries that are supported by the United States and have been certified by the United States as respecting the human rights of their citizens. This use of a euphemism constitutes doublespeak, since it is designed to mislead, to cover up the unpleasant. Its real intent is at variance with its apparent intent. It is language designed to alter our perception of reality.

The Pentagon, too, avoids discussing unpleasant realities when it   8 refers to bombs and artillery shells that fall on civilian targets as "incontinent ordnance." And in 1977 the Pentagon tried to slip funding for the neutron bomb unnoticed into an appropriations bill by calling it a "radiation enhancement device."

Second Kind of Doublespeak

A second kind of doublespeak is jargon, the specialized language of a   9 trade, profession, or similar group, such as that used by doctors, lawyers, engineers, educators, or car mechanics. Jargon can serve an important and useful function. Within a group, jargon functions as a kind of verbal shorthand that allows members of the group to communicate with each other clearly, efficiently, and quickly. Indeed, it is a mark of membership in the group to be able to use and understand the group's jargon.

But jargon, like the euphemism, can also be doublespeak. It can be—   10 and often is—pretentious, obscure, and esoteric terminology used to give an air of profundity, authority, and prestige to speakers and their subject matter. Jargon as doublespeak often makes the simple appear complex, the ordinary profound, the obvious insightful. In this sense it is used not to express but impress. With such doublespeak, the act of smelling something becomes "organoleptic analysis," glass becomes "fused silicate," a crack in a metal support beam becomes a "discontinuity," conservative economic policies become "distributionally conservative notions."

Lawyers, for example, speak of an "involuntary conversion" of prop-   11 erty when discussing the loss or destruction of property through theft, accident, or condemnation. If your house burns down or if your car is stolen, you have suffered an involuntary conversion of your property. When used by lawyers in a legal situation, such jargon is a legitimate use of language, since lawyers can be expected to understand the term.

However, when a member of a specialized group uses its jargon to com-   12 municate with a person outside the group, and uses it knowing that the nonmember does not understand such language, then there is doublespeak. For example, on May 9, 1978, a National Airlines 727 airplane crashed while attempting to land at the Pensacola, Florida, airport. Three of the fifty-two passengers aboard the airplane were killed. As a result of the crash, National made an after-tax insurance benefit of $1.7 million, or an 18¢ extra a share dividend for its stockholders. Now National Airlines had two problems: It did not want to talk about one of its airplanes crashing, and it had to account for the $1.7 million when it issued its annual report to its stockholders. National solved the problem by inserting a footnote in its annual report which explained that the $1.7 million income was due to "the involuntary conversion of a 727." National thus acknowledged the crash of its airplane and the subsequent profit it made from the crash, without once mentioning the accident or the deaths. However, because airline officials knew that most stockholders in the company, and indeed most of the general public, were not familiar with legal jargon, the use of such jargon constituted doublespeak.

Third Kind of Doublespeak

A third kind of doublespeak is gobbledygook or bureaucratese. Basically, such doublespeak is simply a matter of piling on words, of overwhelming the audience with words, the bigger the words and the longer the sentences the better. Alan Greenspan, then chair of President Nixon's Council of Economic Advisors, was quoted in the *Philadelphia Inquirer* in 1974 as having testified before a Senate committee that "It is a tricky problem to find the particular calibration in timing that would be appropriate to stem the acceleration in risk premiums created by falling incomes without prematurely aborting the decline in the inflation-generated risk premiums." 13

Nor has Mr. Greenspan's language changed since then. Speaking to the meeting of the Economic Club of New York in 1988, Mr. Greenspan, now Federal Reserve chair, said, "I guess I should warn you, if I turn out to be particularly clear, you've probably misunderstood what I've said." Mr. Greenspan's doublespeak doesn't seem to have held back his career. 14

Sometimes gobbledygook may sound impressive, but when the quote is later examined in print it doesn't even make sense. During the 1988 presidential campaign, vice-presidential candidate Senator Dan Quayle explained the need for a strategic defense initiative by saying, "Why wouldn't an enhanced deterrent, a more stable peace, a better prospect to denying the ones who enter conflict in the first place to have a reduction of offensive systems and an introduction to defensive capability? I believe this is the route the country will eventually go." 15

The investigation into the Challenger disaster in 1986 revealed the doublespeak of gobbledygook and bureaucratese used by too many involved in the shuttle program. When Jesse Moore, NASA's associate administrator, was asked if the performance of the shuttle program had improved with each launch or if it had remained the same, he answered, "I think our performance in terms of the liftoff performance and in terms of the orbital performance, we knew more about the envelope we were operating under, and we have been pretty accurately staying in that. And so I would say the performance has not by design drastically improved. I think 16 we have been able to characterize the performance more as a function of our launch experience as opposed to it improving as a function of time." While this language may appear to be jargon, a close look will reveal that it is really just gobbledygook laced with jargon. But you really have to wonder if Mr. Moore had any idea what he was saying.

Fourth Kind of Doublespeak

The fourth kind of doublespeak is inflated language that is designed to make the ordinary seem extraordinary; to make everyday things seem impressive; to give an air of importance to people, situations, or things that would not normally be considered important; to make the simple seem complex. Often this kind of doublespeak isn't hard to spot, and it is usually pretty funny. While car mechanics may be called "automotive internists," elevator operators members of the "vertical transportation corps," used cars "pre-owned" or "experienced cars," and black-and-white television sets described as having "non-multicolor capability," you really aren't misled all that much by such language.   17

However, you may have trouble figuring out that, when Chrysler "initiates a career alternative enhancement program," it is really laying off five thousand workers; or that "negative patient care outcome" means the patient died; or that "rapid oxidation" means a fire in a nuclear power plant.   18

The doublespeak of inflated language can have serious consequences. In Pentagon doublespeak, "pre-emptive counterattack" means that American forces attacked first; "engaged the enemy on all sides" means American troops were ambushed; "backloading of augmentation personnel" means a retreat by American troops. In the doublespeak of the military, the 1983 invasion of Grenada was conducted not by the U.S. Army, Navy, Air Force, and Marines, but by the "Caribbean Peace Keeping Forces." But then, according to the Pentagon, it wasn't an invasion, it was a "predawn vertical insertion."   19

◆ ◆ ◆

FIRST RESPONSES

What examples of doublespeak have you come across lately? How do you feel about them after reading Lutz's essay? Jot down any examples of euphemism, jargon, gobbledygook, and inflated language you encounter in the next few days. Pay attention to the language of advertising, the terms used by corporations and politicians, and even some of your textbooks. Bring some examples to discuss with your class.

TAKING A CLOSER LOOK

Exploring *Who:* Voice and Tone

1. How does Lutz feel about doublespeak? Does he feel the same way about each kind of doublespeak? What words and sentences reveal his attitudes?
2. Who uses doublespeak? Is Lutz writing to these people? Or does he have a different audience in mind?
3. Do you ever use deceptive language? What kinds do you use—euphemisms, jargon, inflated language? Why? After reading this article, will you continue to use such language?
4. How do you feel about the examples of inflated language mentioned in the final section of the essay? How do you think Lutz wants you to react to these examples?

Exploring *What:* Content and Meaning

1. According to Lutz, what is doublespeak? What questions help you to identify it?
2. How many kinds of doublespeak does Lutz discuss? List them and give an example of each.
3. What useful functions do euphemisms and jargon serve?
4. ◾⬛ *Using the Internet.* Visit the American Newspeak Web site (http://www.scn.org/ news/newspeak/) to look at samples of doublespeak gathered from current news sources. You will find the most recent examples in the "Top Stories of the Month" section. After reading eight to ten examples, answer these questions: Are Lutz's criticisms still valid? Who is using doublespeak today? What kinds are they using? Why do politicians and government agencies use gobbledygook and inflated language?

Exploring *Why:* Purpose

1. Why does Lutz want you to be able to spot doublespeak? What does he want you to do when you spot it?
2. Why does Lutz say that "the doublespeak of inflated language can have serious consequences"? What are those consequences? Do you agree with him?
3. Why does Lutz include the beneficial and harmless uses of euphemism and jargon?

4. Does the language you use *reflect* your character and values, or does the language you use *influence* and *shape* your character and values?

Exploring *How:* Style and Structure

1. Why does Lutz begin with a series of examples? Is that an effective opening?
2. Explain the function of the question that opens paragraph 4.
3. Why does the author use headings?
4. Are the four kinds of doublespeak presented in any particular order? Why does Lutz end with inflated language?
5. How important are the examples in this essay? Would you have understood the author's explanations without them? Which examples did you find most illuminating and interesting?

WRITING FROM READING ASSIGNMENT

William Lutz writes about the way people use language to accomplish certain purposes and communicate with various audiences. Do you use different language with your friends, your boss, your family, and your professors? Your goal in this writing assignment is to examine the way you change your language when you communicate with different audiences.

A. Begin by brainstorming, with help from friends and classmates if you want it, for ideas about the various audiences you write and talk to. If you have time, take notes about the conversations you have and writing you do for a week or more. Pay particular attention to how you vary your language from situation to situation. Jot down specific examples to use in developing your essay.
B. Classify the language you use—spoken or written—into three to five distinct types. You might make up a label for each type: shop talk, jock talk, party talk, family talk; or academic writing, e-mail messages, business writing, notes and cards.
C. Decide on a purpose for your division and classification. Why do you alter your language? What do these variations tell you about yourself and your relationships with others? Is this process of tailoring your language to fit your audience harmful? useful? beneficial? necessary? hypocritical?
D. Develop a section explaining each kind of language you use. Use specific examples, as Lutz does, to illustrate and define the types.

E. Arrange your sections in some logical order—perhaps from least formal to most formal; or from impersonal to indifferent to casual to intimate. You can point out how each type varies from the others as you go along.

F. Use signals to show when you are moving from one type to the next. You could use headings (as Lutz does) or transitional phrases, such as "The second type of language that I use is . . ."

G. Consider an introduction that uses a collection of examples, as Lutz does, to get your readers' attention and set up your categories.

H. One way to close your essay is with a discussion that draws all the kinds together, explaining why you vary your language for each group and what this practice tells you about yourself and your relationships with different audiences.

I. Use the Checklist for Reading and Writing Division and Classification Essays (on pp. 298–299) when you revise your essay.

◆ ◆ ◆ PREPARING TO READ

How many different types of students do you know? Could you divide them all into two main classes? What would they be?

◆ ◆ ◆

The Power of Two: A New Way of Classifying Everyone

CULLEN MURPHY

Cullen Murphy, the managing editor for *The Atlantic Monthly,* often writes on medicine, science, technology, anthropology, and archeology. He is also the author of the text for the Prince Valiant comic strip. Murphy's latest book, *The Word According to Eve* (1998), surveys the accomplishments of women in the field of biblical studies. Murphy has an interest in everyday curiosities and a fondness for quirky subjects, as the following essay illustrates. It appeared in *The Atlantic Monthly* in 1994.

There is a certain experiment, I have been told, that psychologists use 1 to gauge a person's ability to conceptualize categorically. No psychologist I have consulted is actually familiar with it as a clinical experiment; perhaps it originated as, and remains, a parlor game. Whatever the case, one begins by asking another person to empty the contents of a pocket or a purse onto a table and then to divide the items into two groups. "Two groups based on what?" the subject typically asks. The clinically correct response is simply to shrug. The pocket or purse is duly emptied, and after a moment or two of bafflement the process of sorting begins. It usually goes quickly, powered by some sudden enlightenment.

In the end there are always two piles, but although I have seen this ex- 2 periment conducted five or six times, I have yet to be able to discern the basis for division. A logical basis always turns out to exist. Here are some of the explanations I have heard: "The things in this pile contain at least one piece of plastic, and the things in the other pile don't." "All the things in one pile and not the other have a letter of the alphabet on them." "These things here you could find on anyone, but those things there you could find only on me."

What any of these responses says about the individual involved I 3 won't venture to guess, but I have come to believe that this experiment is a manifestation of one of nature's most overlooked laws—namely, that a reasonable criterion always exists for dividing any group of things or beings into two. This is the General Theory of Divisibility.

All of us pay unthinking tribute to this idea every time we begin a sentence with the familiar words "There are two kinds of people. . . ." Frequently the assertions are rudimentary: "There are two kinds of people—Italians and those who wish they were." But some proposed divisions have a metaphoric power that holds the promise of great utility. A press release from the American Humane Association and other groups, announcing the observance of a Year of the Cat, helpfully set the record straight with respect to a number of myths that have arisen about *felis catus.* (Myth No. 4, according to the press release: "Cats will suck the breath from sleeping infants.") The Humane Association's mailing, which noted that cats had surpassed dogs in popularity as pets, came as a reminder that the classification of people as either dogs or cats in terms of character is one of the most basic divisions there is. Everyone would agree, I think, that T. S. Eliot, Nancy Reagan, Garrick Utley, and Diana Rigg are cats. Walter Matthau, Ted Williams, and Julia Child are dogs. George F. Will is a cat pretending to be a dog. (Like many intellectual cats, Will furthers this subterfuge by maintaining a very public canine interest in baseball.) In contrast, Daniel Patrick Moynihan is a dog pretending to be a cat.

Of course, dividing people into cats and dogs is only one way of cleaving the world's population. There is room for infinite refinement. The pop philosopher Alan Watts, for example, sliced humanity another way—he maintained that people were either prickly or gooey. Adding his classification to the previous one gives us not two kinds of people but four:

prickly dogs	gooey dogs
prickly cats	gooey cats

Oliver Wendell Holmes divided humanity into two groups according to psychological orientation: external versus internal. Adding that distinction increases the number of possible combinations to eight. Ogden Nash once wrote, "There are two kinds of people who blow through life like a breeze, / And one kind is gossipers, and the other kind is gossipees"; the combinations now number sixteen. In Isaiah Berlin's famous taxonomy people are either hedgehogs or foxes, the foxes being those who know many little things and the hedgehogs those who know one big thing. That gives us thirty-two combinations. One of them—gooey canine external gossipee fox—begins to resemble our President.

Indeed, the more layers of dyads one adds, the less one is defining broad demographic groups and the closer one is coming to singling out specific individuals. Surprising as it may seem, a mere twenty dyads yield more than a million possible combinations. A mere fifty yield a quadrillion. Perhaps these dyads can be thought of as the building blocks of personality, with each of us possessing a unique combination of characteristics just as we possess unique sequences of adenine, cytosine, guanine, and thymine, which define our personal genetic maps. The task ahead for science, then, is to begin nailing down a master list.

Here are some suggestions: 7

standard	automatic
white	whole wheat
deciduous	evergreen
dry	wet
saver	tosser
loyalist	secessionist
cook	cleaner
star	planet
hard drive	floppy disk

never tire of Pachelbel's
    "Canon"
	nauseated by Pachelbel's
	    "Canon"

The practical applications of a system like this are not hard to imag-   8
ine. Western society has for decades been looking for something to supplant the failed god of psychoanalysis; surely the dyad project could assume at least part of this role. Also, consider how personal advertisements would be revolutionized. The standard but not all that revealing SWMs and DJFs and BGMs could now be complemented by a whole palette of accessory qualities.

Less happily, thinking about people in this way eventually leads one to   9
a troubling question: What happens if a person with all the characteristics of column A meets a person who has all the characteristics of column B—who is, that is to say, exactly the opposite in every last particular? My brother, playing to the groundlings for a cheap laugh, says, "They get married." A more disturbing possible consequence is that, as with the theorized collision of matter and anti-matter, the universe as we know it would instantly cease to exist. The mathematics, unfortunately, is unassailable on this point: $A + B = 0$. The General Theory of Divisibility did not bring this problem into existence; it has presumably been there all along. But the likelihood that person A would actually meet person B used to be small: people didn't casually brush up against as many total strangers as they commonly do today, what with modern transportation and the voluminous sloshings of population all

over the planet. It is only a matter of time before some chance encounter in Rio, Kampala, or Muncie inadvertently snuffs out the entire human enterprise. As even my clan eventually learned, if anything can go wrong, it will.

◆ ◆ ◆

FIRST RESPONSES

In terms of character and personality, are you a cat or a dog? Are you gooey or prickly? Are you a gossiper or a gossipee? How well does this kind of classification suit you?

TAKING A CLOSER LOOK

Exploring *Who:* Voice and Tone

1. At what point did you realize Murphy was not serious? What tipped you off? How does he make you think he's serious?
2. Murphy is an editor and published author of books and articles about science and technology. In what ways does he reveal his credentials in this essay?
3. How is a reader supposed to respond to an article like this? How did you respond? Do you think you responded in the way that Murphy wanted you to? Explain.

Exploring *What:* Content and Meaning

1. What is a "dyad"? How does this essay illustrate the meaning of that word? Have you heard of other dyads?
2. Which people did you recognize in Murphy's list of "cats" and "dogs" (paragraph 4)? Do you agree with his categorization of any of them? Can you think of some celebrities that would fit into these two categories?
3. What does Murphy mean when he says, "Western society has for decades been looking for something to supplant the failed god of psychoanalysis" (paragraph 8)? Is he making a serious point here? If so, what is it?
4. What does Murphy's last sentence mean? Do you know what Murphy's law is? If you find out, you'll have a better understanding of that last sentence.

Exploring *Why:* Purpose

1. What is the author's reason for writing this essay?
2. Murphy says that in the experiment about classifying the contents of a person's purse or pocket, "there are always two piles" and "a logical basis always turns out to exist." Can you explain why this result would always occur?
3. Did you ever hear anyone begin a sentence with the words, "There are two kinds of people. . ."? Have you ever said something like this? How did you finish the sentence?
4. What human tendencies does Murphy satirize? Did you recognize yourself or anyone you know in this essay?

Exploring *How:* Style and Structure

1. Did Murphy's introduction get your attention?
2. Why does Murphy cite people like Oliver Wendell Holmes, Alan Watts, Ogden Nash, and Isaiah Berlin (paragraph 5)?
3. What do you think of Murphy's suggestions for a "master list" (paragraph 7)? Can you add to this list?
4. Why does Murphy mention "adenine, cytosine, guanine, and thymine" (paragraph 6)? Why does he also include the abbreviations from personal ads (SWMs, DJFs, and BGMs)?
5. Why does Murphy conclude with the "theorized collision of matter and anti-matter"?

IDEAS FOR WRITING A DIVISION AND CLASSIFICATION PAPER

1. Take a group of people you know well—friends, classmates, co-workers, teammates, or family members—and divide them into at least three separate dyads. Explain the basis for each division, and comment on the validity of your categories. Do the groups change much from one division to another? Does this classification process tell you anything about the group of people you know and associate with?
2. Perform the experiment that Murphy describes in his opening paragraphs: ask at least five different people to divide the contents of their purses or pockets into two groups. Observe their behavior and take notes. Also ask them to explain the basis for their division. Then write up the results of your experiment.

3. ▣ *Using the Internet.* Use a search engine to find out the meaning of the following: Murphy's law, Parkinson's law, Gresham's law, and Grimm's law. Which ones are serious and which are humorous? Then make up your own "law"—the way that Murphy did with the General Theory of Divisibility—and explain its meaning and applications.

◆ ◆ ◆ PREPARING TO READ

What stereotypes of Asians do you know? How do you know that they are stereotypes? How are Asians and Asian Americans depicted in movies and on television, in cartoons and on video games?

◆ ◆ ◆

Lotus Blossoms Don't Bleed: Images of Asian American Women

RENEE TAJIMA

Renee Tajima is a filmmaker and writer. She produced the documentary *Adopted Son: The Death of Vincent Chin* for public television. Tajima is also an associate editor for *The Independent Film and Video Monthly,* a freelance writer, and the co-director of the Film News Now Foundation. In the following article, which appeared in *Making Waves: An Anthology of Writings by and about Asian American Women* (1989), Tajima reminds us how much the images presented by film and television can shape our perceptions.

In recent years the media have undergone spectacular technical inno-   1
vations. But whereas form has leaped toward the year 2000, it seems that content still straddles the turn of the last century. A reigning example of the industry's stagnation is its portrayal of Asian women. And the only real signs of life are stirring far away from Hollywood in the cutting rooms owned and operated by Asian America's independent producers.

The commercial media are, in general, populated by stereotyped   2
characterizations that range in complexity, accuracy, and persistence over time. There is the hooker with a heart of gold and the steely tough yet honorable mobster. Most of these characters are white, and may be as one-dimensional as Conan the Barbarian or as complex as R. P. McMurphy in *One Flew Over the Cuckoo's Nest.*

Images of Asian women, however, have remained consistently sim-   3
plistic and inaccurate during the sixty years of largely forgettable screen appearances. There are two basic types: the Lotus Blossom Baby (a.k.a. China Doll, Geisha Girl, shy Polynesian beauty), and the Dragon Lady (Fu Manchu's various female relations, prostitutes, devious madames). There is

little in between, although experts may differ as to whether Suzie Wong belongs to the race-blind "hooker with a heart of gold" category, or deserves one all of her own.

Asian women in American cinema are interchangeable in appearance   4
and name, and are joined together by the common language of non-language—that is, uninterpretable chattering, pidgin English, giggling, or silence. They may be specifically identified by nationality—particularly in war films—but that's where screen accuracy ends. The dozens of populations of Asian and Pacific Island groups are lumped into one homogeneous mass of Mama-sans.

Passive Love Interests

Asian women in film are, for the most part, passive figures who exist to   5
serve men, especially as love interests for white men (Lotus Blossoms) or as partners in crime with men of their own kind (Dragon Ladies). One of the first Dragon Lady types was played by Anna May Wong. In the 1924 spectacular *Thief of Bagdad* she uses treachery to help an evil Mongol prince attempt to win the Princess of Bagdad from Douglas Fairbanks.

The Lotus Blossom Baby, a sexual-romantic object, has been the   6
prominent type throughout the years. These "Oriental flowers" are utterly feminine, delicate, and welcome respites from their often loud, independent American counterparts. Many of them are the spoils of the last three wars fought in Asia. One recent television example is Sergeant Klinger's Korean wife in the short-lived series *AfterMash*.

In the real world, this view of Asian women has spawned an entire   7
marriage industry. Today the Filipino wife is particularly in vogue for American men who order Asian brides from picture catalogues, just as you might buy an imported cheese slicer from Spiegel's. (I moderated a community program on Asian American women recently. A rather bewildered young saleswoman showed up with a stack of brochures to promote the Cherry Blossom companion service, or some such enterprise.) Behind the brisk sales of Asian mail-order brides is a growing number of American men who are seeking old-fashioned, compliant wives, women they feel are no longer available in the United States.

Feudal Asian customs do not change for the made-for-movie women.   8
Picture brides, geisha girls, concubines, and hara-kari are all mixed together and reintroduced into any number of settings. Take for example these two versions of Asian and American cultural exchange:

1. It's Toko Riki on Japan's Okinawa Island during the late 1940s in the film *Teahouse of the August Moon.* American occupation forces nice

guy Captain Fisby (Glenn Ford) gets a visit from Japanese yenta Sakini (Marlon Brando).

Enter Brando: "Hey Boss, I Sonoda has a present for you."

Enter the gift: Japanese actress Machiko Kyo as a geisha, giggling. Ford: "Who's she?"

Brando: "Souvenir. . . introducing Lotus Blossom geisha girl first class."

Ford protests the gift. Kyo giggles.

Brando sneaks away with a smile: "Goodnight, Boss." Kyo, chattering away in Japanese, tries to pamper a bewildered Ford who holds up an instructive finger to her and repeats slowly, "Me. . . me . . . no." Kyo looks confused.

2. It's San Francisco, circa 1981, in the television series "The Incredible Hulk." Nice guy David Banner (Bill Bixby a.k.a. The Hulk) gets a present from Chinese yenta Hyung (Beulah Quo).

Enter Quo: "David, I have something for you."

Enter Irene Sun as Tam, a Chinese refugee, bowing her head shyly.

Quo: "The floating Lotus Company hopes you will be very happy. This is Tam, your mail-order bride."

Bixby protests the gift. Sun, speaking only Chinese, tries to pamper a bewildered Bixby who repeats slowly in an instructive tone, "you. . . must. . . go!" Sun looks confused.

Illicit Interracial Love

On film Asian women are often assigned the role of expendability in situations of illicit Asian-white love. In these cases the most expedient way of resolving the problems of miscegenation has been to get rid of the Asian partner. Thus, some numbers of hyphenated (made-for-television, wartime, wives-away-from-home) Asian women have expired for the convenience of their home-bound soldier lovers. More progressive-minded GI's of the Vietnam era have returned to Vietnam years later to search for the off-spring of these love matches. 9

In 1985 the General Foods Gold Showcase proudly presented a post-Vietnam version of the wilting Lotus Blossom on network television. "A forgotten passion, a child he never knew. . . . All his tomorrows forever changed by *The Lady from Yesterday*." He is Vietnam vet Craig Weston (Wayne Rogers), official father of two, and husband to Janet (Bonnie Bedelia). She is Lien Van Huyen (Tina Chen), whom Weston hasn't seen since the fall of Saigon. She brings the child, the unexpected consequence of that wartime love match, to the United States. But Janet doesn't lose her husband, she gains a son. As *New York Times* critic John J. O'Connor points 10 out, Lien has "the good manners to be suffering from a fatal disease that will conveniently remove her from the scene."

The geographic parallel to the objectification of Asian women is the 11
rendering of Asia as only a big set for the white leading actors. What would *Shogun* be without Richard Chamberlain? The most notable exception is the 1937 movie version of Pearl Buck's novel *The Good Earth*. The story is about Chinese in China and depicted with some complexity and emotion. Nevertheless the lead parts played by Louise Rainer and Paul Muni follow the pattern of choosing white stars for Asian roles, a problem which continues to plague Asian actors.

One film that stands out as an exception because it was cast with 12
Asian people for Asian characters is *Flower Drum Song* (1961), set in San Francisco's Chinatown. Unfortunately the film did little more than temporarily take a number of talented Asian American actresses and actors off the unemployment lines. It also gave birth for a while to a new generation of stereotypes—gum-chewing Little Leaguers, enterprising businessmen, and all-American tomboys—variations on the then new model minority myth. *Flower Drum Song* hinted that the assimilated, hyphenated Asian American might be much more successful in American society than the Japanese of the 1940s and the Chinese and Koreans of the 1950s, granted they keep to the task of being white American first.

The women of *Flower Drum Song* maintain their earlier image with 13
few modernizations. Miyoshi Umeki is still a picture bride. And in *Suzie Wong* actress Nancy Kwan is a hipper, Americanized version of the Hong Kong bar girl without the pidgin English. But updated clothes and setting do not change the essence of these images.

In 1985 director Michael Cimino cloned Suzie Wong to TV news an- 14
chor Connie Chung and created another anchor, Tracy Tzu (Ariane), in the disastrous exploitation film *Year of the Dragon*. In it Tzu is ostensibly the only positive Asian American character in a film that vilifies the people of New York's Chinatown. The Tzu character is a success in spite of her ethnicity. Just as she would rather eat Italian than Chinese, she'd rather sleep with white men than Chinese men. (She is ultimately raped by three "Chinese boys.") Neither does she bat an eye at the barrage of racial slurs fired off by her lover, lead Stanley White, the Vietnam vet and New York City cop played by Mickey Rourke.

At the outset Tzu is the picture of professionalism and sophistication, 15
engaged in classic screen love/hate banter with White. The turning point comes early in the picture when their flirtatious sparring in a Chinese restaurant is interrupted by a gangland slaughter. While White pursues the culprits, Tzu totters on her high heels into a phone booth where she cowers, sobbing, until White comes to the rescue.

The standard of beauty for Asian women that is set in the movies de-   16
serves mention. Caucasian women are often used for Asian roles, which
contributes to a case of aesthetic imperialism for Asian women. When
Asian actresses are chosen they invariably have large eyes, high cheek-
bones, and other Caucasian-like characteristics when they appear on the silver screen. As Judy Chu of the University of California, Los Angeles, has
pointed out, much of Anna May Wong's appeal was due to her Western
looks. Chu unearthed this passage from the June 1924 *Photoplay* which
refers to actress Wong, but sounds a lot like a description of Eurasian
model/actress Ariane: "Her deep brown eyes, while the slant is not pronounced, are typically oriental. But her Manchu mother has given her a
height and poise of figure that Chinese maidens seldom have."

Invisibility

There is yet another important and pervasive characteristic of Asian   17
women on the screen—invisibility. The number of roles in the Oriental
flower and Dragon Lady categories have been few, and generally only supporting parts. But otherwise Asian women are absent. Asian women do not
appear in films as union organizers, or divorced mothers fighting for the cus-
tody of their children, or fading movie stars, or spunky trial lawyers, or farm
women fighting bank foreclosures; Asian women are not portrayed as ordinary people.

Then there is the kind of invisibility that occurs when individual per-   18
sonalities and separate identities become indistinguishable from one another. Some memorable Asian masses are the islanders fleeing exploding
volcanoes in *Krakatoa: East of Java* (1969) and the Vietnamese villagers
fleeing Coppola's airborne weaponry in various scenes from *Apocalypse
Now* (1979). Asian women populate these hordes or have groupings of their
own, usually in some type of harem situation. In *Cry for Happy* (1961),
Glenn Ford is cast as an American GI who stumbles into what turns out to
be the best little geisha house in Japan.

Network television has given Asian women even more opportunities to   19
paper the walls, so to speak. They are background characters in *Hawaii 5-0,
Magnum PI,* and other series that traverse the Pacific. I've seen a
cheongsam-clad maid in the soap *One Life to Live,* and assorted Chinatown
types surface whenever the cops and robbers shows revive scripts about the
Chinatown Tong wars.

The most stunning exceptions to television's abuse of Asian images is   20
the phenomenon of news anchors: Connie Chung (CBS) and Sasha Foo
(CNN) have national spots, and Tritia Toyota (Los Angeles), Wendy Tokuda
(San Francisco), Kaity Tong (New York), Sandra Yep (Sacramento), and

others are reporters in large cities. All of them cover hard news, long the province of middle-aged white men with authoritative voices. Toyota and Yep have been able to parlay their positions so that there is more coverage of Asian American stories at their stations. Because of their presence on screen—and ironically, perhaps because of the celebrity status of today's newscasters—these anchors wield much power in rectifying Asian women's intellectual integrity in the media. (One hopes *Year of the Dragon's* Tracy Tzu hasn't canceled their positive effect.)

Undoubtedly the influence of these visible reporters is fortified by the 21
existence of highly organized Asian American journalists. The West Coast-based Asian American Journalists Association has lobbied for affirmative action in the print and broadcast media. In film and video, the same types of political initiatives have spurred a new movement of independently produced works made by and about Asian Americans.

Small Gems from Independents

The independent film movement emerged during the 1960s as an al- 22
ternative to the Hollywood mill. In a broad sense it has had little direct impact in reversing the distorted images of Asian women, although some gems have been produced. But now Asian American independents, many of whom are women, have consciously set out to bury sixty years of Lotus Blossoms who do not bleed and Mama-sans who do not struggle. These women filmmakers—most of whom began their careers only since the 1970s—often draw from deeply personal perspectives in their work: Virginia Hashii's *Jenny* portrays a young Japanese-American girl who explores her own Nikkei heritage for the first time; Christine Choy's *From Spikes to Spindles* (1976) documents the lives of women in New York's Chinatown; Felicia Lowe's *China: Land of My Father* (1979) is a film diary of the filmmaker's own first reunion with her grandmother in China; Renee Cho's *The New Wife* (1978) dramatizes the arrival of an immigrant bride to America; and Lana PihJokel's *Chiang Ching: A Dance Journey* traces the life of dancer-actress-teacher Chiang. All these films were produced during the 1970s and together account for only a little more than two hours of screen time. Most are first works with the same rough-edged quality that characterized early Asian American film efforts.

Women producers have maintained a strong presence during the 23
1980s, although their work does not always focus on women's issues. Also in this decade veteran filmmakers Emiko Omori and Christine Choy have produced their first dramatic efforts. Omori's *The Departure* is the story of a Japanese girl who must give up her beloved traditional dolls in pre-World War II California. In *Fei Tien: Goddess in Flight*, Choy tries to adapt a

nonlinear cinematic structure to Genny Lim's play *Pigeons,* which explores the relationship between a Chinese American yuppie and a Chinatown "bird lady."

Perhaps the strongest work made thus far has been directed by a male 24 filmmaker, Arthur Dong. *Sewing Woman* is a small, but beautifully crafted portrait of Dong's mother, Zem Ping. It chronicles her life from war-torn China to San Francisco's garment factories. Other films and tapes by Asian men include Michael Uno's *Emi* (1978), a portrait of the Japanese American writer and former concentration camp internee Emi Tonooka; the Yonemoto brothers' neonarrative *Green Card,* a soap-style saga of a Japanese immigrant artist seeking truth, love, and permanent residency in Southern California; and Steve Okazaki's *Survivors,* a documentary focusing on the women survivors of the atomic blasts over Hiroshima and Nagasaki. All these filmmakers are American-born Japanese. *Orientations,* by Asian Canadian Richard Fung, is the first work I've seen that provides an in-depth look at the Asian gay community, and it devotes a good amount of time to Asian Canadian lesbians.

Our Own Image

These film and videomakers, women and men, face a challenge far 25 beyond creating entertainment and art. Several generations of Asian women have been raised with racist and sexist celluloid images. The models for passivity and servility in these films and television programs fit neatly into the myths imposed on us, and contrast sharply with the more liberating ideals of independence and activism. Generations of other Americans have also grown up with these images. And their acceptance of the dehumanization implicit in the stereotypes of expendability and invisibility is frightening.

Old images of Asian women in the mainstream media will likely re- 26 main stagnant for a while. After sixty years, there have been few signs of progress. However, there is hope because of the growing number of filmmakers emerging from our own communities. Wayne Wang in 1985 completed *Dim Sum,* a beautifully crafted feature film about the relationship between a mother and daughter in San Francisco's Chinatown. *Dim Sum,* released through a commercial distributor, could be the first truly sensitive film portrayal of Asian American women to reach a substantial national audience. In quality and numbers, Asian American filmmakers may soon constitute a critical mass out of which we will see a body of work that gives us a new image, our own image.

◆ ◆ ◆

FIRST RESPONSES

Tajima wrote this essay in 1989. Have images of Asian women in the movies changed much since then? Are Tajima's observations and conclusions still valid?

TAKING A CLOSER LOOK

Exploring *Who:* Voice and Tone

1. How would you describe the overall tone of this essay? Does the tone change in any sections? Point out any passages that offer clear instances of **irony,** especially **sarcasm** and **understatement.**
2. How can you tell that Tajima is a filmmaker? How do you respond to her discussion of films and other filmmakers? Are you always able to follow her?
3. Do you share Tajima's views? Do you think you are part of the audience she is writing to in this essay?

Exploring *What:* Content and Meaning

1. What are the two main images of Asian women in Hollywood films (paragraph 3)? What are the three main roles Asian women have played in Hollywood films (paragraphs 5, 6, 9)? Can you think of other examples that confirm or dispute Tajima's claims?
2. How do the roles Asian women play in recent independent productions differ from those generally created for them in Hollywood productions?
3. *Using the Internet.* Find reviews of several of the movies discussed in this essay. A Web source such as the Movie Review Query Engine (http://www.mrqe.com/ lookup?) will help you locate these reviews. Do these reviews corroborate Tajima's observations?
4. What does Tajima mean when she talks about "Mama-sans" (paragraph 4) and "a cheongsam-clad maid" (paragraph 19)?

Exploring *Why:* Purpose

1. What is the author's goal in this essay? Does she want to inform her readers? Does she want to bring about some change?
2. Why does Tajima include the final section "Our Own Image"?

3. How hopeful is Tajima that new images of Asian women will become a reality?

4. What do you think Tajima would think of movies such as *The Joy Luck Club* and *Mulan?*

Exploring *How:* Style and Structure

1. Does Tajima provide a clear description of each category? How might the categories be introduced and defined more clearly? Do the categories overlap? Does Tajima acknowledge this overlapping? Where?

2. Would this essay be more effective if it contained fewer examples? More examples? Evaluate the examples in paragraphs 8 through 20 and 22 through 24. How clear are they? Do they help you to understand the author's ideas?

3. Why does Tajima quote from two different movie scenes (paragraph 8)? How effective is this strategy? What point does it make?

4. Are the examples of work by independent filmmakers convincing? Do they clearly show that these films go beyond the stereotypes?

IDEAS FOR WRITING A DIVISION AND CLASSIFICATION PAPER

1. Films and television programs frequently use stereotypes to depict various ethnic and social groups (such as African Americans, people in their twenties, rural people, gay people). List groups of people who are often represented by stereotypical characters in movies or on television. Choose one or more of these groups to discuss in an essay. Consider classifying the ways a particular group is treated, or sort several different groups into categories based on the way they are represented.

2. Get together with a group of classmates, and discuss various ways that society stereotypes males and females. Think of labels to identify these types, like the Super Mom, the Nagging Wife, the Clinging Vine, the Liberated Woman, the Tramp, the Queen Bee—or for males, the Jock, the Mama's Boy, the Macho Man, the Ladies' Man, Mr. Sensitive, Mr. Mom. Then write an essay describing three or four types (either males or females). You can draw your examples and specific details from movies, television, comic strips, advertising, or videos. Your purpose could be to demonstrate how unfair or misleading these stereotypes are.

3. Classify some sort of media (films, television programs, newspapers, magazines, popular songs, advertisements) according to the way it treats certain ideas (especially political viewpoints or value systems) or certain groups of people.

◆ ◆ ◆ **PREPARING TO READ**

List five or ten people you call "friends." Are they all friends to an equal degree? Do you have a flexible meaning for the word *friend?*

◆ ◆ ◆

What Friends Are For

PHILLIP LOPATE

Phillip Lopate is an acclaimed essayist who has won fellowships from the Guggenheim Foundation and the National Endowment for the Arts. He edited an anthology representing his writing specialty, *The Art of the Personal Essay* (1994). The following essay first appeared in *Against Joie de Vivre* (1989), a collection of Lopate's writings.

Is there anything left to say about friendship after so many great essayists have picked over the bones of the subject? Aristotle and Cicero, Seneca and Montaigne, Francis Bacon and Samuel Johnson, William Hazlitt, Ralph Waldo Emerson, and Charles Lamb have all taken their cracks at it.

Friendship has been called "love without wings." On the other hand, the Stoic definition of love ("Love is the attempt to form a friendship inspired by beauty") seems to suggest that friendship came first. Certainly a case can be made that the buildup of affection and the yearning for more intimacy, without the release of sexual activity, keeps friends in a state of sweet-sorrowful itchiness that has the romantic quality of a love affair. We know that a falling-out between two old friends can leave a deeper and more perplexing hurt than the ending of a love affair, perhaps because we are more pessimistic about the affair's endurance from the start.

Our first attempted friendships are within the family. It is here we practice the techniques of listening sympathetically and proving that we can be trusted, and learn the sort of kindness we can expect in return.

There is something tainted about these family friendships, however. My sister, in her insecure adolescent phase, told me, "You love me because I'm related to you, but if you were to meet me for the first time at a party, you'd think I was a jerk and not worth being your friend." She had me in a bind: I had no way of testing her hypothesis. I should have argued that even if our bond was not freely chosen, our decision to work on it had been. Still, we are quick to dismiss the partiality of our family members when they tell us we are talented, cute, or lovable; we must go out into the world and seduce others.

It is just a few short years from the promiscuity of the sandbox to the tormented, possessive feelings of a fifth grader who has just learned that his best and only friend is playing at another classmate's house after school. There may be worse betrayals in store, but probably none is more influential than the sudden fickleness of an elementary school friend who has dropped us for someone more popular after all our careful, patient wooing. Often we lose no time inflicting the same betrayal on someone else, just to ensure that we have got the victimization dynamic right.

What makes friendships in childhood and adolescence so poignant is that we need the chosen comrade to be everything in order to rescue us from the gothic inwardness of family life. Even if we are lucky enough to have several companions, there must be a Best Friend.

I clung to the romance of the Best Friend all through high school, college, and beyond, until my circle of university friends began to disperse. At that point, in my mid-twenties, I also acted out the dark, competitive side of friendship that can exist between two young men fighting for a place in life and love by doing the one unforgivable thing: sleeping with my best friend's girl. I was baffled at first that there was no way to repair the damage. I lost this friendship forever, and came away from that debacle much more aware of the amount of injury that friendship can and cannot sustain. Perhaps I needed to prove to myself that friendship was not an all-permissive resilient bond, like a mother's love, but something quite fragile. Precisely because best friendship promotes such a merging of identities, such seeming boundarylessness, the first major transgression of trust can cause the injured party to feel he is fighting for his violated soul against his darkest enemy. There is not much room to maneuver in a best friendship between unlimited intimacy and unlimited mistrust.

Still, it was not until the age of thirty that I reluctantly abandoned the best friend expectation and took up a more pluralistic model. At present, I cherish a dozen friends for their unique personalities, without asking that any one be my soul-twin. Whether this alteration constitutes a movement toward maturity or toward cowardly pragmatism is not for me to say. It may be that, in refusing to depend so much on any one friend, I am opting for self-protection over intimacy. Or it may be that, as we advance into middle age, the life problem becomes less that of establishing a tight dyadic bond and more one of making our way in a broader world, "society." Indeed, since Americans have so indistinct a notion of society, we often try to put a network of friendships in its place.

If a certain intensity is lost in the pluralistic model of friendship, there is also the gain of being able to experience all of one's potential, half-buried selves, through witnessing all the spectacle of the multiple fates of our friends. As it happens, the harem of friends, so tantalizing a notion, often translates into feeling pulled in a dozen different directions, with the guilty sense of having disappointed everyone a little. It is also a risky, contrived enterprise to try to make one's friends behave in a friendly manner toward each other. If the effort fails, one feels obliged to mediate; if it succeeds too well, one is jealous.

Whether friendship is intrinsically singular and exclusive or plural and   10 democratic is a question that has vexed many commentators. Aristotle distinguished three types of friendship: "friendship based on utility," such as businessmen cultivating each other for benefit; "friendship based on pleasure," like young people interested in partying; and "perfect friendship." The first two categories Aristotle calls "qualified and superficial friendships," because they are founded on circumstances that could easily change. The last, which is based on admiration for another's good character, is more permanent, but also rarer, because good men "are few." Cicero, who wrote perhaps the best treatise on friendship, also insisted that what brings true friends together is "a mutual belief in each other's goodness." This insistence on virtue as a precondition for true friendship may strike us as impossibly demanding: Who, after all, feels himself good nowadays? And yet, if I am honest, I must admit that the friendships of mine that have lasted longest have been with those whose integrity, or humanity, or strength to bear their troubles I continue to admire. Conversely, when I lost respect for someone, however winning he or she otherwise remained, the friendship petered away almost immediately. "Remove respect from friendship," said Cicero, "and you have taken away the most splendid ornament it possesses."

Friendship is a long conversation. I suppose I could imagine a nonver-   11 bal friendship revolving around shared physical work or sport, but for me, good talk is the point of the thing. Indeed, the ability to generate conversation by the hour is the most promising indication, during the uncertain early stages, that a possible friendship will take hold. In the first few conversations there may be an exaggeration of agreement, as both parties angle for adhesive surfaces. But later on, trust builds through the courage to assert disagreement, through the tactful acceptance that differences of opinion will have to remain.

Some view like-mindedness as both the precondition and the product   12 of friendship. Myself, I distrust it. I have one friend who keeps assuming that we see the world eye-to-eye. She is intent on enrolling us in a flattering aristocracy of taste, on the short "we" list against the ignorant "they." Sometimes I do not have the strength to fight her need for consensus with my own stubborn disbelief in the existence of any such inner circle of privileged, cultivated sensibility. Perhaps I have too much invested in a view of myself as idiosyncratic to be eager to join any coterie, even a coterie of two. What attracts me to friends' conversation is the give and take, not necessarily that we come out at the same point.

"Our tastes and aims and views were identical—and that is where the essence of a friendship must always lie," wrote Cicero. To some extent, perhaps, but then the convergence must be natural, not, as Emerson put it, "a mush of concession. Better be a nettle in the side of your friend than his echo." 13

Friendship is a school for character, allowing us the chance to study, in great detail and over time, temperaments very different from our own. These charming quirks, these contradictions, these nobilities, these blind spots of our friends we track not out of disinterested curiosity: We must have this information before knowing how far we may relax our guard, how much we may rely on them in crises. The learning curve of friendship involves, to no small extent, filling out this picture of the other's limitations and making peace with the results. Each time I hit up against a friend's inflexibility I am relieved as well as disappointed: I can begin to predict, and arm myself in advance against repeated bruises. I have one friend who is always late, so I bring a book along when I am to meet her. I give her a manuscript to read and she promises to look at it over the weekend. I prepare for a month-long wait. 14

Though it is often said that with a true friend there is no need to hold anything back ("A friend is a person with whom I may be sincere. Before him I may think aloud," wrote Emerson), I have never found this to be entirely the case. Certain words may be too cruel if they are spoken at the wrong moment—or may fall on deaf ears, for any number of reasons. I also find with all my friends, as they must with me, that some initial resistance, restlessness, some psychic weather must be overcome before that tender ideal attentiveness may be called forth. 15

I have a good friend, Charlie, who is often very distracted whenever we first get together. If we are sitting in a café, he will look around constantly for the waiter, or be distracted by a pretty woman or the restaurant's cat. It would be foolish for me to broach an important subject at such moments, so I resign myself to waiting the half hour or however long it takes until his jumpiness subsides. Or else I draw this pattern grumpily to his attention. Once he has settled down, however, I can tell Charlie virtually anything, and he me. But the candor cannot be rushed. It must be built up to with the verbal equivalent of limbering exercises. 16

The friendship scene—a flow of shared confidences, recognitions, humor, advice, speculation, even wisdom—is one of the key elements of modern friendships. Compared to the rest of life, this ability to lavish one's best energies on an activity utterly divorced from the profit motive and free 17 from the routines of domination and inequality that affect most relations (including, perhaps, the selfsame friendship at other times) seems idyllic. The friendship scene is by its nature not an everyday occurrence. It represents the pinnacle, the fruit of the friendship, potentially ever present but not always arrived at. Both friends' dim yet self-conscious awareness that they are wandering conversationally toward a goal that they have previously accomplished but that may elude them this time around creates a tension, an obligation to communicate as sincerely as possible, like actors in an improvisation exercise struggling to shape their baggy material into some climactic form. This very pressure to achieve "quality" communication may induce a sort of inauthentic epiphany, not unlike what sometimes happens in the last ten minutes of a psychotherapy session. But a truly achieved friendship scene can be among the best experiences life has to offer.

Contemporary urban life, with its tight schedules and crowded appointment books, has helped to shape modern friendship into something requiring a good deal of intentionality and pursuit. You phone a friend and make a date a week or more in advance; then you set aside an evening, as if for a tryst, during which to squeeze in all your news and advice, confession and opinion. Such intimate compression may add a romantic note to modern friendships, but it also places a strain on the meeting to yield a high quality of meaning and satisfaction, closer to art than life. If I see busy or out-of-town friends only once every six months, we must not only catch up on our lives but also convince ourselves within the allotted two hours together that we still share a special affinity, an inner track to each other's psyches, or the next meeting may be put off for years. Surely there must be another, saner rhythm of friendship in rural areas—or maybe not? I think about "the good old days" when friends would go on walking tours through England together, when Edith Wharton would bundle poor Henry James into her motorcar and they'd drive to the south of France for a month. I'm not sure my friendships could sustain the strain of travel for weeks at a time, and the truth of the matter is that I've gotten used to this urban arrangement of serial friendship "dates," where the pleasure of the rendezvous is enhanced by the knowledge that it will only last, at most, six hours. If the two of us don't happen to mesh that day (always a possibility)—well, it's only a few hours. And if it should go beautifully, one needs an escape hatch from exaltation as well as disenchantment. I am capable of only so much intense, exciting communication before I start to fade; I come to these encounters equipped with a six-hour oxygen tank. Is this an evolutionary pattern of modern friendship, or just a personal limitation? 18

Perhaps because I conceive of the modern friendship scene as a somewhat theatrical enterprise, a one-act play, I tend to be very much affected by the "set." A restaurant, a museum, a walk in the park through the zoo, even 19 accompanying a friend on shopping errands—I prefer public turf where the stimulation of the city can play a backdrop to our dialogue, feeding it with details when inspiration flags.

I have a number of *chez moi* friends who always invite me to come to   20
their homes while evading offers to visit me. What they view as hospitality I see as a need to control the mise-en-scène of friendship. I am expected to fit in where they are most comfortable, while they play lord of the manor, distracted by the props of decor, the pool, the unexpected phone call, the swirl of children, animals, and neighbors. Indeed, *chez moi* friends often tend to keep a sort of open house, so that in going over to see them—for a tête-à-tête, I had assumed—I will suddenly find their other friends and neighbors, whom they have also invited, dropping in all afternoon. There are only so many Sundays I care to spend hanging out with a friend's entourage before I become impatient for a private audience.

Married friends who own their own homes are apt to try to draw me   21
into their domestic fold, whereas single people are often more sensitive about establishing a discreet space for the friendship to occur. Perhaps the married assume that a bachelor like me is desperate for home cooking and a little family life. I have noticed that it is not an easy matter to pry a married friend away from mate and milieu. For married people, especially those with children, the home often becomes the wellspring of all their nurturing feelings, and the single friend is invited to partake in the general flow. Maybe there is also a certain tendency on their part to kill two birds with one stone: They don't see enough of their spouse and kids, and they figure they can visit with you at the same time.

From my standpoint, friendship is a jealous goddess. Whenever a   22
friend of mine marries, I have to fight to overcome the feeling that I am being "replaced" by the spouse. I don't mind sharing a friend with his or her family milieu—in fact I like it, up to a point—but eventually I must get the friend alone, or else, as a bachelor at a distinct power disadvantage, I risk becoming a mere spectator of familial rituals instead of a key player in the drama of friendship.

A person who lives alone usually has more energy to give to friend-   23
ship. The danger is investing too much emotional energy in one's friends. When a single person is going through a romantic dry spell, he or she often tries to extract the missing passion from a circle of friends. This works only up to a point: The frayed nerves of protracted celibacy can lead to hypersensitive imaginings of slights and rejections, and one's platonic friends seem to come particularly into the line of fire.

Today, with the partial decline of the nuclear family and the search for   24
alternatives to it, we also see attempts to substitute the friendship web for intergenerational family life. Since psychoanalysis has alerted us to regard

the family as a mine field of unrequited love, manipulation, and ambivalence, it is only natural that people may look to friendship as a more supportive ground for relation. But in our longing for an unequivocally positive bond, we should beware of sentimentalizing friendship, as saccharine "buddy" movies and certain feminist novels do, and of neutering its problematic aspects. Besides, friendship can never substitute for the true meaning of family: If nothing else, it will never be able to duplicate the family's wild capacity for concentrating neurosis.

In short, friends can't be your family, they can't be your lovers, they   25
can't be your psychiatrists. But they can be your friends, which is plenty.

When I think about the qualities that characterize the best friendships   26
I've known, I can identify five: rapport, affection, need, habit, and forgiveness. Rapport and affection can only take you so far; they may leave you at the formal, outer gate of goodwill, which is still not friendship. A persistent need for the other's company, for the person's interest, approval, opinion, will get you inside the gates, especially when it is reciprocated. In the end, however, there are no substitutes for habit and forgiveness. A friendship may travel for years on cozy habit. But it is a melancholy fact that unless you are a saint you are bound to offend every friend deeply at least once in the course of time. The friends I have kept the longest are those who forgave me time and again for wronging them unintentionally, intentionally, or by the plain catastrophe of my personality. There can be no friendship without forgiveness.

◆ ◆ ◆

FIRST RESPONSES

Do you require "like-mindedness" in your friends? If not, what sort of differences are you comfortable with, and how do you deal with these differences?

TAKING A CLOSER LOOK

Exploring *Who:* Voice and Tone

1. How do the first two paragraphs set the general tone for this essay? How would you describe that tone?
2. Lopate uses "we" and "our" throughout the essay. Why does he use these pronouns? What effect does this usage have on you, the reader?
3. How many of Lopate's personal examples could you identify with?

Exploring *What:* Content and Meaning

1. Make a list of the different kinds of friendships discussed in the essay. Is any kind an exception from the others?
2. What are the functions that friends perform, according to this essay? Are there underlying similarities among the types?
3. What is the "pluralistic model of friendship"? When did Lopate take up the pluralistic model of friends? What did he lose, and what did he gain?
4. What are Aristotle's three types of friendships (paragraph 10)? What does Lopate think of Aristotle's categories, especially the last one?
5. Which type of friendship makes the most sense to you? Do you think you will change your mind on this point as you grow older?

Exploring *Why:* Purpose

1. Lopate begins by suggesting that there is nothing more to say about friendship. Why does he start this way? What does this opening tell you about his purpose?
2. Lopate writes "personal" essays. In what ways is this essay "personal"? To what extent is he writing to clarify his own feelings and ideas?
3. Is this essay primarily informative or persuasive? Is the author trying to get you to examine your own friendships? If so, does he succeed?
4. Does Lopate give you any new insights or perspectives on the subject? How much did you find yourself agreeing with his analyses?

Exploring *How:* Style and Structure

1. Why does Lopate cite so many other writers in the course of his discussion? How did you respond to all these references?
2. At the end of paragraph 4, Lopate says "we must go out into the world and seduce others"; and at the beginning of the next paragraph, he mentions "the promiscuity of the sandbox." Explain what the words *seduce* and *promiscuity* mean in those sentences. Do you consider these effective word choices?
3. The author uses a lot of personal examples to develop his discussion. Why does he include so many? Which ones did you find most informative and revealing?

4. Lopate uses a number of **similes** and **metaphors** to describe and explain friendship. Find several of each, and comment on their effectiveness.

5. Comment on the conclusion. Does the essay end on a strong point?

IDEAS FOR WRITING A DIVISION AND CLASSIFICATION PAPER

1. There are probably as many kinds of people you dislike as people you like. Write an essay categorizing the types that drive you crazy.

2. ▉▯ *Using the Internet.* Locate several sites that are devoted to the same topic (such as libraries, drama, encyclopedias, games, grammar, holidays, magazines, music, poetry, travel, geography, schools, or writing), and examine them closely. Then divide them into groups according to some consistent principle (such as types of information, use of graphics, primary purposes, visual style, or kinds of organization). Write an article directed at Internet users, using your classifications to evaluate and recommend the various sites within a particular topic area.

3. Using plenty of specific examples, write an essay disagreeing with Lopate's statement that "friends can't be your family."

◆ ◆ ◆ **PREPARING TO READ**

Is it easy for you to memorize facts and details for class? How well do you remember people's names and faces? Do you have any techniques for helping you to remember information?

◆ ◆ ◆

What We Now Know About Memory

LEE SMITH

Lee Smith (b. 1937) was educated at Yale University. He began his career in journalism with the Associated Press, then moved to *Newsweek* magazine, where he was a reporter for five years. He has been a writer for *Fortune* magazine since 1977 and has served as that publication's bureau chief in Tokyo and Washington, DC. The following article first appeared in the April 1995 edition of *Fortune.*

The alarm finally goes off in your head around 3 P.M. Your face flushes   1
and your hands plow through the papers on your desk. You have accidentally stood someone up for lunch. It gets worse. You can't remember who. And still worse: You can't recall where you left your glasses, so you can't look up the name in your appointment book. This is the afternoon you find yourself at a different place in life. Ten years ago, when you were 40, you would not have—could not have—forgotten anything.

Why do our memories betray us? Is this a precursor of Alzheimer's or   2
some other serious mental disorder? How can some people command a loyal and prodigious memory well into old age? Are there ways to make everyone's memory clear again?

First, reassurance: A momentary loss of memory is most probably not   3
a sign of Alzheimer's, or if so it's a very distant one. People between 65 and 75 face only a 4% chance of suffering from that sad, destructive disease, vs. a frightening 50% chance for those over 85. Yet almost all of us will be tripped up by forgetfulness from time to time as we age. Memory may begin to get a little shaky even in our late 30s, but the decline is so gradual that we don't start to stumble until we're 50ish.

The vanguard of 78 million baby-boomers will be 49 this year, so an 4 ever larger share of the population will be turning desktops upside down. For many, their anxiety in already difficult careers could rise significantly. Moderate memory loss may be easily manageable for those who spend their entire working lives in the same company. In that steady-state universe, new people arrive and rules change slowly. The 45-year-olds who are downsized out and working as consultants, on the other hand, suddenly must master the rosters of half a dozen clients and as many ways of doing business.

Neuroscience, in a timely way, has begun to pay more attention to this 5 condition. Researchers call it AAMI, age-associated memory impairment. The Charles A. Dana Foundation, named for an early manufacturer of differential joints for cars, has given $8.4 million to five major university medical centers to study AAMI. Researchers get the help of powerful instruments like PET (positron emission tomography) scanners that can detect the chemical changes taking place in the brains of subjects as they perform such tasks as memorizing vocabulary lists.

Some 450 middle-aged and elderly volunteers visit Johns Hopkins 6 Hospital in Baltimore once a year to take a series of memory exams, the results of which are tracked over decades. The brains of some of these good sports will be examined after they die to see if their declining scores over the years relate to physical signs of disease and atrophy.

Much about memory is still baffling. "Despite all the noise we scien- 7 tists make about memory, it is remarkable how little we know," says Dr. Arnold Scheibel, director of the UCLA Brain Research Institute. He and his colleagues can be forgiven. The brain has as many as 100 billion neurons, many with 100,000 or more connections through which they can send signals to neighboring neurons. The number of potential pathways would be beyond the ability of the most advanced supercomputers to map.

Some of the predetermined roadways seem bizarre. In early February, 8 for example, researchers discovered that men process language in one part of their brain, women in several. As for memory, the names of natural things, such as plants and animals, are apparently stored in one part of the brain; the names of chairs, machines, and other man-made stuff in another. Nouns seem to be separated from verbs. (That may explain the resistance of some brains to neologisms that turn nouns into verbs, such as "Let's dialogue on this" or "I'll liaise with Helen's team.")

Aspects of memory are scattered throughout the brain, but many re- 9 searchers believe the hippocampus (Greek for "sea horse," the shape of the tiny organ) has an especially important role. That is where new information is turned into memory. How memories are made—and fade—is still mysterious. But this much is known. Neuron No. 28, say, fires an electrical signal, and in the synapse where one of 28's connectors touches a receiver of neuron No. 29, a chemical change takes place that triggers an electrical signal in 29. That signal gets passed on to neuron No. 30, and on and on. If the connection between 28 and 29 is made often enough, the bond between the two neurons grows stronger. This crucial marriage, the stuff that memory seems to be made of, neuroscientists have dubbed, unpoetically, long-term potentiation, or LTP.

Though memories may be created in the hippocampus, they are stored   10
elsewhere. In TV soap operas the amnesiac is the ingenue who has forgotten she is already married to her fiancé's brother in another city, but is otherwise able to function more or less normally. That doesn't happen often, if ever. Real amnesiacs are people who remember the past but not the present. Their hippocampi have been severely damaged, so they are unable to form new memories, but most old memories remain intact.

Daniel L. Schacter, 42, a Harvard psychology professor, played a   11
round of golf with one such victim. M.T., who was 58, remembered the rules and all the lingo from bogie to wedge. But he couldn't recall where he hit his ball. If Schacter drove first and M.T. followed, M.T. had half a chance of holding on to the image of where his ball went long enough to track it down. But if M.T. drove first and had to wait for Schacter to drive, he had no chance. After M.T. walked off one green, Schacter noted in his journal, "the patient was surprised and confused when told he had not yet putted."

Amnesia can be caused by a virus, a blow to the head, a near drowning   12
or stroke that deprives the brain of oxygen for a time, or a faulty gene that programs parts of the brain to deteriorate early. Stress can play a part as well. Lab animals exposed to low levels of shock they cannot control produce glucosteroids that damage their hippocampi. Marilyn Albert, 51, a researcher at Massachusetts General Hospital, notes that among the elderly she is studying in the Boston area, those who are less educated, are less active physically, and feel less able to influence what happens to them day to day tend to experience greater memory loss than the better educated who regard themselves as more commanding. (This kind of stress is not the same as pressure to finish a job or perform well. Pressure can stir strong emotions that actually help imprint memories more deeply.)

As we age, most of us will experience at least some slowdown in abili-   13
ty to remember. What do we have to fear and how do we avoid it? Laypeople are accustomed to distinguishing between long-term and short-term memory. That oversimplifies the phenomenon. Dr. Murray Grossman, 43, a University of Pennsylvania Medical Center neurologist, has helped develop a model that separates memory into five types. He assigns each a locale, or a possible locale, in the brain and assesses the likelihood of each type's decaying over time. In order of durability, the memory types are as follows:

SEMANTIC. The memory of what words and symbols mean is highly re-   14
silient—even some Alzheimer's patients retain much of their semantic
memory. It's unlikely you'll forget what "Tinkertoy," "prom," and
"mess hall" mean even though you haven't used the words in years.
Nor do you forget religious symbols and corporate trademarks or
what distinguishes a cat from a dog. You can add words to your
semantic memory until death.

IMPLICIT. Years ago someone taught you to ride a bike. You may not re-   15
call the specific instructions of those wobbly, knee-banging first out-
ings, but you will not forget all that you have learned about bike riding
over a lifetime—without even being conscious of learning—from turning corners at high speeds to stopping on a dime. How to swim or drive
a car and many other skills that depend on automatic recall of a series
of motions don't disappear either. Nor do conditioned responses. Like
Pavlov's dogs, once you've learned to salivate at the sound of a bell,
you'll do it forever. Nor will you neglect to reach for a handkerchief
when you sense a sneeze, or for a dollar bill when you see a doorman.
Loss of implicit memory is a sure sign of serious mental deterioration.

REMOTE. This is the kind of memory that wins money on Jeopardy. It is   16
data collected over the years from schools, magazines, movies, conversations, wherever. Remote memory appears to diminish with age in
normal people, though the decline could be simply a retrieval problem. "It could be interference," says Johns Hopkins neurologist Dr.
Barry Gordon, 44. "We have to keep sorting through the constant accumulation of information as we age."

When a 60-year-old hears "war," it has many more associations than   17
Vietnam or the Gulf. And compared with the 30-year-old, the 60-year-
old may have to rummage through twice as much data before digging
way back to the lessons of a high school history course and finding the
names of the five Presidents after Lincoln.

WORKING. Now we enter territory that does erode, at least for most   18
people. This is extremely short-term memory, lasting for no more than
a few seconds. It is the brain's boss, telling it what to cling to. In conversation, working memory enables you to hang on to the first part of
your companion's sentence while she gets to the end. It also lets you
keep several things in mind simultaneously—to riffle through your
mail, talk on the phone, and catch the attention of a colleague walking
by the door to ask him if he wants to go to lunch—all without losing
your place.

For reasons that aren't altogether clear, working memory in many 19
people starts to slow down noticeably between 40 and 50. "Certain environments become more difficult, like the trading floor of a stock exchange, where you have to react very fast to a lot of information," says Richard Mohs, 45, a psychiatry professor at Mount Sinai School of Medicine in New York City. Jetfighter combat is out.

EPISODIC. This is the memory of recent experience—everything from 20
the movie you saw last week and the name of the client with whom you booked lunch to where you put your glasses—and it too dwindles over time. This is the form of memory loss, the AAMI, that does, or will, trouble most people. You remember how to drive your car, but that's academic because you can't recall where you parked it.

Episodic memory could begin to dwindle in the late 30s, but the 21
downward glide is so gentle that unless you are trying to memorize the *Iliad* or pass a bar exam, you probably won't notice for a couple of decades. At 50, however, you are likely to feel a little anxiety as you watch the younger people in the office, even the non-techies, learn how to operate the new computer software much more quickly than you do.

Several years ago a Massachusetts insurance company, observing that 22
malpractice suits are brought against old doctors more often than young ones, asked researchers to develop tests for identifying physicians at risk. Dean K. Whitla, 69, a Harvard psychologist, was on a team that examined 1,000 doctors, ages 30 to 80. In one test the subjects were seated in front of computers and asked to read stories crammed with details, such as street addresses. A few minutes later they took a multiple-choice test.

Ability declined steadily with age, says Whitla. Though some of the 80- 23
year-olds were as good as the 30s, on average the 80s could remember only half as much as the 30s. But there were also some 80s who on further investigation couldn't match the patients they had seen that day with their complaints. (The insurance company has not yet disclosed whether it plans to act on the results.)

What's going on up there? Unlike cells elsewhere in the body, neurons 24
don't divide. They age, and at the rate of 100,000 a day they die, says Dr. Daniel Alkon, 52, chief of the neural science lab at the National Institutes of Health. By the time someone reaches 65 or 70, he may have lost 20% of his 100 billion. Return to the hippocampus, where episodic memory is first recorded. Neuron 28 and some of its neighbors may be dead or so feeble they no longer transmit electrical charges efficiently.

Still, 80 billion remaining neurons is a lot. And even though the brain 25
cannot grow new ones, the neurons can likely sprout new synapses late into

life and thereby form new connections with one another. William Greenough, 50, a researcher at the University of Illinois, supplied lab rats with new balls, dolls, and other toys to play with daily and changed the chutes and tunnels in their cages. When he cut open their brains, he counted many more synapses than in rats that got no toys and no new decor.

It's a good guess that the human brain, too, grows more synapses   26 when stimulated and challenged. So the brain—even while shrinking—may be able to blaze ever more trails for laying down memory. If the neuron 28 path is no longer easily passable, the number of alternate routes may be virtually limitless. The trick is to force the brain to make them.

The habits of highly intelligent people offer a clue as to how to do   27 that. By and large, says Harvard's Schacter, the higher people score on the Wechsler Adult Intelligence Scale (100 is the mean), the higher they score on the Wechsler Memory Scale. "Memory depends on processing," he says. "Very smart people process information very deeply." Perhaps they relate a magazine article on memory to a book on artificial intelligence and a play about prison camp survivors. Doing so, they could be laying networks of neuron highways that will make the recollection of the article, book, or play accessible by multiple routes.

With effort, people with average intellects can boost their memories   28 substantially. For example, most people have trouble remembering numbers of more than seven digits or so, a limitation long recognized by telephone companies. But a decade ago, researchers at Carnegie Mellon University trained otherwise undistinguished undergraduates to memorize hundred-digit numbers. Focusing hard on that long string of digits, the students found patterns they could relate to meaningful number series, such as birthdays.

Forgetting names bedevils most people, the more so as they age. So   29 meet Harry Lorayne, 68, a memory coach and theatrical wonder already familiar to many insomniacs. His half-hour TV infomercials with Dick Cavett run at 4 A.M. and other off-price times. Lorayne has also appeared on *The Tonight Show* and memorized the names of as many as 500 people in the audience. His gift is that he can quickly invent a dramatic, often grotesque, image to slap on the face of everyone he encounters. "I meet Mr. Benavena, and I notice he has a big nose," rasps Lorayne in a voice that was trained on New York's Lower East Side. "So I think 'vane,' like weather vane, a nose that's a bent weather vane." Lorayne's Memory Power package of videotapes, audiotapes, and a book sells for $115.

Frank Felberbaum, 58, refers to himself as a corporate memory   30 consultant. "Think of bottles of beer falling like bombs," he introduces himself unforgettably. Felberbaum's clients include GE Capital, Condé Nast, and some Marriott hotels. For about $6,000, Felberbaum trains a group of 20 or so executives in a two-day course that instructs them on how to retain such critical data as a range of interest rates and the names of hotel guests.

The methods of Lorayne and Felberbaum are legitimate, say the neu-   31 roscientists. The routines they teach—fastening names and other information to vivid pictures—have been around since the ancient Greeks. Lorayne likes to trace his intellectual roots to Aristotle, who taught that in order to think, we must speculate with images. Matteo Ricci, a 16th-century Jesuit missionary to China, "built" a memory palace in his mind and wandered the halls, storing the dosage for a new medicine in one room, perhaps, and retrieving a Thomistic proof for the existence of God from another.

There are modest ways to build, if not a palace, at least a comfortable   32 home for memory. College students may be superior at memorizing not only because their neurons are young but also because they develop mnemonic devices to survive exams. That's an easy practice to resume. For example, memory is WIRES—working, implicit, remote, episodic, and semantic. One of the clichéd pieces of advice for improving your brain, including memory, is to marry someone smarter than yourself. If that's inconvenient, at least hang out with challenging, fast-thinking company. Or study accounting, zoology or a new language.

Coming someday, perhaps, is a memory pill. Cortex Pharmaceuticals,   33 founded by three neuroscientists from the University of California at Irvine, claims to have developed a class of drugs called ampakines that revive tired neurons. Gary Lynch, 52, one of the founders and a prominent LTP researcher, says ampakines heighten the ability of the remaining receptors in weakened neurons to carry on after some of their synapses have died. "We know that this works in middle-aged and old rats," says Lynch. "If you give them ampakines, they will remember in the afternoon where they found food in the morning."

Cortex President Alan Steigrod, 57, says that preliminary clinical trials   34 on humans in Germany have been encouraging. The company hopes to test the drugs soon on about 100 Alzheimer's victims in the U.S. Ampakines, or another series of drugs, may eventually prove to be the easy, safe, and effective way to freshen old memories. Or they may not. A Salk Institute researcher questions whether they are any more useful than caffeine. And they might have dangerous side effects. So the Food and Drug Administration could approve ampakines for Alzheimer's sufferers, who don't have much to lose, but keep them off the market for a long time for those afflicted by normal memory loss. Waiting for the FDA's okay, you could probably learn Chinese.

◆ ◆ ◆

FIRST RESPONSES

Why are the causes of memory disorders still so mysterious? Do you know anyone with a memory problem? How does it affect their day-to-day existence?

TAKING A CLOSER LOOK

Exploring *Who:* Voice and Tone

1. Is Smith a scientist himself? How can you tell from his writing?
2. Who is the audience for this essay?
3. How does Smith attempt to relate to his readers? What details of language and presentation are used to draw you into the discussion? Do you feel the author is talking down to you at any time?
4. How does reading about this topic make you feel? Does Smith do anything to influence your feelings?

Exploring *What:* Content and Meaning

1. Find the examples Smith uses to illustrate each memory type. How well do these examples help you to understand each type? Provide an example of your own for each kind of memory.
2. What is the relationship between intelligence and memory? Why is this relationship important to the research into memory retention for ordinary people?
3. What evidence supports the claim that people with average intelligence can boost their memories substantially?
4. ▮▯ *Using the Internet.* What's a mnemonic device (paragraph 32)? Does the one that Smith gives (WIRES) seem helpful? Do you know any others? Look on the Internet for Web sites on mnemonics. You'll find that a number of people and groups collect mnemonics as a hobby or as study aids. See, for instance, Amanda's Mnemonics Page (http://www.frii.com/ ~geomanda/mnemonics.html) or the Mnemonics Page of the American Medical Student Association (http://uhsweb.edu/rb/mn.htm).

Exploring *Why:* Purpose

1. Is Smith trying to inform you or give you practical advice—or both?

2. Look at the four questions in paragraph 2. What do these questions reveal about Smith's purpose? Does he answer them all?
3. Why does Smith discuss the causes of amnesia?

Exploring *How:* Style and Structure

1. Why does Smith begin with an anecdote about "you" and "your" memory lapses? Is this a good way to open?
2. What principle does the author use to arrange the five memory types?
3. Smith discusses the mechanics of memory before he discusses ways to improve it. Why is this an effective organization?
4. What is the function of the **rhetorical question** in paragraph 13?
5. Why does Smith give the age of every researcher he mentions?

IDEAS FOR WRITING A DIVISION AND CLASSIFICATION PAPER

1. Write an essay that classifies several different types of intelligence. Brainstorm (with help from friends or classmates if you want it) for ideas about the various kinds of "smarts" you see around you. Divide them into types, and discuss their usefulness and relative importance.
2. Return to the Web pages you found on mnemonics (in *What* question 4), and examine them more closely. What are the aims of these sites? How do they sort and present the mnemonics? For an audience of readers who have not viewed these sites, write an essay in which you describe the various sites and discuss their designs and purposes.
3. Write an essay in which you classify the types of lies people tell. For example, you could discuss the lies people tell to save others' feelings, the lies people tell to save their own pride, and so on. You might get together with friends or classmates to think of categories and examples.

◆ FURTHER IDEAS FOR USING DIVISION AND CLASSIFICATION

1. ◼ *Using the Internet.* What different methods of managing money do you see among your friends and family members? For help in developing this topic, locate some sites on the Internet that give advice and information about managing finances; see what kinds of problems and approaches they mention. Then write an essay classifying several types of money managers. Be sure to give plenty of specific examples to identify each type. You might conclude by offering a few tips of your own for managing money.

2. Perhaps you have had contact with a culture that is "foreign" to you. It may be a culture that is different due to class background, ethnic customs, sex or sexual orientation, religious belief, hierarchy of values, or intellectual persuasion. Write about the categories of differences you see between your culture and the foreign one. If you have not had this experience, interview someone who has—perhaps an exchange student—with the goal of writing about cultural differences.

3. COLLABORATIVE WRITING. Classify and explain the types of stress that distinguish a certain period of life. Get together with a group of classmates to brainstorm lists of the stresses associated with the teenage years, the first year of college, marriage, parenthood, or retirement. Review the lists and decide which area to write about. Then have each group member gather examples, details, causes, and effects by interviewing at least three people. Assemble your ideas and materials, and write a group report on the topic.

4. COMBINING STRATEGIES. Even the best-integrated person has different selves that come out in different situations. Write an essay telling about your different selves: describe the environments that bring them out, narrate some experiences that show these selves in action, and explain the effects that these roles have on your life.

Strategies for Examining Connections

Comparison and Contrast

◆ ◆ ◆ ◆ ◆

Comparison and contrast writing purposefully directs a reader's attention to similarities and differences.

- ◆ Writers use comparison and contrast to clarify, decide, and persuade.
- ◆ Effective comparison and contrast is organized clearly in either a point by point or block by block pattern.
- ◆ Points of comparison or contrast are developed consistently from section to section.

One of the fundamental ways we learn new things is by finding similarities and differences between them and the things we already know. "You'll like Jose," a friend tells you. "He's funny in the same way Ellen is." Here the familiar is used to clarify the unfamiliar. Immediate comparisons of this sort are called **analogies.** Teachers use them frequently, especially to help make abstract or difficult concepts more concrete. A biology professor, for example, might compare the human eye to a camera.

Sometimes analogies are used to persuade. Your English tutor will remind you that practicing the various writing strategies is a lot like standing in the batter's cage for a few hours before a big game: in both cases the result will be that the skills will be there when you need them the most. The test of an analogy, of course, is its accuracy. Learning to play racquetball is made much easier if a player realizes early in the process that regardless of the seeming similarities, there are significant differences between it and tennis.

More broadly, **comparison and contrast** is a strategy people use on a daily basis to make choices in their lives, to persuade themselves or others, and to help themselves and others select the best of many options. We weigh the pros and cons and consider advantages and disadvantages. What movie should you see, the new hit comedy or the drama based on the novel you just finished reading? Factors that might affect your decision include who the actors are, whether you liked one of the director's films in the past, and who the people are who have given you the rave and pan reviews.

In general, comparisons seek the likeness between objects or ideas, and contrasts highlight the differences. Although an essay might serve primarily to compare or contrast, the two approaches are quite frequently combined, with a few contrasting points reminding readers of the unique nature of each of the two things being compared, or with a striking comparison serving to undercut an overly general or simplistic contrast. In "Day to Night," Maya Angelou contrasts the cotton pickers' early morning hope to their evening despair, with a few significant comparisons helping to underscore the consistent dignity that defines all of their activities.

Day to Night: Picking Cotton

MAYA ANGELOU

Poet, autobiographer, actress—Maya Angelou (b. 1928) has sought and found success in many roles. Raised in rural, segregated Arkansas as well as in urban St. Louis and San Francisco, Maya found strength, inspiration, and vision in her complex and varied immediate family, as well as in the black and white authors she read so avidly. The first of five volumes of her autobiography, *I Know Why the Caged Bird Sings* (1970), brought her national attention and was made into a television movie in 1979. Angelou's most public role came in 1992, when President-elect Bill Clinton asked her to compose a poem for his inauguration. Her reading of *On the Pulse of Morning* brought her additional fame when the recording was awarded a Grammy. In addition to continuing her work as a writer, Angelou has spent the last several years traveling to university campuses lecturing, singing, and inspiring the next generation.

Early in the century, Momma (we soon stopped calling her Grand- 1
mother) sold lunches to the sawmen in the lumberyard (east Stamps) and the seedmen at the cotton gin (west Stamps). Her crisp meat pies and cool lemonade, when joined to her miraculous ability to be in two places at the same time, assured her business success. From being a mobile lunch counter, she set up a stand between the two points of fiscal interest and supplied the workers' needs for a few years. Then she had the Store built in the heart of the Negro area. Over the years it became the lay center of activities in town. On Saturdays, barbers sat their customers in the shade on the porch of the Store, and troubadours on their ceaseless crawlings through the South leaned across its benches and sang their sad songs of The Brazos while they played Jew's harps and cigar-box guitars.

The formal name of the Store was the Wm. Johnson General Mer- 2
chandise Store. Customers could find food staples, a good variety of colored thread, mash for hogs, corn for chickens, coal oil for lamps, light bulbs for the wealthy, shoestrings, hair dressing, balloons, and flower seeds. Anything not visible had only to be ordered.

Each year I watched the field across from the Store turn caterpillar 3
green, then gradually frosty white. I knew exactly how long it would be before the big wagons would pull into the front yard and load on the cotton pickers at daybreak to carry them to the remains of slavery's plantations.

During the picking season my grandmother would get out of bed at 4
four o'clock (she never used an alarm clock) and creak down to her knees and chant in a sleep-filled voice, "Our Father, thank you for letting me see this New Day. Thank you that you didn't allow the bed I lay on last night to be my cooling board, nor my blanket my winding sheet. Guide my feet this day along the straight and narrow, and help me to put a bridle on my tongue. Bless this house, and everybody in it. Thank you, in the name of your Son, Jesus Christ, Amen."

Before she had quite arisen, she called our names and issued orders, 5
and pushed her large feet into homemade slippers and across the bare lye-washed wooden floor to light the coal-oil lamp.

The lamplight in the Store gave a soft make-believe feeling to our 6
world which made me want to whisper and walk about on tiptoe. The odors of onions and oranges and kerosene had been mixing all night and wouldn't be disturbed until the wooded slat was removed from the door and the early morning air forced its way in with the bodies of people who had walked miles to reach the pickup place.

"Sister, I'll have two cans of sardines."   7

"I'm gonna work so fast today I'm gonna make you look like you   8
standing still."

"Lemme have a hunk uh cheese and some sody crackers."   9

"Just gimme a coupla them fat peanut paddies." That would be from a   10
picker who was taking his lunch. The greasy brown paper sack was stuck behind the bib of his overalls. He'd use the candy as a snack before the noon
sun called the workers to rest.

In those tender mornings the Store was full of laughing, joking, boast-   11
ing, and bragging. One man was going to pick two hundred pounds of cotton, and another three hundred. Even the children were promising to bring
home fo' bits and six bits.

The champion picker of the day before was the hero of the day. If he   12
prophesied that the cotton in today's field was going to be sparse and stick
to the bolls like glue, every listener would grunt a hearty agreement.

The sound of the empty cotton sacks dragging over the floor and the   13
murmurs of waking people were sliced by the cash register as we rang up
the five-cent sales.

If the morning sounds and smells were touched with the supernatural,   14
the late afternoon had all the features of the normal Arkansas life. In the
dying sunlight the people dragged, rather than their empty cotton sacks.

Brought back to the Store, the pickers would step out of the backs of   15
trucks and fold down, dirt-disappointed, to the ground. No matter how
much they had picked, it wasn't enough. Their wages wouldn't even get
them out of debt to my grandmother, not to mention the staggering bill that
waited on them at the white commissary downtown.

The sounds of the new morning had been replaced with grumbles   16
about cheating houses, weighted scales, snakes, skimpy cotton, and dusty
rows. In later years I was to confront the stereotyped picture of gay song-
singing cotton pickers with such inordinate rage that I was told even by fellow Blacks that my paranoia was embarrassing. But I had seen the fingers
cut by the mean little cotton bolls, and I had witnessed the backs and shoulders and arms and legs resisting any further demands.

Some of the workers would leave their sacks at the Store to be picked   17
up the following morning, but a few had to take them home for repairs. I
winced to picture them sewing the coarse material under a coal-oil lamp with
fingers stiffening from the day's work. In too few hours they would have to
walk back to Sister Henderson's Store, get vittles and load, again, onto the
trucks. Then they would face another day of trying to earn enough for the
whole year with the heavy knowledge that they were going to end the season
as they started it. Without the money or credit necessary to sustain a family

for three months. In cotton-picking time the late afternoons revealed the harshness of Black Southern life, which in the early morning had been softened by nature's blessing of grogginess, forgetfulness, and the soft lamplight.

◆ ◆ ◆

◆ ◆ ◆ *Writer's Workshop I* ◆ ◆ ◆
Responding to Comparison and Contrast

Use the *Who, What, Why,* and *How* questions (see pp. 3–4) to explore your own understanding of the ideas and the writing strategies employed by Maya Angelou in "Day to Night." Your instructor may ask you to record these responses in a journal or bring them to class to use in small group discussions.

◆ WRITING FROM READING

While working her way through the *Who, What, Why,* and *How* questions, student writer Kara Kitner concluded that, "The details she [Angelou] focused on in different stages throughout the essay not only made me feel as if I were there, but also created within me the feeling of a childhood memory. When this feeling is contrasted with the reality of the workers' lives, it makes the harshness more startling and lends it more weight." Kara recognized that beneath the most obvious contrast in Angelou's essay—the morning and evening behaviors of the cotton pickers—lay many additional contrasts: Angelou's own childhood idealism vs. her adult anger, and the reality of rural poverty against the racist stereotype of the happy cotton picker. Kara decided to brainstorm about her own evolving attitudes toward childhood, and ended by writing "Life: It's All About Choices."

Kara Kitner
English 1001
April 23, 1998

Life: It's All About Choices

Still lying in bed after I have shut off the alarm   1
that insisted that I get out of bed, I suddenly

remember other mornings much like this one. Well, sort
of like this one. On those days, however, it wasn't an
alarm that woke me up.

"Rise and shine! It is 7:15--time to get up," my   2
mother would shout.

I would open my eyes at the sound and squint   3
against the morning light. Growing accustomed to the
sudden brightness, my eyes would flit over the contents
of the room: the antique desk my dad had found and
refinished for me, the long lace curtains my mom knew
I would like, and the old wooden dresser I've had
since I was a child. These items were a familiar part
of my everyday life, but while I appreciated their
existence and the thoughtfulness of those who had
procured them for me, I knew I had never actively
chosen them for myself. Finally, I would get up and
head for the shower. On my way, my mom would stop
me before she left for work: "I've got to go--have a
good day!"

"You too," I would respond sleepily. Emerging from 4
the bathroom fifteen minutes later, fully awake, I
would begin to hurry to get ready so I would not be
late for school. Rushing in from the parking lot to
the crowded, noisy hallways of the high school, I
would check the clock and always find a few minutes
to talk to friends before the beginning of my formal
day, regularly signaled by the authority of the
bell. The day was divided into eight periods, which
included classes, study hall, lunch, and physical
education. There were specific times to learn, to
study, to eat, and to play. Almost every day the
schedule would be the same, and, again, someone else
had chosen it for me.

After school I would drive down the street to my   5
after-school job, work for about an hour and a half,
and then go home to study. It wasn't too much later
when my mom would arrive, asking me in the same breath
about my day and what I wanted for dinner. If I had
play rehearsal that night, we would decide on
something quickly. Then I'd go back to school, to the
exciting atmosphere exuded by the lights, red velvet
curtains, and hardwood floors of the auditorium. When

rehearsal was over, my friends and I would go for ice cream or a coke, but none of us could stay out very long because we had ten o'clock curfews. Home again, I would turn on the television and call my boyfriend. We would talk until mom knocked on the door telling me it was time to get off the phone, and soon afterwards I went to bed.

Hearing my roommate leave the apartment for her 6 first class, I am startled from my memory. I am now more aware of my current surroundings. I notice my new desk, which I had to put together myself, along with the papasan chair I had always wanted to buy. Not wanting to be late for class, I quickly get up, take a shower, and throw my hair up into a ponytail, dashing off to class and putting in my backpack the muffins I will eat for breakfast in the hour break between my first two classes. An hour at work is next, and then I walk back home for lunch break--a luxurious two hours.

My day is still scheduled, but it's now 7 completely up to me. With this choice comes more freedom, but also more responsibility. I decide what and when to eat, when to study, when to just relax with friends, even when to take my classes. Every day is what I make it. It is now up to me to make time for all of the events I feel are important in my life.

I walk home from class at the end of the day, 8 considering those high school memories I'd had in the morning and realize the old cliché is true: life is all about choices. Even more importantly, they are now all my choices. During the time I've spent away from home, I have really had to take stock of the values and traditions I was raised with, and decide which of these to carry over into my adult life and which to leave behind. I know that I could skip class tomorrow. No one would check up on me or call my parents. But I will choose to go anyway, because it is something I have made important in my life, something on which I place great value.

◆ GETTING STARTED ON COMPARISON AND CONTRAST

Comparison and contrast is used to *clarify* a point, to *decide* between several options, and to *persuade* you or someone else that one thing might be better than another. Your purpose for turning to this strategy, as well as who your readers might be, should guide you in making early choices about what you will compare or contrast, which points you will base the comparison or contrast on, how you will arrange the essay, and how many illustrations you will use.

Begin by turning your reason for writing into a sentence or question. Maya Angelou, for example, might have started writing "Day to Night" to clarify the reality of the cotton pickers' lives. Kara Kitner, on the other hand, began with the question, "How is my daily life now different from life at home?"

Next it's time to use brainstorming, freewriting, or perhaps clustering to generate answers to your question, points you might compare and contrast to make your point, and examples of your points. Kara brainstormed a list of all the things she heard, saw, and did over the course of her days at home and then did the same for her days now.

After you have generated your options, points, and examples, you'll need to review your reason for writing and decide if research is necessary to supplement your personal experience. The autobiographical nature of both Angelou's and Kara's essays did not require research. Either, however, might have expanded the scope of her essay by surveying others like her or by researching the opinions of professional sociologists or psychologists— as political scientist Andrew Hacker did to support his thesis in "Dividing American Society," as you will see later in the chapter.

When you have generated sufficient material, it's time to decide on a working **thesis**—a sentence that captures the clarification you hope to accomplish or that asserts the decision you would suggest or the position you would persuade your readers to take. With this generalization in mind, you can determine what, exactly, you will need to compare and contrast to accomplish your purpose. Finally, you need to decide the best points upon which to base the comparison and contrast. Angelou wanted to persuade her readers that, "In cotton-picking time the late afternoons revealed the harshness of Black Southern life, which in the early morning had been softened by nature's blessing of grogginess, forgetfulness and the soft lamplight." What she wished to contrast was implied in her thesis, and her strong memories of the sights and sounds of her grandmother's store provided her with her points of comparison—the way the workers looked and the things they talked about.

◆ ORGANIZING COMPARISON AND CONTRAST

Once you have determined what you are going to compare or contrast and the points upon which those comparisons or contrasts will be based, you then need to determine how to arrange the essay. You have two primary choices—**point by point** or **block by block.** The material to be covered remains essentially the same; however, the pattern variations provide opportunities to fulfill your purpose and meet your readers' needs more precisely. Regardless of which plan you choose, consistency is the key to successful implementation.

Block Comparison

Both Angelou and Kara decided on a block by block organization. In this pattern, readers are given complete information about one of the things being compared before moving on to the next thing. Angelou first writes all about the morning's events and then all about the evening's activities. Kara describes her teen years at home and then brings us up to date on her days at college. Looking closely, however, you'll discover that both have a subplan as well. Within each block or section of their essays are the points that meaningfully connect the things being compared or contrasted. In fact, during her prewriting, Kara produced this outline of Angelou's essay:

DAY	NIGHT
The plentifulness of goods at the store	The lack of goods in the worker's homes
Hope and promise of the new day	Bleakness and despair of the evening
Make-believe world of child—oranges, etc.	Real world of adults—cut fingers, etc.
Workers making purchases	Workers talking about bills
Positive, hopeful discussion of wages	Negative, disillusioned view of wages
"hero of the dawn"	"dirt disappointed" workers
"joking, boasting, and bragging"	"grumbles" and "heavy knowledge"
dragging cotton sacks	dragging workers
daybreak	dusk

This thoughtful analysis of Angelou's careful structuring provided Kara with a model for paralleling the development of each section of the blocked essay to persuade readers of the accuracy and value of the contrast being described.

In the block method of organization, you can either imply the point of the comparison or contrast, leaving the readers to draw their own conclusions, or direct the readers' attention to the points of comparison. Angelou does the latter in a transitional paragraph between the two sections—and as she develops the parallel points in the second half of her essay. One danger here is that the second block of the comparison may require too much repetition of the material already covered.

Similarities and Differences

A variation on the block by block method is to cluster the points of comparison and contrast around similarities and differences. Consider, for example, the proverbial apples and oranges. An advertising executive for the apple industry might organize a fact sheet promoting apples by clustering the similarities between apples and oranges—their nutritional value and availability, for example—and then emphasizing their differences after that—more varied uses for apples and their lower cost. Her purpose, to sell apples, is best served by admitting the comparison but emphasizing the contrasts.

Point by Point Comparison

Point by point development places responsibility for the comparison or contrast more directly into the hands of the writer. Each major section of the paper covers one point in terms of both or all of the things being compared or contrasted. A nutritionist, for example, without the profit motive of the advertising executive, might organize the fact sheet on apples and oranges by drawing conclusions one section at a time about relative cost, nutritional value, availability, and use, covering both apples and oranges under each of these points. For ease of use and consistency, either apples or oranges would be discussed first in each section. An outline of this arrangement would look like this:

APPLES VS. ORANGES

1. Relative cost
   a. Orange prices remain relatively constant throughout the year.
   b. Apples are least expensive during the fall harvest season.
2. Nutritional value
   a. Oranges contain significant amounts of vitamins A and C and have 62 calories.
   b. Apples offer fiber and have 81 calories.

3. Availability
   a. Oranges are generally available year round.
   b. Apples are best during the fall season.
4. Use
   a. Oranges can be used as snacks, & in salads, main dishes, desserts.
   b. Apples can be used as snacks, & in salads, main dishes, desserts.

◆ DEVELOPING COMPARISON AND CONTRAST

Having determined what will be compared or contrasted, the points with which to accomplish this, and the best organizing principle, you may want to do additional brainstorming, freewriting, or clustering to ensure the best development of your points. A review of the discussion in Chapter 5 of providing appropriate, relevant, and sufficiently detailed examples might be useful as you generate this additional supporting material. It's also time to reconsider the needs of your readers. Their experience with your topic or level of education might help you to select the right **analogy** or comparison to clarify your idea. The extent to which you expect readers to agree or disagree will indicate how many supporting points are needed and the extent to which they will need to be developed. Knowing that most of her readers would be more familiar with the stereotype than with the reality of picking cotton, Angelou provides in-depth descriptions and a wide range of sights and sounds. Kara, on the other hand, assumes her fellow classmates are familiar with college life and so concentrates on her unique behaviors and choices.

One pitfall of comparison and contrast essays can be the overuse of direct transitional phrasing—*but, and, however, on the other hand, in contrast.* The effect is to produce sing-song-like sentences that become annoying to read. Instead, you want to vary your style and allow the ideas themselves to provide the implied comparison or contrast, saving the transitions for strategic turning points within and between paragraphs. If you find yourself beginning each new sentence or every few sentences with a transition, it also may indicate that you are not fully developing your individual points. This kind of paragraph reads more like a list than an essay.

◆ OPENING AND CLOSING COMPARISON AND CONTRAST

As with all the strategies, the introductions to comparison and contrast essays are written to provide readers with any background that might be required to understand the points to be developed, to reveal the writer's purpose, to forecast the essay's pattern of development, and to create reader interest.

Angelou chooses to delay her purpose in favor of developing a context for her comparison and contrast. Her own authority for writing about her topic is established in the descriptions of Momma's store, while readers are drawn into the world through the same sensory descriptions that are subsequently used to compare and contrast the cotton pickers. Later, her block by block organization allows Angelou a natural spot to state her thesis—at the turning point from the morning section of the essay to the evening section.

Although Kara chose the same block by block organization and delayed providing a direct thesis, she decided to emphasize her comparison and contrast strategy in her introduction. Readers are left with the expectation that by the end of the essay they'll understand the value of Kara's memories. Wanting to know the unknown is a great reason to keep reading.

Deborah Tannen's "Sex, Lies, and Conversation," a point by point essay, begins with an anecdote that recurs throughout her essay. By providing readers with a familiar scene and recognizable people, she prepares doubting readers for her controversial thesis, which appears in paragraph 2, immediately before the actual point by point comparisons.

Only two of the essays in this chapter begin with direct theses. Both Denise Noe and Andrew Hacker illustrate why challenging or provocative comparisons might best begin with a straightforward purpose and design. Because readers might easily dismiss Noe's claim for a similarity between rap and country music, she must hit the ground running and immediately convince them of at least one substantial point of comparison. Similarly, Hacker's very topic implies his problem as a writer—many white readers will resist facing the problem of race in America. As a result, he realizes he must act quickly. In strong, concrete language, within a single, introductory paragraph, he moves readers across the history of slavery to the present and his central claim that history is itself the foundation of the problem.

Conclusions to comparison and contrast essays depend on the complexity of the material covered, the type of introduction chosen, and the structure of the essay. Only in the most difficult and technical essays will readers require a summary of the points of comparison and contrast. Instead, most essays, such as Kara's, use the conclusion to reveal a delayed thesis, or to state directly a previously implied thesis, as Angelou does. Scott Russell Sanders uses his last paragraph to reinforce the value of his comparisons to others. His seemingly personal tirade against the empty urban life in favor of a rich and full rural one is given broader social significance in his conclusion—and thus its value for any reader, regardless of background, is brought home.

◆ USING THE MODEL

Maya Angelou's interest in writing about the cotton pickers begins with an emotional response to what she believes is a misperception of them. She returns to her own concrete memories to sustain her argument against the stereotype. Though Kara, too, compares past impressions to present understandings, she comes to the conclusion that, in her case, "the old cliché is true: life is all about choices."

We grow up and grow old reacting to and against such commonly held beliefs. Identify some popular perception with which you strongly agree or disagree based on your own experience. Consider whether or not your feelings about the perception have changed as you've grown up. Then interview others and record their responses to this same belief and write a comparison or contrast essay based on your results.

◆ ◆ ◆ *Writer's Workshop II* ◆ ◆ ◆
Analyzing Comparison and Contrast

Working individually or with a small group of classmates, read through Kara Kitner's essay "Life: It's All About Choices," and respond to the following questions.

1. Which of her personal values does Kara hope to emphasize in her essay? Is there sufficient detail to explain what these values are and how they developed?
2. Are Kara's experiences typical? What evidence is there that she believes they are?
3. What do you think of Kara's parents? Will Kara be a similar kind of parent?
4. Does Kara's conclusion suggest that she hopes to influence her readers in any concrete way? Does she succeed?
5. Why does Kara provide more extensive description of her childhood than of her current routine? Did you need additional information to understand the contrast between the two?

◆ ◆ ◆ *Checklist for Reading and Writing* ◆ ◆ ◆
Comparison and Contrast Essays

1. Is a purpose for comparison or contrast made clear through either a direct or implied thesis?

2. Are the things being compared, contrasted, or developed through analogy logically connected to one another?
3. Are the points of comparison useful and sufficient, and are they consistently developed?
4. Is the pattern of development appropriate for the writer's purpose and readers' needs?
5. Are transitions provided where needed but not overused?

Does someone you live with or know make you listen to a type of music that is significantly different from your favorite type of music? What makes the two styles of music so different? Can you find any similarities?

◆ ◆ ◆

Parallel Worlds: The Surprising Similarities (and Differences) of Country-and-Western and Rap

DENISE NOE

Denise Noe seems to have chosen just the right career. Being a journalist allows her to pursue her widely diverse interests, from dinosaurs to the value of technology in the everyday lives of the disabled. Throughout her work, she seeks connections where others may only find differences. The titles of a few of the magazines in which she has been published give some insight into her unusual view of the world: *Gauntlet, Chrysalis, Metis, The Gulf War Anthology, Exquisite Corpse,* and *Nuthouse.* "Parallel Worlds" first appeared in *The Humanist* in the summer of 1995.

In all of popular music today, there are probably no two genres that are more apparently dissimilar than country-and-western and rap: the one rural, white, and southern; the other urban, black, and identified with the two coasts ("New York style" versus "L.A. style"). Yet C&W and rap are surprisingly similar in many ways. In both C&W and rap, for example, lyrics are important. Both types of music tell stories, as do folk songs, and the story is much more than frosting for the rhythm and beat. 1

The ideologies espoused by these types of music are remarkably similar as well. We frequently stereotype country fans as simple-minded conservatives—"redneck," moralistic super-patriots à la Archie Bunker. But country music often speaks critically of mainstream American platitudes, especially in such highly charged areas as sexual morality, crime, and the Protestant work ethic. 2

The sexual ethos of C&W and rap are depressingly similar: the men of both genres are champion chauvinists. Country singer Hank Williams, Jr., declares he's "Going Hunting Tonight," but he doesn't need a gun since he's 3 hunting the "she-cats" in a singles bar. Male rappers such as Ice-T, Ice Cube, and Snoop Doggy Dogg are stridently misogynist, with "bitches" and "hos" their trademark terms for half of humanity; their enthusiastic depictions of women raped and murdered are terrifying. Indeed, the sexism of rap group NWA (Niggaz with Attitude) reached a real-life nadir when one member of the group beat up a woman he thought "dissed" them—and was praised for his brutality by the other members.

On a happier note, both rap and C&W feature strong female voices as   4 well. Women rappers are strong, confident, and raunchy: "I want a man, not a boy / to approach me / Your lame game really insults me. . . . I've got to sit on my feet to come down to your level," taunt lady rappers Entice and Barbie at Too Short in their duet/duel, "Don't Fight the Feeling." Likewise, Loretta Lynn rose to C&W fame with defiant songs like "Don't Come Home a-Drinkin' with Lovin' on Your Mind" and "Your Squaw Is on the Warpath Tonight."

Country music can be bluntly honest about the realities of sex and   5 money—in sharp contrast to the "family values" rhetoric of the right. "Son of Hickory Hollow's Tramp" by Johnny Darrell salutes a mother who works as a prostitute to support her children. "Fancy" by Bobbie Gentry (and, more recently, Reba McEntire) describes a poverty-stricken woman's use of sex for survival and her rise to wealth on the ancient "gold mine." Both tunes are unapologetic about the pragmatic coping strategies of their heroines.

More startling than the resemblances in their male sexism and "uppi-   6 ty" women are the parallels between C&W and rap in their treatment of criminality. Country-and-western music is very far from a rigid law-and-order mentality. The criminal's life is celebrated for its excitement and clear-cut rewards—a seemingly promising alternative to the dull grind of day-to-day labor.

"Ain't got no money / Ain't got no job / Let's find a place to rob," sings   7 a jaunty Ricky Van Shelton in "Crime of Passion." In "I Never Picked Cotton," Roy Clark is more subdued but still unrepentant when he says: "I never picked cotton / like my mother did and my sister did and my brother did / And I'll never die young / working in a coal mine like my daddy did." Waylon Jennings' "Good Ole Boys" boast gleefully of having "hot-wired a city truck / turned it over in the mayor's yard."

Similarly, rap songs like "Gangsta, Gangsta" and "Dopeman" by   8 NWA and "Drama" by Ice-T tell of the thrill and easy money offered by a life of crime. "Drama" records the dizzying high of the thief; "Gangsta, Gangsta," the rush of adrenaline experienced by a murderer making a quick getaway. Of course, both C&W and rap songs do express the idea that in the long run crime doesn't pay. The sad narrator of Merle Haggard's "Mama

Tried" "turned 21 in prison / doing life without parole," while the thief of Ice-T's "Drama" is forced to realize that "I wouldn't be here if I'd fed my brain / Got knowledge from schoolbooks / 'stead of street crooks. / Now all I get is penitentiary hard looks."

Though both C&W and rap narrators are often criminals, their atti-   9
tudes toward law enforcement differ radically. The Irish Rovers' "Wasn't That a Party?" ("that little drag race down on Main Street / was just to see if the cops could run") pokes light-hearted fun at the police, while the Bobby Fuller Four's "I Fought the Law and the Law Won" expresses the most common C&W attitude: an acceptance that criminals must be caught, even if you are one. Neither song displays any anger toward the police, who are, after all, just doing their job.

To rappers, on the other hand, cops are the enemy. Two of the most   10
notorious rap songs are Ice-T's "Cop Killer" and NWA's "Fuck tha Police" (which angrily asserts, "Some police think they have the authority to kill a minority"). Despite ample evidence of police brutality in the inner city, "Fuck tha Police" was almost certainly regarded by nonblack America as a paranoid shriek—until the world witnessed the infamous videotape of several of Los Angeles' finest brutally beating Rodney King while a dozen other "peace officers" nonchalantly looked on.

Interestingly, although the C&W view of law enforcement naturally   11
sits better with the general public (certainly with the police themselves), the fact remains that country-and-western music contains a good deal of crime, violence, and casual sex. Yet it is easily accepted by white Americans while rap arouses alarm and calls for labeling. Why?

I believe there are three major reasons. The first, and simplest, is lan-   12
guage. Rappers say "bitch," "ho," "fuck," and "motherfucker"; C&W artists don't. Country singers may say, "I'm in the mood to speak some French tonight" (Mary Chapin-Carpenter, "How Do") or "There's two kinds of cherries / and two kinds of fairies" (Merle Haggard, "My Own Kind of Hat"), but they avoid the bluntest Anglo-Saxon terms.

A second reason is race. African Americans have a unique history of   13
oppression in this country, and rap reflects the inner-city African American experience. Then, too, whites expect angry, frightening messages from blacks and listen for them. Many blacks, on the other hand, hope for uplifting messages—and are dismayed when black artists seem to encourage or glorify the drug abuse and violence in their beleaguered communities. Thus, the focus on violence in rap—and the dismissal of same in C&W.

While the differing attitudes toward law enforcement are real enough,   14
much of the difference between violence in country-and-western music and in rap lies not in the songs themselves but in the way they are heard. Thus, when Ice Cube says, "Let the suburbs see a nigga invasion / Point-blank,

smoke the Caucasian," many whites interpret that as an incitement to violence. But when Johnny Cash's disgruntled factor worker in "Oney" crows, "Today's the day old Oney gets his," it's merely a joke. Likewise, when Ice Cube raps, "I've got a shotgun and here's the plot / Taking niggas out with the fire of buckshot" ("Gangsta, Gangsta"), he sends shudders through many African Americans heartbroken by black-on-black violence; but when Johnny Cash sings of an equally nihilistic killing in "Folsom Prison Blues"—"Shot a man in Reno / just to watch him die"—the public taps its feet and hums along. It's just a song, after all.

There is a third—and ironic—reason why rap is so widely attacked: 15
rap is actually closer to mainstream American economic ideology than country-and-western is. While C&W complains about the rough life of honest labor for poor and working-class people, rap ignores it almost entirely. "Work your fingers to the bone and what do you get?" asks Hoyt Axton in a satirical C&W song, then answers sardonically with its title: "Bony Fingers." Likewise, Johnny Paycheck's infamous "Take This Job and Shove It" is a blue-collar man's bitter protest against the rough and repetitive nature of his life's work. Work in C&W is hard and meaningless; it keeps one alive, but leaves the worker with little time or energy left to enjoy life.

Songs by female country singers reinforce this point in a different   16
way; they insist that love (with sex) is more important than affluence. The heroine of Reba McEntire's "Little Rock" says she'll have to "slip [her wedding ring] off," feeling no loyalty to the workaholic husband who "sure likes his money" but neglects his wife's emotional and physical needs. Jeanne Pruett in "Back to Back" lampoons the trappings of wealth and proclaims, "I'd trade this mansion / for a run-down shack / and a man who don't believe in sleeping back to back."

Rap's protagonists, on the other hand, are shrewd, materialistic, and ra-   17
bidly ambitious—although the means to their success are officially proscribed in our society. Not for them a "life that moves at a slower pace" (Alabama, "Down Home"); unlike the languorous hero of country-and-western, "catching these fish like they're going out of style" (Hank Williams, Jr., "Country State of Mind"), rap singers and rap characters alike are imbued with the great American determination to get ahead.

Rap's protagonists—drug dealers, burglars, armed robbers, and   18
"gangstas"—live in a society where success is "a fistful of jewelry" (Eazy E, "No More ?s"), "Motorola phones, Sony color TVs" (Ice-T, "Drama"), where "without a BMW you're through" (NWA, "A Bitch Iz a Bitch"). In NWA's "Dopeman," sometimes cited as an anti-drug song, the "Dopeman" is the archetypal American entrepreneur: clever, organized, ruthless, and not ruled by impulse—"To be a dopeman you must qualify / Don't get high off your own supply."

The proximity of rap to our success ethic arouses hostility because 19
America is torn by a deep ideological contradiction: we proudly proclaim
ourselves a moral (even religious) nation and tout our capitalist economic
system. But the reality of a successful capitalist system is that it undermines
conventional morality. A glance at the history books shows how our sup-
posedly moral nation heaped rewards upon the aptly named "robber
barons": the Rockefellers, Vanderbilts, Carnegies, and Morgans. The crack
dealer is a contemporary version of the bootlegger—at least one of whom,
Joe Kennedy, Sr., founded America's most famous political dynasty. (Indeed, I would not be surprised if history repeated itself and the son—or
daughter—of a drug lord becomes this country's first African American
president.)

Capitalism is unparalleled in its ability to create goods and distribute 20
services, but it is, like the hero of "Drama," "blind to what's wrong."
The only real criterion of a person's worth becomes how much money she
or he has—a successful crook is treated better than a poor, law-abiding
failure.

In short, the laid-back anti-materialist of country-and-western can be 21
dismissed with a shrug, but the rapper is attacked for that unforgivable sin:
holding a mirror up to unpleasant truths. And one of them is that amoral
ambition is as American as apple pie and the Saturday Night Special.

◆ ◆ ◆

FIRST RESPONSES

Is Noe correct in assuming that most of her readers will be surprised
by her observations? Has she changed your response to either country-and-
western or rap music? Are you interested in paying closer attention to the
lyrics now? Why?

TAKING A CLOSER LOOK

Exploring *Who:* Voice and Tone

1. When are Noe's personal political views most directly expressed?
   Going back, can you find more subtle evidence of her views in early
   paragraphs?
2. As Noe observes in paragraph 12, many readers will find the strong
   language of rap difficult to accept, yet as early as paragraph 3 she illustrates her point about rap's sexism with some very explicit lyrics.

How did you respond to the examples? Why would Noe make such a risky move?

3. Do a close reading of paragraph 14. How many different "ways of hearing" does the paragraph explore? What does this variety of perspectives tell you about the care Noe took in writing about the complex problem of race?

4. In paragraph 5, Noe describes country music's opposition to "family values," but she doesn't provide a similar discussion of rap's position on the topic. Why not? What is she assuming about her probable readers here? Is she correct?

Exploring *What:* Content and Meaning

1. List the major "surprising similarities (and differences)" between country-and-western and rap music. Which of these did you already know and which were new to you? Do you agree with the list? Could you add to it?

2. How familiar were you with the lyrics Noe uses to illustrate her points? Which did you find most convincing or dramatic? Why?

3. ■ *Using the Internet.* Use a search engine such as Yahoo to locate a relevant Web site for each of the styles of music discussed in the essay. Read some of the descriptions of recent songs and artists. How well do Noe's ideas apply to current songs in each style?

4. Did you know that Joseph Kennedy, Sr., had been associated with bootlegging? How does Noe hope this information will affect you? Is her purpose to justify crime?

Exploring *Why:* Purpose

1. Which one of the similarities does Noe believe is the most important? Why?

2. Has this essay changed your feelings about issues such as record labeling? How?

3. What is the effect of using Rodney King to justify the accuracy of some of the rap lyrics? Why does Noe place "peace officers" in quotation marks in the same sentence?

4. In the closing paragraphs of the essay, Noe makes some bold claims about American society. What were your responses to these observations? Can you think of other forms of popular culture that might confirm or contradict her claims?

Exploring *How:* Style and Strategy

1. Why does Noe dedicate the first half of the essay to similarities before moving onto the differences? For example, try reading paragraph 9 as if it were the second paragraph of the essay to evaluate the effect of changing its placement.
2. What does Noe mean when she describes women rappers as being "raunchy"? What would the country-and-western equivalent be?
3. In paragraph 15, what does Noe mean when she describes her third point as being "ironic"? Is this why she lists it third rather than first?

WRITING FROM READING ASSIGNMENT

In "Parallel Worlds," Noe finds similarities where the casual observer would find only differences. She then digs deep for what she believes are the more important contrasts. In this writing project, you will identify a misunderstanding that you believe is caused by a superficial response to similarities and/or differences.

A. Use a prewriting activity to identify possible topics. Focus on misunderstandings or errors in judgment that might be corrected if the thing being misjudged was compared to something that the readers already understand. You might consider different high school cliques, types of hobbies, forms of sports, popular heroes, even other styles of music. Be open to all the possibilities, however off the wall or startling they may seem. Clearly Noe thought her topic would make a good essay in part *because of* its unusual pairing.

B. Now, pick the topic you already know the most about or feel most strongly about. Unless this is a longer paper, you will want to limit yourself to comparing only two or three things so that you can fully develop your ideas. Noe, for example, didn't add folk music to her essay, even though she indicates in her introduction that it has something fundamental in common with country-and-western and rap.

C. Write out a generalization that captures your purpose for writing. Make a list of the similarities and differences that will help you to achieve that purpose. Review your answer to question 1 in the *What* section to get a sense of the kinds and number of comparisons you might want to cover.

D. Brainstorm to identify your own storehouse of information about the things to be compared. What additional information will you need? Noe probably used artists and song titles she was already familiar with, but she may have read articles to evaluate the accuracy of her impressions or to identify titles she might add to ensure a responsible discussion of country-and-western and rap. She also may have listened to CDs or used the Internet to track down the lyrics she needed to illustrate her points more precisely.

E. Review your evaluations of Noe's motives for organizing her paper according to similarities and differences and for ordering her subpoints as she did. Do your purpose and your audience's current attitudes require you to use either the point by point or block by block pattern? Do you need to arrange the points within the pattern in a particular way? Can you assume that your audience already knows some of what you plan to say, as Noe does in her discussion of family values?

F. Noe chose to introduce her essay with a very direct statement of her topic but developed the implications of her comparisons throughout the essay itself. She saved her underlying social criticism for the conclusion. Decide how and where you will introduce your topic and reveal your purpose. As you plan your comparison or draft the paper, additional insights into the misunderstanding may emerge and provide a generalization like the one Noe uses to conclude your essay.

G. Return to the "Checklist for Reading and Writing Comparison and Contrast Essays" (pp. 354–355) for a final revision of your essay, paying special attention to the need for appropriately used transitions.

◆ ◆ ◆ PREPARING TO READ

Did you have a very favorite childhood food? What made it so enjoyable? What memories do you associate with it and how do you feel about that food and those memories now?

◆ ◆ ◆

Guavas

ESMERALDA SANTIAGO

Autobiographer and novelist Esmeralda Santiago has the gift of turning difficult personal experiences into art. Born in rural Puerto Rico into a family that struggled each day for its economic and emotional well-being, Santiago survived, in part, by finding pleasure and meaning in the sights, sounds, and tastes of her island. This fascination with the world around her later provided a connection to the strange new people and their alien language when she moved to New York City and attended first the famed High School for the Performing Arts and later Harvard and Sarah Lawrence College. Her first two books, *When I Was Puerto Rican* (1993), a memoir, and *America's Dream* (1996), a novel, move fluidly between the diverse cultures of Puerto Rico and America. "Guavas" is the opening chapter of her memoir.

There are guavas at the Shop & Save. I pick one the size of a tennis   1
ball and finger the prickly stem end. It feels familiarly bumpy and firm. The
guava is not quite ripe; the skin is still a dark green. I smell it and imagine a
pale pink center, the seeds tightly embedded in the flesh.

A ripe guava is yellow, although some varieties have a pink tinge. The   2
skin is thick, firm, and sweet. Its heart is bright pink and almost solid with
seeds. The most delicious part of the guava surrounds the tiny seeds. If you
don't know how to eat a guava, the seeds end up in the crevices between
your teeth.

When you bite into a ripe guava, your teeth must grip the bumpy sur-   3
face and sink into the thick edible skin without hitting the center. It takes
experience to do this, as it's quite tricky to determine how far beyond the
skin the seeds begin.

Some years, when the rains have been plentiful and the nights cool,   4
you can bite into a guava and not find many seeds. The guava bushes grow
close to the ground, their branches laden with green then yellow fruit that
seem to ripen overnight. These guavas are large and juicy, almost seedless,

their roundness enticing you to have one more, just one more, because next year the rains may not come.

As children, we didn't always wait for the fruit to ripen. We raided the 5
bushes as soon as the guavas were large enough to bend the branch.

A green guava is sour and hard. You bite into it at its widest point, be- 6
cause it's easier to grasp with your teeth. You hear the skin, meat, and seeds crunching inside your head, while the inside of your mouth explodes in little spurts of sour.

You grimace, your eyes water, and your cheeks disappear as your lips 7
purse into a tight O. But you have another and then another, enjoying the crunchy sounds, the acid taste, the gritty texture of the unripe center. At night, your mother makes you drink castor oil, which she says tastes better than a green guava. That's when you know for sure that you're a child and she has stopped being one.

I had my last guava the day we left Puerto Rico. It was large and juicy, 8
almost red in the center, and so fragrant that I didn't want to eat it because I would lose the smell. All the way to the airport I scratched at it with my teeth, making little dents in the skin, chewing small pieces with my front teeth, so that I could feel the texture against my tongue, the tiny pink pellets of sweet.

Today, I stand before a stack of dark green guavas, each perfectly 9
round and hard, each $1.59. The one in my hand is tempting. It smells faintly of late summer afternoons and hopscotch under the mango tree. But this is autumn in New York, and I'm no longer a child.

The guava joins its sisters under the harsh fluorescent lights of the ex- 10
otic fruit display. I push my cart away, toward the apples and pears of my adulthood, their nearly seedless ripeness predictable and bittersweet.

◆ ◆ ◆

FIRST RESPONSES

Have you ever seen a guava or eaten one? Does Santiago make you want to try one? As an adult and an American, can you fully enjoy the experience the way Santiago did as a Puerto Rican child?

TAKING A CLOSER LOOK

Exploring *Who:* Voice and Tone

1. How well does the adult Santiago remember the details and recapture the feelings of her childhood experience? What challenges does she face in doing so?

2. What does paragraph 8 reveal about Santiago's personality?
3. *Using the Internet.* Visit the Voices in America Web site (http://www.humanities-interactive.org/vocesamericanas/ex097_02.html). How does the background it provides on Latino writers in the United States help you to understand Santiago's feelings about her subject?

Exploring *What:* Content and Meaning

1. How many different ways of eating a guava are described in this essay? What, exactly, makes each experience different?
2. How does Santiago feel about having left Puerto Rico? About her life now, in New York?
3. What attitude toward adults is revealed in paragraphs 7 and 9?

Exploring *Why:* Purpose

1. Why does Santiago open her essay at a "Shop & Save"?
2. Does Santiago expect her readers to have eaten or even seen a guava before? By contrast, will most of them have eaten apples and pears? How does this knowledge suit her purpose of sharing this memory with her readers?
3. As a child, Santiago felt the guavas "enticing" her "to have one more, just one more, because next year the rains might not come." What does this memory reveal about her way of life in Puerto Rico?

Exploring *How:* Style and Strategy

1. How many of your senses does Santiago appeal to in her description?
2. What is the effect of telling you that the guava in New York costs "$1.59"? Why does Santiago tell us that "The guava joins its sisters under the harsh fluorescent lights of the exotic fruit display"?
3. Why does Santiago spend only the first and the last two paragraphs describing the New York supermarket guava? Why begin and end the essay with that half of the comparison?

IDEAS FOR WRITING COMPARISON AND CONTRAST

1. In a brief essay, compare and contrast two familiar things that are similar in kind—two types of fruit, two models of bicycles, two breeds of cats or dogs, for example. Consider what is learned about each type by noticing both its similarities to and its differences from the other kind.

2. Write an essay comparing and contrasting your experience of visiting a particular place as a child and later as an adult—perhaps a family vacation destination, a relative's home, or a grade school classroom. Concentrate on describing the place as well as analyzing any changes in the place and in you.

3. Sometimes people feel nostalgic about old ways, customs, techniques, or things. Write an essay about something old that you feel nostalgic about and that has been replaced with something new. Be sure to tell whether the new thing is really an improvement or really a decline— or both.

◆ ◆ ◆ PREPARING TO READ

When you share a personal problem with a friend of the same sex, what kinds of things do you expect him or her to say and do? Does your expectation change when you tell a problem to someone of the opposite sex? Why?

◆ ◆ ◆

Sex, Lies, and Conversation

DEBORAH TANNEN

Deborah Tannen, Professor of Linguistics at Georgetown University, writes academic and popular articles on how men and women communicate—and fail to communicate—with one another. She is the author of several books on the subject, including *That's Not What I Meant! How Conversational Style Makes or Breaks Relationships* (1986) and *You Just Don't Understand: Women and Men in Conversation* (1990). The following article originally appeared in the *Washington Post* in 1990.

I was addressing a small gathering in a suburban Virginia living   1
room—a women's group that had invited men to join them. Throughout the evening, one man had been particularly talkative, frequently offering ideas and anecdotes, while his wife sat silently beside him on the couch. Toward the end of the evening, I commented that women frequently complain that their husbands don't talk to them. This man quickly concurred. He gestured toward his wife and said, "She's the talker in our family." The room burst into laughter; the man looked puzzled and hurt. "It's true," he explained. "When I come home from work I have nothing to say. If she didn't keep the conversation going, we'd spend the whole evening in silence."

This episode crystallizes the irony that although American men tend   2
to talk more than women in public situations, they often talk less at home. And this pattern is wreaking havoc with marriage.

The pattern was observed by political scientist Andrew Hacker in the   3
late '70s. Sociologist Catherine Kohler Riessman reports in her new book *Divorce Talk* that most of the women she interviewed—but only a few of the men—gave lack of communication as the reason for their divorces. Given the current divorce rate of nearly 50 percent, that amounts to millions of cases in the United States every year—a virtual epidemic of failed conversation.

In my own research, complaints from women about their husbands 4
most often focused not on tangible inequities such as having given up the
chance for a career to accompany a husband to his, or doing far more than
their share of daily life-support work like cleaning, cooking, social arrangements, and errands. Instead, they focused on communication: "He doesn't
listen to me," "He doesn't talk to me." I found, as Hacker observed years before, that most wives want their husbands to be, first and foremost, conversational partners, but few husbands share this expectation of their wives.

In short, the image that best represents the current crisis is the stereo- 5
typical cartoon scene of a man sitting at the breakfast table with a newspaper held up in front of his face, while a woman glares at the back of it,
wanting to talk.

Linguistic Battle of the Sexes

How can women and men have such different impressions of commu- 6
nication in marriage? Why the widespread imbalance in their interests and
expectations?

In the April issue of *American Psychologist,* Stanford University's 7
Eleanor Maccoby reports the results of her own and others' research showing that children's development is most influenced by the social structure of
peer interactions. Boys and girls tend to play with children of their own gender, and their sex-separate groups have different organizational structures
and interactive norms.

I believe these systematic differences in childhood socialization make 8
talk between women and men like cross-cultural communication, heir to all
the attraction and pitfalls of that enticing but difficult enterprise. My research on men's and women's conversations uncovered patterns similar to
those described for children's groups.

For women, as for girls, intimacy is the fabric of relationships, and talk 9
is the thread from which it is woven. Little girls create and maintain friendships by exchanging secrets; similarly, women regard conversation as the
cornerstone of friendship. So a woman expects her husband to be a new and
improved version of a best friend. What is important is not the individual
subjects that are discussed but the sense of closeness, of a life shared, that
emerges when people tell their thoughts, feelings, and impressions.

Bonds between boys can be as intense as girls', but they are based less 10
on talking, more on doing things together. Since they don't assume talk is
the cement that binds a relationship, men don't know what kind of talk
women want, and they don't miss it when it isn't there.

Boys' groups are larger, more inclusive, and more hierarchical, so boys 11
must struggle to avoid the subordinate position in the group. This may play

a role in women's complaints that men don't listen to them. Some men really don't like to listen, because being the listener makes them feel one-down, like a child listening to adults or an employee to a boss.

But often when women tell men, "You aren't listening," and the men   12
protest, "I am," the men are right. The impression of not listening results from misalignments in the mechanics of conversation. The misalignment be-gins as soon as a man and a woman take physical positions. This became clear when I studied videotapes made by psychologist Bruce Dorval of children and adults talking to their same-sex best friends. I found that at every age, the girls and women faced each other directly, their eyes anchored on each other's faces. At every age, the boys and men sat at angles to each other and looked elsewhere in the room, periodically glancing at each other. They were obviously attuned to each other, often mirroring each other's movements. But the tendency of men to face away can give women the impression they aren't listening even when they are. A young woman in college was frustrat-ed: Whenever she told her boyfriend she wanted to talk to him, he would lie down on the floor, close his eyes, and put his arm over his face. This signaled to her, "He's taking a nap." But he insisted he was listening extra hard. Nor-mally, he looks around the room, so he is easily distracted. Lying down and covering his eyes helped him concentrate on what she was saying.

Analogous to the physical alignment that women and men take in   13
conversation is their topical alignment. The girls in my study tended to talk at length about one topic, but the boys tended to jump from topic to topic. The second-grade girls exchanged stories about people they knew. The second-grade boys teased, told jokes, noticed things in the room, and talked about finding games to play. The sixth-grade girls talked about problems with a mutual friend. The sixth-grade boys talked about 55 different topics, none of which extended over more than a few turns.

Listening to Body Language

Switching topics is another habit that gives women the impression   14
men aren't listening, especially if they switch to a topic about themselves. But the evidence of the 10th-grade boys in my study indicates otherwise. The 10th-grade boys sprawled across their chairs with bodies parallel and eyes straight ahead, rarely looking at each other. They looked as if they were riding in a car, staring out the windshield. But they were talking about their feelings. One boy was upset because a girl had told him he had a drink-ing problem, and the other was feeling alienated from all his friends.

Now, when a girl told a friend about a problem, the friend responded   15
by asking probing questions and expressing agreement and understanding. But the boys dismissed each other's problems. Todd assured Richard that

his drinking was "no big problem" because "sometimes you're funny when you're off your butt." And when Todd said he felt left out, Richard responded, "Why should you? You know more people than me."

Women perceive such responses as belittling and unsupportive. But the boys seemed satisfied with them. Whereas women reassure each other by implying, "You shouldn't feel bad because I've had similar experiences," men do so by implying, "You shouldn't feel bad because your problems aren't so bad." 16

There are even simpler reasons for women's impression that men don't listen. Linguist Lynette Hirschman found that women make more listener-noise, such as "mhm," "uhuh," and "yeah," to show "I'm with you." Men, she found, more often give silent attention. Women who expect a stream of listener-noise interpret silent attention as no attention at all. 17

Women's conversational habits are as frustrating to men as men's are to women. Men who expect silent attention interpret a stream of listener-noise as overreaction or impatience. Also, when women talk to each other in a close, comfortable setting, they often overlap, finish each other's sentences, and anticipate what the other is about to say. This practice, which I call "participatory listenership," is often perceived by men as interruption, intrusion, and lack of attention. 18

A parallel difference caused a man to complain about his wife, "She just wants to talk about her own point of view. If I show her another view, she gets mad at me." When most women talk to each other, they assume a conversationalist's job is to express agreement and support. But many men see their conversational duty as pointing out the other side of an argument. This is heard as disloyalty by women, and refusal to offer the requisite support. It is not that women don't want to see other points of view, but that they prefer them phrased as suggestions and inquiries rather than as direct challenges. 19

In his book *Fighting for Life*, Walter Ong points out that men use "agonistic" or warlike, oppositional formats to do almost anything; thus discussion becomes debate, and conversation a competitive sport. In contrast, women see conversation as a ritual means of establishing rapport. If Jane tells a problem and June says she has a similar one, they walk away feeling closer to each other. But this attempt at establishing rapport can backfire when used with men. Men take too literally women's ritual "troubles talk," just as women mistake men's ritual challenges for real attack. 20

The Sounds of Silence

These differences begin to clarify why women and men have such different expectations about communication in marriage. For women, talk creates intimacy. Marriage is an orgy of closeness: you can tell your feelings 21 and thoughts, and still be loved. Their greatest fear is being pushed away. But men live in a hierarchical world, where talk maintains independence and status. They are on guard to protect themselves from being put down and pushed around.

This explains the paradox of the talkative man who said of his silent 22 wife, "She's the talker." In the public setting of a guest lecture, he felt challenged to show his intelligence and display his understanding of the lecture. But at home, where he has nothing to prove and no one to defend against, he is free to remain silent. For his wife, being home means she is free from the worry that something she says might offend someone, or spark disagreement, or appear to be showing off; at home she is free to talk.

The communication problems that endanger marriage can't be fixed 23 by mechanical engineering. They require a new conceptual framework about the role of talk in human relationships. Many of the psychological explanations that have become second nature may not be helpful, because they tend to blame either women (for not being assertive enough) or men (for not being in touch with their feelings). A sociolinguistic approach by which male-female conversation is seen as cross-cultural communication allows us to understand the problem and forge solutions without blaming either party.

Once the problem is understood, improvement comes naturally, as it 24 did to the young woman and her boyfriend who seemed to go to sleep when she wanted to talk. Previously, she had accused him of not listening, and he had refused to change his behavior, since that would be admitting fault. But then she learned about and explained to him the differences in women's and men's habitual ways of aligning themselves in conversation. The next time she told him she wanted to talk, he began, as usual, by lying down and covering his eyes. When the familiar negative reaction bubbled up, she reassured herself that he really was listening. But then he sat up and looked at her. Thrilled, she asked why. He said, "You like me to look at you when we talk, so I'll try to do it." Once he saw their differences as cross-cultural rather than right and wrong, he independently altered his behavior.

Women who feel abandoned and deprived when their husbands won't 25 listen to or report daily news may be happy to discover their husbands trying to adapt once they understand the place of small talk in women's relationships. But if their husbands don't adapt, the women may still be comforted that for men, this is not a failure of intimacy. Accepting the difference, the wives may look to their friends or family for that kind of talk. And husbands who can't provide it shouldn't feel their wives have made unreasonable demands. Some couples will still decide to divorce, but at least their decisions will be based on realistic expectations.

In these times of resurgent ethnic conflicts, the world desperately   26
needs cross-cultural understanding. Like charity, successful cross-cultural
communication should begin at home.

◆ ◆ ◆

FIRST RESPONSES

Can you remember a specific difficult conversation you had with
someone of the opposite sex? How might you have used Tannen's advice to
help resolve that conversation more positively?

TAKING A CLOSER LOOK

Exploring *Who:* Voice and Tone

1. How does Tannen achieve a personal voice in the essay while maintaining her professional credibility? Did this voice help to maintain
   your interest as you read?
2. Clearly, Tannen has done extensive primary research on her topic.
   Why, then, does she quote several other researchers? Did you recognize the names of these scholars? What other strategies does Tannen
   use to establish their authority?
3. What evidence is there that Tannen hopes that both men and women will be interested in her topic? Did this point of view surprise
   you?
4. ▌⌐ *Using the Internet.* Visit the Web page of the *Washington Post,*
   where this essay originally appeared. What in the essay reflects that
   Tannen had the readers of this major national newspaper in mind as
   she wrote?

Exploring *What:* Content and Meaning

1. Make a point by point list of the causes of women's and men's differing feelings about communicating. Now make a list of the behaviors
   these differences create.
2. Do you recognize yourself in the styles of communication Tannen describes? If not, does this negate her conclusions?
3. Reread the last sentence of paragraph 24. What, exactly, do you believe allowed the boyfriend to change his behavior?

Exploring *Why:* Purpose

1. Has Tannen convinced you that this problem is "a virtual epidemic"? Can you identify any marriages where "this pattern is wreaking havoc"?
2. What is Tannen's purpose in describing the cartoon she recalls in paragraph 5 as "stereotypical"? How does her essay change the way you respond to that cartoon?
3. In paragraphs 8 through 11, Tannen traces gender differences to childhood socialization. In what ways is she working with an awareness of the powerful nature of these formative years when she formulates her hopeful suggestions in the closing paragraphs of the essay?
4. In paragraphs 8 and 26, Tannen makes an **analogy** between male/female miscommunication and the problems of cross-cultural communication. What does she mean? Why does she choose this comparison? Does your greater understanding of gender miscommunication also help you, in turn, to better understand cross-cultural problems?

Exploring *How:* Style and Strategy

1. Why does Tannen begin her essay with the anecdote about the husband and wife? What was your response to their predicament? By the time she returns to this couple in paragraph 22, had your response changed? How about your response to the couple in paragraphs 12 and 24?
2. Tannen occasionally uses the jargon of a professional linguist, such as "listener-noise" and "participatory listenership." Did you find this terminology useful or confusing? Why did she choose to use it?
3. Identify the two parallel phrases that Tannen uses in paragraph 22. What is the effect of this comparison strategy?

IDEAS FOR WRITING COMPARISON AND CONTRAST

1. Visit a playground. Observe both boys and girls—playing alone and interacting with one another. Then, focusing on gender or the type of play engaged in, write a brief essay describing a surprising or significant similarity or difference that you observe in the children's behaviors.
2. Will either men or women find it easier to adapt to the other gender's communication style? Write an essay comparing and contrasting the suggestions you would give to women with those you would give to

men. Use personal examples as well as ideas from Tannen's essay to support your ideas. Be sure to acknowledge Tannen's ideas through appropriate citations.

3. What other differences might account for miscommunication between friends? Consider, for example, country versus city or suburban childhoods, having blue-collar versus white-collar parents, or being an only child versus growing up in a family of ten. Using personal experience and perhaps interviews with friends or family members, write an essay in which you compare and contrast the ways in which these childhood experiences might shape adult behaviors. Like Tannen, be aware of the realities behind the stereotypes as you write.

◆ ◆ ◆ **PREPARING TO READ**

What do you feel and think when you hear a rural accent, especially a southern accent? How has popular culture—television, movies, music— contributed to these responses?

◆ ◆ ◆

Coming from the Country

SCOTT RUSSELL SANDERS

In addition to teaching college English, Scott Russell Sanders has had an active career as a freelance journalist with magazines such as *Audubon,* the *Utne Reader,* and the *Georgia Review.* As a regionalist, he explores everyday life in search of meaningful connections between individual well-being and the common good. In addition to essay collections, which include *Staying Put: Making a Home in a Restless World* (1994) and *Writing from the Center* (1995), Sanders writes children's books, such as his recent *A Place Called Freedom* (1997), a 19th-century pioneer story.

When my family packed up and moved from the backwoods of Ten- 1
nessee to the backwoods of Ohio I was not quite six years old. Like most children at that age I was still a two-legged smudge. Hardly a thing about me was definite except my way of talking, and that soon landed me in trouble. The kids in Ohio took one listen to my Tennessee accent and decided I was a hick. They let me know their opinion by calling me not only hick but hillbilly, ridge runner, clodhopper, and hayseed. (Our language provides about as many ways of calling somebody a yokel as of calling him a drunkard.) To my southern ears, *they* were the ones who sounded funny. But they had me outnumbered. So with cheerful cruelty they danced in circles around me and mimicked my drawl. In school, whenever I had to answer a teacher's question, they would echo my words and hoot with laughter. The only southerners they had met before were Kentuckians and West Virginians who had moved north when the Appalachian coal mines shut down. These Ohio kids lumped all southerners together under the heading of hillbillies, and regarded us all as the scum of the earth.

I wasn't comfortable in the role of scum of the earth. At first I tried 2
fighting, swinging at anyone of any size who mocked me. The mockers gleefully hit back, of course. After having better sense pounded into me, I made

a discovery that chameleons and turncoats have known for ages: I would be safer if I blended in. From that time on, whatever the Ohio kids mimicked in my speech, I simply erased. Out went "you all," "I reckon," "rode a fur piece," and "tote a poke of taters." I quit saying my southern "Yes, Ma'am" and "No, Ma'am" to the teacher, who had labeled me a smart aleck for pretending such politeness. Before long I was talking like a Midwesterner, bland and cautious, as if I were cupping a marble on my tongue. It is the dialect I still speak, although when I'm tired, or telling stories, or visiting with my southern kinfolk, or feeling amorous, I slip back into the accents of Tennessee.

When my playmates quit mocking my speech, I thought I must surely   3 have graduated from being a hick. But I had only quit sounding like a southern variety in order to begin sounding like a northern one; I had left one backwoods for another. In the years since that move to Ohio I've met enough purebred city people to realize that, however many layers of travel and booklearning I wear on my outside, down inside I am pure country. Since I'm now reasonably grown up, and still inwardly a yokel, I no longer expect to mature into a cosmopolitan. For better or worse, I come from the country, and lately I've begun to reflect on what this means.

Being a hick is less of a handicap than I once thought. It amuses my   4 urban friends, it means I can leave my windows rolled down when I drive by pig farms, it allows me to ignore about half of what passes for modernity, and it supplies an excuse for a good many of my crotchets. Consider my habits of sleep, for example. I like to get up roughly when the sun does, and if sloth or a faulty alarm keeps me abed much later than seven I stumble through the day feeling out of sorts. This habit of rising early also means I turn into a sack of sawdust around ten o'clock at night, when my town friends want to go dancing. Knowing I'm a hick, they rib me a little and then let me shuffle off to bed.

Or consider—on my long list of rural crotchets—my dread of taxis. I   5 will carry a suitcase and walk any distance to avoid hiring a cab. The first time I ever had the chance of hiring one was at the age of seventeen, when I went away to college in Providence. Fresh off the Greyhound bus after a ride of forty-eight hours, lugging a year's supply of goods in my grandfather's sea chest, I asked a ticket-seller where I would find the university. He pointed up a hill, but said it was too far to walk hauling such a big trunk, so I'd better get a cab. I glanced warily at the row of dented yellow cars, each with its bubble on top and its flanks inscribed with the prices of various distances, then hefted the sea chest and trudged on up the hill. I haven't outgrown this phobia. Recently, in Baltimore, I was going out to dinner with some friends. Since there were nine of us, somebody ordered three taxis.

Shy and backward, I stood aside while four of my friends got in the first cab and the remaining four piled into the second; when the last car drew up beside me I spun around and fled.

Now as it happens I enjoy using my legs and saving a dollar—two good 6
reasons for avoiding cabs. But my difficulties with taxis lie deeper. I like to know where I'm going, and like to choose my own path for getting there. I hate sitting behind a driver who treats a crowded avenue as his private racetrack, shouting threats and blaring the horn. It is a torture for me to hear the meter tick and watch the odometer spin its numbers. I can't stand having time and distance parceled out that way, so many cents per click.

What bothers me even more, and not just in taxis, is to hire strangers 7
to serve my needs. I don't like turning myself over to bellhops, waitresses, museum guides, barbers, or doctors unless I am on familiar territory and know the people I am dealing with. When I can't avoid staying in hotels, I mark myself out as a yokel by opening my own doors and carrying my own bags. I read the room service brochures with dismay. Imagine, leaving your dirty socks in the hallway and having them come back, discreetly perfumed, in a plastic sack the next morning. Imagine, ringing for a glass of milk at midnight. It's as if, through room service, you're invited to become a child again, to be waited on hand and foot without the trouble of coming down with fever.

When I can't avoid going to a restaurant, I sit there with my plate full 8
of food cooked by somebody I've never seen, I watch the frazzled waitress dashing between tables with a coffee pot, her bangs stringy from sweat, and I feel like getting up and giving her my chair. For me there is something shameful in being pampered and catered to by hirelings, a hint almost of slavery. And there is something craven in paying others to do what you could perfectly well do yourself.

Now you will not get very far or rise very high in a city if you refuse to 9
have people wait on you. Foolish as it may be, this inhibition has stuck with me from my country upbringing. Lack of money and distance from town meant that we looked after ourselves; we shopped once a week, and otherwise made do with what was in the house; we fixed what broke. My father and mother between them could mend anything from bluejeans to banjos, from televisions to fishing tackle. We never used the yellow pages. If some job needed doing that we lacked the skills or the tools for—shoeing our ponies, cleaning a septic tank—we got a neighbor to do it, sometimes for money, sometimes for labor or a bushel of sweet corn or a jar of strawberry jam. There was no bragging attitude of self-sufficiency behind this. It was simply how we lived, and how I learned to live. In the country most children are taught to see to their own needs, and when they can't handle the job alone they hunt up a friend.

If you're used to fixing and patching and making-do, you need spare   10
parts, which is why a lot of country places look like salvage yards, with discouraged cars up on blocks, disemboweled washing machines and cement
mixers on the porch, coils of wire and stacks of wood under tarps by the
barn. Stores are a long way off, they may not have the part you need, and
anyway they'll charge you for it. Better keep every scrap of metal and plastic and wood you can lay your hands on. And if you started to build a house
but ran out of money and strength after finishing the basement and you're
living down there under ground, or if you're cramped inside a sixteen-foot
trailer and hope one day to surround it with weathertight rooms, that's all
the more reason for saving junk. To a pair of city eyes, such a place looks
squalid. To the folks living at the center of that pile, it's neither ugly nor
lovely; it's just there, an orchard of human fruits ready for plucking in season. Since I don't have much land around me these days, I've turned my
basement into a junkyard. Down there you will find pieces from every machine that has ever failed me, sheets of plywood and plasterboard, tiles,
bricks, blocks, switches, parts I can't name from gizmos I've forgotten.

The more I scavenge, the less I have to buy, which saves me confusion   11
as well as money. When it comes to buying goods and services—the correct
wine at dinner, a rental car, a shoeshine—city people always seem to me
like clairvoyants, knowing every in and out, and I feel like an ignoramus.
Take mixed drinks, for example. Everything I know about cocktails has to
do with roosters. I come from a long line of drinkers, but whatever they
drank came straight out of the bottle—beer, wine, whiskey. The first time I
was roped into attending a fancy reception, I arrived hot and thirsty from a
hard walk (avoiding taxis again), and a waiter sidled up to me with a trayful
of drinks. It was plain he meant for me to take *something,* so I grabbed a
glass of clear liquid and, thinking it was water, took an eager swig. It wasn't
water. As nearly as I could figure, it was some concoction built around
vodka. I held it in, but dared not speak for a long while.

The list of things I don't know how to buy is nearly as long as the list   12
of things for sale. Digital stereos, lingerie for my wife, insurance, carpet,
cheese. I find the ordering of meals especially grueling. My city friends
know this instinctively, and so whenever I pay them a visit the first thing
they say is, "Where shall we eat?" I suggest the kitchen, but they ignore me
and begin reciting the names of ethnic restaurants. Even plain old American cafes are a trial and tribulation to me. If there are more than seven
items on the menu I'll have to choose by pointing with my eyes shut. And
even with seven dishes, chances are that five will be utter mysteries to me. I
would rather plant and grow the food than figure out how to order it.

I'm also hopeless at buying clothes. My twelve-year-old daughter says   13
I dress like somebody out of a time-capsule. It is true my wardrobe hasn't

changed much except in the size of collars and pants-legs since I turned eight. (I have heard rumors that men these days sometimes go without collars altogether, but I started with collars and am sticking by them.) The only time I'm *à la mode* is when I eat ice cream on pie. In my defensive moods—which come over me occasionally, like the flu—I repeat Thoreau's dictum: "beware of all enterprises that require new clothes, and not rather a new wearer of clothes." Like many folks whose tastes were formed in the boondocks, I'm not so much hostile to fashion as oblivious to it. The breezes of fashion blow hardest where people have time and money on their hands—two items in short supply in the country.

What I learned from growing up in the country is not how to buy things but how to *do* things: carpentry, plumbing, grafting, gardening, pruning, sewing, making hay with or without sunshine, cooking, canning, felling and planting trees, feeding animals and fixing machines, electrical wiring, plastering, roofing. There is a rude balance in effect here, which prevents me from understanding half of what my city friends are talking about when I stay with them, but enables me to fix their toaster and jump-start their car. My clothes may be stodgy, but I can mend them. Restaurants may baffle me, but I know something about the raising of the cows and cabbages that appear under such mystifying aliases on the menu. 14

If I don't know how to do a job that needs doing in our household, my first thought is always to hunt up somebody who can teach me. To this day I still feel responsible for overhauling my house and car and for repairing whatever comes inside my four walls. This policy soon leads to grief. The second law of thermodynamics declares that entropy is on the increase everywhere, and the whole universe is drifting toward disorder. I can't vouch for the universe, but I know for sure that old houses and cheap cars fall apart faster than any mortal can patch them up. There are a great many more gadgets in my adult house than there were in my childhood one, and they break down in bafflingly novel ways. On the rear panels of most appliances, as you will have noticed, a label warns you not to remove the cover because there are no user serviceable parts inside. Instead, you are to ship the item off to qualified personnel, whose address, if provided at all, is usually in a city five hundred miles away. It galls me about as much to play the ignorant user as to play the scum of the earth. So when a gadget breaks down I brazenly undo the cover and poke about in the forbidden parts; and, lo and behold, about two-thirds of the time I can fix it. The other one-third of the time I am driven to despair. 15

My city friends avoid despair by renting apartments and turning their cars over to mechanics. Those brash enough to live in houses keep lists of plumbers, exterminators, chimney sweeps, handymen, painters, electricians, gardeners, a whole army of attendants. When anything needs tending, 16 they reach for the phone. I keep no such list. Occasionally, in a panic, I will open the yellow pages, but I quickly shut them again without dialing, appalled by the mere thought of all those strangers waiting out there to serve me. Actually, I don't like using a phone at all. Not because I have any grudge against the instrument itself—I can fix a telephone—but because I like to see the folks I'm talking to. Without a face and a breath attached to speech, I grow uneasy. It's like eating when you have a cold and can taste nothing.

Pushed to its ugly extreme, this cleaving of the world between neighbors and strangers becomes tribalism, a disease common in the country. I have seen crosses burning on the lawns of integrated schools, have listened to slander against Jews and Italians and Hispanics, have watched factory workers beat imported strike-breakers with shovels. I have been an outsider in too many places myself to underestimate the dangers of tribalism. But the prejudices of country people are limited by ignorance; you can't very well hate nations or religions you've never heard tell of. The crazy-quilt mixture of peoples in a metropolis may lead to wise tolerance, or it may lead to a more comprehensive brand of bigotry. I once knew a Chicago doctor, a descendant of the Old Testament Assyrians, whose roster of enemies included such Biblical remnants as Chaldeans, Babylonians, and Mesopotamians, as well as Zoroastrians and Swedenborgians. 17

This business of neighbors and strangers touches on another of my country oddities. My city friends describe their glee in watching eccentrics perform on street corners, in subways, in the lobbies of skyscrapers. The shaggy old man who wears a sandwich board and drools in his beard and proclaims the end of the world is a source of entertainment for them, part of the urban spectacle. But the sight of him makes me ache. I feel my way inside his dingy hide and share his apocalyptic dread. Mind you, I don't sidle up and talk with him. I keep my distance, afraid he might lay on me some enormous claim. By the end of a day in the city, identifying with drunks and prophets and twitching zombies, unable to help a single one of them, I feel battered and drained. 18

Back in my country childhood, there were so few people around that every one of them stood out for me as a person. The local eccentrics were also neighbors; I went to school with their children, picked apples for them, stood beside them in the hardware store, listened to their harangues on our front porch. I knew their life histories and learned, often, what ill wind had turned their minds in strange directions. To meet derelicts I didn't have to go cruising through the Bowery, or dress up in rags like George Orwell and sneak into a Parisian flophouse; there were derelicts enough living on our road, squirreled away in trailers and tarpaper shacks. 19

Our local prophet of doom was a carpenter with five children, one of   20
whom, a gawky boy, was in my class at school. Every crazy word from the father left a shadow on the face of the son. When the carpenter received his
message that the world was about to end, he stopped work on the family
house, which was half-built, quit his other jobs, and withdrew his children
from school. As the date announced for the earth's demise drew near, the
prophet grew frenzied, surrounded as he was by skeptics and sinners, and
eventually he landed in jail. After the date passed and the world survived,
the father was set free, but he never finished his house, never unbent from
God's stiff wind; and the face of his son, my classmate, never uncrimped
from the pain.

My trouble is, I hate turning other people into a spectacle, as if human   21
beings were two-dimensional figures in a mural. For a short while I exult in
the city's million faces; but soon those faces become as indistinguishable to
me as dewdrops on the morning grass, and then I hurry back to a place where
people are rare enough to have features and names. This withdrawal troubles
my city friends. How can I survive without getting a daily look at Afghans or
Sikhs? They count upon seeing the costumes and complexions of two dozen
nationalities on their ride to work each morning. I will grant there is pleasure
and the chance of wisdom in observing that human display. I say a chance
rather than a certainty, because I notice that most of my friends do no more
than look at these colorful strangers, never so much as exchange a word with
them, and rarely see the same mysterious face two days running. I'm not convinced there is more pleasure or wisdom to be had from glimpsing two dozen
nationalities of *homo sapiens* than from encountering on a day's walk fifty
species of plants and animals. Do we have to stretch ourselves farther to appreciate a Tibetan, say, than to appreciate a turtle or a trillium? Notice I'm
not saying that a wildflower is deeper or nobler than a Buddhist monk, but
that a flower's inwardness is further from our own. When all is said and done,
despite its heady mix of peoples, the city is filled with versions of ourselves;
the country is likelier to confront us with true otherness.

I think we all could stand a good dose of otherness, to tell you the truth.   22
I think we are far too full of ourselves. Walk around in a city, and everything
you see, even the sickly tree corseted in an iron grate or the dog on a leash, is
there by human design or sufferance. What wizards we are! Look at those
skyscrapers! Listen to the roar of those engines in our concrete canyons! Behold the wonders for sale behind the plateglass windows! The executives
who make the decisions that shape our lives gaze down from gleaming towers onto that scene. How can they help but regard themselves as gods?

You may point to museums and open-air markets—places I love to   23
visit—but I believe the city's pure essence shows in office towers and shopping malls. Deep in the architects who design these enclosures and in the

enthusiasts who frequent them—the skyscraper addicts and mall zealots—there is a horror of the nonhuman. A shopping mall is a space-age Garden of Eden. Everything needful sprouts on the shelves of stores, as if by spontaneous generation, lights defy the cycles of day and night, windows keep out bugs, and overhead the arched roof shuts out weather and wildness. Push the shopping mall one degree further and you have Disneyland, the urban dream of nature: sterilized dirt, paved walkways, rivers that flow in circles and never flood, mechanical beasts that roar on signal, grass and flowers chastened into purity by chemicals.

24   It is easy to pretend, in a city, that humans have made the world and dwell there alone. In the country, you know better. It's the difference between living in a creation and living in *the* creation. Life in the boondocks discourages you from claiming with a straight face that humans are omnipotent. If you think our works are mighty and permanent, drive down any back road and study the caved-in barns, the cellar holes grown up in thickets. If you begin to doubt we have companions on spaceship earth, try clearing a patch of ground beside a woods and gardening for a summer. Insects and worms and rabbits and raccoons and possums and beasts you never identify will gobble your plants; weeds and forest seedlings will sprout between your neat rows. Go away for a month and when you come back the woods will be occupying your garden plot. Of course we have devised ways of discouraging rabbits and chickweed. The manufacturers of poisons sell brews that snuff out everything except what we suffer to live—brews that incidentally, and more slowly, snuff us out as well. But this very willingness to poison whatever obstructs our schemes is a symptom of the arrogance for which life in the country is a good antidote.

25   When Hamlet speaks to Ophelia of "country matters," he means sex, fertility, the old sashay of the flesh. What else could the Prince of Denmark know about the backwoods? City people often think of the land rolling beyond the last streetlight as one vast breeding ground for soybeans and mistletoe, pulpwood and hogs. The folks who make their lives out there seem, from the city, more like pigs and pines than humans. When a writer needs a character to symbolize the animal within us—think of D. H. Lawrence, Tennessee Williams—he's likely to drag in a bumpkin with muddy boots and rural twang. If you write a novel about the backwaters and hope to make a splash in the metropolis, you had better feature incest and idiots.

26   Of course things do breed in the country—otherwise neither Hamlet nor the rest of us would have a bite to eat. And of course rural kids don't have to wait for high school health class or a chat with Mom and Dad to learn the alphabet of sex. I learned the rudiments with a bang, long before I was in a position to apply the knowledge, by raising rabbits. I observed the mechanics on a large scale every time we took one of our mares to visit the

stud. I tassled corn and helped pollinate squash by poking the flowers with a feather. This knowledge of how animals and plants go about their business has not kept me from greatly enjoying the human version. If anything, it has deepened my pleasure to know that my loving a woman, and the whole amazing edifice of romance, is raised on such sturdy foundations.

It's true that culture is stretched pretty thin in the sticks. If you can't   27
get through the week without seeing an opera or visiting an art gallery, you had better stay in the metropolis. I've noticed that my city friends are most-ly consumers of culture, not creators, buying their way in just as they buy their groceries. Sometimes they talk as though a season ticket to the ballet makes them bearers of Western Civilization. Because the human net is spread so thin in the countryside, you realize you must help make and sus-tain it. Whatever happens on the back roads and in small towns—carnivals and spelling bees, parades and horse races, bluegrass concerts, open air theatricals—happens because people you know, or you yourself, make it happen. It is do-it-yourself culture, homely to be sure, but heartfelt and sprung from local talent.

In the country, if things go undone, you can't blame officials. I know a   28
carpenter who didn't see the point of joining the volunteer fire department until one day his barn started to smoke. His wife called the emergency num-ber, a siren went off and pretty soon the neighbors turned up with their pumper and hoses. They held off spraying long enough for the chief to ask, "What do you think about volunteering now?" and for the carpenter to reply, "I think now's a real good time." So he joined on the spot, grabbed a hose, and has remained a loyal volunteer ever since. It's good to feel re-sponsible for the place you inhabit, and easier to feel that responsibility when the place is thinly settled.

Marx and Engels, those two quintessential urban visionaries, pro-   29
mised in their Communist manifesto that the world revolution would free all hicks and yokels from "rural idiocy." As someone who inherited a good dose of rural idiocy, I have to admit there is a core of truth in this contemp-tuous phrase. When I work all day in the sun pitching hay or driving nails or splitting wood, I slump down at night and live wholly in my body. On those nights the neighborhood dogs have livelier thoughts than I do. With or without a revolution, I'll remain backward and countrified. I'll never be urbane—the very word a reminder of how we equate refinement with the city. I'll never feel at ease living where the glare of lights keeps me from see-ing the stars and where fear of strangers keeps me from walking out at night. A Tennessee ridgerunner accent still underlies my Midwestern prairie tones, a dirt-road soul shows through cracks in the paving of my education. The pleasures and knowledge that come to those of us who grew up in the

country may be small potatoes compared to what city breeding offers, but in the long cold winter of cruelty and want that lies ahead for the world, we'll need all the potatoes we can find.

FIRST RESPONSES

What similarities and differences are there between Sanders's pictures of city and country life and your experiences with these places?

TAKING A CLOSER LOOK

Exploring *Who:* Voice and Tone

1. Sanders refers to himself as a "yokel" throughout the essay. How did you respond to the term the first time he used it? Had your response changed by the time he used it in the conclusion? Can you think of other such terms that have been reclaimed by the groups they were meant to demean?
2. Sanders begins paragraph 2 with, "I wasn't comfortable in the role of scum of the earth." What is his tone of voice in this sentence, and how well did it prepare you for the rest of the essay?
3. How did your own background, either rural or urban, affect your responses to Sanders's feelings about city life?
4. Why might Sanders have decided to include the sentence, "The second law of thermodynamics declares that entropy is on the increase everywhere, and the whole universe is drifting toward disorder"?

Exploring *What:* Content and Meaning

1. What urban behaviors most irritate Sanders? Why?
2. List all of the advantages Sanders gives for having country habits. When and where do these advantages become disadvantages?
3. Why does Sanders lapse into his southern dialect, "when [he's] tired, or telling stories, or visiting with my southern kinfolk, or feeling amorous"? Do you remember ever changing your accent around people who have an accent different from yours?
4. Do you know people who are pack rats like Sanders? Do they have some of his other traits as well?

5. In paragraph 8, Sanders describes having someone wait on him as having "a hint almost of slavery." What stereotypes might he be challenging here?

Exploring *Why:* Purpose

1. ▣ *Using the Internet.* Has Sanders convinced you of his claim that, "What I learned from growing up in the country is not how to buy things but how to *do* things"? The Orion Society, an environmental educational group, fosters grassroots and community organizing. Visit its Web site at http://orionsociety.org/index.html. As you browse the site, identify goals and projects that Sanders would link to country values.

2. How well does Sanders prepare you for his belief that "the prejudices of country people are limited by ignorance: you can't very well hate nations or religions you've never heard of"? What is your response to this view of the causes of prejudice?

3. In paragraph 20, Sanders provides an extended example of a country eccentric. Why does he describe him from the son's point of view? How does the example prepare you for his judgment that city outsiders become "two dimensional figures in a mural"?

4. What does Sanders mean by "we all could stand a good dose of otherness"? How is his intention clarified by the examples in paragraph 22?

Exploring *How:* Style and Strategy

1. How would you describe Sanders's method of comparison and contrast? What advantage does his organization give to his country point of view?

2. In the extended story Sanders tells in paragraph 11, he seems to be making fun of himself. What else is he mocking here?

3. When his city friends ask Sanders, "Where shall we go to eat?" his response is, "I suggest the kitchen." Can you find other one-liners? Why does Sanders use them?

4. What is the effect of Sanders quoting Thoreau?

5. What feelings are created by Sanders's use of this **metaphor** in the conclusion: "A Tennessee ridgerunner accent still underlies my Midwestern prairie tones, a dirt-road soul shows through cracks in the paving of my education"?

IDEAS FOR WRITING COMPARISON AND CONTRAST

1. Write an essay comparing the opportunities and experiences of an urban versus a rural childhood. If your experiences are limited to only one environment, you will need to do interviews or research to provide concrete information and a fair perspective about the other.

2. What are the advantages and disadvantages to living on campus versus living off campus? Write an essay supporting one of the two choices by examining their similarities and differences.

3. Write an essay analyzing significant differences between the daily life of two people who appear on the surface to lead very similar lives— two students in the same major, two employees working the same job, or two athletes in the same sport, for example.

◆ ◆ ◆ PREPARING TO READ

Into what racial or ethnic category or categories would you place yourself if given total freedom to choose? Can you remember any specific experiences—at home, with friends, or at school—that led you to this conclusion or that challenged it?

◆ ◆ ◆

Dividing American Society

ANDREW HACKER

Andrew Hacker is a political scientist who teaches at Queens College in New York and writes regularly on race, family, and health care issues for the influential *New York Review of Books*. Two of Hacker's most recent books reflect his life-long personal and professional efforts to reveal the powerful relationship between economics and social justice: *Two Nations: Black and White, Separate, Hostile, Unequal* (1992), from which the following essay was taken, and *Money: Who Has How Much and Why* (1998).

Race has been an American obsession since the first Europeans   1
sighted "savages" on these shores. In time, those original inhabitants would be subdued or slaughtered, and finally sequestered out of view. But race in America took on a deeper and more disturbing meaning with the importation of Africans as slaves. Bondage would later be condemned as an awful injustice and the nation's shame, even as we have come to acknowledge the stamina and skill it took to survive in a system where humans could be bought and sold and punished like animals. Nor are these antecedents buried away in the past. That Americans of African origin once wore the chains of chattels remains alive in the memory of both races and continues to separate them.

Black Americans are Americans, yet they still subsist as aliens in the   2
only land they know. Other groups may remain outside the mainstream—some religious sects, for example—but they do so voluntarily. In contrast, blacks must endure a segregation that is far from freely chosen. So America may be seen as two separate nations. Of course, there are places where the races mingle. Yet in most significant respects, the separation is pervasive and penetrating. As a social and human division, it surpasses all others—even gender—in intensity and subordination.

If white Americans regard the United States as their nation, they also   3
see it beset with racial problems they feel are not of their making. Some
contrast current conditions with earlier times, when blacks appeared more
willing to accept a subordinate status. Most whites will protest that they
bear neither responsibility nor blame for the conditions blacks face. Neither
they nor their forebears ever owned slaves, nor can they see themselves as
having held anyone back or down. Most white Americans believe that for at
least the last generation blacks have been given more than a fair chance and
at least equal opportunity, if not outright advantages. Moreover, few white
Americans feel obliged to ponder how membership in the major race gives
them powers and privileges.

America is inherently a "white" country: in character, in structure, in   4
culture. Needless to say, black Americans create lives of their own. Yet, as a
people, they face boundaries and constrictions set by the white majority.
America's version of *apartheid,* while lacking overt legal sanction, comes
closest to the system even now being reformed in the land of its invention.

That racial tensions cast a pall upon this country can hardly be denied.   5
People now vent feelings of hostility and anger that in the past they re-
pressed. Race has become a national staple for private conversation and
public controversy. So it becomes necessary to ask what in recent decades
has brought the issue and reality of race to the center of the stage.

The idea of race is primeval. Humans have given names to their varied   6
strains since physical differences first began to appear. Nor are there signs
that racial lines have grown dimmer in modern times. On the contrary, race
continues to preoccupy the public mind, a reminder of a past that cannot be
willed away.

Since race is part of common parlance, people have used the term in   7
many ways. Little will be gained by asking for clear-cut definitions; or, for
that matter, trying to decide exactly how many different races occupy this
planet. Anthropologists have their lists, but even they disagree on criteria
and classifications. Still, some major groupings recur: Negroid, Mongoloid,
Australoid, Caucasoid, and Indic, with American Indians and Pacific Islanders added as two encompassing categories. But there are also finer
racial divisions, such as Aryans and Semites and Dravidians. Tribes like the
Watusi and Navahos have also been given racial designations. Indeed, since
there is no consensus when it comes to defining "race," the term has been
applied to a diversity of groups. The Irish have been called a race in their
own right, as have Jews and Hindus. Many find these ambiguities unsettling,
but then so is much of life. In the United States, what people mean by "race"
is usually straightforward and clear, given the principal division into black
and white. Yet, as it happens, not all Americans fit into "racial" designations.

In theory, Native Americans taken together belong to what most an-   8
thropologists would call a basic race. Yet on the whole, they tend to be a
loose residue of tribes, rather than a racial entity. A single primal consciousness cannot be said to bind the aspirations and interests of Chippewas and
Seminoles and Aleuts. As it happens the Native American population has
undergone an unusual increase. Between 1970 and 1990, the number of persons claiming tribal antecedents rose from 827,268 to 1,516,540, which
works out to more than three times the growth rate for the nation as a
whole. The chief reason is that a lot of people who had concealed their native origins are now reclaiming them as their primary identity. As it happens, another group can claim an even firmer racial cohesion. It consists of
descendants of Hawaii's original inhabitants, most of whom have Polynesian origins. Their growth has mirrored the Native American model, doubling from 100,179 in 1970 to 210,907 in 1990.

Until just a decade or so ago, Americans spoke of "Orientals," and the   9
individuals so described are certainly members of what the anthropologists
call the "Mongoloid" race. However, these terms—along with "yellow"—
are now hardly ever heard. For one thing, many of those subsumed under
the "Oriental" rubric never liked that designation. After all, it was invented
and imposed by Europeans, who saw their own continent as the center of
civilization, and relegated the "Orient" to Europe's eastern horizon.

Today, we have the generic term "Asian," which includes not only   10
Japanese and Chinese and Koreans, but also Indonesians and Indians, along
with Burmese and Thais, plus Filipinos and Pakistanis. Geographically
speaking, Asia extends from the Kurile Islands to Istanbul and Israel. In
fact, "Asian Americans" did not choose this title for themselves. Rather, the
larger society has found it convenient to collect them into a single category
that mingles racial and national origins. For this reason, obviously, "Asian"
itself cannot be a race, since it embraces not only persons once described as
"Mongoloid," but also Indics and Dravidians and Caucasians. Even the Koreans and Chinese and Japanese, who belong to the common "Mongoloid"
race, seldom mix with one another and have few activities or interests in
common. Rather than racial, their images of their identities are almost
wholly national. So while in textbook terms, most Americans of Asian origin have specific racial origins, in social and political terms those identities
have only a residual significance. In 1970, the census counted 1,438,544 people in what is now the Asian category. By 1990, due mainly to immigration,
that group had grown fivefold to 7,273,662.

Nor can it be contended that Americans of Hispanic—or Chicano or   11
Latino—heritage comprise a race. On the contrary, among their numbers
can be found persons of almost pure European ancestry, as well as some of
partial but visible African origins, along with individuals of unblemished

Indian descent. But far outnumbering them are people of such varied parentages as to render any talk of race impossible. Since 1970, the Hispanic group has increased from 9,072,602 to 22,354,059, almost three times the rate for the population as a whole.

In fact, the "nonracial" character of Hispanics has been reflected in   12
recent census reports, where individuals are allowed to describe themselves as they choose. Accordingly, in one census question, individuals may indicate that they are Latin or Hispanic. In another place, they may also fill in a race. Thus in 1990, the census located 7,687,938 residents of California who selected the Latin or Hispanic designation. Within this group, just under half—49.5 percent—chose to say that they also had a race: black or white, or, in a few cases, Asians or Native Americans. However, the other 50.5 percent told the census that in their own view, they had no "race" at all. For them, to be Hispanic was a sole and sufficient identity. (The same eschewal of "race" may be observed among Islamic immigrants from the Middle East.)

So it would seem that the country's fastest-growing groups prefer to   13
emphasize their cultural and national identities rather than traits associated with race. However, the same cannot be said for the rest of the nation, which remains either black or white.

To give the names "black" and "white" to races might seem, on its   14
face, quite ludicrous. Clearly, no human beings have skins of either color. Indeed, very few come even close to those tones. But then "white" and "black" stand for much more than the shades of epidermal coverings. To start, they refer to the "Caucasian" and "Negroid" races, whose facial appearances differ as prominently as their colors.

But more is involved than color or facial features or skeletal structure.   15
The terms also carry cultural connotations. In its basic meaning, "white" denotes European antecedents, while "black" stands for Africa. Since the human species began in Africa, we can say that black people are those whose ancestors remained on that continent, while whites descend from those who embarked on migrations to cooler climates. This has led some to the presumption that the races are at different levels of evolutionary development. For at least half a dozen centuries, and possibly longer, "white" has implied a higher civilization based on a superior inheritance.

Europeans who colonized the western hemisphere sought to recreate   16
it in their image, and to transform North and South America into "white" continents. With conquest comes the power to impose your ways on territories you have subdued. The treatment of the Native Americans simply ratified that view. (In some places, the native populations remained large enough to exert a reciprocal influence, as in India and most of Africa. This

was not to be the case in the United States.) Still, something can be learned by looking at how "white" was originally conceived, and the changes it has undergone.

From the colonial period through the Jacksonian era, most white   17
Americans were of English ancestry. Alexis de Tocqueville, during his visit in the 1830s, found he could characterize the country and its people as "Anglo-Americans."

Given the expansion of the population, this epithet could not last.   18
Even so, the Anglo-American model has remained remarkably durable, with most subsequent immigrants adapting to its canons. They not only learned English, the single national language, but also adjusted their lives to the economy and technology associated with that prototype. This does not mean that the majority of white Americans regard themselves as "English" in a literal sense. They can and do identify with other origins. Even so, it could be argued that most contemporary citizens associate themselves to a greater degree with Anglo-American culture than with their actual country of origin.

To say this would seem to resurrect the conception of the melting pot,   19
which argued that immigrants would shed their older identities and assimi-late to the new culture they encountered. That view has been challenged in many quarters. Rather than as a cauldron, many commentators today prefer to see America as a mosaic or even a lumpy stew. At best, the pot still con-tains plenty of unmelted pieces. Hence the renewed emphasis on "ethnicity," with its focus on the country's racial and national and religious diversity.

Even so, assimilation has taken place and it continues apace. One of   20
the earliest examples came with Germans, who in terms of sheer numbers made up the nation's largest immigrant group. Yet for at least a generation, it has been hard to find many people who qualify as "German-Americans" in any serious sense. Soon after their arrival, which gathered momentum following 1848, Germans quickly learned English and studied the customs of their new land. Many were merchants or farmers, familiar with the rules of a market economy. In addition, it became evident that they were not par-ticularly committed to the country they had left behind. (In fact, there was no unified Germany at that time.) Each generation saw more intermarriage, accompanied by moves to mixed neighborhoods. Service in the Union Army during the Civil War speeded the assimilation process, which was ef-fectively completed during the First World War. With the suburbanization of Milwaukee, only Cincinnati retains the vestiges of a German flavor.

What also eased acceptance of German immigrants was the reali-   21
zation by Americans of English origin that they needed an ally. For one thing, their own stock was not being renewed by immigration. And, as often

happens with groups that arrive early, the offspring they produce begin to feel they should no longer have to do society's less pleasant chores. German-Americans could see why they were being co-opted, and they welcomed the chance to show their ambitions and skills. The English had a further motive: encouraging the Germans, who were mainly Protestant, helped to hold the Catholic Irish at bay.

It took the Irish longer to shed an alien identity. Although they arrived already knowing English, rural folkways slowed their adjustment to an urban world. Furthermore, at the time of their arrival, Catholics were not regarded as altogether "white." (Thomas Nast's political cartoons gave Irish immigrants subhuman features.) Italians may have been less fervidly Catholic than the Irish, but their acceptance was hampered by peasant habits. Many chose to return to Italy after brief sojourns here, and some of those who chose to stay took their time learning the new language.

Jews, who arrived in large numbers at the turn of the century, were at first kept at the margin of "white" America simply because they were not Christians. Still, by a generation after their arrival, they had set themselves to mastering the tests for college admission, civil service posts, and many professions. World War II speeded the process of assimilation. At its end, people from every corner of Europe were considered fully "white." By 1990, two Americans of Irish extraction had been elected President, and being a Catholic was seldom a bar to promotion or preferment. The Chrysler Corporation has had a Lee (from Lido) Iacocca for its chairman, while an Irving Shapiro headed DuPont, and several Ivy League universities have had Jewish presidents.

By this time, it should be clear that the question is not "Who *is* white?" It might be more appropriate to ask "Who *may* be considered white?" since this suggests that something akin to permission is needed. In a sense, those who have already received the "white" designation can be seen as belonging to a club, from whose sanctum they ponder whether they want or need new members, as well as the proper pace of new admissions.

Recent immigration from Asia and Latin America complicates any discussion of race. To start, we might ask if persons arriving from countries like Korea or Pakistan might somehow "become white." (Nor is this to say that they might desire the designation.) As was noted earlier, Koreans and others who were once portrayed as belonging to the "yellow" race now reject that description. Their membership in the "Asian" category conjoins them with people as far west as Istanbul. Armenians are now considered "white," as are most Lebanese and Iranians. While in theory, some Asian Indians might be thought too dark to be "white," the appellation has shown itself to possess remarkable elasticity.

In many respects, therefore, color is becoming less important. Most   26
Asian immigrants arrive in this country ready to compete for middle-class
careers. Many come with a level of educational preparation at least as good
as our own. Schools in Seoul and Bombay now offer coursework as sophisticated as any in Seattle or Baltimore. As hardly needs repeating Asia has
been catapulting itself into the modern world; so if most Asians are not literally "white," they have the technical and organizational skills expected by
any "Western" or European-based culture.

How Asians are currently being viewed has much in common with the   27
ways earlier generations co-opted new talents and energies as their own
were winding down. To cite a single example, studies show that white students today spend less time on homework than their Asian classmates. At
college, white undergraduates tend to select easier majors, and are opting for
comfortable careers in the more sociable professions. Right now, it is in science and technology where Asian talents are being co-opted. But a glance at
the list of editors of the *Harvard Law Review* suggests that they are destined
for broader representation in the professions and management.

As Asians find places in the economy, they are allowed to move up-   28
ward on social and occupational ladders. Middle-class whites do not object
if Asian children attend their local schools or populate their neighborhoods.
Even now, we are beginning to see an increasing incidence of intermarriage,
although with the caveat that the first pairings will most usually involve an
Asian woman and a white man. The grandchildren will undoubtedly be regarded as a new variant of white.

Much the same process can be observed among Hispanics. Of course,   29
large numbers are already quite "white." This is clearly the case with
Cubans, a prominent example being Roberto Goizueta, the Yale-educated
chairman of the Coca-Cola Corporation. Most Central and South Americans can claim a strong European heritage, which eases their absorption
into the "white" middle class. While skin color and features still figure in social grading, they are less obstacles to mobility than was once the case. More
at issue is the divide between unskilled laborers, who will continue pouring
across the border for the foreseeable future, and others with the skills and
schooling that allow them to enter legally.

With the absorption of increasing numbers of Hispanics and Asians,   30
along with Middle Eastern immigrants, being "white" will cease to carry
many of the connotations it did in the past. The future population will reflect
a more varied array of national origins rather than races, since—as has been
stressed—the new groups cannot be easily assigned to racial classifications.

Nor should we be too quick in proclaiming that America will become   31
"multicultural" as well. True, one can point to exotic neighborhoods, with
their parades and festivals, to foreign-language newspapers and television

channels, along with calls for new kinds of courses in colleges and schools. It would be more accurate to say that the United States will continue to have a single dominant culture. It doesn't really matter whether it is called "white" or "Western" or European or Anglo-American or by another title. It would be better simply to describe it as a structure of opportunities and institutions that has been willing to use the energies and talents of people from various origins. The reception given to recent immigrants is essentially similar to that accorded to successive waves of Europeans. In neither case have the newcomers been given a very cordial welcome. Indeed, they have often met with mistrust, not to mention violence and hostility. Despite the felicitous words on the Statue of Liberty, immigrants are allowed entry on the condition that they serve as cheap labor and live unobtrusively. Many will tell you that now, as in the past, they find their religions scorned, their customs ridiculed, and their features caricatured.

Throughout this nation's history, the expectation has been that new-   32
comers will adapt to the models they encounter on their arrival. If that means relinquishing old-country customs, there are signs that many are prepared to do just that, or at least watch as their children assimilate. Perhaps the first instance of the expanded purview of "white" was when the English founders sought the services of two talented Scots—James Madison and Alexander Hamilton—to help found this nation. The process is still going on.

As with "white," being "black" is less one's particular shade of color   33
than physical features and continent of ancestry. Of course, very few Americans are entirely African in origin. As is well known, slave owners and other whites felt free to force themselves on black women. Still, no matter how light their skin tones, if they retained any vestige of African features, they and their descendants continue to be delineated as "black."

The United States, unlike other countries and cultures, no longer uses   34
terms specifying finer gradations. Hence "mestizo" and "mulatto" have disappeared from our parlance, as have "creole" and "quadroon." Nor has this country retained the generic term "colored" for people whose ancestries are obviously mixed. (The last use of an intermediate term was in the 1910 census, in which interviewers identified about 20 percent of the "Negro" group as "Mulattoes.") It has been far from accidental that this country has chosen to reject the idea of a graduated spectrum, and has instead fashioned a rigid bifurcation.

For all practical purposes, "whites" of all classes and ethnicities now   35
prefer to present a common front. Unlike in the past, there are no pronounced distinctions of "purer" versus "lesser" whites, or of those with older claims as against newer arrivals. While immigrants from Colombia

and Cyprus may have to work their way up the social ladder, they are still allowed as valid a claim to being "white" as persons of Puritan or Pilgrim stock.

Americans of African ancestry were never given that indulgence. The   36
reason is not that their coloration was too "dark" to allow for absorption into the "white" classification. After all, the swarthiness of some Europeans did not become a barrier to their admission. Had white America really believed in its egalitarian declarations, it would have welcomed former slaves into its midst at the close of the Civil War. Indeed, had that happened, America would not be two racial nations today. This is not to suggest how far blacks themselves would have assimilated, since a lot depends on how far members of a group want to preserve their special heritage. The point is that white America has always had the power to expand its domain. However, in the past and even now, it has shown a particular reluctance to absorb people of African descent.

How do blacks feel about this bifurcation? Today, most express pride   37
in their African origins, especially those who make a point of calling themselves African-Americans. While, like it or not, a lighter color remains an advantage for women, social advantage is no longer gained by alluding to white elements in one's ancestry. Black Americans are aware that much in the "black" designation represents how whites have defined the term. Still, despite attempts by whites to describe and define them, black Americans have always sought to create their own lives and sustain their sentiments and interests. It started when the first slaves created a culture of their own. Similarly, the drive to replace "colored" with "negro," followed by the move to "Negro," and then on to "black" and "African-American," have all reflected a desire to maintain an autonomous identity.

For most black Americans to be an African-American means literally   38
that in that continent lies the primal origin of your people. The experiences of capture and transportation, of slavery and segregation, never diminished or erased the basic culture and character of tribal ancestries. Yet it is also instructive that blacks from the West Indies and other islands of the Caribbean seek to retain an independent history. Their forebears also originated in Africa and served as slaves, but blacks born in Barbados and Jamaica, or Haiti and Martinique, make clear the British or French connections that distinguish them from others of their race. This emphasis is not intended to render Haitians or Jamaicans "less black" in terms of color. Rather, they wish it known that their antecedents are not exclusively African, but also bear a European imprint.

Black Americans came from the least-known continent, the most ex-   39
otic, the one remotest from American experience. Among the burdens blacks bear is the stigma of "the savage," the proximity to lesser primates.

Hence the question in many minds: Can citizens of African origin find acceptance in a society that is dominantly white, Western, and European?

Even at a time when Americans of European backgrounds are giving   40
less emphasis to their ancestries, it is not as easy for black men and women
to assimilate into the American mainstream. Even those who aspire to careers in white institutions, and emulate white demeanor and diction, find
that white America lets them only partly past the door.

Arguably, this is because the "Africa" in African-American contrasts   41
with much of the European structure of technology and science, of administrative systems based on linear modes of reasoning. Today, Africa is the
least developed and most sorrow-ridden of continents. It has more than its
share of malnutrition and debilitating diseases, and at least its share of tribal rancor and bloodshed. It seems always to be petitioning the rest of the
world for aid. Since the close of the colonial era, over a generation ago,
there have not been many African success stories.

Yet the actual Africa of today is not really the model black Americans   42
have in mind. Of much greater significance is how the continent is construed as a symbol: what it says about the human spirit, what it connotes as
a way of life. It is more the Africa of history, before the imperial powers arrived. It is also an Africa of the imagination, of music and dance and stories.
This Africa speaks for an ancestral humanity, for an awareness of the self,
the bonds of tribe and family and community. If the European heritage imposes the regimens of standardized tests, the African dream inspires discursive storytelling celebrating the soul and the spirit.

But as much as anything, being "black" in America bears the mark of   43
slavery. Even after emancipation, citizens who had been slaves still found
themselves consigned to a subordinate status. Put most simply, the ideology
that had provided the rationale for slavery by no means disappeared.
Blacks continued to be seen as an inferior species, not only unsuited for
equality but not even meriting a chance to show their worth. Immigrants
only hours off the boat, while subjected to scorn, were allowed to assert
their superiority to black Americans.

And in our own time, must it be admitted at the close of the twentieth   44
century, that residues of slavery continue to exist? The answer is obviously
yes. The fact that blacks are separated more severely than any other group
certainly conveys that message. Indeed, the fear persists that if allowed to
come closer they will somehow contaminate the rest of society.

What other Americans know and remember is that blacks alone were   45
brought as chattels to be bought and sold like livestock. As has been noted,
textbooks now point out that surviving slavery took a skill and stamina that
no other race has been called upon to sustain. Yet this is not what others
choose to recall. Rather, there remains an unarticulated suspicion: might

there be something about the black race that suited them for slavery? This is not to say anyone argues that human bondage was justified. Still, the facts that slavery existed for so long and was so taken for granted cannot be erased from American minds. This is not the least reason why other Americans—again, without openly saying so—find it not improper that blacks still serve as maids and janitors, occupations seen as involving physical skills rather than mental aptitudes.

The recollections of the past that remain in people's minds continue to shape ideas about the character and capacities of black citizens. Is it possible to erase the stigmas associated with slavery? After all, a very considerable number of black Americans have achieved impressive careers, winning many of the rewards bestowed by white America. Still, there is no way that even the most talented of these men and women will be considered eligible for the honorific of "white." They are, and will remain, accomplished blacks, regarded as role models for their race. But white Americans, who both grant and impose racial memberships, show little inclination toward giving full nationality to the descendants of African slaves. . . .   46

Put most simply, none of the presumptions of inferiority associated with Africa and slavery are imposed on other ethnicities. Moreover, as has also been noted, second and subsequent generations of Hispanics and Asians are merging into the "white" category, partly through intermarriage and also by personal achievement and adaptation. Indeed, the very fact that this is happening sheds light on the tensions and disparities separating the two major races.   47

◆ ◆ ◆

FIRST RESPONSES

What were your reactions to the Rodney King beating and the O. J. Simpson trial? How does either or both relate to Hacker's belief that, "The recollections of the past that remain in people's minds continue to shape ideas about the character and capacities of black citizens"?

TAKING A CLOSER LOOK

Exploring *Who*: Voice and Tone

1. How directly does Hacker reveal his personal feelings about race within the first few paragraphs? What were your responses to this point of view? Why would he choose to be so direct so early in the essay?

2. How does Hacker establish his professional credibility on this topic? Did you find his credentials convincing?

3. Where was your understanding of your own racial or ethnic identity reinforced as you read the essay? Where was this understanding brought into question?

Exploring *What:* Content and Meaning

1. ■▯ *Using the Internet.* Hacker claims that racial division in the United States is "pervasive and penetrating." What does he mean? Does this accurately reflect your experience of the relationship between black and white Americans? Visit the Web site of one of the national African-American organizations, such as the NAACP or the Rainbow Coalition, to evaluate how its programs and goals reinforce or challenge Hacker's point of view.

2. What does Hacker believe are the predominant attitudes among white Americans toward black Americans? Have you heard people say things that reflect such attitudes? Were they privately or publicly expressed?

3. What paradox is Hacker exploring when he says, "Bondage would later be condemned as an awful injustice and the nation's shame, even as we have come to acknowledge the stamina and skill it took to survive in a system where humans could be bought and sold and punished like animals"?

4. Why do some people now describe the "melting pot" concept as more accurately being "a mosaic or even a lumpy stew"? Which version makes the most sense to you?

5. According to Hacker, all major immigrant groups, regardless of skin color, have had or now have the potential to become "white." What was required of these groups in the past and what is required now? Reread paragraph 31 and discuss to what extent Hacker believes this success is positive.

Exploring *Why:* Purpose

1. Young golf pro Tiger Woods has often been identified as an African American golfer, even though his mother is Asian American and only his father is African American. How does this support Hacker's view of the complexities of racial categorization?

2. Were you convinced that race is more about "cultural connotations" than biology? Which arguments or examples did you find most persuasive?

3. In what ways does our popular culture—movies, television, and music—support Hacker's belief that we live in a culture of "rigid bifurcation"?

4. According to Hacker, what is the primary reason that black Americans have not been allowed to assimilate? What is his evidence for this claim?

Exploring *How:* Style and Strategy

1. How quickly does Hacker reveal his thesis? Why?

2. What was the effect of Hacker's use of the term *apartheid* in paragraph 4? What associations did it create for you?

3. To what experts does Hacker turn to support his belief that, "Little will be gained by asking for clear-cut definitions" of race? Why does he spend such a significant part of the essay proving this point?

4. Hacker uses both point by point and block by block methods of comparison and contrast. Find examples of each.

5. What functions do paragraphs 13 and 24 serve in the organization of Hacker's essay?

IDEAS FOR WRITING COMPARISON AND CONTRAST

1. After interviewing your parents and perhaps other members of your extended family, write an essay comparing and contrasting the ways in which various members of your family consider race or ethnicity in their definitions of who they are and what they can be.

2. Compare and contrast two movies, television series, short stories, or songs that have very similar plots (such as love stories or family tragedies) but whose primary characters belong to different racial or ethnic groups. Concentrate on identifying important similarities and significant differences.

3. Do you and someone you know disagree about something, at least in part, because of a difference in your ages? Compare your positions on the topic and explain how age helps to create your differences. Music, education, and relationships are possible topics.

◆ FURTHER IDEAS FOR USING COMPARISON AND CONTRAST

1. Compare and contrast a job you enjoyed doing to one that you considered quitting on a daily basis. What in you and what in the job created the positive and negative feelings? What did you learn about yourself and your work from these experiences?

2. ▣ *Using the Internet.* Visit two similar Web sites—two museums, two zoos, or two children's museums, for example. When you have finished exploring these two sites, write a comparison and contrast essay analyzing the site's ease of use and any other features you believe make such a "visit" interesting and worthwhile.

3. COMBINING STRATEGIES. Write an essay in which you recommend one specific vacation destination over another. Use narration and description to develop this essay in the block pattern. Make your direct recommendations in the introduction and conclusion of the essay. For example, you might write an article for your school newspaper in which you recount two different Spring Break trips in order to encourage other students to visit your favorite one.

4. COMBINING STRATEGIES. Compare and contrast your process for making an important decision with the way a family member or friend makes such a decision. What are the consequences of the similarities and differences?

5. COLLABORATIVE WRITING/COMBINING STRATEGIES. In small groups, brainstorm a list of the ways in which your concepts of friendship have changed or remained the same since coming to college. After this session, decide which of these changes accurately capture your experience of friendship. Next, freewrite, cluster, or brainstorm examples of childhood, high school, and college friendships. Use these examples to compare and contrast your pre-college and college definitions of the term.

Strategies for Interpreting Meaning

Cause and Effect

◆ ◆ ◆ ◆ ◆

Cause and effect writing traces the *why*—to reveal the root of a problem or to illuminate the consequence of an action.

◆ Writers use cause and effect to explain both immediate and indirect connections.

◆ Effective cause and effect depends on logical connections and clear, consistent patterns of organization.

Reflection is an essential human act. People want to know *why* and *what if.* It helps us to understand our past and, in turn, to attempt a happier, more successful future. In your personal life, this reflection might involve understanding how you ended up becoming a biology major and how well this choice connects with your future goals. Investigating **causes and effects** is also a basic pursuit in many professional fields, such as marketing and psychology. What will it take to make consumers shift their loyalties from one product to another? Do girls and boys play with different toys because of their genes or the color of the blankets they were placed in at birth?

In all cases, figuring out why things happen takes intellectual effort since your logic can get so tangled, and some causes and effects are quite subtle. Distance, objectivity, and sustained analysis can help. Glossy ads for Disneyland make it difficult for anyone to arrive at a quick conclusion about the consequences of taking a summer vacation rather than working full time. And it might be comforting to think that failing an examination was the result of staying out too late the night before, but not looking for additional causes can mean continued poor study skills and habits—and more failed exams.

That problems can be solved only by going beyond the obvious and exploring all possibilities fully is illustrated in the following professionally written essay, where E. M. Forster ponders the effects of owning a piece of land.

My Wood

E. M. FORSTER

A prolific essayist, fiction writer, and social critic, E. M. Forster (1879–1970) is highly regarded for both originality of voice and subtlety of style. His stories of early twentieth-century British culture, and especially the transition from youth to adulthood, have been rediscovered by a modern audience through their film adaptations, including *A Passage to India, A Room with a View, Maurice,* and *Howards End.*

A few years ago I wrote a book which dealt in part with the difficulties of the English in India. Feeling that they would have had no difficulties in India themselves, the Americans read the book freely. The more they read it the better it made them feel, and a check to the author was the result. I bought a wood with the check. It is not a large wood—it contains scarcely any trees, and it is intersected, blast it, by a public footpath. Still, it is the first property that I have owned, so it is right that other people should participate in my shame, and should ask themselves, in accents that will vary in horror, this very important question: What is the effect of property upon the character? Don't let's touch economics; the effect of private ownership upon the community as a whole is another question—a more important question, perhaps, but another one. Let's keep to psychology. If you own things, what's their effect on you? What's the effect on me of my wood?

In the first place, it makes me feel heavy. Property does have this effect. Property produces men of weight, and it was a man of weight who failed to get into the Kingdom of Heaven. He was not wicked, that unfortunate millionaire in the parable, he was only stout; he stuck out in front, not to mention behind, and as he wedged himself this way and that in the crystalline entrance and bruised his well-fed flanks, he saw beneath him a comparatively slim camel passing through the eye of a needle and being woven into the robe of God. The Gospels all through couple stoutness and slowness. They point out what is perfectly obvious, yet seldom realized: that if you have a lot of things you cannot move about a lot, that furniture requires dusting, dusters require servants, servants require insurance stamps, and the whole tangle of them makes you think twice before you accept an invitation to dinner or go for a bathe in the Jordan. Sometimes the Gospels proceed further and say with Tolstoy that property is sinful; they approach the difficult ground of asceticism here, where I cannot follow them. But as to the immediate effects of property on people, they just show straightforward logic. It produces men of weight. Men of weight cannot, by definition, move like the lightning from the East unto the West, and the ascent of a fourteen-stone bishop into a pulpit is thus the exact antithesis of the coming of the Son of Man. My wood makes me feel heavy. 2

In the second place, it makes me feel it ought to be larger. 3

The other day I heard a twig snap in it. I was annoyed at first, for I 4 thought that someone was blackberrying, and depreciating the value of the undergrowth. On coming nearer, I saw it was not a man who had trodden on the twig and snapped it, but a bird, and I felt pleased. My bird. The bird was not equally pleased. Ignoring the relation between us, it took flight as soon as it saw the shape of my face, and flew straight over the boundary hedge into a field, the property of Mrs. Henessy, where it sat down with a loud squawk. It had become Mrs. Henessy's bird. Something seemed grossly amiss here, something that would not have occurred had the wood been larger. I could not afford to buy Mrs. Henessy out, I dared not murder her, and limitations of this sort beset me on every side. . . .

In the third place, property makes its owner feel that he ought to do 5 something to it. Yet he isn't sure what. A restlessness comes over him, a vague sense that he has a personality to express—the same sense which, without any vagueness, leads the artist to an act of creation. Sometimes I think I will cut down such trees as remain in the wood, at other times I want to fill up the gaps between them with new trees. Both impulses are pretentious and empty. They are not honest movements toward money-making or beauty. They spring from a foolish desire to express myself and from an inability to enjoy what I have got. Creation, property, enjoyment form a sinister trinity in the human mind. Creation and enjoyment are both very,

very good, yet they are often unattainable without a material basis, and at such moments property pushes itself in as a substitute, saying, "Accept me instead—I'm good enough for all three." It is not enough. It is, as Shakespeare said of lust, "The expense of spirit in a waste of shame"; it is "Before, a joy proposed; behind, a dream." Yet we don't know how to shun it. It is forced on us by our economic system as the alternative to starvation. It is also forced on us by an internal defect in the soul, by the feeling that in property may lie the germs of self-development and of exquisite or heroic deeds. Our life on earth is, and ought to be, material and carnal. But we have not yet learned to manage our materialism and carnality properly; they are still entangled with the desire for ownership, where (in the words of Dante) "Possession is one with loss."

And this brings us to our fourth and final point: the blackberries.　6

Blackberries are not plentiful in this meager grove, but they are easily　7
seen from the public footpath which traverses it, and all too easily gathered. Foxgloves, too—people will pull up the foxgloves, and ladies of an educational tendency even grub for toadstools to show them on the Monday in class. Other ladies, less educated, roll down the bracken in the arms of their gentlemen friends. There is paper, there are tins. Pray, does my wood belong to me or doesn't it? And, if it does, should I not own it best by allowing no one else to walk there? There is a wood near Lyme Regis, also cursed by a public footpath, where the owner has not hesitated on this point. He had built high stone walls each side of the path, and has spanned it by bridges, so that the public circulate like termites while he gorges on the blackberries unseen. He really does own his wood, this able chap. And perhaps I shall come to this in time. I shall wall in and fence out until I really taste the sweets of property. Enormously stout, endlessly avaricious, pseudo-creative, intensely selfish, I shall weave upon my forehead the quadruple crown of possession until those nasty Bolshies come and take it off again and thrust me aside into the outer darkness.

◆ ◆ ◆

◆ ◆ ◆ **Writer's Workshop I** ◆ ◆ ◆
Responding to Cause and Effect

Use the *Who, What, Why,* and *How* questions (see pp. 3–4) to explore your own understanding of the ideas and the writing strategies employed by E. M. Forster in "My Wood." Your instructor may ask you to record these responses in a journal or bring them to class to use in small group discussions.

◆ WRITING FROM READING

After writing her own responses to the *Who, What, Why,* and *How* questions, student writer Ami Krumery chose to work very closely with the Forster model, in her case asking what effect owning her first car had on her.

Ami Krumery
English 1001
April 23, 1994

My Car

In our society big cars, big yachts, and big   1
houses symbolize power and prestige; in fact, a
critical component of the "American Dream" is the
pursuit of property and wealth. However, novelist and
essayist E. M. Forster has advocated an opposing point
of view. In his essay "My Wood," Forster described the
burdens that ownership put upon him and the
transformation of his personality that ownership
caused. I understand how Forster was affected by his
property. My first possession, a used car presented
to me on my sixteenth birthday, caused me much
confusion. At first, I was excited about having a car
of my own, but later I realized that the car changed
me. Like Forster, I became more self-centered and
self-glorifying.

Of course, in the beginning I enjoyed being able   2
to go anywhere at any time in my own car; however,
soon after I got it, I viewed the car less positively.
It became a responsibility that I loathed at times. I
enjoyed cruising around town--until the gas gauge read
"E." Then, I realized, I was the person responsible
for refueling it. Because I had to save my money for
gas and car repair bills instead of spending it on
clothes and cassette tapes, I felt like the car
disrupted my life. I pitied myself because I did not
have enough money to buy a leather jacket or the
latest Bon Jovi tape, and I blamed the car. Forster

experienced the same feelings with his wood. He described how owning the wood burdened him. He felt "heavy" because of the wood; owning a car gave me that same feeling of oppression.

Although I felt burdened, and sometimes, disgusted 3 by my possession, I also became obsessed with it. I felt like I had to have more; my baby-blue four-speed no longer satisfied me. Likewise, Forster defined the second burden of his wood as greed. Owning the acres of wooded land made him want to own more; he felt "it ought to be larger." I hated myself for wanting to have more because when I first received the slightly used Dodge Omni, I was perfectly happy. At first I wasn't concerned with the fact that it didn't have power steering or cruise control, and I didn't care that the music from the radio was often interrupted by static or that the heater made a clanking noise all winter. But when I saw my friends driving brand new Camaros and Trans Ams, my Omni no longer seemed like the perfect car I had thought it was. During the years that I owned that car, I never stopped comparing it to others. I was always jealous of the faster, fancier, sportier cars.

My unhappiness with my possession did not end with 4 my greed; it extended to include the feeling that the car was not totally mine. Forster experienced the same feeling with his wood. Just as he wanted to cut down trees or maybe plant some, I, too, wanted to drastically alter the appearance of the car to reflect my own personality. I did not want any remaining trace of the previous owners, and I did not want my 1983 Dodge Omni to look like all the other 1983 Dodge Omnis in the world. I attached stuffed animals with suction cups to the windows and stuck humorous bumper stickers on the fenders, but those only made my car look cluttered. I laid down floor mats to hide the faded blue carpet and hung scented ornaments from the rear view mirror to make my car smell like strawberries. However, these attempts failed also. I always knew that the car was not completely mine. Someone else had washed it, driven it, and even dented the door a little, and I could always smell a faint

odor of cigar that the imitation strawberry could
not conceal.

Finally, I discovered that the car had made me   5
selfish. Until I got the car, I had been a generous
person, but my generosity wilted when my dad drove the
car into the driveway for the first time. I hated the
thought of ever having to let someone else drive it,
even to pull it into the garage. I would never let my
classmates drive it, and I was even careful to offer
rides to only my very closest friends. I really wanted
my own private garage where no one could even look at
my car if I didn't want them to, but the only defense
I had was to hide my keys from the world, just as
Forster wanted to hide the blackberries that grew
along the footpath of his wood.

After reading E. M. Forster's essay, I discovered   6
that I had undergone a similar experience when I
acquired my first big possession. I discovered some
sobering truths about myself from owning my first car.
I realized that I was capable of being a person I
would normally not like. I turned back into my old
self when I sold the car, but the knowledge of who
I had become still haunts me sometimes. I suppose,
like Forster, I will have to wear the "quadruple crown
of possession" until I learn to resist "the sweets
of property."

◆ GETTING STARTED ON CAUSE AND EFFECT

Cause and effect writing often starts because of a desire to understand
a problem or the meaning of an event. Both E. M. Forster and Ami
Krumery, for example, wrote to figure out why something that seemed so
positive on the surface ended up having negative consequences.

Prewriting begins with jotting down what the writer already knows
and what he or she hopes to know by the end of the writing project. Is the
effect known or the cause, and what, then, must be uncovered—effects or
causes? Forster knew the cause—he'd acquired private property—and he
wished to discover what the effects of this change in his life might be.

Focused discovery writing provides writers the opportunity to seek a
wide range of appropriate causes and/or effects. The obvious or **immediate**

causes and effects should come easily. It's the subtle or **indirect causes and effects** that will take more time and care to discover. A fight with your best friend from high school might seem to explain the fact that you didn't want to see him or her the last time you went home for a weekend. But if you reflect on the situation, you may discover that the alienation had begun long before that fight, a result of the different choices you've made since high school and the new friendships you've each formed. If you find yourself unable to generate in-depth answers or indirect possibilities, because you are too close to the problem or do not have sufficient information, it's time to turn to conversations with others or go to the library.

Having achieved an understanding, you are then ready to shift your attention to your audience and your purpose. The goal of understanding shifts to explanation as you turn your original questions into a thesis or generalization. To narrow the thesis you will need to sort through the causes and effects identified in your prewriting. Objectively analyzing these causes and effects is essential to this process of selecting which ones are most useful and directly relevant to understanding. If, for example, you look thoughtfully at your high school friendship and decide to write to your friend to suggest some changes in the relationship, you will need to choose your evidence carefully to explain the changes that have taken place and to anticipate the effects your suggestions will have on your friendship.

◆ ORGANIZING CAUSE AND EFFECT

In modeling her essay after Forster's, Ami chose exactly the same organizational scheme, which looks like this:

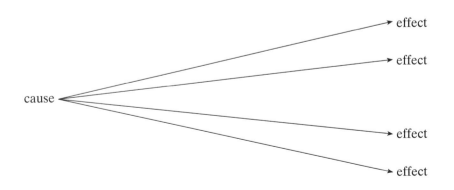

Filling in the context, the two essays look like this:

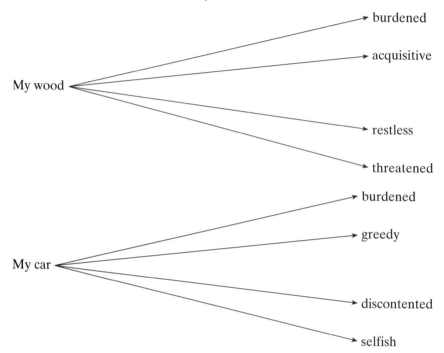

However, there are more possibilities for the investigation of causes and effects. For example, you might want to focus on several causes for one effect, backwards from Forster's strategy, looking like this:

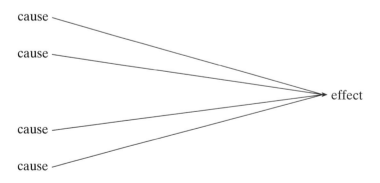

In this case, the effect would be introduced in your opening, and each cause would be developed in sequence in the body of the essay. For example, in the case of tracing the failure of your high school friendship, you can link the present state of things to several causes, each of which could be developed into a paragraph. It might be pictured like this:

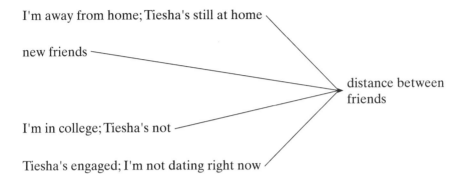

I'm away from home; Tiesha's still at home

new friends

distance between friends

I'm in college; Tiesha's not

Tiesha's engaged; I'm not dating right now

Later in this chapter you will notice that Kathy A. Svitil, too, effectively illustrates the multiple-cause structure in her explanation for a "Greenland Viking Mystery" (page 421).

In the readings in this chapter, you will also see a few other organizational schemes for cause and effect writing. In her exploration of the myths of the Latina woman, for example, Judith Ortiz Cofer offers a chain of causes and effects ("The Myth of the Latin Woman," page 427). Alberto Alvaro Rios uses a circular organization, moving back and forth among causes and effects to weave together the origins and consequences of his process of becoming a poet ("Becoming and Breaking: Poet and Poem," page 435).

◆ DEVELOPING CAUSE AND EFFECT

Having established your major points and the structure of your discussion, you must next determine the order in which you will present your causes and effects. Chronology and order of importance—least to most or most to least—are effective choices for this strategy. Or, perhaps, there will be one primary cause or effect to be developed extensively and several secondary ones that might be clustered. If you take a chronological approach, take care to check for faulty or unchallenged connections. Simply because one event precedes or follows another does not necessarily prove that a meaningful link exists between the two. If you wake up ill in the night, it might have been those onion rings you ate, and then again it might just be a flu bug you picked up several days earlier.

Transitions will help you to communicate your plan to your readers. Notice that in their essays, both Forster and Ami give clear indications of their strategies and announce when they are moving from one effect to the next. Forster writes, "In the first place," "In the second place," and so on; he also uses single-sentence paragraphs to mark transitions. Ami uses "in the beginning," "also," "it extended," and "finally," as she piles one effect upon another. In either case, you are never left wondering when a new effect is coming.

◆ OPENING AND CLOSING CAUSE AND EFFECT

Forster begins his essay with some humorous chiding of Americans, who enjoyed feeling superior to the British so much that they bought enough copies of his book that he could afford a piece of property. Then he brings forth his main question quite bluntly: "What is the effect of property upon the character?" Ami Krumery follows Forster's lead in briefly stating how she came to own her used car. In this way, both writers swiftly reveal their intent to explore the multiple effects of a particular event or experience. Ami chooses to put hers into a statement rather than posing a question: "I realized that the car changed me." Your duty in the introduction to your essay is to do these two tasks: (1) provide an appropriate setting, and (2) state your main point or main question, perhaps forecasting the specific cause and effect pattern you will employ. Reread both introductory paragraphs. If you had stopped reading there, you would still have a pretty good idea of what the essays are about.

Forster and Ami demonstrate two different tactics to close their writing. Continuing in a humorous vein, Forster looks into an exaggerated future as a bloated and piggish landowner ripe for unseating by communists. Ami takes a serious look back at her whole experience: "I realized that I was capable of being a person I would normally not like." The tones could be altered: Forster could take a serious look at the future, perhaps deciding not to buy any more land, and Ami could take a humorous look back at her youthful self-centeredness. Whatever tone fits with your own essay, consider looking forward or looking back as ways to close the piece gracefully.

◆ USING THE MODEL

Because Ami chose to write a piece so parallel to Forster's, she decided to incorporate Forster's ideas directly into her essay. She explicitly shows how her experience relates to Forster's, sometimes using direct quotations.

That's not the only way she could have done it. Look again at her essay. You can see how easily the references to the model essay could be deleted, leaving Ami's writing to stand alone. In paragraph 5, for instance, only the last part of the last sentence would have to go.

You may decide to use the model essays we provide in a more indirect way. For example, Forster's essay may make you feel argumentative if you have acquired a possession that improved your character rather than degraded it. You could either use Forster's statements and refute them with your own experience, or you could not refer to his essay at all. You may decide just to copy the structure of the model and put in content that has nothing to do with the effect of possession on character. For example, you might write about several effects of global warming. In such a case, you would not mention Forster's essay at all.

It's a testament to Forster's wisdom that almost any belonging could be substituted as the "cause" and still produce an accurate, interesting essay: my house, my computer, my wardrobe, my sound system, my fiancé, my new baby, my gold medal. He answers his main question with uncanny generality and makes us think twice about ownership of anything. You might choose to write a close imitation of Forster's and Ami's essays using a possession of your own on the "cause" side.

◆ ◆ ◆ *Writer's Workshop II* ◆ ◆ ◆ *Analyzing Cause and Effect*

Working individually or with a small group of classmates, read through Ami Krumery's essay "My Car," and respond to the following questions.

1. Ami chooses to share a not terribly flattering side of herself in this essay. Why does she take this risk, and how did you respond to her self-criticisms? What does her tone of voice have to do with your responses?
2. Could you recognize yourself in any of Ami's behaviors? Would you explain your responses in the same way Ami has explained hers?
3. Why does Ami include so many of the details of Forster's essay within her essay?
4. Are Ami's reasons for writing this essay exactly the same as Forster's? Explain any differences you find.
5. Reread the first sentences of the body paragraphs (2 through 5). What strategies do they share?

◆ ◆ ◆ *Checklist for Reading and Writing* ◆ ◆ ◆
Cause and Effect Essays

1. Is there a clear thesis that reveals the exact cause and effect relationship under consideration?
2. Are all causal connections logical, and is that logic sufficiently explained?
3. Is there an evident pattern of development that is consistently followed, avoiding confusing shifts between causes and effects?
4. Are transitions provided to assist readers in seeing and following the cause and effect connections?
5. Are all appropriate causes and effects, both immediate and indirect, included and fully developed? If there is a chain of causes and effects, are all links included?

◆ ◆ ◆ **PREPARING TO READ**

What were your favorite toys when you were a child? Why? Were there toys you would have liked but were discouraged from playing with by your family or friends?

◆ ◆ ◆

Why Boys Don't Play with Dolls

KATHA POLLITT

Poet and essayist Katha Pollitt's writing has been described as "lucid, gutsy, funny, and just." Her very first book of poetry, *Antarctic Traveller* (1982), brought her wide recognition, including the National Book Critics Circle Award. A number of her essays, which first appeared in *The New Yorker,* the *New York Times,* and the *Nation,* were recently published in the collection *Reasonable Creatures: Essays on Women and Feminism* (1994). With sharp humor and insight, Pollitt grapples with many of our most challenging problems—abortion, the media surrogate motherhood. "Why Boys Don't Play with Dolls" was written in 1995 for the *New York Times Magazine.*

It's twenty-eight years since the founding of NOW, and boys still like   1
trucks and girls still like dolls. Increasingly, we are told that the source of these robust preferences must lie outside society—in prenatal hormonal influences, brain chemistry, genes—and that feminism has reached its natural limits. What else could possibly explain the love of preschool girls for party dresses or the desire of toddler boys to own more guns than Mark from Michigan.

True, recent studies claim to show small cognitive differences between   2
the sexes: he gets around by orienting himself in space, she does it by remembering landmarks. Time will tell if any deserve the hoopla with which each is invariably greeted, over the protests of the researchers themselves. But even if the results hold up (and the history of such research is not encouraging), we don't need studies of sex-differentiated brain activity in reading, say, to understand why boys and girls still seem so unalike.

The feminist movement has done much for some women, and some-   3
thing for every woman, but it has hardly turned America into a playground free of sex roles. It hasn't even got women to stop dieting or men to stop interrupting them.

Instead of looking at kids to "prove" that differences in behavior by   4
sex are innate, we can look at the ways we raise kids as an index to how unfinished the feminist revolution really is, and how tentatively it is embraced
even by adults who fully expect their daughters to enter previously male-
dominated professions and their sons to change diapers.

I'm at a children's birthday party. "I'm sorry," one mom silently   5
mouths to the mother of the birthday girl, who has just torn open her
present—Tropical Splash Barbie. Now, you can love Barbie or you can hate
Barbie, and there are feminists in both camps. But *apologize* for Barbie? Inflict Barbie, against your own convictions, on the child of a friend you know
will be none too pleased?

Every mother in that room had spent years becoming a person who   6
had to be taken seriously, not least by herself. Even the most attractive, I'm
willing to bet, had suffered over her body's failure to fit the impossible
American ideal. Given all that, it seems crazy to transmit Barbie to the next
generation. Yet to reject her is to say that what Barbie represents—being
sexy, thin, stylish—is unimportant, which is obviously not true, and children
know it's not true.

Women's looks matter terribly in this society, and so Barbie, however   7
ambivalently, must be passed along. After all, there are worse toys. The Cut
and Style Barbie styling head, for example, a grotesque object intended to
encourage "hair play." The grown-ups who give that probably apologize, too.

How happy would most parents be to have a child who flouted sex   8
conventions? I know a lot of women, feminists, who complain in a comical,
eyeball-rolling way about their sons' passion for sports: the ruined weekends, obnoxious coaches, macho values. But they would not think of discouraging their sons from participating in this activity they find so foolish.
Or do they? Their husbands are sports fans, too, and they like their husbands a lot.

Could it be that even sports-resistant moms see athletics as part of   9
manliness? That if their sons wanted to spend the weekend writing up their
diaries, or reading, or baking, they'd find it disturbing? Too antisocial? Too
lonely? Too gay?

Theories of innate differences in behavior are appealing. They let par-   10
ents off the hook—no small recommendation in a culture that holds moms,
and sometimes even dads, responsible for their children's every misstep on
the road to bliss and success.

They allow grown-ups to take the path of least resistance to the dom-   11
inant culture, which always requires less psychic effort, even if it means
more actual work: just ask the working mother who comes home exhausted
and nonetheless finds it easier to pick up her son's socks than make him do
it himself. They let families buy for their children, without too much guilt,

the unbelievably sexist junk that the kids, who have been watching commercials since birth, understandably crave.

But the thing the theories do most of all is tell adults that the *adult* 12
world—in which moms and dads still play by many of the old rules even as they question and fidget and chafe against them—is the way it's supposed to be. A girl with a doll and a boy with a truck "explain" why men are from Mars and women are from Venus, why wives do housework and husbands just don't understand.

The paradox is that the world of rigid and hierarchical sex roles 13
evoked by determinist theories is already passing away. Three-year-olds may indeed insist that doctors are male and nurses female, even if their own mother is a physician. Six-year-olds know better. These days, something like half of all medical students are female, and male applications to nursing school are inching upward. When tomorrow's three-year-olds play doctor, who's to say how they'll assign the roles?

With sex roles, as in every area of life, people aspire to what is possi- 14
ble, and conform to what is necessary. But these are not fixed, especially today. Biological determinism may reassure some adults about their present, but it is feminism, the ideology of flexible and converging sex roles, that fits our children's future. And the kids, somehow, know this.

That's why, if you look carefully, you'll find that for every kid who fits 15
a stereotype, there's another who's breaking one down. Sometimes it's the same kid—the boy who skateboards *and* takes cooking in his afterschool program; the girl who collects stuffed animals *and* A-pluses in science.

Feminists are often accused of imposing their "agenda" on children. 16
Isn't that what adults always do, consciously and unconsciously? Kids aren't born religious, or polite, or kind, or able to remember where they put their sneakers. Inculcating these behaviors, and the values behind them, is a tremendous amount of work, involving many adults. We don't have a choice, really, about whether we should give our children messages about what it means to be male and female—they're bombarded with them from morning till night.

The question, as always, is what do we want those messages to be?   17

◆ ◆ ◆

FIRST RESPONSES

How would you feel about your daughter playing with a toy bulldozer? Would you let your son play with a Tropical Splash Barbie? Can both boys and girls play with beanie babies? Why or why not?

TAKING A CLOSER LOOK

Exploring *Who:* Voice and Tone

1. Reread paragraph 1. By the end of the paragraph, do you know whether Pollitt is a liberal or a conservative? What is the effect of her strategy?
2. Find several examples of phrases that reveal Pollitt's explicitly feminist perspective. Did her tone of voice reinforce your views of feminists or challenge them? Did that affect your openness to her ideas?
3. Describe the group of people Pollitt seems most interested in reaching with this essay. How does paragraph 16 help to answer this question?
4. Is Pollitt discouraged by the fact that traditional gender roles continue three decades after NOW was founded? Where does she place her hope? Do you share any of her feelings?

Exploring *What:* Content and Meaning

1. What has science concretely proven about the influence of genetics on gender behavior? Does Pollitt dispute this research? Why or why not?
2. Pollitt locates one of the primary causes for the continuation of traditional gender roles in "adults who fully expect their daughters to enter previously male-dominated professions and their sons to change diapers." Did this claim surprise you? What proof does she offer? Can you add other causes or think of additional examples to support her viewpoint?
3. Why does Pollitt feel that a boy's love of sports is a sign of a "sex convention"? Has Title IX, which mandates equal opportunity in school athletics, had any effect on this traditional division of interests? How does popular culture, such as the television sitcom, reinforce or challenge the norm?
4. What does Pollitt mean when she says, "Theories of innate differences in behavior are appealing. They let parents off the hook . . ."?

Exploring *Why:* Purpose

1. Pollitt believes that "The feminist movement has done much for some women, and something for every woman . . . ." Name some changes that she might be thinking of when she says this.
2. ◼ *Using the Internet.* When you watch younger children at play or see commercials for children's toys, what similarities and what

differences do you see between now and when you were a child? Use a search engine to find an Internet site for children's toys (company sites, such as Disney, or organizations that evaluate the quality of toys, for example), and note the extent to which gender is part of the presentation. Do you think gender considerations have become more important in the toy business than they used to be?

3. Exactly what changes does Pollitt hope to encourage? Has she affected your attitudes toward parenting?

4. Why are children changing their habits despite their parents' attitudes?

Exploring *How:* Style and Strategy

1. Outline Pollitt's chain of causes and effects. Why did she choose this in-depth approach rather than offering a wider variety of causes for gender differences? What explains the order of her points?

2. What is the effect of saying that boys' liking trucks and girls' playing with dolls are "robust preferences"?

3. Why does Pollitt use the word "hoopla" to describe the opposition's viewpoint in paragraph 2?

4. What is Pollitt's intention when she uses questions in paragraph 5? How is it different from her use of a question as the conclusion to her essay?

WRITING FROM READING ASSIGNMENT

Katha Pollitt took what she saw as a superficial response to the problem of gender-role preferences in children and uncovered several sites of responsibility in a surprising place—parents who themselves have struggled to lead nontraditional lives. By doing so, she hoped to contradict her opposition and to encourage genuine change for children.

In this writing assignment, your goal is to dig beneath the surface to trace not only the *immediate* but also the *indirect* and interrelated causes for a current problem. One place to look is your campus—the lack of a day-care center, a parking crisis, a refusal to fund a new student group, or trouble getting the courses needed to graduate. You might also write about a problem in your family, if understanding the nature of the problem would be valuable to your readers in some way. If formal research is allowed or required, you might consider writing about a problem in your local community, such as an increase in sexual assaults.

A. Brainstorming is a productive way to discover the best topic for this assignment. Don't stop at the first problem that comes to mind, but remember that unless you will be doing formal research, the topic must be one you know well enough that you can discuss it in some depth. If nothing comes to mind, review a few weeks of your campus newspaper or chat with family and friends to identify possibilities. You might also glance through the readings in this book for inspiration.

B. Once you've decided what to write about, you'll want to list all the causes that you and others have thought of so far—even the ones you don't necessarily see as primary or correct. Again, conversations with others and research might be useful to extend the possibilities.

C. Clustering the points on your list will help you to start the process of seeing connections among the causes: immediate or easily observable causes in one group, indirect or less easily seen in another. Next, cluster around the indirect causes, trying to identify where those causes might originate. Pollitt's search for causes led her to where children learn their gender roles, which led her to the parents, which led her to the social pressures the parents themselves face.

D. Like Pollitt, you now will need to select the few most important causes for the problem in order to allow you the space to develop each one fully. Consider which lines of analysis are least familiar, even surprising, to your readers and most likely to influence their thinking on the problem. A new perspective can sometimes move those with set opinions to reconsider their views.

E. A sketch outline of your chain of causes will let you know how fully prepared you are to begin your draft. If the chain reveals a need for more examples or explanation than you are prepared for, return to brainstorming or research to fill in the gaps.

F. Before you begin the draft, you also might wish to review Pollitt's organization. Do you want to introduce the essay as she does, with causes that inaccurately or inadequately account for the problem? Will you begin with the most immediate causes to trace your way back or vice versa? Your readers' familiarity with the problem and attitudes toward it will help you to make these decisions.

G. In your conclusion, consider using Pollitt's technique of placing the next step in the hands of your readers: What will they or can they do with the insights you have provided them?

H. Focus your first-stage revisions on the logic of your connections and the adequacy of your supporting examples and analysis. Before the last round of editing, consider how clearly you have guided the readers through the logical connections. Are there appropriate transitional words and phrases?

◆ ◆ ◆ PREPARING TO READ

Have you ever been in a difficult situation where you really needed help, but for some reason you were unable to ask for or accept assistance? What explains your behavior? Would you act differently now?

◆ ◆ ◆

The Greenland Viking Mystery

KATHY A. SVITIL

Kathy A. Svitil writes for *Discover* magazine, a Disney publication that brings recent scientific research and insights to a popular audience. Svitil's interests encompass the past, present, and future, from the disappearance of the dinosaurs, to our current struggles with global warming, to how robotics will shape our lives in days to come. "The Greenland Viking Mystery," which first appeared in June 1997, calls on the wonders of modern technology to help explain the disappearance of two separate groups of Icelandic colonists in the Middle Ages.

1   To the Norse men and women living in Iceland in the tenth century, an island called Greenland must have sounded like Eden. At the time, the North Atlantic was in the throes of a warm spell, and parts of southern Greenland were actually green and fertile, at least by Icelandic standards. Enticed by the promise of truly greener pastures, a group of Norse Icelanders established two settlements on Greenland—the Eastern, as archeologists call it, on the southern tip of the island; and the Western, along the southwest coast near the modern capital of Nuuk. The settlers built farms and large stone churches, raised animals, hunted seals and walrus, traded with Europe, and struggled to survive.

2   Survive they did, for centuries, even as the temperatures chilled at the end of the thirteenth century with the onset of a prolonged European cooling trend often called the little ice age. Then, mysteriously, the Norse Greenlanders—some 5,000 to 6,000 strong at their peak—disappeared. The Western Settlement succumbed first, sometime in the mid-1300s; Eastern settlers hung on longer, until the mid-fifteenth century. Almost ever since the settlers' demise, historians and archeologists have speculated about what happened to them. Were they killed by invaders from arctic Canada? Were they carried off by Basque pirates? Or did they starve to death in the bitter cold?

Now a diverse body of research is shedding new light on those final des-   3
perate years. Pirates and war weren't the agents of doom, according to the
emerging view. Rather, an unlikely combination of changing climate and ethnocentrism probably brought down the Norse colonies in Greenland.

The Norse colonists couldn't have had a better start. Both the Eastern   4
and Western settlements were ideally placed—located on inner fjords miles
from the sea, nestled up against the ice sheet and sheltered from fierce winds.
A persistent high-pressure zone over the ice cap made for warm summers on
the fjords by deflecting coastal storms out to sea. From archeological excavations, researchers know that the Greenlanders subsisted on a diet of harp and
harbor seal (and sometimes caribou), which were hunted in the summer on
the outer fjords near the ocean, along with food from cows, sheep, and goats.
The domestic animals pastured year-round along the inner fjords that produced grasses during the brief summer growing season. Despite their closeness to the sea, the Greenlanders, for unknown reasons, apparently didn't fish.

A model of that economy, created by archeologist Thomas McGovern   5
of the City University of New York and his colleagues, indicates that the
summer growth of fodder for those domestic animals—and, in turn, the survival of the Greenlanders—was critically linked to climate change. "The
model showed that the kind of climate change that would be most damaging would not be the once-every-500-years very bad year," McGovern says,
or even a record-breaking cold winter. "The most difficult thing for them to
cope with would be a string of especially cold summers."

That conclusion is supported by the findings of Lisa Barlow, a paleo-   6
climatologist at the University of Colorado in Boulder who has analyzed
cores from the Greenland ice sheet. To measure temperature change, Barlow looked at the ratio of deuterium (a heavy isotope of hydrogen) to normal hydrogen in sections of the ice core covering the last 700 years.
Ocean-borne water molecules made up of normal hydrogen evaporate at
slightly lower temperatures than do water molecules made with the heavier
deuterium. But as the temperature goes up, more heavy hydrogen evapo-
rates, eventually precipitating out over Greenland.

Barlow managed to trace the fluctuations of the two forms of hydro-   7
gen and found that the fourteenth century suffered four periods with summer temperatures cooler than average. The longest cold spell lasted for
about twenty grim years, from 1343 to 1362, give or take a year—the same
period during which the Western Settlement is believed to have collapsed.
(In one historical account, a seafaring Norwegian priest finds the Western
Settlement eerily abandoned sometime before 1361.)

"In a cool summer the settlement is not going to get as much   8
grass growth as it needs to get through the winter," Barlow says. "If that
consistently happened for a number of years, then they probably reached a

breaking point. When you are dealing with a colony that was living at a subsistence level anyway, it wouldn't take much to put them over the edge."

Did the Norse in the Western Settlement all die, or could some have 9 evacuated? "It would be nice to think that there were survivors" who fled to the Eastern Settlement or perhaps to Europe, says McGovern. "But the problem is that there is absolutely no evidence of that. In many parts of Europe at that time you could have a few boatloads of people show up and disappear into the population, but I think a formal abandonment of the Greenland colony would have been sufficiently newsworthy that it would have ended up in the annals of Iceland and the continent."

And yet it seems that the Europeans were totally unaware of the fate 10 of the Greenland settlements. In the late thirteenth and early fourteenth centuries, vast amounts of sea ice began to clog navigation lanes, making travel to and from Greenland difficult even during the summer. "As late as the 1600s the Pope was still appointing bishops to Greenland, who of course never left Rome," says McGovern. "As far as he was concerned, Greenland was then still a functioning part of Christendom."

McGovern suspects a bleaker fate. "As far as we can tell, they starved 11 to death." Excavations have turned up many expensive portable items, like crucifixes, that would probably have been removed by the settlers in an evacuation. And had the colony's population gradually diminished, McGovern says, the wood in many of the farms—a valuable commodity in a place with few trees—would have been scavenged by the remaining settlers. Such was not the case. "At least one of the farms we've examined shows evidence of a tough winter," McGovern says. "We find the bones of a number of cows—about the same number that lived in the barn—and mixed in with them are a bunch of ptarmigan feet, also famine food. Mixed in with that are the bones of one of the big hunting dogs." Cut marks on the bones suggest the dogs were butchered; even the cow hooves were eaten. "It looks as though they ate the cows and then ate the dogs. It looks like hard times."

Other evidence supports this grim scenario. Entomologist Peter Skid- 12 more of the University of Sheffield in England uncovered an orderly succession of fossil flies in a Western Settlement farmhouse. In the lower layers he found warm-temperature houseflies; in the layers above, cold-tolerant, indoor carrion-eaters that might have moved in when the homestead could no longer be kept warm; and in the final layer, outdoor flies. At that point, the roof of the farmhouse had probably caved in.

This was no Jamestown: the Norse toughed it out for generations under 13 steadily worsening conditions. The Greenlanders became more isolated from Europe. Yet they apparently clung steadfastly to a European way of life, shunning contact with the Thule Inuit peoples who began immigrating to the island from northern Canada in A.D. 1100. "There is indication on the

Thule side of interest in the Norse and their technology. Inuit excavations contain quite a lot of material," McGovern says. The Norse, on the other hand, suspiciously avoided contact with the Thule. "You don't have this kind of barrier between cultures for so long without someone working very hard to maintain it."

The Norse could have learned from the Thule. After all, there was   14
food to be had, even in winter—under the ice. "What has kept the Inuit communities alive through the winters, all through history, has been hunting through the ice or at the ice edge for ring seals," McGovern says. "They have developed this complex hunting technology—harpoons and all sorts of other gadgets—that allows them to do this successfully." But the Norse never learned to use harpoons, and their animal-bone collections are strikingly absent of ring seals. "Out of several thousand bones, there are two or three ring seal bones," says McGovern.

"They didn't adopt harpoons, they didn't adopt skin clothing, and they   15
didn't adopt skin boats," says McGovern. "The extinction of the Norse in Greenland, aided certainly as it was by climatic change, possibly could have been avoided if they had picked up more of those arctic adaptations from the Inuit. You could argue that these folks managed to maintain ethnic purity at the expense of survival."

◆ ◆ ◆

FIRST RESPONSES

Can you imagine yourself in the situation these Norse colonists faced? Why or why not?

TAKING A CLOSER LOOK

Exploring *Who:* Voice and Tone

1. How would you describe Svitil's role in this essay? Do you know her personal opinions about this mystery or her views about the researchers' explanations?
2. How many different types of professional researchers does Svitil call on to develop her topic? Reread some of their quotations. Describe the feelings these researchers reveal about their work and their topic.
3. Is your background in science sufficient to understand the evidence Svitil provides? How easily did you follow her explanations for the disappearance?

Exploring *What:* Content and Meaning

1. What has been the predominant theory used to explain why the colonists starved to death? What kinds of evidence support it?
2. What is the more recent theory of what caused the crisis? What new evidence supports it?
3. Are scientists equally certain about both theories? What were your responses to the two theories?
4. How have scientists disproved other speculations about the extinction?

Exploring *Why:* Purpose

1. What is "ethnocentrism"?
2. Why was the Greenland situation "no Jamestown"? And why does Svitil use this historical reference to make her point?
3. What does Svitil mean by "ethnic purity" in the last paragraph? Can you think of other past or current problems that can be explained by the same cause?

Exploring *How:* Style and Strategy

1. Svitil's thesis does not appear until paragraph 3. Why?
2. In how many different ways does Svitil attempt to draw in readers who might love a good "mystery" but don't usually read about science?
3. ◼ *Using the Internet.* How much did Svitil assume you already knew about Greenland's history and climate? Visit the Web site of the Tourist Board of Greenland, and use the links to answer any questions or pursue any interests that the essay might have raised for you: http://www.greenland.guide.dk/visit/.
4. Try going through the whole essay reading just the first sentence of each paragraph that doesn't begin with a quotation. How much of her topic does Svitil outline through these lead sentences?

IDEAS FOR WRITING CAUSE AND EFFECT

1. Is there a prejudice or preconception that especially bothers you? Write an essay explaining why people might think in this way and why you are offended by it.
2. What is currently the most popular daytime show among your friends or on campus? Write an essay explaining what causes the show to

appeal to this particular group of people. You might interview people to gather supporting evidence.

3. Review the "Preparing to Read" discovery writing that you did for this essay. If you want, discuss your responses with other members of your class. Then write an essay tracing the causes of a difficult situation that you have found yourself in, one from which you learned something about how to avoid a similar problem or difficulty in the future.

◆ ◆ ◆ PREPARING TO READ

Were you ever embarrassed by your family—by having to be seen with them, by something one of them did? What caused those feelings at the time? How do you feel about the experience now?

◆ ◆ ◆

The Myth of the Latin Woman: I Just Met a Girl Named Maria

JUDITH ORTIZ COFER

Most of Judith Ortiz Cofer's books, including *Silent Dancing: A Partial Remembrance of a Puerto Rican Childhood* (1990) and *The Year of Our Revolution: Selected and New Stories and Poems* (1998), mix poetry, folk-tales, and stories to bring to life her native Puerto Rico and the American barrios, or neighborhoods, to which many Puerto Ricans emigrate. In *The Latin Deli* (1993), Cofer wrote, "I was born a white girl in Puerto Rico but became a brown girl when I came to live in the United States." The challenge of living between two cultures is the focus of her essay "The Myth of the Latin Woman."

On a bus trip to London from Oxford University where I was earning some graduate credits one summer, a young man, obviously fresh from a pub, spotted me and as if struck by inspiration went down on his knees in the aisle. With both hands over this heart he broke into an Irish tenor's rendition of "Maria" from *West Side Story*. My politely amused fellow passengers gave his lovely voice the round of gentle applause it deserved. Though I was not quite as amused, I managed my version of an English smile: no show of teeth, no extreme contortions of the facial muscles—I was at this time of my life practicing reserve and cool. Oh, that British control, how I coveted it. But Maria had followed me to London, reminding me of a prime fact of my life: you can leave the Island, master the English language, and travel as far as you can, but if you are a Latina, especially one like me who so obviously belongs to Rita Moreno's gene pool, the Island travels with you.

This is sometimes a very good thing—it may win you that extra minute of someone's attention. But with some people, the same things can make *you* an island—not so much a tropical paradise as an Alcatraz, a place nobody wants to visit. As a Puerto Rican girl growing up in the United States and wanting like most children to "belong," I resented the stereotype that my Hispanic appearance called forth from many people I met.

Our family lived in a large urban center in New Jersey during the six-   3
ties, where life was designed as a microcosm of my parents' casas on the island. We spoke in Spanish, we ate Puerto Rican food bought at the bodega, and we practiced strict Catholicism complete with Saturday confession and Sunday mass at a church where our parents were accommodated into a one-hour Spanish mass slot, performed by a Chinese priest trained as a missionary for Latin America.

As a girl I was kept under strict surveillance, since virtue and modesty   4
were, by cultural equation, the same as family honor. As a teenager I was instructed on how to behave as a proper señorita. But it was a conflicting message girls got, since the Puerto Rican mothers also encouraged their daughters to look and act like women and to dress in clothes our Anglo friends and their mothers found too "mature" for our age. It was, and is, cultural, yet I often felt humiliated when I appeared at an American friend's party wearing a dress more suitable to a semiformal than to a playroom birthday celebration. At Puerto Rican festivities, neither the music nor the colors we wore could be too loud. I still experience a vague sense of letdown when I'm invited to a "party" and it turns out to be a marathon conversation in hushed tones rather than a fiesta with salsa, laughter, and dancing—the kind of celebration I remember from my childhood.

I remember Career Day in our high school, when teachers told us to   5
come dressed as if for a job interview. It quickly became obvious that to the barrio girls, "dressing up" sometimes meant wearing ornate jewelry and clothing that would be more appropriate (by mainstream standards) for the company Christmas party than as daily office attire. That morning I had agonized in front of my closet, trying to figure out what a "career girl" would wear because, essentially, except for Marlo Thomas on TV, I had no models on which to base my decision. I knew how to dress for school: at the Catholic school I attended we all wore uniforms; I knew how to dress for Sunday mass, and knew what dresses to wear for parties at my relatives' homes. Though I do not recall the precise details of my Career Day outfit, it must have been a composite of the above choices. But I remember a comment my friend (an Italian-American) made in later years that coalesced my impressions of that day. She said that at the business school she was attending the Puerto Rican girls always stood out for wearing "everything at once." She meant, of course, too much jewelry, too many accessories. On that day at school, we were simply made the negative models by the nuns who were themselves not credible fashion experts to any of us. But it was painfully obvious to me that to the others, in their tailored skirts and silk

blouses, we must have seemed "hopeless" and "vulgar." Though I now know that most adolescents feel out of step much of the time, I also know that for the Puerto Rican girls of my generation that sense was intensified. The way our teachers and classmates looked at us that day in school was just a taste of the culture clash that awaited us in the real world, where prospective employers and men on the street would often misinterpret our tight skirts and jingling bracelets as a come-on.

Mixed cultural signals have perpetuated certain stereotypes—for example, that of the Hispanic woman as the "Hot Tamale" or sexual firebrand. It is a one-dimensional view that the media have found easy to promote. In their special vocabulary, advertisers have designated not only the foods but also the women of Latin America. From conversations in my house I recall hearing about the harassment that Puerto Rican women endured in factories where the "boss men" talked to them as if sexual innuendo was all they understood and, worse, often gave them the choice of submitting to advances or being fired.   6

It is custom, however, not chromosomes, that leads us to choose scarlet over pale pink. As young girls, we were influenced in our decisions about clothes and color by the women—older sisters and mothers—who had grown up on a tropical island where the natural environment was a riot of primary colors, where showing your skin was one way to keep cool as well as to look sexy. Most important of all, on the island, women perhaps felt freer to dress and move more provocatively, since, in most cases, they were protected by the traditions, mores, and laws of a Spanish/Catholic system of morality and machismo whose main rule was: *You may look at my sister, but if you touch her I will kill you.* The extended family and church structure could provide a young woman with a circle of safety in her small pueblo on the island; if a man "wronged" a girl, everyone would close in to save her family honor.   7

This is what I have gleaned from my discussions as an adult with older Puerto Rican women. They have told me about dressing in their best party clothes on Saturday nights and going to the town's plaza to promenade with their girlfriends in front of the boys they liked. The males were thus given an opportunity to admire the women and to express their admiration in the form of *piropos:* erotically charged street poems they composed on the spot. I have been subjected to a few piropos while visiting the island, and they can be outrageous, although custom dictates that they must never cross into obscenity. This ritual, as I understand it, also entails a show of studied indifference on the woman's part; if she is "decent," she must not acknowledge the man's impassioned words. So I do understand how things can be lost in translation. When a Puerto Rican girl dressed in her idea of what is attractive meets a man from the mainstream culture who has been trained to react to certain types of clothing as a sexual signal, a clash is likely to take   8 place. The line I first heard based on this aspect of the myth happened when the boy who took me to my first formal dance leaned over to plant a sloppy overeager kiss painfully on my mouth, and when I didn't respond with sufficient passion said in a resentful tone: "I thought you Latin girls were supposed to mature early"—my first instance of being thought of as a fruit or vegetable—I was supposed to *ripen,* not just grow into womanhood like other girls.

It is surprising to some of my professional friends that some people, including those who should know better, still put others "in their place." Though rarer, these incidents are still commonplace in my life. It happened to me most recently during a stay at a very classy metropolitan hotel favored by young professional couples for their weddings. Late one evening after the theater, as I walked toward my room with my new colleague (a woman with whom I was coordinating an arts program), a middle-aged man in a tuxedo, a young girl in satin and lace on his arm, stepped directly into our path. With his champagne glass extended toward me, he exclaimed, "Evita!" 9

Our way blocked, my companion and I listened as the man half-recited, half-bellowed "Don't Cry for Me, Argentina." When he finished, the young girl said: "How about a round of applause for my daddy?" We complied hoping this would bring the silly spectacle to a close. I was becoming aware that our little group was attracting the attention of the other guests. "Daddy" must have perceived this too, and he once more barred the way as we tried to walk past him. He began to shout-sing a ditty to the tune of "La Bamba"—except the lyrics were about a girl named Maria whose exploits all rhymed with her name and gonorrhea. The girl kept saying "Oh, Daddy" and looking at me with pleading eyes. She wanted me to laugh along with the others. My companion and I stood silently waiting for the man to end his offensive song. When he finished, I looked not at him but at his daughter. I advised her calmly never to ask her father what he had done in the army. Then I walked between them and to my room. My friend complimented me on my cool handling of the situation. I confessed to her that I really had wanted to push the jerk into the swimming pool. I knew this same man—probably a corporate executive, well educated, even worldly by most standards—would not have been likely to regale a white woman with a dirty song in public. He would perhaps have checked his impulse by assuming that she could be somebody's wife or mother, or at least *somebody* who might take offense. But to him, I was just an Evita or a Maria: merely a character in his cartoon-populated universe. 10

Because of my education and my proficiency with the English language, I have acquired many mechanisms for dealing with the anger I experience. This was not true for my parents, nor is it true for the many Latin women working at menial jobs who must put up with stereotypes about our 11 ethnic group such as "They make good domestics." This is another facet of the myth of the Latin woman in the United States. Its origin is simple to deduce. Work as domestics, waitressing, and factory jobs are all that's available to women with little English and few skills. The myth of the Hispanic menial has been sustained by the same media phenomenon that made "Mammy" from *Gone with the Wind* America's idea of the black woman for generations; Maria, the housemaid or counter girl, is now indelibly etched into the national psyche. The big and the little screens have presented us with the picture of the funny Hispanic maid, mispronouncing words and cooking up a spicy storm in a shiny California kitchen.

This media-engendered image of the Latina in the United States has been documented by feminist Hispanic scholars, who claim that such portrayals are partially responsible for the denial of opportunities for upward mobility among Latinas in the professions. I have a Chicana friend working on a Ph.D. in philosophy at a major university. She says her doctor still shakes his head in puzzled amazement at all the "big words" she uses. Since I do not wear my diplomas around my neck for all to see, I too have on occasion been sent to that "kitchen," where some think I obviously belong. 12

One such incident that has stayed with me, though I recognize it as a minor offense, happened on the day of my first public poetry reading. It took place in Miami in a boat-restaurant where we were having lunch before the event. I was nervous and excited as I walked in with my notebook in my hand. An older woman motioned me to her table. Thinking (foolish me) that she wanted me to autograph a copy of my brand new slender volume of verse, I went over. She ordered a cup of coffee from me, assuming that I was the waitress. Easy enough to mistake my poems for menus, I suppose. I know that it wasn't an intentional act of cruelty, yet of all the good things that happened that day, I remember that scene most clearly, because it reminded me of what I had to overcome before anyone would take me seriously. In retrospect I understand that my anger gave my reading fire, that I have almost always taken doubts in my abilities as a challenge—and that the result is, most times, a feeling of satisfaction at having won a convert, when I see the cold, appraising eyes warm to my words, the body language change, the smile that indicates that I have opened some avenue for communication. That day I read to that woman and her lowered eyes told me that she was embarrassed at her little *faux pas,* and when I willed her to look up at me, it was my victory, and she graciously allowed me to punish her with my full attention. We shook hands at the end of the reading, and I never saw her again. She has probably forgotten the whole thing but maybe not. 13

Yet I am one of the lucky ones. My parents made it possible for me to acquire a stronger footing in the mainstream culture by giving me the chance at an education. And books and art have saved me from the harsher forms of 14 ethnic and racial prejudice that many of my Hispanic *compañeras* have had to endure. I travel a lot around the United States, reading from my books of poetry and my novel, and the reception I most often receive is one of positive interest by people who want to know more about my culture. There are, however, thousands of Latinas without the privilege of an education or the entree into society that I have. For them life is a struggle against the misconceptions perpetuated by the myth of the Latina as whore, domestic, or criminal. We cannot change this by legislating the way people look at us. The transformation, as I see it, has to occur at a much more individual level. My personal goal in my public life is to try to replace the old pervasive stereotypes and myths about Latinas with a much more interesting set of realities. Every time I give a reading, I hope the stories I tell, the dreams and fears I examine in my work, can achieve some universal truth which will get my audience past the particulars of my skin color, my accent, or my clothes.

I once wrote a poem in which I called us Latinas "God's brown daugh-   15
ters." This poem is really a prayer of sorts, offered upward, but also, through the human-to-human channel of art, outward. It is a prayer for communication, and for respect. In it, Latin women pray "in Spanish to an Anglo God / with a Jewish heritage," and they are "fervently hoping / that if not omnipotent, / at least He be bilingual."

◆ ◆ ◆

FIRST RESPONSES

Are there myths that have led to misunderstandings about you—myths about farm people, red-haired people, or tall people, for example?

TAKING A CLOSER LOOK

Exploring *Who:* Voice and Tone

1. What aspect of her identity does Cofer choose to reveal in the first sentence of the essay? Why? How is this choice further explained at the end of the essay in paragraph 14?
2. The word "Daddy" is used three times in paragraph 10. How does its tone change?
3. In paragraph 11, Cofer tells us she has "acquired many mechanisms for dealing with the anger" in her life. How many ways of coping can you find in this essay?

4. ■ *Using the Internet.* Visit the official Web site of MANA: The National Latina Organization (http://www.hermana.org/) to learn more about issues of importance to Hispanic American women. How does Cofer's essay support the need for the types of projects undertaken by this group?

Exploring *What:* Content and Meaning

1. Have you seen advertisements that support Cofer's claims about the "Hot Tamale" stereotype? What other images of Latina women have you noticed on television?
2. What caused the problems Cofer and her friends faced on Career Day? Can you remember any similar confusions about appropriate behavior in a new situation?
3. Why are Latina women "freer to dress and move more provocatively" in Puerto Rico? How does Cofer explain the reactions of American men to this behavior?
4. What "myth of the Latin woman" led to Cofer's traumatic experience at her "first formal dance"? Can you name other kinds of myths that create problems for young men and women on such occasions?

Exploring *Why:* Purpose

1. What does Cofer mean when she says, "It is custom, however, not chromosomes, that leads us to choose scarlet over pale pink," in paragraph 7?
2. Both of the public male assaults on Cofer result in part from the man's experience with popular culture—*West Side Story, Evita, La Bamba.* What was responsible for the experience with the woman at the poetry reading? Can you speculate about the gender differences revealed here?
3. Why does Cofer speak to the daughter, not the father, at the conclusion of the hotel experience?
4. How does Cofer expand her topic by including a reference to "Mammy" from *Gone with the Wind*?
5. Did you identify with Cofer or with the woman at the poetry reading? Why? How does the way Cofer handled her anger about being mistaken for a waitress connect to her purpose for writing this essay?

Exploring *How:* Style and Strategy

1. Cofer cites several myths as the cause for mainstream American responses to Latina women. How many additional strategies of development does she use to support this thesis?

2. How did you respond to the opening anecdote about the young British singer? Would you have applauded? Why did Cofer begin with this story?

3. How did Cofer's "island" **metaphor** in paragraph 2 prepare you for the rest of her essay?

4. Why do the first five paragraphs focus on Cofer's personal experiences? How does the decision to take this approach relate to the author's analysis of her readers?

IDEAS FOR WRITING CAUSE AND EFFECT

1. One of Cofer's reactions to stereotypical thinking was to take any "doubts in my abilities as a challenge." Write an essay about a negative experience that you turned into a positive one. What in your past enabled you to turn bad into good?

2. Write an essay based on your responses to the second part of question 2 in the "Exploring *What*" section. Consider what caused your confusion, as well as the effects the experience had on you.

3. Have you ever hid something about yourself because you feared the reactions you might get? Write an essay explaining what caused your fears and the effects of your decision not to reveal the truth.

◆ ◆ ◆ PREPARING TO READ

Is there a talent or an ability that you have discovered about yourself since starting college? How did you become aware of it? Why were you not aware of it before that time?

◆ ◆ ◆

Becoming and Breaking: Poet and Poem

ALBERTO ALVARO RIOS

Poet and short story writer Alberto Alvaro Rios teaches English in his native Arizona. Recently, his stories have been collected in the book *Pig Cookies and Other Stories* (1995) and his poetry in *Teodoro Luna's Two Kisses* (1990). Individual poems are also found in major anthologies such as *The Norton Anthology of Modern Poetry* and *The Morrow Anthology of Younger American Poets*. The quality and importance of his writing have been recognized by a Guggenheim Fellowship in poetry, a National Endowment for the Arts Award, and the Walt Whitman Award.

Maybe 1971 it was, summer, inside my parents' house, in Nogales, on the Arizona border with Mexico. I was doing one day what many, if not all, my friends were: filling out preregistration forms—a recent innovation—for my second year at the University of Arizona. I had two spots left to fill. I was a political science major, but only because my adviser taught it. Yet I did have a focus, a purpose: I spent the entire day thumbing through the catalog for the two easiest courses I could find. 1

And I found them. Thinking "these are for me," I signed up for first-level classes in poetry writing and fiction writing. How hard could these be? And they were not hard; they were what I was looking for exactly; they were the mythical "easy classes." At least in the beginning. 2

Then something happened, a small moment, issuing almost from a single phrase. Up to now I had done well in school, and in making the transition to college; though I was the first in my family to go, I didn't have to make many adjustments. The formula was not magic—one simply had to follow through. If someone asked me a question about astronomy, I went to an astronomy book. If a teacher asked me about biology, I went to a different 3

biology teacher and asked. If a report was called for, I went to the encyclopedia and copied it. Like that, school. I could play this.

But the rules changed midstream, and I was unprepared—which, in   4
retrospect, means entirely ready. After the first two or three weeks in these
easy classes, getting the jargon and the cool and the rules on spelling, I was
asked almost simultaneously in both classes to now go *write one.* A poem. A
prose sketch.

There was no reference book, no biology teacher. I could copy things   5
down, of course, but both teachers had expressed thoughts on that ahead of
time. There was no place to go. At that moment, school changed for me—
and life, if I may be so dramatic. School had always come at me; I was the
back wall to a tennis player, and I simply let things bounce back. But now,
for the first time, school would have to come *from* me, from the inside. From
the flick of my wrist, my racquet.

I rebelled, of course; surely I had missed out on some technique along   6
the way, a certain knack, a locker room secret; surely there was some way
around this. My first efforts were a kind of treading water, waiting for help.
I wrote things never earlier than the night before and often in a Spanish mix
so as not to be so easily understood. Buying time. And it worked.

It worked in the sense that no real time could be bought. The more I   7
wrote, the more I realized I had been writing almost all my life—I simply
had had no name for it. To get away from schoolwork, I had always written
things in the backs of my notebooks. Words, phrases, *things*. Not stories. And
certainly not poems; I knew better. The town was hard, and people who
wrote were called names, especially if they were guys. And especially if they
wrote poems. Not me. I kept it hidden, called it nothing, and didn't tell anyone about it. You know, smart.

2

I was born in Nogales, on the border of Mexico. My father is from   8
Tapachula, Chiapas, Mexico, and my mother from Warrington, Lancashire,
England. I grew up around my father's family but I look like my mother,
which means I got to see two worlds from the beginning, and could even
physically experience the difference growing up where I did: I could put,
every day of my life, one foot in Mexico and one foot in the United States,
at the same time.

Growing up around my father's family and in that town, for all practi-   9
cal purposes my first language was Spanish. My mother, who was the only
one who spoke English entirely, was ignored by everyone; not on purpose,
but because no one knew what else to do with her. I joke about this, and I
must have been learning English, but it is the Spanish I remember hearing.

There was no problem with this until first grade. That little kids can't   10
make some very big decisions is not true. When we got to that first-grade
classroom, my friends and I, we were told: you can't speak Spanish. That was
crazy, of course, and we all raised our hands, saying *seguro que sí,* "we can,
yes." But no: Spanish is bad, don't speak it here. "Bad" was perhaps an unfortunate word choice, but this was a strange time in educational history,
and I believe that hearts were in the right place, even if methods weren't.
We got swats for speaking Spanish, even on the playground. As children, we
had a choice right then. One gets swatted for doing something bad—
certainly our parents had taught us that. So if we got swatted for speaking
Spanish, Spanish must be bad. This was the bargain, and here was the other
side: what we saw when we got to that first-grade classroom was clay, black-
boards, cubbyholes, fingerpaints, kickballs that weren't flat. And when we
got home that day, we looked around—and didn't see any of that stuff. The
decision was easy. We knew what we wanted. And if learning English was
going to do it, we weren't dumb, we could go along.

But we learned something else in the bargain of these games. If we   11
spoke Spanish and got swatted for that, Spanish was bad. Okay. We, then,
must be bad kids. So. And our parents still spoke Spanish, our grandparents,
and everyone. They, then, must be bad people. This was easy enough; we
learned to be ashamed of them. We loved them, but we knew the truth. We
had no PTA meetings—none of us ever took notes home. By the time I was
in junior high school and the beginning of high school, I could no longer
speak Spanish—which is to say, I didn't want to, I was embarrassed, and I
didn't practice. Not until my later years of high school and college did I relearn Spanish, but that is what I had to do, relearn. It was more than words.

Things have changed since then. I know they have in my hometown. But   12
here is a poem about that time, when I couldn't, or wouldn't, speak Spanish.

I was still going to my grandmother's house once a week at least for   13
lunch, always meatballs with mint from the garden, and she did not then and
still does not speak English. What we had to do, essentially, is invent for ourselves, so that neither one of us would suffer, a third language, one that was
all our own. Pablo Neruda spoke often about this. We came up with something many will understand. It was simple and it worked. Our language was
this, the language of grandmother and grandson: she would cook and I
would eat. In this way, with love, we talked. The poem is "Nani," our name,
as grandchildren, for her—different from the Refugio, or Doña Cuca, or la
Señora de Rios, that older people used.

> Sitting at her table, she serves
> the sopa de arroz to me
> instinctively, and I watch her,

the absolute *mamá,* and eat words
I might have had to say more
out of embarrassment. To speak,
now-foreign words I used to speak,
too, dribble down her mouth as she serves
me *albóndigas.* No more
than a third are easy to me.
By the stove she does something with words
and looks at me only with her
back. I am full. I tell her
I taste the mint, and watch her speak
smiles at the stove. All my words
make her smile. Nani never serves
herself, she only watches me
with her skin, her hair. I ask for more.

I watch the *mamá* warming more
tortillas for me. I watch her
fingers in the flame for me.
Near her mouth, I see a wrinkle speak
of a man whose body serves
the ants like she serves me, then more words
from more wrinkles about children, words
about this and that, flowing more
easily from these other mouths. Each serves
as a tremendous string around her,
holding her together. They speak
Nani was this and that to me
and I wonder just how much of me
will die with her, what were the words
I could have been, was. Her insides speak
through a hundred wrinkles, now, more
than she can bear, steel around her,
shouting, then, What is this thing she serves?

She asks if I want more.
I own no words to stop her.
Even before I speak, she serves.

3

    I wrote the poem in the early 1970s, and by the late 1970s I was doing   14
a good deal of work in the Arizona Artists-in-Education Program, traveling

all over the state. As an offshoot and partner to that program, founding the Central Arizona College Community Writing Project, in 1980 I did a week-long residency in Florence, a small town in the middle of the state, not un-like my hometown.

I did the residency as I normally do, giving students a range of exer-   15
cises, interchange, anecdote. On Friday I read some works of my own, a number of poems, beginning with "Nani" and the story of its making. The event passed simply enough.

The next year I did a second residency in Florence. Friday came and I   16
had decided to again read some of my own work. I jokingly asked if anyone had any requests. A young Mexican girl in the back of the class who had not said a word all week raised her hand.

"Yes?"   17

"Read the poem you read last year, the one about your grandmother,   18
Nani."

In one sentence she remembered that I had been to the school before,   19
remembered the subject matter of a poem, and remembered its title. Flo-rence, Arizona. A Friday. Hot outside, late September just after my birthday, with the sounds of setting up for a football game later that evening. *I could not remember her name.*

4

"Nani" is not the first poem I wrote, nor the best. But it is the first im-   20
portant one in that the words were important to someone else, this before other things. Someone like me, in a town like mine, a place where no one came to talk about writing poems and what literature could be. I had writ-ten, in essence, the first poem to myself.

I would not learn these things about the poem until many years   21
later, of course, not learn that it was a breakthrough poem until long after, when it was no longer breaking through. Yet I knew it was different when I wrote it: more work, more than I had done on anything up to that point. And it came from the inside, the new book. The work was on things I knew, so it wasn't a real kind of work at all. It was, instead, if not a game, a kind of earnest demand, finally, from somewhere inside. I had a story, a real story, for the first time, no fooling around, and I wanted someone else to know it, and sonofagun best of all there it was in front of me all the time. And wasn't this easy, and wasn't life good once again now that I'd found the answer?

Except that it didn't work, not right away and not like I expected. I   22
could not be accurate in the telling. I would have had to include everything. Instead I had to opt for the truth, for a kind of freedom in the telling, for a

kind of selective vision that was mine only, had to leave out and shore up, simplify and shine up. I could not have had a better introduction to the Muse if I had shaken hands.

And so I wrote, and with the freedom of this new writing went on to a companion sestina about my grandfather, whom I had never met, and another about great-aunts. There was no stopping me now that I had found this new angle on truth. I had in fact found the way once again. And it *was,* after all, easy; it's just that it was hard.   23

I chose the sestina form because it was hard, and I'd just learned about it and this seemed the thing to match the new small epiphany I was going through. Well, and also, it was an assignment. The truth of the whole thing is that the best parts of the story—the realizations about the poem's importance, and all the rest—came well after the poem. But the poem carried those things in it, had a kind of prescience. A good thing to discover; it keeps one from having to invent things about the work.   24

I think too that the sestina came as a kind of car to me. I became a writer because I could do it, if I may simplify. My brother could fix cars, my father could do everything, my mother could be a nurse and cook. They all came home greasy in their various ways. I had to find something, and took comfort in the kind of car a sestina was, could work at fixing its engine, polishing its fins, calling it a Dodge.   25

Sestina later began to mean simply working at a poem. But it was nice to call work something else, and to enjoy it. To find I had been doing it all along. To call it poetry. And I could find, though I tried, no other job where I could use those snags and bits, those things—"the cereal smell of urine"— that kept haunting me.   26

◆ ◆ ◆

FIRST RESPONSES

Has Rios confirmed or challenged your image of a poet? Do you think you would enjoy attending one of his poetry workshops?

TAKING A CLOSER LOOK

Exploring *Who:* Voice and Tone

1. Make a list of all of the words you can think of to describe the persona Rios uses in this essay—especially in his attitudes toward himself, his topic, and his readers.

2. What image of himself does Rios give in the two opening paragraphs? Why is it important for his readers to see his motivations at this stage of his life?

3. What is Rios's tone of voice at the end of paragraph 2, when he says, "At least in the beginning"? What did you think he meant by this remark when you first read the essay?

4. How does Rios feel about the people who made him stop speaking Spanish? Has his essay affected your feelings about bilingual education?

Exploring *What:* Content and Meaning

1. What was Rios's approach to college when he first arrived? Why did it work so well for him? How does what you learn about his pre-college education explain this approach?

2. ▣ *Using the Internet.* Exactly what about his creative writing classes caused Rios's life to change? Visit the Poet's Directory Web site (http://dir.yahoo.com/arts/humanities/literature/poetry/poets/). Select a poet, perhaps one you've read and enjoyed, and browse the site to gather information about influences on that poet's career. Do any seem similar to Rios's?

3. Why had Rios kept his attraction to language and writing secret before coming to college? From your experience, were his fears justified?

4. How many different **immediate** and **indirect** effects were there? How did being told that speaking Spanish was bad affect Rios's life?

Exploring *Why:* Purpose

1. What is the difference between school coming "at" a student and coming "from" a student (paragraph 5)? Have you had both kinds of educational experiences? What accounts for the differences?

2. How did Rios's own student days prepare him to work with the Arizona Artists-in-Education program?

3. Why does Rios tell us that he cannot remember the student's name who remembers his poem "Nani"? And why does he call this poem "the first poem to myself"?

4. Explain the **paradox,** "And it *was,* after all, easy; it's just that it was hard."

Exploring *How:* Style and Strategy

1. Read the last three sentences of paragraph 3. How would you describe the style of these sentences and the effect Rios hopes to have in writing in that style?
2. What **metaphor** does Rios use in paragraph 5 for his changed attitude toward education? Does it seem appropriate for the kind of change he experienced? How does paragraph 21 extend the meaning of that metaphor?
3. In the poem "Nani," Rios writes that smiles and wrinkles "speak," skin and hair "watch," and backs "look." How does this help you define Rios's term "the language of the grandmother and grandson"?
4. How does "selective vision" offer Rios "a kind of freedom in the telling" in his poetry? Does this help you to understand the organization of this essay?
5. Explain how thinking of a sestina as a kind of car allows Rios to understand his place in the world.

IDEAS FOR WRITING CAUSE AND EFFECT

1. Write an essay tracing the most significant influences on your decision to pursue your current career path. Consider narrating specific experiences that illustrate these influences.
2. Write an essay identifying the sources of your greatest strengths and challenges as a writer. Consider specific classes you took, assignments you wrote, and the teachers you had.
3. What experiences—with teachers, librarians, family, friends—shaped the kind of reader you are and the kind of reading you most enjoy?

◆ ◆ ◆ PREPARING TO READ

What was your favorite story when you were very little? Try to remember everything you can about reading or being read the story—the place, the people, the feelings. What was your favorite part of the story?

◆ ◆ ◆

The Most Human Art:
Ten Reasons Why We'll Always
Need a Good Story

SCOTT RUSSELL SANDERS

In addition to teaching college English, Scott Russell Sanders has an active career as a freelance journalist with magazines such as *Audubon,* the *Utne Reader,* and the *Georgia Review.* As a regionalist, he explores everyday life in search of meaningful connections between individual well-being and the common good. In addition to essay collections, which include *Staying Put: Making a Home in a Restless World* (1994) and *Writing from the Center* (1995), Sanders writes children's books, such as his recent *A Place Called Freedom* (1997), a 19th–century pioneer story.

We have been telling stories to one another for a long time, perhaps 1
for as long as we have been using language, and we have been using language, I suspect, for as long as we have been human. In all its guises, from words spoken and written to pictures and musical notes and mathematical symbols, language is our distinguishing gift, our hallmark as a species.

We delight in stories, first of all, because they are a playground for lan- 2
guage, an arena for exercising this extraordinary power. The spells and enchantments that figure in so many titles remind us of the ambiguous potency in words, for creating or destroying, for binding or setting free. Italo Calvino, a wizard of storytelling, described literature as "a struggle to escape from the confines of language; it stretches out from the utmost limits of what can be said; what stirs literature is the call and attraction of what is not in the dictionary." Calvino's remark holds true, I believe, not just for the highfalutin modes we label as literature, but for every effort to make sense of our lives through narrative.

Second, stories create community. They link teller to listeners, and   3
listeners to one another. This is obviously so when speaker and audience
share the same space, as humans have done for all but the last few centuries
of our million-year history; but it is equally if less obviously so in our literate age, when we encounter more of our stories in solitude, on page or
screen. When two people discover they have both read *Don Quixote,* they
immediately share a piece of history and become thereby less strange to
one another.

The strongest bonds are formed by sacred stories, which unite entire   4
peoples. Thus Jews rehearse the events of Passover; Christians tell of a
miraculous birth and death and resurrection; Buddhists tell of Gautama
meditating beneath a tree. As we know only too well, sacred stories may
also divide the world between those who are inside the circle and those who
are outside, a division that has inspired pogroms and inquisitions and wars.
There is danger in story, as in any great force. If the tales that captivate us
are silly or deceitful, like most of those offered by television and advertising, they waste our time and warp our desires. If they are cruel, they make
us callous. If they are false and bullying, instead of drawing us into a
thoughtful community they may lure us into an unthinking herd or, worst of
all, into a crowd screaming for blood—in which case we need other, truer
stories to renew our vision. So *The Diary of Anne Frank* is an antidote to
Mein Kampf. So Ralph Ellison's *Invisible Man* is an antidote to the paranoid yarns of the Ku Klux Klan. Just as stories may rescue us from loneliness, so, by speaking to us in private, they may rescue us from mobs.

This brings me to the third item on my list: Stories help us to see   5
through the eyes of other people. Here my list overlaps with one compiled
by Carol Bly, who argues in "Six Uses of Story" that the foremost gift from
stories is "experience of *other.*" For the duration of a story, children may
sense how it is to be old, and the elderly may recall how it is to be young;
men may try on the experiences of women, and women those of men.
Through stories, we reach across the rifts not only of gender and age, but
also of race and creed, geography and class, even the rifts between species
or between enemies.

Folktales and fables and myths often show humans talking and work-   6
ing with other animals, with trees, with rivers and stones, as if recalling or
envisioning a time of easy commerce among all beings. Helpful ducks and
cats and frogs, wise dragons, stolid oaks, all have lessons for us in these old
tales. Of course no storyteller can literally become hawk or pine, any more
than a man can become a woman; we cross those boundaries only imper-
fectly, through leaps of imagination. "Could a greater miracle take place
than for us to look through each other's eyes for an instant?" Thoreau asks.
We come nearer to achieving that miracle in stories than anywhere else.

A fourth power of stories is to show us the consequences of our actions. To act responsibly, we must be able to foresee where our actions might lead; and stories train our sight. They reveal the patterns of human conduct, from motive through action to result. Whether or not a story has a moral purpose, therefore, it cannot help but have a moral effect, for better or worse. 7

An Apache elder, quoted by the anthropologist Keith Basso, puts the case directly: "Stories go to work on you like arrows. Stories make you live right. Stories make you replace yourself." Stories do work on us, on our minds and hearts, showing us how we might act, who we might become, and why. 8

So we arrive at a fifth power of stories, which is to educate our desires. Instead of playing on our selfishness and fear, stories can give us images for what is truly worth seeking, worth having, worth doing. I mean here something more than the way fairy tales repeat our familiar longings. I mean the way *Huckleberry Finn* makes us want to be faithful, the way *Walden* makes us yearn to confront the essential facts of life. What stories at their best can do is lead our desires in new directions—away from greed, toward generosity; away from suspicion, toward sympathy; away from an obsession with material goods, toward a concern for spiritual goods. 9

One of the spiritual goods I cherish is the peace of being at home, in family and neighborhood and community and landscape. Much of what I know about becoming intimate with one's home ground I have learned from reading the testaments of individuals who have decided to stay put. The short list of my teachers would include Lao-tzu and Thoreau and Faulkner, Thomas Merton, Black Elk, Aldo Leopold, Rachel Carson, Gary Snyder, and Wendell Berry. Their work exemplifies the sixth power of stories, which is to help us dwell in place. 10

According to Eudora Welty, herself a deeply rooted storyteller, "the art that speaks most clearly, explicitly, directly, and passionately from its place of origin will remain the longest understood." So we return to the epic of Gilgamesh, with its brooding on the forests and rivers of Babylonia; we return to the ancient Hebrew accounts of a land flowing with milk and honey; we follow the Aboriginal songs of journeys over the continent of Australia—because they all convey a passionate knowledge of place. 11

Native American tribes ground their stories in nearby fields and rivers and mountains, and thus carry their places in mind. As the Pueblo travel in their homeland, according to Leslie Marmon Silko, they recall the stories that belong to each mesa and arroyo, and "thus the continuity and accuracy of the oral narratives are reinforced by the landscape—and the Pueblo interpretation of that landscape is *maintained.*" 12

Stories of place help us recognize that we belong to the earth, blood and brain and bone, and that we are kin to other creatures. Life has never 13 been easy, yet in every continent we find tales of a primordial garden, an era of harmony and bounty. In *A God Within,* René Dubos suggests that these old tales might be recollections "of a very distant past when certain groups of people had achieved biological fitness to their environment." Whether or not our ancestors ever lived in ecological balance, if we aspire to do so in the future, we must nourish the affectionate, imaginative bond between person and place.

Mention of past and future brings us to the seventh power of stories,   14
which is to help us dwell in time. I am thinking here not so much of the mechanical time parceled out by clocks as of historical and psychological time. History is public, a tale of influences and events that have shaped the present; the mind's time is private, a flow of memory and anticipation that continues, in eddies and rapids, for as long as we are conscious. Narrative orients us in both kinds of time, private and public, by linking before and after within the lives of characters and communities, by showing action leading on to action, moment to moment, beginning to middle to end.

Once again we come upon the tacit morality of stories, for moral   15
judgment relies, as narrative does, on a belief in cause and effect. Stories teach us that every gesture, every act, every choice we make sends ripples of influence into the future. Thus we hear that the caribou will only keep giving themselves to the hunter if the hunter kills them humbly and respectfully. We hear that all our deeds are recorded in some heavenly book, in the grain of the universe, in the mind of God, and that everything we sow we shall reap.

Stories gather experience into shapes we can hold and pass on   16
through time, much the way DNA molecules in our cells record genetic discoveries and pass them on. Until the invention of writing, the discoveries of the tribe were preserved and transmitted by storytellers, above all by elders. "Under hunter-gatherer conditions," Jared Diamond observes, "the knowledge possessed by even one person over the age of 70 could spell the difference between survival and starvation for a whole clan."

Aware of time passing, however, we mourn things passing away, and   17
we often fear the shape of things to come. Hence our need for the eighth power of stories, which is to help us deal with suffering, loss, and death. From the Psalms to the Sunday comics, many tales comfort the fearful and the grieving; they show the weak triumphing over the strong, love winning out over hatred, laughter defying misery. It is easy to dismiss this hopefulness as escapism, but as Italo Calvino reminds us, "For a prisoner, to escape has always been a good thing, and an individual escape can be a first necessary step toward a collective escape."

Those who have walked through the valley of the shadow of death tell   18
stories as a way of fending off despair. Thus Aleksandr Solzhenitsyn tells of

surviving the Soviet gulag; Toni Morrison recounts the anguish of planta-
tion life; Black Elk tells about the slaughter of the buffalo, the loss of his
Lakota homeland. Those of us who have not lived through horrors must still
face losing all that we love, including our own lives. Stories reek of our obsession with mortality. As the most enchanting first line of a tale is "once
upon a time," so the most comforting last line is "and they lived happily ever
after." This fairy-tale formula expresses a deep longing not only for happiness, but also for ever-afterness, for an assurance that life as well as happiness will endure, that it will survive all challenges, perhaps even the grave.
We feel the force of that longing, whether or not we believe that it can ever
be fulfilled.

The ninth item on my list is really a summation of all that I have said   19
thus far: Stories teach us how to be human. We are creatures of instinct, but
not solely of instinct. More than any other animal, we must *learn* how to
behave. In this perennial effort, as Ursula Le Guin says, "story is our nearest and dearest way of understanding our lives and finding our way on-
ward." Skill is knowing how to do something; wisdom is knowing when and
why to do it, or to refrain from doing it. While stories may display skill
aplenty, in technique or character or plot, what the best of them offer is wisdom. They hold a living reservoir of human possibilities, telling us what has
worked before, what has failed, where meaning and purpose and joy might
be found. At the heart of many tales is a test, a riddle, a problem to solve;
and that, surely, is the condition of our lives, both in detail—as we decide
how to act in the present moment—and in general, as we seek to understand what it all means. Like so many characters, we are lost in a dark wood,
a labyrinth, a swamp, and we need a trail of stories to show us the way back
to our true home.

Our ultimate home is the Creation, and anyone who pretends to com-   20
prehend this vast and intricate abode is either a lunatic or a liar. In spite of
all that we have learned through millennia of inquiry, we still dwell in mystery. Why there is a universe, why we are here, why there is life or consciousness at all, where if anywhere the whole show is headed—these are
questions for which we have no final answers. Not even the wisest of tales
can tell us. The wisest, in fact, acknowledge the wonder and mystery of Creation—and that is the tenth power of stories.

In the beginning, we say, *at the end of time,* we say, but we are only   21
guessing. "I think one should work into a story the idea of not being sure of
all things," Borges advised, "because that's the way reality is." The magic
and romance, the devils and divinities we imagine, are pale tokens of the
forces at play around us. The elegant, infinite details of the world's unfolding, the sheer existence of hand or tree or star, are more marvelous than
anything we can say about them.

A number of modern physicists have suggested that the more we learn   22
about the universe, the more it seems like an immense, sustained, infinitely
subtle flow of consciousness—the more it seems, in fact, like a grand story,
lavishly imagined and set moving. In scriptures we speak of God's thoughts
as if we could read them; but we read only by the dim light of a tricky brain on
a young planet near a middling star. Nonetheless, we need these cosmic narratives, however imperfect they may be, however filled with guesswork. So
long as they remain open to new vision, so long as they are filled with awe,
they give us hope of finding meaning within the great mystery.

◆ ◆ ◆

FIRST RESPONSES

Do you prefer stories that "dwell in mystery" or that try to fill in all
the details and answer all the questions? Why?

TAKING A CLOSER LOOK

Exploring *Who:* Voice and Tone

1. Would you like to have Sanders as a friend or neighbor? Why?
2. Sanders quotes a number of writers, past and present. How many did
   you recognize? Which of them might you want to look up and read
   based on their quotations?
3. From reading this essay, would you say that Sanders is an ecologist? A
   spiritual person?
4. How do you think these ten reasons affect Sanders when he sits down
   to tell his own stories?

Exploring *What:* Content and Meaning

1. Briefly and in your own words, list Sanders's ten reasons.
2. When are stories harmful? What standards help you to recognize such
   stories?
3. ◼ *Using the Internet.* Sanders's second reason, that "stories create
   community," is strongly supported by the amount of storytelling on
   the Internet. Visit the National Storytelling Association's Web site (at
   http://www.storynet.org/) to see the various activities of only one of
   the many groups keeping storytelling an active part of modern life.

How many of Sanders's other reasons appear to be part of the Association's goals?

4. What does Sanders mean in paragraph 19 when he says that the great stories provide "wisdom"? Where and how do you usually hear that word being used?

Exploring *Why:* Purpose

1. What kinds of human relationships does this essay encourage?
2. Has a story that you've read ever given you such a dramatic "experience of *other*" that it significantly changed your attitude toward that group or thing?
3. What does Sanders mean when he says stories "help us dwell in place"? Is there a story that captures how you feel about your favorite place?
4. How might a parent or a teacher or a librarian be helped by reading Sanders's essay? How about a counselor or minister?
5. Are you "comforted" by the line "and they lived happily ever after"? Why or why not?

Exploring *How:* Style and Strategy

1. What are the effects of using the terms "playground" and "arena" in paragraph 2? Do these words capture your feelings about either telling or hearing stories?
2. What does Sanders mean when he says that *"The Diary of Anne Frank* is an antidote to *Mein Kampf"?*
3. What does the DNA **analogy** in paragraph 16 help to explain?
4. As the title suggests, Sanders set out to give his readers ten reasons. What strategies does he use to help you keep track of those reasons? How does he avoid making it read like a simple list of points?

IDEAS FOR WRITING CAUSE AND EFFECT

1. Explain how a favorite book has affected the way you think and live.
2. Does your family or social group tell and even retell stories? Write an essay explaining the purposes these stories serve.
3. Write an essay developing a short list of reasons why your readers should or should not do something that is a common human activity—shop, watch television, listen to music, have pets. Focus on the effects the activity has on individuals as well as on society as a whole.

◆ FURTHER IDEAS FOR USING CAUSE AND EFFECT

1. What are the major challenges being experienced by your generation? Select one that you feel strongly about, and write an essay explaining what created the challenge and what immediate and indirect effects it is having on you and the people around you.

2. Discuss the effects of television portrayals of some group (men, women, parents, police officers, teenagers, doctors, etc.).

3. ▮▯ *Using the Internet.* Does playing video games shape values and personality? Is it an addiction or does it teach meaningful lessons and important skills? Brainstorm your own thinking on the topic and then gather other ideas by using a search engine to browse sites on the Internet—those where video games are advertised and played, as well as those where other points of view might be provided, such as sites created by Parent-Teacher Associations.

4. COLLABORATIVE WRITING. With a small group of classmates, discuss the following questions about your daily life: Why do you dress the way you do, eat the foods you do, and hope to live in a certain kind of neighborhood or house? What values do these habits or goals reflect? Next choose one or two of the values you identified during the discussion. Write an essay connecting the habits to the values and explaining the influences that created them.

5. COMBINING STRATEGIES. Write an essay narrating a major change in your life—a move to a new place, a friendship with someone very different from you, or a marriage, for example. Concentrate on how well or ill prepared you were to make the change, as well as how the change affected your life.

6. COMBINING STRATEGIES. Is there a special relationship you had with someone—a parent, a child, an aunt, a teacher, a coach—that significantly affected the person you are? Write an essay about the development of that effect by describing or narrating important interactions you had with this person.

CHAPTER 11

Strategies for Influencing Opinion

Argument

◆ ◆ ◆ ◆ ◆

Argumentation seeks to persuade readers to think and act in agreement with the writer's opinion.

◆ Arguments are organized according to the nature of the writer's material and purpose: point-by-point *for*, point-by-point *against*, point-by-point *refutation*, or *problem-solution*.

◆ Writers use strategies of all kinds to develop their points of argument: cause and effect, comparison and contrast, logical reasoning, description, narration, definition, and classification.

Persuasion is one of the most powerful uses of the written word. Think of a time when you chose to express yourself in a letter rather than having a conversation. We usually choose to express ourselves in writing when we want a chance to present our side of an issue carefully, with plenty of thought and control over what we have to say, with no unplanned interruptions from the other side. We also have a record of our thinking and proof of what we said—a major improvement over our slips of memory in recalling conversations, especially heated ones.

While these letters usually have an audience of one, the written **arguments** you compose in college and thereafter have a larger readership. The purpose is the same: to persuade others to consider your opinion on an issue and perhaps to take some action. Cookbook author Laurel Robertson used her forum to convince readers that regular bread-baking is worth the trouble. Student writer Sean Stangland, spurred to thoughts about human values by reading Robertson's essay, defended the source of his own ethical development—films. Notice that in neither case does the everyday connotation of *argument* apply: a negative, confrontational emotional tone is absent from both essays.

Bake Your Bread at Home

LAUREL ROBERTSON

Laurel Robertson became famous with her first down-to-earth vegetarian cookbook, *Laurel's Kitchen,* published in 1976. Her sensible advice about vegetarian cooking and nutrition is carried in "Notes from Laurel's Kitchen," a column published in more than twenty newspapers across the country. In *The Laurel's Kitchen Bread Book* (1984), Robertson combines recipes and detailed directions with brief essays on the art and science of bread-baking. The selection we reprint here is an excerpt from one of these thought-provoking essays.

Watch a four-year-old burst in the door after a long morning with his   1
buddies, still exultant, talking nonstop, but exhausted, too, from the sustained stress of it all. Watch him fall with instinctive good sense on a pile of play-dough, and pull, push, pummel and squeeze until finally all the tension has flowed out through his fingertips and he is at peace. Watch him, and wonder why on earth grownups shouldn't have access to the same very healing, very basic kind of activity. And in fact, they can. For kneading bread dough, forming it into coffee-cake wreaths or cottage loaves or long baguettes affords exactly this kind of satisfaction.

Good breadbaking is much more, though, than just a good outlet. At   2
certain critical junctures, you really have got to block out extraneous goings-on and attend meticulously to small details. Far from being onerous,

these more exacting phases of the baking process can also be the most calming—precisely because they do require such powerful concentration. And the very fact that so much of oneself is called upon, in the way of artistry and resourcefulness, makes the whole business that much more gratifying—enhances the quality of life overall.

That breadbaking—as well as gardening, spinning, beekeeping, and animal husbandry—is in fact creative and exacting is often overlooked. Instead, they are regarded as "subsistence skills"—what you have to deal with to scratch out a bare living, reeling, as you do, from the endless labor entailed. You can hardly blame our parents and grandparents for having set firmly behind them so rigorous and chancy a way of life, and for thinking a bit daft those of us who cast a rueful glance backwards. For it was with full, trusting, and grateful consent that people began to buy what they needed, use "convenience foods," and adopt a full complement of helpful household machines. Hardly a voice was raised in protest when our traditionally home-centered, small-scale system of food production gave way, little by little, to what has been called "the corporate cornucopia."   3

Today, though, there is good reason to question whether our present food system can be sustained—so profoundly dependent on petroleum is it, and so flagrantly wasteful of other resources as well. Good reason, too, to seek out more direct ways of meeting our food needs, and to breathe a little easier when you find them. This ease of mind is yet another source of satisfaction that comes of being a competent whole grains baker. Revival of what is, yes, a subsistence skill, means you know yourself able to turn just about any flour or grain that might come your way into something that will nourish and even delight. Knowing this, you feel that much less vulnerable to circumstance. It's a subtle change, but it goes deep.   4

Reinstate breadbaking as a home-based activity, and you begin to change the home, too. Once you have established a regular baking pattern and the people who live with you *know* that on, say, Tuesday evenings and Saturday mornings there will be fresh bread, and good smells, and you there, too, manifestly enjoying yourself, there begins to be more reason for *them* to be there as well. The place starts to exert its own gentle tug, a strong counterforce to the thousand-and-one pulls that would draw them out and away.   5

The creature comfort of a warm kitchen and people to chat with accounts only in part for this magnetic force. It's the baking itself: the artistry, the science, the occasional riddle of it. People of all ages, but particularly children, seem to draw immense satisfaction from hanging around a place where work is taken as seriously as we've come to take baking. We observed this when we first began the kitchen research that preceded *Laurel's Kitchen,* and had a chance to reaffirm it just last year, when we constructed the oven where our beloved "desem" bread is baked.   6

Building the oven, which extended along the top of an enormous fire- 7
place as part of a large new kitchen, was a formidable undertaking. It drew
in an architect, bricklayers, carpenters, a blacksmith, and several master
bakers. It also drew in every toddler in the vicinity. At every opportunity,
there they'd be, watching unblinking as each brick was laid in place and
each fitting was forged. My own son was among them and for months afterward, once the oven was working he would watch twice weekly with equal
fascination as the bread itself came out of the oven—loaf after round,
brown loaf sliding out on a wooden paddle we learned to call a "peel,"
caught in leather-gauntleted hands and then pitched onto racks to cool.
Back in his room later, he would re-enact the entire sequence, molding
loaves out of clay, using a spatula and my old driving gloves to unload the
"oven" he'd built out of wooden blocks.

Now, at four, Ramesh proudly brings in firewood for the baking—and 8
he's not likely to stop there. He is as crazy about the desem bread as we are,
and he's well aware how much care goes into its making. To him, a kitchen
is a place where unquestionably important things go on, and where everyone has a contribution to make. I'm profoundly glad he feels that way.

Much of what gives traditional communities their special character 9
and form has to do with the way they go about meeting basic life needs. In
the past, to get crops harvested, wheat ground, or a well dug and maintained, people had to come together in respectful cooperation, suspending
for the moment any private grievances they might be nursing. Often, they
even managed to get some fun out of what they were doing—enough, even,
to lay some of those grievances to rest. It was in the course of carrying out
all that work—the "bread labor" of which Leo Tolstoy was so enamored—
that the essential values of a particular society got hammered out and then
transmitted to the young people growing up and working in its midst.

Until quite recently, this has been true for families as well as commu- 10
nities. Just about everything people ate, wore, slept under, and sat on was
produced at home. Everyone took part in the producing and everyone
knew he or she was needed. It was in work carried out together that relationships deepened and values were handed on. Kitchens, gardens,
woodshops—workshops of any sort that aren't dominated by machines too
loud to talk over—are ideal places to exchange confidences as well as acquire skills. There's no more effective situation to impart "the way we do
things here" than in the throes of a specific job—no better place to show by
example the patience to see out a task, or the good humor and ingenuity to
set things right when they go awry.

In today's world, the home tends not to be as productive a place as it once 11
was. We take jobs elsewhere, earn money, buy things, and bring them home to
use. If we want our families to benefit from work undertaken together, we have

deliberately to set up situations where that can happen. A great many families are doing just that today, in a variety of ways. Breadbaking maybe, or a vegetable garden, the tasks assigned by age and skill. One family of friends maintains a cottage-scale spinning and weaving industry using wool from their goats. The proceeds from what they sell go into a college savings fund.

Still another friend, a single mother and full-time librarian, missing the fine, fresh milk of her native Scotland and feeling vaguely that something was missing in her admittedly hectic life, decided that what she and her teenaged daughter needed more than anything . . . was a cow. Skeptical friends like me have been chastened to observe that she may have been right. Having the common, and thoroughly endearing focal point of a soft-eyed Jersey cow, knowing that she's got to be milked no matter who's overslept or who has a cold, having to arrange for grain, and hay, and visits from the vet, actually has not stressed the relationship of mother and daughter to the breaking point or sent either of them into exhaustion. Rather, it seems to have compelled them to stay in closer touch than they would have otherwise, and they both find the outdoor work, the contact with the animal herself, to be a perfect restorative. Not for everyone, a cow, but it does illustrate the principle and makes a twice-weekly baking seem small potatoes by comparison!   12

◆ ◆ ◆

◆ ◆ ◆ Writer's Workshop 1 ◆ ◆ ◆
Responding to an Argument

Use the *Who, What, Why,* and *How* questions (see pp. 3–4) to explore your own understanding of the ideas and writing strategies employed by Laurel Robertson in "Bake Your Bread at Home." Your instructor may ask you to record these responses in a journal or bring them to class to use in small group discussions.

◆ WRITING FROM READING

Student writer Sean Stangland was caught up in the idea of how "the essential values of a particular society got hammered out and then transmitted to the young people growing up and working in its midst" when he read Robertson's essay. He began to think about how knowledge, wisdom, and values had been imparted to him. He realized that this process, for him, did not come from sharing work with his family, but from his absorption in movies. Sean brainstormed a list of films that had affected him in different ways and wrote some notes about each one of them. These notes became the following essay.

Sean Stangland
English 101
February 2, 1998

The Educational Value of Film

Picture this: The young boy pulls the drawer open,   1
looking for his favorite compact disc. He searches for
a while and finally finds it; there are a lot of CDs in
there. He reaches up to press the button marked
OPEN/CLOSE, and the CD tray shoots out with a
mechanical whir. The CD is placed carefully in the
tray, and the button is pressed again, sending the
shiny disc of music into the player. He cues up track
seven, his very favorite selection.

The piece is called "Eine Kleine Nachtmusik,"   2
which, when translated from German, means "A Little
Night Music." It is one of Wolfgang Amadeus Mozart's
most famous pieces of music. The child has no
background in German, nor do his parents force a love
for classical music upon him. This child loves the
movies, in fact, and the CD that contains this
particular version of "Eine Kleine Nachtmusik" is the
second volume of the soundtrack of *Amadeus,* the 1984
Academy Award winning film about the famed composer.

That kid was me. At age seven or eight, I had   3
earned an appreciation for classical music and even
had enough knowledge to tell someone what three words
in German could translate to. At this young age, I was
spellbound by Milos Forman's movie that told a tragic
story about one of the world's most heralded
composers, a child prodigy whose playful nature and
immature lifestyle led him to a young death. On the
surface, *Amadeus* appeared to be a stuffy costume
drama, something that no one but the haughtiest of

critics would want to watch. In reality, *Amadeus* is a
grand teaching tool, a work of art so wonderful that
it can open the eyes of even a seven-year-old.

My sisters and I used to watch Forman's movie two   4
or three times a week. We marveled at the period
costumes, the grand scale of the Austrian opera
houses, and the sheer power of Mozart's music. In a
time when most elementary school kids were listening
to Michael Jackson and watching *Diff'rent Strokes,* the
Stangland kids were absorbed in the music of a man who
had died two hundred years ago. *Amadeus* is the prime
example of how the movies are an educational tool, a
way of conveying ideas and facts that will captivate
and excite viewers everywhere.

As I got older and watched *Amadeus* more and more,   5
I took an active interest in Mozart's life. The
encyclopedia had plenty of information to offer, but
it also gave me a new perspective on the film. The
incredible story and music of Mozart became more real,
more tangible to me. I also discovered that the film's
opposition between Mozart and fellow composer Antonio
Salieri was pretty much an imaginative fiction on the
part of the filmmakers. I learned my first lesson about
"creative license."

Films based on historical fact are almost always a   6
valid teaching tool, whether the film is accurate or
not. When I first saw *Braveheart,* Mel Gibson's epic
about Scottish freedom fighter William Wallace, I
immediately went home and looked up his name in the
World Book. It turns out that Gibson and writer
Randall Wallace took a lot of license and created most
of the story off the tops of their heads. Very little
is known about the real William Wallace, but Gibson's
film will serve as a historical document for all. The
movie is full of passion, courage, and life, even
though it's all wrong. Still, the film conveyed the
horror of the battlefield and the frustration that
Scotland's people must have felt being under the
constant rule of the English King.

Of course, some movies are dead on in their   7
historical accounts, like Milos Forman's *The People
vs. Larry Flynt*. This movie about a pornographer's

struggle against society and the Reverend Jerry
Falwell was very accurate. The writers, Scott
Alexander and Larry Karaszewski, went so far as to
include the statement that Flynt's lawyer, Alan
Isaacman, made to the Supreme Court--with no Hollywood
alterations. The film teaches a lot about the way our
country works, a lot about freedom of expression in
the United States, and a fair amount about the rules
of libel and obscenity.

But such films are not the only ones with value.   8
Any movie can be of value, even something as
sophomoric and silly as John Landis's *Three Amigos!*,
starring Martin Short, Chevy Chase, and Steve Martin
as a band of would-be heroes in Mexico. How can a film
so stupid have value? Well, at one point, the villain,
El Guapo (Alfonso Arau), proclaims that he has a
"plethora of piñatas." "A plethora?" his sidekick
asks. When El Guapo explains that "plethora" means
"many," the viewer has learned a new word. Somehow,
that word has stuck with me forever since the first
time I saw that silly little film.

In fact, any time I hear an unfamiliar word in a   9
movie, I want to find out what it means. Nothing
bothers me more than not knowing what the characters
are talking about in a movie. This attention to
language and how it is used has benefited me today. I
truly believe that I would not be a good writer were
it not for my continued focus on film dialogue. I
remember the way that a sentence is structured, and
try to imitate that structure in my writing. Learning
new words and new techniques has improved all of my
scholastic abilities.

But most of all, films have taught me about people,   10
about the way the world works. A great film can portray
humanity at its finest, like *The Shawshank Redemption*
(directed by Frank Darabont). The hope and love
inside all humans have never been more powerfully
conveyed than in this film about the friendship
between two inmates at a Maine prison. *The Shawshank
Redemption* examines how humanity, at its best, never
gives up hope, never stops trying. Even in the worst
of times, when life is hardest, the human spirit can

go on, and I'd like to think that that's in all of us (especially in me).

Another such film is Steven Spielberg's *Schindler's List*, arguably the most powerful movie ever made. This story of a factory owner who defied Nazi Germany and worked tirelessly to save the lives of over a thousand Jews during World War II portrays the human race at both its best and its worst. Even in the face of the most terrible event in history, Oskar Schindler (Liam Neeson) was able to conquer tyranny and save lives that would have surely been lost without his help. *Schindler's List* is more a documentary than a movie; it is an honest, well-researched account of history and humanity. 11

So I think that everyone should sit down and enjoy a great movie with frequency. Parents should encourage their children to learn more about the people and events depicted in what they watch, and adults should never underestimate a child's ability to learn and to think. Films, like books, capture the raw emotion and experience of life and tell a story. Every story we take in, every line of dialogue we soak up, every powerful image that our eyes witness represents another memory, another lesson. The more we are exposed to, the more we will know about our world and our existence. The movies are more than a diversion, more than light entertainment; they are pieces of our lives. 12

◆ GETTING STARTED ON AN ARGUMENT

Since the whole point of an argument is to persuade, your starting point must be a belief, opinion, or idea that you hold strongly enough to want others to share it, and usually even to act on it. This is your thesis. Your paper will be more effective if your idea is controversial, but it doesn't have to be controversial in the usual sense, like the arguments for and against capital punishment. Both Laurel Robertson and Sean Stangland argue for activities that few people would come to harsh words over. However, for each one there is another side that gives the topic some dynamic tension: Robertson may be facing an audience who thinks that the time and effort involved in baking bread weekly is just not worthwhile; Sean may address readers who believe that immersing themselves (or their children) in movies is harmful or at least frivolous. Once you have decided on your main point, ask yourself, "What is the point of view on the other side?" Even if you never directly refer to the opposite point of view, the question will help you firm up your own.

One way to think of an idea for an argumentative essay is to look at your own life, the way Sean did when he read the bread-baking piece. He asked himself what had transmitted knowledge and values in his past, since it wasn't weekly bread baking with the family. Follow yourself through a normal week as though you were viewing a documentary about yourself. Your activities each day, from the most obvious to the smallest detail, reflect your beliefs about what is important and how your values are prioritized. One of these beliefs and values is probably worth supporting in a persuasive piece of writing. For example, what goods and services do you pay for rather than making them or doing them yourself, and vice versa? Why?

Sean started by making a list of films off the top of his head. Then he made notes on what he had learned from each one of them. As he wrote, he remembered more titles that would support his points—for example, thinking about the made-up elements of *Amadeus* brought to mind other films that had varying levels of historical accuracy and what he learned from that. When you start out with an idea, you don't need to have all your points firmly in mind to consider it a good topic for argument. You will discover more points as you play around with the idea, both on paper and in your mind as you go about your business. You might discuss your idea with other people, either with those who you know have a different point of view or with those who agree with you. If Sean had gotten stuck in the prewriting phase, he could have talked with his sisters, who obviously shared his love of movies, or his parents, who must have had their own reasons for letting their children become entranced by the silver screen.

◆ ORGANIZING AN ARGUMENT

Most arguments, no matter what the topic is, involve one or more points—sub-arguments that build up to prove the main idea. When you scribble down your ideas on your subject as they come into your mind, as you talk to other people, and as you do research, the ideas begin to congregate in groups that belong together logically. On your notes, use arrows and lassos to show which jottings seem to hang together. Sometimes you need to take a new piece of paper to re-organize your notes in a visibly sensible form. Laurel Robertson probably sat down while her bread was rising and listed all the benefits she could think of for baking your own bread. As she wrote, she probably noticed two clusters of ideas: one about how the activity benefits an individual and another about how it benefits a household or family. She used this **clustering** as a basis for organization. The micro- to macro-structure—from small to large concerns—is a common way to structure ideas. And, in fact, the continuation of Robertson's chapter, which we do not print here, takes up the political implications of domestic self-sufficiency.

Within each of the two clusters, individual and family, Robertson still had to decide an order for her sub-arguments. This part of her organization is more subtle, but if you look closely you can see that in both sections she works from fairly concrete points to larger, more abstract ideas:

INDIVIDUAL BENEFITS	FAMILY BENEFITS
Concrete: tension release of pounding dough	Concrete: human attraction of a warm, busy kitchen
Abstract: lack of dependence on "the corporate cornucopia"	Abstract: transmittal of values

You, too, can look at your notes and see whether you can organize them along some range, like small to big, concrete to abstract, trivial to important, or personal to global.

You will see the point-by-point organization that you see in Robertson's piece in other forms within this chapter. For example, while Robertson writes a series of points *for* a social activity, Jeanne Heaton provides a series of points *against* another one ("Tuning in Trouble"). David Cole ("Five Myths About Immigration") and Lindsy Van Gelder ("Marriage as a Restricted Club") define their points by envisioning what people on the other side would say and by talking back to them, organizing according to counter-argument or **refutation.** Finally, Arlie Hochschild ("Time for Change") and Gary Howard ("Whites in Multicultural Education") develop points on *both* sides of their issues to explain the pros and cons of a controversial topic; then they propose points of remedy, in a **problem-solution** structure. These four approaches constitute the primary ways to organize an argument essay:

- ◆ point-by-point *for*
- ◆ point-by-point *against*
- ◆ point-by-point *refutation*
- ◆ *problem-solution*

The student writer, Sean Stangland, also uses a point-by-point organization to defend movies as teaching tools. However, his structure proceeds film by film rather than benefit by benefit. An outline of his essay would include the headings *Amadeus, Braveheart, The People vs. Larry Flynt, Three Amigos!, The Shawshank Redemption,* and *Schindler's List.* Under each of these, he discusses the film's educational role in his life. This structure gives the essay a loose, conversational feel.

◆ DEVELOPING AN ARGUMENT

Within your argument, each point needs to be developed in order to be convincing. Laurel Robertson has some complex and abstract ideas, and she usually develops these in paragraphs of around 150 words, mostly following **cause-and-effect** reasoning. Look at paragraph 3, for example. The point is that bread baking, properly done, is not just a physical outlet for tension. After making this claim, Robertson anticipates the reader's question, "Why?" Well, pounding out the dough, which she describes as the physical release in paragraph 2, is not all there is. Several aspects of the process require mental focus and concentration, which calm by blocking out "extraneous goings-on." The cause-and-effect reasoning is that concentration leads to calm. The next development of the topic is also cause-and-effect: putting a great deal of oneself into a project leads to gratification, which leads to enhanced quality of life. Most readers can follow these lines of reasoning and agree. Robertson assumes knowledge of bread baking on the part of her readers. Otherwise, she would have to provide specific details about which parts of baking require concentration and artistry.

Sean Stangland, on the other hand, does not assume that his readers have seen the films he discusses. Therefore, in his development he needs to give us the relevant details and show how they contributed to his education. Each film is described briefly; the inclusion of writers' and directors' names helps establish Sean's credibility as a serious film fan. The main development tactic he uses is **exemplification,** with his own learning experiences from each film serving as arguments. By analogy, readers are encouraged to believe that all children would gather knowledge about history, creative license, public affairs, language, and human values from watching movies.

◆ OPENING AND CLOSING AN ARGUMENT

Both pieces we are analyzing here open with a *scene* to place the topic in a context. Robertson puts us in the kitchen with a group of enthusiasts; Stangland opens with a peek at a seven-year-old choosing his favorite CD, unexpectedly a classical composition by Mozart. These openings give the readers immediate visual images. One of our colleagues in composition says, "The first sentence should put a picture in the reader's mind." These openings do so. Robertson very quickly moves to her thesis, "the subtle, far-reaching, and distinctly positive changes that can take place when you begin to bake regularly. . . ." Sean develops his opening scene fully before coming to his thesis statement in paragraph 3: "the movies are an educational tool, a way of conveying ideas and facts that will captivate and excite viewers everywhere." He can get away with this delayed thesis because his first example is "the prime example" and begins to develop the argument in a clear direction before the thesis is stated.

Robertson closes her argument similarly, with a "prime example." Her conclusion takes a step back from the activity of bread baking in order to emphasize a broader point: the restorative nature of home production. In the same way, many experienced writers use the conclusion to suggest the larger implications or applications of the thesis. Sean Stangland's conclusion is much more traditional. He restates the main point and touches upon each of his arguments, in a summary. He also includes a conventional *call to action* by encouraging everyone to "sit down and enjoy a great movie with frequency."

◆ USING THE MODEL

Laurel Robertson and Sean Stangland both suggest ways of passing along knowledge and values that most people don't usually consider when they think about education. The fact that the two writers chose topics so remote from each other is proof that following a model does not result in a cookie-cutter similarity. It's hard to imagine Robertson tuning in *Die Hard* while waiting for her dough to rise, and Sean probably enjoys without guilt his mass-produced Ding-Dongs during a movie. Yet Stangland's chain of thought began when he considered how he received knowledge and values in his own life, a consideration that came from reading "Bake Your Bread at Home." Ask yourself where, outside of school, your own education took place. Was there an unusual or unexpected site of learning? Could you encourage others to think of this site as educational, as an essay topic?

◆ ◆ ◆ *Writer's Workshop II* ◆ ◆ ◆
Analyzing an Argument

Working individually or with a group of classmates, read through Sean Stangland's essay "The Educational Value of Film," and respond to the following questions.

1. Imagine how the essay would be different if Sean had organized it benefit by benefit instead of film by film. Make a scratch outline of how the essay would look. Would any changes in order be called for? For example, how would he arrange the topics along some range like small to large, minor to major, or concrete to abstract? Would the benefit-by-benefit structure be an improvement?

2. Did the title of the essay catch your interest? Did it capture the tone of the piece? Make up a title that would be more effective.

3. Were there enough examples to convince you of the main point? Did the essay make you think about examples from your own movie-watching experience? What tactics other than exemplification could you use to develop the thesis that films are learning tools? Review the previous chapter titles in this book to get ideas.

4. Stangland's essay does not deal with arguments on the other side— that is, it does not include *refutation.* What are some points against frequent movie-watching or against films as educational? If you were Sean, how would you argue back against these points? Where in the essay would you put your *refutation?*

◆ ◆ ◆ *Checklist for Reading and Writing* ◆ ◆ ◆ *Argument Essays*

1. Is the main point of the argument clear? Where is it stated? How directly is it stated?

2. Is there an identifiable plan of organization: point-by-point *for,* point-by-point *against,* or point-by-point *refutation?* Does the essay instead establish a problem and then argue for a solution (*problem-solution* structure)?

3. Is the argument convincing? What contributes to either agreement or disagreement with the author's main point? Have any important arguments been omitted? Have serious counter-arguments been refuted?

4. What strategies were used to develop the points? What other strategies could be used?

5. Who is the intended audience for this essay? Are the tone and approach appropriate for this audience?

◆ ◆ ◆ PREPARING TO READ

Many single people complain that our social world in the United States seems to be designed for couples. Have you ever noticed this arrangement? As you go about your business for the next couple of days, pay attention to places where coupledom seems to be the norm. Make lists of places where it seems all right to be alone or in same-sex pairs or groups and where it seems customary to be in traditional male-female couples.

◆ ◆ ◆

Marriage as a Restricted Club

LINDSY VAN GELDER

Lindsy Van Gelder (b. 1944) is an old hand at writing about controversial topics for various audiences: she has contributed to *Esquire, Rolling Stone,* the *Village Voice, Redbook,* and *Ms.,* where the selection we reprint here originally appeared. The daughter of a railroad freight agent and a receptionist, Van Gelder has worked as a UPI reporter, a TV news commentator, and a professor of journalism. Her articles and essays often make use of her personal experience to illuminate larger public issues.

Several years ago, I stopped going to weddings. In fact, I no longer celebrate the wedding anniversaries or engagements of friends, relatives, or anyone else, although I might wish them lifelong joy in their relationships. My explanation is that the next wedding I attend will be my own—to the woman I've loved and lived with for nearly six years. 1

Although I've been legally married to a man myself (and come close to marrying two others), I've come, in these last six years with Pamela, to see heterosexual marriage as very much a restricted club. (Nor is this likely to change in the near future, if one can judge by the recent clobbering of what was actually a rather tame proposal to recognize "domestic partnerships" in San Francisco.) Regardless of the *reason* people marry—whether to save on real estate taxes or qualify for married student housing or simply to express love—lesbians and gay men can't obtain the same results should they desire to do so. It seems apparent to me that few friends of Pamela's and mine would even join a club that excluded blacks, Jews, or women, much less assume that they could expect their black, Jewish, or female friends to toast their new status with champagne. But probably no other 2 stand of principle we've ever made in our lives has been so misunderstood, or caused so much bad feeling on both sides.

Several people have reacted with surprise to our views, it never having 3 occurred to them that gay people can't legally marry. (Why on earth did they think that none of us had bothered?) The most common reaction, however, is acute embarrassment, followed by a denial of our main point—that the about-to-be-wed person is embarking on a privileged status. (One friend of Pamela's insisted that lesbians are "lucky" not to have to agonize over whether or not to get married.) So wrapped in gauze is the institution of marriage, so ingrained the expectation that brides and grooms can enjoy the world's delighted approval, that it's hard for me not to feel put on the defensive for being so mean-spirited, eccentric, and/or politically rigid as to boycott such a happy event.

Another question we've fielded more than once (usually from our 4 most radical friends, both gay and straight) is why we'd want to get married in the first place. In fact, I have mixed feelings about registering my personal life with the state, but—and this seems to me to be the essence of radical politics—I'd prefer to be the one making the choice. And while feminists in recent years have rightly focused on puncturing the Schlaflyite myth of the legally protected homemaker, it's also true that marriage does confer some very real dollars-and-cents benefits. One example of inequity is our inability to file joint tax returns, although many couples, both gay and straight, go through periods when one partner in the relationship is unemployed or makes considerably less money than the other. At one time in our relationship, Pamela—who is a musician—was between bands and earning next to nothing. I was making a little over $37,000 a year as a newspaper reporter, a salary that put me in the 42 percent tax bracket—about $300 a week taken out of my paycheck. If we had been married, we could have filed a joint tax return and each paid taxes on half my salary, in the 25 or 30 percent bracket. The difference would have been nearly $100-a-week in our pockets.

Around the same time, Pamela suffered a months'-long illness which 5 would have been covered by my health insurance if she were my spouse. We were luckier than many; we could afford it. But on top of the worry and expense involved (and despite the fact that intellectually we believe in the ideal of free medical care for everyone), we found it almost impossible to avoid internalizing a sense of personal failure—the knowledge that *because of who we are, we can't take care of each other.* I've heard of other gay people whose lovers were deported because they couldn't marry them and enable them to become citizens; still others who were barred from intensive-care units where their lovers lay stricken because they weren't "immediate family."

I would never begrudge a straight friend who got married to save a 6 lover from deportation or staggering medical bills, but the truth is that I no longer sympathize with most of the less tangible justifications. This includes the oft-heard "for the sake of the children" argument, since (like many gay people, especially women) I *have* children, and I resent the implication that some families are more "legitimate" than others. (It's important to safeguard one's children's rights to their father's property, but a legal contract will do the same thing as marriage.)

But the single most painful and infuriating rationale for marriage, as   7
far as I'm concerned, is the one that goes: "We wanted to stand up and show the world that we've made a *genuine* commitment." When one is gay, such sentiments are labeled "flaunting." My lover and I almost never find ourselves in public settings outside the gay ghetto where we are (a) perceived to be a couple at all (people constantly ask us if we're sisters, although we look nothing like each other), and (b) valued as such. Usually we're forced to choose between being invisible and being despised. "Making a genuine commitment" in this milieu is like walking a highwire without a net—with most of the audience not even watching and a fair segment rooting for you to fall. A disproportionate number of gay couples do.

I think it's difficult for even my closest, most feminist straight women   8
friends to empathize with the intensity of my desire to be recognized as Pamela's partner. (In fact, it may be harder for feminists to understand than for others; I know that when I was straight, I often resented being viewed as one half of a couple. My struggle was for an independent identity, not the cojoined one I now crave.) But we are simply not considered *authentic,* and the reminders are constant. Recently at a party, a man I'd known for years spied me across the room and came over to me, arms outstretched, big happy-to-see-you grin on his face. Pamela had a gig that night and wasn't at the party; my friend's wife was there but in another room, and I hadn't seen her yet. "How's M——?" I asked the man. "Oh, she's fine," he replied, continuing to smile pleasantly. "Are you and Pam still together?"

Our sex life itself is against the law in many states, of course, and like   9
all lesbians and gay men, we are without many other rights, both large and small. (In Virginia, for instance, it's technically against the law for us to buy liquor.) But as a gay couple, we are also most likely to be labeled and discriminated against in those very settings that, for most heterosexual Americans, constitute the most relaxed and personal parts of life. Virtually every tiny public act of togetherness—from holding hands on the street to renting a hotel room to dancing—requires us constantly to risk humiliation (I think, for example, of the two California women who were recently thrown out of a restaurant that had special romantic tables for couples), sexual harassment (it's astonishing how many men can't resist coming on to a lesbian couple), and even physical assault. A great deal of energy goes into just expecting possible trouble. It's a process which, after six years, has become

second nature for me—but occasionally, when I'm in Provincetown or someplace else with a large lesbian population, I experience the *absence* of it as a feeling of virtual weightlessness.

What does all this have to do with my friends' weddings? Obviously, I   10 can't expect my friends to live my life. But I do think that lines are being drawn in this "profamily" Reagan era, and I have no choice about what side I'm placed on. My straight friends do, and at the very least, I expect them to acknowledge that. I certainly expect them to understand why I don't want to be among the rice-throwers and well-wishers at their weddings; beyond that, I would hope that they would commit themselves to fighting for my rights—preferably in personally visible ways, like marching in gay pride parades. But I also wish they wouldn't get married, period. And if that sounds hard-nosed, I hope I'm only proving my point—that not being able to marry isn't a minor issue.

Not that my life would likely be changed as the result of any individ-   11 ual straight person's symbolic refusal to marry. (Nor, for that matter, do all gay couples want to be wed.) But it's a political reality that heterosexual live-together couples are among our best tactical allies. The movement to repeal state sodomy laws has profited from the desire of straight people to keep the government out of *their* bedrooms. Similarly, it was a heterosexual New York woman who went to court several years ago to fight her landlord's demand that she either marry her live-in boyfriend or face eviction for violating a lease clause prohibiting "unrelated" tenants—and whose struggle led to the recent passage of a state rent law that had ramifications for thousands of gay couples, including Pamela and me.

The right wing has seized on "homosexual marriage" as its bottom-   12 line scare phrase in much the same way that "Would you want your sister to marry one?" was brandished twenty-five years ago. *They* see marriage as their turf. And so when I see feminists crossing into that territory of respectability and "sinlessness," I feel my buffer zone slipping away. I feel as though my friends are taking off their armbands, leaving me exposed.

◆ ◆ ◆

FIRST RESPONSES

Do you have any strong opinions that your close friends do not share? Do you identify with Van Gelder's reactions to such a disagreement? Are there ever times that your strong opinions set you apart in public—for example, asking that your companions eat at a restaurant that serves some vegetarian choices, or refusing to go into a strip club for a drink? What is this experience like? What is it like to be in the group that does not hold a strong opinion when one individual among you does?

TAKING A CLOSER LOOK

Exploring *Who:* Voice and Tone

1. What personal experiences does Van Gelder draw on in her argument? How might the essay be different if she did not identify herself as a lesbian in paragraph 1?
2. How do you think that Van Gelder's straight friends reacted when they read this essay? Did Van Gelder do anything to help them accept her arguments?
3. Was the essay successful in changing your attitude toward heterosexual marriage? Will it have any repercussions in your behavior? Why or why not?
4. Do you think you were able to read the essay objectively, or did your preconceived ideas lead you to agree or disagree from the beginning?

Exploring *What:* Content and Meaning

1. What benefits does marriage confer on heterosexual couples?
2. What social, psychological, and legal drawbacks does Van Gelder find in being in a lesbian couple?
3. What image is Van Gelder trying *not* to project in her argument? Why does she want to avoid this image?
4. Van Gelder refers to the question, "Would you want your sister to marry one?" from twenty-five years ago. What does she mean? What is the question's relationship to the topic of this essay?
5. What are the "armbands" that the marrying friends seem to be taking off (paragraph 12)?

Exploring *Why:* Purpose

1. *Using the Internet.* If this essay had a call to action, what would it be? Could there be more than one call to action possible? Use the Internet to explore the topic of same-sex marriage. Try to find out what actions, if any, are being taken by advocates and opponents.
2. What are Van Gelder's reasons for wanting to marry? Which reason is most compelling for her? Which reason is most convincing to you?

3. This essay appeared in *Ms.* magazine. If Van Gelder had wanted to write an essay with the same purpose for *Esquire* or *Newsweek* or *USA Today,* how might it be different?

Exploring *How:* Style and Strategy

1. What is the analogy used to support the thesis in paragraph 2? What similarity is the basis of the analogy?
2. "Several years ago, I stopped going to weddings." How does this short opening sentence serve to grab your attention?
3. Find examples of the following development techniques: statistics, examples, comparison/contrast, and logical reasoning. Which technique is used most often in the essay?
4. The writer uses "I" and "we" and contractions *(can't, it's, we've),* usually signs of informality. Why do you think she chose this informal level? In what situation do you think she would have chosen a more formal style? What about an even less formal style?

WRITING FROM READING ASSIGNMENT

"Marriage as a Restricted Club" explains why the author refuses to celebrate weddings and anniversaries, even among her friends. In this writing assignment, you will write about some principle you hold strongly enough to deny yourself a pleasure or to set you apart from your group of friends. For example, you may be a vegetarian among meat-eaters, or you may take the letter of the law very seriously and refuse to engage in even minor infractions, or you may be more scrupulously honest or hardworking or religious or studious than your friends are. You may be more cautious with money or more generous in your spending than the norm, or you may be more accepting or limiting about choosing members of your social group. (If you cannot think of a way you are set apart by your principles, ask your friends for ideas. You may finally have to write about someone else instead of yourself, in which case you will have to interview the other person extensively.)

A. Begin by writing a sentence expressing the principle (or set of related principles) you hold strongly.
B. Brainstorm about various situations when acting on your principle made your difference from other people obvious. Do additional freewriting about each situation so that you will be able to develop it with details if you decide to use it in your essay.

C. List as many reasons as you can, explaining why you stick to your principle. As you make the list, some of the reasons will go together or overlap. Draw lines and lassos to show which ones belong together. Put a star by the reason that you consider most important.

D. Van Gelder explains many drawbacks to being different. List the drawbacks you have noticed related to your own difference. Van Gelder discusses social, psychological, and legal drawbacks, and you may find some structure like this for your list. If possible, connect the drawbacks to the situations you brainstormed in step B.

E. Van Gelder also provides the advantages that come to people who are in the mainstream. What benefits are enjoyed by those who don't hold your principle strongly? What benefits would you get if you compromised your principle? Jot down these ideas and connect these to concrete situations from step B as well.

F. You now have several sheets of prewriting material including reasons, situations, drawbacks, and advantages and their interrelationships. The next step is to organize these into a point-by-point structure. For example, you could decide on a paragraph that describes one of the drawbacks of your different stance, compares and contrasts it with the advantages of the mainstream stance, gives an example from your experience to develop the point, and explains the reason why you stick to your principle. Put together four or five of these "packages" of points and related evidence, and write the body paragraphs from the "packages."

G. Choose an order for the paragraphs you have written. As we have noted earlier, usually you can organize them along some range of values, like least to most important, concrete to abstract, or personal to political.

H. Begin your essay with a short, arresting sentence that forces your readers to ask, "Why?" as Van Gelder does.

I. Close your essay by reflecting on how you feel when you see your friends ignoring the principle that you hold dear. Review Van Gelder's closing for an example.

◆ ◆ ◆ PREPARING TO READ

Do you think daytime television talk shows are helpful, harmful, or just silly? In the next few days, watch a daytime talk show and talk with friends who watch them regularly to help you evaluate the following essay.

◆ ◆ ◆

Tuning in Trouble: Talk TV's Destructive Impact on Mental Health

JEANNE A. HEATON

Jeanne A. Heaton is a psychologist and a professor of guidance and counseling at Ohio University. The essay we reprint here is an excerpt from a 1995 book of the same title. Heaton sees the proliferation of nationally syndicated daytime talk shows (more than twenty at last count) as a threat to the soundness of the audience's world view.

In 1967, *The Phil Donahue Show* aired in Dayton, Ohio, as a new day-   1
time talk alternative. Donahue did not offer the customary "women's fare." On Monday of his first week he interviewed atheist Madalyn Murray O'Hair. Tuesday he featured single men talking about what they looked for in women. Wednesday he showed a film of a baby being born from the obstetrician's point of view. Thursday he sat in a coffin and interviewed a funeral director. And on Friday he held up "Little Brother," an anatomically correct doll without his diaper. When Donahue asked viewers to call in response, phone lines jammed.

For eighteen years daytime talk *was* Donahue. His early guests re-   2
flected the issues of the time and included Ralph Nader on consumer rights, Bella Abzug on feminism, and Jerry Rubin on free speech. Never before had such socially and personally relevant issues been discussed in such a democratic way with daytime women viewers. But his most revolutionary contribution was in making the audience an integral part of the show's format. The women watching Donahue finally had a place in the conversation, and they were determined to be heard. The show provided useful

information and dialogue that had largely been unavailable to house-bound women, affording them the opportunity to voice their opinions about everything from politics to sex—and even the politics of sex.

No real competition emerged until 1985, when *The Oprah Winfrey Show* went national. Her appeal for more intimacy was a ratings winner. She did the same topics Donahue had done but with a more therapeutic tone. Donahue seemed driven to uncover and explore. Winfrey came to share and understand. In 1987, Winfrey's show surpassed Donahue's by being ranked among the top twenty syndicated shows. Phil and Oprah made it easier for those who followed; their successors were able to move much more quickly to the top.   3

At their best, the shows "treated the opinions of women of all classes, races, and educational levels as if they mattered," says Naomi Wolf in her book *Fire with Fire:* "That daily act of listening, whatever its shortcomings, made for a revolution in what women were willing to ask for; the shows daily conditioned otherwise unheard women into the belief that they were entitled to a voice." Both Donahue and Winfrey deserve enormous credit for providing a platform for the voices of so many who needed to be heard, and for raising the nation's consciousness on many important topics, including domestic violence, child abuse, and other crucial problems. But those pioneering days are over. As the number of shows increased and the ratings wars intensified, the manner in which issues are presented has changed. Shows now encourage conflict, name-calling, and fights. Producers set up underhanded tricks and secret revelations. Hosts instruct guests to reveal all. The more dramatic and bizarre the problems the better.   4

While more air time is given to the problems that women face, the topics are presented in ways that are not likely to yield change. The very same stereotypes that have plagued both women and men for centuries are in full force. Instead of encouraging changes in sex roles, the shows actually solidify them. Women viewers are given a constant supply of the worst images of men, all the way from garden-variety liars, cheats, and con artists to rapists and murderers.   5

If there is a man for every offense, there is certainly a woman for every trauma. Most women on talk TV are perpetual victims presented as having so little power that not only do they have to contend with real dangers such as sexual or physical abuse, but they are also overcome by bad hair, big thighs, and beautiful but predatory "other" women. The women of talk are almost always upset and in need. The bonding that occurs invariably centers around complaints about men or the worst stereotypes about women. In order to be a part of the "sisterhood," women are required to be angry with men and dissatisfied with themselves. We need look no further than at some of the program titles to recognize the message. Shows about   6 men bring us a steady stream of stalkers, adulterers, chauvinistic sons, abusive fathers, and men who won't commit to women.

The shows provide a forum for women to complain, confront, and cajole, but because there is never any change as a result of the letting loose, this supports the mistaken notion that women's complaints have "no weight," that the only power women have is to complain, and that they cannot effect real changes. By bringing on offensive male guests who do nothing but verify the grounds for complaint, the shows are reinforcing some self-defeating propositions. The idea that women should direct their energies toward men rather than look for solutions in themselves is portrayed daily. And even when the audience chastises such behavior, nothing changes, because only arguments and justifications follow.   7

On *The Jenny Jones Show* a woman was introduced as someone who no longer had sex with her husband because she saw him with a stripper. Viewers got to hear how the stripper "put her boobs in his face" and then kissed him. The husband predictably defended his actions: "At least I didn't tongue her." The next few minutes proceeded with insult upon insult, to which the audience "oohed" and "aahed" and applauded. To top it all off, viewers were informed that the offense in question occurred at the husband's birthday party, which his wife arranged, *stripper and all.* Then in the last few minutes a psychologist pointed out the couple weren't wearing rings and didn't seem committed. She suggested that their fighting might be related to some other problem. Her comments seemed reasonable enough until she suggested that the wife might really be trying to get her husband to rape her. That comment called up some of the most absurd and destructive ideas imaginable about male and female relationships—yet there was no explanation or discussion.   8

It is not that women and men don't find lots of ways to disappoint each other, or that some women and some men don't act and think like the women and men on the shows. The problem is talk TV's fixation on gender war, with endless portrayals of vicious acts, overboard retaliations, and outrageous justifications. As a result, viewers are pumped full of the ugliest, nastiest news from the front.   9

When issues affecting people of color are dealt with, the stereotypes about gender are layered on top of the stereotypes about race. Since most of the shows revolve around issues related to sex, violence, and relationships, they tend to feature people of color who reflect stereotypical images—in a steady stream of guests who have children out of wedlock, live on welfare, fight viciously, and have complicated unsolvable problems. While there are less than flattering depictions of white people on these shows, white viewers have the luxury of belonging to the dominant group, and therefore are more often presented in the media in positive ways.   10

On a *Ricki Lake* show about women who sleep with their friends' 11
boyfriends, the majority of the guests were African American and Hispanic
women who put on a flamboyant display of screaming and fighting. The pro-
fanity was so bad that many of the words had to be deleted. The segment
had to be stopped because one guest yanked another's wig off. For many
white viewers these are the images that form their beliefs about "minority"
populations.

The shows set themselves up as reliable sources of information about 12
what's really going on in the nation. And they often cover what sounds like
common problems with work, love, and sex, but the information presented
is skewed and confusing. Work problems become "fatal office feuds" and
"back-stabbing coworkers." Problems concerning love, sex, or romance become "marriage with a fourteen-year-old," "women in love with the men
who shoot them," or "man-stealing sisters." TV talk shows suggest that
"marrying a rapist" or having a "defiant teen" are catastrophes about to
happen to everyone.

Day in and day out, the shows parade all the myriad traumas, betray- 13
als, and afflictions that could possibly befall us. They suggest that certain issues are more common than they actually are, and embellish the symptoms
and outcomes. In actuality, relatively few people are likely to be abducted as
children, join a Satanic cult in adolescence, fall in love with serial rapists,
marry their cousins, hate their own race, or get sex changes in midlife, but
when presented over and over again the suggestion is that they are quite
likely to occur.

With their incessant focus on individual problems, television talk 14
shows are a major contributor to the recent trend of elevating personal concerns to the level of personal rights and then affording those "rights" more
attention than their accompanying responsibilities. Guests are brought on
who have committed villainous acts (most often against other guests). The
host and audience gratuitously "confront" the offenders about their wrong-
doing and responsibilities. The alleged offenders almost always refute their
accountability with revelations that they too were "victimized." On *Sally
Jessy Raphael,* a man appeared with roses for the daughter he had sexually
molested. He then revealed that he had been molested when he was five,
and summed it up with "I'm on this show too! I need help, I'll go through
therapy."

His sudden turnabout was not unusual. Viewers rarely see guests 15
admit error early in the show, but a reversal often occurs with just a few
minutes remaining. This works well for the shows because they need the
conflict to move steadily to a crescendo before the final "go to therapy" res-
olution. But before that viewers are treated to lots of conflict and a heavy
dose of pseudo-psychological explanations that are really nothing more

than excuses, and often lame ones at that. The guests present their problems, the hosts encourage them to do so with concerned questions and occasional self-disclosures, and the audience frequently gets in on the act with their own testimonies. Anything and everything goes.

The reigning motto is "Secrets keep you sick." On a *Jerry Springer*   16 show about confronting secrets, a husband revealed to his wife that he had been having an affair. Not only was the unsuspecting wife humiliated and speechless, but Springer upped the ante by bringing out the mistress, who kissed the husband and informed the wife that she loved them both. Conflict predictably ensued, and viewers were told this was a good idea because now the problem was out in the open. When Ricki Lake did a similar show, a man explained to his very surprised roommate that he had "finally" informed the roommate's mother that her son was gay, a secret the roommate had been hiding from his family.

Referring to these premeditated catastrophes as simply "disclosures"   17 softens their edges and affords them a kind of legitimacy they do not deserve. On a program about bigamy, Sally Jessy Raphael invited two women who had been married to the same man at the same time to appear on the show. The man was also on, via satellite and in disguise. His nineteen-year-old daughter by one of the wives sat on the stage while these women and her father tore each other apart. Sally and the audience encouraged the fight with "oohs" and "aahs" and rounds of applause at the ever-increasing accusations. A "relationship therapist" was brought on to do the postmortem. Her most notable warning was that all this turmoil could turn the daughter "to women," presumably meaning that she could become a lesbian. The scenario was almost too absurd for words, but it was just one more show like so many others: founded on stereotypes and capped off with clichés. From the "catfight" to the "no-good father" to archaic explanations of homosexuality— cheap thrills and bad advice are dressed up like information and expertise.

These scenarios are often legitimized by the use of pseudo-psychologi-   18 cal explanations, otherwise known as psychobabble. This is regularly used as a "disclaimer," or as a prelude to nasty revelations, or as a new and more sophisticated way of reinforcing old stereotypes: "men are cognitive, not emotional," or "abused women draw abusive men to them." This not only leaves viewers with nothing more than platitudes to explain problems and clichés to resolve them, but it fails to offer guests with enormous conflicts and long histories of resentment and betrayals practical methods for changing their circumstances. The "four steps to get rid of your anger" may sound easy enough to implement, but what this kind of ready-made solution fails to acknowledge is that not all anger is the same, and certainly not everyone's anger needs the same treatment. Sometimes anger is a signal to people that they are being hurt, exploited, or taken advantage of, and it can motivate change.

Rather than encouraging discussion, exploration, or further under-   19
standing, psychobabble shuts it off. With only a phrase or two, we can believe that we understand all the related "issues." Guests confess that they
are "codependents" or "enablers." Hosts encourage "healing," "empowerment," and "reclaiming of the inner spirit." In turn, viewers can nod know-
ingly without really knowing at all.

Talk TV initially had great potential as a vehicle for disseminating ac-   20
curate information and as a forum for public debate, although it would be
hard to know it from what currently remains. Because most of these talk
shows have come to rely on sensational entertainment as the means of increasing ratings, their potential has been lost. We are left with cheap shots,
cheap thrills, and sound-bite stereotypes. Taken on its own, this combination
is troubling enough, but when considered against the original opportunity
for positive outcomes, what talk TV delivers is truly disturbing.

◆ ◆ ◆

FIRST RESPONSES

Have you witnessed any of the negative effects Heaton warns of
among people you know, including yourself? If so, describe the effects. If
not, why not?

TAKING A CLOSER LOOK

Exploring *Who:* Voice and Tone

1. What is the tone of the essay—that is, what emotion does the writer
   convey?
2. What can you infer about Heaton's attitude toward television?
3. What tone do you usually hear when people discuss daytime talk
   shows?
4. Did the author's attitude change your own? Do you view the issue
   more seriously than you did before?

Exploring *What:* Content and Meaning

1. According to Heaton, what are the positive contributions of TV talk
   shows such as those hosted by Oprah Winfrey and Phil Donahue?
2. List Heaton's main points against daytime TV talk shows.

3. What stereotypes does the writer accuse today's talk shows of reinforcing? Did you see this reinforcement when you watched a sample show?

4. When Heaton writes that the shows emphasize individual problems but not individual responsibilities, what does she mean? Was there an example on the show you watched?

5. What is the difference between "psychobabble" and psychological explanations? Why do the talk shows lean toward psychobabble? Why is this damaging to audiences?

6. What danger lies in overestimating the frequency of common problems (paragraphs 12 and 13)? Do you know people who overestimate the risk of getting robbed, experiencing violence, or being cheated? What is the source of their overestimation?

Exploring *Why:* Purpose

1. Was this essay written to persuade fans of daytime talk shows? What evidence did you see to decide your answer?

2. If the author had included a direct call to action, what might it be?

3. Was the point suggested by the title—that daytime talk shows destroy mental health—proven in this selection?

4. What do you know about the author? How does her profession affect her goals and intentions in writing about talk shows?

Exploring *How:* Style and Strategy

1. Given the title, were you surprised by the first three paragraphs? How do these three paragraphs affect the way you read the rest of the piece?

2. What are the two main types of supporting evidence used? What other types of evidence would be persuasive?

3. Identify two or three places where Heaton uses strong, emotional language. If her editor asked her to tone down her word choice, how could she defend its vividness?

4. If you were writing a critique of the daytime talk show you recently watched, which of Heaton's main points would you follow? What points would you add and develop that are not covered in Heaton's essay?

IDEAS FOR WRITING AN ARGUMENT

1. Choose some other form of media, communication, or art that once served a positive purpose or had promise (e.g., cartoons, music videos, rap music, call-in radio, political comics, public access TV, performance art, comedy clubs, Internet chat rooms). Argue that it went downhill instead of fulfilling its early potential.

2. ▪▫ *Using the Internet.* Defend your favorite talk show. To gather specific information and help develop your arguments, consult the show's Web page (most of them have one), or look at The Talkshow Page (http://www.eden.com/~johnny/letstalk.html), which has links to all the major talk shows.

3. Defend some other type of TV show that often comes under negative criticism (sitcoms, soap operas, sports coverage, MTV, etc.).

4. Write about a course, seminar, or workshop you have attended that looked educational, helpful, and inviting, but ultimately conveyed negative or disappointing messages.

◆ ◆ ◆ PREPARING TO READ

Do you know the history of how your forebears came to live in this country? Is it a family story that is told with pride, humor, sorrow, regret, or some other prevailing emotion? If you are not aware of your ancestors' immigration, why not?

◆ ◆ ◆

Five Myths About Immigration

DAVID COLE

David Cole is a graduate of Yale University and Yale Law School and is a professor of constitutional law. He frequently writes articles both for general audiences in newspapers like the *New York Times* and the *Washington Post* and for legal experts in journals such as *Legal Times* and the *Stanford Law Review*. The following essay appeared in the *Nation* in the fall of 1994.

For a brief period in the mid-nineteenth century, a new political move-   1
ment captured the passions of the American public. Fittingly labeled the "Know-Nothings," their unifying theme was nativism. They liked to call themselves "Native Americans," although they had no sympathy for people we call Native Americans today. And they pinned every problem in American society on immigrants. As one Know-Nothing wrote in 1856: "Four-fifths of the beggary and three-fifths of the crime spring from our foreign population; more than half the public charities, more than half the prisons and almshouses, more than half the police and the cost of administering criminal justice are for foreigners."

At the time, the greatest influx of immigrants was from Ireland, where   2
the potato famine had struck, and Germany, which was in political and economic turmoil. Anti-alien and anti-Catholic sentiments were the order of the day, especially in New York and Massachusetts, which received the brunt of the wave of immigrants, many of whom were dirt-poor and uneducated. Politicians were quick to exploit the sentiment: There's nothing like a scapegoat to forge an alliance.

I am especially sensitive to this history: My forebears were among   3
those dirt-poor Irish Catholics who arrived in the 1860s. Fortunately for them, and me, the Know-Nothing movement fizzled within fifteen years.

But its pilot light kept burning, and is turned up whenever the American public begins to feel vulnerable and in need of an enemy.

Although they go by different names today, the Know-Nothings have 4 returned. As in the 1850s, the movement is strongest where immigrants are most concentrated: California and Florida. The objects of prejudice are of course no longer Irish Catholics and Germans; 140 years later "they" have become "us." The new "they"—because it seems "we" must always have a "they"—are Latin Americans (most recently, Cubans), Haitians, and Arab-Americans, among others.

But just as in the 1850s, passion, misinformation, and short-sighted 5 fear often substitute for reason, fairness, and human dignity in today's immigration debates. In the interest of advancing beyond know-nothingism, let's look at five current myths that distort public debate and government policy relating to immigrants.

§ *America is being overrun with immigrants.* In one sense, of course, this 6 is true, but in that sense it has been true since Christopher Columbus arrived. Except for the real Native Americans, we are a nation of immigrants.

It is not true, however, that the first-generation immigrant share of our 7 population is growing. As of 1990, foreign-born people made up only 8 percent of the population, as compared with a figure of about 15 percent from 1870 to 1920. Between 70 and 80 percent of those who immigrate every year are refugees or immediate relatives of U.S. citizens.

Much of the anti-immigrant fervor is directed against the undocu- 8 mented, but they make up only 13 percent of all immigrants residing in the United States, and only 1 percent of the American population. Contrary to popular belief, most such aliens do not cross the border illegally but enter legally and remain after their student or visitor visa expires. Thus, building a wall at the border, no matter how high, will not solve the problem.

§ *Immigrants take jobs from U.S. citizens.* There is virtually no evi- 9 dence to support this view, probably the most wide-spread misunderstanding about immigrants. As documented by a 1994 ACLU Immigrants' Rights Project report, numerous studies have found that immigrants actually create more jobs than they fill. The jobs immigrants take are of course easier to see, but immigrants are often highly productive, run their own businesses, and employ both immigrants and citizens. One study found that Mexican immigration to Los Angeles County between 1970 and 1980 was responsible for 78,000 new jobs. Governor Mario Cuomo reports that immigrants own more than 40,000 companies in New York, which provide thousands of jobs and $3.5 billion to the state's economy every year.

§ *Immigrants are a drain on society's resources.* This claim fuels many 10 of the recent efforts to cut off government benefits to immigrants. However, most studies have found that immigrants are a net benefit to the economy because, as a 1994 Urban Institute report concludes, "immigrants generate significantly more in taxes paid than they cost in services received." The Council of Economic Advisers similarly found in 1986 that "immigrants have a favorable effect on the overall standard of living."

Anti-immigrant advocates often cite studies purportedly showing the   11
contrary, but these generally focus only on taxes and services at the local or state level. What they fail to explain is that because most taxes go to the federal government, such studies would also show a net loss when applied to U.S. citizens. At most, such figures suggest that some redistribution of federal and state monies may be appropriate; they say nothing unique about the costs of immigrants.

Some subgroups of immigrants plainly impose a net cost in the short   12
run, principally those who have most recently arrived and have not yet "made it." California, for example, bears substantial costs for its disproportionately large undocumented population, largely because it has on average the poorest and least educated immigrants. But that has been true of every wave of immigrants that has ever reached our shores; it was as true of the Irish in the 1850s, for example, as it is of Salvadorans today. From a long-term perspective, the economic advantages of immigration are undeniable.

Some have suggested that we might save money and diminish incen-   13
tives to immigrate illegally if we denied undocumented aliens public services. In fact, undocumented immigrants are already ineligible for most social programs, with the exception of education for schoolchildren, which is constitutionally required, and benefits directly related to health and safety, such as emergency medical care and nutritional assistance to poor women, infants and children. To deny such basic care to people in need, apart from being inhumanly callous, would probably cost us more in the long run by exacerbating health problems that we would eventually have to address.

§ *Aliens refuse to assimilate, and are depriving us of our cultural and*   14
political unity. This claim has been made about every new group of immigrants to arrive on U.S. shores. Supreme Court Justice Stephen Field wrote in 1884 that the Chinese "have remained among us a separate people, retaining their original peculiarities of dress, manners, habits, and modes of living, which are as marked as their complexion and language." Five years later, he upheld the racially based exclusion of Chinese immigrants. Similar claims have been made over different periods of our history about Catholics, Jews, Italians, Eastern Europeans and Latin Americans.

In most instances, such claims are simply not true; "American culture"   15
has been created, defined, and revised by persons who for the most part are descended from immigrants once seen as anti-assimilationist. Descendants of the Irish Catholics, for example, a group once decried as separatist and alien, have become Presidents, senators, and representatives (and all of these in one family, in the case of the Kennedys). Our society exerts tremendous pressure

to conform, and cultural separatism rarely survives a generation. But more important, even if this claim were true, is this a legitimate rationale for limiting immigration in a society built on the values of pluralism and tolerance?

§ *Noncitizen immigrants are not entitled to constitutional rights.* Our government has long declined to treat immigrants as full human beings, and nowhere is that more clear than in the realm of constitutional rights. Although the Constitution literally extends the fundamental protections in the Bill of Rights to all people, limiting to citizens only the right to vote and run for federal office, the federal government acts as if this were not the case. 16

In 1893 the executive branch successfully defended a statute that required Chinese laborers to establish their prior residence here by the testimony of "at least one credible white witness." The Supreme Court ruled that this law was constitutional because it was reasonable for Congress to presume that nonwhite witnesses could not be trusted. 17

The federal government is not much more enlightened today. In a pending case I'm handling in the Court of Appeals for the Ninth Circuit, the Clinton Administration has argued that permanent resident aliens lawfully living here should be extended no more First Amendment rights than aliens applying for first-time admission from abroad—that is, none. Under this view, students at a public university who are citizens may express themselves freely, but students who are not citizens can be deported for saying exactly what their classmates are constitutionally entitled to say. 18

Growing up, I was always taught that we will be judged by how we treat others. If we are collectively judged by how we have treated immigrants—those who appear today to be "other" but will in a generation be "us"—we are not in very good shape. 19

◆ ◆ ◆

FIRST RESPONSES

Which of the myths that Cole discusses have you heard before? Do you think you could argue against the myths in a conversation, after reading the essay? What else would you need to know to argue effectively, if anything?

TAKING A CLOSER LOOK

Exploring *Who:* Voice and Tone

1. What level of education does the writer expect his readers to possess? How can you tell?
2. Why does Cole include information about his own family background?

3. Reread the headnote about David Cole. Was this information important to you as you read his argument? Would knowing these things
   about him affect most readers' evaluation of his points?

Exploring *What:* Content and Meaning

1. Make a list of the five myths about immigration.
2. Each myth is refuted, and some are refuted in more than one way.
   Summarize the refutation for each myth.
3. What does Cole mean in paragraph 19 when he refers to "those who
   appear today to be 'other' but will in a generation be 'us' "? How does
   this reference relate to the essay as a whole?
4. Are there other generalizations you have heard about immigrants that
   Cole does not refute? Why do you think he chose the myths he did?

Exploring *Why:* Purpose

1. Paragraphs 1 through 4 give some historical background about attitudes
   toward immigrants, and Cole invokes historical facts throughout his
   essay. How does understanding history illuminate the current situation?
2. In paragraph 2, Cole gives the examples of Irish and German immigrants in the nineteenth century and suggests why they immigrated.
   What difference do these reasons make in the way you look at the
   topic? How are you encouraged to think about the reasons for current
   immigration?
3. Think about the use of the word *myths* in the title and in the essay.
   What other words could be used instead? What is meaningful about
   the word choice?

Exploring *How:* Style and Strategy

1. The organization of Cole's essay is made clear by italicizing and marking the five myths. When is this type of highlighting useful in writing?
   When would you *not* want to use this method of emphasis?
2. Notice the plentiful use of statistics as supporting evidence. Did any of
   these statistics surprise you? Why?
3. Look for other types of supporting evidence for the refutations. Identify at least one analogy, one use of expert testimony, and one use of
   logical reasoning.
4. Why is the point-by-point *refutation* a good choice of structure for this
   topic?

IDEAS FOR WRITING AN ARGUMENT

1. In a short essay, refute three myths about something else you happen to know about—sex, polar bears, intelligence, or Asian women, for example.

2. Interview an immigrant or an immigrant's child about his or her experience in the United States. Write about this experience and whether stereotypes or myths came into play.

3. Develop an analogy between some earlier period of history and our own. Argue that there is a lesson to be learned from the analogy.

4. *Using the Internet.* Use a search engine to research how some other country deals with regulating immigration and obtaining citizenship. Look, for example, at Canada: An Immigration Index (http://www/escapeartist.com/canada/canada.htm), which provides help for people interested in moving to Canada. Write an essay arguing for the strength or weakness of this other system in comparison to the U.S. system.

◆ ◆ ◆ PREPARING TO READ

Have you ever felt a conflict between your paid work and your responsibilities at home? Have you heard your parents complain about such a conflict? How do people you know resolve this conflict, or do they?

◆ ◆ ◆

Time for Change

ARLIE RUSSELL HOCHSCHILD

Arlie Russell Hochschild is a sociologist well known for her book *The Second Shift: Working Parents and the Revolution at Home* (1989), which investigated family life in homes where both parents worked outside jobs. She found that 75 percent of the housework and 80 percent of the child care were still performed by women. In the essay we reprint here, Hochschild reflects on the research she did for her latest book on the family-work conflict, *The Time Bind: When Work Becomes Home and Home Becomes Work* (1997).

On the twenty-fifth anniversary of *Ms.*, we can look back on much   1
good news and some bad. The good news is that women make up nearly half
the U.S. paid workforce, and there is no conceivable going back. Millions
more women are in the educational pipelines. We closed some of the wage
gap, lifted some glass ceilings, and raised women's income. The earnings gap
between men and women is closing, and not just because men's real earnings have declined. So we're developing skills, taking home paychecks, and
we are, as always, holding up half the sky.

The bad news is that, despite our best intentions, the workplace has   2
changed women more than we have changed it. Many more women are fitting themselves into the ironclad work schedules their dads worked by,
while few men have gotten out of them. Some of us have been working rigid
schedules all along, of course, but now most of us do. All this is understandable, given the power of companies to set the terms of work, but it also takes
us away from an important original feminist goal: to humanize the workplace as we join it. A major part of that goal involved finding a way to make
work more compatible with family life. Our failure to do this really hit
home for me when I visited a child care center associated with a Fortune
500 company I researched for my book *The Time Bind*. It opened its doors
to toddlers at 7:00 A.M., served breakfast, lunch, and snacks, and offered

puzzles, dress-up clothes, and toys. But as the late afternoon wore on, I found my heart going out to a four-year-old who had arrived at 7:45 A.M.; by late afternoon she could be found sucking her thumb, waiting to be picked up, which usually happened around 6:00.

Good child care is great for children. But for this child, ten hours was 3 a long day. Scenes like this often evoke guilt—but it's a guilt that misses its mark. It presumes that working mothers *are* a problem, rather than that working mothers *and* fathers *have* a problem—indeed, two. For one thing, we often work in inflexible workplaces that require us to be there long hours if we want to get ahead, or even keep our jobs. For another, we sometimes unconsciously accommodate a traditional workplace culture, in which we identify with our employers and take on their priorities as our own. The combination of these two factors inhibits our political resolve for change.

Nationwide, work absorbs more of a parent's time than it did 25 years 4 ago. Women go back to work earlier after childbirth—in the 1960s, one in eight women returned to work less than a year after childbirth; in 1996, it was approximately one in two. Once back, more mothers now work full-time, year-round. Studies on hours vary, but one national study conducted by Families and Work Institute found that, of workers with children age 12 and under, only 4 percent of men and 13 percent of women worked less than 40 hours a week.

This is part of a larger pattern I refer to as a "stalled revolution." In 5 the last 25 years, women have changed, but everything else has not changed as fast or as much. Thus, tens of millions of women go out to work in offices and plants that demand long hours and inflexible schedules, live in a world without widespread quality child care, and come home to mates who don't share the domestic load. The family has become the shock absorber for the strains between faster-changing women and slower-changing men and workplaces. This was already true for some families in the 1950s and 1960s, but now it's true for most. And we've come to think of the family under these strained conditions as the "normal" family. Then we wonder why young people are scared to death to become working parents and why our divorce rate is one of the world's highest.

Thoughtful public discussion about this state of affairs has been oddly 6 silenced by two opposing parties, both of which divert our attention from the project of transforming the workplace. First, there are what I call the "accusatory traditionals," who have an eagle eye out for the problems of working mothers. If working mothers are tired, have troubled kids or tense marriages, the traditionals admonish women to junk their careers and stay home. Men, they don't touch.

Responding to these scolding traditionals are the "sunshine moderns," 7 who get cornered into saying, "Two-, three-, and four-year-olds in nine and ten-hour child care? Fine." "Middle-school children home alone after school? Let's call it 'self-care.'" The sunshiners' motto is "Don't bring me any bad news." Or at least no news that isn't strictly about the external world. Anything internal—like the idea that we can become complicit in the very cultural pressures that end up hurting us—is too dangerous, because if you admit such a thing, you're playing into the hands of the scolding traditionals and you're back to square one.

As in a boxer's clinch, each side immobilizes the other. As a result, no   8
one feels safe to explore what's really going on. Neither group lays out any compelling reason to change the workplace—the traditionals, because they believe that mothers, if not all women, should either take some dinky job on the side or quit; the sunshiners because they admit to no problems except getting more women into higher positions. If the traditionals ignore the fact that most women work to put bread on the table and many find work fulfilling as well, the sunshiners ignore how much women have assimilated to a dominant male culture at work.

In *The Time Bind,* I explore this culture by looking at parents whose   9
time has been pumped out of the home and into work. Why, I ask, at a company offering family-friendly work schedules, do so few use them? There were many reasons, but mixed with them all, so basic as to be hidden from view, was the very importance and appeal of the workplace—as a place to feel appreciated, competent, socially engaged, even relaxed. The "village," once centered around home and church, I argue, has gone to work.

Meanwhile, at home, parents often lack support for dealing with prob-   10
lems. For about a fifth of the people I talked to, work had become a substitute "home," while home had become a place of unwashed dishes, uncleaned laundry, unmade meals, and perplexing human relationships. The other four-fifths were in a time bind even though they felt neutral to negative about work; or they weren't in a time bind because they had flexible jobs or shorter hours. Indeed, some parents were in a time bind because they were afraid of being considered "unserious" if they asked for time off. Some women worked long hours to ward off the "evil eye" of male resentment, as if to say, "I deserve this job; look at the hours I put in." Some workers had bosses who wouldn't allow flexible hours. Or they were afraid of layoffs, which did hit the company I studied, a shocking reminder to the 10 percent laid off not to mistake a workplace for a home, and a covert speedup for the 90 percent who remained. In interviews with managers, clerical workers, and assembly-line workers, I saw glimmerings of a theme: work as home, home as work.

In the twinkling of an eye, the media picked up this idea of reversal, and   11
everyone saw in it what they wanted to see. Some publications, like *Working USA,* rightly saw a call for a movement to reduce hours of work—i.e., to

reshape the workplace. Others, including *U.S. News & World Report*—scolding traditionals—saw an alarmist report on women's "choice" to put in long hours at work and neglect their children at home. The sunshiners got upset at the traditionals' scolds, and at their version of *The Time Bind.* This exchange took on a momentum of its own that led right back into the boxer's clinch.

This standoff has produced much nervous talk, but also a curious si-   12 lence precisely where an open, deep, honest, think-big, solution-oriented conversation about changing the workplace should be. In order to open up this larger conversation, it would help to remember that progressive change is completely possible.

Other societies—Sweden, Norway, Canada—have led the way. And a   13 number of organizations, inspired by the women's movement, are fighting the good fight here. The Women's Legal Defense Fund, for example, is trying to expand the 1993 Family and Medical Leave Act to cover more working people and more family needs, such as minor illnesses. It is also trying to make these leaves paid for low-wage workers. We can begin to think about a broader movement pressing for a shorter workweek and work-sharing as an alternative to layoffs. And we need men to join us in taking pressure off kids and putting it on the workplace. These are all ways we can unstall the feminist revolution in the next 25 years.

◆ ◆ ◆

FIRST RESPONSES

Were you convinced that there is a problem with the incompatibility of work and family life? What points did you find most convincing?

TAKING A CLOSER LOOK

Exploring *Who:* Voice and Tone

1. Despite the fact that this essay focuses on a problem, the first paragraph lists positive changes for working women. Why do you think Hochschild chose to begin with the bright side?

2. In paragraph 2, the author reports that her heart went out to a four-year-old at a company day care. Why did she feel this way? How does the incident affect your evaluation of the writer?

3. Were you an appropriate audience for this essay? Why or why not?

Exploring *What:* Content and Meaning

1. What does Hochschild mean when she says that women "are, as always, holding up half the sky"?
2. What are two problems of working mothers and fathers, according to paragraph 3?
3. What positions do the two opposing sides take on the problems of working women? What is wrong with each position?
4. Even when family-friendly work schedules are available, they are not widely used. Why not?
5. How would a shorter workweek and work sharing help solve the problems discussed in the essay?

Exploring *Why:* Purpose

1. In this problem-solution essay, the solution section is very brief in contrast with the problem section. Can you justify this lack of balance?
2. Do you think that part of Hochschild's purpose was to encourage you to read *The Time Bind?* Why or why not?
3. What tactics does Hochschild use to avoid alienating men in her audience? If you are a man, do the tactics work?

Exploring *How:* Style and Strategy

1. How does Hochschild establish the fact that a problem exists? Were you convinced?
2. Point out the use of statistical evidence to support points. Where else could statistics effectively be used in the essay? What other types of support are presented?
3. Hochschild labels the two sides as "accusatory traditionals" and "sunshine moderns." Why does she give them these labels as well as describing their positions? When might you consider giving types of people or their arguments labels in your own writing?
4. In paragraph 5, the author describes the family as a "shock absorber." Explain this metaphor.
5. Hochschild avoids mentioning other possible solutions for the problem of working couples, such as encouraging child-free marriages or pay for parents who care for children at home. Why do you think she offers such minimal development of solutions?

IDEAS FOR WRITING AN ARGUMENT

1. ▇ *Using the Internet.* Argue for your own ideas about how to make work more compatible with family life. You can find sources on the Internet to help you choose and develop a specific topic for this assignment. For example, if you look at the Work & Family page of the Parenting Q&A site (http://www.parenting-qa.com/), you will find fact sheets and other resources for working parents. The National Parent Information Network (NPIN) at http://ericps.ed.uiuc.edu/npin/ index. html lists numerous relevant sources, including the Special Feature of Parent News for November 1996 on work and family.

2. Choose another workplace issue, and write a problem-solution essay. Such issues include runaway companies, the role of labor unions, tenure in academia, company loyalty, sex bias, and downsizing.

3. Would you rather do domestic work in your home or go to a workplace for a job? Defend your choice.

4. Interview a working woman about how she manages to juggle work and family duties. Ask about the dilemmas described in paragraph 10 of Hochschild's essay. Argue that your interviewee is an example for the "accusatory traditional" or the "sunshine modern" position, or for neither.

5. Identify a problem, other than women's work and family conflict, where there seems to be a "boxer's clinch" stand-off between two opposing viewpoints. Establish the existence of the problem, and explain both viewpoints.

◆ ◆ ◆ PREPARING TO READ

How strongly do you identify with your ethnic or cultural heritage? Does your family follow customs or celebrate holidays from a country of origin other than the United States? Growing up, did you ever feel that your home was culturally different from your classmates' homes?

◆ ◆ ◆

Whites in Multicultural Education: Rethinking Our Role

GARY HOWARD

Gary Howard is the founder and executive director of REACH Center, a national curriculum and staff development project that concentrates on multicultural education for kindergarten through twelfth grade, based in Seattle, Washington. This essay first appeared in the *Phi Kappa Deltan* journal in 1993 and was reprinted in a collection from Columbia University entitled *Multicultural Education, Transformative Knowledge, and Action* (1996).

How does an ethnic group that has historically been dominant in its society adjust to a more modest and balanced role? Put differently, how do white Americans learn to be positive participants in a richly pluralistic nation? These questions have always been a part of the agenda of multicultural education but are now coming more clearly into focus. Most of our work in race relations and multicultural education in the United States has emphasized—and appropriately so—the particular cultural experiences and perspectives of black, Asian, Hispanic, and American Indian groups. These are the people who have been marginalized to varying degrees by the repeated assertion of dominance by Americans of European ancestry. As the population of the United States shifts to embrace ever-larger numbers of previously marginalized groups, there is an emerging need to take a closer look at the changing role of white Americans. 1

Part of this need is generated by the growing evidence that many white Americans may not be comfortable with the transition from their dominant status. As our population becomes more diverse, we have seen an alarming increase in acts of overt racism. The number and size of hate groups in the United States is rising. Groups such as the Aryan Nation, neo-Nazis, and 2 skinheads tend to play on the anger, ignorance, and fears of the more alienated, disenfranchised, and uneducated segments of white society.

Too many segments of our white American population remain committed to their position of dominance; they are willing to defend it and legitimize it, even in the face of overwhelming evidence that our world is rapidly changing. Taken as a whole, these realities strongly suggest that a peaceful transition to a new kind of America, in which no ethnic or cultural group is in a dominant position, will require considerable change in education and deep psychological shifts for many white Americans. Attempting to effect these changes is part of the work of multicultural education, and that challenge leads us to a central question: What must take place in the minds and hearts of white Americans to convince them that now is the time to begin their journey from dominance to diversity? 3

There is much that needs to be said to help us understand our collective past, as well as the present. In a sense we are all victims of our history, some more obviously and painfully than others. It is critical that we white Americans come to terms with our reality and our role. What does it mean for white people to be responsible and aware in a nation where we have been the dominant cultural and political force? What can be our unique contribution, and what are the issues we need to face? How do we help create a nation where all cultures are accorded dignity and the right to survive? 4

I explore these questions here from the perspective of a white American. Each nation, of course, has its own special history to confront and learn from, but the depth and intensity of our struggle with diversity in the United States has significant lessons to teach both our own people and the rest of the world. 5

American Immigrants

European Americans share at least one commonality: we all came from somewhere else. In my own family, we loosely trace our roots to England, Holland, France, and perhaps Scotland. However, with five generations separating us from our various "homelands," we have derived little meaning from these tenuous connections with our ancestral people across the water. This is true for many white Americans, who are often repulsed by the appellation "European American" and would never choose such a descriptor for themselves. They simply prefer to be called "American" and to forget the past. 6

On the other hand, many white Americans have maintained direct and strong ties with their European roots. They continue after many generations to draw meaning and pride from those connections. In the Seattle region 7 there is an Ethnic Heritage Council composed of members of one hundred and three distinct cultural groups, most of them European. These people continue to refer to themselves as Irish American, Croatian American, Italian American, or Russian American—terminology that acknowledges the two sides of their identity.

European Americans are a diverse people. We vary broadly across extremely different cultures of origin, and we continue here in the United States to be diverse in religion, politics, economic status, and lifestyle. We also vary greatly in the degree to which we value the notion of the melting pot. Many of us today are ignorant of our ethnic history because our ancestors worked so hard to dismantle their European identity in favor of what they perceived to be the American ideal. The further our immigrant ancestors' cultural identities diverged from the white Anglo-Saxon Protestant image of the "real" American, the greater was the pressure to assimilate. Jews, Catholics, Eastern Europeans, Southern Europeans, and members of minority religious sects all felt the intense heat of the melting pot. From the moment they arrived on American soil, they received a strong message: Forget the home language, make sure your children don't learn to speak it, change your name to sound more American—or, if the immigration officials can't pronounce it, they'll change it for you.   8

In dealing with the history and culture of European Americans, it is important to acknowledge the pain, suffering, and loss that were often associated with their immigrant experiences. For many of these groups, it was a difficult struggle to carve out a niche in the American political and economic landscape and at the same time to preserve some sense of their own ethnic identity. Some white Americans resist the multicultural movement today because they feel that their own history of suffering from prejudice and discrimination has not been adequately addressed.   9

Family Realities

Like many white Americans, I trace my roots in this country back to the land—the Minnesota farm my mother's great-grandparents began working in the 1880s. My two uncles still farm this land, and I spent many of the summers of my youth with them. It was there that I learned to drive trucks and tractors at the age of twelve. I learned the humor and practical wisdom of hard-working people. I learned to love the land—its smell and feel; its changing moods and seasons; its power to nurture the crops, the livestock, and the simple folks who give their lives to it. On this land and with these people I have known my roots, my cultural heritage, much more deeply than through any connection with things European. The bond of my Americanness has been forged in my experience with the soil.   10

Yet, as I have grown to understand more of the history of this country,   11
a conflict has emerged in my feelings about our family tradition of the land.
I have a close friend and colleague, Robin Butterfield, whose traditional
Ojibwa tribal lands once encompassed the area now occupied by my family's farm. This farm, which is the core experience of my cultural rootedness
in America, is for her people a symbol of defeat, loss, and domination. How
do I live with this? How can I incorporate into my own sense of being an
American the knowledge that my family's survival and eventual success on
this continent were built on the removal and near extermination of an entire race of people?

And to bring the issue closer to the present, many of my relatives today   12
hold narrow and prejudicial attitudes about cultural differences. The racist
jokes they tell at family gatherings and the ethnic slurs that punctuate their
daily chatter have been an integral part of my cultural conditioning. It was
not until my college years, when I was immersed in a rich multicultural living
situation, that these barriers began to break down for me. Most of my relatives
have not had that opportunity. They do not understand my work in multicultural education. "You do what?" The racist jokes diminish in my presence, but
the attitudes remain. Yet, I love these people. They are my link with tradition
and the past, even though many of their beliefs are diametrically opposed
to what I have come to know and value about different cultures.

My family is not atypical among white Americans. Internal contradic-   13
tions and tensions around issues of culture and race are intrinsic to our collective experience. For most white Americans, racism and prejudice are not
theoretical constructs; they are members of the family.

When we open ourselves to learning about the historical perspectives   14
and cultural experiences of other races in America, much of what we discover is incompatible with our image of a free and democratic nation. We
find conflicting realities that do not fit together easily in our conscious
awareness, clashing truths that cause train wrecks in the mind. In this sense,
white Americans are caught in a classic state of cognitive dissonance. Our
collective security and position of economic and political dominance have
been fueled in large measure by the exploitation of other people. The physical and cultural genocide perpetrated against American Indians, the en-
slavement of African peoples, the exploitation of Mexicans and Asians as
sources of cheap labor—on such acts of inhumanity rests the success of the
European enterprise in America.

This cognitive dissonance is not dealt with easily. We can try to be   15
aware. We can try to be sensitive. We can try to deal with the racism in our
own families, yet the tension remains. We can try to dance to the crazy
rhythms of multiculturalism and race relations in the U.S., but the dissonant
chords of this painful past and present keep intruding.

The Luxury of Ignorance

Given the difficulty of dealing with such cognitive dissonance, it is no   16
mystery why many white Americans simply choose to remain unaware. In
fact, the possibility of remaining ignorant of other cultures is a luxury
uniquely available to members of any dominant group. Throughout most of
our history, there has been no reason why white Americans, for their own
survival or success, have needed to be sensitive to the cultural perspectives
of other groups. This is not a luxury available to people of color. If you are
black, Indian, Hispanic, or Asian in the United States, daily survival depends on knowledge of white America. You need to know the realities that
confront you in the workplace, in dealing with government agencies, in relation to official authorities like the police. To be successful in mainstream institutions, people of color in the U.S. need to be bicultural—able to play by
the rules of their own cultural community and able to play the game according to the rules established by the dominant culture. For most white
Americans, on the other hand, there is only one game, and they have traditionally been on the winning team.

The privilege that comes with being a member of the dominant group,   17
however, is invisible to most white Americans. Social research has repeatedly demonstrated that if Jessie Myles, an African American friend, and I
walk into the same bank on the same day and apply for a loan with the same
officer, I will be more likely to receive my money—and with less hassle, less
scrutiny, and less delay. This is in spite of the fact that Jessie has more education and is also more intelligent, better looking, and a nicer person. Likewise, if I am turned down for a house purchase, I don't wonder whether it
was because of the color of my skin. And if I am offered a new job or promotion, I don't worry that my fellow workers may feel that I'm there not
because of my qualifications, but merely to fill an affirmative action quota.
Such privileged treatment is so much a part of the fabric of our daily existence that it escapes the conscious awareness of most white Americans.
From the luxury of ignorance are born the Simi Valley neighborhoods of
our nation, which remain painfully out of touch with the experiences and
sensibilities of multicultural America.

Emotions That Kill

The most prevalent strategy that white Americans adopt to deal with   18
the grim realities of history is denial. "The past doesn't matter. All the talk
about multicultural education and revising history from different cultural
perspectives is merely ethnic cheerleading. My people made it, and so can
yours. It's an even playing field and everybody has the same opportunities,

so let's get on with the game and quit complaining. We've heard enough of your victim's history."

Another response is hostility, a reaction to cultural differences that we   19
have seen resurfacing more blatantly in recent years. The Aryan Nation's organizing in Idaho, the murder of a black man by skinheads in Oregon, the killing of a Jewish talk show host by neo-Nazis in Denver, cross burnings and Klan marches in Dubuque, and the increase in racist incidents on college campuses all point to a revival of hate crimes and overt racism in the U.S. We can conjecture why this is occurring now: the economic downturn, fear of job competition, the rollback on civil rights initiatives by recent administrations. Whatever the reason, hostility related to racial and cultural differences has always been a part of American life and was only once again brought into bold relief by the first Rodney King decision and its violent aftermath in Los Angeles.

Underlying both the denial and the hostility is a deep fear of diversity.   20
This fear is obvious in the Neanderthal violence and activism of white supremacist groups. Because of their personal and economic insecurities, they seek to destroy that which is not like them.

The same fear is dressed in more sophisticated fashion by Western tra-   21
ditionalists and neoconservatives who campaign against multicultural education. They fear the loss of European and Western cultural supremacy in the school curriculum. With their fraudulent attempt to characterize "political correctness" as a new form of McCarthyism and with their outcries against separatism, particularism, reverse racism, and historical inaccuracy in multicultural texts, they defend cultural turf that is already lost. The United States was never a white European Christian nation and is becoming less so every day. Most public school educators know the curriculum has to change to reflect this reality, but many guardians of the traditional canon still find it frightening to leave the Old World.

Denial, hostility, and fear are literally emotions that kill. Our   22
country—indeed, the world—has suffered endless violence and bloodshed over issues of racial, cultural, and religious differences. And the killing is not only physical, but emotional and psychological as well. With this hostility toward diversity, we threaten to destroy the precious foundation of our national unity, which is a commitment to equality, freedom, and justice for all people. It is not multiculturalism that threatens to destroy our unity—as some neoconservative academics would have us believe—but rather our inability to embrace our differences and our unwillingness to honor the very ideals we espouse.

Ironically, these negative responses to diversity are destructive not   23
only for those who are the targets of hate but also for the perpetrators themselves. Racism is ultimately a self-destructive and counter-evolutionary

strategy. As is true for any species in nature, positive adaptation to change requires a rich pool of diversity and potential in the population. In denying access to the full range of human variety and possibility, racism drains the essential vitality from everyone, victimizing our entire society.

Another emotion that kills is guilt. For well-intentioned white Americans guilt is a major hurdle. As we become aware of the realities of the past and the present—of the heavy weight of oppression and racism that continues to drag our nation down—it is natural for many of us of European background to feel a collective sense of complicity, shame, or guilt. On a rational level, of course, we can say that we didn't contribute to the pain. We weren't there. We would never do such things to anyone. Yet, on an emotional level, there is a sense that we were involved somehow. And our membership in the dominant culture keeps us connected to the wrongs, because we continue to reap the benefits of past oppression. 24

There is a positive side to guilt, of course. It can be a spur to action, a motivation to contribute, a kick in the collective conscience. Ultimately, however, guilt must be overcome, along with the other negative responses to diversity—for it, too, drains the lifeblood of our people. If we are finally to become one nation of many cultures, then we need to find a path out of the debilitating cycle of blame and guilt that has occupied so much of our national energy. 25

Responses That Heal

How do we as white Americans move beyond these negative responses to diversity and find a place of authentic engagement and positive contribution? The first step is to approach the past and the present with a new sense of honesty. Facing reality is the beginning of liberation. As white Americans we can face honestly the fact that we have benefited from racism. The point is simply to face the reality of our own privilege. We can also become supportive of new historical research aimed at providing a more inclusive and multidimensional view of our nation's past. Scholars and educators are searching for the literature, the experiences, the contributions, and the historical perspectives that have been ignored in our Eurocentric schooling. It is important that white Americans become involved in and supportive of this endeavor, which is, of course, highly controversial. 26

Many white Americans feel threatened by the changes that are coming. One of our responsibilities, therefore, is to help them understand that our nation is in a time of necessary transition. This is part of the honesty we are trying to address. It took five hundred years to evolve our present curriculum, which, in spite of its many fine qualities, is still flawed and inaccurate and excludes most non-European perspectives and influences. The new 27 multicultural curricula will also have to go through a process of evolution toward balance and accuracy. The appropriate role for aware white Americans is to participate in this evolution, rather than to attack it from the outside, as many critics of multicultural education have chosen to do.

Along with this honesty must come a healthy portion of humility. It is 28 not helpful for white Americans to be marching out in front with all the answers for other groups. The future belongs to those who are able to walk and work beside people of many different cultures, lifestyles, and perspectives. The business world is embracing this understanding. We now see top corporate leaders investing millions of dollars annually to provide their employees with skills to function effectively in a highly diverse work force. They are forced to make this expenditure because schools, frankly, have not done an adequate job. Diversity is a bottom line issue for employers. Productivity is directly related to our ability to deal with pluralism. Whenever power, truth, control, and the possibility of being right are concentrated in only a few people, a single perspective, one culture, or one approach, the creativity of an entire organization suffers.

Honesty and humility are based on respect. One of the greatest con- 29 tributions white Americans can make to cultural understanding is simply to learn the power of respect. In Spanish, the term *respeto* has a deep connotation. It goes far beyond mere tolerance or even acceptance. *Respeto* acknowledges the full humanness of other people, their right to be who they are, their right to be treated in a good way. When white Americans learn to approach people of different cultures with this kind of deep respect, our own world becomes larger and our embrace of reality is made broader and richer. We are changed by our respect for other perspectives. It is more than just a nice thing to do. In the process of respecting other cultures, we learn to become better people ourselves.

But all of this is not enough. As members of the majority population, 30 we are called to provide more than honesty, humility, and respect. The race issue for white Americans is ultimately a question of action: What are we going to do about it? It is not a black problem or an Indian problem or an Asian problem or a Hispanic problem—or even a white problem. The issue of racism and cultural diversity in the U.S. is a human problem, a struggle we are all in together. It cannot be solved by any one group. We have become embedded in the problem together, and we will have to deal with it together.

This brings us to the issue of co-responsibility. The way for us to over- 31 come the denial, hostility, fear, and guilt of the past and present is to become active participants in the creation of a better future. As white Americans, once we become aware of the heavy weight of our oppressive past, our role is not to fall into a kind of morose confessionalism about the sins of our ancestors. The healing response for ourselves, as well as for those who have been the victims of oppression, is involvement, action, contribution, and responsibility. The healing path requires all of us to join our efforts, resources, energy, and commitment. No one group can do it alone. Together we are co-responsible for the creation of a new America.

The Search for Authentic Identity

Before white Americans can enter fully into this active partnership for change, however, we need to come to terms with who we are as a people. One problem that arises from an honest appraisal of the past is that it sometimes becomes difficult for us as white people to feel good about our own history. Where do we turn to find positive images for ourselves and our children? In the 1960s and early 1970s we saw a revolution in positive identity for blacks, American Indians, Hispanics, and Asians. During this period there was an explosion of racial and cultural energy—what James Banks refers to as the ethnic revitalization movement. What were white youths doing at this time? There was a revolution happening with them as well: a revolution of rejection. As the civil rights movement, the antiwar movement, and the women's liberation movement were bringing to the public's attention many of the fundamental flaws of a culture dominated by white males, the youths of white America were searching for an alternative identity.   32

At this time in our history, white America was at war with itself. The children of affluence and privilege, the very ones who had benefited the most from membership in the dominant culture, were attacking the foundation of their own privilege. In creating a new counterculture of rebellion and hope, they borrowed heavily from black, Indian, Hispanic, and Asian traditions. Their clothing, ornamentation, hairstyles, spiritual explorations, jargon, values, and music defined an eclectic composite culture that symbolized identification with the oppressed. In their rejection of the dominant culture, they sought to become like those whom the dominant culture had historically rejected.   33

Thus we have the essence of the "wannabe" phenomenon: white Americans trying to be someone else. When the limitations of privilege, of affluence, of membership in the dominant group become apparent to us as white Americans, we often turn to other cultural experiences to find identity, purpose, meaning, and a sense of belonging. When the truth of our collective history is brought home to us, we turn to other traditions for a new place to be.   34

But there is another alternative for white identity, one that resides within our own cultural roots. It became clear to me during my sabbatical study tour around the world in 1990–1991. I began the trip with the goal of gaining some new insights about education from the First Peoples in   35 several countries. During a seven-month period I was immersed in the rich contexts of the Navajo, Hopi, Maori, Australian aboriginal, Balinese, and Nepalese cultures. I gained much from my exposure to the traditional perspectives of these cultures, but the most powerful personal experiences came for me in the place I least expected them—my own ancestral Europe.

In the Basque country of northern Spain, in the Pyrenees Mountains   36
near the French border, I entered a prehistoric cave that was one of the sacred sites of the ancient people of Europe. I was amazed by the beauty and the power this cave held for me. I had been in the sacred caves of the Anasazi, those people who preceded the Navajo and Hopi in what is now Arizona and New Mexico. I had been in the ceremonial caves of the aboriginal people of Australia. In both of these previous experiences, I had been drawn to the handprints on the walls, created there by ancient artists blowing pigment through a bone or reed to leave images of their hands on the surface of the stone.

When I discovered, in the deepest part of a cave in the Pyrenees,   37
twenty-one handprints created by ancient Europeans in the exact style of the Anasazi and the aborigine, I knew I had connected with a profound source of my own identity. There was a sense of the universality of all human experience. In the projection of our hands on stone walls, in the desire to express ourselves and find meaning in life, we are all one. And then came an even deeper lesson. In my journey around the world, I had been searching for meaning in other people's cultures. Here in a cave in Europe was a connection with my own.

After leaving the Pyrenees, I spent the next three weeks exploring the   38
ancient sacred sites of England and Scotland. In the company of Peter Vallance, a storyteller, dancer, and modern version of the old Celtic bard, I continued to grow more deeply into a sense of rootedness in my own past. I learned that the old Celts and other ancient ones of Great Britain were a fascinating people. They had spread over a large area in Europe and were, in fact, some of the people who worshiped in those magnificent caves in northern Spain.

I also learned that the Celts became the victims of the imperialistic expansion of Roman Christianity. Their culture was overwhelmed by the   39
twofold aggression of the Roman army and the church. Consequently, much of their history is lost to us today. The amazing stone circles, like Stonehenge, which are still evident throughout the British Isles, stand as powerful reminders of the Celtic vision of nature and of the people's sacred connection with both the earth and the sky.

What does my experience in Europe mean for us as white Americans?   40
First, there is no need to look to other cultures for our own sense of identity. Any of us who choose to look more deeply into our European

roots will find there a rich and diverse experience waiting to be discovered. Second, the history of oppression and expansionism perpetrated by European nations is only part of our past. It is a reality that must be acknowledged and dealt with, but it is not our only heritage as white Americans. In fact, many of our own ancestral groups, like the Celts, have themselves been the victims of the same kind of imperialistic drives that have been so devastating to other indigenous populations around the world. And third, when we push the human story back far enough, we come to a place of common connection to this earth, to a place where people of all races are brothers and sisters on the same planet. It is in this recognition of both our uniqueness as European Americans and our universality as human beings that we can begin to make an authentic contribution to the healing of our nation.

Who Are My People?

As a result of my world tour and of my lengthy struggle with the issues   41
discussed here, I have come to a new sense of my own identity as a white American. I have seen that I have deep connections with this earth through my own cultural ancestry. I have also become aware of a complex, painful, yet rich history of connections to all other peoples. I have seen that white Americans can be drawn together with people everywhere who are struggling with the questions of cultural and human survival. We can develop a deep commitment to and a strong stake in the preservation and strengthening of diversity at home and throughout the world. We can become aware that our energy and vision, along with those of other Americans of all cultures, are essential to the healing that must take place if we are to survive as a pluralistic and just nation.

It is time for a redefinition of white America. As our percentage of the   42
population declines, our commitment to the future must change. It is neither appropriate nor desirable to be in a position of dominance. Even though we are undeniably connected by history and ethnicity with a long legacy of oppression, this identification with the oppressor is not our only means of defining ourselves. We can choose now to contribute to the making of a new kind of nation. Young white students need to see that they, too, can be full participants in the building of a multicultural America.

Because the music of the United States is propelled by such a rich   43
mixture of cultural rhythms, it is time for all of us to learn to move with grace and style to the new sounds. The future calls each of us to become partners in the dance of diversity, a dance in which everyone shares the lead. And because we have been separated by race and ethnicity for so long, we may all feel awkward at first with the new moves. It will take time to learn to fully embrace our emerging multicultural partnerships. But with a

little help from our friends in other cultures, even white folks can learn to dance again, as we once did among the great stone circles of ancient Europe. Rather than being isolated in the dance hall of the dominant, we now have an exciting opportunity to join with Americans of all cultures in creating a nation that actually tries to move to the tune of its own ideals. These are my people, and this could be our vision.

◆ ◆ ◆

FIRST RESPONSES

How does your own experience with multicultural education relate to Howard's essay? Do you believe that Howard's vision of "the creation of a new America" is possible?

TAKING A CLOSER LOOK

Exploring *Who:* Voice and Tone

1. Who is the audience for this essay? How does the title reflect the audience?
2. How does Howard manage to address readers who probably feel some of the hostility toward multiculturalism that he describes? What strategies does he use in his attempt to get through to them?
3. Look at the words Howard uses to describe the new role of white people in America. List them. What **connotations** do they have?
4. Why does Howard include information about his own heritage and experience?

Exploring *What:* Content and Meaning

1. Why do many white Americans resist the multicultural movement, according to Howard? Can you think of reasons he does not mention?
2. Howard writes that racism and prejudice "are members of the family" for many Americans. What does he mean? Do you find this to be true?
3. What is "the luxury of ignorance"?
4. What harmful strategies do white Americans use to deal with the grim realities of history? Why are these harmful?
5. What positive strategies does Howard suggest to move beyond negative responses and build a new nation?

Exploring *Why:* Purpose

1. This essay appeared in a book about multicultural education. Who might read such a book? How does Howard appeal to such people? Why are they important as an audience for this message?
2. What does Howard think of the multicultural movement at this point in history? How can you tell?
3. A theme of "dominance versus diversity" unifies this essay. What is the writer's goal in identifying the theme this way? How could the same theme be phrased by Howard's opponents?
4. Why does Howard dwell on the topic of fear?

Exploring *How:* Style and Strategy

1. This is a *problem-solution* argument. What section establishes that a problem exists? What section suggests a solution to the problem?
2. Why do you think that this essay presents a *thesis question* rather than a *thesis statement?*
3. Were the headings helpful to you as you read the essay the first time? How? When do you think it would be appropriate to use headings in your own writing?
4. Why does Howard include a section about European Americans and their diversity?
5. ▆▌ *Using the Internet.* What action does Howard call for? Is his call to action effective—did it make you feel like behaving differently than before? You can find out more about what's being done on this front by using links from the Multicultural Home Page (http://pasture.ecn. purdue.edu/~agenhtml/agenmc/) or consulting the multicultural resources found on the Diversity site (http://execpc.com/~ dboals/diversit.html/).

IDEAS FOR WRITING AN ARGUMENT

1. Howard writes about how white Americans often prefer to cling to an image of a free and democratic nation than to face the reality. Choose some other situation in which people cling to an image rather than the reality—for example, an image of one's family, marriage, childhood, or home town. Discuss the effects of clinging to the image, and suggest solutions for any problems that result.
2. Howard discusses the phenomenon of "cognitive dissonance" in the "Family Realities" section of the essay. Do some research into

psychological sources to expand your knowledge of what cognitive dissonance is and how it operates. Write an informative essay about it, and argue that it explains many different human behaviors (or a particular human behavior).

3. Under "Emotions That Kill," the author brings up denial, hostility, and fear as negative responses to diversity. Identify another issue that brings up these emotions, and argue that they are emotionally and psychologically destructive.

4. Write an essay from your own experience explaining how you deal with an attitude held in your family that is opposed to what you know and value.

◆ FURTHER IDEAS FOR USING ARGUMENT

1. Argue for the value of some particular domestic activity, as Laurel Robertson does in "Bake Your Bread at Home." Then, explain how the world of work prevents or hinders people from engaging in this activity (refer to Arlie Hochschild's "Time for Change" for ideas). Suggest a solution to the dilemma if you can.

2. ■ *Using the Internet.* Use the Internet's subject directory search tools, such as Inter-Links (<http://www.nova.edu/Inter-Links>), to find recent statistics about the U.S. workforce. Use some of these statistics to develop a topic about trends in the workforce and their potential effects on life off the job (such as family life or friendships).

3. COMBINING STRATEGIES. Write an essay modeled on David Cole's, "Five Myths About _____" (you fill in the blank). You might choose a public issue like welfare, a workplace topic like flextime or profit sharing, a social science subject like unemployment, or a psychological topic like schizophrenia. You also might enjoy writing a humorous essay with a title like, "Five Myths About Computer Nerds," or "Five Myths About Life at Texas Christian University." This essay will require you to collect and *classify* beliefs about your subject; then you will *argue* that each general classification is a myth.

4. COLLABORATIVE WRITING. Meet with a small group of students to discuss popular types of television shows. Write a list of interview questions that you will ask fans of a chosen type of show. After you each perform two interviews and type your notes on them, develop a collaborative essay that argues for either the positive or negative effects of this type of show. Use Heaton's essay on daytime talk shows for inspiration.

5. COMBINING STRATEGIES. Narrate an experience that practically single-handedly led you to take a side on some issue. For example, a car accident might convince you that seat belt laws are justified. Looking for an apartment in a predominantly white community, when you are African American, might persuade you that racist stereotypes are alive and thriving. Unexpectedly losing your job might give you a different point of view on the unemployment problem. Be sure to use your narrative as an extended argument for your opinion on the issue.

♦ ♦ ♦ ♦ ♦ ♦ ♦ CHAPTER 12 ♦ ♦ ♦ ♦ ♦ ♦ ♦

Combining Strategies

Further Readings

♦ ♦ ♦ ♦ ♦

This chapter provides you with additional reading selections. Although some of these readings are developed by one controlling strategy, most of them illustrate combinations of various strategies. As you read, use the following questions to analyze how a writer combines strategies:

- ♦ What are the purpose and thesis of the essay? Who is the intended audience?
- ♦ Which strategy controls or dominates the essay?
- ♦ How does this strategy help readers to understand the essay's thesis and purpose?
- ♦ What other strategies appear in the essay?
- ♦ What do these strategies contribute to the readers' understanding of the essay's thesis and purpose?

Also keep in mind our suggestions for being an engaged reader: marking the text and using the *Who, What, Why,* and *How* questions to explore your reactions, understand the content, and analyze the writer's strategies. Then write something of your own that relates to the reading. When possible, discuss the readings with your classmates and consult with them about your written responses.

We have annotated the first reading in the chapter—"Coming to America, to Clean"—to give you a visual guide to the strategies at work.

Here is a review of those strategies, along with comments about their use in the essay.

1. *Narration:* The essay tells what happens when Antonia and her cousin decide to leave Mexico and take jobs as illegal domestic workers in the United States (paragraphs 3 through 11).

2. *Description:* Many passages include specific details about how things look, act, sound, smell, and feel—especially in the house where Antonia works (paragraphs 12 through 14, 19).

3. *Exemplification:* The essay contains numerous examples of how the young women live and what they do in their jobs (paragraphs 13 through 14, 18 through 19).

4. *Process analysis:* A significant part of this essay explains how undocumented workers from Mexico are smuggled into the United States (paragraphs 6 through 9).

5. *Definition:* In the end, Antonia describes "the famous American dream" and gives her own interpretation of it (paragraph 20).

6. *Division and classification:* In discussing her new life in America, Antonia divides her remarks into two parts—what she does at work and what she does in her own apartment (paragraphs 12 through 14).

7. *Comparison and contrast:* Antonia compares her dreams with her cousin's (paragraph 15); she also contrasts housekeeping in her Mexican village to the cleaning she does in America (paragraphs 16 through 18).

8. *Cause and effect:* In the opening, Antonia explains why she decided to leave Mexico.

9. *Argument:* At one point, Antonia summarizes the argument that her cousin used to justify leaving home and going to America (paragraph 3).

Coming to America, to Clean

"ANTONIA" (TRANSLATED BY ANA MARIA CORONA)

Ana Maria Corona collected interviews in Spanish with illegal domestic workers in California. She translated and edited these workers' stories, making a collection called *Like a Flower in the Dust: What They Really Think While They Wax Your Floors,* which first appeared in the *San Diego Reader* in 1993. The following selection, reprinted in *Harper's* magazine, is narrated by a Mexican housekeeper, "Antonia."

I grew up in a *pueblito* in Sinaloa, in the country- 1
side not far from Rosamorada. I was happy enough, but
my friends always talked about getting married or leaving town and going someplace more exciting. My
friends told me I was too pretty to stay there, that I
should go where I would be appreciated by real men,
have a fine life. Even my uncle told me I should go out
into the world, not stay there. "Like a flower in the
dust," he said. But how was I to make my way?

Cause and effect

There was one way. Go to the border and find 2
work as a maid in a foreign household. Every year some
of the girls would catch the bus to Tijuana or Ciudad
Juárez and try to get jobs on the other side of the fron-
tier. Some came back to visit with nice clothes and
money. Some never came back.

My cousin Blanca was the one who first made the 3
decision to go to Tijuana. She was pretty wild, but even
she wouldn't travel alone, so she asked me to go with
her. Her argument was that if we didn't leave when we
were young, we would be trapped. Our families wanted

Argument

us to stay, because they didn't want to lose us as workers
and producers of more workers. She said, "If we are
going to clean house, we might as well get paid for it." I
thought about it and realized she was right. I begged my
uncle to loan me money to go to Tijuana. I had a little
money of my own, and we could stay with Blanca's aunt
in Tijuana. He gave me the money but made me
promise not to tell my mother he had given it to me. I

left without saying good-bye to her; I just left a letter. Blanca and I caught a ride to Rosamorada and bought tickets to Tijuana. We were two very excited girls, giggling but scared half to death. I'll never forget stepping off the bus into that huge station full of men looking us over and *coyotes* offering us rides to Los Angeles. I was very excited and glad that I had come.

Blanca found us both jobs in homes in San Diego 4 in less than a month—with the help of our aunt and a thousand of her friends, of course. That's how it works: it's all word of mouth. Young girls move on or get married or make enough money to go back home, so they give word to their friends and the news passes around. There's a huge network of relatives, friends, inquiries, lost phone messages, old women carrying tales.

Once Blanca and I had jobs, we had to find a way 5 to get across the border to claim them. Our future *patrones* were not willing to smuggle us across in their cars, which would have been the safest way for us. We would have to report to work through our own efforts.

We had heard the usual terrible stories of difficult 6 crossings through dangerous terrain, of people being betrayed and sold, of people being robbed and raped and killed. But we were lucky. We met an excellent *coyote* named Javier, who said he could take us across as easily as we could cross a street downtown. He wanted

$300 apiece, which my uncle said was a high price but fair enough if Javi was as good as he said. Blanca's aunt loaned her the fee and mine would be paid by my *patrones* when Javi delivered me. In return, I would work the first month for them without pay. This had all been arranged through the network of calls and whispers and customs.

Narrative

On the night we were to go, I was terrified. If Blanca   7
hadn't been going with me, I wouldn't have left the house. We met Javi at La Dichosa, a large open-air taco stand in lower Libertad. I was nervous and scared, and couldn't eat a thing. There were eight of us—five men in their twenties and another girl, the fiancée of one of the men. We waited in La Dichosa, everyone nervous, until after midnight. Finally a big red-and-black taxi came, and we all got in.

At first we seemed to be just driving around. No-   8
body was talking except Javi and the taxi driver. We   Process
were driving without headlights and we stopped several times while Javi and the driver stared across into the dark and said things that made no sense to me. Then we entered a short alley that led to a fence. I looked at it, wondering if I could climb it. Javi got out, walked over to the fence, and just opened it up like a door.

The fence had been neatly cut and hooked on   9
nails so that the cuts could not be seen from the other   Narrative
side. Javi motioned us out of the taxi and through the opening in the fence. He told us, very casually, to walk

behind him and keep quiet. But if he said "Drop," we were to fall flat on the ground, and if he said "Back," we should run back to the fence, where the taxi driver would be waiting to open it for us. But there was no need. We walked across the weeds like we were strolling through a park. When we reached the highway a van pulled over, Javi opened the door, and we jumped in and drove off. Javi smiled at me and said, "See? You could have worn your high heels." I realized that we were in the United States, and that I was an outlaw.

When we got to the parking lot where I was to meet my new *patrones,* Javi walked me over to a huge blue Cadillac. The people in the car looked like good people to me, a middle-aged couple that you could tell had been married a long time by the way they sat.

10

Narrative

Javi took money from the man, counted it, then told me, "Get in, go with them. They just bought you for a month, a year, who knows how long." I got in the back seat of the Cadillac, and the lady turned around and smiled at me. She said, "*Bienvenidos.*" She kept on talking to me, but I couldn't understand her. I felt like I'd jumped off a bridge and was washing down the river. It was two weeks before Christmas. I had just turned sixteen.

11

My *patrones* are very fine people and treat me very well, almost as if I were a relative and not a stranger from another country who does not even speak

12

Division

their language. I have a comfortable room with my own television and bath, and I am free to move in the house and to eat from their kitchen. The *señora* has learned some Spanish and is always trying to learn more. She also encourages me to learn English, but I find it very difficult. I feel at home in their house, except for having nobody to really talk to. They pay me $300 a month. In dollars. This is a lot of money, and I never have to spend any for food or soap or any of those things. The oldest daughter is my age and sometimes loans or gives me clothes, so I save most of what I earn.

I usually spend my free time in local Mexican places with Blanca and some other girls who work in houses. We have rented an apartment together, eight or ten of us—I don't really know how many. All friends of friends. We share the rent, which is only thirty dollars apiece. It's a place where we can go on our free days. We have parties there and invite boys from Chula Vista. I keep some nice clothes there in case I want to go out.

I've spent a week of vacation right there in the apartment, laughing and drinking with the other girls, sometimes going to the mall or the movies if somebody has a boyfriend with a car and speaks good English. I like being in the apartment alone, just fooling around, listening to the radio, smoking cigarettes on the bed. I've never had my own house, but when I'm there alone, I can imagine what it would be like. Doing what I want,

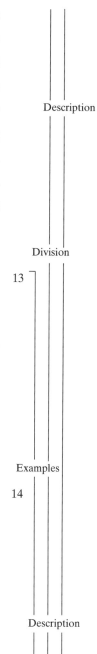

Description

Division

13

Examples

14

Description

walking around naked, singing in the shower, dropping ashes on the floor, dancing in front of the mirror. I like lying around in a bubble bath and drinking coffee, but only if there's nobody around. At times like that, I feel like I'm a long, long way from where I was born.

Blanca's only dream is to marry a boy who is a citizen and get a place of her own. (And get pregnant and fat, clean house, and raise children.) I'm not so sure. Maybe I will go to school, learn English and computers. I like the life you can have here. I just haven't learned how I can make it my own place. But I've only been here three years. I'm still learning a lot of things.

As far as working goes, it's not bad. In some ways it was harder to keep house in my village. Most of our houses were made of posts with palm-thatch roofs, which would get full of spiders and scorpions. The walls were split cane, nailed to the posts with bottle caps to keep the nails from tearing through. The dust came right in whenever the goats or burros or trucks went by.

On the other hand, there was no need to wash or wax the floors; I would use a broom to sweep the inside, then the patios, then the yard. Spills just soaked into the floor. There were not so many dishes or things to clean. There were maybe three towels in the house; in the house where I work now, there are dozens, and they take a long time to wash and dry.

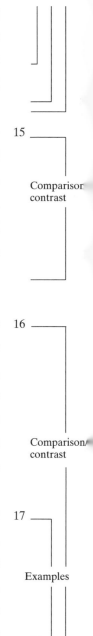

15 Comparison/contrast

16 Comparison/contrast

17 Examples

It takes hours just to keep the bathroom all shiny. 18
The first time I was in the house, that was what amazed
me the most—the bathroom. The bowl and toilet and tub
are all the same color of ceramic. The floor is carpeted—
even the toilet seat is carpeted. One whole wall is
mirror—you can study yourself while using the toilet.
Everything is silvery and shiny. A fan comes on to blow
away smells; a red light in the ceiling warms you when
you get out of the shower. There are mountains of clean,
soft towels in beautiful colors. There is a rack for magazines to read while you are there, even a telephone.

Examples

The kitchen is also incredible. Everything is elec- 19
tric; there are no flames. So it isn't so hot to cook in the
summer, but it never feels nice and warm in there
either. There are tables and chairs in the kitchen, but nobody ever eats there. During parties, everyone ends up
standing in the kitchen, even though the house has large
beautiful sitting rooms like in a movie. There is a radio
that is always on, usually on Radio Latina. There are
small electrical things to do everything: open cans, make
popcorn, peel vegetables, make pancakes, cook a single
hamburger, melt cheese. When my *patrona* cooks, she
uses dozens of dishes and pans and gadgets. Of course,
all of these things must be cleaned and put away. And
everything must be sprayed with poisons and germ-
killers and insecticides. This is in a house with doors
sealed with rubber, with no cracks in the walls, with
floors covered by a single piece of linoleum, where the

Description

Examples

windows have screens and are never opened because of the air-conditioning.

It's a dream world really, like the advertisements ╎20 on television. Everything snowy white, everything soft, everything new, everything bright. The *señora* watches   Definition Mexican television sometimes, to improve her Spanish. She is learning well for a person of her years. She has asked me a few times about the commercials on the programs she watches. They always have tall, blond people in expensive houses wrapping blue-eyed babies up in wonderfully white clothes. She knows that very few people in Mexico live like that and has asked me how people could believe in a commercial where things are so unrealistic. I told her, Of course things are beautiful and perfect—it's television. Who'd want to buy soap or toilet paper if they showed a lot of ugly *negros* using it in filthy shacks? She doesn't understand. I believe that Americans think what they see on television is real, maybe even more real than their own lives. They want to live in *Dallas* or *Dynasty* and think they can get there if they buy the right things. Maybe that's the famous American dream. I don't know. For the rest of the world, the American dream is just to live in America. I live here now. So I know it's real.

◆ ◆ ◆

Coming Home Again

CHANG-RAE LEE

Chang-Rae Lee, a creative writing teacher at the University of Oregon, contributes occasional essays, especially about food and cooking, to *The New Yorker* and other magazines. His first novel, *Native Speaker* (1995)—about a Korean-American detective who struggles to achieve a sense of self—received wide critical acclaim. He also won the Barnes & Noble new writer award in 1996. The following essay appeared in *The New Yorker* in the fall of 1995.

1   When my mother began using the electronic pump that fed her liquids and medication, we moved her to the family room. The bedroom she shared with my father was upstairs, and it was impossible to carry the machine up and down all day and night. The pump itself was attached to a metal stand on casters, and she pulled it along wherever she went. From anywhere in the house, you could hear the sound of the wheels clicking out a steady time over the grout lines of the slate-tiled foyer, her main thoroughfare to the bathroom and the kitchen. Sometimes you would hear her halt after only a few steps, to catch her breath or steady her balance, and whatever you were doing was instantly suspended by a pall of silence.

2   I was usually in the kitchen, preparing lunch or dinner, poised over the butcher block with her favorite chef's knife in my hand and her old yellow apron slung around my neck. I'd be breathless in the sudden quiet, and, having ceased my mincing and chopping, would stare blankly at the brushed sheen of the blade. Eventually, she would clear her throat or call out to say she was fine, then begin to move again, starting her rhythmic *ka-jug;* and only then could I go on with my cooking, the world of our house turning once more, wheeling through the black.

3   I wasn't cooking for my mother but for the rest of us. When she first moved downstairs she was still eating, though scantily, more just to taste what we were having than from any genuine desire for food. The point was simply to sit together at the kitchen table and array ourselves like a family again. My mother would gently set herself down in her customary chair near the stove. I sat across from her, my father and sister to my left and right, and crammed in the center was all the food I had made—a spicy codfish stew, say, or a casserole of gingery beef, dishes that in my youth she had prepared for us a hundred times.

4   It had been ten years since we'd all lived together in the house, which at fifteen I had left to attend boarding school in New Hampshire. My mother

would sometimes point this out, by speaking of our present time as being "just like before Exeter," which surprised me, given how proud she always was that I was a graduate of the school.

My going to such a place was part of my mother's not so secret plan to   5
change my character, which she worried was becoming too much like hers. I was clever and able enough, but without outside pressure I was readily given to sloth and vanity. The famous school—which none of us knew the first thing about—would prove my mettle. She was right, of course, and while I was there I would falter more than a few times, academically and otherwise. But I never thought that my leaving home then would ever be a problem for her, a private quarrel she would have even as her life waned.

Now her house was full again. My sister had just resigned from her job   6
in New York City, and my father, who typically saw his psychiatric patients until eight or nine in the evening, was appearing in the driveway at four-thirty. I had been living at home for nearly a year and was in the final push of work on what would prove a dismal failure of a novel. When I wasn't struggling over my prose, I kept occupied with the things she usually did— the daily errands, the grocery shopping, the vacuuming and the cleaning, and, of course, all the cooking.

When I was six or seven years old, I used to watch my mother as she   7
prepared our favorite meals. It was one of my daily pleasures. She shooed me away in the beginning, telling me that the kitchen wasn't my place, and adding, in her half-proud, half-deprecating way, that her kind of work would only serve to weaken me. "Go out and play with your friends," she'd snap in Korean, "or better yet, do your reading and homework." She knew that I had already done both, and that as the evening approached there was no place to go save her small and tidy kitchen, from which the clatter of her mixing bowls and pans would ring through the house.

I would enter the kitchen quietly and stand beside her, my chin lodg-   8
ing upon the point of her hip. Peering through the crook of her arm, I beheld the movements of her hands. For *kalbi,* she would take up a butchered short rib in her narrow hand, the flinty bone shaped like a section of an airplane wing and deeply embedded in gristle and flesh, and with the point of her knife cut so that the bone fell away, though not completely, leaving it connected to the meat by the barest opaque layer of tendon. Then she methodically butterflied the flesh, cutting and unfolding, repeating the action until the meat lay out on her board, glistening and ready for seasoning. She scored it diagonally then sifted sugar into the crevices with her pinched fingers, gently rubbing in the crystals. The sugar would tenderize as well as sweeten the meat. She did this with each rib, and then set them all aside in a large shallow bowl. She minced a half-dozen cloves of garlic, a stub of gingerroot, sliced up a few scallions, and spread it all over the meat. She wiped

her hands and took out a bottle of sesame oil, and, after pausing for a moment, streamed the dark oil in two swift circles around the bowl. After adding a few splashes of soy sauce she thrust her hands in and kneaded the flesh, careful not to dislodge the bones. I asked her why it mattered that they remain connected. "The meat needs the bone nearby," she said, "to borrow its richness." She wiped her hands clean of the marinade except for her little finger, which she would flick with her tongue from time to time, because she knew that the flavor of a good dish developed not at once but in stages.

Whenever I cook, I find myself working just as she would, readying 9
the ingredients—a mash of garlic, a julienne of red peppers, fantails of shrimp—and piling them in little mounds about the cutting surface. My mother never left me any recipes, but this is how I learned to make her food, each dish coming not from a list or a card but from the aromatic spread of a board.

I've always thought it was particularly cruel that the cancer was in her 10
stomach, and that for a long time at the end she couldn't eat. The last meal I made for her was on New Year's Eve, 1990. My sister suggested that instead of a rib roast or a bird, or the usual overflow of Korean food, we make all sorts of finger dishes that our mother might fancy and pick at.

We set the meal out on the glass coffee table in the family room. I pre- 11
pared a tray of smoked-salmon canapés, fried some Korean bean cakes, and made a few other dishes I thought she might enjoy. My sister supervised me, arranging the platters, and then with some pomp carried each dish in to our parents. Finally, I brought out a bottle of champagne in a bucket of ice. My mother had moved to the sofa and was sitting up, surveying the low table. "It looks pretty nice," she said. "I think I'm feeling hungry."

This made us all feel good, especially me, for I couldn't remember the 12
last time she had felt any hunger or had eaten something I cooked. We began to eat. My mother picked up a piece of salmon toast and took a tiny corner in her mouth. She rolled it around for a moment and then pushed it out with the tip of her tongue, letting it fall back onto her plate. She swallowed hard, as if to quell a gag then glanced up to see if we had noticed. Of course we all had. She attempted a bean cake, some cheese, and then a slice of fruit, but nothing was any use.

She nodded at me anyway, and said "Oh, it's very good." But I was al- 13
ready feeling lost and I put down my plate abruptly, nearly shattering it on the thick glass. There was an ugly pause before my father asked me in a weary, gentle voice if anything was wrong, and I answered that it was nothing, it was the last night of a long year, and we were together, and I was simply relieved. At midnight, I poured out glasses of champagne, even one for my mother, who took a deep sip. Her manner grew playful and light, and I

helped her shuffle to her mattress, and she lay down in the place where in a brief week she was dead.

My mother could whip up most anything, but during our first years of living in this country we ate only Korean foods. At my haranguelike behest, my mother set herself to learning how to cook exotic American dishes. Luckily, a kind neighbor, Mrs. Churchill, a tall, florid young woman with flaxen hair, taught my mother her most trusted recipes. Mrs. Churchill's two young sons, palish, weepy boys with identical crewcuts, always accompanied her, and though I liked them well enough, I would slip away from them after a few minutes, for I knew that the real action would be in the kitchen, where their mother was playing guide. Mrs. Churchill hailed from the state of Maine, where the finest Swedish meatballs and tuna casserole and angel-food cake in America are made. She readily demonstrated certain techniques—how to layer wet sheets of pasta for a lasagna or whisk up a simple roux, for example. She often brought gift shoeboxes containing curious ingredients like dried oregano, instant yeast, and cream-of-mushroom soup. The two women, though at ease and jolly with each other, had difficulty communicating, and this was made worse by the often confusing terminology of Western cuisine ("corned beef," "devilled eggs"). Although I was just learning the language myself, I'd gladly play the interlocutor, jumping back and forth between their places at the counter, dipping my fingers into whatever sauce lay about.   14

I was an insistent child, and, being my mother's firstborn, much too prized. My mother could say no to me, and did often enough, but anyone who knew us—particularly my father and sister—could tell how much the denying pained her. And if I was overconscious of her indulgence even then, and suffered the rushing pangs of guilt that she could inflict upon me with the slightest wounded turn of her lip, I was too happily obtuse and venal to let her cease. She reminded me daily that I was her sole son, her reason for living, and that if she were to lose me, in either body or spirit, she wished that God would mercifully smite her, strike her down like a weak branch.   15

In the traditional fashion, she was the house accountant, the maid, the launderer, the driver, the secretary, and, of course, the cook. She was also my first basketball coach. In South Korea, where girls' high-school basketball is a popular spectator sport, she had been a star, the point guard for the national high-school team that once won the all-Asia championships. I learned this one Saturday during the summer, when I asked my father if he would go down to the school yard and shoot some baskets with me. I had just finished the fifth grade, and wanted desperately to make the middle-school team the coming fall. He called for my mother and sister to come along. When we arrived, my sister immediately ran off to the swings, and I   16 recall being annoyed that my mother wasn't following her. I dribbled clumsily around the key, on the verge of losing control of the ball, and flung a flat shot that caromed wildly off the rim. The ball bounced to my father, who took a few not so graceful dribbles and made an easy layup. He dribbled out and then drove to the hoop for a layup on the other side. He rebounded his shot and passed the ball to my mother, who had been watching us from the foul line. She turned from the basket and began heading the other way.

"*Urn-mah,*" I cried at her, my exasperation already bubbling over,   17
"the basket's over here!"

After a few steps she turned around, and from where the professional   18
three-point line must be now, she effortlessly flipped the ball up in a two-handed set shot, its flight truer and higher than I'd witnessed from any boy or man. The ball arced cleanly into the hoop, stiffly popping the chain-link net. All afternoon, she rained in shot after shot, as my father and I scrambled after her.

When we got home from the playground, my mother showed me the   19
photograph album of her team's championship run. For years, I kept it in my room, on the same shelf that housed the scrapbooks I made of basketball stars, with magazine clippings of slick players like Bubbles Hawkins and Pistol Pete and George (the Iceman) Gervin.

It puzzled me how much she considered her own history to be imma-   20
terial, and if she never patently diminished herself, she was able to finesse a kind of self-removal by speaking of my father whenever she could. She zealously recounted his excellence as a student in medical school and reminded me, each night before I started my homework, of how hard he drove himself in his work to make a life for us. She said that because of his Asian face and imperfect English, he was "working two times the American doctors." I knew that she was building him up, buttressing him with both genuine admiration and her own brand of anxious braggadocio, and that her overarching concern was that I might fail to see him as she wished me to—in the most dawning light, his pose steadfast and solitary.

In the year before I left for Exeter, I became weary of her oft-   21
repeated accounts of my father's success. I was a teen-ager, and so ever inclined to be dismissive and bitter toward anything that had to do with family and home. Often enough, my mother was the object of my derision. Suddenly, her life seemed so small to me. She was there, and sometimes, I thought, *always* there, as if she were confined to the four walls of our house. I would even complain about her cooking. Mostly, though, I was getting more and more impatient with the difficulty she encountered in doing everyday things. I was afraid for her. One day, we got into a terrible argument when she asked me to call the bank, to question a discrepancy she had

discovered in the monthly statement. I asked her why she couldn't call herself. I was stupid and brutal, and I knew exactly how to wound her.

"Whom do I talk to?" she said. She would mostly speak to me in Korean, and I would answer in English.   22

"The bank manager, who else?"   23

"What do I say?"   24

"Whatever you want to say."   25

"Don't speak to me like that!" she cried.   26

"It's just that you should be able to do it yourself," I said.   27

"You know how I feel about this!"   28

"Well, maybe then you should consider it *practice,*" I answered lightly,   29
using the Korean word to make sure she understood.

Her face blanched, and her neck suddenly became rigid, as if I were   30
throttling her. She nearly struck me right then, but instead she bit her lip
and ran upstairs. I followed her, pleading for forgiveness at her door. But it
was the one time in our life that I couldn't convince her, melt her resolve
with the blandishments of a spoiled son.

When my mother was feeling strong enough, or was in particularly   31
good spirits, she would roll her machine into the kitchen and sit at the table
and watch me work. She wore pajamas day and night, mostly old pairs of
mine.

She said, "I can't tell, what are you making?"   32

"Mahn-doo filling."   33

"You didn't salt the cabbage and squash."   34

"Was I supposed to?"   35

"Of course. Look, it's too wet. Now the skins will get soggy before you   36
can fry them."

"What should I do?"   37

"It's too late. Maybe it'll be O.K. If you work quickly. Why didn't you   38
ask me?"

"You were finally sleeping."   39

"You should have woken me."   40

"No way."   41

She sighed, as deeply as her weary lungs would allow.   42

"I don't know how you were going to make it without me."   43

"I don't know, either. I'll remember the salt next time."   44

"You better. And not too much."   45

We often talked like this, our tone decidedly matter-of-fact, chin up,   46
just this side of being able to bear it. Once, while inspecting a potato-fritter
batter I was making, she asked me if she had ever done anything that I
wished she hadn't done. I thought for a moment, and told her no. In the next

breath, she wondered aloud if it was right of her to have let me go to Exeter, to live away from the house while I was so young. She tested the batter's thickness with her finger and called for more flour. Then she asked if, given a choice, I would go to Exeter again.

I wasn't sure what she was getting at, and I told her that I couldn't be 47 certain, but probably, yes, I would. She snorted at this and said it was my leaving home that had once so troubled our relationship. "Remember how I had so much difficulty talking to you? Remember?"

She believed back then that I had found her more and more ignorant 48 each time I came home. She said she never blamed me, for this was the way she knew it would be with my wonderful new education. Nothing I could say seemed to quell the notion. But I knew that the problem wasn't simply the *education;* the first time I saw her again after starting school, barely six weeks later, when she and my father visited me on Parents Day, she had already grown nervous and distant. After the usual campus events, we had gone to the motel where they were staying in a nearby town and sat on the beds in our room. She seemed to sneak looks at me, as though I might discover a horrible new truth if our eyes should meet.

My own secret feeling was that I had missed my parents greatly, my 49 mother especially, and much more than I had anticipated. I couldn't tell them that these first weeks were a mere blur to me, that I felt completely overwhelmed by all the studies and my much brighter friends and the thousand irritating details of living alone, and that I had really learned nothing, save perhaps how to put on a necktie while sprinting to class. I felt as if I had plunged too deep into the world, which, to my great horror, was much larger than I had ever imagined.

I welcomed the lull of the motel room. My father and I had nearly 50 dozed off when my mother jumped up excitedly, murmured how stupid she was, and hurried to the closet by the door. She pulled out our old metal cooler and dragged it between the beds. She lifted the top and began unpacking plastic containers, and I thought she would never stop. One after the other they came out, each with a dish that travelled well—a salted stewed meat, rolls of Korean-style sushi. I opened a container of radish kimchi and suddenly the room bloomed with its odor, and I revelled in the very peculiar sensation (which perhaps only true kimchi lovers know) of simultaneously drooling and gagging as I breathed it all in. For the next few minutes, they watched me eat. I'm not certain that I was even hungry. But after weeks of pork parmigiana and chicken patties and wax beans, I suddenly realized that I had lost all the savor in my life. And it seemed I couldn't get enough of it back. I ate and I ate, so much and so fast that I actually went to the bathroom and vomited. I came out dizzy and sated with the phantom warmth of my binge.

And beneath the face of her worry, I thought, my mother was smiling.   51

From that day, my mother prepared a certain meal to welcome me   52
home. It was always the same. Even as I rode the school's shuttle bus from
Exeter to Logan airport, I could already see the exact arrangement of my
mother's table.

I knew that we would eat in the kitchen, the table brimming with plates.   53
There was the *kalbi,* of course, broiled or grilled depending on the season.
Leaf lettuce, to wrap the meat with. Bowls of garlicky clam broth with miso
and tofu and fresh spinach. Shavings of cod dusted in flour and then dipped
in egg wash and fried. Glass noodles with onions and shiitake. Scallion-and-
hot-pepper pancakes. Chilled steamed shrimp. Seasoned salads of bean
sprouts, spinach, and white radish. Crispy squares of seaweed. Steamed rice
with barley and red beans. Homemade kimchi. It was all there—the old
flavors I knew, the beautiful salt, the sweet, the excellent taste.

After the meal, my father and I talked about school, but of course I   54
could never say enough for it to make any sense. My father would often recall his high-school principal, who had gone to England to study the methods and traditions of the public schools, and regaled students with stories of
the great Eton men. My mother sat with us, paring fruit, not saying a word
but taking everything in. When it was time to go to bed, my father said good
night first. I usually watched television until the early morning. My mother
would sit with me for an hour or two, perhaps until she was accustomed to
me again, and only then would she kiss me and head upstairs to sleep.

During the following days, it was always the cooking that started our   55
conversations. She'd hold an inquest over the cold leftovers we ate at lunch,
discussing each dish in terms of its balance of flavors or what might have
been prepared differently. But mostly I begged her to leave the dishes
alone. I wish I had paid more attention. After her death, when my father
and I were the only ones left in the house, drifting through the rooms like
ghosts, I sometimes tried to make that meal for him. Though it was too
much for two, I made each dish anyway, taking as much care as I could. But
nothing turned out quite right—not the color, not the smell. At the table,
neither of us said much of anything. And we had to eat the food for days.

I remember washing rice in the kitchen one day, and my mother's say-   56
ing in English, from her usual seat, "I made a big mistake."

"About Exeter?"   57

"Yes. I made a big mistake. You should be with us for that time. I   58
should never let you go there."

"So why did you?" I said.   59

"Because I didn't know I was going to die."   60

I let her words pass. For the first time in her life, she was letting herself   61
speak her full mind, so what else could I do?

"But you know what?" she spoke up. "It was better for you. If you   62
stayed home, you would not like me so much now."

I suggested that maybe I would like her even more.   63

She shook her head. "Impossible."   64

Sometimes I still think about what she said, about having made a mis-   65
take. I would have left home for college, that was never in doubt, but those
years I was away at boarding school grew more precious to her as her illness
progressed. After many months of exhaustion and pain and the haze of the
drugs, I thought that her mind was beginning to fade, for more and more it
seemed that she was seeing me again as her fifteen-year-old boy, the one she
had dropped off in New Hampshire on a cloudy September afternoon.

I remember the first person I met, another new student, named Zack,   66
who walked to the welcome picnic with me. I had planned to eat with my
parents—my mother had brought a coolerful of food even that first day—
but I learned of the cookout and told her that I should probably go. I wanted to go, of course. I was excited, and no doubt fearful and nervous, and I
must have thought I was only thinking ahead. She agreed wholeheartedly,
saying I certainly should. I walked them to the car, and perhaps I hugged
them, before saying goodbye. One day, after she died, my father told me
what happened on the long drive home to Syracuse.

He was driving the car, looking straight ahead. Traffic was light on the   67
Massachusetts Turnpike, and the sky was nearly dark. They had driven for
more than two hours and had not yet spoken a word. He then heard a
strange sound from her, a kind of muffled chewing noise, as if something inside her were grinding its way out.

"So, what's the matter?" he said, trying to keep an edge to his voice.   68

She looked at him with her ashen face and she burst into tears. He   69
began to cry himself, and pulled the car over onto the narrow shoulder of
the turnpike, where they stayed for the next half hour or so, the blank-faced
cars droning by them in the cold, onrushing night.

Every once in a while, when I think of her, I'm driving alone some-   70
where on the highway. In the twilight, I see their car off to the side, a blue
Olds coupe with a landau top, and as I pass them by I look back in the mirror and I see them again, the two figures huddling together in the front seat.
Are they sleeping? Or kissing? Are they all right?

◆ ◆ ◆

The Long Good-bye: Mother's Day in Federal Prison

AMANDA COYNE

Amanda Coyne was a graduate student in the Master of Fine Arts writing program at the University of Iowa when she wrote this article about a visit with her sister, an inmate of the Federal Prison Camp for women in Pekin, Illinois. This is Coyne's first published article; it appeared in the May 1997 edition of *Harper's* magazine.

You can spot the convict-moms here in the visiting room by the way   1
they hold and touch their children and by the single flower that is perched in front of them—a rose, a tulip, a daffodil. Many of these mothers have untied the bow that attaches the flower to its silver-and-red cellophane wrapper and are using one of the many empty soda cans at hand as a vase. They sit proudly before their flower-in-a-Coke-can, amid Hershey bar wrappers, half-eaten Ding Dongs, and empty paper coffee cups. Occasionally, a mother will pick up her present and bring it to her nose when one of the bearers of the single flower—her child—asks if she likes it. And the mother will respond the way that mothers always have and always will respond when presented with a gift on this day. "Oh, I just love it. It's perfect. I'll put it in the middle of my Bible." Or, "I'll put it on my desk, right next to your school picture." And always: "It's the best one here."

But most of what is being smelled today is the children themselves.   2
While the other adults are plunking coins into the vending machines, the mothers take deep whiffs from the backs of their children's necks, or kiss and smell the backs of their knees, or take off their shoes and tickle their feet and then pull them close to their noses. They hold them tight and take in their own second scent—the scent assuring them that these are still their children and that they still belong to them.

The visitors are allowed to bring in pockets full of coins, and today that   3
Mother's Day flower, and I know from previous visits to my older sister here at the Federal Prison Camp for women in Pekin, Illinois, that there is always an aberrant urge to gather immediately around the vending machines. The sandwiches are stale, the coffee weak, the candy bars the ones we always pass up in a convenience store. But after we hand the children over to their mothers, we gravitate toward those machines. Like milling in the kitchen at a party. We all do it, and nobody knows why. Polite conversation ensues around

the microwave while the popcorn is popping and the processed-chicken sandwiches are being heated. We ask one another where we are from, how long a drive we had. An occasional whistle through the teeth, a shake of the head. "My, my, long way from home, huh?" "Staying at the Super 8 right up the road. Not a bad place." "Stayed at the Econo Lodge last time. Wasn't a good place at all." Never asking the questions we really want to ask: "What's she in for?" "How much time's she got left?" You never ask in the waiting room of a doctor's office either. Eventually, all of us—fathers, mothers, sisters, brothers, a few boyfriends, and very few husbands—return to the queen of the day, sitting at a fold-out table loaded with snacks, prepared for five or so hours of attempted normal conversation.

Most of the inmates are elaborately dressed, many in prison-crafted   4
dresses and sweaters in bright blues and pinks. They wear meticulously applied makeup in corresponding hues, and their hair is replete with loops and curls—hair that only women with the time have the time for. Some of the better seamstresses have crocheted vests and purses to match their outfits. Although the world outside would never accuse these women of making haute-couture fashion statements, the fathers and the sons and the boyfriends and the very few husbands think they look beautiful, and they tell them so repeatedly. And I can imagine the hours spent preparing for this visit—hours of needles and hooks clicking over brightly colored yards of yarn. The hours of discussing, dissecting, and bragging about these visitors—especially the men. Hours spent in the other world behind the door where we're not allowed, sharing lipsticks and mascaras, and unraveling the occasional hair-tangled hot roller, and the brushing out and lifting and teasing. . . and the giggles that abruptly change into tears without warning—things that define any female-only world. Even, or especially, if that world is a female federal prison camp.

While my sister Jennifer is with her son in the playroom, an inmate's   5
mother comes over to introduce herself to my younger sister, Charity, my brother, John, and me. She tells us about visiting her daughter in a higher-security prison before she was transferred here. The woman looks old and tired, and her shoulders sag under the weight of her recently acquired bitterness.

"Pit of fire," she says, shaking her head. "Like a pit of fire straight from   6
hell. Never seen anything like it. Like something out of an old movie about prisons." Her voice is getting louder and she looks at each of us with pleading eyes. "My daughter was there. Don't even get me started on that place. Women die there."

John and Charity and I silently exchange glances.   7

"My daughter would come to the visiting room with a black eye and   8
I'd think, 'All she did was sit in the car while her boyfriend ran into the
house.' She didn't even touch the stuff. Never even handled it."

She continues to stare at us, each in turn. "Ten years. That boyfriend   9
talked and he got three years. She didn't know anything. Had nothing to tell
them. They gave her ten years. They called it conspiracy. Conspiracy? Aren't
there real criminals out there?" She asks this with hands outstretched, waiting for an answer that none of us can give her.

The woman's daughter, the conspirator, is chasing her son through the   10
maze of chairs and tables and through the other children. She's a twenty-
four-year-old blonde, whom I'll call Stephanie, with Dorothy Hamill hair and
matching dimples. She looks like any girl you might see in any shopping mall
in middle America. She catches her chocolate-brown son and tickles him,
and they laugh and trip and fall together onto the floor and laugh harder.

Had it not been for that wait in the car, this scene would be taking   11
place at home, in a duplex Stephanie would rent while trying to finish her
two-year degree in dental hygiene or respiratory therapy at the local community college. The duplex would be spotless, with a blown-up picture of
her and her son over the couch and ceramic unicorns and horses occupying
the shelves of the entertainment center. She would make sure that her son
went to school every day with stylishly floppy pants, scrubbed teeth, and a
good breakfast in his belly. Because of their difference in skin color, there
would be occasional tension—caused by the strange looks from strangers,
teachers, other mothers, and the bullies on the playground, who would
chant after they knocked him down, "Your Momma's white, your Momma's
white." But if she were home, their weekends and evenings would be spent
together transcending those looks and healing those bruises. Now, however,
their time is spent eating visiting-room junk food and his school days are
spent fighting the boys in the playground who chant, "Your Momma's in
prison, your Momma's in prison."

He will be ten when his mother is released, the same age my nephew   12
will be when his mother is let out. But Jennifer, my sister, was able to spend
the first five years of Toby's life with him. Stephanie had Ellie after she was
incarcerated. They let her hold him for eighteen hours, then sent her back to
prison. She has done the "tour," and her son is a well-traveled six-year-old.
He has spent weekends visiting his mother in prisons in Kentucky, Texas,
Connecticut (the Pit of Fire), and now at last here, the camp—minimum security, Pekin, Illinois.

Ellie looks older than his age. But his shoulders do not droop like his   13
grandmother's. On the contrary, his bitterness lifts them and his chin higher
than a child's should be, and the childlike, wide-eyed curiosity has been

replaced by defiance. You can see his emerging hostility as he and his mother play together. She tells him to pick up the toy that he threw, say, or to put the deck of cards away. His face turns sullen, but she persists. She takes him by the shoulders and looks him in the eye, and he uses one of his hands to swat at her. She grabs the hand and he swats with the other. Eventually, she pulls him toward her and smells the top of his head, and she picks up the cards or the toy herself. After all, it is Mother's Day and she sees him so rarely. But her acquiescence makes him angrier, and he stalks out of the playroom with his shoulders thrown back.

Toby, my brother and sister and I assure one another, will not have   14
these resentments. He is better taken care of than most. He is living with relatives in Wisconsin. Good, solid, middle-class, churchgoing relatives. And when he visits us, his aunts and his uncle, we take him out for adventures where we walk down the alley of a city and pretend that we are being chased by the "bad guys." We buy him fast food, and his uncle, John, keeps him up well past his bedtime enthralling him with stories of the monkeys he met in India. A perfect mix, we try to convince one another. Until we take him to see his mother and on the drive back he asks the question that most confuses him, and no doubt all the other children who spend much of their lives in prison visiting rooms: "Is my Mommy a bad guy?" It is the question that most seriously disorders his five-year-old need to clearly separate right from wrong. And because our own need is perhaps just as great, it is the question that haunts us as well.

Now, however, the answer is relatively simple. In a few years, it won't   15
be. In a few years we will have to explain mandatory minimums, and the war on drugs, and the murky conspiracy laws, and the enormous amount of money and time that federal agents pump into imprisoning low-level drug dealers and those who happen to be their friends and their lovers. In a few years he might have the reasoning skills to ask why so many armed robbers and rapists and child-molesters and, indeed, murderers are punished less severely than his mother. When he is older, we will somehow have to explain to him the difference between federal crimes which don't allow for parole, and state crimes, which do. We will have to explain that his mother was taken from him for five years, not because she was a drug dealer but because she made four phone calls for someone she loved.

But we also know it is vitally important that we explain all this with-   16
out betraying our bitterness. We understand the danger of abstract anger, of being disillusioned with your country, and, most of all, we do not want him to inherit that legacy. We would still like him to be raised as we were, with the idea that we live in the best country in the world with the best legal system in the world—a legal system carefully designed to be immune

to political mood swings and public hysteria; a system that promises to fit the punishment to the crime. We want him to be a good citizen. We want him to have absolute faith that he lives in a fair country, a country that watches over and protects its most vulnerable citizens: its women and children.

So for now we simply say, "Toby, your mother isn't bad, she just did a bad thing. Like when you put rocks in the lawn mower's gas tank. You weren't bad then, you just did a bad thing."   17

Once, after being given this weak explanation, he said, "I wish I could have done something really bad, like my Mommy. So I could go to prison too and be with her."   18

We notice a circle forming on one side of the visiting room. A little boy stands in its center. He is perhaps nine years old, sporting a burnt-orange three-piece suit and pompadour hair. He stands with his legs slightly apart, eyes half-shut, and sways back and forth, flashing his cuffs and snapping his fingers while singing: 19

> . . . Doesn't like crap games with barons and earls.
> Won't go to Harlem in ermine and pearls.
> Won't dish the dirt with the rest of the girls.
> That's why the lady is a tramp.

He has a beautiful voice and it sounds vaguely familiar. One of the visitors informs me excitedly that the boy is the youngest Frank Sinatra impersonator and that he has been on television even. The boy finishes his performance and the room breaks into applause. He takes a sweeping bow, claps his miniature hands together, and points both little index fingers at the audience. "More. Later. Folks." He spins on his heels and returns to the table where his mother awaits him, proudly glowing. "Don't mess with the hair, Mom," we overhear. "That little boy's slick," my brother says with true admiration.   20

Sitting a few tables down from the youngest Frank Sinatra is a table of Mexican-Americans. The young ones are in white dresses or button-down oxfords with matching ties. They form a strange formal contrast to the rest of the rowdy group. They sit silently, solemnly listening to the white-haired woman, who holds one of the table's two roses. I walk past and listen to the grandmother lecture her family. She speaks of values, of getting up early every day, of going to work. She looks at one of the young boys and points a finger at him. "School is the most important thing. *Nada mas importante.* You get up and you go to school and you study, and you can make lots of money. You can be big. You can be huge. Study, study, study."   21

The young boy nods his head. "Yes, *abuelita.* Yes, *abuelita,*" he says.   22

The owner of the other flower is holding one of the group's three in-   23
fants. She has him spread before her. She coos and kisses his toes and nuz-
zles his stomach.

When I ask Jennifer about them, she tells me that it is a "mother and   24
daughter combo." There are a few of them here, these combos, and I notice
that they have the largest number of visitors and that the older inmate, the
grandmother, inevitably sits at the head of the table. Even here, it seems the
hierarchical family structure remains intact. One could take a picture, replace the fast-food wrappers with chicken and potatoes, and these families
could be at any restaurant in the country, could be sitting at any dining room
table, paying homage on this day to the one who brought them into the world.

Back at our table, a black-haired Middle Eastern woman dressed in   25
loose cottons and cloth shoes is whispering to my brother with a sense of ur-
gency that makes me look toward my sister Charity with questioning eyes
and a tilt of my head. Charity simply shrugs and resumes her conversation
with a nineteen-year-old ex-New York University student—another conspirator. Eight years.

Prison, it seems, has done little to squelch the teenager's rebellious na-   26
ture. She has recently been released from solitary confinement. She wears
new retro-bellbottom jeans and black shoes with big clunky heels. Her hair is
short, clipped perfectly ragged and dyed white—all except the roots, which
are a stylish black. She has beautiful pale skin and beautiful red lips. She
looks like any midwestern coed trying to escape her origins by claiming New
York's East Village as home. She steals the bleach from the laundry room, I
learn later, in order to maintain that fashionable white hue. But stealing the
bleach is not what landed her in the hole. She committed the inexcusable act
of defacing federal property. She took one of her government-issue T-shirts
and wrote in permanent black magic marker, "I have been in your system. I
have examined your system." And when she turned around it read, "I find it
very much in need of repair."

But Charity has more important things to discuss with the girl than re-   27
belling against the system. They are talking fashion. They talk prints versus
plains, spring shoes, and spring dresses. Charity informs the girl that sling-
back, high-heeled sandals and pastels are all the rage. She makes a disgusted
face and says, "Damn! Pinks and blues wash me out. I hate pastels. I don't
have any pastels."

This fashion blip seems to be putting the girl into a deep depression.   28
And so Charity, attempting to lighten up the conversation, puts her nose toward the girl's neck.

"New Armani scent, Gio," my sister announces.   29

The girl perks up. She nods her head. She calls one of the other in-   30
mates over.

Charity performs the same ritual: "Coco Chanel." And again: "Paris,   31
Yves St. Laurent."

The line gets longer, and the girls talk excitedly to one another. It   32
seems that Charity's uncanny talent for divining brand-name perfumes is
perhaps nowhere on earth more appreciated than here with these sensory-
starved inmates.

As Charity continues to smell necks and call out names, I turn back to   33
my brother and find that the woman who was speaking to him so intensely
has gone. He stares pensively at the concrete wall ahead of him.

"What did she want?" I ask.   34

"She heard I was a sculptor. She wants me to make a bust, presented   35
in her name, for Qaddafi."

"A bust of what?"   36

"Of Qaddafi. She's from Libya. She was a freedom fighter. Her kids   37
are farmed out to strangers here—foster homes. It's Qaddafi's twenty-
eighth anniversary as dictator in September. She knows him. He's mad at
her now, but she thinks that he'll get over it and get her kids back to Libya
if she gives him a present."

"Obsession. Calvin Klein," I hear my sister pronounce. The girls cheer   38
in unison.

I get up and search for the girl. I want to ask her about her crime. I   39
look in the book room only to find the four-foot Frank Sinatra crooning
"Somewhere over the Rainbow" to a group of spellbound children.

I ask Ponytail, one of the female guards, where the woman went.   40
"Rule," she informs me. "Cannot be in the visiting room if no visitor is present. Should not have been here. Had to go back to unit one." I have spoken
to Ponytail a few times while visiting my sister and have yet to hear her use
a possessive pronoun, a contraction, or a conjunction.

According to Jennifer, Ponytail has wanted to be a prison guard since   41
she was a little girl. She is one of the few female guards here and she has
been here the longest, mainly because the male guards are continuously
being fired for "indiscretions" with the inmates. But Ponytail doesn't mess
around. She is also the toughest guard here, particularly in regard to the
federal rules governing exposed skin. She is disgusted by any portion of the
leg showing above the required eight-inch shorts length. In summer, they
say, she is constantly whipping out her measuring tape and writing up those
who are even a fraction of an inch off.

Last summer posed a particular problem for Ponytail, though. It seems   42
that the shorts sold in the commissary were only seven inches from crotch to
seam. And because they were commissary-issued, Ponytail couldn't censor
them. So, of course, all the women put away their own shorts in favor of
the commissary's. This disturbed Ponytail—a condition that eventually,

according to one of the girls, developed into a low-grade depression. "She walked around with that sad old tape in her hands all summer, throwing it from one hand to the other and looking at our legs. After a while, not one of us could get her even to crack a smile—not that she's a big smiler, but you can get those corners to turn sometimes. Then she started looking downright sad, you know real depressed like."

Ponytail makes sure that the girls get proper medical care. Also none   43
of the male guards will mess with them when she's around. But even if those things weren't true, the girls would be fond of Ponytail. She is in a way just another woman in the system, and perhaps no other group of women realizes the absolute necessity for female solidarity. These inmates know with absolute certainty what women on the outside only suspect—that men still hold ultimate power over their bodies, their property, and their freedom.

So as a token of this solidarity, they all agreed to slip off their federal   44
shorts and put on their own. Ponytail perked up, the measuring tape appeared again with a vengeance, and quite a few of the shorts owners spent much of their free time that summer cleaning out toilet bowls and wiping the scuffs off the gym floor.

It's now 3:00. Visiting ends at 3:30. The kids are getting cranky, and the   45
adults are both exhausted and wired from too many hours of conversation, too much coffee and candy. The fathers, mothers, sisters, brothers, and the few boyfriends, and the very few husbands are beginning to show signs of gathering the trash. The mothers of the infants are giving their heads one last whiff before tucking them and their paraphernalia into their respective carrying cases. The visitors meander toward the door, leaving the older children with their mothers for one last word. But the mothers never say what they want to say to their children. They say things like, "Do well in school," "Be nice to your sister," "Be good for Aunt Betty, or Grandma." They don't say, "I'm sorry I'm sorry I'm sorry. I love you more than anything else in the world and I think about you every minute and I worry about you with a pain that shoots straight to my heart, a pain so great I think I will just burst when I think of you alone, without me. I'm sorry."

We are standing in front of the double glass doors that lead to the out-   46
side world. My older sister holds her son, rocking him gently. They are both crying. We give her a look and she puts him down. Charity and I grasp each of his small hands, and the four of us walk through the doors. As we're walking out, my brother sings one of his banana songs to Toby.

"Take me out to the—" and Toby yells out, "Banana store!"   47
"Buy me some—"   48
"Bananas!!"   49
"I don't care if I ever come back. For it's root, root, root for the—"   50

"Monkey team!"   51

I turn back and see a line of women standing behind the glass wall.   52
Some of them are crying, but many simply stare with dazed eyes. Stephanie
is holding both of her son's hands in hers and speaking urgently to him. He
is struggling, and his head is twisting violently back and forth. He frees one
of his hands from her grasp, balls up his fist, and punches her in the face.
Then he walks with purpose through the glass doors and out the exit. I look
back at her. She is still in a crouched position. She stares, unblinking,
through those doors. Her hands have left her face and are hanging on either
side of her. I look away, but before I do, I see drops of blood drip from her
nose, down her chin, and onto the shiny marble floor.

◆ ◆ ◆

The Way We Weren't:
The Myth and Reality
of the "Traditional" Family

STEPHANIE COONTZ

Stephanie Coontz teaches at Evergreen State College in Olympia,
Washington, and is the recipient of the Washington Governor's Writers
Award. Coontz has written several books about the American family, including *The Way We Never Were: American Families and the Nostalgia Trap*
(1993) and *The Way We Really Are: Coming to Terms with America's Changing Families* (1997). The following article was first published in the *Phi
Kappa Phi Journal* in 1995.

Families face serious problems today, but proposals to solve them by   1
reviving "traditional" family forms and values miss two points. First, no single
traditional family existed to which we could return, and none of the many varieties of families in our past has had any magic formula for protecting its
members from the vicissitudes of socioeconomic change, the inequities of
class, race, and gender, or the consequences of interpersonal conflict. Violence, child abuse, poverty, and the unequal distribution of resources to
women and children have occurred in every period and every type of family.

Second, the strengths that we also find in many families of the past   2
were rooted in different social, cultural, and economic circumstances from

those that prevail today. Attempts to reproduce any type of family outside of its original socioeconomic context are doomed to fail.

Colonial Families

American families always have been diverse, and the male breadwinner- 3 female homemaker, nuclear ideal that most people associate with "the" traditional family has predominated for only a small portion of our history. In colonial America, several types of families coexisted or competed. Native American kinship systems subordinated the nuclear family to a much larger network of marital alliances and kin obligations, ensuring that no single family was forced to go it alone. Wealthy settler families from Europe, by contrast, formed independent households that pulled in labor from poorer neighbors and relatives, building their extended family solidarities on the backs of truncated families among indentured servants, slaves, and the poor. Even wealthy families, though, often were disrupted by death; a majority of colonial Americans probably spent some time in a stepfamily. Meanwhile, African Americans, denied the legal protection of marriage and parenthood, built extensive kinship networks and obligations through fictive kin ties, ritual co-parenting or godparenting, adoption of orphans, and complex naming patterns designed to preserve family links across space and time.

The dominant family values of colonial days left no room for senti- 4 mentalizing childhood. Colonial mothers, for example, spent far less time doing child care than do modern working women, typically delegating this task to servants or older siblings. Among white families, patriarchal authority was so absolute that disobedience by a wife or child was seen as a small form of treason, theoretically punishable by death, and family relations were based on power, not love.

The Nineteenth-Century Family

With the emergence of a wage-labor system and a national market in 5 the first third of the nineteenth century, white middle-class families became less patriarchal and more child-centered. The ideal of the male breadwinner and the nurturing mother now appeared. But the emergence of domesticity for middle-class women and children depended on its absence among the immigrant, working class, and African American women or children who worked as servants, grew the cotton, or toiled in the textile mills to free middle-class wives from the chores that had occupied their time previously.

Even in the minority of nineteenth-century families who could afford 6 domesticity, though, emotional arrangements were quite different from nostalgic images of "traditional" families. Rigid insistence on separate spheres for men and women made male-female relations extremely stilted, so that women commonly turned to other women, not their husbands, for their most intimate relations. The idea that all of one's passionate feelings should go toward a member of the opposite sex was a twentieth-century invention—closely associated with the emergence of a mass consumer society and promulgated by the very film industry that "traditionalists" now blame for undermining such values.

Early Twentieth-Century Families

Throughout the nineteenth century, at least as much divergence and   7
disruption in the experience of family life existed as does today, even though divorce and unwed motherhood were less common. Indeed, couples who marry today have a better chance of celebrating a fortieth wedding anniversary than at any previous time in history. The life cycles of nineteenth-century youth (in job entry, completion of schooling, age at marriage, and establishment of separate residence) were far more diverse than they became in the early twentieth century. At the turn of the century a higher proportion of people remained single for their entire lives than at any period since. Not until the 1920s did a bare majority of children come to live in a male breadwinner-female homemaker family, and even at the height of this family form in the 1950s, only 60 percent of American children spent their entire childhoods in such a family.

From about 1900 to the 1920s, the growth of mass production and   8
emergence of a public policy aimed at establishing a family wage led to new ideas about family self-sufficiency, especially in the white middle class and a privileged sector of the working class. The resulting families lost their organic connection to intermediary units in society such as local shops, neighborhood work cultures and churches, ethnic associations, and mutual-aid organizations.

As families related more directly to the state, the market, and the   9
mass media, they also developed a new cult of privacy, along with heightened expectations about the family's role in fostering individual fulfillment. New family values stressed the early independence of children and the romantic coupling of husband and wife, repudiating the intense same-sex ties and mother-infant bonding of earlier years as unhealthy. From this family we get the idea that women are sexual, that youth is attractive, and that marriage should be the center of our emotional fulfillment.

Even aside from its lack of relevance to the lives of most immigrants,   10
Mexican Americans, African Americans, rural families, and the urban poor, big contradictions existed between image and reality in the middle-class family ideal of the early twentieth century. This is the period when many Americans first accepted the idea that the family should be sacred from

outside intervention; yet the development of the private, self-sufficient family depended on state intervention in the economy, government regulation of parent-child relations, and state-directed destruction of class and community institutions that hindered the development of family privacy. Acceptance of a youth and leisure culture sanctioned early marriage and raised expectations about the quality of married life, but also introduced new tensions between the generations and new conflicts between husband and wife over what were adequate levels of financial and emotional support.

The nineteenth-century middle-class ideal of the family as a refuge 11 from the world of work was surprisingly modest compared with emerging twentieth-century demands that the family provide a whole alternative world of satisfaction and intimacy to that of work and neighborhood. Where a family succeeded in doing so, people might find pleasures in the home never before imagined. But the new ideals also increased the possibilities for failure: America has had the highest divorce rate in the world since the turn of the century.

In the 1920s, these contradictions created a sense of foreboding about 12 "the future of the family" that was every bit as widespread and intense as today's. Social scientists and popular commentators of the time hearkened back to the "good old days," bemoaning the sexual revolution, the fragility of nuclear family ties, the cult of youthful romance, the decline of respect for grandparents, and the threat of the "New Woman." But such criticism was sidetracked by the stock-market crash, the Great Depression of the 1930s, and the advent of World War II.

Domestic violence escalated during the Depression, while murder 13 rates were as high in the 1930s as in the 1980s. Divorce rates fell, but desertion increased and fertility plummeted. The war stimulated a marriage boom, but by the late 1940s one in every three marriages was ending in divorce.

The 1950s Family

At the end of the 1940s, after the hardships of the Depression and war, 14 many Americans revived the nuclear family ideals that had so disturbed commentators during the 1920s. The unprecedented postwar prosperity allowed young families to achieve consumer satisfactions and socioeconomic mobility that would have been inconceivable in earlier days. The 1950s family that resulted from these economic and cultural trends, however, was hardly "traditional." Indeed, it is best seen as a historical aberration. For the first time in 100 years, divorce rates dropped, fertility soared, the gap between men's and women's job and educational prospects widened (making middle-class women more dependent on marriage), and the age of marriage fell—to the point that teenage birth rates were almost double what they are today.

Admirers of these very nontraditional 1950s family forms and values   15
point out that household arrangements and gender roles were less diverse
in the 1950s than today, and marriages more stable. But this was partly because diversity was ruthlessly suppressed and partly because economic and
political support systems for socially-sanctioned families were far more
generous than they are today. Real wages rose more in any single year of
the 1950s than they did in the entire decade of the 1980s; the average thirty-
year-old man could buy a median-priced home on 15 to 18 percent of his income. The government funded public investment, home ownership, and job
creation at a rate more than triple that of the past two decades, while 40 percent of young men were eligible for veteran's benefits. Forming and maintaining families was far easier than it is today.

Yet the stability of these 1950s families did not guarantee good out-   16
comes for their members. Even though most births occurred within wedlock, almost a third of American children lived in poverty during the 1950s,
a higher figure than today. More than 50 percent of black married-couple
families were poor. Women were often refused the right to serve on juries,
sign contracts, take out credit cards in their own names, or establish legal
residence. Wife-battering rates were low, but that was because wife-beating
was seldom counted as a crime. Most victims of incest, such as Miss America of 1958, kept the secret of their fathers' abuse until the 1970s or 1980s,
when the women's movement became powerful enough to offer them the
support denied them in the 1950s.

The Post-1950s Family

In the 1960s, the civil rights, antiwar, and women's liberation move-   17
ments exposed the racial, economic, and sexual injustices that had been papered over by the Ozzie and Harriet images on television. Their activism
made older kinds of public and private oppression unacceptable and helped
create the incomplete, flawed, but much-needed reforms of the Great Society. Contrary to the big lie of the past decade that such programs caused our
current family dilemmas, those antipoverty and social justice reforms
helped overcome many of the family problems that prevailed in the 1950s.

In 1964, after fourteen years of unrivaled family stability and eco-   18
nomic prosperity, the poverty rate was still 19 percent; in 1969, after five
years of civil rights activism, the rebirth of feminism, and the institution of
nontraditional if relatively modest government welfare programs, it was
down to 12 percent, a low that has not been seen again since the social welfare cutbacks began in the late 1970s. In 1965, 20 percent of American children still lived in poverty; within five years, that had fallen to 15 percent.
Infant mortality was cut in half between 1965 and 1980. The gap in nutrition

between low-income Americans and other Americans narrowed significantly, as a direct result of food stamp and school lunch programs. In 1963, 20 percent of Americans living below the poverty line had never been examined by a physician; by 1970 this was true of only 8 percent of the poor.

Since 1973, however, real wages have been falling for most Americans. 19 Attempts to counter this through tax revolts and spending freezes have led to drastic cutbacks in government investment programs. Corporations also spend far less on research and job creation than they did in the 1950s and 1960s, though the average compensation to executives has soared. The gap between rich and poor, according to the April 17, 1995, *New York Times,* is higher in the United States than in any other industrial nation.

Family Stress

These inequities are not driven by changes in family forms, contrary to 20 ideologues who persist in confusing correlations with causes; but they certainly exacerbate such changes, and they tend to bring out the worst in all families. The result has been an accumulation of stresses on families, alongside some important expansions of personal options. Working couples with children try to balance three full-time jobs, as employers and schools cling to policies that assume every employee has a "wife" at home to take care of family matters. Divorce and remarriage have allowed many adults and children to escape from toxic family environments, yet our lack of social support networks and failure to forge new values for sustaining intergenerational obligations have let many children fall through the cracks in the process.

Meanwhile, young people find it harder and harder to form or sustain 21 families. According to an Associated Press report of April 25, 1995, the median income of men aged twenty-five to thirty-four fell by 26 percent between 1972 and 1994, while the proportion of such men with earnings below the poverty level for a family of four more than doubled to 32 percent. The figures are even worse for African American and Latino men. Poor individuals are twice as likely to divorce as more affluent ones, three to four times less likely to marry in the first place, and five to seven times more likely to have a child out of wedlock.

As conservatives insist, there is a moral crisis as well as an economic 22 one in modern America: a pervasive sense of social alienation, new levels of violence, and a decreasing willingness to make sacrifices for others. But romanticizing "traditional" families and gender roles will not produce the changes in job structures, work policies, child care, medical practice, educational preparation, political discourse, and gender inequities that would permit families to develop moral and ethical systems relevant to 1990s realities.

America needs more than a revival of the narrow family obligations   23
of the 1950s, whose (greatly exaggerated) protection for white, middle-class
children was achieved only at tremendous cost to the women in those families and to all those who could not or would not aspire to the Ozzie and
Harriet ideal. We need a concern for children that goes beyond the question
of whether a mother is waiting with cookies when her kids come home from
school. We need a moral language that allows us to address something besides people's sexual habits. We need to build values and social institutions
that can reconcile people's needs for independence with their equally important rights to dependence, and surely we must reject older solutions that
involved balancing these needs on the backs of women. We will not find our
answers in nostalgia for a mythical "traditional family."

◆ ◆ ◆

Let's Get Rid of Sports

KATHA POLLITT

Katha Pollitt's writing has been described as "lucid, gutsy, funny, and
just." A number of her essays, which first appeared in *The New Yorker,* the
New York Times, and the *Nation,* were recently published in the collection
Reasonable Creatures: Essays on Women and Feminism (1994). In her regular column for the *Nation,* "Subject to Debate," Pollitt grapples with many
of society's most challenging problems—abortion, the media, and surrogate
motherhood. The following article was written for that column in the summer of 1995.

There ought to be a rule that bold proposals for the social and politi-   1
cal betterment of mankind be accompanied by explanations of how these
ideas will be brought to reality and why, if they're so brilliant and beneficial
as all that, they haven't already been implemented. I figure this requirement
would put most pundits out of business within weeks, which would be all to
the good. Imagine, for example, if the many who facilely advocate adoption
over abortion actually had to explain how it would work: where the millions
of would-be parents would come from; how women with unplanned preg-
nancies, who overwhelmingly reject adoption no matter how desperate
their circumstances, will be brought to embrace it; how mass adoption will

sit with current notions of genetic determinism, father's rights, cultural and racial identity. Are Tennessee Baptists really prepared to see their grand-children shipped off to be raised by New York Jews—or vice versa? To spell out what it would really involve is to make clear what a crackpot idea it is—which is, of course, why its advocates tend to move right along to the next "thought experiment," like orphanages over A.F.D.C.

But why criticize the right alone? Our own pages are full of visionary   2 schemes. Let's tell Clinton to abolish the C.I.A.! Let's permit noncitizens to vote! Let's raise children to be noncompetitive! Missing is a serious discussion of what organized interests are served by the status quo, how those interests are to be defeated and by whom. Lots of good ideas have no constituency in a position to bring them about: Think of all those Op-Ed articles that crop up every four years advocating the abolition of the Electoral College.

Well, I'm no better than the next pundit, so here's my big idea: Let's get   3 rid of sports. Baseball, basketball, football, boxing—especially boxing—tennis, gymnastics, Little League, high school, college, professional, Olympic, the whole schmear. Away with them!

Fans say athletics promote values, and so they do—the wrong values,   4 like the childish confusion of physical prowess with "character" that is such a salient feature of the O.J. Simpson trial. Sports pervert education, draining dollars from academic programs and fostering anti-intellectualism. They skew the priorities of the young, especially the poor, black young, by offering them the illusory hope of wealth and fame. Sports scholarships, often touted as a poor kid's only chance, just mean less money available to other poor kids, like girls, and ones with O.K. grades and no trophies. Besides, without the will-o'-the-wisp incentive of a scholarship, physically gifted kids might not be so ready to blow off their schoolwork. Why not give scholarships for art or music instead?

Although women are becoming more involved in sports, it's still a male   5 world, which actively encourages and protects the worst forms of male privilege and jerkiness. Athletes are disproportionately represented in reported campus sex crimes, and the pros' reputation for violence, against women or otherwise, is legendary. Without sports, we never would have heard of Ty Cobb, O.J. Simpson, Mike Tyson, Billy Martin, Darryl Strawberry.

Being a sports fan is even worse than being an actual athlete, since instead of getting all that exercise, one simply watches TV, punches the chair   6 and curses. But for both fans and players, sports are about creating a world from which women are absent. Men who follow sports, which means most men, have a realm of conversation that allows them to bond across classes effortlessly but superficially. Lefty sports advocates like to tout this cross-class appeal as a virtue—How about those Knicks?—but, even setting aside the fact that it's based on the exclusion of women, why would a leftist think it's good for class divisions to be smoothed over?

Sports fandom trains the young in group identification, passivity, spectatorship and celebrity-worship. I know men whose entire lives are mediated through sports, like my cousin who brings a little TV to family gatherings to catch The Game, or my writing student whose efforts at autobiography consisted entirely of play-by-play of long-ago Little League tournaments. Maybe once, sports functioned as a family, communal activity—the whole town out at the ballpark for a good time. Now it's just another form of isolation: every man in his own living room, staring at the screen. Women who object to pornography should be even more upset about sports. After all, whatever else porn may do, it does encourage sexual interest, which is why couples rent those videos. But sports are basically a way for men to avoid the claims of other people. That's one of several reasons why David ("Fatherless America") Blankenhorn's idea of promoting fatherhood by getting athletes to endorse it is such a joke: A guy who spends half the year on the road with the team pitches family life to men who are watching him expressly because he symbolizes the footloose and fancy-free life.

But what about the game, you cry, the thwack of ball against bat, the arc of football on its way to touchdown, the swish of ball into net? O.K., let's keep sports—but let's have only women play. Women can thwack and throw and swish too, after all. Turning sports over to women would change their meaning—you can't have bimbo cheerleaders if the athletes are women too—and, instead of promoting the worst qualities of men, they'd counteract the worst qualities of women, like defining themselves through men and wearing three-inch fake fingernails.

I know what you're thinking: Sports is a billion-dollar industry, deeply woven into the fabric of American life, avidly followed by millions who would go berserk if deprived. Besides, all-female football wouldn't be football. Right. Forget the whole thing. I don't know what came over me. And the next time a pundit comes up with a big idea—Let's bring back shame! Let's not let parents divorce!—you can probably forget that too.

◆ ◆ ◆

Back in the Hot Zone

RICHARD PRESTON

Richard Preston (b. 1954) earned a Ph.D. from Princeton in 1983 and began his career as a freelance writer in 1985. He specializes in scientific nonfiction. In 1992, Preston published a long article in *The New Yorker* that recounted the history of the extremely deadly Ebola viruses, including the 1989 outbreak in a suburban Washington, DC, animal laboratory. The expanded version of this article became a national best seller—*The Hot Zone* (1995). The following selection takes up where those earlier works left off.

1   We live in a kind of biological Internet, in which viruses travel like messages, moving at high speed from node to node, moving from city to city. Last week, reports reached the World Health Organization, in Geneva, that some kind of lethal unknown infectious agent, some kind of African hemorrhagic fever, possibly Ebola virus, was burning in Kikwit, Zaire, a poor city with a population of half a million. The city has grown in recent years. It is a transportation center some two hundred and fifty miles east of Kinshasa, the capital of Zaire, sprawling at the end point of the paved section of the Kinshasa Highway, the road that crosses Africa and along which the AIDS virus has spread. Kikwit is situated in rolling savannah threaded by slow rivers the color of chocolate milk, lined with gallery forest.

2   The city was in a panic. The Army had sealed off roads and wasn't allowing anyone to leave. The unknown infectious agent was causing people to die with hemorrhages flooding from the natural orifices of the body. That is, victims were bleeding out. The local people were calling it "the red diarrhea." The agent is now reported to be very similar to the Ebola Zaire strain that erupted in 1976 in villages near the Ebola River, five hundred miles north of Kikwit, where it killed nine out of ten of its infected victims. It is too early at this point to gauge how long it will take the Kikwit strain to burn itself out. It passes from person to person through blood and secretions, and it may also travel by sexual contact. It is quite contagious. There is no treatment and no cure for it.

3   Ebola is an emerging virus from the rain forest; it seems to come out of tropical ecosystems. It lives in some natural host, some type of fly, rodent, monkey, African cat—who knows? Where Ebola hides in the rain forest is a mystery. In the past couple of decades, it has been popping into the human species in different places and in different strains. It keeps touching the human biological Internet. Probing it, so to speak.

In the initial report received at the W.H.O., the agent was said to have   4
infected seventy-two people and killed fifty-six. There were rumors that a
medical technician had become sick, had been taken into surgery, and had
essentially exploded in the O.R.—had bled all over the place. A number of
people on the surgical team, it was said, had later died. Whatever was happening, it seemed that the Kikwit agent had zeroed in on the city's medical
personnel and was taking them out.

When this scary news in its unreliable shapes reached the W.H.O., it   5
happened that a W.H.O. scientific team was preparing to fly to Ivory Coast,
in West Africa, to investigate a confirmed case of a new strain of Ebola virus
there. Ebola had returned—this time to Ivory Coast. The W.H.O. Ebola
team consisted of a scientist from the Institut Pasteur in Paris named
Bernard Le Guenno and a French virologist named Pierre Rollin, who is
currently with the Centers for Disease Control in Atlanta. Le Guenno and
Rollin were diverted from their mission to Ivory Coast, and were sent to
Zaire instead; they joined a ten-member W.H.O. team of doctors from
South Africa, from France, from Zaire, and from the United States.

One of the South African doctors is a gigantic figure in the history of   6
infectious-disease outbreaks named Margaretha Isaacson. She is a grandmotherly woman who retired a couple of years ago from the South African
Institute for Medical Research and went to live in a retirement community
outside Johannesburg. Last week, she left a message on her home answering
machine that went, "Dr. Isaacson is not available," and she came out of retirement and flew to Zaire, and joined the team. She is in Kikwit now. During the
1976 Ebola eruption in Zaire, Margaretha Isaacson once took off her biohazard respirator because it interfered with her treatment of an Ebola patient,
and afterward she washed up two blood-splashed rooms by hand.

The Ivory Coast Ebola case occurred some six months ago, in Novem-   7
ber, 1994, when a woman scientist from Switzerland was studying a troop of
wild chimpanzees in the National Park of Tai. The Tai Forest is one of the
last pristine rain forests in West Africa. The troop of chimpanzees became
infected with a virus and many of them died. The Swiss woman, extremely
concerned about her chimps, dissected one of the dead animals, trying to
find out what had killed it, and, having come into contact with the dead
chimp's blood, she developed the symptoms of Ebola virus.

Severely ill, she was flown on a commercial airliner to Switzerland for   8
treatment. In other words, the Swiss woman entered the biological Internet.
Her doctors in Switzerland did not realize that she had Ebola. They suspected the illness was dengue fever, a virus carried by mosquitoes. Nevertheless, she survived, and no other infections were reported. Bernard Le
Guenno isolated the virus and, with backup confirmation from the Special
Pathogens Branch of the C.D.C., identified it as a new Ebola strain, and

also confirmed that the Tai Forest chimpanzees were infected with the same strain. It is known as Ebola Ivory Coast. It lives in the Tai Forest. The Tai chimps hunt colobus monkeys and eat them. Perhaps chimps are catching Ebola from colobus monkeys. Perhaps colobus monkeys are the original host of Ebola virus. Or perhaps the colobus monkeys are eating something that is the original host, and Ebola could be thereby moving up the food chain.

There was another curious case. In January, 1991, a twenty-one-year-old Swedish medical student who had been travelling in Kenya returned to Sweden. He had lived for about a month in the town of Kitale, which is at the base of Mt. Elgon, about twenty-five miles from Kitum Cave, a site that may be a hiding place of Ebola's cousin the Marburg virus. He did not visit the cave during his time near Mt. Elgon. Five days after his flight home to Sweden, he became deathly ill, and he ended up in the University Hospital in Linköping—a topnotch research hospital. He was showing all the signs of African hemorrhagic fever. His blood was clotting up internally, he had a high fever, and then he began to bleed out of the openings of his body.   9

In this type of illness, the patient may reach a crisis point, and can go into irreversible terminal shock. This is the so-called "crash." The student went into crisis, he seemed to be crashing, and a medical team at the Linköping hospital did everything it could to save his life. A nurse was bending over his face when he suddenly vomited blood into the nurse's eyes. Two other members of the team accidentally stuck themselves with needles—possibly they were scared and shaky or, far more likely, they were working fast and the needles slipped. These accidents with blood and needles did not happen because the medical staff at Linköping were incompetent. They were highly trained. The accidents happened because they rushed in to save a patient's life, forgetful of their own safety, which is what the best doctors tend to do with a patient in crisis.   10

The man lived. Meanwhile, Sweden called on the United States for help—this being a suspected case of African hemorrhagic fever—and a team from the United States Army Medical Research Institute for Infectious Diseases, or USAMRIID, in Frederick, Maryland, flew into Sweden carrying biohazard spacesuits and other gear, to help contain the agent and investigate it. The investigation revealed that fifty-five medical personnel at the Linköping hospital had been exposed to the patient's blood and bodily fluids; they were all at risk of being infected. Almost unbelievably, no one became sick, including the nurse who had got a faceful of blood. The researchers were never able to identify an infectious agent in the student. It remains a case of "suspected Marburg virus." Despite the happy outcome, good doctors and good hospitals are extremely vulnerable in the face of any infectious agent that turns humans into bleeders.   11

Knowing all this, I began to wonder what is really happening to the   12
local doctors, male nursing staff, and nuns on the ground in Kikwit, who are
struggling in clinics and hospitals that are wretched, run-down cauldrons,
virtually abandoned by government authorities, currently as hot as hell in a
biological sense, and unequipped with even the most basic medical supplies,
such as rubber gloves, waterproof gowns, or clean needles. For the local
medical people in Kikwit the situation is a working nightmare—at least, for
those who are still alive. The doctors and staff are literally up to their elbows
in blood, black vomit, and shit the color of beet soup.

Seeking some perspective, I spoke on the telephone with a doctor   13
named Bill Close, who lived in Zaire for sixteen years, was there during the
terrifying 1976 Ebola outbreak, and helped organize the effort to stop Ebola
then. Dr. Close (who happens to be the father of the actress Glenn Close)
was the chief doctor of the Congolese Army, and he rebuilt and ran the
Mama Yemo General Hospital, a two-thousand-bed facility in the capital. He
is now in effect the liaison between the Zairean government and the C.D.C.
He scoffed at reports coming over the wire services that medical personnel
are "fleeing" from the hospitals in the area. He said, "I can tell you that we
have at least one local doctor and two nurses in Kikwit who have gone back
into the hospital to work, *knowing* they are going to die. The greatest need in
Kikwit right now is for rubber aprons to protect the doctors, because the
blood and vomit is soaking through their operating gowns."

("That's correct," an official at the C.D.C. told me. "The surgical gowns   14
they are using are not high-quality material. They're not plastic, and they're
soaking through. And the other thing the Kikwit doctors desperately
need right now is needles. Clean needles.")

"This is a huge, lethal African hemorrhagic virus," Dr. Close went on.   15
"We all sort of feel that Ebola comes out of its hiding place when something
occasionally alters the very delicate balance of the ecosystems, in a region
where things grow as they would in a warm petri dish. But if there are
lessons to be learned here, they are the human lessons. This is about people
doing their duty. It's about doctors doing what has to be done, right now,
without a whole lot of heroics. Have you ever been absolutely petrified with
fear? Real fear? Possessed by naked fear, where you have no hope of control over your fate? When the die is cast, the fear goes away, and you do
what you have to do—you get to work. That's what's happening with the
medical people in Zaire right now. There are things happening there. . ."
He paused. "Magnificent human things . . . How can I explain this? In
Zaire in 1976, there was a nun who died of Ebola. There was a priest who
gave her her last rites as she died. She had a terrible fever, sweat was pouring down her face. And blood was coming out of her eyes. She was weeping
blood. Bloody tears were running down her cheeks. The priest took out his

handkerchief and wiped the sweat from her forehead and the blood from her cheeks. Then, unthinkingly, he took the bloody handkerchief and wiped his own face with it. Ten days later, he was dead. One of the doctors in '76—he was a Belgian—delivered a baby in the middle of it all. There were people dying of Ebola all around in that hospital, and there was a woman in childbirth. His patient. The baby was stuck—too big for the birth canal. So the doctor performed the Zarat procedure on the woman. That's a simple and rather crude but very effective way of enlarging the outlet to remove the baby. With a knife, you split the symphysis pubis."

"What is the symphysis pubis?" I asked.   16

"That's the front of the pelvis. The pelvic bones. You split them. You   17
press a scalpel through the cartilage. The bones go *pop* and the pelvis springs open, and you pull the baby out. The hospital had run out of anesthetics. So he did it without giving her an anesthetic."

"My God."

"He did have a sedative, and he gave it to her to calm her down, but she was conscious. By the time he got the baby out, the baby had stopped breathing, because of the sedative. The baby was in breathing arrest and drenched with the woman's blood. He held up the baby and put the baby's mouth to his mouth and gave the baby mouth-to-mouth resuscitation. The baby started to breathe. He pulled away, and his face and mouth were smeared with blood. There was a nurse standing by, and when she saw his face she said, 'Doctor, *do you realize what you've done?*'"

"'I do now,' he said."   18

◆ ◆ ◆

The Case Against Babies

JOY WILLIAMS

Joy Williams is the author of three novels and two collections of short stories, as well as a history and guide to the Florida Keys. Her stories and essays appear frequently in prize anthologies and textbooks. Williams is the recipient of the Strauss Living Award from the American Academy of Arts and Letters. She lives in Key West. "The Case Against Babies" first appeared in *Granta* in 1996; it was subsequently selected for inclusion in *The Best American Essays of 1997*.

Babies, babies, babies. There's a plague of babies. Too many rabbits   1
or elephants or mustangs or swans brings out the myxomatosis, the culling
guns, the sterility drugs, the scientific brigade of egg smashers. Other
species can "strain their environments" or "overrun their range" or clash
with their human "neighbors," but human babies are always welcome at
life's banquet. Welcome, Welcome, Welcome—Live Long and Consume!
You can't draw the line when it comes to babies because . . . where are
you going to draw the line? *Consider having none or one and be sure to
stop after two,* the organization Zero Population Growth suggests politely.
Can barely hear them what with all the babies squalling. Hundreds of
them popping out every minute. Ninety-seven million of them each year.
While legions of other biological life forms go extinct (or, in the creepy
phrase of ecologists, "wink out"), human life bustles self-importantly on.
Those babies just keep coming! They've gone way beyond being "God's
gift"; they've become entitlements. Everyone's having babies, even women
who can't have babies, *particularly* women who can't have babies—they're
the ones who sweep fashionably along the corridors of consumerism with
their double-wide strollers, stuffed with twins and triplets. (Women push
those things with the effrontery of someone piloting a bulldozer, which
strollers uncannily bring to mind.) When you see twins or triplets, do you
think *awahhh* or *owhoo* or *that's sort of cool, that's unusual,* or do you
think *that woman dropped a wad on in vitro fertilization, twenty-five, thirty
thousand dollars at least. . . ?*

The human race hardly needs to be more fertile, but fertility clinics are   2
booming. The new millionaires are the hotshot fertility doctors who serve
anxious gottahavababy women, techno-shamans who have become the most
important aspect of the baby process, giving women what they want:
BABIES. (It used to be a mystery what women wanted, but no more . . .
Nietzsche was right . . .) Ironically—though it is far from being the only
irony in this baby craze—women think of themselves as being *successful, personally fulfilled* when they have a baby, even if it takes a battery of men in
white smocks and lots of hormones and drugs and needles and dishes and
mixing and inserting and implanting to make it so. Having a baby means *individual completion* for a woman. What do boys have to do to be men? Sleep
with a woman. Kill something. Yes, killing something, some luckless deer,
duck, bear, pretty much anything large-ish in the animal kingdom, or even
another man appropriate in times of war, has ushered many a lad into man-
hood. But what's a woman to do? She gets to want to have a baby.

While much effort has been expended in Third World countries educat-   3
ing women into a range of options that do not limit their role merely to bear-
ing children, well-off, educated, and indulged American women are
clamoring for babies, babies, babies to complete their status. They've had it

all, and now they want a baby. And women over thirty-five want them NOW. They're the ones who opt for the aggressive fertility route, they're impatient, they're sick of being laissez-faire about this. Sex seems such a laborious way to go about it. At this point they don't want to endure all that intercourse over and over and maybe get no baby. What a waste of time! And time's awasting. *A life with no child would be a life perfecting hedonism,* a forty-something infertile woman said, now the proud owner of pricey twins. Even women who have the grace to submit to fate can sound wistful. *It's not so much that I wish that I had children now,* a travel writer said, *but that I wish I had had them. I hate to fail at anything.* Women are supposed to wish and want and not fail....

The eighties were a decade when it was kind of unusual to have a baby.   4
Oh, the lower classes still had them with more or less gusto, but professionals did not. Having a baby was indeed so quaintly rebellious and remarkable that a publishing niche was developed for men writing about babies, *their* baby, their baby's first year in which every single day was recorded (he slept through the night . . . he didn't sleep through the night . . .). The writers would marvel over the size of their infant's scrotum; give advice on how to tip the obstetrician (not a case of booze; a clock from Tiffany's is nicer); and be-musedly admit that their baby exhibited intelligent behavior like rolling over, laughing, and showing fascination with the TV screen far earlier than normal children. Aside from the talk about the poopie and the rashes and the cat's psychological decline, these books frequently contained a passage, an overheard bit of Mommy-to-Baby monologue along these lines: *I love you so much I don't ever want you to have teeth or stand up or walk or go on dates or get married. I want you to stay right here with me and be my baby. . .* Babies are one thing. Human beings are another. We have way too many human be-ings. Almost everyone knows this.

Adoption was an eighties thing. People flying to Chile, all over the   5
globe, God knows where, returning triumphantly with their BABY. It was difficult, adventurous, expensive, and generous. It was trendy then. People were into adopting bunches of babies in all different flavors and colors: Ko-rean, Chinese, part Indian (part Indian was very popular), Guatemalan (Guatemalan babies are way cute). Adoption was a fad, just like the Cab-bage Patch dolls, which fed the fad to tens of thousands of pre-pubescent girl consumers.

Now it is *absolutely* necessary to digress for a moment and provide an   6
account of this marketing phenomenon. These fatuous-faced soft-sculpture dolls were immensely popular in the eighties. The gimmick was that these dolls were "born"; you couldn't just buy the damn things—if you wanted one, you had to "adopt" it. Today they are still being born and adopted, although at

a slower rate, in Babyland General Hospital, a former medical clinic right on the fast-food and car-dealership strip in the otherwise unexceptional north Georgia town of Cleveland. There are several rooms at Babyland General. One of them is devoted to the premies (all snug in their little gowns, each in its own spiffy incubator) and another is devoted to the cabbage patch itself, a suggestive mound with a fake tree on it from which several times a day comes the announcement CABBAGE IN LABOR! A few demented moments later, a woman in full nurse regalia appears from a door in the tree holding a brand-new Cabbage Patch Kid by the feet and giving it a little whack on the bottom. All around her in the fertile patch are happy little soft heads among the cabbages. Each one of these things costs $175, and you have to sign papers promising to care for it and treasure it forever. There are some cheesy dolls in boxes that you wouldn't have to adopt, but children don't want those—they want to sign on the line, want the documentation, the papers. The dolls are all supposed to be different, but they certainly look identical. They've got tiny ears, big eyes, a pinched rictus of a mouth, and lumpy little arms and legs. The colors of the cloth vary for racial verisimilitude, but their expressions are the same. They're glad to be here and they expect everything.

But these are just dolls, of course. The *real* adopted babies who rode   7 the wave of fashion into many hiply caring homes are children now, an entirely different kettle of fish, and though they may be providing (just as they were supposed to) great joy, they are not darling babies anymore. A baby is not really a child; a baby is a baby, a cuddleball, representative of virility, wombrismo, and humankind's unquenchable wish to outfox Death.

Adoptive parents must feel a little out of it these days, so dreadfully   8 dated in the nineties. Adoption—how foolishly sweet. It's so Benetton, so kind of naive. With adopted babies, you just don't know, it's too much of a crapshoot. Oh, they *told* you that the father was an English major at Yale and that the mother was a brilliant mathematician and harpsichordist who was just not quite ready to juggle career and child, but what are you going to think when the baby turns into a kid who rather than showing any talent whatsoever is trying to drown the dog and set national parks on fire? Adoptive parents do their best, of course, at least as far as their liberal genes allow; they look into the baby's *background,* they don't want just any old baby (even going to the dog and cat pound you'd want to pick and choose, right?); they want a pleasant, healthy one, someone who will appreciate the benefits of a nice environment and respond to a nurturing and attentive home. They steer away (I mean, one has to be realistic, one can't save the world) from the crack and smack babies, the physically and mentally handicapped babies, the HIV and fetal-alcoholic-syndrome babies.

Genes matter more and more, and adoption is just too . . . where's   9 the connection? Not a single DNA strand to call your own. Adoption signifies you didn't do everything you could; you were too cheap or shy or lacked the imagination to go the energetic fertility route, which, when successful, would come with the assurance that some part of the Baby or Babies would be a continuation of you, or at the very least your companion, loved one, partner, whatever.

I once prevented a waitress from taking away my martini glass, which   10
had a tiny bit of martini remaining in it, and she snarled, *Oh, the precious liquid,* before slamming it back down on the table. It's true that I probably imagined that there was more martini in the glass than there actually was (what on earth could have happened to it all?), but the precious liquid remark brings unpleasantly to mind the reverent regard in which so many people hold themselves. Those eggs, that sperm, oh precious, precious stuff! There was a terrible fright among humankind recently when some scientists suggested that an abundance of synthetic chemicals was causing lower sperm counts in human males—awful, awful, awful—but this proves not to be the case; sperm counts are holding steady and are even on the rise in New York. Los Angeles males don't fare as well (do they drink more water than beer?), nor do the Chinese who, to add insult to insult, are further found to have smaller testicles, a finding that will undoubtedly result in even more wildlife mutilation in the quest for aphrodisiacs. Synthetic chemicals *do* "adversely affect" the reproductive capabilities of nonhuman animals (fish, birds), but this is considered relatively unimportant. It's human sperm that's held in high regard, and in this overpopulated age it's become more valuable—*good* sperm, that is, from intelligent, athletic men who don't smoke, drink, do drugs, have AIDS, or a history of homicide—because this overpopulated age is also the donor age. Donor sperm, donor womb, donor eggs. Think of all the eggs that are lost to menstruation every month. The mind boggles. Those precious, precious eggs, lost. (Many egg donors say they got into the business because they didn't like the idea of their eggs "going to waste.") They can be *harvested* instead and frozen for a rainy day, or sold nice and fresh. One woman interviewed in the *New York Times* early this year has made it something of a career. *I'm not going to just sit home and bake cookies for my kids, I can accomplish things,* she says. No dreary nine-to-five desk job for her. She was a surrogate mother for one couple, dishing up a single baby; then she donated some eggs to another couple who had a baby; now she's pregnant with twins for yet another couple. *I feel like a good soldier as if God said to me, "Hey girl, I've done a lot for you, and now I want you to do something for Me,"* this entrepreneurial breeder says. (It's sort of cute to hear God invoked, sort of for luck, or out of a lingering folksy superstition.) Egg donors are regular Jenny Appleseeds, spreading joy, doing the Lord's work, and earning a few bucks all at once, as well as attaining an odd sense of empowerment (I've got a bunch of kids out there, damned if I know who they all are . . .).

One of the most successful calendars of 1996 was Anne Geddes's   11
BABIES. Each month shows the darling little things on cabbage leaves,
cupped in a tulip, as little bees in a honeycomb, and so on—solemn, bright-
eyed babies. They look a little bewildered, though, and why shouldn't they?
How did they get here? They were probably mixed up in a dish. Donor eggs
(vacuumed up carefully through long needles); Daddy's sperm (maybe . . .
or maybe just some high-powered New York dude's); gestational carrier;
the "real" mommy waiting anxiously, restlessly on the sidelines (want to get
those babies home, start buying them stuff!). Baby's lineage can be a little
complicated in this one big worldwebby family. With the help of drugs like
Clomid and Pergonal there are an awful lot of eggs out there these days—
all being harvested by those rich and clever, clever doctors in a "simple procedure" and nailed with bull's-eye accuracy by a spermatozoon. One then
gets to "choose" among the resulting cell clumps (or the doctor gets to
choose, he's the one who knows about these things), and a number of them
(for optimum success) are inserted into the womb, sometimes the mother's
womb and sometimes not. These fertilized eggs, unsurprisingly, often result
in multiple possibilities, which can be decreased by "selective reduction."
They're not calendar babies yet, they're embryos, and it is at this point, the
multiple-possibility point, that the mother-to-be often gets a little overly ec-
static, even greedy, thinking ahead perhaps to the day when they're not babies any longer, the day when they'll be able to amuse themselves by
themselves like a litter of kittens or something—if there's a bunch of them
all at once there'll be no need to go through that harrowing process of finding appropriate playmates for them. She starts to think, *Nannies probably
don't charge that much more for three than for two* or *Heaven knows we've
got enough money or we wouldn't have gotten into all this in the first place.*
And many women at the multiple-possibility point, after having gone
through pretty much all the meddling and hubris that biomedical technology has come up with, say demurely, *I don't want to play God* (I DON'T
WANT TO PLAY GOD?) or *It would be grotesque to snuff one out to improve the odds for the others* or *Whatever will be will be.*

So triplets happen, and even quads and quints (network television is   12
still interested in quints). And as soon as the multiples, or even the less prestigious single baby, are old enough to toddle into daycare, they're responsibly taught the importance of their one and only Earth, taught the three
R's—Reduce, Reuse, Recycle. Too many people (which is frequently considered undesirable—gimme my space!) is caused by too many people (it's
only logical), but it's mean to blame the babies, you can't blame the babies,
they're innocent. Those poor bean counters at the United Nations Population Fund say that at current growth rates, the world will double its population in forty years. Overpopulation poses the greatest threat to all life on

earth, but most organizations concerned with this problem don't like to limit their suggestions to the most obvious one—DON'T HAVE A BABY!—because it sounds so negative. Instead, they provide additional, more positive tips for easing the pressures on our reeling environment, such as car-pooling or tree-planting. (A portion of the proceeds from that adorable best-selling BABIES calendar goes to the Arbor Day Foundation for the planting of trees.)

Some would have it that not having a baby is *disallowing* a human life,   13
horribly inappropriate in this world of rights. Everyone has rights; the un-born have rights; it follows that the *unconceived* have rights. (Think of all those babies pissed off at the fact that they haven't even been thought of yet.) Women have the *right* to have babies (we've fought so hard for this), and women who can't have babies have an even bigger right to have them. These rights should be independent of marital or economic status, or age. (Fifty- and sixty-something moms tend to name their babies after the gyne-cologist.) The reproduction industry wants fertility treatments to be avail-able to *anyone* and says that it wouldn't all be so expensive if those recalcitrant insurance companies and government agencies like Medicare and Medicaid weren't so cost-conscious and discriminatory and would just cough up the money. It's not as though you have to take out a *permit* to have a baby, be *licensed* or anything. What about the rights of a poor, elderly, fem-inist cancer patient who is handicapped in some way (her car has one of those stickers . . .) who wants to assert her right to independent mother-hood and feels entitled to both artificial insemination into a gestational "hostess" and the right to sex selection as a basis for abortion should the fetus turn out to be male when she wants a female? Huh? What about her? Or what about the fifteen-year-old of the near future who kind of wants to have her baby even though it means she'll be stuck with a kid all through high school and won't be able to go out with her friends anymore, who dis-covers through the wonders of amniocentesis and DNA analysis that the baby is going to turn out fat, and the fifteen-year-old just can't deal with fat and shouldn't have to . . .? Out goes the baby with the bathwater.

But these scenarios are involved merely with messy political or ethical   14
issues, the problematical, somewhat gross byproducts of technological and marketing advances. Let the philosophers and professional ethicists drone on and let the baby business boom. Let the courts figure it out. Each day brings another, more pressing problem. Implanted with their weak-cervixed daughter's eggs and their son-in-law's sperm, women become pregnant with their own grandchildren; frozen embryos are inadvertently thawed; eggs are pirated; eggs are harvested from aborted fetuses; divorced couples battle over the fate of cryo-preserved material. "We have to have better

regulation of the genetic product—eggs, sperm, and embryos—so we can legally determine who owns what," a professor of law and medicine at a California university says plaintively. (Physicians tend to oppose more regulation, however, claiming that it would "impede research.")

While high-tech nations are refining their options eugenically and quibbling litigiously, the inhabitants of low-tech countries are just having babies. The fastest growth in human numbers in all history is going to take place in a single generation, an increase of almost five billion people (all of whom started out as babies). Ninety-seven percent of the surge is going to take place in developing countries, with Africa alone accounting for 35 percent of it (the poorer the country, the higher the birth rate, that's just the way it is). These babies are begotten in more "traditional," doubtless less desperate ways, and although they are not considered as fashion statements, they're probably loved just as much as upper-class Western babies (or that singular one-per-family Chinese boy baby) and are even considered productive assets when they get a little older and can labor for the common good of their large families by exploiting more and more, scarcer and scarcer resources.

15

The argument that Western countries with their wealth and relatively low birth rates do not fuel the population crisis is, of course, fallacious. France, as national policy, urges its citizens to procreate, giving lots of subsidies and perks to those French who make more French. The U.S. population is growing faster than that of eighteen other industrialized nations, and in terms of energy consumption, when an American couple stops spawning at two babies, it's the same as an average East Indian couple stopping at sixty-six, or an Ethiopian couple drawing the line at one thousand.

16

Yet we burble along, procreating, and in the process suffocating thousands of other species with our selfishness. We're in a baby glut, yet it's as if we've just discovered babies, or invented them. Reproduction is sexy. Assisted reproduction is cool. The announcement that a movie star is going to have a baby is met with breathless wonder. A BABY! Old men on their third marriage regard their new babies with "awe" and crow about the "ultimate experience" of parenting. Bruce Springsteen found "salvation" with the birth of his son. When in doubt, have a baby. When you've tried it all, champagne, cocaine, try a baby. Pop icons who trudged through a decade of adulation and high living confess upon motherhood, This Baby Saved My Life. Bill Gates, zillionaire founder of Microsoft, is going to have (this is so wonderful) a BABY. News commentators are already speculating: Will fatherhood take away his edge, his drive; will it diminish his will to succeed, to succeed, to succeed? National Public Radio recently interviewed other high-powered CEO dads as to that ghastly possibility.

17

It's as though, all together; in the waning years of this dying century, we collectively opened the Door of our Home and instead of seeing a friend

18

standing there in some sweet spring twilight, someone we had invited over for drinks and dinner and a lovely civilized chat, there was Death, with those creepy little black seeds of his for planting in the garden. And along with Death we got a glimpse of ecological collapse and the coming anarchy of an overpeopled planet. And we all, in denial of this unwelcome vision, decided to slam the door and retreat to our toys and make babies—those heirs, those hopes, those products of our species' selfishness, sentimentality, and global death wish.

◆ ◆ ◆

◆ IDEAS FOR COMBINING WRITING STRATEGIES

1. *Description, narration, and argument.* Using "The Long Good-bye" as a model, write an essay in which the main rhetorical technique is description. Choose a setting that has firm boundaries—physical, temporal, or psychological, or a combination. Immerse your reader in description and in brief narrative sequences that capture the culture and atmosphere of the setting, as Coyne does in her essay. However, mere immersion is not your purpose: you also need to make a persuasive point about some issue the setting evokes. For example, Coyne clearly wants to lead us to believe that these women should not be incarcerated, though she never makes such a bald statement. So, you might take your readers "backstage" at a wedding, with an unspoken agenda of undermining its sacred image. You might bring readers into the culture of some all-male setting like a locker room or a bachelor party, or an all-female environment like a beauty parlor or a sorority house—to expose what's going on there.

2. *Cause and effect, and comparison and contrast.* Several of the readings in this chapter endeavor to debunk some social belief or institution that people might see as stable or universal, but is not. "The Case Against Babies," "Let's Get Rid of Sports," and "The Way We Weren't" take on conventional ways of thought and suggest that there are other ways to look at things. Choose something in our culture that you generally believe has always been about the same as it is now, and do some research on the history of the social institution or belief, using Internet sources if you wish. You will probably find, as Coontz did in looking at the history of the family, that a complex system of cause-and-effect relationships determines the shifting status of a social "universal." Explain some of these relationships and compare and contrast the past with the present.

3. *Comparison and contrast, classification, and persuasion.* Many of the readings in this textbook highlight the differences between male and female experience. Do some field work at your school to investigate the nature of men's and women's fears, whether they differ, and what point can be made about them. With a group of classmates, devise a list of common fears—like fear of never finding a partner, fear of repercussions for holding an unpopular belief, and fear of violence. Make sure you list twenty or more fears. Use this list to help you perform interviews with women and men on your campus. Make tapes or notes to record what your interviewees have to say about what their biggest fears are. Reconvene with your classmates to go over your notes and come to some conclusions about what types of things the people around you are afraid of, whether the sexes differ, and what action is implied by your conclusions. Make a call to such action your persuasive edge in a paper called "Why People Get the Willies."

4. *Description, exemplification, and process analysis.* A strong presence in the readings in this textbook is the world of work, whether it be in the home (as in Chang-Rae Lee's cooking in "Coming Home Again") or at a workplace (as in Richard Preston's "Back in the Hot Zone" or Ana Maria Corona's "Coming to America, to Clean"). For an informative essay, do some research concerning one of the occupations in one or more of these readings. Put together your essay using at least three different types of sources. Some choices are career-center offerings such as the *Occupational Outlook Handbook,* Internet sites about the field and important people in it, interviews with people in the job, observations you make by visiting a worksite, and visions of the work portrayed in popular culture, such as TV shows, songs, and films. Your goal is to present a thorough and accurate account of this career or job to someone thinking of pursuing it. You might consider choosing a job that's unfamiliar to most readers or, in contrast, a job that most readers *think* they know about but probably don't.

5. *Description, narration, and comparison and contrast.* A number of readings in this book explore the theme of exclusion or displacement. Write about a personal or family experience of being displaced or excluded; and compare or contrast it with the experiences you have read about in such essays as "Coming to America, to Clean," "The Long Good-bye," "Coming Home Again," "The Myth of the Latin Woman," "Coming from the Country," "A Weight That Women Carry," or "Marriage as a Restricted Club."

6. *Argument, cause and effect, and exemplification.* Following Katha Pollitt's lead in "Let's Get Rid of Sports," write your own "bold proposal

for the social and political betterment of mankind." Use examples and cause-effect reasoning to recommend a change or plan that you know is unreasonable or unworkable.

7. *Using the Internet.* Search the Internet for more information on one of the subjects discussed in the essays in this chapter: undocumented workers, Korean cooking, women in prison, the status of American families, the place of sports in American culture, emerging viruses, fertility clinics, or overpopulation. Choose something that interests you, gather the ideas and information, narrow the topic, and decide what strategies you will need to develop it. Then write an essay that presents your views and analysis.

Glossary

◆ ◆ ◆ ◆ ◆

Abstract words: language that refers to ideas, conditions, and qualities that cannot be observed directly through the five senses. Words such as *beauty, love, joy, wealth, cruelty, power,* and *justice* are abstract. In his essay (p. 277), Andrew Holleran explores the abstract term "fear," offering a series of concrete examples and incidents to make the meaning clearer. *Also see* Concrete words.

Active reading: *See* Engaged Reading.

Allusion: a passing reference to a familiar person, place, or object in history, myth, or literature. Writers use allusions to enrich or illuminate their ideas. For instance, in his essay about African-American men, Michel Marriott makes an allusion to lynching when he describes his father as "a proud Black man dangling from a leafless tree of opportunities denied" (p. 273). And when Jessica Mitford writes "Alas, Poor Yorick!" (p. 211), she's alluding to the skull of an old friend that Shakespeare's Hamlet discovers in the graveyard.

Analogy: a comparison that uses a familiar or concrete item to explain an abstract or unfamiliar concept. For example, a geologist might compare the structure of the earth's crust to the layers of an onion, or a nature writer might describe the effect of pollution on the environment by comparing it to cancer in the human body. See the introduction to Chapter 9.

Anecdote: a brief story about an amusing or interesting event, usually told to illustrate an idea or support a point. Writers also use anecdotes to begin essays, as Rebecca Kirkendall does in "Who's a Hillbilly?" (p. 253), or Deborah Tannen does in "Sex, Lies, and Conversation" (p. 368).

Antonym: a word that has the opposite meaning of another word. For example, *wet* is an antonym of *dry; coarse* is an antonym of *smooth; cowardly* is an antonym of *brave*.

Argumentation: a type of writing in which the author tries to influence the reader's thinking on a controversial topic. See the introduction to Chapter 11.

Audience: the readers for whom a piece of writing is intended. Many essays are aimed at a general audience, but a writer can focus on a specific group of readers. For example, Anne Lamott directs her essay "Shitty First Drafts" (p. 152) to writers and would-be writers, while Bud Herron is addressing cat owners in "Cat Bathing as a Martial Art" (p. 188).

Block by block pattern: an organizational pattern used in comparison and contrast writing. In this method, a writer presents, in a block, all the important points about the first item to be compared and then presents, in another block, the corresponding points about the second item to be compared. See the introduction to Chapter 9.

Brainstorming: a method for generating ideas for writing. In brainstorming, a writer jots down a list of as many details and ideas on a topic as possible without stopping to evaluate or organize them. See Chapter 2.

Cause and effect: the rhetorical strategy that allows a writer to interpret the meaning of events by focusing on reasons and/or consequences. See the introduction to Chapter 10.

Causes: the reasons or explanations for why something happens. Causes can be *immediate* or *indirect*. See the introduction to Chapter 10.

Chronological order: the arrangement of events according to time—that is, in the sequence in which they happened.

Classification: the process of sorting items or ideas into meaningful groups or categories. See the introduction to Chapter 8.

Cliché: a phrase or expression that has lost its originality or force through overuse. To illustrate, novelist and teacher Janet Burroway writes: "Clichés are *the last word* in bad writing, and it's *a crying shame* to see all you *bright young things* spoiling your *deathless prose* with phrases *as old as the hills.* You must *keep your nose to the grindstone,* because the *sweet smell of success* only comes to those who *march to the tune of a different drummer.*"

Clustering: a method of exploring a topic and generating material in which a writer groups ideas visually by putting the main point or topic in the center of a page, circling it, and surrounding it with words or phrases that identify the major points to be discussed. The writer creates new clusters by circling these points and surrounding them with additional words and phrases. See Chapter 2.

Coherence: the logical flow of ideas in a piece of writing. A writer achieves coherence by having a clear thesis and by making sure that all the supporting details relate to that thesis. Coherence within paragraphs is established with a clear topic sentence and maintained with transitions, pronoun reference, parallelism, and intentional repetition. *Also see* Unity.

Colloquial language: conversational words and expressions that are sometimes used in writing to add color and authenticity. Peg Bracken (p. 206), Judy Brady (p. 259), and Mike Royko (p. 44) use colloquial language to good effect in their writing. *Also see* Informal writing.

Comparison and contrast: a strategy of writing in which an author points out the similarities and differences between two or more subjects. See the introduction to Chapter 9.

Conclusion: the sentences and paragraphs that bring an essay to its close. In the conclusion, a writer may restate the thesis, sum up complex and important ideas, emphasize the topic's significance, make a generalization, offer a solution to a problem, or encourage the reader to take some action. Whatever the strategy, a conclusion should end the essay in a firm and definite way.

Concrete words: language that refers to real objects that can be seen, heard, tasted, touched, or smelled. Words like *tree, desk, car, orange, Chicago, Roseanne,* or *jogging* are concrete. Concrete examples make abstractions easier to understand, as in "Contentment is a well-fed cat asleep in the sun." *Also see* Abstract words.

Connotation and denotation: terms used to describe the different kinds of meaning that words convey. **Denotation** refers to the most specific or direct meaning of a word—the dictionary definition. **Connotations** are the feelings or associations that attach themselves to words. For example, *assertive* and *pushy* share a similar denotation—both mean "strong" or "forceful." But their differing connotations suggest different attitudes: an assertive person is admirable; a pushy person is offensive.

Controlling idea: *See* Thesis.

Conventions: customs or generally accepted practices. The conventions of writing an essay require a title, a subject, a thesis, a pattern of organization, transitions, and paragraph breaks.

Definition: a method of explaining a word or term so that the reader understands what the writer means. Writers use a variety of methods for defining words and terms; see the introduction to Chapter 7.

Denotation: *See* Connotation and denotation.

Description: writing that uses sensory details to create a word picture for the reader. See the introduction to Chapter 4.

Details: specific pieces of information (examples, incidents, dates, statistics, descriptions, and the like) that explain and support the general ideas in a piece of writing.

Development: the techniques and materials that a writer uses to expand and build on a general idea or topic.

Dialogue: speech or conversation recorded in writing. Dialogue, which is commonly found in narrative writing, reveals character and adds life and authenticity to an essay.

Diction: choice of words in writing or speaking.

Discovery: the first stage in the writing process. It may include finding a topic, exploring the topic, determining purpose and audience, probing ideas, doing reading and research, and planning and organizing material. Discovery usually involves writing and is aided considerably by putting preliminary thoughts and plans in writing. See the introduction to Chapter 3.

Division: the process of breaking a large subject into its components or parts. Division is often used in combination with classification. See the introduction to Chapter 8.

Dominant impression: the main idea or feeling that a writer wants to convey in an extended description—that a teacher is competent and well liked, for example, or that an event is terrifying. See the Introduction to Chapter 4.

Drafting: the stage in the writing process during which the writer puts ideas into complete sentences, connects them, and organizes them into a meaningful sequence.

Editing: the last stage in the writing process, during which the writer focuses on the details of mechanics and correctness.

Effects: the results or outcomes of certain events. Effects can be *immediate* or *indirect*. Writers often combine causes and effects in explaining why something happens. See the introduction to Chapter 10.

Ellipsis: an omission of words that is signaled by three equally spaced dots.

Emphasis: the placement of words and ideas in key positions to give them stress and importance. A writer can emphasize a word or idea by putting it at the beginning or end of a paragraph or essay. Emphasis can also be achieved by using repetition, parallelism, and figurative language to call attention to an idea or term.

Engaged reading: the process of getting involved with the reading material. An engaged reader surveys the text, makes predictions, asks questions, writes notes and responses in the margins or in a notebook, rereads difficult passages, and spends time afterward summarizing and reflecting.

Essay: a short prose work on a limited topic. Essays can take many forms, but they usually focus on a central theme or thesis and often convey the writer's personal ideas about the topic.

Euphemism: an inoffensive or polite term used in place of language that readers or listeners might find distasteful, unpleasant, or otherwise objectionable: *passed on* is a euphemism for *died*.

Evidence: *See* Supporting material.

Examples: specific cases or instances used to illustrate or explain a general concept. See the introduction to Chapter 5.

Exemplification: the strategy of development in which a writer uses particular instances to support a general idea or thesis. See the introduction to Chapter 5.

Extended definition: a lengthy exploration of a controversial term or an abstract concept, developed by using one or more of the rhetorical strategies discussed in this book.

Figurative language: words that create images or convey symbolic meaning beyond the literal level. Truman Capote, for example, uses figurative language to portray the dramatic effect of gun fire: "Bullets rained in the trees like the rattle of castanets, and the train, with a wounded creak, slowed to a halt" (see "A Ride Through Spain," p. 104).

Figures of speech: deliberate departures from the ordinary, literal use of words in order to provide fresh perceptions and create lasting impressions. *See* Metaphor, Paradox, Personification, *and* Simile.

First person: the use of *I, me, we,* and *us* in speech and writing to express a personal view or present a firsthand report. *Also see* Point of view.

Flashback: a narrative device that presents material that occurred prior to the opening scene. Various flashback methods can be used: recollections of characters, narration by characters or the narrator, dream sequences, reveries.

Focus: the narrowing of a topic to a specific aspect or set of features.

Freewriting: a procedure for exploring a topic that involves writing without stopping for a set period of time. See Chapter 2.

General and specific: a way of referring to the level of abstraction in words. A *general* word names a group or a class; a *specific* word refers to an individual member of a group or class. The word *nature* is general, the word *flower* is more specific, and the word *orchid* is even more specific.

Generalization: a broad assertion or conclusion based on specific observations. The value of a generalization is determined by the number and quality of the specific instances.

Illustration: the use of examples, or a single long example, to support or explain an idea. See the introduction to Chapter 5.

Image: a description that appeals to the readers' senses of sight, smell, sound, touch, or taste. Images add interest and clarify meaning. See the introduction to Chapter 4.

Immediate causes and effects: the reasons and consequences that are the most obvious; these are also called *direct* or *proximate* causes and effects. See the introduction to Chapter 10.

Indirect causes and effects: the reasons and consequences that are less easily perceived. Indirect causes are also called *remote* or *underlying* causes; indirect effects may also be called *long-term* effects. See the introduction to Chapter 10.

Inference: a conclusion drawn by a reader from the hints and suggestions provided by the writer. Writers sometimes express ideas indirectly rather than stating them outright; readers must use their own experience and knowledge to read between the lines and make inferences to gather the full meaning of a selection.

Informal writing: the familiar, everyday level of usage, which includes contractions and perhaps slang but requires standard grammar and punctuation.

Introduction: the beginning or opening of an essay, which usually presents the topic, arouses interest, and prepares the reader for the development of the thesis.

Irony: the use of words to express the opposite of what is stated. Writers use irony to expose unpleasant truths or to poke fun at human weakness.

Jargon: the specialized or technical language of a trade, profession, or similar group. To readers outside the group, however, jargon can be inaccessible and meaningless.

Journalistic style: the kind of writing found in newspapers and popular magazines. It normally employs informal diction with relatively simple sentences and unusually short paragraphs. Many of the selections in this book first appeared as columns and articles in magazines or newspapers.

Logical order: arrangement of points and ideas according to some reasonable principle or scheme (e.g., from least important to most important).

Main idea: *See* Thesis.

Metaphor: a figure of speech in which a word or phrase that ordinarily refers to one thing is applied to something else, thus making an implied comparison. For example, Mark Twain writes of "the language of this water" and says the river "turned to blood" ("Two Views of the Mississippi," p. 98). Similarly, Phillip Lopate says "Friendship is a long conversation" (p. 325), and Scott Russell Sanders writes about "the breezes of fashion" that "blow hardest where people have time and money on their hands" (p. 380).

An **extended metaphor** may serve as a controlling image for a whole work, as indicated in this opening sentence from Sue Hubbell's essay about truck stops: "In the early morning there is a city of the mind that stretches from coast to coast, from border to border. Its cross streets are the interstate highways. . . . Its citizens are all-night divers, the truckers, and the waitresses at the stops" (p. 146).

A **dead metaphor** is an implied comparison that has become so familiar that we accept it as literal: the arm of a chair, the leg of a table, the hands of a clock. A **mixed metaphor** runs two metaphors together in an illogical way: "the wheels of justice are coming apart at the seams."

Modes: *See* Rhetorical strategies.

Narration: writing that recounts an event or series of interrelated events; presentation of a story in order to illustrate an idea or make a point. See the introduction to Chapter 3.

Objective and subjective: terms that refer to the way a writer handles a subject. Objective writing presents the facts without including the writer's own feelings and attitudes. Subjective writing, on the other hand, reveals the author's personal opinions and emotions.

Onomatopoeia: the use of words that suggest or echo the sounds they are describing—*hiss, plop,* or *sizzle,* for example.

Order: the sequence in which the information or ideas in an essay are presented. *Also see* Chronological order *and* Logical order.

Parable: an illustrative story that teaches a lesson or points out a moral. In Christian countries, the most famous parables are those told by Jesus, the best known of which is that of the Prodigal Son.

Paradox: a seeming contradiction that may nonetheless be true. For example, "Less is more" or "The simplest writing is usually the hardest to do."

Paragraph: a series of two or more related sentences. Paragraphs are units of meaning; they signal a division or shift in thought. In newspapers and magazines, paragraph divisions occur more frequently, primarily to break up the narrow columns of print and make the articles easier to read.

Parallelism: the presentation of two or more equally important ideas in similar grammatical form. Writers use parallelism to organize their ideas and give them force, as Gary Howard does in this sequence of parallel sentences: "We can try to be aware. We can try to be sensitive. We can try to deal with the racism in our own families, yet the tension remains. We can try to dance to the crazy rhythms of multiculturalism and race relations in the U.S., but the dissonant chords of this painful past and present keep intruding" (p. 495).

Patterns of organization: *See* Rhetorical strategies.

Person: *See* Point of view.

Personification: a figure of speech in which an inanimate object or an abstract concept is given human qualities. For example, "Hunger sat shivering on the road"; "Flowers danced on the lawn." In "Two Views of the Mississippi" (p. 97), Mark Twain refers to the "river's face" and describes the river as a subtle and dangerous enemy.

Persuasion: writing that attempts to move readers to action or to influence them to agree with a position or belief.

Point by point pattern: an organizational pattern used in comparison and contrast writing. In this method (also called the *alternating method*), the writer moves back and forth between two subjects, focusing on particular features of each in turn: the first point or feature of subject *A* is followed by the first point or feature of subject *B,* and so on. See the introduction to Chapter 9.

Point of view: the angle or perspective from which a story or topic is presented. Personal essays often take a first-person (or "I") point of view and sometimes address the reader as "you" (second person). The more formal third person ("he," "she," "it," "one," "they") is used to create distance and suggest objectivity.

Previewing: the first step in engaged reading in which the reader prepares to read by looking over the text and making preliminary judgments and predictions about what to expect.

Prewriting: the process that writers use to prepare for the actual drafting stage by gathering information, considering audience and purpose, developing a provisional thesis, and mapping out a tentative plan.

Problem-solution: a strategy for analyzing and developing an argument in which the writer identifies a problem within the topic and offers a solution (or solutions) to it. See the introduction to Chapter 11.

Process writing: a rhetorical strategy in which a writer explains the step-by-step procedure for doing something. See the introduction to Chapter 6.

Purpose: the writer's reasons for writing; what the writer wants to accomplish in an essay.

Refutation: in argumentation, the process of acknowledging and responding to opposing views. See the introduction to Chapter 11.

Revision: the stage in the writing process during which the author makes changes in focus, organization, development, style, and mechanics to make the writing more effective. See Chapter 2.

Rhetorical question: a question that a writer or speaker asks to emphasize or introduce a point and usually goes on to answer. Lee Smith uses a series of rhetorical questions to launch his discussion of memory: "Why do our memories betray us? Is this a precursor of Alzheimer's or some other serious mental disorder? How can some people command a loyal and prodigious memory well into old age? Are there ways to make everyone's memory clear again?" (p. 332).

Rhetorical strategies: patterns for presenting and developing ideas in writing. Some of these patterns relate to basic ways of thinking (classification, cause and effect, problem-solution), whereas others reflect the most common means for presenting material (narration, comparison and contrast, process) or developing ideas (exemplification, definition, description) in writing.

Sarcasm: obviously insincere and biting irony, often used to express strong disapproval.

Satire: writing that uses wit and irony to attack and expose human folly, weakness, and stupidity. Cullen Murphy (p. 308) and Judy Brady (p. 259) use satire to question human behavior and criticize contemporary values.

Sexist language: words and phrases that stereotype or ignore members of either sex. For example, the sentence "A doctor must finish his residency before he can begin to practice" suggests that only men are doctors. Writing in the plural will avoid this exclusion: "Doctors must finish their residencies before they can begin to practice." Terms like *mailman, stewardess, manpower,* and *mothering* are also sexist; gender-neutral terms are preferred: *mail carrier, flight attendant, workforce, parenting.*

Simile: a figure of speech in which two essentially unlike things are compared, usually in a phrase introduced by *like* or *as.* For example, in "Shitty First Drafts," Anne Lamott uses several similes to make the point that few writers know what they want to say before they begin to write: "[Writers] do not type a few stiff warm-up sentences and then find themselves bounding along *like* huskies across the snow. . . . We all often feel *like* we are pulling teeth, even those writers whose prose ends up being the most natural and fluid. The right words and sentences just do not come pouring out *like* ticker tape most of the time" (p. 153).

Slang: the informal language of a given group or locale, often characterized by racy, colorful expressions and short-lived usage.

Specific: *See* General and specific.

Structure: the general plan, framework, or pattern of a piece of writing.

Style: individuality of expression, achieved in writing through selection and arrangement of words, sentences, and punctuation.

Subject: what a piece of writing is about.

Subjective: *See* Objective and subjective.

Supporting material: facts, figures, details, examples, reasoning, expert testimony, personal experiences, and the like, which are used to develop and explain the general ideas in a piece of writing.

Symbol: a concrete or material object that suggests or represents an abstract idea, quality, or concept. The lion is a symbol of courage; a voyage or journey can symbolize life; water suggests spirituality; dryness stands for the absence of spirituality. In E. B. White's "Once More to the Lake" (p. 125), the lake comes to symbolize the author's awareness of his own mortality.

Synonym: a word that means the same or nearly the same as another word. *Sad* is a synonym of *unhappy. Also see* Antonym.

Thesis: the main point or proposition that a writer develops and supports in an essay. The thesis is often stated early, normally in the first paragraph, to give the reader a clear indication of the essay's main idea.

Third person: the point of view in which a writer uses *he, she, it, one,* and *they* to give the reader a less-limited and more seemingly objective account than a first-person view would provide. *Also see* Point of view.

Title: the heading a writer gives to an article or essay. The title usually catches the reader's attention and indicates what the selection is about.

Tone: the attitude that a writer conveys toward the subject matter. Tone can be serious or humorous, critical or sympathetic, affectionate or hostile, sarcastic or soothing, passionate or detached—or any of numerous other attitudes.

Topic sentence: the sentence in which the main idea of a paragraph is stated. Writers often state the topic sentence first and develop the rest of the paragraph in support of this main idea. Sometimes a writer will build up to the topic sentence and place it at the end of a paragraph.

Transitions: words and expressions such as *for example, on the other hand, next,* or *to illustrate* that help the reader to see the connections between points and ideas. Pronouns, repeated words and phrases, and parallel structure also help to link sentences or paragraphs and to point out relationships within them.

Understatement: a type of irony that deliberately represents a point or idea as less than it is in order to stress its importance or seriousness.

Unity: the fitting together of all elements in a piece of writing; sticking to the point. *Also see* Coherence.

Usage: the accepted manner of using language.

Voice: the expression of a writer's personality in his or her writing; an author's distinctive style or manner of writing.

Writing process: the series of steps that most writers follow in producing a piece of writing. The five major stages in the writing process are finding a topic and generating ideas (discovering), focusing on a main idea and mapping out an approach (organizing), preparing a rough draft (drafting), reworking and improving the draft (revising), and proofreading and correcting errors (editing).

Acknowledgments

Amanda Coyne, "The Long Good-bye: Mother's Day in Federal Prison" from *Harper's* (May 1997). Copyright © 1997 by Harper's Magazine. Reprinted with the permission of *Harper's*.

Andre Dubus, "A Quiet Siege: The Death and Life of a Gay Naval Officer" from *Harper's Magazine* (June 1993). Copyright © 1993 by Harper's Magazine. Reprinted with the permission of *Harper's*.

M. F. K. Fisher, "Let the Sky Rain Potatoes" from *The Art of Eating*. Copyright © 1990. Reprinted with the permission of Simon & Schuster.

E. M. Forster, "My Wood" from *Abinger Harvest*. Copyright © 1936 and renewed 1964 by Edward Morgan Forster. Reprinted with the permission of Harcourt Brace and Company, King's College, Cambridge, and The Society of Authors as the literary representatives of the E. M. Forster Estate.

Anne Frank, excerpts from *The Diary of Anne Frank: The Definitive Edition,* edited by Otto H. Frank and Mirjam Pressler, translated by Susan Massotty. Copyright © 1995 by Doubleday, a division of the Bantam Doubleday Dell Publishing Group, Inc. Reprinted with the permission of the publishers.

Ian Frazier, "Street Scene: Minor Heroism in a Major Metropolitan Area" from *The Atlantic Monthly* (February 1995). Copyright © 1995 by Ian Frazier. Reprinted with the permission of the author.

Emilie Gallant, "White Breast Flats" from Beth Brant (ed.), *A Gathering of Spirit: A Collection by North American Indian Women*. Copyright © 1984 by Emilie Gallant. Reprinted with the permission of Firebrand Books, Ithaca, New York.

Henry Louis Gates, Jr., "In the Kitchen" from *Colored People: A Memoir*. Copyright © 1994 by Henry Louis Gates, Jr. Reprinted with the permission of Alfred A. Knopf, Inc.

Malcolm Gladwell, "The Alzheimer's Strain" from *The New Yorker* (October 20 & 27, 1997). Copyright © 1997 by Malcolm Gladwell. Reprinted with the permission of the author.

Ellen Goodman, "The Company Man" from *Close to Home*. Copyright © 1979 by The Washington Post Company. Reprinted with the permission of Simon & Schuster.

William Grider, "Mock Democracy" from *Who Will Tell the People*. Copyright © 1992 by William Grider. Reprinted with the permission of Simon & Schuster.

Andrew Hacker, "Dividing American Society" from *Two Nations*. Copyright © 1992 by Andrew Hacker. Reprinted with the permission of Scribner, a division of of Simon & Schuster.

Jeanne Heaton and Nona Wilson, "Tuning in Trouble: Talk TV's Destructive Impact on Mental Health" from *Ms.* (September/October 1995). Originally published in *Tuning in Trouble: Talk TV's Destructive Impact on Mental Health.* Copyright © 1995 by Jossey-Bass, Inc. Reprinted with the permission of the publishers.

Arlie Russell Hochschild, "Time for Change" from *Ms.* (September/October 1997). Copyright © 1997. Reprinted with permission.

Lee Smith, "What We Now Know About Memory" [Editors' title. Originally titled "Memory: Why You're Losing It, How to Save It."] from *Fortune* (April 17, 1995). Copyright © 1995 by Time, Inc. Reprinted with the permission of *Fortune*.

Brent Staples, "Just Walk on By: A Black Man Ponders His Ability to Alter Public Space" from *Ms.* (September 1986). Copyright © 1986 by Brent Staples. Reprinted with the permission of the author.

Kathy A. Svitil, "The Greenland Viking Mystery" from *Discover* (July 1997). Copyright © 1997 by Kathy A. Svitil. Reprinted with the permission of *Discover Magazine*.

Renee Tajima, "Lotus Blossoms Don't Bleed: Images of Asian American Women" from *Making Waves: An Anthology of Writings By and About Asian American Women*. Copyright © 1989 by Asian United Women of California. Reprinted by permission.

Deborah Tannen, "Gender Gap in Cyberspace" from *Newsweek* (May 16, 1994). This article is based in part on material from *You Just Don't Understand* (Ballantine, 1990). Copyright © 1994 by Deborah Tannen. Reprinted with the permission of the author.

Deborah Tannen, "Sex, Lies and Conversation" from *The Washington Post* (June 14, 1990). This article is based in part on material from *You Just Don't Understand* (Ballantine, 1990). Copyright © 1990 by Deborah Tannen. Reprinted with the permission of the author.

Sallie Tisdale, "A Weight That Women Carry" from *Harper's Magazine* (March 1993). Copyright © 1993 by Harper's Magazine. Reprinted with the permission of *Harper's*.

Calvin Trillin, "The Extendable Fork." Copyright © 1995 by Calvin Trillin. Reprinted with the permission of the author.

Lindsy van Gelder, "Marriage as a Restricted Club" from *Ms. Magazine* (February 1984). Copyright © 1984 by Lindsy van Gelder. Reprinted with the permission of the author.

E. B. White, "Once More to the Lake" from *One Man's Meat*. Copyright © 1941 by E. B. White. Reprinted with the permission of Tilbury House, Publishers, Gardiner, Maine.

Joy Williams, "The Case Against Babies" from *Granta* 55 (Autumn 1996). Copyright © 1996. Reprinted with permission.

Dereck Williamson, "Wall Covering" from *The Complete Book of Pitfalls: A Victims Guide to Repairs, Maintenance, and Repairing the Maintenance*. Copyright © 1971 by Dereck Williamson. Reprinted with the permission of the author.

Index

Able Writer: A Rhetoric and Handbook, The (Broderick), 32–33
Abstraction, extended definition to explain, 248
Abstract words, 558
Active reading. *See* Engaged reading
African American Web Connection Web site, 123
AIDS, Web sites about, 285
Allusion, 558
Alternating method, 566
"Alzheimer's Strain: How to Accommodate Too Many Patients, The" (Gladwell), 234–39
  responses to, 239–40
American Newspeak Web site, 305
American Way of Death, The (Mitford), 211
America's Dream (Santiago), 364
Analogies, 342–43, 352, 374, 449, 558
  defining through, 250
Anecdote, 257, 374, 559
Angelou, Maya, 349, 350, 352, 353, 354
  "Day to Night: Picking Cotton," 343–46
Antonym, 559
Argumentation, 451–506, 508, 559
  analyzing, 463–64
  checklist for reading and writing, 464
  combining strategies with, 505, 506, 555, 556–57
  defined, 451
  developing, 462
  examples of, 452–59
  getting started on, 459–60
  ideas for using, 479, 485, 491, 504–6
  opening and closing, 462–63
  organizing, 451, 460–62
  purpose of, 451, 452
  selected readings and responses to, 465–504
  using Internet, 469, 479, 485, 491, 504, 505
  using model, 463
Art of Eating, The (Fisher), 264
As, use of, 95. *See also* Similes
Attributing characteristics, defining through, 250
Audience, 18, 144, 559
  languages used to communicate with, 306–7
  process analysis and, 193

Awareness, extended definition to increase, 248

"Back in the Hot Zone" (Preston), 543–47
"Bake Your Bread at Home" (Robertson), 452–55
Barry, Dave, 568
"Becoming and Breaking: Poet and Poem" (Rios), 435–40
  responses to, 440–42
Blair, Eric. *See* Orwell, George
Block by block pattern, 559
Block comparison, 350–51
Bracken, Peg, 560
  "Company Menu No. 1," 206–8
Brady, Judy, 248, 560, 568
  "I Want a Wife," 259–61
Brainstorming, 19–20, 141, 420, 559
Broderick, John P., 32–33
Bryans, James R., 195, 197
  "Buying Land: Easier Said Than Done," 191–93
Burroway, Janet, 560
"Buying Land: Easier Said Than Done" (Bryans), 191–93

Canada: An Immigration Index Web site, 485
Capote, Truman, 563
  "Ride Through Spain, A," 102–6
"Case Against Babies, The" (Williams), 547–55
"Cat Bathing as a Martial Art" (Herron), 188–90
  writing assignment based on, 190–93
Cause-and-effect reasoning, argument developed by, 462
Cause and effect writing, 402–50, 508, 559
  analyzing, 413
  checklist for reading and writing, 414
  combining strategies with, 450, 555, 556–57
  defined, 402
  developing, 411–12
  examples of, 403–8
  getting started on, 408–9
  ideas for using, 425–26, 434, 442, 449, 450
  immediate, 408–9, 441
  indirect, 409, 441
  opening and closing, 412
  organizing, 409–11
  selected readings and responses to, 415–49

using Internet, 418–19, 425, 433, 441, 448–49, 450
using model, 412–13
Causes, 559. *See also* Cause and effect writing
China Men (Kingston), 63
Chronological order, 559
    in developing cause and effect, 411–12
    in narration, 41
Chronological process writing, 188
Clarification, comparison and contrast for, 349
Classification, 559. *See also* Division and classification writing
Clemens, Samuel. *See* Twain, Mark
Cliché, 560
Clinton, Bill, 343
Clustering, 23, 24, 420, 461, 560
Cofer, Judith Ortiz, 411
    "Myth of the Latin Woman: I Just Met a Girl Named Maria, The," 427–32
Coherence, 560
Cole, David, 461
    "Five Myths about Immigration," 480–83
Collaborative writing
    for argumentation, 505
    for cause and effect, 450
    for comparison and contrast essays, 401
    for definition essay, 286
    for description, 132
    for division and classification, 341
    for exemplification, 185
    for narration, 84
    for process analysis, 241
Colloquial language, 560
Colored People (Gates), 116
Combining strategies
    analyzing, 507
    in argumentation, 505, 506, 555, 556–57
    in cause and effect writing, 450, 555, 556–57
    in comparison and contrast essays, 401
    in definition essay, 286
    in description, 133, 186, 555, 556
    in division and classification, 341
    in exemplification, 185–86
    ideas for, 555–57
    in process analysis, 241
    selected readings illustrating, 507–57
"Coming from the Country" (Sanders), 376–85
    responses to, 385–86
"Coming Home Again" (Lee), 517–25
"Coming to America, to Clean" (translated by Corona), 508–16

"Company Man, The" (Goodman), 243–45
"Company Menu No. 1" (Bracken), 206–8
    responses to, 208–9
Comparison and contrast, 342–401, 508, 560
    analyzing, 354
    around similarities and differences, 351
    block comparison, 350–51
    checklist for reading and writing, 354–55
    combining strategies with, 555, 556
    defined, 342, 343
    developing, 352
    examples of, 343–48
    getting started on, 349
    ideas for writing, 366–67, 374–75, 387, 400, 401
    opening and closing, 352–53
    organizing, 350–52
    point by point comparison, 351–52
    selected readings and responses to, 356–400
    using Internet, 361, 366, 373, 386, 399, 401
    using model, 354
Composition Site on the World Wide Web, 33
Concept, extended definition to explain, 248
Conclusions, 560
    in argumentation, 463
    in cause and effect writing, 412
    in comparison and contrast essays, 353
    in division and classification writing, 297
    in exemplification, 144
    in extended definition, 251
    in narration, 42–43
    in process analysis, 196–97
Concrete words, 560
Connotations, 257, 503, 561
Contrasts, defining through, 250. *See also* Comparison and contrast
Controlling idea. *See* Thesis
Controversial term, extended definition to interpret, 248
Conventions, 561
Coontz, Stephanie, "Way We Weren't: The Myth and Reality of the 'Traditional' Family, The," 534–40
Corona, Ana Maria (translator), 556
"Coming to America, to Clean," 508–16
Counterdefinition, essays offering, 253–55
    writing, 257–58
Coyne, Amanda, 555
    "Long Good-bye: Mother's Day in Federal Prison, The," 526–34
Coyote v. Acme (Frazier), 50
Crooked Little Heart (Lamott), 152

"Day to Night: Picking Cotton" (Angelou), 343–46
Dead metaphor, 565
"Dealing with Death, Coping with Life" (Hoff), 25–30
Decision making, comparison and contrast for, 349
Defining terms, 195
Definitions, 242–86, 508, 561
  checklist for reading and writing definition essays, 252
  defined, 242
  developing, 250
  examples of, 242–47
  extended, 248, 250–51
  ideas for using, 268, 275–76, 285–86
  opening and closing, 250–51
  organizing, 249
  purpose of, 247–48
  using Internet, 256, 263, 268, 274–75, 285, 286
  using model, 251
Denotation, 561
Description, 86–132, 508, 561
  analyzing, 96
  checklist for reading and writing, 95
  combining strategies in, 133, 186, 555, 556
  defined, 86
  developing, 93–94
  examples of, 87–92
  expressive, 92–93
  extended examples as, 143
  getting started, 92–94
  ideas for using, 107, 115, 124, 132–33
  objective, 92
  organizing, 93
  reasons for using, 92–93
  selected readings and responses to, 97–132
  using Internet, 100, 107, 114, 123, 124, 131, 133
  using model, 94
Details, 561
  emphasis through, 41–42
  sufficient, in examples, 142
Development, 561
Dialogue, 42, 95, 561
Diary, keeping, 35–37
Diction, 561
Direct transitional phrasing, 352
Discovery, 18–20, 561
Discovery writing. *See also* Narration
  defined, 34
  focused, 37–38, 408–9
  informal, 35–37
  relating discoveries to readers, 38–40

Diversity site, 504
"Dividing American Society" (Hacker), 388–98
  responses to, 398–400
Division, 562
Division and classification writing, 287–341, 508
  analyzing, 298
  checklist for reading and writing, 298–99
  combining strategies in, 341, 556
  defined, 287, 288
  developing, 296
  examples of, 288–93
  getting started on, 293–94
  ideas for using, 312–13, 322, 331, 340–41
  opening and closing, 296–97
  organizing, 294–95
  selected readings and responses, 300–340
  using Internet, 305, 313, 321, 331, 339
  using model, 297–98
Dominant impression, 107, 562
"Doublespeak" (Lutz), 300–304
  responses to, 304–6
Drafting, 22–23, 562
Dubus, Andre, 42
  "Quiet Siege: The Death and Life of a Gay Naval Officer, A," 54–60

Editing, 24–25, 562
"Educational Value of Film, The" (Stangland), 456–59
Effects, 562. *See also* Cause and effect
Ellipsis, 562
"Embalming Mr. Jones" (Mitford), 211–16
  responses to, 216–18
Emphasis, 562
Engaged reading, 1–16, 562
  example of, 4–9
  getting started, 1–2
  making reading-writing connection, 14–16
  marking text, 2
  questions to develop habits of, 2–16
Essay, constructing, 18–30, 562. *See also specific types of essays*
  drafting, 22–23
  editing, 24–25
  idea generation, 18–20
  organizing ideas, 20–22
  revision, 23–24, 25
  sample essay with comments, 25–30
  steps in, 18
  thesis, 20, 141, 142, 249, 349, 353, 459
Euphemisms, 184, 562
Evidence. *See* Supporting material

Examples, 134, 563. *See also* Exemplification
defining through, 250
Exemplification, 134–86, 508, 563
analyzing, 145
argument developed by, 462
checklist for reading and writing, 145
combining strategies in, 556–57
defined, 134
developing, 143
examples of, 135–41
getting started on, 141–42
ideas for using, 150–51, 157, 164, 185–86
opening and closing, 144
organizing, 142–43
selected readings and responses to, 146–85
using Internet, 150, 156, 163, 171, 184, 185
using model, 144
Expressive description, 92–93
"Extendable Fork, The" (Trillin), 288–90
writing assignment based on, 290–93
Extended definitions, 248, 250–51, 563
Extended metaphor, 565

Family (Frazier), 50
Far Flung Hubbell (Hubbell), 146
"Father Hunger" (Marriott), 269–74
responses to, 274–75
"Fear, The" (Holleran), 277–83
responses to, 283–84
Figurative language, 563
Figure of speech, 62, 563
First person, 563
Fisher, M.F.K., 251
"Let the Sky Rain Potatoes," 264–67
"Five Myths about Immigration" (Cole), 480–83
responses to, 483–84
Flashbacks, 41, 193, 563
Focus, 563
Focused discovery writing, 37–38, 408–9
Forster, E.M., 412
"My Wood," 403–5
Frank, Anne, 35–37
Frazier, Ian, "Street Scene: Minor Heroism in a Major Metropolitan Area," 50–52
Freewriting, 22, 141, 563
"Friend, Foe, Or ???" (Shamhart), 291–93

Gallant, Emilie, "White Breast Flats," 108–13
Gates, Henry Louis, Jr., "In the Kitchen," 116–22
Gathering of Spirits, A, 108
"Gender Gap in Cyberspace" (Tannen), 4–9
Generalization, 141, 144, 563
General word, 563

Gilford, Chuck, 32
Gladwell, Malcolm, "Alzheimer's Strain: How to Accommodate Too Many Patients, The," 234–39
Global Gastronomer: Cuisines of the World Web site, 268
Glossary, 558–70
Goodman, Ellen, 248, 250, 251
"Company Man, The," 243–45
Great Plains (Frazier), 50
"Greenland Viking Mystery, The" (Svitil), 421–24
responses to, 424–25
Greider, William, "Mock Democracy," 143, 158–62
Ground Zero (Holleran), 277
"Guavas" (Santiago), 364–65
responses to, 365–66
Guide to Grammar and Writer, 33

Hacker, Andrew, 353
"Dividing American Society," 388–98
Heaton, Jeanne A., 461
"Tuning in Trouble: Talk TV's Destructive Impact on Mental Health," 472–77
Herron, Bud, 195, 196, 197, 559
"Cat Bathing as a Martial Art," 188–90
Hochschild, Arlie Russell, 461
"Time for Change," 486–89
Hoff, Jennifer, "Dealing with Death, Coping with Life," 25–30
Holleran, Andrew, 248, 251, 558
"Fear, The," 277–83
Howard, Gary, 461, 566
"Whites in Multicultural Education: Rethinking Our Role," 492–503
"How to Write a Personal Letter" (Keillor), 220–22
responses to, 222–24
Hubbell, Sue, 565
"On the Interstate: A City of the Mind," 143, 146–49
Hull, Jon D., "Slow Descent into Hell," 144, 165–70

Ideas
for argumentation, 479, 485, 491, 504–6
for cause and effect, 425–26, 434, 442, 449, 450
for combining strategies, 555–57
for comparison and contrast, 366–67, 374–75, 387, 400, 401
for definitions, 268, 275–76, 285–86
for description, 107, 115, 124, 132–33

Ideas *(cont.)*
  for division and classification, 312–13, 322,
    331, 340–41
  for exemplification, 150–51, 157, 164,
    185–86
  generation of, 18–20
  for narration, 53, 62, 75, 83, 84–85
  organizing, 20–22
  for process analysis, 210, 219–20, 224,
    232–33, 240–41
I Hate to Cook Book, The (Bracken), 206
I Know Why the Caged Bird Sings
    (Angelou), 343
Illustration, 564
Images, 94–95, 564
Immediate causes and effects, 408–9, 441, 564
In Cold Blood (Capote), 102
Indirect causes and effects, 409, 441, 564
Inference, 564
Informal discovery writing, 35–37
Informal writing, 564
Inkspots Internet Web site, 156
Internet
  activities on, 16
  searches on, 30–33
  sources for writers, 32–33
Internet, using
  for argumentation, 469, 479, 485, 491, 504,
    505
  for cause and effect, 418–19, 425, 433, 441,
    448–49, 450
  for combining strategies, 557
  for comparison and contrast, 361, 366, 373,
    386, 399, 401
  for definitions, 256, 263, 268, 274–75, 285,
    286
  for description, 100, 107, 114, 123, 124, 131,
    133
  for division and classification, 305, 313,
    321, 331, 339
  for exemplification, 150, 156, 163, 171, 184,
    185
  for ideas for writing, 340–41
  for narration, 48, 53, 61, 82, 84–85
  for process analysis, 209, 219, 223, 232–33,
    240–41
"In the Kitchen" (Gates), 116–22
  responses to, 122–23
Introduction, 564
  in argumentation, 462–63
  in cause and effect writing, 412
  in comparison and contrast essays, 352–53
  in division and classification writing,
    296–97
  in exemplification, 144

in extended definition, 250–51
in narration, 42
in process analysis, 196
"In Tune with His Students" (Quick), 245–47
Irony, 321, 564
"I Want a Wife" (Brady), 259–61
  responses to, 261–63

"Jackie's Debut: A Unique Day" (Royko),
    44–46
  responses to, 46–48
  writing assignment based on, 48–49
Jargon, 374, 564
Jaroff, Leon, "To Hell and Back," 225–30
Jones, Mark, "Looking Up from the
    Bottom," 139–41
Journalistic style, 564
"Just Walk on By: A Black Man Ponders His
    Power to Alter Public Space" (Staples),
    135–38

Keillor, Garrison, "How to Write a Personal
    Letter," 220–22
Kidder, Tracy, 95
  "Mrs. Zajac," 87–89
Kingston, Maxine Hong, 42
  "No Name Woman," 63–73
Kirkendall, Rebecca Thomas, 250–51, 559
  "Who's a Hillbilly?," 253–55
Kitner, Kara, 349, 350
  "Life: It's All about Choices," 346–48
Krumery, Ami, 412, 413
  "My Car," 406–8

Lamott, Anne, 559, 568
  "Shitty First Drafts," 152–56
Laurel's Kitchen Bread Book, The
    (Robertson), 452
Laurel's Kitchen (Robertson), 452
Lee, Chang–Rae, 556
  "Coming Home Again," 517–25
"Let's Get Rid of Sports" (Pollitt),
    540–42
"Let the Sky Rain Potatoes" (Fisher),
    264–67
  responses to, 267–68
"Life: It's All about Choices" (Kitner),
    346–48
Life on the Mississippi (Twain), 100
Like, use of, 95. *See also* Similes
"Lisa" (Moroney), 90–92
Logical order, 565
Logical process writing, 188, 194
"Long Good–bye: Mother's Day in Federal
    Prison, The" (Coyne), 526–34

"Looking Up from the Bottom" (Jones), 139–41
Lopate, Phillip, 293, 565
   "What Friends Are For," 323–29
"Lotus Blossoms Don't Bleed: Images of Asian American Women" (Tajima), 314–20
   responses to, 321–22
Lutz, William, "Doublespeak," 300–304

Main idea. *See* Thesis
Marking text, 2
"Marriage as a Restricted Club" (Van Gelder), 465–68
   responses to, 468–70
   writing assignment based on, 470–71
Marriott, Michel, 250, 558
   "Father Hunger," 269–74
Maxwell, Bruce, "Twelve Tips to Search the Internet Successfully," 30–33
Metaphors, 95, 100, 331, 386, 434, 442, 565
Micro- to macro-structure, 461
Mistakes, cautioning readers against, 195
Mitford, Jessica, 558
   "Embalming Mr. Jones," 211–16
Mixed metaphor, 565
Mnemonics, Web sites on, 339
"Mock Democracy" (Greider), 143, 158–62
   responses to, 163–64
Modes. *See* Rhetorical strategies
Moroney, Ann, "Lisa," 90–92
"Most Human Art: Ten Reasons Why We'll Always Need a Good Story, The" (Sanders), 443–48
   responses to, 448–49
Movie Review Query Engine Web site, 321
"Mrs. Zajac" (Kidder), 87–89
Multicultural Home Page, 504
Murphy, Cullen, "Power of Two: A New Way of Classifying Everyone, The," 308–11
"My Car" (Krumery), 406–8
"Myth of the Latin Woman: I Just Met a Girl Named Maria, The" (Cofer), 427–32
   responses to, 432–34
"My Wood" (Forster), 403–5

Narration, 34–85, 508, 565
   checklist for reading and writing, 43
   combining strategies in, 133, 186, 555, 556
   developing, 41–42
   extended examples as, 143
   focused discovery writing and, 37–38
   getting started, 40–41
   ideas for using, 53, 62, 75, 83, 84–85
   informal discovery writing and, 35–37
      opening and closing, 42–43
      organizing, 41
      relating discoveries to readers, 38–40
      selected readings and responses to, 44–83
      using Internet, 48, 53, 61, 82, 84–85
      using model, 43
National Gay and Lesbian Task Force Web site, 61
National Parent Information Network (NPIN), 491
National Partnership for Women and Families Web site, 263
National Storytelling Association Web site, 448
Noe, Denise, 353
   "Parallel Worlds: The Surprising Similarities (and Differences) of Country-and-Western and Rap," 356–60
"No Name Woman" (Kingston), 63–73
   responses to, 73–75
Notes, making, 2

Objective description, 92
Objective writing, 565
"Once More to the Lake" (White), 125–30
   responses to, 130–32
Online Slang Dictionary, 257
Onomatopoeia, 565
"On the Interstate: A City of the Mind" (Hubbell), 143, 146–49
   responses to, 149–50
On the Pulse of Morning (Angelou), 343
Order, 565
Organization
   of argumentation, 451, 460–62
   of cause and effect writing, 409–11
   of comparison and contrast, 350–52
   of definition essays, 249
   of description, 93
   of division and classification writing, 294–95
   of exemplification, 142–43
   of ideas, 20–22
   of narration, 41
   of process analysis, 193–94
   questions to ask about, 4
Orion Society, 386
Orwell, George, 41
   "Shooting an Elephant," 76–82

Parables, 83, 566
Paradigm Online Writing Assistant (Gilford), 32
Paradox, 441, 566
Paragraph, 566

Parallelism, 566
"Parallel Worlds: The Surprising Similarities
    (and Differences) of Country-and-
    Western and Rap" (Noe), 356–60
    responses to, 360–62
    writing assignment based on, 362–63
Parenting Q&A site, 491
Patterns of organization. *See* Organization;
    Rhetorical strategies
Person. *See* Point of view
Personification, 100, 566
Persuasion, 451–52, 566. *See also*
    Argumentation
    combining strategies with, 556
    comparison and contrast for, 349
Pitfalls, mentioning possible, 195–96
Poet's Directory Web site, 441
Point-by-point argumentation, 461
Point by point comparison, 351–52
Point by point pattern, 566
Point of view, 566–67
Pollitt, Katha, 556
    "Let's Get Rid of Sports," 540–42
    "Why Boys Don't Play with Dolls," 415–17
"Power of Two: A New Way of Classifying
    Everyone, The" (Murphy), 308–11
    responses to, 311–12
Preston, Richard, 556
    "Back in the Hot Zone," 543–47
Previewing, 567
Prewriting, 408, 567
Problem-solution structure, 461, 567
Process writing/analysis, 187–241, 508, 567
    analyzing, 197
    checklist for reading and writing, 198
    chronological process writing, 188
    combining description and exemplification
        with, 556
    defined, 188
    developing, 194–96, 204–5
    examples of, 188–93
    getting started on, 193
    ideas for using, 210, 219–20, 224, 232–33,
        240–41
    logical process writing, 188, 194
    opening and closing, 196–97
    organizing, 193–94
    selected readings and responses to,
        199–240
    using Internet, 209, 219, 223, 232–33,
        240–41
    using model, 197
Purpose, 18, 567
    of argumentation, 451, 452
    choice of definition and, 247–48

in exemplification, 141
of narration, 40–41
questions to ask about, 3–4

Questions/questioning
    to develop habits of engaged reading, 2–16
    in drafting stage, 23
    in revision stage, 23–24
    rhetorical, 340, 567
Quick, Megan, 248, 249, 250, 251
    "In Tune with His Students," 245–47
"Quiet Siege: The Death and Life of a Gay
    Naval Officer, A" (Dubus), 54–60
    responses to, 60–62

Reader–writer interaction, 17–33. *See also*
    Essay, constructing
Reading–writing connection, making, 14–16
Reasons in process writing, including, 195
Refutation, 461, 567
Relevance, 142
Revision, 23–24, 25, 567
Rhetorical questions, 340, 567
Rhetorical strategies, 567. *See also* Strategies
    for writing
"Ride Through Spain, A" (Capote), 102–6
    responses to, 106–7
Rios, Alberto Alvaro, 411
    "Becoming and Breaking: Poet and
        Poem," 435–40
Robertson, Laurel, 452, 461, 462, 463
    "Bake Your Bread at Home," 452–55
Rosie (Lamott), 152
Royko, Mike, 560
    "Jackie's Debut: A Unique Day," 44–46

Sanders, Scott Russell, 353, 565
    "Coming from the Country," 376–85
    "Most Human Art: Ten Reasons Why
        We'll Always Need a Good Story, The,"
        443–48
Santiago, Esmeralda, "Guavas," 364–65
Sarcasm, 321, 568
Satire, 218, 568
*Second Shift: Working Parents and the
    Revolution at Home, The* (Hochschild),
    486
"Sex, Lies, and Conversation" (Tannen),
    368–73
    responses to, 373–74
Sexist language, 568
Shamhart, Brian, 297–98
    "Friend, Foe, Or ???," 291–93
"Shitty First Drafts" (Lamott), 152–56
    responses to, 156–57

"Shooting an Elephant" (Orwell), 76–82
    responses to, 82–83
Similarities and differences, clustering, 351
Similes, 74, 95, 100, 157, 331, 568
Slang, 568
"Slow Descent into Hell" (Hull), 144, 165–70
    responses to, 170–72
Smith, Lee, "What We Now Know about
    Memory," 332–38
Specificity, 195, 563
Stangland, Sean, 452, 455–62, 463
    "Educational Value of Film, The," 456–59
Staples, Brent, 142, 143, 144
    "Just Walk on by: A Black Man Ponders
    His Power to Alter Public Space,"
    135–38
Stereotypes, 296
Strategies for writing. *See also* Combining
    strategies; *specific strategies*
    argumentation, 451, 459–64, 508
    cause and effect, 408–14, 508
    comparison and contrast, 349–55, 508
    definition, 247–52, 508
    description, 92–96, 508
    division and classification, 293–99, 508
    exemplification, 141–45, 508
    narration, 38–43, 508
    process analysis, 193–98, 508
"Street Scene: Minor Heroism in a Major
    Metropolitan Area" (Frazier), 50–52
    responses to, 52–53
Structure, 568
Style, 568
Subjective writing, 565
Subject (topic), 18–20, 568
    thesis vs., 20
Subtopics, 94
Summarization, emphasis through, 41–42
Supporting material, 568
Svitil, Kathy A., 411
    "Greenland Viking Mystery, The," 421–24
Symbol, 569
Synonym, 569

Tajima, Renee, "Lotus Blossoms Don't
    Bleed: Images of Asian American
    Women," 314–20
Talkshow Page, The, 479
Tannen, Deborah, 353, 559
    "Gender Gap in Cyberspace," 4–9
    "Sex, Lies, and Conversation," 368–73
Thesis, 20, 569
    in argumentation, 459
    in comparison and contrast writing, 349,
    353

in definition essay, 249
    in exemplification, 141, 142
Third person, 569
"Time for Change" (Hochschild), 486–89
    responses to, 489–90
Tisdale, Sallie, 143
    "Weight That Women Carry, A," 173–82
Title, 569
"To Hell and Back" (Jaroff), 225–30
    responses to, 231–32
Tone, 18, 569
Topic, generating ideas for, 18–20. *See also*
    Thesis
Topic sentence, 569
Transitions, 142, 569
    in developing cause and effect, 411–12
    direct transitional phrasing, 352
Trillin, Calvin, 293, 297, 298
    "Extendable Ford, The," 288–90
Tripmaster Monkey (Kingston), 63
"Tuning in Trouble: Talk TV's Destructive
    Impact on Mental Health" (Heaton),
    472–77
    responses to, 477–78
Twain, Mark, 565
    "Two Views of the Mississippi," 97–99
"Twelve Tips to Search the Internet
    Successfully" (Maxwell), 30–33
"Two Views of the Mississippi" (Twain),
    97–99
    responses to, 99–100
    writing assignment based on, 100–101

Understatement, 321, 569
Unity, 569
University of Victoria's Hypertext Writer's
    Guide, The, 32
Usage, 570

Vagrant Gaze Web site, 171
Van Gelder, Lindsy, 461
    "Marriage as a Restricted Club," 465–68
Voice, 3, 10, 570
Voices in America Web site, 366

"Wall Covering" (Williamson), 199–202
    responses to, 202–4
"Way We Weren't: The Myth and Reality of
    the 'Traditional' Family, The" (Coontz),
    534–40
We Are Still Married (Keillor), 220
Web sites. *See* Internet
"Weight That Women Carry, A" (Tisdale),
    173–82
    responses to, 183–84

"What Friends Are For" (Lopate), 323–29
responses to, 329–31
"What We Now Know about Memory"
(Smith), 332–38
responses to, 339–40
When I Was Puerto Rican (Santiago), 364
White, E.B., 569
"Once More to the Lake," 125–30
"White Breast Flats" (Gallant), 108–13
responses to, 113–14
"Whites in Multicultural Education:
Rethinking Our Role" (Howard),
492–503
responses to, 503–4
"Who's a Hillbilly?" (Kirkendall), 253–55
responses to, 255–57
*Who Will Tell the People: The Betrayal of
American Democracy* (Greider), 158

"Why Boys Don't Play with Dolls" (Pollitt),
415–17
responses to, 417–19
writing assignment based on, 419–20
Williams, Joy, "Case Against Babies, The,"
547–55
Williamson, Dereck, "Wall Covering,"
199–202
Woman Warrior, The (Kingston), 63
Woolf, Virginia, 35
Word According to Eve, The (Murphy), 308
Writer's Web, 32
Writing process, 570. *See also* Essay,
constructing
Writing skills, developing, 17
WWWebster Dictionary, 257